SOCIETIES AND LANGUAGES OF THE ANCIENT NEAR EAST

I. M. DIAKONOFF

Societies and Languages of the Ancient Near East

STUDIES IN HONOUR OF

I. M. DIAKONOFF

ARIS & PHILLIPS LTD – WARMINSTER – ENGLAND

British Library Cataloguing in Publication Data

Societies and languages of the ancient Near East.
1. Diakonoff, I.M. 2. Linguistics – Near East – History – Addresses, essays, lectures
3. Near East – History – to 622 – Addresses, essays, lectures
I. Postgate, J.N. II. Diakonoff, I.M.
470'.939 P63

ISBN 0 85668 205 5

Printed and published by ARIS & PHILLIPS LTD, Warminster, Wilts, England.

CONTENTS

PREFACE

Although Igor Michailovitch's sixtieth and sixty-fifth birthdays have not passed unnoticed in his own country*, his international standing calls for some recognition of his academic achievements from the scholars of other countries as well. We could easily have filled another volume as large as this, and to accomplish the invidious task of selecting contributors we have had to restrict invitations to those with close personal links with Prof. Diakonoff, or whose work has been on subjects close to his own interests, in particular the fields of language and social history. To those we could not invite, and to those who were prevented from contributing by the very short notice given by the editors, we can only tender our apologies and entreat their understanding. Sadly, we also have to record that R. Ghirshman died before he could contribute, although he wrote "Je suis de coeur avec cette entreprise".

We would like to acknowledge very warmly the generous contribution towards the costs of the volume made by the Yarshater Fund. Despite the length of the book, which results from the very full response to our invitation, this has helped significantly in our efforts to keep its price within reasonable limits. Unfortunately its length has also prevented us from including a full bibliography of I.M. Diakonoff. However, one will be given in the forthcoming collection of his works edited in Budapest by G. Komoróczy, called *Studies in Assyriology and Ancient Oriental Philology*. Our thanks also go to the Deutsches Archäologisches Insitut, and to Dr. W. Kleiss, for generously enabling us to use Dr. Trümpelmann's photograph of the Behistun relief.

There is little to add of a technical nature. For bibliographical abbreviations in general, see W. von Soden, *Akkadisches Handwörterbuch*, I and II, or *The Assyrian Dictionary* (CAD), Vol. M. When not found in either place, they are noted after each individual article. For typographical reasons Russian titles are transliterated.

M.A. Dandamayev
I. Gershevitch
H. Klengel
G. Komoróczy
M.T. Larsen
J.N. Postgate

*See VDI 1975/1, 245; *Drevnii Vostok* 2 [1976]; *Narody Azii i Afriki* 1975/1, 227-32; *Peredneaziatskii Sbornik* 3 [1979].

I.M. DIAKONOFF

Igor Michailovitch was born in Petrograd (Leningrad) on 12th January, 1915. His father, Michail Alexeyevitch, was born in Tomsk, Siberia, as the son of a bank clerk; he was an economist, and from 1921 to 1929 was in Norway with his family as chief of the financial department of the commercial delegation of the U.S.S.R. His mother, Maria, was born in Tashkent as the daughter of an artillery officer, and became a physician. Igor's elder brother, Michail Michailovitch (1907-1954) was himself a distinguished scholar in Iranian history and archaeology, and was the author of "Ancient History of Iran". His younger brother, Alexei, was an engineer, but fell in the war (30th December 1941).

Diakonoff attended Secondary School in Oslo, 1928-29, and in Leningrad, 1930-31, with teachers in English and German. In 1931 he worked as a geography teacher for the children of English and American workers in Leningrad. At the Historical Faculty of the University of Leningrad he attended the Department of History of Arabic Countries, studying Arabic under N.V. Yushmanov. In 1932 Alexandr P. Riftin founded the Institute of Assyriology and Hebrew Studies, and Diakonoff was among its first students. In 1933 he was present at the great lecture of V.V. Struve, and decided that it was pointless to study ancient oriental history without a philological grounding. He studied Akkadian and Sumerian under Riftin, Hebrew under I.G. Frank-Kamenetsky and A. Yu. Borisov, Phoenician and Aramaic (including the Babylonian Talmud) under Borisov, and Arabic with I. Yu. Krachkovsky.

During 1935 he worked on the N.P. Likhachev collection, which was known as the Museum of the History of Writing of the Academy of Sciences of the U.S.S.R., and met Likhachev himself. In 1936 his first article was published, and he started work at the Hermitage as Curator of the tablet collection, an experience which he felt to be a "second university" and in which he "learned to regard Babylonians as living creatures"; his teacher here was Miss Nathalie Flittner. In 1938 Diakonoff started teaching at the University, in the Philological and Historical Faculties, in Akkadian and the history of Babylonia and Assyria, and published further papers.

On 22nd June, 1941, he took part in the evacuation of the Hermitage, and after serving for a week as a volunteer private in the beginning of July was recalled to continue the evacuation. On 5th September, 1941, he was mobilized, and served until December 1945, as staff officer in the north, within the Arctic Circle, finishing his war service with the rank of Captain.

Six months after demobilization in 1946 he took his Candidature, and from 1946 to 1950 taught Akkadian, Sumerian, Cuneiform Literature, and the History of Babylonia and Assyria. From 1945 to 1959 he was Curator of the Babylonian Collection at the Hermitage. In 1959 he received his Doctorate ("Habilitation") for the book *Sumer*. In 1952 he worked for a short time for the Academy of Sciences of Azerbaijan, and at their request wrote his *History of Media*. From 1953 he has been at the Oriental Institute (Institut Vostokovedeniya) of the Academy of Sciences, as a Senior Research Worker (i.e. Professor). In 1963 he went for three months to Chicago as a Visiting Professor at the Oriental Institute. When the XXV International Congress of Orientalists was held in Moscow in 1960, I.M. Diakonoff was appointed its Secretary General. In 1969 he was elected Soviet representative to the Bureau of the International Association of Economic Historians, serving until 1971, and he organized the Ancient Near Eastern section of its Congresses at Paris (1967),

Leningrad (1971), Copenhagen (1974) and Edinburgh (1978). An honorary member of the Royal Asiatic Society since 1962, of the American Oriental Society since 1973, of the Société Asiatique since 1976, he was elected in 1975 a Corresponding Fellow of the British Academy.

Only a full bibliography can do justice to the full scope of Diakonoff's academic output, but we cannot pass over in silence a few of his major contributions. His two biggest works in the social and economic history of the ancient Orient are *Razvitie zemel'nykh otnošenii v Assirii* (Development of Agrarian Conditions in Assyria; 1949), and *Obščestvennyi i gosudarstvennyi stroi drevnevo Dvureč'ya: Šumer* (Society and State in Ancient Mesopotamia: Sumer; 1959). His interest in philology is reflected in his systematic description of the languages of Western Asia (*Yazyki drevnei Perednei Azii;* 1967), and in studies in Sumerian and other non-Semitic languages (e.g. *Hurrisch und Urartäisch*; 1971). Recently he has also been much engaged with Afrasian linguistics. A particularly important landmark for western scholars was his edition of a volume of articles by Soviet authors on *Ancient Mesopotamia* (1969). Recent major articles of his own are "Die hethitische Gesellschaft" (*Mitt. des Instituts für Orientforschung* XIII, 1967, 313-366), and "Slaves, helots and serfs in early antiquity" (*Acta Antiqua Academiae Scientiarum Hungaricae* XXII, 1974, 45-78). His translations and editions of major cuneiform texts in Russian include in particular the Codex Hammurapi and other law codes, and the Epic of Gilgamesh.

As a result of his vigorously developing the Iranological legacy of his elder brother, Diakonoff's name has become a household word also among Iranianists. We have mentioned above his *Istoriya Midii* (1956), which was the first detailed treatment of the subject. It is brought up to date in the chapter on Media which he wrote for Volume 2 (shortly to appear) of the *Cambridge History of Iran*. His major contribution to the study of the origin of the Old Persian script was published in 1970 (see below, p. 107, n.6). Students of Iranian prehistory have much to gain from his authoritative support and refinement of the arguments by which Annelies Kammenhuber brought about "the end of the myth" of Aryan predominance in ancient Western Asia (*Orientalia* NS 41, 1972, 91-120). The publication of the pioneering work he did in collaboration with V.A. Livshits in deciphering and identifying language and contents of the 2758 Parthian ostraca from Nisa, is still in progress (see below, p. 107, n.4).

Apart from his own academic output, Diakonoff has had the satisfaction of seeing his students and colleagues spread cuneiform studies across the Soviet Union. Of his pre-war students the first four died in the fighting, and the fifth was Dunayevskaya. Later he taught Sarkisian, Jankowska and Batsieva. His later colleagues and graduate students at Leningrad include: Afanasjeva, Dandamayev, Gamkrelidze, Golovleva, Harouthouniyan, Jakobson, Kaneva, Kashkay, Khačikjan, Kločkov, Kozyreva, Melikischwili, Papazyan, and Yusifov. From abroad he has taught J. Zabłocka (Poznań) and M.A. Powell (DeKalb), but this Festschrift will bear witness that his influence, as well as his reputation, is world-wide.

ADDENDUM

(to p. 291)
On second consideration, the relation of the star-shaped design in one of the two imprints is much closer to Egyptian button seals (Petrie, *Buttons and Design Scarabs,* London 1925, Pl. IV: 212, 213) than to the Bactrian examples here cited. While the relation between Bactria and Nubia should therefore be dropped, the sea route from East Iran to Egypt should still be considered as a possible alternative to the land routes.

PROPERTY RIGHTS AND FUNCTIONAL TENURE IN MESOPOTAMIAN RURAL COMMUNITIES

Robert McC. Adams (Chicago)

No one has done more than Professor Diakonoff to deepen our understanding of the major socioeconomic undercurrents in ancient Mesopotamian society, as well as to sensitize his colleagues to the many lines of indirect, sometimes ambiguous evidence that must be drawn together from diverse sources in order to expose them to view at all. Hence it may be not inappropriate to honor him by seeking to cast a net over a portion of one of his own favorite subjects, but with somewhat different intent and from an unfamiliar direction.

Diakonoff has succinctly identified a major feature of his theoretical approach as the distinguishing of social classes from one another on the basis of their differing socio-political interests. Contributing to these differences, he maintains, are historically conditioned differences in access to means of production, different roles in the social organization of labor, and of course ensuing differences in wealth. For the third and early part of the second millennia B.C. he sketches an admittedly generalized picture in which an upper stratum of citizenry derived its living primarily from a much larger mass of "slave-type dependent persons" while between these two sharply opposed (if not necessarily or equally self conscious) groups there survived a class of freeholding peasants subsisting largely on the produce of their own labor. Others have taken issue with him over whether it is proper to group chattel slaves and technically free, not wholly propertyless laborers in the state sector within a single category. Different levels of generalization are useful for different purposes, and there is little to be added by reconsidering in the abstract the respective advantages of tripartite and quadripartite schemes of social stratification. In a sense anterior to the contention over this issue is a doubt over the grounds on which it has been based. I believe it is fair to characterize its main focus hitherto as having been the concept of formal ownership of the means of production, and above all land, rather than the broad relationship of forces within the society at large.[1]

The difficulty with the narrower concentration of interest is that the idea of property, no less in land than in anything else, is itself only to be understood as a historically conditioned social construct. Access to and control over property has always been conditioned by successive accretions of rights and obligations that may survive or be altered only slowly according to the at least partly autonomous dynamics of all conceptual systems. Some of these accretions originate in local custom or in prevailing patterns of kin loyalty, with shadings of moral or legal authority introduced by the rich diversity of oppositions and alliances that go on within any generalized set of norms. Others set the interests of the individual or his family off against those of all or part of a community, while still others involve individuals, families or communities with the supervening powers of the state. But behind the misleadingly unifying facade of codes and constitutions, the whole corpus of such accretions cannot constitute a harmonious, balanced system of legal precepts together with their applications. That would seem to be a fairly neutral historical generalization, but should be particularly apparent to anyone who views contending classes as the driving force of change and hence recognizes that no society can remain a smoothly functioning, timeless equilibrium.

To make ancient principles of property most salient in the study of class stratification is, I suggest, to risk losing sight of the changing complexities of historical reality by following normative definitions that may have a trajectory of their own. Diakonoff's upper stratum (and the state institutions with which it must have come into being in an interactive process) indeed found it expedient to codify and cite prescriptive principles. Much less clear, however, is how widely and uniformly such principles ever prevailed. Taken for granted in both private and official transactions was a wider context of social relationships that surely always exercised an important, often decisive influence on their outcome. Recorded rights and obligations were only parts of a much larger spectrum of relationships that was mostly not recorded, selected according to criteria that were never made explicit. As Miguel Civil has recently put it,

> ...il y a des renseignements, souvent essentiels pour la solution de nos problèmes, qui ne figurent pas dans les textes non parce qu'ils n'étaient point *perçus* par les scribes mais tout au contraire parce qu'ils étaient *trop connus* des scribes.... Une conclusion assez pessimiste s'impose: plus un fait culturel se situe près du noyau central d'activités humaines, moins il y a de chances qu'il apparaisse dans les textes.[2]

What is perhaps most importantly and pervasively missing is an acknowledgement of the relative power, extending far beyond any specific relationship or transaction, of members of social elites to impose their will on inferior social segments or even on one another. Lacking this, all too often discouragingly little can be said in other than stereotypical terms about the attribution of motives to actions, and hence about the interplay and selection between alternatives. And without this, little real social depth can be detected, leaving us with testimony more pertinent to the elaboration of a series of stylized chronicles than to history as an interpretive and explanatory undertaking.

One approach to overcoming these difficulties proceeds primarily from the analysis of variant practices and terminology directly attested to within the textual corpus. Ultimately Assyriologists will no doubt overcome many present ambiguities in this fashion, of course to some extent depending on the recovery of more and more broadly representative bodies of documentary evidence. But much more problematical is a determination of the role of the largely silent mass of Diakonoff's lower social strata from purely documentary sources. Archaeological data is potentially more helpful in this respect, although the potential will not be realized until this is more widely acknowledged among my archaeological colleagues as a central responsibility. But also of some slight help can be a consideration of the conditions of life and forms of association of the working agricultural population of other places as well as periods, in order to take advantage of types of documentation for which there is as yet no cuneiform parallel.

Let us first briefly consider the frequently associative character of peasant village agricultural holdings, which are not necessarily to be identified with the more formal, state-recognized features of land tenure systems. The classic form of communal systems of this type, at least in terms of its recognition and intensive study by historians, is the "open field" village agriculture that, together with the manorial domains exercising control over most of it, was dominant in much of western Europe throughout the medieval period.[3] Recently this has begun to receive the attention of a new "cliometric" group of economic historians who are prepared to do battle with the rich manorial data (and with one another) by invoking a sophisticated, sometimes even explicitly "counterfactual" battery of assumptions and quantitative methodologies. Naturally, I do not imply that historical, social and environmental conditions in the two world regions were so similar as to justify any uniformity of explanation. Two premises common to the cliometricians working on this problem may further limit the wider applicability of their findings. One is that medieval peasants' behavior can be adequately understood by regarding them as "selfish", knowing, rational, entirely economically motivated individualists. Second, the present group of investigators seems to hold that the role of the larger political system may be assumed (at least over the long run) to have been static, benign, and in any case ultimately irrelevant. Most of us would regard these as crude, first-order approximations at best. Even to a skeptic, however, they have indeed been made to serve as the founding hypotheses of an explicitly deductive, quantitatively testable approach that persuasively organizes and interprets much of the available data and that promises yet further insights. Hence the findings are useful in identifying various features of an explanatory model that should apply to communal systems of cultivation and tenure more generally.

Two principal positions have been enunciated, regarded as to some degree antithetical by their protagonists but for present purposes potentially complementary. One holds that there were prevailingly low yields, unpredictable weather, high variability in soil fertility due to such problems as poor drainage, high losses associated with storage, very limited and high cost facilities for transporting agricultural surpluses over any distance, poorly developed futures markets, and limited as well as expensive access to credit on the part of cultivators. Associating at least some modest cost with any scattering of individual plots of land within larger, communally held "open fields", this position seeks to demonstrate that the dominant factor in the dispersal of plots must have been a reduction of the risks to the individual from those forms of disaster that were strictly localized. The second position sharply challenges some elements of the earlier one, arguing in particular that there was greater reliance on storage as a means of risk aversion and that fluid exchanges of credit within a peasant community could serve the same end. Further, the second position credits positive advantages to field dispersal, outweighing additional costs for time lost in transit between plots. These are said to have taken the form of improvements in the scheduling of agricultural activities throughout the year, since scattering meant that sowing, cultivating and harvesting times could be somewhat staggered rather than simultaneous.[4]

The applicability of considerations like these to any type of traditional agriculture, the Near East included, is reasonably apparent. True, there are obvious differences. Climatic unpredictability in Europe would be moderated in Mesopotamia by the use of irrigation, although there is no lack of other -- human as well as natural -- elements of unpredictability in irrigation. Storage, too, assumes a somewhat different aspect in a region with fallow land available for forage and without harsh winters to decimate herds. Near Eastern pastoralism surely must be understood at least in part as a form of capital investment that could smooth the effects of crop fluctuations. In general, however, the factors held uppermost in the medieval debate are ones that surely also deserve close attention when we turn to the ancient

Orient. Some, like scheduling, may even take on greater force when considered in connection with the periodicities of an irrigation regime than they seem to have in medieval Europe. What is most obviously missing, as we shall see presently, is a place in the cliometricians' system for what economists might call political "externalities".

Elegant as the cliometricians' models are in other respects, their use with different sets of measured variables is made exceedingly difficult by disparities in the available data. The voluminous cuneiform sources simply fall short of the standards of medieval record-keeping (at least from the thirteenth century onwards) in comprehensiveness. There is less emphasis in manorial records on purely routine transactions, and more on fully listing holdings, rents, services, annual yields, disbursements, and even some descriptive information on the tenantry. With some proceedings of manor courts also available to shed additional light on the latter, the relations of feudal or monastic superiors to communities of cultivators hence can be relatively more fully and clearly specified. Not all of this may lie permanently beyond the reach of Assyriologists, to be sure, but for the present the differences are substantial. How then can we come to grips with what may have been Near Eastern equivalents for opportunities and constraints in communal agriculture like those that can be dealt with directly in medieval Europe? One way is to use relatively recent, much more adequately documented conditions in the Near Eastern countryside as a point of departure. My primary field of geographic concern in doing so is obviously southern Iraq, although ampler data from adjacent areas is necessary to supplement what can be said of the Mesopotamian alluvium in recent times. The relevant temporal span begins roughly in the mid-nineteenth century, and terminates with the massive reforms and land redistribution that followed in the wake of the revolution of 1958.

Apart from the sustaining areas immediately surrounding the main towns of the time, the mid-nineteenth century pattern of landholding was based on a tribal territory or *dira* within which tenure was for the most part regarded as held in common. Sections might be set aside to be cultivated on behalf of the paramount tribal leadership or for heads of tribal divisions, but these attached to the responsibilities of their offices rather than to themselves or their immediate families as persons. Some prescriptive rights also were connected with orchards, water lifting machinery, and other forms of capital improvement, but it must be stressed that the prevailing insecurity of the times discouraged such improvements. Irrigation was of course essential for agriculture, but it was prevailingly of a localized, small scale character that could be abandoned under military pressure (from other tribes or Ottoman authorities) and replaced at little cost. Plots under cultivation within the *dira* were continually shifted, in response not only to the diversions and interruptions characteristic of a wholly acephalous system of water control but also to the greater attachment of the bulk of the population to fighting in support of tribal interests rather than to agriculture. Yet for all of the insecurity and lack of consistent economic advance associated with these chaotic conditions, it must be recognized that this type of social and subsistence system was at least a highly flexible or resilient one. It permitted, if only at low population levels, rapid adaptation or recovery of its constituent tribal groups in the face of a wide variety of severe ecological pressures.[5]

Little need be said here in detail of the formal categories of land ownership that were recognized by the Ottoman authorities. The Land code of 1858 envisioned the vesting of permanent *tapu* rights on all those who had settled and cultivated the *miri* or state domain, but explicitly forbade communal tenure. This proved largely inapplicable in the vast areas still under tribal control. Sufficient continuity of settlement and use to meet the terms of the Code could seldom be demonstrated by individual cultivators. Tribal shaykhs, since they were not themselves cultivators and since their claims were merely those of the tribes they represented, also had difficulties in proving their eligibility. Moreover, the prevailing mistrust between the tribes and the Ottoman government, coupled with well justified fears of conscription and other forms of governmental encroachment, forestalled any general movement by the shaykhs toward purchasing these rights. Hence the primary acquisition of them was by townsmen, who in effect speculated on finding a profitable niche between the tribes and the government. Subsequent to the departure of Midhat Pasha as Governor of Baghdad (1869-71) all efforts to transfer land titles to occupants were simply abandoned in favor of a more passive (as well as more profitable) policy of state landlordism on the remaining four-fifths of the cultivable terrain. Clearly, the formal patterns of ownership that emerged from this process reflected a shifting, heterogeneous relationship of forces, and they are further obscured by the "absolute confusion and anarchy" reigning in the departments responsible for Ottoman land survey and registration.[6]

More important for present purposes is the informal, unrecorded pattern that prevailed throughout the region. Great estates generally were leased by the shaykhs from the state institution or private individual with some semblance of title to them. Subdivisions of these, called *qitʿa*, were the primary operational units. In strong, centralized tribes the paramount leader might retain considerable authority over tribal sections occupying individual *qitʿa*. Elsewhere subordinate shaykhs came independently to terms with title holders. In the detribalized sustaining areas around the major towns the title holders increasingly undertook to operate their own estates independently, acting indirectly through subordinate agents or managers. Agricultural activities there were of course carried on by fellahin on a sharecropping basis. Where the *qitʿa* holder and the cultivators formed a single tribal unit, they were bound together by a complex, reciprocal set of military and social as well as economic obligations that could not be readily broken. At the other end of a fluid continuum of disintegrating tribes, easily ruptured, essentially contractual relations prevailed in the vicinity of towns between fragmented, rootless groups of fellahin and shaykhs whose functions and social position had become those of private landlords.[7]

Had other conditions held constant, it might have been expected that the decay of tribalism would continue in the years after World War I. Improvements in the technology of communications worked toward this end, as did the strengthening of the government's capacity to extend at least some aspects of its administrative apparatus into the countryside. Less directly, changed world conditions that greatly accelerated the growth of towns had the same effect. By creating urban and foreign markets for agricultural products, they increased the incentives for shaykhs to adopt the stance of private landlords rather than tribal leaders. Yet there were powerful sociopolitical considerations of a very familiar, traditional kind that counteracted this seemingly "natural" trend, and that continued to prevail not only under the British Mandate but under the monarchy that succeeded it. An imposed government without a secure and well established base of regional or popular support found a readier community of interest with the great landed shaykhs with some remaining claims on their tribal followers than it could identify with any other group of remotely comparable influence. The shaykhs helped to strengthen the chain of authority, moreover, by which additional revenues could be extracted from the by no means docile countryside. As early as 1919 the terms of the alliance were clearsightedly set forward by the Revenue Commissioner: "We must recognize that it is primarily our business not to give rights to those who have them not, but to secure their rights to those who have them." Even earlier but along similar lines, a Political Officer had written that his policy was to "go straight for getting the power in each tribe into the hands of one man". Thus it was that the four decades ensuing after World War I saw not the devolution of tribal tenure into more atomistic, private patterns of ownership but instead "the growth of a new *commercial* shaikhly semifeudalism".[8]

Such developments obviously found some reflection in urban record-keeping. Yet the level at which they occurred was largely detached from peasant life in the villages and the routine associations involved in the conduct of agriculture. It has already been noted that there was a screen of intermediaries between holders of formal titles and the cultivators. Sometimes this was composed of lesser shaykhs still primarily linked to the cultivators, while at other times it was composed of agents acting primarily on behalf of the owners in dealing with sharecroppers or hired laborers. What lay on the further, rural side of this screen was at or beyond the peripheries of urban interest and competence. In particular, local arrangements for the allotment of land to cultivators, the concrete articulation of the formally recognized large holdings with agricultural production, seem to have largely escaped any substantial administrative attention. That had to await the arrival upon the scene after World War II of specialists with an entirely unprecedented set of objectives, including both planners of agricultural development schemes and anthropologists.

What emerges from a number of reports of these latter kinds is the existence of a system of periodic land redistribution, not infrequently coupled with the scattering of individual parcels of land within larger holdings that are partly worked in common. An account of agricultural practices along the Hilla branch of the Euphrates and the Daghara canal, for example, refers concisely to tenants having

> ...received a piece of land every year. The landowner decided which part of his property would be cultivated in a definite year. Under supervision of the representatives the tenants organized a ballot as a result of which equal pieces were allocated. In this allocation waste and idle lands were not considered.[9]

On the other hand, a much fuller anthropological account of a particular town and its hinterlands in the same region describes a different as well as a more differentiated picture. Only a small proportion of the cultivable land around Daghara was registered jointly in the names of all of the members of a particular tribal section, and this especially included date orchards. Most commonly fields were also jointly owned, but only by brothers or by brothers and patri-cousins together rather than by larger agnatic groups. And there were numerous individual holdings, which in fact were regarded as preferable. Joint ownership in this case was a strategy for maintaining units large enough to cultivate through successive generations of fractionating inheritance, as well as for assuring access to irrigation water across a checkerboard of adjoining fields. The data appear to be limited, however, to tribally organized freeholders enjoying a stability of tenure that would have been rarely if ever attainable by their ancestors in Ottoman times. Moreover, information is not available on how fields were allocated among others of the same shaykh's tribal followers who had been reduced to the status of sharecropping tenants on his own lands. Preferences for individual ownership do not, in any case, overcome pressures that continually force most of the group in the opposite direction. As the anthropologist observes, "owners must do the best they can with the land they inherit or are able to purchase; micro-variations in population densities throughout the region cannot be accommodated through expansion or contraction of tribal holdings".[10]

A partial transition toward parcelling of land among tenant tribesmen has been attested in the southern Mesopotamian marshes. Its circumscribed extent is suggested in one published account by the fact that the *sirkal* of the clan in question had 350 cultivable (and 2,750 uncultivable) hectares of land at his direct disposal (through lease of state domain lands) while assigning less than thirty hectares to members of his own clan in return for a third of their crop. In this case,

> The cultivating unit is usually the family. Sometimes two or more families, usually of one lineage, cultivate jointly, sharing the seeds and the crop. Frequently, a lineage may cultivate jointly. If so, they may share according to the number of *habil* (0.25 ha.) cultivated by every family, the money spent and the crop produced. Clans tend to hold adjacent patches of land, usually near their dwelling islands. In the days of the feudal shaikhdom, the lineages received land direct from the shaikh and no doubt their corporate solidarity was derived from this as well as from other institutions. To-day lineages or clans (except one) have no corporate rights to land. Inheritance is from father to son.[11]

Stability of tenure among cultivating families in the foregoing cases is clearly related to the ties of tribal solidarity that continue to exist between them and the shaykh or his representative, the holders of formal title. As specifically noted for the southern marshmen, "the user cannot be evicted unless he has failed to cultivate or to pay the *sirkal's* share" and can mortgage, share and even sell his right of occupancy. Conditions were quite different among sharecropping tenants in detribalized areas. In such an area on the lower Diyala plains east of Baghdad, for example,

> At present (this was in 1956) the sharecropping system does not provide for the tenant receiving any specific block of land, since he is moved about from field to field each season according to the pattern of the fallow rotation and the random method of allocating land at the beginning of each new season. This method, which consists of allocating to a tenant several strips of land, each individual locality being chosen by lot, is useful in so far as it ensures that the tenants on a property have more chance of receiving a fair proportion of the better land.[12]

Fuller details (including mapped holdings) are available for a village near the right bank of the Tigris, between Baghdad and Kut. A local shaykh "organizes all agricultural production, determines what crops shall be grown in which fields, allocates the land to the cultivators, owns the water pump and pays for its maintenance, taking in return a half share of all crops grown.... The size of the area allocated to each family depends on two main factors, primarily the working capacity of the family, secondarily the needs of the family. The number of strips into which the total area is divided and their size depends upon the importance put upon ensuring a fair distribution of good and bad land between families".[13] It cannot be concluded, however, that this process of subdivision of plots is limited in its application to tenant farmers only. Another well documented example refers to an extended family of freeholders owning more than 70 irrigated hectares:

> The distribution of land among the farmers, even though they are all relations, follows the same pattern as in other holdings in the area... Each field...is devoted to a particular crop, and subdivided among the cultivators, into strips. Sometimes each cultivator merely has one strip in each field; sometimes the field is split up into blocks and each cultivator has one strip in each block. This system has striking similarities to the old English open-field system. In this particular village this system appears to have reached an extreme situation. The fields are divided up into blocks of approximately 1½ acres (0.6 ha.) in size and each block is subdivided into three strips; the sheikh's son Hassan has one, rather larger than the other two, which go to his brothers, Hussein and Karmel. The sheikh himself farms an occasional strip at the ends of the fields.
>
> The unit of measurement is the local long-handled digging shovel (*mishah*) some 6-8 ft. (2-2½ m.) long, the width of the block corresponding to approximately 20 handle lengths, 8 of these going to Hassan and 6 each to Hussein and Karmel. The object of this elaborate subdivision is to ensure that each person gets an equal share of the good and bad land.[14]

The pattern encountered here is immediately recognizable as a variant of the *musha*ʿ system of common village tenure, widely known during the late Ottoman period in Syria and Palestine and persisting on a diminishing scale thereafter. Unrecognized in Islamic law as a prescriptive system, its essential features also included periodic reallocations of land to equalize the cultivators' risks and opportunities. The basic allocational unit, named after a yoke of oxen or *faddan*, was the amount of land such a team could plow in a day.[15] *Musha*ʿ villages generally were to be found in transitional areas between fully sedentary, intensively cultivated regions around the larger towns and regions further to the east that were given over to pastoral nomads, and there is some evidence that reallocation occurred most frequently where adequate precipitation to support dry agriculture was most problematical. Larger tribal groupings were little in evidence, but highly fragmented communal fields are described as having been jointly cultivated by *hamula* or clan members whose village residences also tended to coalesce into separate quarters.[16]

The details of the *musha*ʿ system are not of further concern for present purposes. Most of the documented examples of it are geographically as well as culturally distant from southern Iraq, and are found in particular under conditions of dry agriculture rather than irrigation. Yet there are persuasive similarities in the broadly adaptive strategy to which the same institution contributed in contrastive settings. Most immediately apparent to those who have described the system (because this was uppermost in the minds of their informants?) is the equalizing of risks and opportunities. Levelling mechanisms of this kind have much in common with attributes regularly found in what elsewhere have been termed "closed corporate peasant communities".[17] Their essentially defensive functions, in so-called dual societies with central governments exercising repressive control over large, subordinate and impoverished groupings of their subjects, must include helping to maintain the internal solidarity of the latter as a contribution to their common productive needs and even survival.

Yet there is more to be said of the specific adaptive features of *musha*ᶜ villages. A recent, comprehensive analysis of them[18] points out that communal tenure served effectively for a time, in the wake of the enactment of the Ottoman Land Code but surely also earlier, as a strategy of resistance to the state. In particular, it permitted withdrawal, at some cost that could only be met by an institutionalized pattern of sharing that involved the whole community, from the threats of predatory tax-farming and conscription that were concentrated in better favored, intensively settled areas. The *musha*ᶜ pattern also was associated with a careful balance between pastoral and agricultural activities, preserving herding as an alternative mode of subsistence that could be fully supportive during times of crop failure. Both of these features were also of vital importance in the Iraqi setting, although agricultural failure there was linked to the undependability of stream flow and an anarchically maintained irrigation system rather than to variations in rainfall.

At least in Palestine, the *musha*ᶜ strategy must be described as ultimately having failed. Land registration through surrogates and other forms of evasion eventually led to the control of titles not by villagers but by Ottoman officials and urban notables. Large estates were assembled on this basis in the early years of this century, the process gradually spreading outward from the larger towns. All that survived for a time under the new conditions were the traditional methods of rotating land allocation and joint cultivation. In the end, rising market pressures led to the replacement of these too by more rationalized field patterns and other forms of intensification.

However, it should be mentioned that there is at least one strikingly different variant to this process of devolution under the special challenges imposed by modern conditions. Turkmen nomads who settled on the Amik (Amouq) plain in what is now Turkish Hatay in late Ottoman times are today found divided into what another anthropologist has called core and fringe villages. While these physically resemble one another, the fringe villages, like the *musha*ᶜ villages of Palestine, have tended to become socially heterogeneous and to lose control over their lands to outside groups and urban landlords. The core villages, on the other hand, have prospered and increased the lands under their control. What distinguishes the core villages is that they form highly endogamous, corporate units, each built around a strong lineage. Two related strategies apparently contribute to this successful outcome. Internally, egalitarianism is limited to the dominant lineage; others are forced into out-migration or into a dependent, sharecropping status. Externally, the leadership in the core villages has forged effective, vertically oriented alliances with urban officials and notables. Probably the strength and durability of these alliances is only explainable on the basis of the consolidated wealth and power of the core villages themselves, but in any case it has enabled them to withstand repeated government efforts to force the issuance of individual land titles and to stabilize rotation. At least under some circumstances, in other words, a *musha*ᶜ-like strategy apparently can serve not merely as a passive and transitory defense against urban powers but as a more positive and effective response that, beyond survival, even allows expansion and upward mobility.[19]

It is not surprising, in light of these diverse forms of adaptive potential, that various patterns of plot subdivision and reallocation, coupled with a sharing of some cultivation responsibilities by corporate groups, are very widespread in the Near and Middle East. Lambton has catalogued the variant terminology and practices that are found in Khuzistan and all across the Iranian plateau, with the basic term, *juft*, again referring to a yoke of oxen. A particularly full description of local variants is available for the plains around ancient Susa, where both the voluntarily formed groups of tenants and the land they subdivide and cultivate on two- or three-field rotation systems is referred to by the term *bonku*.[20] However, none of this variability can yet be related to differing environmental or historical opportunities and constraints. Hence it serves here merely to underline that communal forms of *de facto* tenure, as distinguished from whatever forms of titular ownership of land may be formally recognized by law, are surely a very ancient, complex and widely occuring institution. They deserve to be taken fully into account in any reconstruction of early Mesopotamian agriculture.

Professor Diakonoff is of course in the forefront of those who in recent decades have made impressive progress toward such a reconstruction. His designation of what he combines to call a "communal-and-private sector" aptly alludes to the fluid continuum between these conceptually distinct forms, corresponding to the recent conditions that have been described above. His primary concern, however, has been to identify the substantial place of this sector in Mesopotamian society of the early and mid-third millennium, although he acknowledges that family communes and other types of corporate communities continued to exist in the Babylonian countryside through the second millennium as well. Thus his general conclusion is that the communal element in this combined sector progressively declined from the terminal third millennium onward, being

> gradually superseded -- at least in the cities -- by individual households, the process starting in the richer strata of society. The communal property rights became more and more dormant, and the process of development tended apparently toward the formation of individual private property.[21]

The foregoing sections of this paper prompt two reflections on this generalization. First, Diakonoff's caveat that the replacement of communal by individual forms of tenure may have been largely concentrated in the cities, unfortunately still the sources of almost all of the evidence, is clearly an essential one. Second, it is once again worth noting with some concern that his focus is rather narrowly on formal property rights, as distinguished from informal, legally unrecognized rights and customs covering access to landed property like those that prevailed until very recently in the Iraqi countryside. Symbolizing the disjunction in legal norms that can occur are the Tribal Disputes Regulations that were first imposed by British authorities in 1918 and then incorporated in the Iraqi Constitution under the monarchy. In having found it administratively necessary to exclude the countryside from the purview of the national law (in spite of considerable agitation against this in the cities), as one authority notes, "Iraq would thus remain legally subject to two norms -- one for the cities and one for the tribal countryside".[22]

Thus there is an alternative possibility deserving consideration, that the role of corporate communities in Mesopotamian agriculture continued to remain a substantial one not only through the second millennium but long beyond it. Their numbers and influence on the course of events were surely subject to fluctuations, but while individually weak such communities seem collectively almost indestructible. They were, in short, both regularly undermined and continually generated anew by a larger context of ecological uncertainty, pressures toward subordination to urban credit and power and resistance to those pressures, and the cyclical coalescence and decay of political and administrative controls imposed by successive dynasties. This alternative reconstruction implies that there may have been only the appearance of a progressive, cumulative decline in the importance of the communal sector after the third millennium.[23] We could largely account for that appearance by reference to the likelihood of an increasing separation between a rigid and artificial legal tradition embodying urban-based definitions of rights to property and the quite different usages with regard to land that continued to be exercised in the villages.

It is the resilience of the system and not its individual components which is critical. Individual villages and even groups of villages were at all times at risk of being more or less forcibly incorporated into larger estates and otherwise losing their corporate character. But we must not lose sight of the inherent biases of the documentary material. It was natural for urban officials or notables to preserve records of transactions in which they took over rights and titles that earlier had been communally held. Such is the case with a group of Middle Assyrian tablets that Diakonoff and others have discussed.[24] But while he stresses the "archaic nature" of a form of land ownership by extended family groups, with both periodic reallocation of plots and provision for substitutability of plot boundaries upon transfer, this combination of features comes persuasively close to constituting an antecedent of the *musha*ᶜ system -- a system, it will be recalled, that was still widespread and vigorous more than three millennia after the time of the documents. Much less to be expected is the presence in urban archives of documents recording the reversals of this process, but that emphatically cannot be taken to mean that such reversals did not occur. Included among them, for example, would have been the slow loss of effective control over their outlying possessions by landowning urban families subject to downward mobility for any reason, not to speak of the erosion on a greater scale affecting a dynasty in the years of its decadence.[25]

The central argument of this paper concerns the probability of rural forms of organization that are not adequately attested in texts. The predisposition of cuneiform sources to focus primarily on urban concerns, and on legally rather than customarily defined rights and obligations, has already been suggested. But incautiously sweeping though the discussion may already have been, it is perhaps worthwhile in conclusion briefly to extend the same approach to social statuses. Just as there is likely to have been a bifurcation between the customary basis of rural tenure and the refracted view of tenure obtained through legal prisms, so the features of individual status that are highlighted in cuneiform sources are likely to be those that conform to the perceptions and limitations -- the 'class view' or even 'ideology', for those who prefer that formulation -- of the groups responsible for ordering and writing the tablets. Characteristic of those perceptions and limitations, it may be suggested, was an overemphasis on criteria of status that articulated closely with the activities and powers of state institutions in an urban setting, and a corresponding underemphasis on less institutionally defined criteria that prevailed among the agricultural peasantry beyond the city walls.

Consider in this light the perennial problem of the coupling of *awīlu* and *muškēnu*. The former is ordinarily identified as a full, relatively high status member of an urban community while definitions of the latter specify not merely his low status and limited civic rights but also obligations of state or temple servitude. These correlates of status may indeed adequately reflect the entire body of known textual references to both terms. But neither definition includes any reference to a fundamental reality of Mesopotamian life in every historic period -- the great social gulf between urban institutions and their rural counterparts. It may well be that this was the way urban elites would have seen the world; for them, what lay beyond the walls probably was mainly more ignorant and primitive, sometimes dangerous, and always potentially exploitable. But must modern scholarship maintain the same skewed perception?

One obvious alternative begins with the realization that the requisite for a *muškēnu* of dependent service within state institutions could not have applied uniformly (if at all) to the entire population of full time cultivators. It would have been far more frequently imposed, of course, on villagers who had been more or less involuntarily brought within the routinely recorded scope of urban-dominated economic or administrative activities than on the surely much larger proportion of the peasant population to whom (as individuals) there are few or no textual references. But more generally, there is very likely to have been a close association of the term *muškēnu* not merely with inferior status but with the outlook and cultural patterns that particularly characterized rural life. If so, apart from presently recognized connotations of the term, it also surely would have had connotations rather like those of modern Iraqi "tribesmen", involving participation in a separate, kin-based, largely extra-urban web of customary allegiances.

My colleague John A. Brinkman has pointed out to me, on the other hand, that a case could conceivably be made for an almost exactly contrary hypothesis. The *awīlu* might have been seen as an individual deriving his rights and revenues from land that he at least participated in cultivating, and the *muškēnu* as a committed urbanite although of inferior status. According to the CAD, he observes in briefly sketching this position,

> the customary opposition in Old Babylonian and earlier times is between the palace/king and the *muškēnu* (primarily an urban opposition) and not between the *awīlu* and the *muškēnu* (which is attested only once or twice outside the Codex Hammurabi and then only in the Old Babylonian period). These terms are not used for designating social classes after Old Babylonian times; *muškēnu* is then used as a synonym for *lapnu*, 'poor', in a poor-rich comparison (*lapnu-šarû*), while *awīlu*/*amīlu* survives as a socio-economic term almost entirely in its abstract form *amīlūtu*, which refers to the person and status of a slave, commonly in an agricultural context. A rather unexpected context for an urbanite?[26]

A definitive choice between these two (and perhaps other) alternatives is unnecessary for present purposes, although the former is certainly easier to reconcile with preponderant concentrations of wealth and status in the cities. Both are at least responsive to the wide ramifications of urban-rural differences in ancient just as in modern Mesopotamia. Both hypothesize corresponding differences in customary usage, only partly or indirectly reflected in most textual references to status. Both seek ways to transcend a strictly scribal viewpoint, even though the best available evidence for doing so will always consist of the material residues of that viewpoint in the form of texts. And both imply that *textual* progress along any of these lines is likely to be more apparent than real unless it is linked to continuing efforts at a generalizing, *contextual* clarification of the relations between cities and their hinterlands.

Already during the formative epoch of Assyriology a great pioneer in modern history and social theory called attention to what he termed "die Scheidung von Stadt und Land". "Mann kann sagen", he continued, "dass die ganze ökonomische Geschichte der Gesellschaft sich in der Bewegung dieses Gegensatzes resümiert".[27] There he broke off, unable at the time to develop the theme further. Perhaps now, more than a century later and with studies of the ancient Orient in full maturity, it should be taken up again on his behalf.

---

1 I.M. Diakonoff, "Socio-economic classes in Babylonia and the Babylonian concept of social stratification" pp. 41-49 (with following discussion) in D.O. Edzard, ed., *Gesellschaftsklassen im Alten Zweistromland und in den angrenzenden Gebieten -- XVIII. Rencontre assyriologique internationale.* [Munich: Bayerische Akademie der Wissenschaften, 1972].

2 M. Civil, "Les limites de l'information textuelle" paper to be included in *L'archéologie de l'Iraq du début de l'époque néolithique à 333 avant notre ère -- Perspectives et limites de l'interprétation anthropologique des documents, Colloque International C.N.R.S. No. 580*, M.T. Barrelet, ed. [Paris: Editions du C.N.R.S.].

3 M. Bloch, *French Rural History,* pp. 35-56 [Berkeley: University of California Press, 1966]; M.M. Postan, ed., "The Agrarian Life of the Middle Ages" pp. 41-42, *The Cambridge Economic History of Europe,* vol. 1, 2nd ed. [Cambridge: Cambridge University Press, 1966]; W.A. Ault, *Open-Field Farming in Medieval England* [London: Allen und Unwin Ltd., 1972].

4 D.N. McCloskey, "English open fields as behavior toward risk" pp. 124-70 in P. Uselding, ed., *Research in Economic History*, vol. 1 (Greenwich, Connecticut: JAI Press, 1976); S. Fenoaltea, "Risk, transaction costs, and the organization of Medieval agriculture" *Explorations in Economic History*, 13 [1976] 129-51; reply and rejoinder *loc. cit.*, 14 [1977] 402-10.

5 A. Jwaideh, "Midhat Pasha and the land system of lower Iraq" pp. 106-36 in *St. Antony's Papers, no. 16, Middle Eastern Affairs,* vol. 3 [1963]; R.McC. Adams and H.J. Nissen, *The Uruk Countryside*, chapter 5 [Chicago: University of Chicago Press, 1972]; R.McC. Adams, "Strategies of maximization, stability, and resilience in Mesopotamian society, settlement, and agriculture", *Proceedings of the American Philosophical Society*, vol. 122 [1978] 329-35.

6 G. Baer, "Land tenure in Egypt and the Fertile Crescent, 1800-1950", pp. 79-90 in C. Issawi, ed., *The Economic History of the Middle East, 1800-1914*, p. 87 [Chicago: University of Chicago Press].

7 S. Haider, "Land Problems of Iraq", pp. 164-78 in Issawi, *op.cit.*

8 P. Sluglett, *Britain in Iraq 1914-1932*, p. 239 [London: Ithaca Press, 1976]; D. Pool, "From elite to class: the transformation of Iraqi political leadership", pp. 63-87 in A. Kelidar, ed., *The Integration*

of Modern Iraq, p. 75 [London: Croom Helm, 1979]; H. Batatu, *The Old Social Classes and the Revolutionary Movements of Iraq*, pp. 78, 86-102 [Princeton: Princeton University Press, 1978].

9 A.P.G. Poyck, "Farm studies in Iraq", *Mededelingen van de Landbouwhogeschool te Wageningen*, vol. 62, no. 1, pp. 56-57.

10 R.A. Fernea, *Shaykh and Effendi*, pp. 43, 97-99 [Cambridge: Harvard University Press].

11 S.M. Salim, *Marsh Dwellers of the Euphrates Delta*, p. 84 [London: Athlone Press].

12 Government of Iraq, Development Board, *Diyala and Middle Tigris Projects. Report No. 2, Lower Diyala Development*, part 3, p. 100 [London: Sir M. MacDonald & Partners].

13 P.E. Naylor, "Farming organization in central Iraq", *Empire Journal of Experimental Agriculture*, vol 29, pp. 19-34, pp. 27, 29.

14 *ibid.*, pp. 24-26.

15 E. Grant, *The People of Palestine*, p. 132 [Philadelphia: J.B. Lippincott, 1921 (reprinted 1976)].

16 D. Warriner, *Land and Poverty in the Middle East*, p. 66 [London: Royal Institute of International Affairs]; A. Granott, *The Land System in Palestine: History and Structure*, pp. 215, 217 [London: Eyre and Spottiswoode].

17 E.R. Wolf, "Closed corporate peasant communities in Mesoamerica and central Java", *Southwestern Journal of Anthropology*, vol. 13 [1957] 1-18.

18 J.D. Held, "The effects of the Ottoman land laws on the marginal population and *musha*ʿ village of Palestine, 1858-1914", Unpublished M.A. thesis, Department of Geography and Center for Middle Eastern Studies, University of Texas, Austin, 1979.

19 B.C. Aswad, "Property Control and Social Strategies in Settlers in a Middle Eastern Plain", pp. 43-44. *Anthropological Papers* No. 44 [Ann Arbor: Museum of Anthropology, University of Michigan, 1971].

20 A.K.S. Lambton, *Landlord and Peasant in Persia*, pp. 5-6, 367-74 [Oxford: Oxford University Press, 1953]; E. Ehlers, "Traditionelle und moderne Formen der Landwirtschaft in Iran", pp. 107-31 *Marburger Geographische Schriften*, Heft 64 [1975].

21 Diakonoff, *op. cit.*, p. 48.

22 Batatu, *op. cit.*, p. 24.

23 Evidence from archaeological surveys may lend some indirect support to this alternative, since it suggests a massive, continuing increase in the proportion of the total settlement area given over to smaller communities from the mid-third millennium until the early first millennium B.C. Cf. R.McC. Adams, *Heartland of Cities: Surveys of Ancient Settlement and Land Use on the Central Floodplain of the Euphrates* [Chicago: University of Chicago Press (in press)].

24 I.M. Diakonoff, "Agrarian conditions in Middle Assyria", pp. 204-34 in I.M. Diakonoff, ed., *Ancient Mesopotamia* [Moscow: Nauka Publishing House, 1969]; cf. J.N. Postgate, "Land tenure in the Middle Assyrian Period: A reconstruction", pp. 496-520 in *Bulletin of the School of Oriental and African Studies*, vol. 34 [1971].

25 N. Yoffee, "The economic role of the crown in the Old Babylonian period", *Bibliotheca Mesopotamica*, vol. 5 [Los Angeles: Undena, 1977].

26 Personal communication.

27 K. Marx, *Das Kapital*, vol. 1, chapter 12, p. 373 [Leipzig: Europäische Verlagsanstalt, 1968].

ZU DEN METAPHERN IN EINEM LIED DER "HEILIGEN HOCHZEIT"

V. Afanasjeva (Leningrad)

S.N. Kramer, der den sumerischen Text UM 29-16-37 veröffentlichte und in einer Gruppe weiterer Texte zum Ritual der sog. "heiligen Hochzeit" bearbeitete,[1] rechnete diese kurze Dichtung zu den Liedern über die "voreheliche Liebeswerbung" ("premarital courting"). Er hat die Schwierigkeiten in der Interpretation der zweiten, symbolisch anmutenden Hälfte des Textes klar gesehen und vermutete dabei eine sexuelle Symbolik der mit den Worten ^{na_4}š u b a, "š u b a-Stein" und u r$_{11}$(URU$_4$ = APIN), "pflügen" gebildeten Ausdrücke.[2]

Wohl trifft seine Deutung des Textes im ganzen zu. Die erste Hälfte der Dichtung (Z. 1-22) trägt einen allgemein-alltäglichen Charakter: Es wird in diesen Zeilen die Liebesneckerei der Göttin Inanna/Innin mit ihrem Geliebten Amaušumgalanna (Dumuzi) beschrieben. Die zweite Hälfte (Z. 23-45) ist weniger verständlich, vor allem wegen der kaum durchsichtigen Wendungen, die verschiedene Handlungen andeuten. Diese Handlungen beziehen sich alle irgendwie auf den š u b a-Stein.

Auf den ersten Blick hat man den Eindruck, die zweite Hälfte des Textes hängt nicht unmittelbar mit der ersten zusammen,[3] obwohl die Z. 23 f. eindeutig als Verbindung oder Überführung dienen, sie erklären nämlich, was geschah und was noch kommen wird:[4]

"Die Worte, die gesprochen wurden, sie sind Worte der Begierde, mit dem Streit kommt Begierde im Herzen auf."

Die zweite Hälfte des Textes ist in Metaphern und Wortspielen aufgebaut, deren nähere Betrachtung -- die Entzifferung ihres Sinnes -- erlaubt uns erst, die inneren Zusammenhänge der beiden Textteile aufzudecken.

Wenden wir uns zuerst den Z. 25 f. zu, die das Thema der š u b a-Steine einführen:[5]

^{na_4}š u b a - k e$_4$ ^{na_4}š u b a - k e$_4$ ^{na_4}š u b a n a - u r$_{11}$- r u

^{d}a m a - u š u m g a l - a n - n a ^{na_4}š u b a - k e$_4$ ^{na_4}š u b a n a - u r$_{11}$- r u

S.N. Kramer gibt zu dieser Stelle die folgende Übersetzung:[6]

"He of the š u b a-stones, he of the š u b a-stones, plows the š u b a-stones.

Amaušumgalanna, he of the š u b a-stones, he of the š u b a-stones, plows the š u b a-stones."

Diese Übersetzung lässt sich ohne weiteres etwas verbessern. Die Verwendung des Ergativs (Agentivs),[7] ferner die ganz folgerichtige grammatische Unterscheidung zwischen dem "Subjekt" und dem "Objekt" der Handlung (die beide mit dem Wort ^{na_4}š u b a ausgedrückt sind) als ^{na_4}š u b a - k e$_4$ und ^{na_4}š u b a, veranlässt uns, diese Worte hier für zwei verschiedene Begriffe zu halten. Die

Frage ist, ob beide Bedeutungen ermittelbar sind.

Die Zusammensetzungen mit dem Wort ^{na4}š u b a sind in der monumentalen Wortliste u r_5(ḪAR) - r a = *ḫubullu*, Taf. XVI und Vorläufer,[8] unter den verschiedensten Amulettsteinen und Siegeln[9] aufgezählt.[10] ^{na4}š u b a(ZA-MÚŠ) = *šubû* heisst eine Art Stein, wohl ein (Halb-) Edelstein, vielleicht Achat,[11] aus welchem u. a. Rollsiegel, Amulette usw. geschliffen wurden.

Das Verb u r_{11}(URU_4 = APIN), welches an dieser Stelle neben dem Wort ^{na4}š u b a gebraucht wird, heisst eigentlich, wie auch das Wortzeichen in seiner ursprünglichen Form zeigt,[12] "pflügen", aber wohl auch "aufbrechen", "durchbohren" u. ä., d. h. "durchbrechen", "etwas hindurchbekommen". Man kann annehmen, dass hier die Rede über bestimmte Steinzylinder ist,[13] mit deren Hilfe andere Steine durchbohrt werden können.[14]

Das Wort (^{na4})š u b a hat ferner noch eine andere Bedeutung, zumindest im Akkadischen: es wird ebenfalls mit dem Wort *ḫalpû*, "Brunnen" übersetzt.[15] Dem dritten Vorkommen des Wortes ^{na4}š u b a der hier behandelten Zeile, dem "Objekt" der Handlung, liegt, wie wir annehmen können, eben diese Bedeutung des Wortes zugrunde. "Brunnen" verstehen wir hier als "Steinöffnung".

Wenn unsere Vermutung zutrifft, lassen sich die Z. 25 f. auf folgende Weise übersetzen:

"Der Steinzylinder, der Steinzylinder durchbricht die Steinöffnung,
Amaušumgalanna, der Steinzylinder, durchbricht die Steinöffnung."

Für diese Deutung spricht u.E. auch der Umstand, dass das Wort *ḫalpû* eine Assoziation mit *ḫaštu/ḫaltu*, "Loch", "Grube"[16] hervorrufen können hat. In diesem Fall hat, meinen wir, keine entscheidende Bedeutung, dass die betreffenden Worte akkadisch sind: Der Text stammt sowieso aus der Zeit der umfassenden sumerisch-akkadischen Zweisprachigkeit, wenn nicht gerade seine Abfassung, doch die vorliegende Abschrift.

Auf diese Weise kann man für sicher halten, dass unser Text Metapher verwendet, und zwar Metapher mit sexueller Bedeutung: er spricht über den Verlust der Jungfräulichkeit;[17] dies wird mit dem Durchbohren des Steines verglichen.

Im gleichen Sinn können auch die Z. 29 f. interpretiert werden:

[... a ù r] - r a l á - l á a ù r - r a m u - n a - a b - l á -*[l á]*

[... a b à d] - d a l á - l á a b à d - d a m u - n a - a b - l á - l á

"Wasser, das Dach bespritzendes, Wasser wird für sie spritzen,
Wasser, die Wand bespritzendes, Wasser wird für sie spritzen."

Auch in diesen Zeilen wird der geschlechtliche Akt gemeint, nur gebraucht der Dichter statt der Beschreibung die Metapher. Das Wort a, "Wasser", kann übrigens auch "Samen" o. ä. bedeuten, es sei hier nur auf Wendungen wie etwa a - r i - a = *reḫû*, "begatten, zeugen, sich ergiessen" hingewiesen. Es ist ferner nicht ausgeschlossen, dass auch hier die durch Homonymie verursachte Assoziation der Wörter u r_{11}, "'pflügen'" (des Hauptwerbs dieses Abschnittes), ù r, "Dach" und ú r, "Schoss" bzw. b à d, "Wand" und b a d, "öffnen", "Öffnung" usw. mit in Kauf genommen werden kann. Die metaphorische Bedeutung der angeführten Ausdrücke ist jedoch auch ohnehin klar und eindeutig.

Und nun bekommt die im Text nächstfolgende Z. 31 einen ganz konkreten und genauen Sinn:

d a[m - a - n i[18] ... ^{d}]a m a - u š u m g a l - a n - n a - r a gù - m u - n a - d é -[e]

"[Seine Ehe]frau [...] sprich[t] zu Amaušumgalanna."

In den darauffolgenden Zeilen wird weiterhin mit dem Motiv gespielt; es folgen Fragen und Antworten der Neuverheirateten. Die parallel gebauten Z. 34 f.[19] verdienen eine besondere Aufmerksamkeit:

na_4 š u b a -[n a] na_4 š u[b a] - t u r - t u r - b i š i - p a - ág - m e NE - a

na_4 š u b a - n a na_4 š u[b a] - g a l - g a l - b i g a b a - k ù - m e NE - a

"(... für wen 'pflügt' er)
die kleineren unter seinen š u b a-Steinen, die unsere Kehle geschmückt haben,
die grossen unter seinen š u b a-Steinen, die unsere helle Brust geschmückt haben?"[20]

Diese Zeilen beziehen sich auf das Durchbohren der kleineren und grösseren Steine, Schmuck für den Hals ("Kehle") und Brust.[21] Dieser kann eventuell auch eine symbolische Bedeutung haben, vielleicht als Brautschmuck, der erst nach Vollführung des Heiratsaktes angezogen werden konnte.[22] In diesem Zusammenhang möchten wir uns auf ethnographische Parallelen berufen, etwa auf das Kopftuch der russischen Frauen, oder die beiden Frauenzöpfe, im Unterschied zu dem einzigen Zopf der jungen Mädchen, der Jungfrauen.

Eine ähnlich konkrete Bedeutung gewinnt auch die Z. 37:

n u - u_8- g i g - g a - àm d a m - m u n u - u_8- g i g - g a - àm ...

"Von jetzt an/Wahrlich ist sie Hierodule, meine Frau, sie ist Hierodule ..."

Diese Worte klingen wie eine Formel der Eheschliessung, die bei dem Heiratsakt gesprochen wird.

Die Z. 38-45 enthalten wieder einen spielerischen Streit zwischen Inanna und ihrem Geliebten, aber der Wechsel im Gebrauch des pronominalen Elements weist auf Teilnahme einer anderen Person, nämlich des Anführers,[23] oder auch eines Chors hin.

Gleich am Beginn zeigt der Text, dass an der Handlung mehrere Personen teilnehmen.[24] Drei von diesen sind ganz leicht fassbar: die Göttin Inanna, ihr Geliebter Amaušumgalanna und der Anführer. Die Textabschnitte des Anführers können aber ohne weiteres in zwei Teile getrennt werden: auf Partien des Anführers selbst und auf solche eines Chors; zu den letzteren könnten eventuell die Refrains gehören. Oder man könnte gleich an zwei Chöre denken: an den Chor des Bräutigams und den der Braut.[25] Manches davon, was hier der Göttin Inanna zugeschrieben wird, kann mit gleichem Recht als Worte eines Frauenchors aufgefasst werden, so z. B. die Z. 1 f. (s. - m e, "unser"), Z. 34 f. (s. wiederum - m e) u. a.

Auf Grund dieser Überlegungen möchten wir den Text auf die folgende Weise in elementare Abschnitte zerlegen:

Z. 1-6: Der Monolog Inannas (bzw. Z. 1-2: Frauenchor; Z. 3-6: Die Worte Inannas).
Z. 7-22: Die Antwort Amaušumgalannas an Inanna, von welcher jede vierte Zeile

von einem männlichen Chor übernommen oder wiederholt werden könnte.
Z. 23-24: Die Worte des Anführers.
Z. 25-30: Die Partien des Chors oder der beiden Chöre (bei der letzteren Möglichkeit: Z. 25-28: männlicher Chor; Z. 29-30: Frauenchor).
Z. 31: Der Anführer.
Z. 32-35: Die Rede Inannas; es kann aber sein, dass der Göttin nur die Z. 32 gehört, und Z. 33-35 werden in diesem Fall von dem Frauenchor vorgetragen.
Z. 36: Der Anführer.
Z. 37: Amaušumgalanna.
Z. 38-42: Der Chor bzw. die beiden Chöre.
Z. 43-44: Inanna.
Z. 45: Die abschliessenden Worte des Chors.

Die Annahme eines Frauenchors wird eigentlich dadurch erschwert, dass der Text nur wenige Emesal-Formen[26] gebraucht; s. jedoch Z. 1-6, den Monolog Inannas bzw. des Frauenchors und der Göttin, beide mit eindeutigen Emesal-Formen wie etwa das Phonem |g̃| in den Präfixketten,[27] Z. 3 f. mit g a š a n statt n i n, "Herrin", Z. 43 f., ebenso die Worte Inannas, mit m e - a - a m statt s i p a, "Hirte".[28] Dabei kommt der Emesal-Form š i - p a - á g statt z i - p a - á g, "Kehle",[29] eine besondere Bedeutung in Z. 34 zu: gerade hinsichtlich dieser Zeile haben wir an einen Frauenchor gedacht.

ANET = J.B. Pritchard (ed.), *Ancient Near Eastern Texts relating to the Old Testament, Supplement* [Princeton 1969].

PAPS = *Proceedings of the American Philosophical Society*

SRT = E. Chiera, *Sumerian Religious Texts* [Upland, Pa. 1924]

---

1 S.N. Kramer, *Cuneiform Studies and the History of Literature: The Sumerian Sacred Marriage Texts*, PAPS 107 [1963] 485-527, bes. 490a (Bemerkungen zum Inhalt), 493 ff., Nr. 1 (Umschrift, Übersetzung und kurzer Kommentar), 517 f., Fig. 1-2 (Foto). Siehe noch seine Übersetzung allein in ANET, Suppl. [1969] 637 f., ferner die z. T. paraphrasierende Übersetzung in seinem Buch, *The Sacred Marriage Rite, Aspects of Faith, Myth, and Ritual in Ancient Sumer* [Bloomington - London 1969] 72 f. - Den Text hat kürzlich C. Wilcke neubearbeitet: *Formale Gesichtspunkte in der sumerischen Literatur*, in *Sumerological Studies in Honor of Th. Jacobsen* (AS 20) [Chicago - London 1976], 205-316, bes. 293 ff.: "*Exkurs: Ein* k u n - g a r-*Lied Inanna's*".

2 Gegen diese Deutung wendet sich C. Wilcke, AS 20, 315. Siehe bereits W.H. Ph. Römer, in *lišān mithurti, Festschrift W. F. v. Soden*... (AOAT 1) [Kevelaer - Neukirchen-Vluyn 1969] 294.

3 Für die scharfe Zweiteilung des Textes s. C. Wilcke, AS 20, 304 ff.

4 Die deutsche Übersetzung in Anlehnung an unsere russische Übersetzung des Textes in: *Poèzija i proza drevnego Vostoka* [Moskva 1973] 141 f. (Übersetzung), 666 f. (Kommentar).

5 Die Lautwerte in der Umschrift nach R. Borger. *Assyrisch-babylonische Zeichenliste* (AOAT 33) [Kevelaer - Neukirchen-Vluyn 1978].

6 S.N. Kramer. PAPS 107, 494.

7 Zum Ergativ im Sumerischen s. I.M. Diakonoff, *Jazyki drevnej Perednej Azii*

[Moskva 1967] 29 ff.; ders., *The Ergative Construction in the Languages of the Ancient East* (XXVII International Congress of Orientalists. Papers Presented by the U.S.S.R. Delegation) [Moscow 1967]; ders., *Hurrisch und Urartäisch* [München 1971] 1-4; ders., in AS 20 [1976] 116 ff.; ferner D.A. Foxvog: *The Sumerian Ergative Construction*, Or NS 44 (1975) 395-425.

8 B. Landsberger - M. Civil - E. Reiner, MSL X [Roma 1970].

9 Vgl. die sich ständig wiederholende Gruppe n a$_4$-/^{na_4}k i š i b-..., n a$_4$-/^{na_4}l a g a b-..., n a$_4$-/^{na_4}é l l a g-..., d. h. *kunukku*, *šibirtu*, *takpītu*, "Siegel", "Stück, Block", "eine ... Gemme" (zu den akkadischen Worten s. W. v. Soden: AHw 507 f., 1227, 1308 resp.), die mit verschiedensten Gesteinsnamen erweitert sein konnte.

10 Siehe die "^{na_4}š u b a-Sektionen" in den Wortlisten: u r$_5$- r a XVI 162 ff. (MSL X, S. 9, vgl. S. 20 f. mit Kommentar); Ras Shamra Recension 126 ff. (MSL X, S. 42); Late Old Babylonian Forerunner 13 ff. (MSL X, S. 51) und 67 ff. (MSL X, S. 52); Forerunner from Nippur 8 ff. (MSL X, S. 54 f.) und 65 ff. (MSL X, 56 f.); Miscellaneous Forerunner from Kisurra II 4 ff. (MSL X, S. 62, vgl. kürzlich B. Kienast, *Die altbabylonischen Briefe und Urkunden aus Kisurra* [Wiesbaden 1978] I, Taf. 76, Nr. 181); Uruanna, Chapter n a$_4$- k a l a g - g a, Rec. A-B 11 f. (MSL X, S. 69); Rec. C 40 und 42 f. (MSL X, S. 71); Rec. D 15′ f. (MSL X, S. 72); vgl. ausserdem die Liste von Amulettsteinen A 231 I 19, 23, 30, II 18, 27 (K. Yalvaç. *Eine Liste von Amulettsteinen im Museum zu Istanbul*, in *Studies in Honor of B. Landsberger* (AS 16) [Chicago 1965] 329-333, s. 332 f.); das Wort kommt auch in einem geographischen Namen vor: Miscellaneous Geographical List 2 R 50 Rs. (!) III 12 (MSL XI, S. 56): íd šu-ba!$_{\text{š u b a}}$ = íd ^{d}DUMU.ZI (s. auch ŠL 586,41).

11 Vgl. Akk. *šubû* (s. dazu W. v. Soden: AHw 1258 s. v.); Hebr. *šᵉbō* (Ex. 28: 19; 39:12); s. [G. G.] Boson, in: RLA 2 [1938] 268a. -- In Ausdrücken wie *d u$_6$- š u b a heisst das Wort š u b a doch wohl "Achat" o. ä. (anders Å. W. Sjöberg, *The Collection of the Sumerian Temple Hymns* (TCS 3) [Locust Valley, N.Y. 1969] 96). Dagegen ist der Ausdruck ^{d}u t u ... *š u b a - k a l a m - m a u. ä. (Å. W. Sjöberg: a. a. O.), in welchem š u b a nur "Licht" u. ä. bedeuten kann, u. E. als (fehlerhafte) sumerische Interpretation aufzufassen; es sind vielleicht *šūpû* (*wapû* Š) und *šubû* verwechselt worden.

12 R. Labat. *Manuel d'épigraphie akkadienne* [Paris 1976] Nr. 56.

13 C. Wilcke, AS 20, 315 kommt auch zu dem Schluss, das Wort "pflügen" ist "eindeutig auf die Gewinnung der Steine bezogen -- freilich in einem Bild, das der Feldbestellung entlehnt ist". Er denkt dabei an "das Auffädeln der Edelsteine zu einer Halskette" (ebd.).

14 Zur Technik der Durchbohrung härterer Steine s. den für uns exemplarischen Fall des Lazursteins bei M. Tosi -- M. Piperno, *Lithic Technology behind the Ancient Lapis Lazuli Trade*, *Expedition* 16 [1973] 15-23: M. Tosi, *Gedanken über den Lasursteinhandel des 3. Jahrtausends v. u. Z. im iranischen Raum*, *Acta Ant. Hung.* 22 [1974] = Wirtschaft und Gesellschaft im alten Vorderasien [Budapest 1976] 33-43, bes. Abb. 1-2; vgl. Ph. L. Kohl, *A Note on Chlorite Artefacts from Shahr-i Sokhta*, *East and West* NS 27 [1977] 111-127.

15 Zu *ḫalpû*, "Brunnen" s. CAD Ḫ 49b s. v. *ḫalpû* B; W. v. Soden: AHw 313a s.

v. *ḫalpium*, *ḫalpû* II. Zu den sumerischen Entsprechungen s. auch CAD 49b s. v. *ḫalpû* C, discussion (vgl. W. v. Soden: AHw 313b und 518b s. v. *kutpû*; s. dazu CAD K 610 s.v. *kutpû*).

16 Zu *ḫaštu/ḫaltu* s. CAD Ḫ 143 s. v.; vgl. W. v. Soden: AHw 334.

17 Im allgemeinen s. B. Landsberger: *Jungfräulichkeit...*, in *Symbolae ... M. David*, II [Leiden 1968] 41-105.

18 C. Wilcke, AS, 295: 31 und 300 s. v. möchte M[UNUS ...] lesen; u. M. n. passt aber die Lesung S.N. Kramers d a[m - a - n i ...] besser in den Zusammenhang. DAM beginnt sowieso mit MUNUS.

19 Von Z. 32 an steht uns auch ein Duplikat zur Verfügung: PRAK C 94, identifiziert von J. Krecher, in *Heidelberger Studien zum Alten Orient* [Wiesbaden 1967] 106 (PRAK C 49 ist hier Druckfehler für 94!) und (unabhängig) B. Alster, RA 67 [1973] 109: "Notes brèves, Nr. 1"; s. auch C. Wilcke, AS 20, 294: "Text B".

20 Für die Übersetzung s. C. Wilcke, AS 20, 296.

21 Wohl gehört in diesen Zusammenhang die bereits von W.H. Ph. Römer in *lišān mitḫurti*, *Festschrift W. F. v. Soden...* (AOAT 1) [Kevelaer -- Neukirchen-Vluyn 1969] 293 ff. hinzugezogene Stelle im Nininsina-Hymnus SRT 6 // 7, nämlich Z. 66-69 (SRT 6, II 26-29 = 7, 3-6):

u$_4$- b a ú n u - š u b a n u - g á l - l a - à m
ú n u - š u b a g ú - a n u - g á l - l a - à m
^{d}n i n - i n - s i - n a - k e$_4$ i n i m - e b í - i b - s ì - g e
š u b a n a - u r u$_4$^{ru} n u m u n - e - e š n a - g á - g á

"Damals gab es keinen Schmuck aus š u b a-Stein,
es wurde kein Schmuck aus š u b a-Stein am Hals getragen,
Nininsina erfindet ihn,
š u b a-Steine pflügt sie, macht sie zu Samen."

(Umschrift und Übersetzung, mit schlichten Modifizierungen, nach W.H. Ph. Römer, a. W. 293; zur lexikalischen Deutung s. ebd. 293 f.) Hier ist eindeutig über die Erfindung (*i n i m - a s ì (g), s. J. van Dijk, JCS 19 [1965] 12; W.H. Ph. Römer. a. W. 294) des Schmuckes aus š u b a-Stein die Rede; "pflügen" ist dabei, wie in unserem Text, etwa "durchbohren" o. ä.; n u m u n, "Same" ist etwa der Prototyp aller ähnlichen Schmucke. (Für parallele Bildungen s. J. Krecher, *Sumerische Kultlyrik* [Wiesbaden 1966] 206.)

22 Zu den Heiratszeremonien in Mesopotamien s. S. Greengus, *Old Babylonian Marriage Ceremonies and Rites*, JCS 20 [1966] 55-72.

23 Man denke etwa an den n i m g i r - s i = *susapinnu*, für dessen Rolle in Heiratszeremonien s. S. Greengus, JCS 20 [1966] 68 ff. Für Worte, die Personen mit einer ähnlichen Rolle bezeichnen könnten, s. Erimḫuš V 75 ff. u. Parallelen (zitiert von W.G. Lambert, *Babylonian Wisdom Literature* [Oxford 1960] 339f.; CAD A II, 144 s. v. *ansamullu*).

24 Siehe gleich das erste Wort des Textes: a m a - m e, "unsere Mutter".

25 Vgl. C. Wilcke, AS 20, 310 ff.: "Sprecher und Haltungen", wo ausser Inanna und Amaušumgalla mit einer oder mehreren ungenannten Schwester(n) der Göttin, ferner mit einem "Sprecher" gerechnet wird. Sein "ungenannter Sprecher" entspricht eigentlich unserem Anführer. Die "Schwestern" Inannas bei C. Wilcke, d. h. die Begleiterinnen der Göttin, könnten dem von

uns vermuteten Frauenchor zugerechnet werden. Das Wort "Schwester" ist ja nicht buchstäblich zu nehmen. Zu den Schwestern Inannas s. A. Falkenstein, ZA 56 (NF 22) [1964] 45, Anm. 7; W.H. Ph. Römer, a. W. 293.

26 Zum Begriff Emesal s. J. Krecher, *Sumerische Kultlyrik* [Wiesbaden 1966] 12 ff.; ders., *Zum Emesal-Dialekt des Sumerischen*, In *Heidelberger Studien zum Alten Orient* [Wiesbaden 1967] 87-110; und bes. I.M. Diakonoff, in AS 20 [1976] 113 ff.

27 Siehe J. Krecher, in *Heidelberger Studien zum Alten Orient* [Wiesbaden 1967] 105 (auch zu unserer Stelle).

28 Vgl. C. Wilcke, AS 20, 309 f.: "Dialekt-Ebene".

29 Siehe C. Wilcke, AS 20, 310.

TWO IRANIAN WORDS, GEORGIAN *ZVARA* AND *VARZ-I*

H.W. Bailey (Cambridge)

I am pleased to make this small offering to Professor I.M. Diakonoff, for, though he is an Assyriologist primarily, he has worked at the Parthian Nisa Documents and may have an interest in these two contributions to the material life of early Iran.

I

There is a word[1] which has baffled scholars for many years, found in various forms of Iranian origin, but in every case unusually transmitted. The Georgian had taken from the Armenian *zuarak'-i*, *zvarak'-i*, and without the *k'*, as often[2], has also *zvara* used of the young bullock used for sacrifice, in the Old Testament translation. The Swanetian has *zorāk'*. But Georgian has also a word direct from Parthian Iranian, not via Armenian, in *azaver-i*, *azavir-i* 'ox, bullock as beast of burden', explained by *samušak'o xari* 'working ox' and *sabargo xari* 'loaded ox'. In the epic Vepxis t'qaosani 464 *azavrebi vaazavre* 'I loaded the oxen' has the verbal *azavreba* (misprinted *azarveba* in Chubinov, ed. 2).

From this *azaver-* the Parthian can be reconstructed as **uz-bara-* or **uz-bārya-* (in final position Iranian *-ar-* was taken over as *-er-* distinct from *-ār-* to *-ar-*). Parthian has developed the old preverb *uz-* to *az-* (or possibly *əz-*), written *ʻz-* and *ʼz-*. The intrusive *-a-* between *-z-* and *-v-* is like that in Armenian loan-word *čaxarak* 'wheel'.

The Armenian had *zouarak* 'bullock for sacrifice' in the Old Testament.

Such an Iranian *uz-bar-* 'to bear up, lift up' could mean 'to load', although neither Avestan *uz-bar-* 'to put on (clothes)' nor Old Indian *ud-bhar-* seems to be known as 'to load'. For 'to load' Khotan Saka has *drays-* (*darz-*, *draz-*) which renders Buddhist Sanskrit *upanāmaya-* and *āropaya-*. From *uz-bar-* 'load' either **uz-bāra-*, or **uz-bara-* or **uz-baraθra-* could result in *uzβār* or *uzbahr*. The second case is like Georgian *bar-i* and Armenian *bah* 'spade' from **barθra-* (see on *bēl*, in the *Henning Memorial Volume* 31).

The expected form in Zoroastrian Pahlavī would be **uzbār* or **uzbahr*. It occurs however spelled *zbhl* (or *zb'l*), that is, without the initial *u-*, as if it had developed like the Parthian to *əz-* and then lost the vowel. The Pāzand, *zabar*, if it has any basis, would suit rather **uzbahra-*. For the Georgian passage the Ossetic translation has *samadton uärγtä äz galtil* 'I placed loads on the oxen'. For the beast of burden the Khotan Saka had the epithet *vgstairma* for the *stūra-* 'large beasts', from **ava-stārmya-*.

The huge Shire Horses of England would suit the **(u)zβahr* horse whom the context states to be the largest (*mas*).

This recognition of the largest horse is a gain for the world of workers in ancient Iran, Georgia and Armenia.

II

The replacement of Old Iranian initial *u̯-* is various in later sources. The New Persian has *b-* in *bad-*, *vata-* 'bad', *bād*, *vāta-* 'wind', but also *gurz* 'club', *vazra-*, and *gurāz* 'boar', *varāza-*. For *vi-*, *vr̥-*, *gu-* was developed as in *gurg* 'wolf', Avestan *vəhrka-*, Khotan Saka *birgga-*, *bärga-*, and *guzīdan* 'to choose', *vi-čai-*. Balōčī has *gw-* in *gwat*, *gwāt* and *gi-* from *vi-*, *gičinag*. Khotan Saka has usually *b-* (= β) *birgga-* 'wolf', *bāta-* 'wind', but *gu-* from *vi-* as in *gvar-* 'to open' from *vi-var-*, and sometimes without change in *vara* 'courtyard'. For *vart-s-* 'turn' both *gęs-* and *bęs-* occur. In Ossetic the *u̯-* normally remains. But there are some words with *b-* as *biyun* 'twist', *bedun* 'appear', *barä* 'will', *särē-barä* 'free'. From *vi-* the result was Digoron *i-* (with occasional loss of *i-*) and Iron loss, except that after new preverbs the *i̯-* is present. There are also some words with *g-* from *v-*. Thus *goren*, Iron *gärän* 'enclosure', (connected with Abkhaz *gwara* and *bora* 'stall') with Khotan Saka *vara* 'court'; and in *guppur*, older *visa(s)-puθra-* 'sons of the House', a title of nobility.

This *u̯-* to *g-* can be seen also in *gärzä*, Iron *gärz* 'tool', whence also Chechen and Inguš *gerz* 'weapon'. This word is fairly certainly from the base *varz-* 'to work', and so *varza-* 'tool'. The base is very familiar in the Avesta and has survived in one word in Khotan Saka *valys-*, and is in Parthian and Sogdian. From the same base Greek has *ergon* 'work' and *organon* 'tool'.

In Georgian in the 10th century Old Testament translation, *varz-i* translates the Greek *enkheiridion* 'dagger'.

There is also the word *vazr-i* 'a cutting instrument, weapon'. This is Avestan *vazra-* 'a weapon with 100 edges (*satō.dāra-*)'. It became in New Persian *gurz* and is used for a 'club, mace', but still a weapon of war. The Georgian also uses *gurz-i*.

A. Shanidze[3] has thought over the problem of these words *varz-i* and *vazr-i* and decided that there was the one word *vazr-i*. But he has no reference to the Iranian base *varz-*. The 10th century date seems also rather early to suspect confusion of *vazr-* to *varz-*. His article has however important information on the several passages and dictionary references.

---

1 Listed in H. Ačarean, *Hayerēn armatakan bararan*, ed. 2, 1973. Add B.T. Anklesaria, *Zand-ākāsīh*, 1956, p. 119, 10, and D. MacKenzie, *Concise Pahlavi Dictionary*, 1971, both have *zibāl* 'swift' (the latter with note "early New Persian", but without reference). Both ignore the Pāzand, and fail the context.

2 Thus *zirak'-i*, *zira* 'cumin'; *danak'-i*, *dana* 'knife' (base Iranian *dā-* 'to cut' beside *dā-s-* in Ossetic *dāsun* 'to cut', and Armenian *dašnak* 'dagger', New Persian *dašnah*); *ešmak'-i*, *ešma* 'demon', Armenian *hešmak*, Avestan *aēšma-*; *mušak'-i*, *muša* 'workman', Armenian *mšak* 'farmer', to Khotan Saka *miṣa-* 'field'.

3 A. Shanidze, *From the lexicon of old Georgian*, Mecnierebata ak'ademiis xelnac'erta inst'it'ut'is moambe, II, 1960, 56-58.

LA CREATION DE L'HOMME ET SA NATURE DANS LE POEME D'ATRAḪASÎS

J. Bottéro (Paris)

I.M. Diakonoff sait fort bien, comme tous les sages, qu'à la différence de l'Arithmétique, où tout le monde est unanime pour proclamer que deux et deux font quatre, l'Histoire, résultante d'une combinaison: de documents, en bonne règle univoques et immuables, et d'historiens, multiples, divers, prisonniers chacun de son optique, et labiles, ondoie et se multiplie constamment au gré de ces derniers - c'est même un de ses intérêts et de ses charmes! Il ne m'en voudra donc pas si, en hommage à sa compétence et sa curiosité universelles, non moins qu'en témoignage d'une vieille amitié, je ne lui présente ici qu'une nouvelle démonstration de cette variabilité indéfinie, en formulant une opinion de plus à propos d'une *crux* fameuse.

Il s'agit, dans le *Poème* vieux-babylonien d'*Atraḫasîs*[1] (I:[171]-248), plus précisément du passage où *Enki* révèle (I:204-219), puis fait exécuter (220-230) le plan qu'il a conçu pour mettre au point un "instrument de travail" destiné à prendre le relais des "dieux-ouvriers", après le refus des *Igigu* de poursuivre leur lourde et fastidieuse besogne de "producteurs" aux ordres d'une aristocratie de "purs consommateurs".

Ce plan, sans doute l'a-t'il déjà amorcé dans la partie perdue ([171-188]), à la fin de laquelle il en a désigné l'exécutrice: "*Bêlit-ilî*-la-Matrice" (189), et l'objet: "l'Homme (*awîlu*), qui doit assumer la corvée des dieux" (190-1). Et ces derniers, convaincus, ont fait appel à la déesse, qu'ils interpellent comme "la Sage-femme divine, *Mami*-l'Experte" (193; elle porte aussi le nom de *Nintu*: 198; 211; 226....).

De cet Homme (*awîlu*: 197; et cf. 194), il n'est d'abord question de préparer qu'un *prototype*. Dans ce pays de techniciens, on savait qu'avant de lancer la fabrication "standardisée" d'un produit, il était nécessaire d'en agencer avec soin l'étalon, ou le moule. C'est pourquoi, transposant cette précaution usuelle dans la mythologie de l'anthropogonie, on avait imaginé, sorti en premier des mains des créateurs, ce que l'on appelait le *lullû*: "l'original humain" (et non pas simplement "l'homme": *man*, comme traduit CAD L 242a s.v.; dans le mythe sumérien d'Enki et Ninmaḫ: 28 et 34, il porte le nom de s i g $_7$ - e n - s i g $_7$ - š á r). Cet original n'était naturellement pas différent des *awîlû* futurs: ce n'en était, ni un avorton, ni une caricature (*izbu*; *kûbu*), mais seulement l'archétype, réalisé: "fabriqué" (*banû*: 195; aussi II:9 de l'autre version aB: CT 44, 20; et 4 du fragment nA: K 6634 - *Atr.* p.56; dans *Enûma eliš*, on trouve *banû* en VI:7, et son quasi-synonyme *šuzzuzu*: "susciter", à la ligne précédente) en premier, avant que l'on passât à la production en série. Ici, c'est à la déesse désignée par *Enki* qu'il revenait de le façonner. Ensuite, seulement, une fois ledit prototype approuvé (223-248), commencerait la "fabrication en gros" ([271]-306), toujours sous la direction de la "Sage-femme des dieux", en quatorze "Matrices" (277; et cf. K 3399+:5 sqq., dans *Atr.* pp.60-1): sept pour les hommes, et sept pour les femmes, lesquels couples pourraient dès lors propager à eux seuls l'Humanité, par la génération commune.

Pour réaliser le *lullû* que lui réclament les dieux, *Nintu* en appelle à l'inventeur, *Enki*, seul capable, assure-t'elle, de lui fournir en état la *materia ex qua* (198-203). La confection de l'Homme posait en effet un problème: pour accomplir parfaitement et indéfectiblement la tâche à laquelle on le destinait, il devait se trouver, tout ensemble, le plus proche possible des dieux qu'il allait suppléer, mais assez différencié pour qu'il ne lui vînt pas, quelque jour, à l'idée de réclamer, lui aussi, après les *Igigu*, au nom d'une identité de nature, une identité de destin: le droit au non-travail. *Enki* l'a fort bien compris, en calculant la "formule" de l'Homme. C'est pourquoi il entend lui donner pour substance la matière universelle de tout ce qui compose le monde sublunaire: la terre, l'argile (*ṭiddu*: 203; 211; 266, etc.), à la fois l'emblème et la cause du caractère terrestre et périssable des choses, puisque, à la mort, toutes "retourneraient en l'argile" (AHw 1392a s.v.:6). Ainsi sera garantie la mortalité des hommes: leur différence fondamentale d'avec les dieux, leur diversité de *nature*, et par conséquent de *destin*.

Mais puisque, d'autre part, il était indispensable de conférer à l'Homme les prérogatives requises par son état de remplaçant des dieux, Enki va donc introduire en lui quelque chose de divin: il préconise, en humidifiant l'argile humaine pour la pétrir et la modeler, d'y "incorporer", d'y "mélanger" (*balâlu*, *bullulu*: 211//226; et cf. 231; *butallulu*, passif, en 212) "la chair et le sang d'un dieu", autrement dit sa substance (210//225; "la chair", dans 215//228) - un dieu qu'il faudra sacrifier dans ce but. On prendra occasion, car décidément *Enki* pense à tout, d'une fête comportant "lustration avec bain" (206-7//221-2), ce qui permettra aux dieux, non seulement de se retrouver tous réunis, y compris la future victime, mais de se purifier sur le champ du meurtre d'un de leurs semblables. Ainsi obtiendra-t'on "ensemble dans l'argile, du dieu et de l'homme durablement-mélangés (*butallulu*: 212)".

"Dorénavant", il ne restera plus aux dieux qu'à "écouter le tambour(?)" (*uppu*: AHw 1424b:III; 214//227), proposition obscure à *nos* yeux, mais qui, d'une manière ou d'une autre, devait résumer l'avenir sans nuages qu'assurerait à la société divine la mise en marche de son "instrument de production": que ledit "tambour" ait représenté (W.G. Lambert, *Atr.*, p.152:214) une manière de gong pour annoncer des festins désormais servis aux dieux sans autre souci que de se mettre à table, ou qu'il ait symbolisé, par sa musique d'accompagnement, la fête indéfinie qui remplirait leurs jours. Telle est la conclusion attendue et le résultat final du plan de sauvetage élaboré par *Enki*: l'Homme mis en fonctions, les dieux pourront mener une existence oisive, insouciante et opulente (le premier aspect seul, négatif mais fondamental, est évoqué au moment de "l'approbation du prototype" dans 240 sqq.).

Cependant, le discours-programme d'*Enki*, et, par suite, le récit de sa mise en oeuvre, ne s'arrêtent point là: trois lignes s'y ajoutent, où précisément gît notre *crux* (215-217//228-230), d'autant plus irritante que le mot à mot en est parfaitement limpide, sans un seul terme inconnu, sans le moindre problème grammatical insoluble. En voici la teneur, avec, entre parenthèses, la variante la plus notable du manuscrit "E":

215 *ina šîr ili eDimmu(WeDimmu) libši*	228 *ina šîr ili eD[immu ibši]*
216 *balṭa itta-šu lišêdi-šu-ma*	229 *balṭa itta-šu ušê[di-šu-ma]*
217 *aššu lâ muššî eDimmu(WeDimmu) libši*	230 *aššu lâ muššî eDimmu [ibši]*

Si, comme on l'a compris à tout ce qui précède, la "formule" de l'Homme, en qualité de substitut des dieux, est censée désormais au point, il ne saurait être ici question de la modifier ou de la compléter. Il doit donc s'agir d'autre chose. Comme le suggère la remise en tête et en relief de l'élément divin qui compose avec l'argile la nature de l'Homme (*ina šîr ili*), on veut en souligner, dans cette même nature, *un autre résultat substantiel* (215), dont l'effet (216) et l'objectif (217) sont déclinés ensuite, comme pour légitimer sa présence et définir son rôle. Il porte le nom écrit *e-DI-im-mu* en "A", et *we-DI-im-mu* en "E" (on comprendra plus loin pourquoi du signe PI, polyphonique, nous retenons, comme hypothèse de travail, la valeur phonétique: *we*). Et ici commencent les perplexités....

On avait lu d'abord (*Annuaire 1967-1968 de la IVème Section de l'Ecole pratique des Hautes Etudes*, p.119; W.G. Lambert, *Atr.* p.58 et 152:215-6) et presque tous les commentateurs ont gardé depuis: *eṭemmu*, W.G. Lambert (loc. cit.) supposant, pour le PI initial du mot tel que l'écrit le manuscrit "E", une lecture E_x (*e_x-ṭe-em-mu*), parfaitement plausible à côté des valeurs analogues: Å (*Akk. Syll.*, *2. Aufl.*, p.43 et *3. Aufl.*, p.6*: no. 223; déjà à l'époque aB), U_{17} et I_{16} (*2. Aufl.*, p.43), pour peu fréquentes qu'elles soient. C'était évidemment la lecture la plus obvie et la plus vraisemblable.

Elle a pourtant "fortement gêné" (*höchst unbefriedigend*) W. von Soden, comme il l'a expliqué, notamment, pp. 350-1 de son étude *Der Mensch bescheidet sich nicht - Überlegungen zu Schöpfungserzählungen in Babylonien und Israel* (pp. 349-358 des *Symbolae... F.M.T. de Liagre Böhl dedicatae* [Leiden 1973]. Les raisons qu'il en donne sont assez déconcertantes. Tout d'abord, pose-t'il en principe, il s'agit évidemment, dans ce passage, du Premier Homme (*Urmensch*). Or, il est impensable qu'un *eṭemmu* serve ainsi de souche et d'archétype à la race humaine, puisque "c'est un démon (*Dämon*), dans lequel (*in dem*) l'esprit (*Geist*) de morts demeurés sans sépulture, continue d'agir (*weiterwirkt*) pour causer à des survivants des troubles de l'esprit" (p. 350). Il est donc exclu de lire et d'entendre *eṭemmu/weṭemmu* dans le présent contexte et il faut chercher autre chose. Et W. von Soden de préconiser (*w*)*edimmu*/(*w*)*idimmu*, vocable parfaitement inconnu jusqu'ici, et qu'il rattache à IDIM sumérien. Comme ce dernier n'a pas moins de quatorze équivalents accadiens, dont certains passablement contradictoires (*kabtu*: haut personnage, notabilité, et *pisnâqu*: chétif, débile, par exemple), il parvient, en argumentant, à tirer du tout un sens général possible d'"être en ébauche, inachevé, imparfait" (d'esprit ou de corps), ce qui, selon lui, s'entend fort bien du Prototype humain, de l'*Urmensch* (pp. 350 sqq.).

Voilà qui est bien vite dit! Mais comme, en lexicographie au moins autant qu'ailleurs, il est toujours prudent de s'en tenir à la règle d'or des vieux scolastiques: *Non sunt multiplicanda entia sine necessitate*, mieux vaut y réfléchir à deux fois avant d'enregistrer ce vocable inconnu, dont l'existence n'est encore que hautement spéculative, et l'interprétation qu'il nous procure de notre péricope.

Et d'abord, pourquoi les auteurs d'*Atraḫasîs* auraient-ils employé, à quelques vers de distance, et sans nuance appréciable de signification, un double nom pour désigner l'archétype des hommes: *lullû*, bien connu par ailleurs et indubitable, en 195, et le supposé *widimmu* (etc.) ici? W. von Soden le note (p. 350), mais ne le justifie pas.

Est-il bien sûr, du reste, qu'il s'agit en effet ici de l'*Urmensch comme tel*, dont le cas a été réglé auparavant et sur lequel les auteurs seraient donc revenus? Dans quel but? Du moins W. von Soden n'explique-t'il point comment il voit la relation entre ledit Prototype et les effets et objectifs de sa présence, tels qu'ils paraissent ressortir de 216-217.

D'autre part, il semble que pour mieux exorciser d'ici l'*eṭemmu*, W. von Soden le définit d'une façon bien sommaire et encore plus surprenante. L'*eṭemmu*

N'ÉTAIT PAS un démon, même si, lorsqu'il s'agit de ses méfaits, on l'a souvent adjoint à la cohorte des autres personnalités démoniaques, et si l'analogie graphique de son idéogramme (GEDIM) avec celui des *utukkû* (UDUG) suggère que, faute de mieux, on pouvait les imaginer plus ou moins sur le même patron (voir *Annuaire 1979-1980 de la IVème Section de l'Ecole pratique des Hautes Etudes*, à paraître; ainsi que *La Mythologie de la Mort*, pp. 25ss. de *Death in Mesopotamia: Actes de la XXVIème R.A.I.*, à Copenhague). L'activité de l'*eṭemmu* ne se bornait pas à causer ici-bas des désordres psychiques ou autres: si les incantations pertinentes dénoncent avec vigueur sa responsabilité en ce domaine, c'est précisément qu'elles ont été composées pour lutter contre de tels maux. Du reste, pour peu qu'on les lise avec soin, elles nous laissent entrevoir de tout autres capacités, bienveillantes et bienfaisantes (voir les articles cités).

Enfin, et surtout, l'*eṭemmu*, à l'opposé de ce que le raisonnement de W. von Soden laisserait, mot à mot, entendre, n'est pas propre à une certaine catégorie de défunts - ceux qu'on n'a pas mis en terre - , mais à *tous les morts*. Comme la *néfèš* des vieux Israélites et la *psyché* des anciens Grecs, c'était "l'esprit" du défunt, son fantôme, son ombre, son "âme": tout ce qui, outre son cadavre et ses ossements, subsistait de lui après son trépas. Dans un régime de pensée où l'on était incapable (le sommes-nous vraiment moins aujourd'hui?) d'imaginer et de poser le Néant, l'on s'était persuadé que l'Homme, une fois décédé, persistait forcément, d'une manière ou d'une autre, non seulement par cette charpente et quintessence de son être matériel qu'était le squelette (*eṣemtu*), mais surtout par quelque chose qui lui ressemblât formellement davantage, et dont l'existence réelle était démontrée par les visions que l'on pouvait en avoir, en songe ou autrement. Ainsi avait-on imaginé une façon de "double" ombreux, volatil et inconsistant, qui se détachait du cadavre pour rejoindre (si du moins on le lui permettait en le mettant en terre) le Royaume d'En-bas, le Pays-sans-retour, lieu de rassemblement définitif de tous ces "esprits" des Trépassés (voir *La Mythologie de la Mort*, plus haut citée).

L'*eṭemmu* faisait donc partie de la *nature* et du *destin* de l'Homme. Dans la mesure où nos auteurs, traitant de ses *origines*, entendaient du même coup expliquer et définir cette *nature*, ainsi "créée", et ce *destin*, ainsi inauguré, l'*eṭemmu* avait ici sa place. *Enki* nous est présenté comme trop intelligent et sagace pour n'avoir point songé, en calculant la "formule" du composé humain, à cet état final qui devait être le sien.

Car si, non convaincu par les réticences et les spéculations contraires, on en revient à l'*eṭemmu* qu'on n'aurait jamais dû abandonner, notre passage s'éclaire d'autant mieux que l'on y peut découvrir, semble-t'il, une clé pour y entrer de plain-pied.

Après le discours d'*Enki* (204-217), et l'accord unanime des *Anunnaki* (218-9), commence l'exécution du programme. C'est alors que nous est communiqué le "nom propre" du dieu immolé pour fournir sa substance à l'Homme. Ce nom est marqué des deux signes PI+E. On les a lus, avec prudence (W.G. Lambert, *Atr.* p.133: 233) ou intrépidité (G. Pettinato, *Oriens Antiquus* IX [1970] 75-6), PI-*e*, et même W.G. Lambert (loc. cit.) avait senti que la bonne lecture devait être quelque chose comme *We-e*. W. von Soden (op. cit., 352-3) s'y est refusé, pour s'en tenir à GEŠTU-*e*, sans du reste l'expliquer clairement. Peut- être s'est-il fermé, du coup, en en rejetant la clé, l'intelligence de la péricope et de tout un aspect de la "doctrine" du Poème?

Il y a en effet là deux points dont on n'a peut-être pas assez reconnu l'importance. Tout d'abord *Wê* (puisque ainsi nous lisons, on percevra pourquoi tout à l'heure), désigné comme appartenant au monde divin par le déterminatif *ad hoc* (^{d}*We-e*), est en outre qualifié de "dieu" par un terme dont W.G. Lambert (loc. cit.) s'est demandé s'il représentait le complément d'un nom divin composé: ^{d}*We-e-i-la*, ou une apposition au nom simple: ^{d}*We-e i-la ša* ... Il a probablement raison en donnant sa préférence à la première de ces interprétations; mais, en soi, la chose ne semble guère tirer à conséquence, dans la mesure où, comme on le comprendra plus loin, compte moins la relation grammaticale précise entre ces deux mots: *Wê* et *ila*, que leur association étroite et, disons, phonétique.

D'autre part, nous apprend la même ligne 223, le dieu en question est choisi "parce qu'il a du *ṭêmu*", ou bien "en tant que doué de *ṭêmu*" (*ša išû ṭêma*; voir aussi 239, qui le présente "immolé avec = à cause de son *ṭêmu*": *qadu ṭêmi-šu*; comp. également le ms "D":II/vii:33, dans *Atr.* p. 84). Il n'est pas dit qu'il soit le seul parmi les dieux à en avoir, mais seulement qu'il en a, en effet - d'où découle, cela va sans dire, qu'il pourra donc communiquer cette qualité, "par sa chair", à l'Homme qu'il va contribuer à "composer". Car ici W. von Soden (352-3) a parfaitement raison: le *ṭêmu*, capacité de planification et de décision (ibid., et, maintenant, AHw 1385-6), est aussi indispensable aux hommes, pour accomplir au mieux leur tâche native de producteurs et transformateurs des biens utiles, qu'il l'était à leurs prédécesseurs divins en cette même entreprise. Mais la transmission de toutes les vertus nécessaires s'étant déjà trouvée, par force, impliquée dans le "mélange" du divin parmi l'argile humaine, pourquoi diable a-t'on ici détaché et mis en un relief particulier ce *ṭêmu* qui n'était, après tout, que l'une d'entre elles?

W.G. Lambert (loc. cit.) avait déjà senti qu'un tel choix pouvait avoir été commandé par une manière de "jeu de mots" entre *ṭêmu* et *eṭemmu*. Nous connaissons l'insigne faiblesse des vieux lettrés et théologiens de Mésopotamie pour ces sortes d'allitérations, par nous tenues pour un effet du hasard et sans autre portée qu'un amusement de l'esprit, à leurs yeux d'une tout autre valeur: objective et pour ainsi dire *ontologique*. La célèbre partie terminale de l'*Enûma eliš*: la liste des "Cinquante Noms de Marduk", avec son "commentaire", et d'autres pièces encore, nous ont suffisamment révélé ce type de "logique" qui, par l'analyse des *mots* était censée permettre un progrès dans l'intelligence des *choses* (voir *Les Noms de Marduk, l'écriture et la "logique" en Mésopotamie ancienne*, pp. 4 sqq. de *Ancient Near Eastern Studies in Memory of J.J. Finkelstein*). Serait-il vraiment téméraire d'y faire ici appel? D'autant plus que si *wê+ṭêmu* évoque *eṭemmu*, *wê+ilu* fait assitôt penser à *awê/îlu*....

Nous voici donc conduits à nous demander si les auteurs d'*Atraḫasîs* ne seraient point partis de telles assonances pour construire cette portion de leur mythe. Ils auront remarqué que dans *awê/îlu*, comme dans *(w)eṭemmu*, figuraient, et un élément disparate: *ilu* d'un côté, et *ṭêmu* de l'autre; et un élément commun: *(w)ê*. Ils en auront tiré, moyennant leur "logique", que pour *être* ainsi (même successivement) *awêlu*, puis *eṭemmu*, l'Homme devait *avoir en lui* quelque chose de divin (*ilu*) et quelque chose tenant du *ṭêmu*, grâce à la présence originelle, en sa substance même, de "la chair" d'une divinité *Wê*, à la fois "dieu" (*ilu*) et doué de *ṭêmu*. Nous ignorons si ce dieu *Wê* (dont la lecture exacte, dans un pareil contexte, est ainsi surabondamment fixée) était connu par ailleurs, sous cette forme précisément, ou quelque autre, voisine, ou bien s'il a été supposé et comme "déduit" à partir des équations ci-dessus - ce qui, *a priori*, paraît moins vraisemblable. Quiconque s'est tant soit peu familiarisé avec les "règles" de ce type d'exégèse, du mot *écrit* et "traité à la façon d'une substance simple, dont toutes les propriétés se retrouvent intégralement en chacune de ses parcelles" (*Les Noms de Marduk* ...., pp. 16 sqq.), sait à quoi s'en tenir touchant des approximations insupportables à nos propres exigences de rigueur et d'exactitude, comme l'alternance vocalique *e/i* dans *awêlu/awîlu* (art. cité, pp. 17-18: §12; les deux formes du mot sont du reste en usage: CAD A Pt. 2, 48b); le découpement du continu sémantique *(a)-wê-ilu* et *wê-ṭêmu* (art. cité, p. 16: §7); la négligence de la voyelle initiale *a-* de *awê/îlu* (ibid., pp. 18-19: §16) et du redoublement de la deuxième consonne: *eṭeMMu*, au profit d'un allongement de la voyelle qui précède: *ṭêmu* (particularité non attestée au cours de l'art. cité, mais dans le droit fil de sa doctrine; une orthographe "savante" *ṭemmu*, avec deux *M* n'est du reste pas exclue, si l'on tient compte de l'équivalence sumérienne DÍM.MU dans MAOG I/2, p. 27; iii:1-2 = *Nabnîtu* A); voire la dissonance entre l'*eṭemmu* usuel et le *weṭemmu* attendu. Sur ce dernier point, tout au moins, le ms "E" a fait le nécessaire pour accorder sa graphie avec son exégèse, en écrivant carrément *we-ṭe-em-mu*, qu'il ait pensé à une valeur E_x de PI (ci-dessus), ou qu'il ait préservé une forme connue de lui, dans une tradition lexicographique ou dialectale, où le *W* aurait pu rappeler la présence d'une palatale en tête du mot sumérien: GEDIM, accadisé en *eṭemmu*. Pour citer un fait parallèle, tout le monde connait la contiguïté des phonèmes *G* et *M* en sumérien (A. Poebel, GSG §§48, 75 sqq., etc.). Du reste, considéré que ce qui comptait avant tout dans la procédure exégétique à laquelle nous nous référons, c'était le signe *écrit*, duquel "l'on tenait pour sémantiquement équivalentes toutes les valeurs sumérographiques ....comme on les estimait d'autre part phonétiquement interchangeables" (art. cité, p. 20: §21), quelle précisément qu'ait été la prononciation de l'initiale du mot (*eṭemmu* ou *weṭemmu* ....), le choix du signe PI a pu être commandé *aussi* par son champ sémantique (*uznu*: "oreille" et "discernement"; *ḫasîsu*: "pensée" et "jugement"; *nêmequ*: "sagesse" ....), dans lequel entrait directement *ṭêmu*, opération mentale relevant, elle aussi, de "l'intelligence" (comp. du reste l'art. cité de W. von Soden, p. 352. Exemples analogues de telles "constellations sémantiques" dans l'art. cité, p. 220: §25).

Avant de tirer de 215-217//228-230 considérés sous cet angle, des conclusions de fond et d'une tout autre portée que l'identification d'un dieu *Wê* et de l'*eṭemmu*, revenons aux autres questions que soulève ce menu couplet.

215//228 établit donc, comme un effet ultérieur de la "chair du dieu" qui compose l'Homme, l'existence de l'*eṭemmu* de ce dernier, c'est-à-dire de l'état particulier de "fantôme", d'"ombre" et d'"esprit" sous lequel il doit subsister après sa mort:

De par la chair du dieu, il y aura/[il y eut](en outre, dans l'Homme) un "esprit".

Selon 216//229, le premier effet de l'existence de cet "esprit" sera de "démontrer que l'Homme est (toujours) vivant", après sa mort, s'entend, puisque, auparavant, l'*eṭemmu* n'a encore, semble-t'il, dans l'individu dont il représentera la dernière métamorphose, qu'une existence, dirions-nous, "virtuelle". On a traduit, et l'on continuera de traduire de bien des façons *balṭa itta-šu lušêdi/ušêdi-šu-ma*. W.G. Lambert, du moins, avait parfaitement compris (*Atr*., p. 152:216, 229) que le sujet de cette proposition, qu'il jugeait avec raison *extraordinarily important*, devait être l'*eṭemmu*, mentionné juste auparavant, et son objet, marqué par le suffixe verbal *-šu*, l'Homme en personne, dont *balṭa* est l'attribut. Reste *itta-šu*, qui a donné de la tablature à tout le monde. En réalité, B. Landsberger avait raison (WdO III [1964] 69-70: n. 82, et p. 76): l'expression composée *uddû/uteddû/šudû+itta/giskimma*, qui transcrit et traduit le sumérien GISKIM.ZU(.ZU) signifie mot à mot "faire connaître par une marque distinctive/par quelque chose de caractéristique, de significatif" - "dé-signer". Ici, ce "signe" est mis en relations, par le possessif *-šu*, avec le sujet de la phrase, l'*eṭemmu*: "par le signe-caractéristique qu'il constitue lui-même" (*itta-šu*: "son propre-signe"), il doit "le faire reconnaître" (*lišêdi*/*ušêdi-šu*), à savoir l'Homme, pour "vivant" (*balṭa*). Vu la situation: avec l'*eṭemmu* et donc obligatoirement après la mort, il ne s'agit que d'une "vie" particulière, chétive, torpide et morne, comme nous le savons par ailleurs (voir notamment l'art. cité plus haut: *La Mythologie de la Mort*) - plutôt, apparemment, dirions-nous, une simple *subsistance*. Mais après son trépas, et dans son *eṭemmu*, l'Homme perdure, il continue d'exister, et l'*eṭemmu* est à la fois le suppôt et la preuve de cette "vie" qui se poursuit. Un tel privilège, tout modeste qu'il soit, ne saurait être explicable à partir de l "argile", qui fait de l'Homme un être périssable; ce qui en rend raison, c'est la présence, en l'argile, de la "chair du dieu". Elle n'a pas suffi, précisément par l'effet de son "mélange" avec l'argile, à conférer aux hommes cette prérogative des dieux qu'est l'Immortalité: la Vie toujours continuée aussi pleine, débordante, active et heureuse. Une telle "vie", de par l' "argile", il faut que la mort l'interrompe. Mais elle se poursuivra, même réduite, débile et triste, dans l'*eṭemmu* qui subsistera, et qui prouvera ainsi que, du fait de sa "formule" calculée par *Enki*, l'Homme, entre autres avantages qui le rapprochent des dieux, participe, de loin et chétivement, non certes à l'Immortalité, mais à ce pâle reflet qu'en est la Durée, la "Subsistance".

L'existence de l'*eṭemmu* (217//230: *eṭemmu libši*/*[ibši]*) avait une autre finalité (*ana*): "éviter qu'on laisse-choir dans l'oubli" (*ana lâ mušši*, dans la mesure où la forme D de ce verbe *mašû*, par ailleurs peu usitée, a bien une valeur "factitive"). Quoi? Concis à l'extrême, comme souvent, les auteurs du Poème, en omettant ici de préciser l'objet qu'on pouvait ainsi "laisser choir dans l'oubli" ou "la négligence", semblent avoir volontairement procédé par allusion: ce qu'ils avaient en tête n'échappait certainement pas à leur entourage, aux vieux lecteurs et auditeurs du Poème, alors que nous, qui ne vivons plus du tout dans le même univers de pensées, d'images et de sentiments, nous demeurons perplexes. Pour peu que l'on y réfléchisse, pourtant, et vu le contexte: d'*eṭemmu* et d'outre-tombe, qui donne tout son sens au tercet 215-217//228-230, ce que l'on risquait d'oublier et de négliger, c'était précisément la persistance du trépassé en l'état de fantôme, et les devoirs des survivants envers lui (voir l'art. cité plus haut, de l'*Annuaire 1979-1980* ....., non moins que *La Mythologie de la Mort*). Nous savons, en effet, qu'incapables désormais de se suffire, les défunts attendaient, d'abord et surtout, des membres de leur famille et de leur descendance, non seulement qu'ils les ensevelissent selon les rites, leur permettant ainsi de gagner leur nouveau et définitif séjour, mais qu'ils leur assurassent, par des libations, des offrandes, des repas sacrificiels, et en particulier le *kispu* (mêmes articles; voir également M. Bayliss, *The Cult of Dead Kin in Assyria and Babylonia*, pp. 115 sqq. de *Iraq* XXXV [1973]), le filet de "vie" qu'il leur restait en leur infernal habitacle. Si on les négligeait, si on "laissait choir dans l'oubli" leur malheureux "fantôme", totalement dépendant et démuni de tout, ils étaient fort capables, nous le savons aussi (*Annuaire 1979-80*...., surtout), de rappeler durement les négligents à l'ordre, en les persécutant et les tourmentant de multiples manières. Par cette capacité de harceler, de frapper et léser les survivants, et pas seulement par sa seule existence, l'*eṭemmu* avait donc pour office et mission de faire "en sorte qu'ils ne laissent pas choir dans l'oubli" leurs devoirs envers lui: chacun envers ses morts - obligation enracinée dans la propre solidarité familiale et sociale, et par conséquent dans la *nature* et le *destin* des hommes.

Car, au delà du mythe de ses *origines*, ce qui transparaît le plus clairement, dans cette première partie du *Poème d'Atraḫasîs*, c'est l'idée que ses auteurs se faisaient de l'Homme: de sa *nature* et de son *destin*. A leurs yeux, il n'avait de raison d'être que dans la mise en valeur de toutes les richesses d'ici-bas, D'ABORD à l'avantage des dieux: il était essentiellement "théocentrique", comme tout ce qui n'appartenait pas au monde surnaturel. Mieux encore, il était fait: combiné et adapté pour les servir ainsi; et tout ce qu'il avait en lui, tout ce qui le caractérisait et définissait, se trouvait commandé par une telle finalité. C'est dans ce but qu'avait dû être introduit en sa "formule" un élément divin (*Wê+ilu*), grâce à quoi il avait son *nom* et sa *nature* d'Homme: *awêlu*. Mais pour que, sans se prévaloir de cet avantage, il demeurât à jamais radicalement inférieur à ceux au profit de qui il lui fallait oeuvrer, cette parcelle divine, du reste empruntée à une divinité du bas-choeur et quasi inconnue, avait été mêlée à l'argile terrestre: il lui faudrait donc, au bout du compte, par une partie de lui-même, "redevenir argile", "retourner à la terre", et mourir. Alors, il cesserait d'être Homme (*awêlu*): il changerait de nom et d'*état* et, par une vertu particulière de la même divinité (*Wê+ṭêmu*) qui lui avait communiqué ses autres prérogatives, il passerait à celui d "Esprit": *eṭemmu*. Ainsi persévèrait-il dans l'être, poursuivant une certaine "vie" - pâle décalque et dérisoire image de l'Immortalité divine. Dans cette ombreuse, piteuse et définitive existence larvaire, il ne garderait plus rien de sa vocation laborieuse d'*awêlu*. Mais ses survivants, à leur tour, devraient travailler pour lui aussi, pour le nourrir, pour lui fournir de quoi alimenter ce peu de vie indéfinie qu'il lui resterait. Autrement, à la façon des dieux tirant vengeance de ceux qui négligeaient leur culte, il saurait se rappeler durement à leur souvenir. Tels étaient la *nature* et le *destin*, enchâssés dans ses *noms* et par eux intelligibles, de cet être "amphibie", si riche et si complexe: d'abord *awêlu*, actif et au travail pour les dieux, avant sa mort; puis *eṭemmu*, ne faisant guère plus que subsister, et servi à son tour par d'autres *awîlû*, en ses chétifs besoins. Il n'avait fallu rien moins qu'*Enki*, l'Intelligent, le Sagace, le Supertechnicien (voir *Enki/Éa, l'Intelligence et la fonction technique du Pouvoir*, dans le *Dictionnaire des Mythologies* [sous presse, chez Flammarion, Paris]), pour mettre au point une machine aussi complexe et précisément ajustée.

Par là nous rejoignons le *mythe*. Car *Atraḫasîs*, ce n'est pas un traité de théologie, où les choses aient été exposées rationnellement, clairement, bien tranchées en leur abstraction; c'est un *Mythe*, où les explications étaient fournies par des énarrations d'évènements, de mouvements imaginaires de personnages construits par la fantaisie et qui, même lorsqu'ils étaient mis sur le plan surnaturel et omnipotent, dégagés de toutes nos contingences, avaient été empruntés par l'imagination au monde d'ici-bas, et, explicitement ou non, en reflétaient donc *tout* ce qu'en connaissaient et ressentaient créateurs et usagers de l'oeuvre. Celle-ci, et par ce qu'elle disait, et par ce qu'elle ne disait pas, suggérait seulement, ou laissait carrément dans l'ombre, n'était donc perceptible en sa totalité qu'à ses auteurs et à leur entourage. Comme un discours en quelque langue étrangère que nous possédons mal ne nous est pas véritablement intelligible, en toutes ses finesses, mais à ceux-là seuls qui la parlent couramment depuis leur enfance. Nous, qui "parlons une autre langue", qui vivons dans un tout autre univers de pensées, de jugements, de sentiments, comment ne pas hésiter, tâtonner comme des aveugles, avouer souvent (ou dissimuler!) nos perplexités et nos ignorances devant un texte aussi concret, aussi serré, aussi subtil et plein de sous-entendus, aussi laconique et, çà et là, hermétique, et qui n'a pas été écrit pour nous? Pour essayer d'y entrevoir au moins quelques articulations (car, de toute manière, on doit le supposer beaucoup plus riche que nous ne saurions l'imaginer, dans notre position), nous sommes donc contraints de rameuter tout ce que nous croyons avoir appris par ailleurs de ces vieilles gens: chacun de nous en a son propre bagage, sa propre optique, ses propres convictions ....

Voilà pourquoi il sera toujours quasiment impossible, sur l'exégèse d'un document aussi dense et arrivé tout droit de si loin, en dépit de son unité et de sa cohérence, de la masse identique et invariable qu'il présente à nos yeux, et même de toutes nos certitudes proprement philologiques à son sujet, de dégager le moins du monde une unanimité quelconque de notre compagnie assyriologique. Aussi me suis-je bien gardé, en commençant ce discours, d'annoncer autre chose qu'"une opinion de plus"...

---

1 Pour le texte, on ira voir, comme il se doit, W.G. Lambert & A.R. Millard, *Atraḫasîs* [Oxford 1969] (cité ici: *Atr.*). Mais il faut tenir compte de la récente et importante révision de W. von Soden: *Die erste Tafel des altbabylonischen Atramḫasîs-Mythus. 'Haupttext' und Parallelversionen*, dans ZA 68 [1978] 50 sqq. Pour les interprétations multiples, je renvoie simplement à la liste de R. Borger, HKL II, 157. La seule référence importante à y ajouter est l'article de W. von Soden: *Konflikte und ihre Bewältigung in babylonischen Schöpfungs- und Fluterzählungen. Mit einer Teil-Übersetzung des Atramḫasis-Mythos*, dans MDOG 111 [1979] 1 sqq.

THE BIPARTITE SOCIETY OF THE ANCIENT IRANIANS

Mary Boyce (London)

The usages of the Younger Avesta, it is incontrovertibly established, attest the existence of a tripartite society, that of 'priest, warrior and herdsman' (*āϑravan-, raϑaēštar-, vāstryō.fšuyant-*); and the terminology reflects the conditions of the Iranian Bronze Age, in that the fighting man is identified as 'one standing in a chariot', not as a horse-rider, and members of the third estate are called 'pasturers', not tillers of the soil. The horse-drawn chariot appears (on the evidence of grave-goods) to have been known north of the Black Sea by the end of the third millennium B.C., and its use presumably spread across the South Russian steppes in the following centuries. The chariot remained in military and ceremonial use among Persians down to the end of the Achaemenian period; but long before that, from the eighth/seventh centuries B.C., the northern Iranian warrior had become characteristically a rider, sitting his horse, and warrior-horsemen are referred to in passages of the Younger Avesta.

Zoroaster himself knew the horse-drawn chariot, and uses the metaphor of harnessed beasts to convey swiftness,[1] and that of the charioteer (*raiϑya-*) for a controlling force.[2] No specific term occurs, however, in the Gathas for men who fight from chariots, or indeed for fighting men as such. The word *nar-*, 'man', has been identified as the Gathic equivalent of Younger Avesta *raϑaēštar-*;[3] but there is only one passage in Zoroaster's verses where this word appears definitely to be used in a socially distinctive way, i.e. Y.28.8, where the prophet sets it before the name of Frašaoštra. Here it was rendered by Bartholomae as 'wehrhafter Mann, Kriegsmann; kriegerischer Held',[4] and it has generally been translated as 'hero'. It could be understood, however, as distinguishing Frašaoštra the layman from his son-in-law, Zoroaster the priest. In Y.48.10 Bartholomae took the plural *narō* as 'Bezeichnung für den zweiten Stand, Krieger, Ritter'; but although the term has been rendered here as 'noblemen' some scholars have seen it as meaning simply 'men'.[5] Otherwise *nar-* occurs in the Gāthās frequently and indisputably in the ordinary sense of 'man' - 'man' as distinguished from 'woman' (Y.46.10,53.6), and 'man' as 'person' (as in the phrase *narə̄m narəm* 'each man for himself' Y.30.2). The prophet speaks of 'deceitful men' (Y.45.7), and more often of the 'virtuous man' (Y.34.2, 48.7, 51.21); and he applies the word to himself (Y.29.9) and, it seems, to his cousin Maidyōi.må̄ŋha (Y.51.19) - both, it is to be assumed, priests.

If therefore one abandons presuppositions engendered by a study of the Younger Avesta, one finds no firm evidence in Zoroaster's own utterances for a specific social connotation of the word *nar-*. Similarly, there is no evidence that *vāstrya-* 'pasturer', or its virtual equivalent *fšuyant-*, are used by him for a restricted social category. The prophet's use of these two terms strikingly bears out the statement that 'his consideration of life has its concrete foundation in his reflections on pastoral life in the tribe whose priest he was', even though he viewed this life 'in the rays of a gigantic cosmic vision'.[6] So on the concrete level the *vāstrya-* and *fšuyant-* are for him the pasturer and herdsman, law-abiding, honest and peaceable men, who tend the cattle which are theirs by right, and defend them against lawless and brutal marauders. This seems to reflect the actual circumstances of the epoch in which Zarathuštra himself lived, the Iranian Heroic Age, seen from its darker side. (Heroic Ages throughout the world have in general been marked by predatory acts of violence, and indifference on the part of the 'heroes' to the sufferings of the 'non-heroic' members of society.[7]) Metaphorically, the *vāstrya-* appears to represent the just and good person, who cherishes 'good purpose', *vohu- manah-* (symbolized by cattle), and who opposes whoever and whatever is false, wicked and destructive.[8] This is one of the most important metaphors of the Gathas; and there is nothing in Zoroaster's usage to suggest that in thus making the *vāstrya-* the representative of human righteousness he was taking as symbol the poorest and humblest members of a tripartite society. On the contrary, in one verse (Y.53.4) he uses the term *vāstrya-* on the concrete level to represent 'l'ensemble de la population',[9] undertaking for his daughter Pouručista that she will serve 'father, husband, pasturers (*vāstraēibyō*) and family'. On this passage K. Barr wrote: 'In Zarathustra's conception of life, which springs from his dismay at seeing ruin brought to life by the violation of the sacred life of the ox, the herdsmen as the proper guardians of the ox have virtually obtained absolute supremacy over the other two Aryan classes. Thanks to their particular connection with Vohu Manah they may be said to have been raised to be on a level with the two uppermost classes of the community to become in the fullness of time Ahura Mazdāh's one rightful people. As long as the fight for the Kingdom of Happiness is going on, the herdsmen must also be warriors'.[10] It seems probable, however, to judge from Zoroaster's own usages, that this was not merely a symbolic development, but corresponded for him with actuality - that in the society which had shaped his thoughts the herdsman was in fact also the warrior, the *nar-* identical with the *vāstrya-*. The two Avestan terms never occur together in Zoroaster's hymns, and it is first in *Yasna Haptaŋhāiti* that they are juxtaposed, in a verse that runs: 'Then, Mazda Ahura, make the men (*nərəš*) possess truth, be attached to truth; make the herdsmen (*vāstryəng*) apt for long, zealous, firm companionship; (make them) give support to us (priests)' (Y.40.3). These lines have been interpreted as a prayer involving the three divisions of society;[11] but the use of *vāstrya-* here may well be only as a synonym, carrying symbolic overtones, for *nar-*. The priests would thus be praying that society as a whole should be just, harmonious, and supportive to themselves - a threefold wish of the kind characteristic of Zoroastrianism.

An analysis of Gathic society as bipartite (warrior-herdsmen and priests), rather than tripartite needs to take into consideration the role of the Aməša Spənta Khšathra, lord of the first physical creation, sky.[12] Zoroaster evidently accepted the belief current in his day, and long afterwards, that the sky, enclosing the visible world, was a shell of hard stone (cf. Y.30.5); and the link (acknowledged down the centuries by his followers) between Khšathra and fighting men with their weapons, must go back to a pre-metallic age, when weapons - maces, slingstones, flint-tipped arrows and spears, knives and axes - were all of stone. For hundreds of generations the Indo-Iranians had lived with such a culture on the steppes; and down to the third millennium B.C., while the horse was still a wild animal for them, a creature to be hunted, all but the sick and very old (for whom there were perhaps ox-carts) must have progressed by walking. In such a society there can have been few material grounds for social distinctions. All men could readily equip themselves, at the expense only of skill and labour, with weapons, and all would have met on the same physical level. The wealth of the tribe must have been chiefly in its cattle; and comparison with known societies of pastoralists who herd cattle on foot suggest that there would in fact have been little in the way of social divisiveness.[13] 'That economic contrasts between wealthy and poor herdsmen have been existent is highly probable, of course. But they apparently do not find their expression in the Gāthās, nor in the older Zoroastrianized parts of the Avesta. Zarathustra ... considered himself the spokesman of the pastoral tribe as a whole'.[14] The semi-nomadic Iranians, living close to their animals, on whom their lives depended, were likely to have regarded themselves as 'the collectivity of men and cattle together',[15] *pasu vīra* in the Avestan phrase.[16] Apart from priests, adult males are likely to have shared, as the normal activities of manhood, the tasks of herding, hunting and fighting. As herdsmen they would have had to carry weapons against beasts of prey; and if human marauders appeared, it would doubtless have been their accepted duty to stand and fight. In those horseless days it would have been useless to run (as do herdsmen in the Irish sagas) to alert the warriors of the tribe, expecting them to speed after the vanishing foes and cattle. No one could move faster than his own feet would carry him, and so there was no justification for specialised activity.

Khšathra, lord of the protective sky, could therefore be regarded as the especial protector of man, the *nar-*, guardian of the *pasu vīra*. Equally naturally his heavenly partner, Ārmaiti, divinity of the earth which bears and nurtures all things, was venerated as the especial guardian of women - as in the words of *Yasna Haptaŋhāiti*: 'This earth then we worship, her who bears us, together with women' (Y.38.1). Women in a semi-nomadic society are likely to have enjoyed considerable freedom and respect; and the prophet addresses his words explicitly to men and women, *narō jənayō*, seeking to persuade both. Within these two natural groups, only priests seem to have had a distinctive social role, which set them apart among the *nar-*. They as the learned members of society, the repositories of tribal lore, who by their calling had the greatest access to the gods, appear to have had a controlling part in its affairs - to have been in a measure the regents of the tribe;[17] and they felt themselves, it seems, under the especial protection of Ahura Mazdā, the Lord Wisdom, their divine counterpart, who, if a priest were worthy, filled him with his Holy Spirit. What the high priest counselled would then presumably have been carried out by the leading laymen of the tribe, as the behests of Ahura Mazdā were carried out by the lesser Ahuras, Mithra and *Varuna Apąm Napāt.[18]

These appear to be ancient beliefs which were partly inherited, partly developed by Zoroaster, whose own outlook seems to have been moulded by the ancient cohesive pastoral society which gave these concepts birth. The Gāthās appear to mirror, however, the breaking up of that stable society, through the pressures of a new age. To possess a chariot and teams of horses, with charioteer and grooms, and to acquire weapons of mined and wrought metal, demanded means, but once a man had obtained these things, honestly or otherwise, he could acquire more wealth, by combat or raids, and pass it on to his sons; and so there came into being a new class within the ranks of the *nar-*, that of the 'chariot-rider', a man who is no longer accepting the duties of herdsman, but who must often have abandoned his own tribe to seek the service of some noted warrior-chief, devoting himself, with the rest of his retainers, to fighting, feasting and the chase;[19] and thus there evolved the Iranian Heroic Age, with its splendours and miseries. In Zoroaster's terminology such ruthless and acquisitive men were *afšuyantō*, 'non-herdsmen' (Y.49.4), an expression which evidently gained its force from the fact that all honest men had previously borne their part in protecting the tribal herds. To judge from other Heroic Ages, the old authority of the priest would have been diminished at this time, with new military kingships becoming the dominant form of government;[20] and the prophet appears also to denounce those unworthy priests who betrayed the old ways and took service with upstart princes, choosing 'the rule of tyrants and deceit rather than truth'.[21]

These social developments, which led to the creation of a clearly-defined tripartite society, were common to the Indians and Iranians, and were shared too by the ancient Irish and by other members of the Indo-European family of nations; but only, it appears, as a stage in their separate social and economic evolutions, not as part of a common inheritance, as is borne out by the absence of common terms for the three evolved classes of society.[22]

Doctrinal problems arose subsequently for Zoroastrians with the establishment of the three classes. One was that, with the use first of bronze and then of iron weapons, there was no longer a physical link between Khšathra and the warrior-class. The solution found for this by scholar-priests was to identify the 'stone' of the sky as rock-crystal, a substance which they felt able to classify as a metal, presumably because it is found in veins in rock, like metallic ores.[23] So Khšathra, lord of a crystalline sky, could be venerated as lord of metals, and hence the protector still of fighting men. It was clearly not felt to be fitting, however, that 'herdsmen', now more commonly farmers after the settlement within Iran, should look to the same divine patron as their betters; and so, as tillers of the soil, they were in course of time set under the protection of Ārmaiti, divinity of the earth, sharing her guardianship with women. This tardy development does not find expression in the Zoroastrian holy books; but in popular observance Ārmaiti's feast-day, founded probably in the fourth century B.C., came to be celebrated as a farmers' festival as well as a special observance for women.[24] The old clear symbolism of 'Khšathra - the sky - dominion - men' and 'Ārmaiti - the earth - devotion - women' thus became further obscured.

The above considerations make it seem probable that Zoroaster spent his boyhood in an Iranian tribe which was slow to acquire the new techniques and social patterns of the Bronze Age, and which was therefore especially at the mercy of well-armed chariot-riding marauders. His thoughts seem accordingly to have been shaped by the ways and ideals of earlier days, even though, moving to the court of Vištāspa, he probably entered a more progressive society. It is clearly impossible to establish on the basis of such considerations any close dating for the prophet. The Iranian Bronze Age is held to have begun around 1700 B.C., but the use of bronze, with the accompanying social changes, probably spread at an uneven pace among the widely-scattered tribes. It seems, however, increasingly certain that if Zoroaster is to be linked chronologically with the prophet of any other people, it should be with Moses (c.1450 or 1250 B.C.) rather than with the Buddha, Confucius or Jeremiah.

---

1 Y.50.7.

2 Y.50.6 (see the translations of H. Humbach, *Die Gathas des Zarathustra*, Heidelberg 1959, and S. Insler, *The Gāthās of Zarathustra*, Acta Iranica 8, Leiden 1975).

3 See Bartholomae, *Altiranisches Wörterbuch*, 1048; E. Benveniste 'Les classes sociales dans la tradition avestique', JA 1932, 117-34.

4 Loc.cit.

5 So both Humbach and Insler.

6 K. Barr, 'Avest. *drəgu-*, *driγu-*', *Studia Orientalia I. Pedersen ... dicata*, Copenhagen 1953, 26.

7 See, with a wealth of illustration, H.M. Chadwick, *The Heroic Age*, Cambridge 1912, especially Ch. 16, 19.

8 See G.G. Cameron, 'Zoroaster the herdsman', *Indo-Iranian Journal* X, 1968, 261-81.

9 Benveniste, art. cit., 129.

10 Art.cit., 33.

11 See Benveniste, art.cit., 122.

12 See Boyce, *A History of Zoroastrianism* (Handbuch der Orientalistik) I, Leiden 1975, 204, 207-9; and (with revisions) *Zoroastrians : their religious beliefs and practices*, London 1979, 24.

13 See most recently Bruce Lincoln, 'Indo-Iranian **gautra*', *Journal of Indo-European Studies*, III, 1975, 161-71.

14 Barr, art.cit., 27.

15 Lincoln, art.cit., 170.

16 See Benveniste, 'Sur quelques dvandvas avestiques', BSOAS VIII, 1935-1937, 405-7.

17 See Benveniste, *Le vocabulaire des institutions indo-européennes*, Paris 1969, II, 9-15.

18 See Boyce, *A History of Zoroastrianism* I, 24-53.

19 See ibid., 105-8, and more generally Chadwick, op.cit., 348 ff.

20 See Chadwick, op.cit., Ch.17.

21 Y.32.12 (in Insler's translation).

22 Benveniste, art.cit. in n.3, was scrupulous to insist upon this absence, and to confine his own observations to the Indo-Iranians.

23 See Boyce, *History of Zoroastrianism*, I, 132-3 (with this development mistakenly attributed to an archaic period).

24 See Boyce, *A Persian Stronghold of Zoroastrianism*, Oxford 1977, 201-2 with n.26.

THE NEO-BABYLONIAN ELDERS

M.A. Dandamayev (Leningrad)

The role of the Elders in Babylonia in the first millennium BC has never been the subject of research. The word is written LÚ.AB.BA.MEŠ/ LÚ *ši-bu-(u-)tu* (sing. *šību*).[1] Let us turn at once to the documents.

To judge from a text written in 591 BC near the city of Sippar, a certain Šamaš-udammiq was suspected of having received illegally over a period of two years money and some natural products from an official of the temple Ebabbar in Sippar. The case was heard in the presence of some witnesses "and the assembly of the Elders of (the god) Šamaš" (*Nbk.* 104:14 *ù pu-ḫu-ru šá* LÚ *ši-bu-tu šá* ^{d}*šamaš*).[2] The decision was made that if Šamaš-udammiq proved to be guilty, he was to restore thirty-fold the temple property taken by him.

The documents *Cyr.* 328 and 329, written in Sippar in 531 BC, contain a complaint that relatives of a boy who had been given as a pledge for a debt forced the door of the creditor's house, set the pledged boy free, and took 1 mina of silver. The case was heard in the presence of the "Priest (LÚ.ŠID) of Sippar" and the Council of "Elders of the City" (1.4 LÚ *ši-bu-tu šá* URU) of Sippar, but their judicial decision is not known, since the text is in a bad state of preservation.[3]

Cyr. 332 (Sippar, 531 BC) contains a record of proceedings concerning the social status of a person. The Priest of Sippar and "Elders of the City" (1. 21 LÚ.AB.BA.MEŠ *[*URU*]*) read all the relevant documents, heard the evidence of the witnesses and made their decision. According to *Cyr.* 281 (Sippar, 532 BC) a slave of the temple Ebabbar made a statement before the principal temple officials and "Elders of the City" (1.6 LÚ.AB.BA.MEŠ URU) asking them to release from prison a certain slave belonging to the same temple, and declaring that he would go bail for him. As seen from *Camb.* 19 (Sippar, 530 BC), the Priest of Sippar, the governor of the city (1.3 *šá muḫḫi* URU) and the Elders (1.10 LÚ.AB.BA.MEŠ *[...]*) jointly made a decision to dig up the "Canal of (the god) Šamaš".[4]

Camb. 412 (Sippar, 522 BC), which is partly broken, is a record of court proceedings concerning 2 minas of silver belonging to the business capital of two persons. The business had already started in 559 BC, and at the time when the case was heard both contracting parties were dead, so that their sons acted as litigants. The decision in the case was made by the Priest of Sippar and "Elders of the City" (11. 10-11 LÚ.AB.BA.MEŠ URU).[5]

In 555 BC in Babylon "Elders of the City" (1.15 *ši-bu-ut* URU) solved a controversial matter of inheritance of a field by three brothers which was the dowry of their mother (M. Rutten, RA 41 *[*1947*]* 102).

According to *Camb.* 85, in 529 BC at Babylon "the assembly of the Elders of the Egyptians" (1.3 UKKIN LÚ *ši-bu(!)-tu šá* LÚ *mi-ṣir-a-a*) made a decision concerning lands connected with royal service and belonging to Egyptians (among them a certain Hapimenna, son of Piššamiš, is mentioned, whose name and patronymic are Egyptian).

According to the badly broken text BE 8, 29, written in 590 BC, in all probability at Nippur, two persons brought a suit concerning property consisting of a slave-girl, in the presence of five Elders of Nippur (1.6 LÚ *ši-bu-tu šá* EN. LÍL.KI) who solved their lawsuit (1.12 LÚ *ši-bu-tu di-in-šú-nu* ....).

To judge from the letter PBS 1/ii, 87, which seems to come from Nippur,[6] "Elders of the City Abbamantanu" (ll. 5-6 LÚ.AB.BA.MEŠ *šá* URU A.) required some sheep to be sent to a high official (*šandabakku*) as a temple tithe.

BE 8, 80 is a very badly damaged document which records that in the beginning of the reign of Cambyses, Gobryas, the Persian governor in Babylonia, ordered a canal in the vicinity of the town or village Handidi to be given over to the use of some of the king's military colonists of foreign descent. The formal procedure took place in the presence of the governor of the city (*šá muḫḫi* URU) and five "citizens, Elders of the City Handidi" (ll. 6-7 LÚ.DUMU.DÙ. MEŠ LÚ *ši-bu-tu ša* URU ....).

The interpretation of the document UCP 9, p.101, No. 38 is not quite certain because of its bad state of preservation. It seems that a man was to be sentenced to death if he were negligent of his duties in guarding a building, and this statement was made before the "Elders of the City ZAB.ZAB" (1.1 LÚ.AB.BA. MEŠ URU É Z.).

BagMit 5, p.222 No. 15 (the date is destroyed) records a litigation between two persons about their shares in a prebend. The principal administrator (*šatammu*) and the "Elders *[of?]* Eanna" in Uruk (ll. 8-9 LÚ.AB.BA.ME *[šá?] é-an-na*) gave their decision on the case.

In the letter BIN 1, 23 two temple officials inform the principal administrator and the Scribe of the temple Eanna that a certain man has seized a field belonging to the Lady of Uruk, and "all the Elders" (LÚ.AB.BA.MEŠ *gab-bi*) know that the field is the property of the goddess, and these Elders have been informed of this illegal act. According to BIN 1, 46 three Elders (1.14 AB(!). BA.MEŠ) were sent to an official to settle a certain matter.

TCL 9, 137 is a letter sent by Bēl-šarru-uṣur (in all probability the crown-prince, son of Nabonidus) to an official of the Eanna temple, ordering him to come quickly and bring with him "men allowed to enter the temple and Elders who have judgement and hold no offices" (ll. 8-10 LÚ.ERÍN.MEŠ TU.É LÚ.AB.BA.MEŠ *šá mil-ki šá la man-zal-la-ti-šú-nu*).[7] In the letter YOS 3, 6 a Babylonian king, whose name is not given, orders the citizens of Uruk to send ten or fifteen Elders and priests (1.18 LÚ *ši-bu-tú ù* LÚ *ki-niš-ti*) at his disposal.

In one of his inscriptions the king Nabonidus declares that he assembled "Elders of the City, citizens of Babylon" (1.32 *ši-bu-ut* URU DUMU.MEŠ TIN.TIR. KI) in order to ask their advice about the construction of a temple (VAB 4, p.254 No. 6).

The term LÚ.AB.BA.MEŠ/LÚ *ši-bu-tu* is frequently found in the Neo-Babylonian letters of the 7th century BC. For instance, according to ABL 202:rev.15, Elders will come to Babylon and take the oath of the Assyrian king. As seen from ABL 287:12, fifteen Elders came to enquire about the king's welfare. In ABL 517:12 the Elders of the tribe Bīt-Amukanu are mentioned. ABL 576 is a letter sent by the Elders of the Sealand to the king of Assyria.

In VS 6, 101/102 (Babylon, 533 BC) the term under discussion is used to designate a witness instead of *mukinnu*. According to this text at a slave sale the elder son of the seller was present as a witness (ll. 9-10 *a-na* LÚ.AB.BA. MEŠ *ina* IM.DUB KI.LAM *šá* PN *a-sib*).[8]

Sometimes the word LÚ.AB.BA.MEŠ/LÚ *ši-bu-tu* is used in contrast to LÚ.TUR. MEŠ/LÚ *ṣi-ḫi-ru-tu* in the meaning "old and young". For example, as seen from

UCP 9, p.89 No. 24:9, officials of Eanna and the slaves of the same temple "old and young" appointed a certain man as an overseer over the temple slaves. Cf. ABL 293 and 296-7 which are letters of the Assyrian king Assurbanipal to the inhabitants of some cities, "old and young"; in ABL 210 the "old and young" of a city are addressing the Assyrian king; YOS 3, 6 contains an order of the Babylonian king to the citizens of Uruk "old and young" (see CAD Ṣ 184b). Cf. also *il-ta ṣa-ḫi-ir a-di ši-bu-tu* (*Nbk*. 125:1-2) "from youth to old age", and *ši-bu-tu lu-uk-šu-ud* (VAB 4, p.94:49 and p.140:7) "may I attain old age".

From the documents examined we may conclude that the Elders solved important issues of a local nature. In some cases the Elders made their decisions together with the principal temple officials and governors of the cities. Some decisions of the Elders were directly connected with temple affairs (for instance, the collection of the temple tithe) and others were concerned with controversial property cases of private individuals. Sometimes important instructions of the high state officials were announced in the presence of the Elders. Finally, Elders acted before the king as representatives of their own cities.

The assembly where the Elders functioned was called *puḫru* (UKKIN/ *pu-uḫ-ru*, *pu-ḫu-ru*, *pu-ḫur-ru*). In the Babylonian texts of the 7th-4th centuries BC the following kinds of *puḫru* are mentioned: *puḫru ša māti* "the assembly of the country", *puḫur ummāni* "the assembly of the people", and assemblies of cities of Babylon, Kutha, Nippur, Sippar, Uruk, etc.

M. San Nicolò has made valuable observations on the role of the *puḫru* in the Neo-Babylonian period,[9] but this is a subject needing special treatment which it cannot receive here, and we shall only try to outline a general picture of the activity of the *puḫru*. Neo-Babylonian society consisted of fully-fledged citizens (*mār-banī*), of free-born persons deprived of civil rights, of various classes of *glebae adscripti*, and finally of slaves. The citizens were members of the popular assembly (*puḫru*)[10] of the temple community, which was invested with jurisdiction in judging cases involving property and family law. The popular assembly considered civil and criminal cases, including matters in no way related to the temples.[11] In those instances when the popular assembly considered a case, at least in Uruk and Sippar, the principal temple officials directed the court proceedings, since the temple was the heart of the community. Sometimes only Elders, that is the most influential of the citizens, acted as representatives of the assembly, and made decisions, instead of gathering all the members, that is the *mār-banī*.

The centuries-old rivalry between the royal court and popular assembly had already under the Chaldean kings ended in the defeat of the assembly, and only property disputes and private offences of a local nature were now subject to its jurisdiction.

Citizens possessed immovable property within the communal land district which came under the jurisdiction of the popular assembly. Many of them were holders of certain shares of income from the temples. Such citizens included persons of high rank (the upper echelons of the state and temple officials, merchants, prosperous scribes, etc.) as well as craftsmen and peasants, including the poorest strata of the free-born population. From the legal point of view, all citizens were considered equal, and their status was hereditary.

Free-men deprived of civil rights consisted of the king's military colonists, Persian and other foreign officials in the state service (such as tax-collectors, overseers of the palace workmen, dragomans, etc.), and other free-born aliens who lived in Babylonia for different reasons (merchants, craftsmen of various trades, etc.). These persons had no part in city (or temple) self-government because they did not own property within the city's lands, had no access to the Babylonian temples, and consequently could not become members of the popular assembly.

In some cases the aliens in Babylonia were settled in considerable numbers in separate and distinct settlements. Such strangers could establish their own self-government, that is, a popular assembly. For instance, according to the document *Camb.* 85, cited above and dated in the reign of Cambyses, a certain part of the city of Babylon was settled by Egyptians who had their own popular assembly which could decide matters of civil law within their colony. Biblical authors mention Elders of the Jews in Babylonian captivity.[12] Evidently these Elders judged litigations within the Jewish colonies in Babylonia. These self-governing bodies of ethnic minority groups in Babylonia existing alongside the popular assemblies of the citizens in many respects resemble, as Prof. E.J. Bickermann has pointed out to us, the *politeumata* of the Hellenistic period.

---

1 Cf. W. von Soden, AHw 1228f.

2 Cf. M. San Nicolò, *Parerga Babylonica*, VII, in *Archiv Orientální* 4 [1932] p.344.

3 Cf. J. Kohler & F.E. Peiser, *Aus dem babylonischen Rechtsleben*, II [Leipzig 1891] pp. 77f.

4 Cf. Kohler & Peiser, op.cit., IV [1898] p.6.

5 Cf. H. Lanz, *Die neubabylonischen ḫarrânu-Geschäftsunternehmen* [Berlin 1976] pp. 72 and 92.

6 Cf. E. Ebeling, *Neubabylonische Briefe* [München 1949] p.151. The Neo-Babylonian letters were transliterated and translated by E. Ebeling in this book and in *Neubabylonische Briefe aus Uruk*, 1-4 [Berlin 1930-34].

7 See CAD E 291a and M Pt. 2, 68.

8 Cf. *a-na ši-bu-tu a-ši-ib* (VS 4, 197:9-10), *a-na ši-bu-tu ina lìb-bi a-ši-ib / aš-ba-at* (F.E. Peiser, BV XCVII = *Dar.* 463:13; *Nbn.* 903:7-8), *a-na ši-bu-tú ina lìb-bi áš-bi* (M. Rutten, RA 41 [1947] 102:19-20), *a-na* LÚ *ši-bu-ú-tu ina ú-il-tì šá* PN *a-ši-ib* (*Nbn.* 104:9-10). See M. San Nicolò & A. Ungnad, NRVU 103, n.3; A. Ungnad, NRVU Glossar, p. 145.

9 M. San Nicolò, *Babylonische Rechtsurkunden des ausgehenden 8. und des 7. Jahrhunderts v. Chr.* [München 1951] 146-7 (with previous literature).

10 See UKKIN LÚ.DUMU.DÙ.MEŠ (= *puḫur mār-banī* "the assembly of the citizens") in UET 4, 201:3; YOS 7, 167:12, etc.

11 See BE 9, 69; 87; PBS 2/i, 140; M.W. Stolper, JCS 28 [1976] 193; YOS 6, 116; YOS 7, 7; 125; 128; 149; 167; 189, etc.

12 See *Ezekiel* 8:1; 14:1; 20:1. On the Elders in the Bible see H. Reviv, *Elders and "Saviors"*, in *Oriens Antiquus* 16 [1977] 201-4 (with previous literature).

DER AUFBAU DES SYLLABARS "PROTO-EA" *

Dietz Otto Edzard (München)

Welche Schwierigkeiten die Herausgeber der Silbenzeichen-Serie "Proto-Ea"[1] zu bewältigen hatten, wird nur dem klar, der das ausserordentlich spröde Quellenmaterial anhand einer Photosammlung einsehen konnte.[2] Nach ihrer Erstedition durch B. Landsberger 1951 liegt die Serie nun in einer sehr vervollständigten, sehr viel weniger Lücken aufweisenden Edition durch M. Civil vor.[3] Erst hier ist der Grund für weiterführende Studien gelegt.

Wir werden zwar niemals genau wissen, weshalb diese oder jene der zahlreichen lexikalischen und Syllabarserien eine ganz bestimmte Reihenfolge einhielt. Was uns vorliegt, ist ja nur der karge schriftliche Niederschlag eines lebendigen Unterrichts, dessen Ablauf wir nicht rekonstruieren können; dessen Ziel es aber zweifellos n i c h t war, dass der Schüler das Gelernte "schwarz auf weiss getrost nach Hause trug"; er musste es auswendig wissen.[4] Wir können nur versuchen, den Ablauf einer Serie nachzuvollziehen, indem wir Gedankenverbindungen aufspüren, die der antike Kompilator gehabt haben mag.

In diesem Aufsatz, den ich meinem hochverehrten Freunde und Kollegen Igor Michailovič widme, möchte ich einen solchen Versuch wagen. Ob damit etwas "Allgemeines, Theoretisches" geleistet wird, wie es die Herausgeber nahelegten, oder etwas Hochspezialisiertes, Technisches, möge der Jubilar beurteilen. Jedenfalls lohnt sich wohl der Versuch, eines der wichtigsten 'Lehrbücher' der altbabylonischen Schreiberschulen auf seine Struktur und Eigenart hin zu untersuchen.

Die Serie gliedert sich ohne äussere Einteilungsmerkmale[5] in eine grössere Zahl von Abschnitten. Von diesen bilden manche ganz eindeutig in sich geschlossene Einheiten, die scharf gegen das Vorhergehende und Folgende abgesetzt sind; bei manchen anderen müssen wir das Risiko auf uns nehmen, dass wir willkürlich vorgehen. Wir versuchen, die Gliederung zu begründen, so gut es geht. Aber wer in einem Serienwerk der altorientalischen Literatur Systematik in unserem modernen Sinne sucht, verfährt anachronistisch.[6]

Ich habe versucht, die Einteilung an den Quellen nachzuprüfen. Wo beginnen und enden die einzelnen Textzeugnisse, die zum grössten Teil Übungs- oder Auszugstafeln sind?[7] Leider ist das Ergebnis nicht sehr aufschlussreich. Die Texte sind meist so stark beschädigt, dass wir nicht mehr rekonstruieren können, mit welcher Zeile des Gesamtwerkes sie jeweils einsetzten und abschlossen. Die folgende Tabelle führt diejenigen Texte auf, deren Anfangs- und/oder Endzeilen erhalten oder sicher zu rekonstruieren sind. Wir sehen dabei, dass einige Texte eine Stichzeile haben. Die Kolumnen "Zeile davor" und "Zeile danach" sollen über den Kontext orientieren: Beginnt bzw. endet die jeweilige Tafel mit einer Zeichengruppe, die sich deutlich von dem absetzt, was vorausgeht bzw. folgt, oder beginnt (endet) das Exzerpt an einem - wenigstens unserem Verständnis nach - willkürlich herausgegriffenen Punkt?

QUELLE	ANFANGSZEILE	ZEILE DAVOR	ENDZEILE	ZEILE DANACH	STICHZEILE
Ar	-	-	483 U.GA		484 NAM
Cf	45 LAGAB×NUMUN	(44 LAGAB×A)	-	-	-
Co	74 LAL	(73 ME)	-	-	-
Dg	71 ME	(70 U.TÚG)	89 IR	(90 NI)	-
Di	74 LAL	(73 ME)	-	-	-
Dj	74 LAL	(73 ME)	-	-	-
Dr	79 LÁL.KAK	(78 LÁL.LAGAB)	-	-	-
Dl	-	-	198 TAR	(199 DIN)	-
Du	-	-	198 TAR	(199 DIN)	-
Ea	85 ŠITA	(84 SÌLA)	-	-	-
Eb	85 ŠITA	(84 SÌLA)	-	-	-
En	-	-	470 TUR.ZA TUR.ZA	(471 GAL)	-
Eo	-	-	167 ZA	(168 EŠ)	-
Ep	103 BAD	(102 AŠ aufwärts)	108 BAD	(109 BAD.NI)	-
Eq	285 AB	(284 KU$_7$)	108 BAD	(109 BAD.NI)[8]	
Fa	121 ŠÚ	(120 BAR)	-	-	-
Fh	134 AN	(133 BURU$_5$)	145 URI	(146 BA)	-
Fk	125 ḪU	(124 KÉŠ)	-	-	-
Fp	151 UD	(150 SU×A)	-	-	-
Fs	-	-	166 GADA	(167 ZA)	-
Fx	181 SI	(180 LA)	-	-	-
Ga	187 MES	(186 UM.ME)	-	-	-
Ge	[221 É]	(220 KISAL)	-	-	-
Go	285 AB	(284 KU$_7$)	-	-	-
Gy	-	-	328 KA×BAD	(329 KA×ŠU)	-
He	335 KAL	(334a KA×SIG)	-	-	-
Hg	336 da ⟨-an⟩ KAL	(335 KAL)	343 sú-un KAL	(344 mu-ru-uš KAL)	-
Hh	-	-	385 ú-ub UB	(386 wa-ar UB)	-
Hq	-	-	395 NUN NUN	(396 NUN-tenû)	-
Hw	-	-	434 GU	(435 GU× GU)	-
Hx	436 SAL.TUK	(435 GU GU)	-	-	-
Hy	436 SAL.TUK	(435 GU GU)	-	-	-
Ia	680 NAGA inv.	(679 NAGA)	-	-	-
Ig	482 U.GA	(481 GA-gunû)	-	-	-
Ij	616 i-zi NE[9]	(615d še-èm NE)	539 URU GÁNA-tenû	(540 URU×A)	-

QUELLE	ANFANGSZEILE	ZEILE DAVOR	ENDZEILE	ZEILE DANACH	STICHZEILE
Ik	-	-	562 ŠID	(563 GÌR)	-
Il	553 tu-ba ŠID	(552 la-ag ŠID)	-	-	-
Im	-	-	588 GUL	(589 NIMGIR)	-
In	578 LUL	(577 ⟨U.⟩ PIRIG)	-	-	-
Io	583 PÉŠ	(582a LUL)	-	-	-
Ip	589 NIMGIR	(588 GUL)	-	-	-
Iq	589 NIMGIR	(588 GUL)	610 NÍNDA×NE	(611 NÍNDA×Ú+AŠ)	-
Is	Vs.1 Á Rs.606 KUM	 (605 PI)	97 NI.NI 612 NÍNDA×NUN		98 AŠ 613 NE
Iw	623 ŠEŠ	(622 ḪÚB)	-	-	-
Iz	634 TUM	(633 leer) (632 LÚ-šessig)	651 UR-šessig		652 ŠÀ
Ja	-	-	656 ŠÀ×TUR	(657 ŠÀ×⌜NE⌝)	-
Je	681 LI	(680 NAGA-inv.)	-	-	-
Jf	-	-	700 KAD$_5$	(701 ZUR)	-
Ji	652 ŠÀ	(651 UR-šessig)	-	-	-
Jm	750 DAR	(Lücke)	755 MÙŠ-gunû	([756 MÙŠ-gunû], 757 EZEN)	-
Jn	752 MÙŠ	(751 DAR)	756 MÙŠ-gunû		757 EZEN
Jp	791 MUG	(790 ARAD×KUR)	807 GUR$_7$	(808 MUNSUB)	-
Js	-	-	918 (= Ende)	-	-
Jt	-	-	823 NUNUZ.ÁB× ⌜AŠGAB⌝		824 DAG.KISIM [(X)]
Ju	827 DAG.KISIM$_5$× LU.MÁŠ	(DAG.KISIM$_5$× LU.MÁŠ	835 DAG.KISIM$_5$× GÍR	(836 [?])	-
Jw	-	-	873 UR$_4$	(874 MÁ+KAK)	-
Jz	911 si-ki [SÍG?]	(910 [x])	-	-	-
Kg	-	-	76 LÁL		LÁL.DU
Kk	71 ME	(70 ⟨U.⟩ TÚG)	-	-	-
Kl	78 LÁL.LAGAB	(77 LÁL.SAR)	-	-	-
Kp	-	-	79 LÁL.KAK	(80 LÁL.GIŠGAL)	-
Ks	-	-	516b EREN		516c IG

Bemerkungen zur Tabelle: Von den knapp 300 Textzeugen, die M. Civil benutzt hat (s. MSL 14, 17-29), konnten wir nur 62 aufnehmen, d.h. nicht einmal ein Viertel. Von diesen wiederum sind nur 11 so gut erhalten, dass sowohl der Anfang als auch das Ende bestimmt werden können. Es folgen einige Bemerkungen zu einzelnen Texten:

8 Texte (Ar, Is zweimal, Iz, Jn, Jt, Kg, Ks) enthalten eine "Stichzeile", d.h. der letzte aufgeführte Wert gehört nicht mehr zur davor behandelten Zeichengruppe, sondern er bildet den Anfang einer neuen Gruppe. Dies ist besonders augenfällig bei Is Vs., Is Rs. (NE hat 8 Einträge; nur der erste ist angeführt), bei Iz (ŠÀ eröffnet eine neue Reihe), bei Jn (EZEN eröffnet eine neue lange Reihe) und bei Jt (die Stichzeile leitet über zur Gruppe DAG.KISIM$_5$ × Z).

En: Endet 470; GAL (471) ist zwar durch Kontrastassoziation noch mit der TUR-Gruppe verbunden; aber mit 473 BU (472 ist leer) beginnt eindeutig ein neuer Abschnitt.

Ep: Beginnt mit der BAD-Gruppe.

Fh: Endet mit 145 URI: 146 BA eröffnet einen neuen Abschnitt.

Fs: Endet mit 166 GADA; 167 ZA eröffnet einen neuen Abschnitt.

He: Beginnt mit KAL, auf die KA-Gruppe folgend.

Ik: Endet 562 mit dem letzten Eintrag von ŠID; mit 563 GÌR beginnt die "Tierkopf-Gruppe".

Iz: Eröffnet mit 634 TUM (nach Leerzeile) einen neuen Abschnitt; zum Ende mit Stichzeile s. oben.

Jf: 700 KAD$_5$ beendet wahrscheinlich einen Abschnitt; der folgende beginnt mit ZUR.

Jm: Endet mit der MÙŠ-Gruppe; 757 EZEN eröffnet einen neuen Abschnitt.

Dem können wir aber Beispiele gegenüberstellen, wo ein Text mitten in einem von uns als zusammenhängend empfundenen Abschnitt einsetzt oder endet, z.B.:

Jn beginnt mit 752 MÙŠ unter Weglassung des formverwandten DAR (751).

Eq beginnt 285 mit AB unter Weglassung von KU$_7$ (AB-*nutillû*).

Gy endet 328 mitten in der Gruppe KA × Z.

Usw.

Wir beginnen unseren Gliederungsversuch mit A b s c h n i t t 1, den wir von Z.1-80 reichen lassen. Er ist folgendermassen aufgebaut:[10]

1-5 A, 6, 6a A.A, A.A.A, 7-9 Diri's[11] von A (ḪA.A, A.AN), 10-24 KU, 25 KU.KU, 26 KU.AN, 27-33 LAGAB, 34-57 LAGAB mit eingeschriebenem Zeichen, d.h. LAGAB × Z, 58-61 ŠÈ, 61a-c LÙ, 62-63 LU, 64 LU × BAD, 65 DIB, 66-69 TÚG, 70 U.TÚG, 71-73 ME, 74-75 LAL, 76-80 LÁL.Z.

Verkürzt dargestellt, d.h. auf die konstituierenden Zeichen reduziert, sieht dieser Abschnitt so aus:[12]

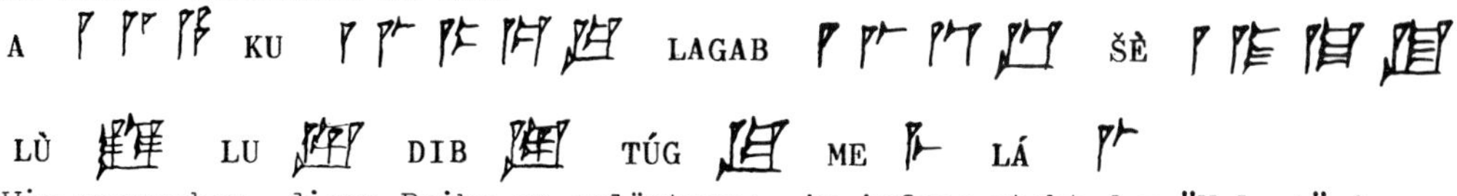

Wir versuchen, diese Reihe zu erläutern: Am Anfang steht der "Urlaut" A, dargestellt durch einen S. und zwei übereinander gestellte S. Die Assoziation mit dem folgenden KU besteht möglicherweise darin, dass dieses Zeichen mit einem S. und zwei kurzen W. beginnt. Nach KU wird unter Weglassung des mittleren W. und leichter Dehnung in die Breite das Quadrat LAGAB gebildet. Dieses LAGAB wird dann 'angefüllt' zum ŠÈ, nachdem eine grosse Zahl von Formen LAGAB × Z vorangegangen waren. Die W. von ŠÈ werden seitwärts verdoppelt, und es entsteht LÙ. Eine weitere Form eines 'angefüllten' LAGAB ist dann LU (gleichsam LAGAB × MAŠ). Füge einen weiteren W. hinzu, und du erhältst DIB. Lasse den mittleren S. von DIB weg, und es bleibt TÚG. Damit ist die "Kästchen"-Gruppe erschöpft, und der Schreiber kehrt zu einfacheren Formen zurück, die mit einem S. beginnen: ME sowie (unter Verschiebung des W.) LAL. Das LAL wird abschliessend noch zu LÁL verdoppelt und bildet den Anfang einiger zusammengesetzter Zeichen.

Dieser erste Abschnitt beschreibt sozusagen einen 'Bogen'. Er beginnt mit einem einfachen Zeichen, schreitet zu komplizierteren fort, um am Ende zu einer einfachen Form zurückzukehren. Wir werden solchen 'Bögen' noch öfter begegnen (s. die *Abschnitte 2, 3, 4, 20-21(?) 23-24* [ideell], *30*).

A b s c h n i t t 2 (81-97) ist viel kürzer: 81-83 PAP samt PAP.E, 83a, 84 QA, 85 ŠITA, 86-88 KAK, 89 IR, 90-97 NI samt NI.NI (*ì-lí*).

PAP
QA
ŠITA
KAK
IR
NI

Der Abschnitt beginnt mit einem einfachen Zeichen, den sich schräg kreuzenden Keilen von PAP. Anfügung eines S. (wobei die Schrägkeile auch spitz aufeinander zulaufen können): QA. Vorn tritt ein kleiner S. an: ŠITA. Der hintere S. fällt weg: KAK. 'Anfüllung' des KAK: IR, NI.

Die Grenze zwischen den *Abschnitten 1* und *2* leuchtet ein: Rechtwinklige Zeichen werden durch solche mit Schrägkeilen abgelöst. *Abschnitt 2* beginnt wie *1* mit einer sehr einfachen Form, und er kehrt zu einer ähnlichen Form zurück.

A b s c h n i t t 3 (98-145) ist komplizierter aufgebaut: 98-100 AŠ, 101 DIŠ, 102 DIŠ-tenû, 102a DIŠ *inversum*, 103-108 BAD, 109 BAD.NI (*be-lí*), 110-111 IDIM, 112-114 U, 115-119 MAŠ samt MAŠ.MAŠ, 120 BAR, 121-124 ŠÚ samt Diri's, 125-128 ḪU samt ḪU.SI, 129-132 RI, 133 BURU$_5$, 134-138 AN samt KÙ.AN und AN.AN, 138a-140 MUL, 141, 141a AN.DÙL, 142-143 ḪAL, 144 TAB und als 'Anhang' 145, 145a URI.

Verkürzt:

AŠ
DIŠ
BAD
IDIM
U
MAŠ
BAR
ŠÚ

ḪU
RI
BURU5
AN
ḪAL
TAB

Der Abschnitt beginnt mit 4 einfachen Keilen, von denen übrigens s a n t a (k) 101 (vgl. 102, 102a) nicht am Anfang unserer Serie steht, wie man das nach "Examenstext A" erwarten könnte.[13] BAD und IDIM sind nur in wenigen Texten voneinander abgesetzt.[14] Beide sind eine Erweiterung von AŠ. Erst dann folgt das einfache U. Sodann werden AŠ und DIŠ gekreuzt: MAŠ. Der W. von MAŠ sinkt hinab: BAR. Er wird zum kurzen Schrägkeil: ŠÚ. ḪU ist *grosso modo* eine Kombination von MAŠ und ŠÚ. ḪU um einen S. bereichert ist RI. BURU$_5$ (von NAM 484, s. *Abschnitt 27*, getrennt) beginnt mit ḪU. Der Übergang zum folgenden AN lässt sich formal nicht befriedigend erklären. Wir dürfen aber vielleicht eine Assoziation BURU$_5$ "Himmelsgetier"[15] > AN "Himmel" annehmen. ḪAL ist AN minus DIŠ. Für ḪAL > TAB kann ich keine unmittelbare graphische Assoziation vorschlagen. TAB steht aber ohne Zweifel in einer Fernbeziehung zu dem *Abschnitt 3* eröffnenden AŠ; es ist seine Verdoppelung, und daher kann beim vorangehenden ḪAL kein 'Bruch' vorliegen. Unser Abschnitt beschreibt wieder einen 'Bogen' vom Einfachen über das Komplizierte zurück zur einfachen Form. Die 'Coda' URI möchte ich so erklären: Das Zeichen besteht in Ur III und altbab. gewöhnlich aus zwei gleichen übereinander gesetzten Elementen, deren jedes mit einem TAB beginnt.[16] (S. Nachtrag.)

A b s c h n i t t 4 (146-166): 146 BA, 147 ZU, 148-150 SU samt SU × A, 151-160 UD samt Diri's, 161 ITU, 162-163 LAGAR-*gunû* (DU$_6$) samt LAGAR-*gunû*.DU (E$_{11}$), 164 LAGAR × ŠE, 165 LAGAR, 166 GADA.

Verkürzt:

BA
ZU
SU
UD
LAGAR
GADA

Abschnitt 4 ist formal klar gegen den vorigen abgesetzt. Für die Folge TAB(-URI-)BA lässt sich vielleicht das geläufige t a b - b a "verdoppelt" verantwortlich machen, d.h. BA wurde durch TAB 'evoziert' (wobei wir von dem Anhang URI absehen). Wir werden noch weitere solche Wortassoziationen kennen lernen (vgl. die Abschnitte 12, 13, 26, 27, 32-3, usw).

BA wird durch Hinzufügung mehrerer S. zu ZU. Ein weiterer W. ergibt SU. UD kann man als Formvariante von BA betrachten, und auch bei LAGAR haben wir es mit einer dem BA ähnlichen Form zu tun; in ein 'Trapez' ist bei BA ein kleiner W., bei LAGAR ein kleiner S. eingezeichnet. GADA ist gleichsam ein LAGAR minus vorderem S. Interessanterweise wird das einfache LAGAR erst nach den mit LAGAR komponierten Zeichen angeführt. Wir beobachten abermals einen 'Bogen', der von einem einfachen Zeichen (BA) auf dem Weg über Komplizierteres wieder zu einem einfachen zurückkehrt.

A b s c h n i t t 5 (167-170): 167 ZA, 168 EŠ, 169 LIMMU$_5$ (ZA), 170 LÍMMU (TAB.TAB).

ZA  EŠ  LIMMU$_5$  LÍMMU 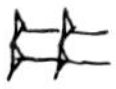

Hier werden, von ZA ausgehend, Zahlzeichen für "drei" und "vier" abgehandelt. Die Auslautsilbe von l i m m u attrahiert dann

A b s c h n i t t 6 (171-178): 171-174 MU, 175 $\frac{\text{MU}}{\text{MU}}$ (DAḪ), 176 U.MU, 177-178 KUL.

MU  KUL 

Der Abschnitt ist formal in sich geschlossen. Der Übergang zu *Abschnitt 7* geschah möglicherweise mit (akk.) *kul-la* "alles" (Akkus.) als Eselsbrücke.

A b s c h n i t t 7 (179-194): 179-180 LA, 181-183a SI samt SI-*gunû* und SI.*[A]*, 184-186 UM samt UM.ME, 187 MES, 188-189 DUB, 190-194 URUDU samt URUDU × U.

LA  SI  UM  MES  DUB  URUDU 

Lassen wir bei einem Ur III-zeitlichen LA die eingeschriebenen S. und W. weg, so bleibt eine dem SI nicht ganz unähnliche Form. Eine Erklärung für den Übergang von SI.A zu UM findet man vielleicht, wenn man die Ligatur SI+A zugrunde legt. Aus UM entsteht MES durch 'Vorschalten' von einem kleinen, und DUB durch 'Vorschalten' von zwei kleinen S. URUDU ist wieder ein MES, das um die eingeschriebenen S. 'entleert' ist. Die Reihe endet also wieder einmal mit einem Zeichen, das seinen Vorgängern gegenüber einfacher ist.

A b s c h n i t t 8 (194a-203): 194a-198 TAR, 199-200 DIN samt 201 I.DIN (= *iddin* in PN), 201a *[*BALAG?*]*, 202-203 BALAG.

TAR 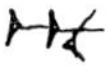 DIN  BALAG 

Dieser Abschnitt setzt (ohne mir erkennbaren Bezug zum vorigen) nochmals mit einem sehr einfachen Zeichen ein und fährt mit dem - formal nicht überzeugend ähnlichen - DIN fort. BALAG ist an DIN angeschlossen, weil DIN das Mittelstück dieses Zeichens bildet.

A b s c h n i t t 9 (204-218): 204-207 TAK$_4$, 208-210 GAR samt 211-213 U.GAR, 214 SUR, 215 BUR, 216-217 E, 218 KÙ.

TAK$_4$  GAR  SUR  BUR  E  KÙ 

TAK$_4$ und GAR könnte man als durch ihren Zeichenbeginn (drei sich nach oben verjüngende S.) verwandt bezeichnen. SUR ist GAR mit vorgesetztem AŠ. BUR ist ähnlich, aber keinesfalls identisch mit einem GAR-*gunû*. E lässt sich formal als ein am Zeichenende 'begradigtes' BUR verstehen. Bei KÙ mag eine vague Formähnlichkeit mit TAK$_4$ oder aber sogar mit E für die Einbeziehung ausschlaggebend gewesen sein. Aber wir wissen nicht, welche Spielart des Zeichens dem Kompilator vorlag. (S. Nachtrag.)

A b s c h n i t t 10 (219-255): 219-220 KISAL, 221-229 É samt É × Z, 230-232 Ú, 233 SA, 234-235 LUḪ, 236-237 DAG, 238-239 KÁ, 240-241 ŠID × A, 242 leer, 243-246 KID samt U.KID, 247-250a IŠ, 251-252 ḪÚL, 253-254 GIDIM und UDUG, 255 GUKKAL, 256-259 leer.

KISAL  É  Ú  SA  LUḪ 

DAG  KÁ  ŠID x A  KID  IŠ 

ḪÚL  GIDIM  UDUG  GUKKAL 

Die Folge KISAL-É-Ú-SA-LUḪ ist einleuchtend. DAG ist ein É mit schräg-gespaltenem Schluss-S. KÁ ist É-*šessig*. ŠID × A wirkt als Fremdkörper,[17] wurde aber vielleicht auf Grund des Zeichenanfangs (drei W. übereinander) aufgenommen. Zu beachten ist die Dissoziation von É und KID (Leerzeile vor KID Zufall?), die in der Ur III-Kursive oft nicht voneinander zu unterscheiden sind. IŠ und ḪÚL sind wohl wegen ihrer zahlreichen übereinander liegenden W. angeschlossen. Für GIDIM und UDUG[18] war der Zeichenanfang von ḪÚL massgebend. GUKKAL schliesslich ist von Hause aus Ligatur UDU+ḪÚL.

A b s c h n i t t 11 (260-264) enthält nur 260-263 DI, 263a-b KI und 264 NA.

DI  KI  NA 

Vielleicht ist der Anfang von DI mit dem rechten Teil von GUKKAL assoziiert. Die Fortsetzung mit KI und NA drängt sich dann auf und bedarf keiner Erläuterung.

A b s c h n i t t 12 (265-275): 265-268 ḪA samt ḪA-*gunû*, 269-271 MA samt MA-*gunû*, 272, 272a TI, 273 BAL, 274-275 SUM.

ḪA  MA  TI  BAL  SUM 

Abschnitt 12 ist der erste, bei dem uns formale Kriterien im Stich lassen. Er stellt eine völlig heterogene Gruppe dar. Zwischen ḪA-MA-TI besteht keine formale Ähnlichkeit. Vielleicht ist es aber nicht zu weit hergeholt, wenn wir an den beliebten Ur III-zeitlichen PN Ḫ a - m a - t i erinnern.[19] Der Übergang von TI zu BAL ist formal plausibel. Da SUM sich schwerlich in den folgenden Abschnitt einfügt, ist wohl an eine Assoziation BAL "übertragen, überweisen" SUM "geben" zu denken. (S. Nachtrag.)

A b s c h n i t t 13 (276-282): 276-279 GUD samt GUD × KUR (AM), 280 GEŠTIN, 281-282 UL.

GUD  GEŠTIN  UL 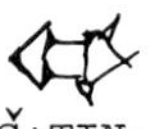

GEŠTIN ist historisch eine Ligatur GIŠ+TIN; es kann aber auch als ein GUD mit zwei eingeschriebenen Winkelhaken aufgefasst werden. UL = U.GUD.

Die Idee "Stier" (GUD) leitet dann - oder ist eine solche Assoziation zu kühn? - zum "Viehmäster" (KU$_7$, k u r u š t a) über, der den nächsten Abschnitt einleitet.[20]

A b s c h n i t t 14 (283-334a): 283-284 KU$_7$, 285-286 AB, 287 AB × PA (ZÉ), 288-290 weitere AB × Z, 291 ZU.AB, 292-302 SAG samt SAG-*gunû*, SAG-*nutillû*, SAG × Z, U.SAG, 303-334a KA samt U.KA, KA × Z.

KU$_7$  AB 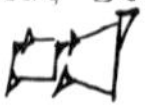 ZU.AB  SAG  KA 

KU$_7$ ist AB-*nutillû* und steht daher vor AB. Zwischenstück zwischen den AB-Komposita und SAG ist ZU.AB (ABZU). SAG liesse sich formal als ein radikal verkürztes ZU.AB verstehen; doch ist die Hypothese kühn. Sonst müssten wir diesen Abschnitt in zwei unabhängige Einzelabschnitte aufteilen. Dass KA auf SAG folgt, ist zu erwarten.

A b s c h n i t t 15 (335-346): 335-344 KAL, 345-346 GUR und U.GUR.

KAL  GUR 

KAL und GUR (das zweite Zeichen ist das einfachere) haben zwar eine gewisse Ähnlichkeit miteinander; aber eine Anlaut-Assoziation KA(Ende 14)-KAL ist nicht ausgeschlossen.

A b s c h n i t t 16 (347-351): 347-350 LUM, 351 $\frac{\text{LUM}}{\text{LUM}}$.

LUM 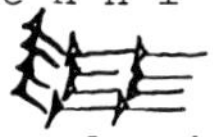

Ich kann das Auftreten von LUM an dieser Stelle nicht erklären. Es hängt formal weder mit vorigem GUR noch mit folgendem BI zusammen.

A b s c h n i t t 17 (352-390): 352-355 BI samt BI.GIŠ, 356-358 leer, 359-363 DUG, 364-384 ḪI samt ḪI × Z, 385-386 UB, 387-390 TE samt TE-*gunû* und TE.A.

BI  DUG  ḪI  UB  TE 

Der Schritt von BI zu DUG ist der einer Vereinfachung. ḪI wird angeschlossen auf Grund des Zeichenendes oder aber wegen des Ähnlichklangs von d u g und d u$_{10}$/d ù g.[21] Unter den Zeichen ḪI × Z findet sich auch AḪ = ḪI × NUN. UB lässt sich als ḪI × DIŠ verstehen (aus der älteren Pentagramma-Form entwickelt) und TE als UB mit anschliessendem S.

Abschnitt 17 stellt, wenn wir den Übergang von DUG zu ḪI richtig gedeutet haben, eine in sich gut geschlossene Gruppe dar.

A b s c h n i t t 18 (391-398b) umfasst nur NUN samt NUN-*tenû* und einigen mit NUN gebildeten Diri's.

NUN 

Ich finde keine Erklärung für die Einordnung an dieser Stelle.

A b s c h n i t t 19 (399-414): 399-402 IGI, 403-404 IGI-*gunû* (nicht = SIG$_7$), 405-406 IGI.IGI, 407 IGI.UR (ḪUL), 408 IGI.DIB (Ù), 409 IGI.ŠÈ (LIBIR), 410 IGI.RU (PÀ), 411-412 IGI.ÉREN, 413-414 SIG$_7$, 415 leer.

IGI  IGI-gunû  SIG$_7$ 

Bemerkenswert ist die Trennung von IGI-*gunû* und dem historisch gleichfalls IGI-*gunû* darstellenden SIG$_7$ (s e$_{12}$, s a$_7$).

A b s c h n i t t 20 (416-416b EN, 417-418 EN × GÁNA-*tenû* samt U.EN × GÁNA-*tenû*, 419-433 SAL.TÚG (NIN) und weitere mit SAL komponierte Zeichen, wobei in 423-424 einfaches SAL eingeschoben ist (425 leer), 434-435 GU samt $\frac{\text{GU}_x}{\text{GU}}$, 436-443 nochmals mit SAL beginnende Zeichen, 444-446 ZUM.

EN  SAL  GU 

Obwohl EN und SAL.Z formal nichts miteinander gemein haben, sind sie doch ideell (e n - n i n) verbunden. Daher beginnt die SAL-Reihe auch nicht mit einfachem SAL.[22] Interessant ist die Aufnahme von GU 434-435 und TILMUN 436 in die SAL-Reihe. Das lässt sich nur erklären, wenn man ein wie SAL beginnendes GU bzw. TILMUN zugrunde legt und nicht die in Ur III übliche Form, die wie ein NI beginnt. Ist dies eine sekundäre Erscheinung in der Liste oder etwa ein Alterskriterium? Vgl. unten S. 57.

A b s c h n i t t 21 (447-450): 447 KUR, 448-449 GAM, 450 NU.

KUR  GAM  NU 

Dieser kurze Abschnitt fügt drei entfernt formverwandte, sehr einfache Zeichen zusammen. Wie gerät er hierher? Ein Übergang zu KUR liesse sich mühelos von einem SAL.KUR (GÉME) aus erklären. Merkwürdigerweise fehlt diese Zeichenverbindung in unserer Serie ganz.[23] Dürfen wir sie interpolieren? Wir könnten dann nicht nur *Abschnitt 21* noch zum vorigen schlagen, sondern wir erhielten auch wieder einen jener 'Bögen' (vgl. oben zu *Abschnitt 1*): Der Schreiber begann theoretisch mit SAL (zog allerdings wegen der Assoziation mit EN das zusammengesetzte NIN und weitere Verbindungen vor), und er hörte mit dem SAL nicht unähnlichen Zeichen NU auf.[24]

A b s c h n i t t 22 (451)

MAH 

ist unerwartet an dieser Stelle, es sei denn, wir nehmen an, dass sich der Kompilator von einer gewissen Verwandtschaft des Zeichenanfangs von MAḪ mit NU orientierte.

A b s c h n i t t 23 (452-461): 452-456 ZI samt $\frac{ZI}{ZI}$ und $\frac{ZI}{ZI}$.LAGAB, 457-459 TIR samt GARADIN, 460-461 GI samt GI-*gunû* (GI_4).

ZI  TIR  GI 

Der Übergang von $\frac{ZI}{ZI}$.LAGAB zu TIR leuchtet zwar ein; denn auch TIR sieht so aus, als sei es aus zwei übereinander stehenden gleichen Elementen aufgebaut. Doch ist zu beachten, dass Text Ia die TIR-Gruppe in *Abschnitt 41* hinter 686 TU anfügt, wo sie formal ebenso gut am Platze ist.

A b s c h n i t t 24 (462-464): 462 DA, 463, 463a Á, 464 KAB.

DA 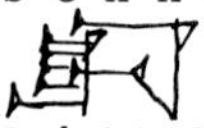 Á  KAB 

Vielleicht darf man die *Abschnitte 23* und *24* zusammenfassen, indem man einen 'Bogen' von "rechts" (ZI 452) nach "links" (KAB = g á b 464) annimmt. Es fällt auf, dass ŠU nicht an der Gruppe DA-Á-KAB teilhat. Es steht vielmehr unten 584 zwischen PÉŠ und GUL, in Fernassoziation mit GÌR.

A b s c h n i t t 25 (465-471): 465-466 I samt IA, 467-470 TUR samt $\frac{TUR.ZA}{TUR.ZA}$ 471 GAL, 472 leer.

I  TUR  GAL 

GAL ist durch Kontrastassoziation mit TUR verbunden.

A b s c h n i t t 26 (473-483): 473-475 BU, 475a-476 SUD, 477-479 DIM_4, 480-483 GA samt GA-*gunû* und U.GA.

BU 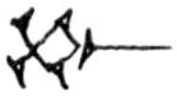 SUD  DIM_4  GA 

Anschluss an GAL vielleicht auf Grund der Ideenverbindung "gross" - "lang", "weit". SUD ist historisch guniertes BU. DIM_4 ist ähnlich wie BU minus W. Text If fügt hinter SUD noch MUŠ an, wie man es der Form nach auch erwartet. Sonst steht MUŠ in *Abschnitt 49* 797 ff. GA, dessen Einordnung zwischen DIM_4 und NAM sich formal nicht begründen lässt, ist vielleicht durch eine Assoziation "aufziehen" (DIM_4) - "Milch" (GA) hierher geraten.

A b s c h n i t t 27 (484-496): 484-486 NAM, 487-496 PA samt einigen mit PA anlautenden Verbindungen.

NAM  PA 

NAM und PA haben formal nichts miteinander zu tun. Ihre Zusammengruppierung könnten wir allenfalls damit erklären, dass beiden Zeichen die Idee der Überordnung (n a m bildet Abstrakta, u g u l a ist der "Obmann") innewohnt. Wie schon bei *Abschnitt 3* bemerkt, ist NAM nicht mit $BURU_5$ (133) zusammengestellt.

A b s c h n i t t 28 (497-514): DU samt DU-*gunû*, DU-*šessig*, $\frac{\text{DU}}{\text{DU}}$ und DU.DU sowie DU.DU.DU.DU.

DU 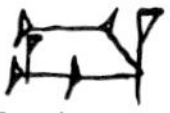

Was hat zur Einordnung von DU an dieser Stelle geführt?

A b s c h n i t t 29 (515-516d): 515, 515a-b SA$_6$, 516, 516a ŠEŠ, 516b EREN, 516c-d IG.

SA$_6$  EREN 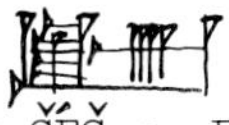 IG 

Der Schritt von SA$_6$ über ŠEŠ zu EREN ist formal leicht erklärt.[24a] Sodann ähnelt das Vorderteil von IG wieder stark dem von EREN. (S. Nachtrag.)

A b s c h n i t t 30 (517-537): 517-518f UŠ samt UŠ × Z, 518g-523 APIN, 524-529 AG samt AG × ÉREN (MÈ), 530-533 DÍM, 534 ḪA-*tenû*, 535 TA, 536 TA × ḪI (LÀL), 537 TA-*gunû*

UŠ 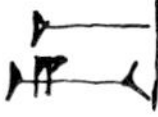 APIN  AG  DÍM  ḪA-tenû  TA 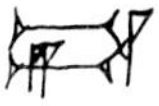

Der Übergang von UŠ zu APIN lässt sich sowohl formal als auch lautlich erklären: a) Einsetzung eines ŠE-artigen 'Kastens' im linken Teil von UŠ unter Weglassung des Winkelhakens rechts, also eine Art Fortsetzung der Reihe UŠ × Z; oder b) dadurch, dass einer der Werte von APIN uš$_8$ ist. AG hat einen ähnlichen Anfang wie APIN. Mit DÍM kehren wir zu einer dem UŠ ähnlichen Form zurück. ḪA-*tenû* ist im Gegensatz zum späteren Ea IV 115 f. (MSL 14, 359) noch nicht mit ḪA zusammengebracht (s. zu diesem *Abschnitt 12*). Es lässt sich ohne grössere Mühe an DÍM anschliessen. TA unterscheidet sich von dem unseren Abschnitt eröffnenden UŠ im Wesentlichen durch einen zusätzlichen Winkelhaken. Der Abschnitt ist also wieder ein Beispiel für einen 'Bogen' (vgl. bei *Abschnitt 1*).

A b s c h n i t t 31 (538-562): 538-550 URU samt URU × Z, 551 RA, 552-562 ŠID.

URU  RA  ŠID 

URU-RA-ŠID folgen in verständlicher Formassoziation.

A b s c h n i t t 32 (563-583): 563-570 GÌR samt GÌR × Z, 571-577 PIRIG samt PIRIG.TUR, PIRIG × Z, U. PIRIG, 578-582a LUL, 583 PÉŠ.

GÌR  PIRIG  LUL  PÉŠ 

Versammelt sind in diesem Abschnitt "Tierkopfzeichen" (historisch gesehen), doch ist die Reihe nicht ganz vollständig. 819 ŠEG$_9$ (*Abschnitt 50'*) und 846 DÀRA (*Abschnitt 52'*) sind von unserem Abschnitt dissoziiert.

A b s c h n i t t 33 (584-585) besteht nur aus ŠU und ŠU.BU.

ŠU 

Wahrscheinlich ist ŠU "Hand", das man formal gern mit DA zusammensehen würde (vgl. oben zu *Abschnitt 24*), durch Fernassoziation mit GÌR "Fuss" des vorigen Abschnitts an seine hiesige Stelle geraten.

A b s c h n i t t 34 (586-596): 586-588 GUL, 589-591 NIMGIR, 592-594 IB, 595-596 UN.

GUL 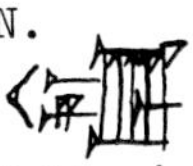 NIMGIR  IB  UN 

Es handelt sich um eine Gruppe rechteckiger Zeichen, wie wir sie auch in *Abschnitt 7* antrafen. In der Tat ist die Dissoziierung von GUL und DUB (188) schwer verständlich. Bei UN ist der ursprüngliche Unterschied von UN = REC

420 und KALAM = REC 421 nicht mehr gewahrt.

A b s c h n i t t 35 (587-605): 597-600 RU, 601-605 PI.

RU  PI 

Sowohl RU als auch PI haben zwei Schrägkeile, die parallel auf einen S. zulaufen.

A b s c h n i t t 36 (606-618): 606-608 KUM samt KUM × ŠE (GAZ), 609-612 NÍNDA samt NÍNDA × Z, 613-618 NE samt NE-*šessig*.

KUM  NÍNDA 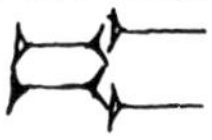 NE 

Der Schritt von KUM zu NÍNDA besteht im Weglassen zweier S. und zweier Winkelhaken. NE hat einen ähnlichen Zeichenanfang wie NÍNDA.

A b s c h n i t t 37 (619-639): 619-620 TUK, 621-622 ḪÚB, 623-624 ŠEŠ, 625-632 LÚ samt LÚ × Z und LÚ-*šessig*, 633 leer, 634-635 TUM, 636 IL, 637 EGIR, 638-639 ZIG.

TUK  ḪÚB  ŠEŠ  LÚ  TUM  IL 

EGIR  ZIG 

In diesem Abschnitt stehen Zeichen zusammen, die als Ganzes oder teilweise durch längliche Dreiecke charakterisiert sind. Hierbei ist ḪÚB eine erweiterte Form von TUK, LÚ ist die logische Folge von ŠEŠ. Es fehlt das seiner Form nach hier zu erwartende AŠGAB (vgl. aber eingeschriebenes AŠGAB in 822f.); ferner fehlt - *horribile dictu* - LUGAL! Bei TUM-IL-EGIR haben wir Zeichen mit zwei Dreiecken vor uns. Man vermisst in unserem Abschnitt die erst in Abschnitt 55 behandelten Zeichen KIN, UR_4, MÁ+KAK und ÙZ.

A b s c h n i t t 38 (640-659): 640-641 GIŠ, 641a GÁNA, 642, 642a GIŠ-*tenû*, 643-644 GIŠ/GIŠ^{x}, 645-651 UR samt UR-*šessig*, 652-657 ŠÀ samt ŠÀ × Z, 658-659 ÚR und ÚR × Ú+AŠ.

GIŠ  GÁNA 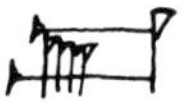 UR  ŠÀ  ÚR 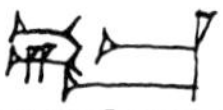

Die Folge GIŠ-GÁNA mag formal im Groben überzeugen, besonders wenn man von einer älteren, länger ausgezogenen Form des GIŠ ausgeht. Doch ist zu beachten, dass der untere W. von GÁNA länger ist als der obere. Für das Weitere ist zu erwägen, dass sich ŠÀ etwa so zu UR verhält wie GIŠ-*tenû* zu GIŠ. ÚR ist dann wohl kaum aus Gründen der Zeichenform angeschlossen. Entweder Lautassoziation UR/ÚR oder Ideenverbindung von ŠÀ "Inneres, Herz" und ÚR "Schoss". Was die Form betrifft, so würden wir ÚR eher in *Abschnitt 36* erwarten.

A b s c h n i t t 39 (660-674): 660-663 IM samt *[I]*M. IM, 664-668 leer, 669 IM(!), 670-672 MI, 673 DUGUD, 674 GIG.

IM 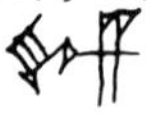 MI  DUGUD  GIG 

Bei der Verbindung von IM mit MI und DUGUD hat - das bedarf keiner Erklärung - der Anzu-Vogel Pate gestanden. DUGUD ist formal MI+AŠ, und GIG = MI+NUNUZ.

A b s c h n i t t 40 (675-676) enthält nur AL.

AL 

Einordnung mir unverständlich. Man könnte meinen, der Kompilator hätte ein Zeichen 'nachgeholt', dessen Anfang dem mancher Zeichen in den *Abschnitten*

36 (KUM), *37* (TUM etc.) und *38* (ÚR) ähnelt. Oder sollte der Kompilator AL und IN (*Abschnitt 41*) als sum. Verbalpräfixe assoziiert haben?

A b s c h n i t t 41 (677-690a): 677 IN, 678-680 NAGA samt NAGA inversum, 681-683 LI, 684-685 TU (REC 147), 686 TU (REC 144?), 687 TU (REC 144)[25], 688, 688a SAR[26], 689, 689a ŠE.

IN  NAGA  LI  TU 

KU_4  SAR  ŠE 

Die Zeichen dieses Abschnitts beginnen mit einer Anhäufung von Winkelhaken. Der Abschnitt endet konsequenterweise mit ŠE. In Text Ia ist auch TIR (457, *Abschnitt 21*) unserem Abschnitt zugeschlagen, und zwar steht es dort hinter TU.

A b s c h n i t t 42 (691-716): 691-692 AD, U.AD, 693-695 GAN samt U.GAN, 696-700 KAD_5, 701-704 AMAR, AMAR.AMAR, AMAR × ŠE.AMAR × ŠE, 705-707 NIM samt [NIM × GÁNA-*tenû*], 708-709 [...], 710-711 GALAM, 712-716 GÚ samt GÚ × Z.

AD  GAN  KAD_5  AMAR 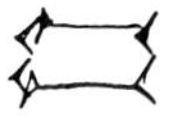 NIM 

[...] GALAM  GÚ 

Vielleicht ist dieser Abschnitt zu weit gefasst; auch ist er mit dem Unsicherheitsfaktor einer Lücke belastet.[27] Er setzt das Thema "Schrägkeile" fort, wobei wir die Zeichen GAN und KAD ebenso gut in *Abschnitt 37* in der Gruppe TUM-IL-EGIR-ZIG erwarten könnten.

A b s c h n i t t 43 (717-719) mit TÙN samt TÙN-*gunû* -

TÙN 

Einordnung mir nicht erklärlich - trennt

A b s c h n i t t 44 (720-722): 720 DU_8, 721-722 GABA ab.

DU_8 

Formal würden wir diesen Abschnitt mit GALAM in *Abschnitt 42* assoziieren. Ist die Unterscheidung in Text Je, wo DU_8 acht, GABA jedoch nur fünf oder sechs Winkelhaken hat, beabsichtigt?

A b s c h n i t t 45 (723-727): 723-725 SIG, 726 LIŠ, 727 NUNUZ.

SIG  LIŠ  NUNUZ 

Der Schritt von SIG zu LIŠ beruht auf Zeichenvereinfachung. Die Assoziation von NUNUZ ist offenbar entfernt formal.

A b s c h n i t t 46 (728-[n]): GÁ samt GÁ × Z.

GÁ 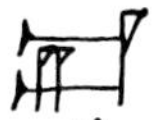

Ich kann die Einordnung von GÁ an dieser Stelle nicht erklären. Man würde das Zeichen eher in *Abschnitt 38* bei GIŠ und GÁNA erwarten, wenn man formale Ähnlichkeit zugrunde legt. Da der Abschnitt aber nicht vollständig erhalten ist, können wir ihn noch nicht endgültig beurteilen.

A b s c h n i t t 47 (750-756): 750-751 DAR, 752-756 MÙŠ samt MÙŠ-*gunû*.

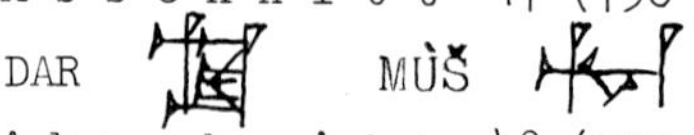

A b s c h n i t t 48 (757-776*[+n]*): EZEN samt EZEN × Z.

In Text Gb ist die EZEN-Gruppe anders eingeordnet. Sie steht (vgl. die Einleitung S. 9) "towards the middle of lines 200-276"; eine genauere Zuweisung ist mangels unmittelbaren Zeilenanschlusses nicht möglich.

A b s c h n i t t 49′ (789-818): 789-790 ARAD, ARAD × KUR, 791-792 MUG, MUG-*gunû* (ZADIM), 793-796 GÍR, 797-798 MUŠ, MUŠ×MUŠ, 799-802 BÚR, 803-804 BULUG, BULUG/BULUG, 805 NAGAR(?), 806-807 GUR$_7$, 808 MUNSUB, 809 SUḪUR, 810 SUMAŠ, 811 LIL, *[...]*, 818 UZU.

Eine komplexe, jedoch in sich geschlossene Gruppe. MUG ist eine reduzierte Form von ARAD, GÍR wieder eine Erweiterung. Bei MUŠ ist der einem DIM$_4$ ähnliche Bestandteil, den wir in GÍR (ohne W. und S.) haben, nach vorne verlegt. Beachte aber, dass Text If das Zeichen MUŠ an der viel eher zu erwartenden Stelle, nämlich hinter SUD, behandelt (vgl. *Abschnitt 26*). Der Anfang von BÚR und BULUG fällt wieder mit dem von MUG zusammen. Bei NAGAR ist am Anfang der W. weggefallen. GUR$_7$ ähnelt den vorangehenden Zeichen in seinem zweiten Bestandteil. Von GÚR$_7$ aus finden wir den Weg zu den folgenden Zeichen. Dabei fällt auf, dass GÁLAM (710, *Abschnitt 42*) trotz starker formaler Anklänge z.B. an LIL von unserem Abschnitt ganz dissoziiert ist. (S. Nachtrag.)

A b s c h n i t t 50′ (819-820): ŠEG$_9$ und ŠINIG.

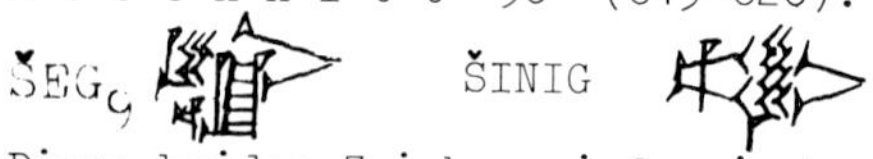

Diese beiden Zeichen sind zwischen UZU und LAḪTAN eingeschoben, bei denen, was den zweiten Zeichenbestandteil betrifft, ein formaler Zusammenhang besteht.

A b s c h n i t t 51′ (821-835*[+n]*): 821-823 NUNUZ.ÁB × Z, 824 ff. DAG.KISIM$_5$ × Z.

Dieser Abschnitt greift auf das Ende des vorvorigen (49′) zurück. Auch UZU (818) endet auf ein KISIM$_5$. Die formale Verwandtschaft zwischen NUNUZ.ÁB und DAG.KISIM$_5$ beruht auf dem zweiten Element: KISIM$_5$ ist ein um einen Winkelhaken erweitertes ÁB.

A b s c h n i t t 52′ (*[840]*-846): *[840-841] [PAP.NÁ]*, 842-843 NÁ, 844 ḪU.NÁ (SA$_4$), 845 ALAM, 846 DÀRA.

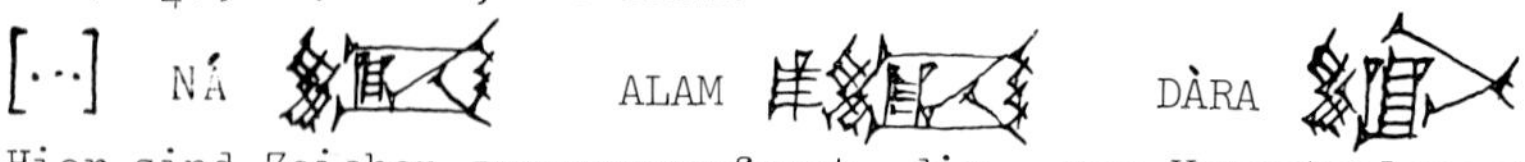

Hier sind Zeichen zusammengefasst, die - von Vorsatzelementen abgesehen - mit U-*gunû* ("GAŠAN") beginnen. Dies mag der Grund sein, weshalb DÀRA hier und nicht in der Gruppe der "Tierkopfzeichen" (*Abschnitt 32*) auftritt.

A b s c h n i t t 53′ (847-848[+n]): TAG, dann Lücke.

TAG  [...]

TAG ist an dieser Stelle unerwartet. Was den Zeichenanfang betrifft, so würde man es eher in den *Abschnitten 36 ff.* einordnen. Da der Kontext jedoch ganz unvollständig ist, müssen wir uns eine genauere Beurteilung versagen.

A b s c h n i t t 54″ ([n]-869): ŠUBUR.

[...] ŠUBUR 

Wohl das Ende eines Abschnittes.

A b s c h n i t t 55″ (870-875[+n]): 870-871 KIN, 872-873 UR$_4$, 874 MÁ+KAK, 875 ÙZ, [...].

KIN  UR$_4$  MÁ+KAK  ÙZ 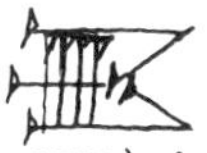 [...]

UR$_4$ ist eine einfachere Form als KIN. MÁ+KAK (nA MÁ+MUG) ist dem UR$_4$ insofern ähnlich, als es mehrere S. aufweist und am Ende in ein 'Dreieck' ausläuft. Bei ÙZ haben wir zwei 'Dreiecke' am Zeichenende. Formal fühlen wir uns an Zeichen in *Abschnitt 37* erinnert.

A b s c h n i t t 56″ ([n]-887-889-[n]): Behandelt wurden u.a. DIM, DIM × ŠE (MUN) und U.DIM × ŠE.

[...] DIM 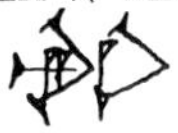 [...]

Man könnte fragen, warum DIM nicht bereits in Abschnitt 49′ bei ARAD und MUG, mit denen es den Zeichenanfang gemeinsam hat, abgehandelt wurde. Aber zur Beantwortung benötigen wir den exakten Listenkontext.

Über das Ende der Serie können wir noch nichts Verbindliches sagen. 911 enthielt höchstwahrwahrscheinlich SÍG, 913 GURUN, 914 LAM, 915 LAM × KUR. Zwischen SÍG, GURUN und LAM lässt sich formal eine Verbindung herstellen. Im Übrigen wird man bei SÍG aber auch an IG (Ende *Abschnitt 29*) erinnert.

SÍG  GURUN  LAM 

L e t z t e r A b s c h n i t t (916-918): LAGAB, ŠU+LAGAB, ŠU+LAGAB+LAGAB.

LAGAB  ŠU+LAGAB  ŠU+LAGAB+LAGAB 

916 greift nochmals auf das schon in 27 ff. (*Abschnitt 1*) behandelte LAGAB zurück, aber interessanterweise mit einem dort nicht notierten - und wohl bewusst für das Ende ausgesparten - Wert k î l i (kurz für k î l i b). Dieser Nachzügler ist sehr leicht zu erklären: Der Kompilator wollte seine Serie mit den Summenzeichen ŠU+LAGAB (ŠU+NÍGIN) und ŠU+LAGAB+LAGAB (ŠU+NIGIN) abschliessen.

Wir können den vorangehenden Gliederungsversuch nur als vorläufig bezeichnen. Die Anzahl der von uns rekonstruierten "Abschnitte" ist vielleicht viel zu gross, und sie wird sich reduzieren lassen, wenn es gelingt, weitere Assoziationen gerade für die formal weder vorwärts noch rückwärts anschliessbaren einzelnen Zeichen zu finden (s. *Abschnitt 16* LUM, *18* NUN, *22* MAḪ, *27* NAM, PA, *28* DU, *40* AL, *43* TÙN, *46* GÁ). Andererseits finden sich in der Rekonstruktion des letzten Drittels der Serie noch einige "weak spots", wie Civil in seiner Einleitung betont (S. 12), so dass Modifikationen in Zukunft nicht ganz auszuschliessen sind. Das würde natürlich auch unseren Gliederungsversuch betreffen. Vielleicht mag aber auch das eine oder andere Ordnungskriterium, das wir ermittelt haben, die Rekonstruktion bestätigen. Damit geraten wir freilich in einen Zirkelschluss, und so muss betont werden, dass wir uns nur vom allergesichertsten Quellenbefund leiten lassen dürfen.

Trotz aller Vorbehalte wollen wir für die *Abschnitte 1-41* eine Zusammenfassung versuchen:

Von A ausgehend werden quadratische Zeichenformen behandelt, die dann wieder auf ME und LÁ reduziert werden (*Abschnitt 1*). Es folgen einfache Zeichen mit zwei aufeinander zu laufenden langen Keilen (*Abschnitt 2*). Der von AŠ bis TAB reichende 'Bogen' (mit Appendix URI) ist eine Variation über das Thema einfacher W. und einfacher S. (*Abschnitt 3*). Es folgen 'trapezförmige' Zeichen (*Abschnitt 4*), einfache Zahlzeichen (*Abschnitt 5*) mit Lautassoziation von MU (samt KUL) (*Abschnitt 6*). Rechteckige Zeichen mit rechteckigen Ausbuchtungen stehen in *Abschnitt 7*. Damit ist der Bestand an geometrisch einfach zu definierenden Zeichen weitgehend erschöpft. Die weiteren Zeichen sind überwiegend geprägt durch ein komplizierteres Zusammenspiel von geraden und schrägen Keilen sowie Winkelhaken. Doch sind Ausnahmen nicht selten.

Abschnitte 8 und *9* sind schwer auf einen Nenner zu bringen. *10* behandelt - *cum grano salis* - längliche Rechtecke, *Abschnitt 11* rautenförmige Zeichen. Der ḪA-MA-TI-*Abschnitt 12* (mit Attraktion von BAL und SUM) entzieht sich einer Formdefinition. *Abschnitt 13* ist durch das Grundelement GUD, *14* durch AB und SAG geprägt. *15* und *16* (KAL, GUR; LUM) sind schwer einzuordnen. *Abschnitt 17* ist durch die Grundelemente DUG und ḪI (DÙG) charakterisiert. Auf die isolierten *Abschnitte 18* (NUN) und *19* (IGI) folgt *20* mit der grossen SAL-Gruppe (vorweg EN attrahiert). Vielleicht gehörte auch *21* ursprünglich zu *Abschnitt 20*.

Über *22* (MAḪ) gelangen wir (Assoziation noch unbekannt) zu *Abschnitt 23* ZI, GI. ZI "rechts" hat möglicherweise den nächsten *Abschnitt 24* "Seite"-"Arm"-"links" attrahiert. *Abschnitt 25* I-TUR-GAL ist in sich erklärbar, doch fehlt uns die Verbindung zu *24*. Bei *26* haben wir einen Übergang "gross" (GAL) -"lang" (BU, g í d) erwogen; innerhalb dieses Abschnittes ist GA "Milch" an DIM_4 "aufziehen" angeschlossen, wenn unsere Vermutung zutrifft. Die *Abschnitte 27* (NAM, PA) und *28* (DU) müssen einstweilen isoliert betrachtet werden, und auch für den Anschluss von *29* (SA_6 usw.) fehlt mir die innere Begründung. *Abschnitt 30* beginnt und endet je mit einem Zeichen, an dessen Anfang zwei W. stehen, durch die zwei S. führen. *31* enthält (ähnlich wie *7*) rechteckige Zeichen mit rechteckigen Ausbuchtungen. In *Abschnitt 32* sind Zeichen untergebracht, die - historisch gesehen - "Tierköpfe" darstellen. *33* ŠU ("Hand") ist wahrscheinlich durch GÌR ("Fuss") fern-attrahiert. Für die *Abschnitte 34* und *35* habe ich keine Erklärung. *36* orientiert sich *grosso modo* an einer Grundkomponente NÍNDA. *37* behandelt Zeichen, die irgendwie durch längliche Dreiecke charakterisiert sind. *Abschnitt 38* enthält rechteckige Zeichen mit den zugehörigen (oder als solche grob definierbaren) *tenû*-Zeichen. Die IM-MI-Gruppe *39* und das isolierte AL (*40*) lassen sich noch nicht einordnen. *Abschnitt 41* schliesslich umfasst Zeichen, die am Anfang eine grössere Anzahl von Winkelhaken haben.

Unser Versuch ist ein Anfang. Weiterer Untersuchung bedarf u.a. die Frage nach konservativem Festhalten auf der einen und Neukonzipierung der Liste auf der anderen Seite. Oben bei *Abschnitt 30* haben wir kurz auf den Fall des Zeichens "ḪA-*tenû*" hingewiesen, das Proto-Ea zwischen DÍM und TA einfügt, während es in der kanonischen Serie zum Abschnitt ḪA gewandert ist. Dies ist kein isolierter Fall. Aber wir müssten idealiter über eine lückenlose Überlieferungskette verfügen, um zu sehen, wie das "Lehrbuch" generationenlang 'in unveränderter Auflage' beibehalten wurde, um von Zeit zu Zeit reformiert zu werden.

Hier sei abschliessend nur noch die Frage nach der Datierung gestellt. Wir können nicht wissen, w e r "Proto-Ea" verfasst hat; doch wir müssen nach Hinweisen suchen, w a n n der Plan entworfen wurde. Bei dieser Frage können wir uns nur zum Teil auf die Zeichenformen berufen, die uns in den Textzeugen vorliegen. Diese Zeichenformen können nämlich bereits eine Formentwicklung innerhalb der Serientradition hinter sich haben (vgl. Anm. 12). Dagegen mag die theoretisch-paläographische Erwägung weiterhelfen, von welchen Formen aus wir die Einordnung bestimmter Zeichen am leichtesten erklären können. Hier sind einige Kriterien:

1) 434 GU (*Abschnitt 20*) fügt sich nur dann sinnvoll in die Reihe mit SAL beginnender Zeichen ein, wenn der Anfang von GU tatsächlich wie SAL aussieht und nicht mehr wie NI, so wie das in Ur III noch überwiegend der Fall ist.[28]

2) 436 TILMUN (*Abschnitt 20*) ist als SAL.TUK unter die SAL-Komposita eingereiht. Es wurde also nicht mehr als NI.TUK aufgefasst, d.h. in der Ur III-zeitlichen und häufig auch noch altbab. Form.[29]

3) Die Zusammenordnung von 465 I und 467 TUR (*Abschnitt 25*) leuchtet ohne weiteres ein, wenn der Kompilator nicht mehr von einer Form des TUR ausging, die mit einem S. beginnt.[30]

4) 128 (U_5) (*Abschnitt 3*) ist als ḪU.SI aufgefasst und offenbar nicht mehr als die in Ur III und oft auch noch altbab. übliche Ligatur, die historisch allerdings auch schon ḪU+SI darstellt.[31]

5) Zeichen, die - nach unserem gegenwärtigen Wissensstand! - erst in der altbab. Zeit auftauchen, während sie in Ur III noch nicht bezeugt sind: Hier können wir ŠEŠ (vgl. *Abschnitt 29*) anführen oder die schon von Landsberger (s. unten) behandelte Produktivierung der Gruppe DAG.KISIM$_5$ × Z (*Abschnitt 51'*).

Von diesen Kriterien haben, genau besehen, nur 1 und 2 entscheidenden Wert. Für 3 beachte, dass möglicherweise auch Ur III schon Formen von TUR ohne S. am Zeichenanfang kannte. Was 4 betrifft, so wäre U_5 (ḪU.SI) wohl auch in seiner älteren Ligaturform im Bereiche von ḪU und RI angesiedelt worden. Zu den altbab. 'neu auftauchenden' Zeichen (5) ist zu sagen, dass wir uns mit dem Ausdruck 'neu auftauchend' zunächst nur am Fundzufall orientieren können. Die Überlieferung von Schriftdenkmälern (zumal literarischen) am Ende der Ur III-Zeit und im ersten Jahrhundert der altbab. Zeit ist bisher noch so dünn, dass wir uns nur ein sehr beschränktes Urteil über Paläographie erlauben dürfen.

Umso mehr Beachtung verdienen die Kriterien 1 und 2 (genau genommen stellen sie nur e i n Kriterium dar). GU und TILMUN können zur Zeit der Listenkompilation am Zeichenanfang nicht mehr wie NI ausgesehen haben; sie hätten sonst unmöglich in der Reihe von SAL und SAL-Komposita erscheinen dürfen.

Wir rechnen daher mit einer Abfassung 'unseres' Proto-Ea in der Zeit n a c h Ur III. Eine solche Datierung ist nicht neu. Landsberger hat sie in MSL 2 implicite vertreten; er hat dort S. 98 den Begriff einer "altbab. Schriftreform" aufgebracht. Er wies besonders auf eine Systematisierungstendenz hin, die sich in der Schaffung von "Rahmenzeichen" wie DAG.KISIM$_5$ äusserte. M.

Powell hat versucht, weitere Argumente für eine solche "Schriftreform" zu liefern.[32] Sind aber die von Landsberger und Powell angeführten Beispiele von so weitreichender Konsequenz, dass man von einer "Reform" sprechen kann, die mehr ist als Tendenz und Entwicklungsfluss?

Wir können diese Frage hier nicht weiter verfolgen. Was jedoch die Abfassungszeit von Proto-Ea betrifft, so ist möglicherweise das letzte Wort noch nicht gesprochen. In einem Kapitel "Secondary Branches of Proto-Ea and Proto-Aa" hat M. Civil in MSL 14, 105 ff. eine Reihe von Fragmenten behandelt, die enge Verwandtschaft mit Proto-Ea aufweisen, aber teilweise eine andere Zeichenreihenfolge erkennen lassen. Da wir uns räumlich beschränken müssen, können wir auf diese Nebenüberlieferung (wir sollten wohl neutral Parallelüberlieferung sagen!) nicht genauer eingehen. Zwei Dinge seien herausgegriffen: 1) Nr. 1.1, 7′ (MSL 14, 112) bucht LAM hinter MÙŠ und vielleicht in Fern-Assoziation mit LUM (Z. 1′-3′), während LAM in Proto-Ea in 914 (hinter *Abschnitt 56″*) steht. 2) Nr. 4 (MSL 14, 113 ff.) bietet in Z. 12-45 die Abfolge GÁ, GÁNA, die formal überzeugender ist als die von Proto-Ea (GIŠ, GÁNA in *Abschnitt 38*) und die Isolierung von GÁ in *Abschnitt 46*. Ein weiteres Studium dieser Parallelüberlieferung ist dringend zu empfehlen.

Vor-altbab. Silbenzeichen-Listen sind m. W. bisher nicht aufgetaucht mit e i n e r Ausnahme: Die bisher wenig beachtete Zeichenliste aus Byblos, die G. Dossin in *Mélanges de l'Université Saint-Joseph* 45, 1969, 245 ff. veröffentlicht hat ("*Fragment de syllabaire de la IIIe dynastie d'Ur*"). Diese Liste (sie ist vielleicht sogar älter als Ur III) lässt hier und da Formassoziation erkennen (z. B. face B V 7-8 GUD, UL) oder manchmal Lautassoziation (z.B. face B III 3-4 TIM, DIM_4 oder I 6-7 GÚ, KU). Sie ist im Ganzen jedoch noch undurchsichtig, was die Reihenfolge der Zeichen betrifft. Mit der Abfolge der Zeichen in Proto-Ea hat sie nicht das Geringste gemein.

Es mag also Vorläufer gegeben haben - das lässt sich nicht abstreiten. Aber solche Vorläufer wären aller Wahrscheinlichkeit nach andere Silbenzeichen-Listen gewesen und noch nicht "Proto-Ea".

---

* Besondere Abkürzungen: S. = senkrechter (Keil), W. = waagerechter (Keil). Auf ein Keilschriftzeichen bezogene Angaben wie "links", "rechts", "oben", "unten" beziehen sich immer auf die uns gewohnte Leserichtung, und die schwierige Frage, in welcher Richtung zu Beginn des II. Jahrtausends v. Chr. geschrieben und gelesen wurde, soll davon unberuhrt bleiben. Vgl. zu dieser Frage zuletzt S.A. Picchioni, Or.NS 49, 1980, und D.O. Edzard, RlA V "*Keilschrift*" §3.

---

1 B. Landsberger, MSL 2 (1951) mit Nachträgen in MSL 3 (1955) 157-223 und 9 (1967) 113-123. Zur Frage der (modernen) Bezeichnung der Serie s. zuletzt M. Civil, MSL 14, 3.

2 Ich danke Miguel Civil herzlich dafür, dass er mir seine Photosammlung im Winter 1979/80 in Chicago zur Verfügung stellte, ebenso für einige nachträgliche briefliche Auskünfte.

3 MSL 14 (1979) 1-81. Der Fortschritt gegenüber der Erstedition und ihren Nachträgen ist beträchtlich: Eine Vervielfachung des Quellenmaterials, was zu einem fast lückenlosen Gesamttext führte (Lücken noch hinter Z.688?, in 708-709, hinter 729, in 777-787, 812-815, 837-839, 849-868, 876-886, 890-909; s. MSL 14, 12 ff. zur Beurteilung dieser Lücken). Wie bei jedem sumerischen Literaturwerk ist auch hier die uns bisher zu-

gängliche Überlieferung gegen Ende am schwächsten, offenbar weil Exzerpte am seltensten vom letzten Drittel oder Viertel eines Werkes gemacht wurden. Vgl. die bequeme Table of Sources MSL 14, 64 ff.

4 Vgl. MSL 14, 15: "... exercises, designed to memorize visual, phonetic, and semantic relationships ...".

5 Die Leerzeilen fügen sich keinem uns erkennbaren System. In einigen Fällen trennen sie zwar "Abschnitte": 256-259 zwischen GUKKAL und DI (unsere *Abschnitte 10* und *11*); 415 zwischen SIG_7 und EN (*Abschnitte 19* und *20*); 472 zwischen GAL und BU (*25* und *26*); 633 zwischen LÚ-*šessig* und TUM (*37* und *38*). Öfter aber finden sie sich innerhalb solcher Abschnitte: 14 (in der Reihe KU); 55 (in der Reihe LAGAB × Z); 242 (zwischen ŠID × A und KID, vgl. *Abschnitt 10*); 320 (in der Reihe KA × Z); 356-358 (zwischen BI.GIŠ und DUG, *Abschnitt 17*); 375 (zwischen AḪ und AḪ.ME); 425 (in der Reihe SAL).

6 H. Petschow, ZA 57, 1963, 146-172, bes. 169 ff., hat auf sehr einleuchtende Weise gezeigt, wie "Systematik und Gesetzestechnik" im Codex Hammurabi funktionieren.

7 Vgl. Landsberger, MSL 2, 2 f.; Civil, MSL 14, 5.

8 Die mit AB beginnende Vs. der Tafel behandelt, gemessen an der Gesamtabfolge der Serie, einen 'späteren' Abschnitt als die Rs. Ähnlich die Texte At, Cm, Dk, Dl, Du, Dy, En, Ez, Fk, Fx, Ib, Ij, Is.

9 Die Zeile davor ist getilgt.

10 Nur Abschnitt 1 ist ausführlich beschrieben. Später müssen wir uns mit einer knapperen Darstellungsweise begnügen.

11 Hier und öfter finden sich Ausnahmen von der Regel, dass Proto-Ea nur einfache Zeichen behandelt. Zur Schwierigkeit, eindeutige Kriterien dafür zu erstellen, was "zusammengesetzt" ist, und folglich für eine angemessene Definition von "Diri" vgl. schon Landsberger, MSL 2, 22 f. In MSL 14, 4 verweist Civil auf die Einleitung zu seiner bevorstehenden Edition der Serie Diri (SI.A) = *watru* (MSL 15).

12 In den Abbildungen habe ich, soweit mir zugänglich, mehr oder weniger normierte Ur III-Zeichenformen verwendet, in einigen besonderen Fällen jedoch auf Formen zurückgegriffen, wie sie in Originaltexten von Proto-Ea vorkommen. Eine vollständige paläographische Dokumentation der Proto-Ea-Tafeln wäre im Prinzip höchst wünschenswert; sie herzustellen, würde aber die Arbeit vieler Monate erfordern. Ur III-Zeichenformen habe ich aus drei Gründen bevorzugt: 1) Es ist denkbar, wenn auch nicht beweisbar, dass dem ersten Kompilator Zeichenformen geläufig waren, die denen von Ur III noch nahe standen (vgl. immerhin unten *Abschnitt 20* und S. 57 zu einem möglichen Gegenargument); 2) im Juni 1979 konnte ich an zwei Tontafelsammlungen (Puškin-Museum, Moskau; Staatl. Eremitage, Leningrad) anhand von Ur III-Tafeln erste Studien zu der Schreib-Reihenfolge der einzelnen Keile in Keilschriftzeichen treiben (mein Dank gilt hierfür Frau Dr. Sv. Hodžaš, Moskau, und Frau Dr. N. Jankowska, Leningrad); dieser zuerst von R.D. Biggs, Or.NS 42 (1973) 40f., betonte Aspekt der Keilschriftpaläographie hat eine grosse Zukunft; 3) während es noch keine frühaltbabylonische Zeichenliste gibt, besitzen wir in N. Schneiders *Keilschrift-Paläographie* 2, 1935, *Die Keilschriftzeichen der Wirtschaftsurkunden von Ur III nebst ihren charakteristischen Schreibvarianten* eine Orientierungshilfe, die wir dankbar zu benutzen haben, solange sie nicht durch ein vollkommeneres Instrumentarium ersetzt ist.

13 Vgl. Å. Sjöberg, ZA 64, 1975, 140 Z.12.

14 Text Dc hat  für Z. 103-109, dagegen 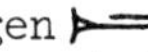 für Z.110 (Z. 111 fehlt); Es hat  für Z. 107-109,  für Z. 110(!) und  für Z. 111; De hat  für Z. 109 und 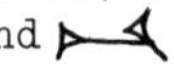 für Z. 110-111. (S. Nachtrag)

15 Vgl. W. Heimpel, *Studia Pohl* 2, 1968, 440 ff.

16 Vgl. die Formenübersicht bei F.R. Kraus, *Sumerer und Akkader*, 1970, Tab. nach S. 62.

17 Vgl. die Fussnote zu Z. 240.

18 Vgl. C. Wilcke, WZKM 68, 1976, 87, für altbab. (Kopien-)Formen von GIDIM. UDUG und GIDIM sind in altbab. Kursive nicht mehr zu unterscheiden (zumindest den Kopien nach zu urteilen). Nach dem Befund von Proto-Ea (freundliche Auskunft von M. Civil) besteht der konstituierende Unterschied offenbar darin, dass GIDIM mit zwei, UDUG mit drei S. beginnt.

19 Vgl. H. Limet, *Anthroponymie*, 1968, 87 und 429; zur Deutung des Namens als "Du-hast(-ihn)-mir-wahrhaftig-leben-lassen" s. Edzard, BiOr. 28, 1971, 164.

20 Beachte allerdings, dass Text Eq mit AB und nicht mit KU_7 einsetzt (vgl. oben die Tabelle).

21 Dagegen muss nicht sprechen, dass die Leseglosse d u - u_4 (Var. d u - g ú, d u - g a) erst an fünfter und letzter Stelle der Reihe ḪI steht.

22 Paläographisch ist folgende Beobachtung wichtig: In Ur III wird der W. von SAL erst gezogen, nachdem der erste S. des folgenden Bestandteils schon geschrieben ist, d.h. 1)  , 2)  , 3)  , 4)  , 5) 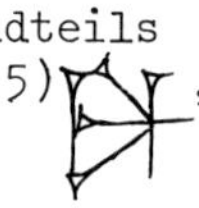 , usw.

23 Leider ist der Abschnitt SAL in Ea V schlecht erhalten (s. MSL 14, 402), so dass wir nicht nachprüfen können, ob und an welcher Stelle GÉME dort stand.

24 NU ist - nicht historisch, aber unter Zugrundelegung einer dreieckigen Form - sozusagen ein horizontal halbiertes SAL.

24a ŠEŠ ist vor der altbab. Zeit bisher nicht bezeugt. Es wird stattdessen EREN (= š e $š_4$) geschrieben; vgl. J. Krecher, *Sum. Kultlyrik*, 1966, 110, der sogar erst nach-altbab. Formausbildung vermutete.

25 Zu beachten ist die Fussnote zu Z. 687, wonach Text Ia die Formen TU(D) und KU_4 auseinanderhält, während Ji für 684 TU = t u - ú die Form KU_4 bietet. Im Ganzen ist die Überlieferung für die betr. Zeilen nicht sehr gut (s. die Tabelle, MSL 14, 80).

26 Eine Lücke hinter Z. 688a ist nicht ausgeschlossen.

27 Civil, MSL 14, 12, begründet seinen Ansatz einer höchstens zweizeiligen Lücke (Landsberger, MSL 9, 113, nahm bis zu 11 Zeilen an) mit einer genauen Überprüfung und Umfangsberechnung der an dieser Stelle einschlägigen Quellen.

28 Vgl. N. Schneider (s. Anm. 12) Nr. 781. Wie mir M. Civil mitteilt, hat GU zwar in e i n e m Text (Hw) die Form  ; doch schreibt just dieser Text einmal auch  für SAL, so dass die besondere Form des GU in ihrem paläographischen Wert relativiert wird.

29 Für altbab. Belege vgl. B. Groneberg, *Répertoire géographique des textes cunéiformes* 3, 1980, 237 f.

30 Allerdings kommen auch in Ur III schon Formen von TUR ohne S. am Anfang vor; s. Schneider (s. Anm. 12) Nr. 801. (S. Nachtrag.)

31 Schneider (s. Anm. 12) Nr. 114.

32 Or.NS 43, 1974, 398-403, besonders Lautwerte betreffend, die durch LÁL-Komposita dargestellt sind.

Nachträge

A b s c h n i t t 3: Der Übergang von BAR zu ŠÚ liesse sich auch als Schritt Schritt von BAR zu BAR-tenû beschreiben (Vorschlag von M. Powell).

A b s c h n i t t 9: Das in Kopie wiedergegebene BUR ist irreführend. Häufiger ist in Ur III und früh-altab. eine Form, die sich aus mehreren übereinanderliegenden W. und GAR zusammensetzt, d.h. eine Art von guniertem GAR. Damit wird die Einbeziehung von E und KÙ problematisch.

A b s c h n i t t 12: Oder etwa BAL "ausgraben"- SUM "Zwiebel"? (Hinweis M. Powell).

A b s c h n i t t 28:Folgt DU auf PA wegen PA.KAS$_4$(DUxŠE) = m a š k i m ? (J. Krecher)

A b s c h n i t t 29: Es lässt sich auch an eine Bedeutungsassoziation "Dattelpalme" - "Zeder" - "Tür" denken, wie mir M. Powell vorschlägt.

A b s c h n i t t 49 : Statt "ARAD" ist als Zeichen-Grundlesung NÍTA vorzuziehen. "ARAD" ist irreführend, weil diese auf akk. *(w)ard-* "Sklave" zurückgehende Lesung von Hause aus nur dem Zeichen NITA x KUR = ir$_{11}$ "Slkave" zukommen kann. - Zwischen MUNSUB und SUḪUR ist auch ein Einschnitt denkbar.

A n m. 14: S. jetzt P. Steinkeller, ZA 71 (1981) 19-28 "Studies in Third Millennium Palaeography, 1: Signs TIL and BAD".

A n m. 30: Die bei Schneider, o.c., wiedergegebenen Formen von TUR ohne anfänglichen S. sehen wenig vertrauenerweckend aus. Textkopien, in denen sie vorkommen, sollten kollationiert werden. (Hinweis M. Powell).

A STANZA FROM THE VERSES OF PRINCE TCŪṂ-TTEHI:

R.E. Emmerick (Hamburg)

With the help of Bailey's *Dict.* it is sometimes possible to obtain his translation of a connected passage of Khotanese that has not yet appeared otherwise in translation. Such is the case with stanza *[28]* from the verses of Prince Tcuṃ-ttehi: published by Bailey in transcription in *KBT* 50 (P 3510. 5.8-9). By combining the information provided by the *Dict.* under the items *prrārū* and *pyerīme* we arrive at the following version:

'What is the contemptible seizing, grasping, may I not really go to the *karma*-acts. I think of limbs of the body, may they (the *kīra* = *karma*-acts) not arise for me by this merit.'

Unfortunately this version does not provide an intelligible interpretation of the stanza. If we try to find out what has gone wrong we are struck at once by the fact that this stanza is considered by Bailey to contain two unusual words: *prrārū* 'grasping' and *pyerīme* 'I think of '. *prrārū* is said to occur only here and as *prrārva* in stanza *[30]* of this same poem. The verb *pyer-* occurs only here.

In stanza *[30]* we have *cu prrārva satvāṃ biṃdä dūkha ṣṭārä kāṣṭi mara*, which Bailey renders: 'what are graspings upon the beings, woes, sorrows here'. That woes and sorrows may be said to stand upon the beings should not surprise us. Thus, we find in Z 3.102 *suhu ni ṣṭe bendä* 'fortune is (lit. stands) upon them (= the Buddhas)'. But that 'graspings' should also stand on them seems unlikely. By its position also *prrārva* looks much more like an adjective referring to *satvāṃ*. The *prrārva satvāṃ* of stanza *[30]* are in fact nothing other than 'ordinary beings' like the *prrāgārätä satvä* of Old Khotanese (Z 23. 7).

If *prrārva* means 'ordinary' in stanza *[30]*, can *prrārū* mean 'ordinary' in stanza *[28]*? According to Bailey *prrārū* is here 'dyadic with Buddhist Sanskrit *āhāra-* "grasping" '. Yet *āhāra-* normally means 'food' in both Buddhist and classical Sanskrit, and that is quite clearly its sense in Old Khotanese (Z 11.46; 13.98, 99). The meaning 'food' allows the description 'ordinary' and suits the context of the body.

ñaśä 'contemptible' could equally well be applied to 'food', especially to 'ordinary food', but *ñaśä* is not necessarily so derogative. Thus in the common phrase *ñaśä bīsä* Bailey usually translates it as 'humble' (see *Dict.* s.v. *nyaśśa-*). We could interpret *prrārū āhārä ñaśä* as 'ordinary, humble food'. However, it is also possible that *ñaśä* refers to the subject of the verb *tsīmä*, namely, Prince Tcūṃ-ttehi:. In that case the meaning would be: 'As for ordinary food, may I, the humble one, not proceed ...'.

According to Bailey *nä tsīmä haiṣṭai kīra* means 'may I not really go to the *karma*-acts'. This is a very strange statement, especially in connection with 'ordinary food'. In order to determine what it may mean it is necessary to consider the use of *tsu-* with *kīra-* in Z. There we find *maṃdrai ni kīru nä tsīndi* (Z 2.97) 'his spells do not do their work', that is, they are ineffective. Similarly, Z 4.41: *ttäna ju mā kīro ni tsīndi* 'therefore they have no effect on us'. The act expressed by *kīra-* is thus the expected act appropriate to the subject. If we further compare Z 22.127: *icche cu ye ūtco paśśäte hīvī kīri u cu rro ūrañi stāma* 'motions, which is when one releases water, one's business, and when there is also the strain in the stomach', it emerges that the natural act appropriate to the subject when the subject is a person may be that of passing solid matter. In the context of 'ordinary food', it is clear that this is what is meant: 'may I not proceed to (my natural) act'.

One word has still to be treated in the first sentence. Bailey does not explain *haiṣṭai*, but his rendering 'really' implies that he regards it as in some way standing for *hārṣṭai*, on which see *Dict.* s.v. *hārṣṭāyä*. *haiṣṭai na* for *hārṣṭai na* occurs in Deśanā 82v3 *KBT* 65. It is possible therefore to interpret *nä tsīme haiṣṭai kīra* as 'may I not proceed at all to (my natural) act'. This is better than looking for Buddhist Sanskrit *heṣṭe* 'below' here until further support for this is found.

That there is particular merit in thinking of the limbs of the body is a little surprising although it is conceivable in certain contexts. Here however in the context of food and the natural act that would normally result, the idea of thinking of the limbs of the body is clearly out of place. Moreover, a subject is required for the verb *hamāṃde*, and it is difficult to supply this from the second line as Bailey does. Additionally there is the difficulty that a verb *pyer-* 'think' is not otherwise known in Khotanese.

All these difficulties can be removed simply by redividing *aga pyerīme* as *agapye rīme* 'unclean filths'. There is of course no word division in the original manuscript. We now have a subject for the verb *hamāṃde* and the sentence means: 'By this merit may there not arise for me the unclean filths of the body'. This is of course a natural result of not proceeding to the natural act after eating ordinary food. Moreover, it accords with the wish expressed in the first line of the next stanza: *sūrai īmä pariśǭdä auṣkä* 'may I be clean, pure always'.

Stanza *[28]* should thus be read:

cu prrārū āhārä ñaśä   nä tsīṃä haiṣṭai kīra
ttaramdarä agapye rīme   nä hamāṃde ma ttanä pauñana

and translated: 'As for ordinary, humble food, may I not proceed at all to the (natural) act. May the unclean filths of the body not arise for me by this merit.'

Dict. = H.W. Bailey, *Dictionary of Khotan Saka*, Cambridge 1979.

KBT = H.W. Bailey, *Khotanese Buddhist texts*, London 1951.

Z = R.E. Emmerick, *The Book of Zambasta*, London 1968.

FERNHANDEL UND WARENPREISE NACH EINER MITTELASSYRISCHEN URKUNDE DES 12. JAHRHUNDERTS v. u. Z.

Helmut Freydank (Berlin/DDR)

Im Vergleich mit der altassyrischen Zeit sind über den Handel der Assyrer gegen Ende des 2. Jahrtausends v. u. Z. bisher recht wenige inschriftliche Quellen bekannt.[1] Der vorliegende Text, dessen Bearbeitung dem Jubilar als bescheidene Festgabe gewidmet sei, bietet einige neue Fakten und zeigt an, daß das Material zu dieser sozialökonomisch bedeutsamen Problematik in den mittelassyrischen Archiven gewiß noch nicht erschöpft ist.

VAT 18062 (Fundnummer Assur 13058 ac!)[2] ist eine fragmentarische Tontafel im Querformat, die vor allem an den Rändern stark beschädigt ist. Erhalten blieb von ihr nur die Rückseite, während die Vorderseite, nach der gleichmäßigen Struktur der Bruchfläche zu urteilen, absichtlich beseitigt worden sein könnte, als der Ton bereits erhärtet war.

Die zeitliche Einordnung der Tafel bereitet Schwierigkeiten, da das Datum bis auf unsichere Zeichen nicht erhalten ist und sich keine direkten Hinweise auf eine Datierung finden. Das Archiv Assur 13058 läßt auf die zweite Hälfte des 12. Jahrhunderts v. u. Z. schließen[3], und auch der Eindruck, den der Schriftduktus vermittelt, scheint diese Datierung zu unterstützen.[4] Inhaltlich zeigt sich insofern eine Verbindung zu den Tafeln aus dem Archiv des *abarakku* Samnuḫa-ašarēd, als diese die Beschaffung von Ausrüstungen verschiedener Art, namentlich auch militärischen, betreffen und der Hauptgegenstand der vorliegenden Urkunde offensichtlich der Ankauf von Pferden ist.[5] - Die Personen bieten bei genauerer Prüfung keinen Anhaltspunkt für eine Datierung. Auffälligerweise ist wohl auch hier ein *tamkāru* namens Uballissu-Marduk (8′) genannt. Seine Identität mit dem gleichnamigen *tamkāru* aus TR 3019[6] ist wegen der Datierung dieses letztgenannten Textes in die Regierungszeit Tukulti-Ninurtas I. sehr fraglich, obwohl beide Tafeln vom Pferdeimport nach Assyrien handeln.[7]

VAT 18062

Rs. 1′ [ ]x x[ ]

2′ [6 GUN 17 5/6 MA.NA ZABA]⌜R(?) 75 G⌝UN 3⌜4⌝ [MA.NA AN.NA
a-ba-ru ŠÀM-*šu-nu*]

3′ [12.TA.ÀM *a-na* AN.NA] *sa-su-ú*[8] *a-na* ŠÀM 20 ANŠE.^{MÍ}ḪÚB$^{\text{M[EŠ}}$
ša ANŠE.KUR.RA^{MEŠ} MU.3 SIG$_5$^{MEŠ}(?)][9]

4′ [ ]x[x]+10 GUN AN.NA *a-ba-ru* ŠÀ[M-*šu*(-*nu*)
a-na ŠÀM ....]

5′ [1 GUN 30 MA.N]A(?) Z[ABAR 1]⌜8?⌝ GUN AN.NA ŠÀM-*šu-nu*
a-na ŠÀM 4 L[Ú^{MEŠ} ....]

6′ 18 MA.NA ZABAR [3] GUN 36 MA.NA AN.NA ŠÀM-*šu-nu a-na* Š[ÀM ....]

7′ 3 MA.NA ZABAR ⌜3⌝[6] MA.NA AN.NA ŠÀM-*šu-nu [a-n]a* ŠÀM 3 ANŠE.x[

8′ *i+na* UGU ^{m}*Ú*-TI-*su*-^{d}A[MAR$^{?}$.UT]U$^{?}$[10] DUMU *Ḫu-zi-ri*[11] ^{md}*La-ab-na-nu-a-tal*$^{?}$[12] DUMU$^{?}$ *M[u*$^{?}$-

9′ ^{m}*Šam-ši*-^{d}ISKUR[13] DUMU *Ki*-x[-x$^{?}$-]x-*JA-e* ^{LÚ}DAM.GÀR^{MEŠ} ^{URU}*Kur-bi-a-JA-e*[14]

10′ *ù* ^{m}EN-ŠEŠ^{MEŠ}-*šu*[15] DUMU ^{d}*Ku-be*$^{?}$-x[ ] ^{URU}*Ṭu-ul-mu-ḫi-a-JA-e*[16]

11′ 2 GUN 31 MA.NA 5 GÍN [A]N.NA B[ABBA]R[17] 37 GUN 45$^{sic!}$ MA.NA 15 [GÍN]

12′ AN.NA *a-ba-ru* ŠÀM-*šu* 15.TA.ÀM *a-n[a]* AN.NA *sa-a-s[u-ú]*

13′ *a-na* ŠÀM 10 ANŠE.KUR.RA^{MEŠ} NITÁ^{MEŠ} MU.3 SIG$_{5}^{MEŠ}$

14′ 3 GUN 8 5/6 MA.NA 5 GÍN ZABAR 37 GUN 47 MA.N[A]

15′ AN.NA *a-ba-ru* ŠÀM-*šu-nu* 12.TA.ÀM *a-n[a* AN].NA *sa-a-su-ú*

16′ *a-na* ŠÀM 10 ANŠE.^{MÍ}ḪÚB^{MEŠ} *ša* ANŠE.KUR.RA$^{[MEŠ]}$ MU.3 ⌜SIG$_{5}$?⌝[MEŠ]

17′ 50 MA.NA AN.NA BABBAR 12 GUN 30 MA.NA AN.NA ŠÀM-*šu* 50 MA.NA ZABAR x[ ]

18′ 10 GUN AN.NA *a-ba-ru* ŠÀM-*šu-nu* ⌜*a-na*⌝ ŠÀM 5 LÚ^{MEŠ} *ši-i-m[e*[18]

19′ 10 MA.NA ZABAR 2 GUN AN.NA ŠÀM-*šu-nu* ⌜*a*⌝-*na* ŠÀM 10 KUŠ GUD^{MEŠ} *dan-nu-t[e*$^{?}$[19]

20′ *i+na* UGU ^{m}*La*-⌜*a*⌝-*lìb-bi*[20] DUMU *Pí-láḫ*-^{d}XXX[21] *ù* LÚ^{MEŠ} ^{URU}*A-za-la-ka-JA-e*[22] *ša il-[te-šu*(?)

21′ ^{LÚ}DAM.GÀR^{MEŠ} *kaṣ-ru-tu*[23] *ù* LÚ^{MEŠ} *ša-ma-la-ú*[24] KÙ.BABBAR-*šu-nu*

22′ *ki-mu-š[u-n]u* ⌈*im*⌉*-ta-aḫ-ru* [?]

23′ ⌈ŠU$^{?}$.N⌉[IGIN$^{?}$ x GUN x+]39 2/3 MA.NA 5 GÍN AN.NA BABBAR 2$^{?}$ (oder: 3$^{?}$) *me*$^{!?}$ x+29 GUN ⌈4⌉[0$^{?}$ MA.NA x GÍN(?) AN.NA

24′ ŠÀM$^{?}$-]*šu* 30 GUN 51 MA.NA 15 GÍN ZABAR^{MEŠ} x[

25′] ⌈MA⌉.NA AN.NA *a-ba-ru* ŠÀM-*šu-nu* [

26′ x+]1 GUN ⌈50$^{?}$⌉+x[MA.NA ZAB]AR$^{?}$ *ša*$^{?}$ *iš-tu na-kám-te* [

Rd. 27′]x ⌈*ša*⌉ [-] ⌈*ú*$^{?}$⌉-*ni-ni*[25]

28′]x x[

l. Rd. 30″]x ⌈ŠÀM⌉ x x[

31″ AN.N]A BABBAR ŠÀM [

32″ [ ]

33″ [^{IT}] ⌈$^{U?}$*al*$^{!??}$-*la*⌉ [-*na-te*(?)

Übersetzung

Rs. 2′ [6 Talent 17 5/6 Minen Bron]ze(?), 75 Talent 34 [Minen Blei (sind) ihr Kaufpreis,]

3′ [- je 12 sind in$^{?}$ Blei] 'ausgerufen' - zum Kauf von 20 [dreijährigen$^{?}$, guten$^{?}$ Pferde]stuten;

4′ [ ]..[..]+10 Talent Blei (sind) [ihr] Kauf[-preis, zum Kauf von .... ;]

5′ [1 Talent 3 Min]en(?) B[ronze, 1]8$^{?}$ Talent Blei (sind) ihr Kaufpreis, zum Kauf von 4 Me[nschen .... ;]

6′ 18 Minen Bronze, [3] Talent 36 Minen Blei (sind) ihr Kaufpreis, zum K[auf .... ;]

7′ 3 Minen Bronze, 3[6] Minen Blei (sind) ihr Kaufpreis, zum Kauf von 3 Eseln[?] ..[

8′ zulasten des Uballissu-M[ardu]k[?], des Sohnes des Ḫuzīru, des Labnanu-atal[?], des Sohnes[?] des M[u[?]. .,]

9′ des Šamšī-Adad, des Sohnes des Ki..[...]..ju, der Kaufleute der Stadt Kurbi(a),

10′ und des Bēl-aḫḫēšu, des Sohnes des Kube[?]-..[ ], (des Mannes) aus der Stadt Ṭulmuḫi(a).

11′ 2 Talent 3 Minen 5 Sekel w[eiße]s [Z]inn, 37 Talent 45 Minen 15 [Sekel]

12′ Blei (sind) sein Kaufpreis, - je 15 sind in[?] Blei 'ausgeru[fen' -]

13′ zum Kauf von 10 dreijährigen, guten Hengsten;

14′ 3 Talent 8 5/6 Minen 5 Sekel Bronze, 37 Talent 47 Min[en]

15′ Blei (sind) ihr Kaufpreis, - je 12 sind i[n[?] Bl]ei 'ausgerufen' -

16′ zum Kauf von 10 dreijährigen, gu[ten[?]] Pferdestuten;

17′ 50 Minen weißes Zinn, 12 Talent 3 Minen Blei (sind) sein Kaufpreis, 50 Minen Bronze, ..[ ]

18′ 10 Talent Blei (sind) ihr Kaufpreis, zum Kauf von 5 gekauft[en (?)] Menschen;

19′ 10 Minen Bronze, 2 Talent Blei (sind) ihr Kaufpreis, zum Kauf von 10 dicken[?] Rinderhäuten;

20′ zulasten des Lā-libbi, des Sohnes des Pilaḫ-Sîn und der

Leute der Stadt Aṣ/zalak(a), die m[it ihm
(sind)(?).]

21′ Die 'organisierten' Kaufleute und die Gehilfen haben
22′ ihr 'Silber' an i[hre]r Statt in Empfang genommen [...(?)]

23′ Ins[gesamt? x Talent x+]39 2/3 Minen 5 Sekel weißes
Zinn, 200? (oder: 300?)+x+29 Talent
4[0? Minen x Sekel(?) Blei]
24′ (sind)]sein [Kaufpreis(?),] 30 Talent 51
Minen 15 Sekel Bronze ..[
25′ x] Minen Blei (sind) ihr Kaufpreis,[
26′ x]+1 Talent 50?+x[Minen Bro]nze?,
die aus dem Vorratshaus [
Rd. 27′].. die?[ ]herge.... haben,
l. Rd. 30″].. Kauf(preis) ....[
31″]weißes [Zin]n (sind)? Kauf(preis)[
33″ [Mon]at? *alla[nate*(?)

Das wesentliche Anliegen der Tafel scheint es zu sein, Käufe zu dokumentieren, die offensichtlich mittels der Metalle Zinn und Bronze zu tätigen waren. Die Beträge in diesen beiden Metallen werden in einem festen Verhältnis, das - womöglich im Bewußtsein eventueller Schwankungen - mehrfach besonders ausgedrückt wird und sich auch rechnerisch bestätigen läßt, in Blei umgerechnet. Angesichts der beträchtlichen Bleimengen ist es nicht sicher, ob dieses Metall unmittelbar als Tauschware diente oder nur als Verrechnungsgrundlage benutzt wurde.

In diesem Text werden sowohl Zinn als auch Blei durch AN.NA wiedergegeben. Zinn ist jedoch regelmäßig durch BABBAR als "weißes Zinn" spezifiziert, während Blei teils als AN.NA *abāru* "*abāru*-Zinn", wörtlich also "Blei-Zinn" (4x), teils als AN.NA "Zinn" (7x) bezeichnet wird.[26] Nach dem Kontext kann es keinen Zweifel daran geben, daß es sich auch in den sieben Fällen um Blei handelt.

Die vollständig erhaltenen Angaben zeigen folgende Mengenverhältnisse der Metalle zueinander:

11′: 2 Talent 31 Minen 5 Sekel Zinn : 37 Talent 46! Minen 15
Sekel Blei

(Das Umrechnungsverhältnis wird Z. 12′ mit 1:15 angegeben.)

14′ : 3 Talent 8 5/6 Minen 5 Sekel Bronze : 37 Talent 47 Minen Blei

(Das Umrechnungsverhältnis wird Z. 15′ mit 1:12 angegeben.)

17′	: 50 Minen Zinn	: 12 Talent 30 Minen Blei	(1:15)
17′f.	: 50 Minen Bronze	: 10 Talent Blei	(1:12)
19′	: 10 Minen Bronze	: 2 Talent Blei	(1:12)

Das Tauschverhältnis von Zinn : Bronze : Blei läßt sich folglich als 1 : 1,25 : 15 ableiten. Wohl seinem Wert entsprechend, erscheint das Zinn in der Summierung (23′ff.) an erster Stelle, wobei seine Gesamtmenge leider nicht erhalten ist und auch nicht errechnet werden kann. Die nicht sicher lesbaren Zeichen in Z. 23′ nach AN.NA BABBAR lassen sich vielleicht als 3 *me*! x bzw. 2 *me*! x deuten, wobei x als Senkrechter für 60 stehen könnte, jedoch davor ein waagerechter Keil sichtbar ist, der nicht zu *me* gehören dürfte. Der Bleimenge würde bei dem Verhältnis 15:1 eine Zinnmenge entsprechen, die zwischen 15 und 26 Talent anzusetzen ist und einem Mehrfachen der Summe der erhaltenen Einzelposten entspricht. Dasselbe gilt für die Gesamtmenge der Bronze, die mit 33 GUN 51 MA.NA 15 GÍN ebenfalls sehr viel größer ist als diejenige, die durch die Addition der auf der Rs. erhaltenen Einzelmengen errechenbar ist. Die sich daraus ergebenden Schlußfolgerungen für den Umfang des verzeichneten Warenaustauschs werden noch zu besprechen sein.

Auffälligerweise wird ZABAR nach der Nennung der jeweiligen Entsprechung in AN.NA (*abāru*) immer durch das Possessivsuffix *-šunu* bei *šīmu*(ŠÁM) "Kaufpreis" aufgenommen (6′, 7′, 14′f., 17′f., 19′, 24′f.). ZABAR^{MEŠ} (24′) unterstreicht dabei die Auffassung von ZABAR als Plural, vielleicht auch hier im Sinne von "Bronzegegenstände" (s. AHw 104b). AN.NA BABBAR ist hier dagegen immer singularisch konstruiert (ŠÁM-*šu*: 11′f., 17′, wohl auch 23′f., fraglich 4′; vgl. für Gegenbeispiele AHw 49b).

Vor dem Versuch, die auf der Rs. der Tafel genannten Bronzebeträge zu addieren, wären die vorgenommenen Ergänzugen zu erläuten, die in Analogie zu den erhaltenen Passagen möglich scheinen.

2′: Da in Z. 14′ die jeweiligen Äquivalente von zehn dreijährigen Stuten in Bronze und Blei angegeben sind und der in Z. 2′ noch lesbare Betrag in Blei doppelt so hoch ist wie der in Z. 14′, andererseits in Z. 3′ von 20 Stuten gesprochen wird, dürfte mit großer Sicherheit in Z. 2′ auch das Doppelte der Bronzemenge aus Z. 14′ zu ergänzen sein, d. h. 6 GUN 17 5/6 MA.NA bzw. 6 GUN 17 MA.NA 50 GÍN ZABAR.

5′: Z. 18′ entsprechend, wo der Kaufpreis für 5 Personen in Zinn und Bronze geteilt ist und ein Gegenwert in Blei je Person von zusammen 4 Talent 30 Minen errechnet werden kann, wären hier 18 Talent Blei zu erwarten, falls der Kaufpreis nur in Bronze entrichtet wird. Bei dem Verhältnis 1:12 für Bronze : Blei ist ein Betrag von 1 Talent 30 Minen Bronze zu veranschlagen.

6′: Nach demselben Verhältnis 1:12 müssen als Entsprechung von 18 Minen Bronze 3 GUN 36 MA.NA AN.NA (*abāru*) ergänzt werden.

7′: Da die Bleimenge weniger als 1 Talent beträgt, darf die Bronzemenge beim üblichen Tauschverhältnisse der Metalle nicht größer als 4 MA.NA sein, so daß vor 3 MA.NA wohl nichts zu ergänzen ist und im folgenden 36 MA.NA AN.NA wahrscheinlich wird.

In den zerstörten Zeilen des ersten Abschnitts der Rs. war vermutlich analog zu Z. 11′-13′ der Kauf der Hengste behandelt worden, der jedoch nach Z. 11 gegen Zinn getätigt wurde. Sollte Zinn als das höherwertige Material regelmäßig zum Ankauf der Hengste verwendet worden sein, so entfiele für diese Zeilen ein Betrag in Bronze. Die Bronzemengen der Rs. wären danach, wie folgt, anzusetzen:

2′:	6 Talent 17 Minen 50 Sekel
4′:	?
5′:	1 Talent 30 Minen
6′:	18 Minen
7′:	3 Minen
14′:	3 Talent 8 Minen 55 Sekel
17′:	50 Minen
19′:	10 Minen
	11 Talent 17 Minen 45 Sekel Bronze

Die so ermittelte Summe, die nur den ohnehin fraglichen Posten in Z. 4′ nicht berücksichtigt, läßt im Vergleich mit der Gesamtsumme in Z. 24′ erkennen, daß die Vorderseite der Tafel die Belege über weitere Käufe für mehr als 22 Talent Bronze enthalten haben muß. Von der vermuteten, aber nicht genauer zu ermittelnden Zinnmenge wären nur zwei Posten der Rs., 2 Talent 31 Minen 5 Sekel (11′) und 50 Minen (17′), zu subtrahieren, so daß möglicherweise mehr als 13 Talent Zinn verblieben, für die ebenso Importgüter erhandelt wurden. Die Annahme liegt nahe, daß die namhaftesten Beträge und Warenposten in den ersten Abschnitten der Tafel aufgeführt waren. Auf eine Abnahme des Volumens deutet im erhaltenen Teil nur die mit 10 Stuten um die Hälfte niedrigere Anzahl in Z. 16′ gegenüber der in Z. 3′ hin. Wenn der Ankauf von Pferden der Hauptgegenstand der hier festgehaltenen kommerziellen Transaktion war, darf man damit rechnen, daß der Text ein Äquivalent in Metall für insgesamt etwa 200 Pferde aufgeführt hat.

Wie bereits deutlich wurde, erlaubt die Tafel, die Preise einiger Waren des Fernhandels zu ermitteln. Bereits in der Anordnung der mittels Metall ertauschten Waren in den beiden erhaltenen Abschnitten spiegeln sich die Rangfolge der Waren und damit auch die Preise.

1. Abschnitt (1′-11′)	2. Abschnitt (11′-22′)
3′: Stuten	13′: Hengste
5′: Menschen	16′: Stuten
6′: ?	18′: Menschen
7′: Esel?	19′: Rinderhäute

Es ergeben sich folgende Stückpreise:

11′-13′: 1 dreijähriger guter Hengst = 15 Minen 6 ½ Sekel Zinn = 3 Talent 46 Minen 37 ½ Sekel Blei

14′-16′: 1 dreijährige gute Stute = 18 Minen 53 ½ Sekel Bronze = 3 Talent 46 Minen 42 Sekel Blei

Zwischen dem Preis eines Hengstes und dem einer Stute zeigt sich ein kaum bedeutender Unterschied von 4 ½ Sekel Blei, der möglicherweise nicht beabsichtigt war. Auch die betreffenden Äquivalente in Blei (11′ u. 14′) weichen trotz der unterschiedlichen Tauschgüter für Hengste (Zinn) und für Stuten (Bronze) unter Zugrundelegung des Tauschverhältnisses von Zinn : Bronze = 1 : 1,25 nur unerheblich voneinander ab.

Wie schon ausgeführt, ist in einem Fall für Personen, die der Text nicht als "Sklaven" (ÌR^{MEŠ}), sondern wohl als "gekaufte? Menschen" (18′: LÚ^{MEŠ} *ši-i-m[e*) bezeichnet, eine aus Zinn und Bronze zusammengesetzte Metallmenge vorgesehen.

17′f.: 1 Mensch = 10 Minen Zinn + 10 Minen Bronze = 4 Talent 30 Minen Blei[27]

Im Fall eines einheitlichen Äquivalents in Bronze (s. o.) läßt sich folgender Preis errechnen:

5′: 1 Mensch = 22 Minen 30 Sekel Bronze = 4 Talent 30 Minen Blei

Als sicher bestimmbare Ware erscheinen noch Rinderhäute:

19′: 1 Rinderhaut (KUŠ GUD *dannu*) = 1 Mine Bronze = 12 Minen Blei

Die für Z. 6′ berechneten 18 Minen Bronze = 3 Talent 36 Minen Blei lassen keinen sicheren Schluß auf die zu kaufende Ware zu. Rinderhäute wären auch hier möglich.

Entsprechend den Überlegungen zur Ergänzung von Z. 7′ (s. o.) ist als letztes folgende Relation festzustellen:

7′: 1 ANŠE.x[= 1 Mine Bronze = 12 Minen Blei

Dieser Preis stimmte mit dem für eine Rinderhaut (19′) überein und schiene für einen Esel angesichts des mehr als das 18fache betragenden Preises für ein Pferd erheblich zu niedrig. Überraschend und kaum zu erwarten wäre andererseits in diesem Zusammenhang ein im Hohlmaß *emāru*(ANŠE) gemessenes Produkt.

Es blieben am Ende die Fragen nach der geographischen Herkunft der Handelswaren und der Kaufleute und nach dem Charakter der in Assur getätigten Handelsgeschäfte. Wegen der Unvollständigkeit der Tafel ist man auch darin auf Vermutungen angewiesen.

Ausdrücklich als Kaufleute und mit ihrem Herkunftsort, einer Stadt Kurbi(a)? (=Kurbaʾil?), sind Uballissu-Marduk?, Labnanu-atal? und Šamšī-Adad genannt, die ausnahmslos keine typisch mA Namen tragen. Der nur nach seinem Herkunftsort Ṭulmuḫi(a) gekennzeichnete Bēl-aḫḫēšu trägt dagegen ebenso wie wohl auch sein Vater einen mA geläufigen Namen. Ebenso spricht nichts dagegen, in Lā-libbi, dem Sohn des Pilaḫ-Sîn, der mit einer unbestimmten Anzahl zusammenfassend als "Leute von Aṣ/zalak(a)" bezeichneter Personen auftritt, einen Assyrer zu erblicken. Sofern die wenigen Anzeichen diesen Schluß zulassen, wäre verallgemeinernd festzustellen, daß an den Geschäften sowohl nichtassyrische Kaufleute als auch Assyrer, die ihrerseits wiederum anscheinend keine Kaufleute waren oder wenigstens nicht als solche bezeichnet sind, beteiligt waren. Die Mittlerfunktion der Kaufleute könnte der Passus 21f. erhellen, der besagt, daß die "organisierten" Kaufleute und die "Gehilfen", also wahrscheinlich die in einer Karawane reisenden Händler, "ihr Silber an ihrer Statt in Empfang genommen haben". Damit hätten die Kaufleute die Aufgabe übernommen, den namentlich bekannten Zulieferern der Ware, an die somit seitens des Hofes eine Forderung bestand, den Gegenwert für die nach Assur zu importierenden Produkte zu überbringen. Soweit der Text einen Einblick gestattet, läßt sich allerdings Silber, das in den vorangegangenen Rechnungen keinerlei Rolle gespielt hat, auf keine Weise in die betreffenden Vorgänge plausibel einbauen. Sehr wahrscheinlich handelt es sich auch hier um "Silber" im Sinne von "Wert(betrag), -gegenstände", wie M. Müller in seinem Beitrag feststellt.[28] Zweifellos sind die Pferde, Menschen usw. als die Waren anzusehen, die in Assur benötigt wurden, denn die umfangreichen und auf die Metalle bezüglichen Angaben der sehr fragmentarischen Zeilen 23′-31′ enthalten den Passus *ša ištu nakamte* "welche aus dem Vorrat(shaus)", der zumindest für einen Teil des Metalls gelten dürfte. Während Blei, als Handelsware oder Verrechnungsgrundlage genommen, in Assur reichlich vorhanden gewesen zu sein scheint, kommen als Bezahlung für die benötigten Waren doch wohl nur Bronze und Zinn in Betracht. Diese Metalle sind nach dem ersten Abschnitt Forderung an die Kaufleute und Bēl-aḫḫēšu, werden also von diesen unmittelbar geschuldet (8′-10′). Dagegen könnte für Lā-libbi und die Leute von Aṣ/zalak(a) die erwähnte Mittlerfunktion der Kaufleute wirksam sein.[29]

Sollten die Städte Kurbi(a) mit Kurbaʾil und Aṣ/zalak(a) mit Azalla/Izalla zu identifizieren sein (s. Anm. 14 u. 22), so wird man die Heimat dieser Pferde jedenfalls im hurritischen Gebiet, in den Gebirgs- und Gebirgsrandzonen nördlich und nordwestlich von Assyrien zu suchen haben. Nur eine ausgedehnte Pferdezucht konnte es einer Stadt ermöglichen, je zehn dreijährige Hengste und Stuten guter Qualität gleichzeitig in den Fernhandel abzugeben.

Man wird die hier behandelte Tafel nur mit Einschränkung als ein Beweisstück für einen allgemein regen Warenumschlag in Assur zur mittelassyrischen Zeit ansehen dürfen, zumal der politische und der ökonomische Zusammenhang, in den das Dokument gehört, unbekannt ist. Wenn jedoch staatlicherseits, und der staatlichen Verwaltung ist die Urkunde zuzuordnen, Mittel aus dem Vorratshaus eingesetzt wurden, um Waren wie Pferde und Sklaven zu erhandeln, die auch im Ergebnis von Kriegszügen als Beute und Tribut nach Assyrien gelangten, so scheint das gegen eine Datierung in das 13. Jahrhundert v. u. Z. zu sprechen. Auch dieses Argument könnte eine Abfassung der Tafel etwa in der Zeit Ninurtatukul(ti)-Aššurs, also in den Jahrzehnten vor dem Regierungsantritt Tiglatpilesars I., befürworten.

AoF = *Altorientalische Forschungen* [Berlin/DDR].

SMEA = *Studi micenei ed egeo-anatolici* [Roma]

---

1 Vgl. C. Saporetti, *La figura del tamkāru nell'Assiria del XIII secolo*, in SMEA 17 [1977], 93-101; H. Freydank, *Eine mittelassyrische Urkunde (KAJ 249) über den Metallhandel*, in AoF VI [1979], 269-271; vgl. ders. zu VAT 16450 demnächst in der Rez. zu J.A. Brinkman, *A Catalogue of Cuneiform Sources ...*, [Chicago 1976], in BiOr.

2 Zu der von E. Weidner, Aus den Tagen eines assyrischen Schattenkönigs, in AfO 10 [1935-1936], 30, irrtümlich mit der Fundnummer 13058 ac versehenen Tafel VAT 15400 s. demnächst H. Freydank, *Bemerkungen zu einigen*

mittelassyrischen Urkunden, in AoF IX. - Es ist beabsichtigt, die Kopie von VAT 18062 in einem der nächsten Bände der "*Vorderasiatischen Schriftdenkmäler*" vorzulegen. Dem Direktor des Vorderasiatischen Museums, Berlin, Frau Dr. L. Jakob-Rost, danke ich für ihr Einverständnis mit der Veröffentlichung des Textes.

3 Die Mehrzahl der bisher publizierten Tafeln dieses Fundkomplexes weist in diese Zeit (vgl. zuletzt VS 19 S. 9; s. demnächst J.N. Postgate, der in Assur 13058 das Archiv des *abarakku* Samnuḫa-ašarēd sieht).

4 Dieser Gesamteindruck ist subjektiv und wäre nur durch eine detaillierte Analyse der Epigraphik zu untermauern.

5 Zu den Aufgaben des Samnuḫa-ašarēd [vgl. Anm. 3] s. demnächst J.N. Postgate.

6 S.D.J. Wiseman, *The Tell al Rimah Tablets, 1966*, in *Iraq* 30 [1968], 183.

7 S.C. Saporetti, SMEA 17 [1977], 96 u. Anm. 19. Bei dem von C. Saporetti als "stagno" gedeuteten AN.NA muß es sich um Blei handeln (s. u. Anm. 27), da ein Betrag von 50 Minen Zinn als "Zoll" mehr als den dreifachen Wert eines guten dreijährigen Tieres darstellt, in Blei aber 50 Minen etwas weniger als ein Viertel des Wertes ausmachen.

8 Die hier eingeschobene Nennung des Tauschverhältnisses könnte eine bindende Regelung dokumentieren, die staatlicherseits getroffen und "ausgerufen" wurde (vgl. AHw 1195b s. v. šasû 6). Der Sinn der Formel ergibt sich aus dem Kontext und erforderte, sie als "je 12 (bzw. 15)(Einheiten), auf Blei bezogen, sind (dafür) ausgerufen (d. h. in Blei zu berechnen)" zu interpretieren und *sa-(a-)su-ú* als Stativ aufzufassen. Wahrscheinlich ist auch die Deutung der Passage ŠÁM MÍ *i-sa-si-ú* (KAJ 168:14; vgl. dazu P. Koschaker, NKRA 105) in dieser Richtung zu suchen, und zwar in dem Sinne, dass ein Preis gemeinsam festgelegt wurde, also der Wert der Sklavin vielleicht "taxiert" wurde.- Die Formel *ana* AN.NA *sasû* findet sich im übrigen, auf Wolle bezogen, wobei unterschiedliche Wollqualitäten mit unterschiedlichen Bleimengen geglichen werden, zweimal in VAT 16450 (Vs.(!) 2 u. 4; vgl. Anm. 1; der Text ist publiziert in E. Weidner, ITn (AfO Beiheft 12) Tafel XI) und belegt die Funktion des Bleis als Wertmesser.

9 Ergänzt nach S. 16'; zu *atānu* "Stute" vgl. AHw 86b und CAD A/ii 481bf. Der Sprachgebrauch in der allgemeineren Bedeutung tritt besonders in den mB und Nuzi-Texten sowie nun auch in den mA hervor.

10 Vgl. C. Saporetti, *Onomastica medio-assira* (OMA), Bd. I [Roma 1970] 489.

11 Der Name ist mA als Maskulinum Ḫuzīru "Schwein" noch nicht belegt (vgl. OMA I 227).

12 Eine Gottheit Labnanu, also wohl das deifizierte Libanon-Gebirge, die hier in einem PN als theophores Element auftritt, ist sonst anscheinend nicht belegt. Sofern richtig gelesen ist, erscheint sie hier mit dem hurritischen Namenselement *-atal* verbunden. Zu Namensbildungen wie Tešup-atal vgl. E. Cassin - J.-J. Glassner, *Anthroponymie et Anthropologie de Nuzi*, Vol. I, *Les Anthroponymes* [Malibu 1977] 146 u. passim.

13 Der Name ist bisher mA nicht belegt (vgl. OMA I 459) und stützt die Vermutung, daß der assyrische Handel dieser Zeit im wesentlichen in den Händen von Nichtassyrern, insbesondere von Babyloniern lag (s. C. Saporetti, SMEA 18 [1977], 97).

14 In ^{URU}*Kur-bi-a-JA-e* ist möglicherweise der vor dem Afformativ *-āju* hier

also schon mA verkürzte Name der Stadt Kurba'il zu erkennen (s. W. von Soden, *Grundriß der akkadischen Grammatik* [Analecta Orientalia 33, Rom 1952] § 56 p. Zu Kurba'il s. noch E. Forrer, *Die Provinzeinteilung des assyrischen Reiches* [Leipzig 1920] 36, und S. Parpola, *Neo-Assyrian Toponyms* (AOAT 6) [Kevelaer - Neukirchen-Vluyn 1970] 217f.

15 Vgl. OMA I 161f.

16 Der Ortsname scheint hier erstmals belegt zu sein.

17 Für weitere Belegstellen s. CAD A/ii 129a. Vgl. Anm. 26 u. 27.

18 Vgl. AHw 1240b šīmu "Gekaufter"?

19 Wahrscheinlich *dannu* im Sinne von "dick" (vgl. AHw 161a u. CAD D 94a).

20 Lā-libbi "gegen den Willen; leider" (vgl. AHw 549bf.; CAD L 172a) ist als PN bisher wohl unbekannt.

21 Pilaḫ-Sîn ist mA neu, jedoch aA bezeugt (vgl. H. Hirsch, *Untersuchungen zur altassyrischen Religion* [AfO, Beih. 13/14, Graz 1961] 21a; AHw 812b).

22 Aṣ/zalak(a) ist vielleicht mit dem jüngeren Azalla/Izalla in Verbindung zu bringen, wobei es wegen der hier erwähnten Rinderhäute kaum von Belang sein wird, daß Aššur-nāṣir-apli II. als Tribut des Landes Izalla neben Wein auch Rinder erhielt (s. zuletzt J.N. Postgate, in RlA Bd. 5, 3./4. Lieferung [Berlin - New York 1977] 225f.). Izalla wird im Hügelland nördlich des Ḫābūr-Tales lokalisiert. Eine Gleichsetzung von Aṣ/zalak(a) mit Ašlakkâ schließen wohl die unterschiedlichen Sibilanten aus (zu Ašlakkâ s. M. Falkner, *Studien zur Geographie des alten Mesopotamien*, in AfO 18 [1957-1958], 5f.).

23 Zu *kaṣru* vgl. CAD K 266.

24 *šamallā'u* ist hier ebenfalls erstmals mA belegt; vgl. AHw 1153bf.

25 Subjunktiv- und Ventivendung deuten auf ein Verbum der Bewegung hin, das wahrscheinlich Art und Richtung der Transaktion wenigstens in Teilen bezeichnet hat.

26 Zu *abāru* s. CAD A/i 36b-38a u. AHw 4a; zu *anāku/annaku* s. AHw 49b u. CAD A/ii 127a-130a.

27 Dieses Ergebnis läßt ernste Zweifel daran aufkommen, ob mA AN.NA mit "Zinn" zu übersetzen ist. Spricht schon der vorliegende Text dagegen, so werden die Zweifel durch KAJ 168 bestätigt. Der Verpflichtungsschein aus der Zeit Tukulti-Ninurtas I.(zum Eponym Libūr-zānin-Aššur s. C. Saporetti, *Gli eponimi medio-assiri* [Bibliotheca Mesopotamica 9, Malibu 1979] 105) sieht einen Betrag von 4 Talent 20 Minen AN.NA (Z. 2) für den Kauf einer Frau vor (Z. 11). Dieser Betrag weicht von dem hier errechneten Preis nur um etwa 4% ab, so daß AN.NA in KAJ 168 als "Blei" aufzufassen ist. Mit einer gewissen Wahrscheinlichkeit sind die CAD A/ii 129a als "Zinn" übersetzten Belege mit der einzigen sicheren Ausnahme der beiden Bezeugungen für AN.NA BABBAR nicht als "Zinn" zu deuten. Leider kann es hier nicht unternommen werden, die Belegstellen im einzelnen zu überprüfen. Zweifel an der Gleichung AN.NA "Zinn" bestehen ohnehin auch für andere Textgruppen (vgl. AHw 49b). Soweit es ein Kontext gestattet, müßte die Gültigkeit einer Übersetzung "Blei" bzw. "Zinn" letztlich aus dem Preisgefüge der Zeit abgeleitet werden, sobald das einmal überschaubar geworden ist. - Zu KAJ 168 s. M. David - E. Ebeling, *Assyrische Rechtsurkunden* [Stuttgart 1929 (= Zeitschrift für ver-

gleichende Rechtswissenschaft 44)] 67 Nr. 74; A.L. Oppenheim, *"Siege-Documents" from Nippur*, in *Iraq* 17 [1955], 74f.

28 M. Müller, dem ich für mehrere Hinweise danke und der mir das Manuskript seines Beitrages zu dieser Festschrift in dankenswerter Weise zur Verfügung gestellt hat, weist überzeugend die Rolle des Bleis als Wertmesser in mittelassyrischer Zeit nach, so daß eine Überlegung, man habe für Blei Zinn und Bronze erhandelt, die etwa ihrerseits, ohne nach Assur zu gelangen, den "Kaufpreis" der betreffenden Waren darstellten, gegen die sie eingetauscht wurden, zu verwerfen ist.

PROBLEMS OF CONSONANTISM OF THE CUNEIFORM HITTITE LANGUAGE *

Th. V. Gamkrelidze (Tbilisi)

In contrast to linguists dealing with modern languages, who have good opportunities for control, scholars analysing ancient languages, which can only be studied from their written records, have peculiar disadvantages. In their case, research into the phonetic repertoire and the grammatical structure of a language has to be based on a previous detailed investigation of the system of writing and the reconstruction of correspondences between graphemes and their phonetic equivalents in the language being studied. Only after such a preliminary analysis of the writing system is it possible to begin the reconstruction of the phonological and morphological system of the ancient language in question.

In this respect, it is of special interest to study the phonological system of the Indo-European Hittite language, which is recorded in written documents by the cuneiform writing system of the so-called "Akkado-Hittite" group. The earliest of these documents belong to the first half of the 17th century BC.[1] The analysis of the cuneiform writing system originating from the North Syrian Akkadian writing[2] has shown a whole series of rules for the representation of Hittite phonetic equivalents by cuneiform signs, and discovered correspondences between certain series of graphemes and phonemes of the Indo-European Hittite language.

It is especially important for the reconstruction of the phonetic repertoire of the Hittite language to define the character and purpose of the graphic reduplication of plosives in the Hittite writing system. According to E. Sturtevant's well-known rule, Indo-Hittite plosives /**p*, **t*, **k*/ appear in Hittite as the voiceless sounds, usually represented in Hittite texts by reduplication of the corresponding consonants, as opposed to "voiced plosives" and "voiced aspirates" which were written single, i.e. with respective consonant realized graphically only once.[3]

The difference between the double and the single writing of the consonants in Hittite texts, which can already be observed in Old Hittite documents, no doubt shows a certain regularity. However, this graphic feature cannot be considered as a uniform means of the realization of certain phonemes. The reduplication of plosives seems to have been used for the marking of single consonants in a different way from that used for the voiced *r*, *l*, *m*, *n*, the spirants *s*, *ḫ*, and the affricate *z* [*ts*], whose graphic reduplication apparently indicated the phonetic reduplication of the relevant consonant.[4] The reduplication of plosives marked in Hittite - according to E. Sturtevant - a voiceless phoneme, while their single writing indicated the corresponding voiced consonant.[5] Such a conclusion could be reached on the basis of the comparison of Indo-European forms with the corresponding Hittite ones, in which Indo-European "voiceless plosives" are equivalent to the plosives which are indicated by the reduplication of the consonant, while Indo-European "voiced plosives" and "voiced aspirates" are equivalent to Hittite phonemes which are realized with the single writing of the consonant in question:

Hitt. *epp-* "to take", "to catch", 1 p. sing. Pret. *e-ip-pu-un*, 3 p. plur. *e-ip-pír*: Lat. *apīscor*; Old Ind. *āpnoti*.

Hitt. *šuppariịa-* "to sleep": Greek ὕπνος, Old Ind. *svápnaḥ*.
Hitt. *kat-ta* "under", "beneath": Greek κατά.
Hitt. *piddāi-* "to run (away)": Greek πέτομαι.
Hitt. *pa-at-tar* "wing": Old Ind. *pátra-*; Greek πτερόν.
Hitt. *ú-it-ti* "year" (Dat.-Loc. sing.): Greek ἔτος.
Hitt. *eku̯-/ aku̯-*"to drink", 3 pers. plur. Pres. *ak-ku-uš-ki-iz-zi*: Lat. *aqua*.
Hitt. *lukk-* "to be dawning": Lat. *luceō*, *lux*.
Hitt. *i-ú-kán*, *i-ú-ga-an* "yoke", "oxbow": Greek ζυγόν ; Lat. *iugum*.
Hitt. *gi-e-nu*, *ki-nu-u̯a-aš* (Dat.-Loc. plur.) "knee": Lat. *genū*; Greek γόνυ, Sanskr. *jānu*.
Hitt. *nekumanza* "naked": Lat. *nudus*.
Hitt. *da-lu-ga-e-eš* "long": Sanskr. *dīrgháḥ*; Greek δολιχός.
Hitt. *kuenzi* (3 pers. sing. Pres), *kunanzi* (3 pers. plur.) "kill": Sanskr. *hanti*/*ghnanti*.
Hitt. *u̯atar*, *u̯etenaš* (Genitive) "water": Greek ὕδωρ, ὕδατος (Genitive).
Hitt. *pedan*, *pí-e-ti/pí-di* (Dat.-Loc.) "place": Greek πέδον.
Hitt. *turiịa-* "to harness", "to team": Old Ind. *dhur-* "harness".
Hitt. *ne-pí-iš* "sky": Greek νέφος ; Sanskr. *nábhaḥ*; Lat. *nebula*; Russian небо.

The correspondences of the Hittite plosives indicated by the graphic reduplication of the consonant with Indo-European "voiceless plosives", and that of the phonemes represented by the single writing with Indo-European "voiced" and "voiced aspirates",[6] do not however tell us anything about the character of the Hittite phonemes themselves, or about the differentiating features by which they were contrasted to each other.

To establish the phonological character of the two series of Hittite plosives indicated by the single or the double writing of the consonant, one must consider the internal phenomena of the Hittite language and its phonological structure, as well as external phenomena reflecting the phonetic character of Hittite words provided by loans of Hittite origin in foreign languages and also the reproductions of foreign forms in Hittite itself.

To define the phonological character of Hittite plosives indicated by the single writing of the consonant, the writing of Hittite names is especially revealing in Egyptian, where Hittite plosives indicated only by the single writing appear consistently as the corresponding voiceless consonants: cf. Hitt. ^{sal}*Pu-du-ḫé-pa* : Eg. *P-ṯ-ḫ-p*; Hitt. *Ha-pa-an-d/ta-li-ia-aš* : Eg. *Ḫr-p-n-t-r-y-s*; Hitt. ^{uru}*Ḫi-eš-ša-aš-ḫa-pa* : Eg. *Ḫ-s-s-p*.[7] In this respect, it is also significant that Old Indian voiceless /*k*/ was indicated in Hittite writing with the single writing of the relevant consonant, for instance in the word *a-i-ka-u̯a-ar-ta-an-na* (KBo III, 5: obv. i.22) in the "Horse Training Texts" where it seems to have been borrowed from the Old Indian hippological *terminus technicus*: Old Ind. **ēka-vartanná-* "single turning"; or in the Hitt. *pa-an-za-u̯a-ar-ta-an-na* (KBo III, 2: rev.58): Old Ind. *pañca-vartanná* "fivefold turning".[8]

This gives us reason to assume that plosives represented in writing by a single consonant could indicate the corresponding voiceless phoneme. This conclusion about the character of Hittite plosives written single, raises the question as to the nature of those Hittite plosives which are represented in writing by reduplicated consonants and which correspond, as mentioned above, to Indo-European voiceless plosives.

The rule of Hittite graphic representation of phonemes corresponding to Indo-European "voiced plosives" by the single writing of the consonant is broken only in the case of such a phoneme resulting from an assimilation with a laryngeal following it. This is denoted in the Hittite texts by the reduplication of the consonant: cf. Hitt. *me-ik-ki* (Acc. sing.), *me-ik-ki-iš* (Nom. sing.), *me-iḳ-ḳa-eš* (plur.) "many", "multiple", corresponding to Greek μέγας, Sanskr. *maha-*; Neuter Greek μέγα, Sanskr. *máhi*.[9]

Although Indo-European *H* is not realized in the Hittite word in question as the consonant *ḫ*,[10] the influence of the "laryngeal" phoneme can still be seen in the fact that the Indo-European plosive which was regularly indicated in Hittite by the single writing of the given consonant (see above), where it precedes an *H* is denoted by the graphic reduplication of *k*. An analogous reduplication can be observed in the realization of the cluster of a plosive and the following *H* in the form *piddāi-* "to pay (marriage portion, tax)": 3 pers. sing. Pres. *píd-da-iz-zi*.[11]

For another example demonstrating the behaviour in Hittite of the "laryngeal" phoneme following the plosive which has a voiced reflection in the historical Indo-European languages, we can cite the adjective *šuppi-* "clean", "holy", compared to Sanskr. *su-bhānu-* "well illuminating" and *bhāti* "shines".[12]

As can be seen, as a result of the assimilation of *H* with the preceding plosive, which yielded a voiced consonant in the historical Indo-European languages, there emerges in Hittite a phoneme which is graphically indicated by the reduplication of the sign used for the relevant consonant. Thus, the difference between voiced and voiceless plosives does not play an important role in such combinations, for the signs for voiced plosives may interchange with signs for the corresponding voiceless ones; so for example beside the form *me-ik-ki-iš* (Nom. sing), we can note the following written forms: *me-ig-ga-e-eš* (Nom. plur.), *me-ig-ga-uš* (Acc. plur.). Consequently, the basic graphic feature of the phoneme which results from the assimilation of a plosive and the following *H* is the reduplication of the plosive in question, without indication of whether it is voiced or voiceless.

To interpret the phonological nature of the Hittite phonemes resulting from the assimilation of a plosive with the following "laryngeal", we can refer to phenomena in other Indo-European languages, specifically Indo-Iranian ones, where analogous assimilations of plosives with the following "laryngeals" yield corresponding plosives with aspiration: cf. Old Ind. *tíṣṭhati* "he stays", Aorist *a-sthā-t*, Past Participle *sthi-táḥ*; *pṛthú* "wide", cf. Greek πλατύς; suffix of 2 pers. sing. Perf. *-tha*, cf. Greek -θα, and Hitt. *-tti*. An analogous development can be noticed in Indo-Iranian for other Indo-European phonemes which yielded voiced plosives: Old Ind. *mahás* (Gen.) "big", *ahám* "I", cf. Greek ἐγω, Lat. *ego*.[13]

In the Akkadian cuneiform writing as adopted for the Hittite language, the double writing of a consonant was used to indicate aspirated sounds as opposed to their single writing which marked a simple (non-aspirated) plosive. However, the reduplication of a consonant is characteristic - as is known - of phonemes which can be traced back to Indo-European plosives which are reflected in the majority of the Indo-European languages in the form of simple (non-aspirated) voiceless plosives. Starting from the fact that the graphic realization of Hittite aspirated phonemes which were formed by the assimilation of plosives and following "laryngeals" was identical with that of the corresponding Indo-European "voiceless plosives", we may infer that these latter phonemes were aspirated consonants in Hittite.[14]

In the light of these facts, Sturtevants's rule acquires a completely different significance: the graphic reduplication of plosives is used to denote not the simple voiceless plosives but the corresponding aspirated phonemes, while their single writing was used for non-aspirated consonants.[15]

Thus we can reach the conclusion that the Hittite phonological system was characterized by two series of plosives: aspirated ones denoted by the graphic reduplication of the relevant consonant on the one hand, and non-aspirated ones on the other, denoted by the single writing of the corresponding consonant.

Three series of Proto-Indo-European plosives: 1) glottalized, 2) voiced (aspirated, and 3) voiceless (aspirated)[16] were reduced in the Hittite phonological system into two series opposed to each other by virtue of aspiration. The differentiating feature for the phonological opposition of plosives is only the factor of aspiration (tenseness), regardless of the original voiced/unvoiced opposition of the plosives, which had phonemic significance in the Proto-Indo-European system. The correlation of Proto-Indo-European plosives depending on whether they were voiced, voiceless or glottalized was replaced in the Hittite phonological system by the correlation on the basis of "aspiration" (tenseness).[17]

The feature of aspiration, which had been phonologically irrelevant with the phonemes of series 2) and 3) in Proto-Indo-European, became a phonologically significant feature in the Hittite system of plosives. In the process, the Proto-Indo-European series 1) and 2) merged into a general series of non-aspirated plosives as opposed to the series of aspirated ones, which derives from the Proto-Indo-European series 3) of voiceless (aspirated) plosives.

With the adoption of the Akkadian cuneiform writing, the two series of Hittite plosives - the simple and the aspirated - were written not by the signs for voiced and voiceless plosives, as these were not differentiated in the early Akkadian writing system, but with the single and double writing of the respective consonants. Accordingly, the *single* writing of a consonant was used to express *simple* plosives, while for the Hittite *aspirated* (tense) plosives a new means of denotation was found, that is the *reduplication* of the consonant in question, by which was solved the problem of how to differentiate graphically between a simple plosive and the corresponding aspirated consonant.[18]

---

* Russian original in: *Peredneaziatski Sbornik* 3, Moscow 1979, 71-77; the Editors wish to thank Prof. W.S. Allen for his help with the English version.

---

1 A. Kammenhuber, *Die Sprachstufen des Hethitischen*, *Zeitschrift für vergleichende Sprachforschung* 83, 1969, 256 sqq.

2 Th. V. Gamkrelidze, *Klinopisnaya sistema akkadsko-khettskoi gruppy i vopros o proiskhoždeni khettskoi pis'mennosti*, VDI 67, 1959/i, 9 sqq.; id., *The "Akkado-Hittite" Syllabary and the Problem of the Origin of the Hittite Script*, *Archiv Orientální* 29, 1961, 411 sqq.

3 E.H. Sturtevant & E.A. Hahn, *A Comparative Grammar of the Hittite Language*, New Haven 1951, 55.

4 The reduplication of *ḫ* determined by its position and the single writing of it seem to have indicated two different allophones (variants) of one and the same phoneme, apparently the velar spirant /*x*/, cf. Th. V. Gamkrelidze, *Hittite and the Laryngeal Theory*, in *Pratidānam: Studies Presented to F.B.J. Kuiper on His Sixtieth Birthday*, 'S-Gravenhage 1969, 92.

5 Cf. E. Benveniste, *Hittite et Indo-Européen*, Paris 1962, 7; A. Kammenhuber is somewhat sceptical in this respect, see her *Hethitisch, Palaisch,*

Luwisch und Hieroglyphenluwisch, in *Handbuch der Orientalistik: Altkleinasiatische Sprachen* [Leiden 1969], 177, with a bibliography.

6 Indo-European "voiceless", "voiced plosive" and "voiced aspirate" here and later mean the Proto-Indo-European phonemes reflected in the historical Indo-European dialects in the respective voiceless and voiced phonemes. These terms, however, are not here assumed to be the definitions of the strict phonological character of these phonemes themselves in the Proto-Indo-European phonological system (on which see later).

7 See S. Langdon & A.H. Gardiner, *Treaty between Hattušili and Ramesses II*, JEA 6, 1920, 179 sqq.

8 On the "Horse Training Texts" and the appearance of the Old Indian terms for horse-breeding in Hittite see the elaborate studies by A. Kammenhuber, *Hippologica hethitica*, Wiesbaden 1961, and *Die Arier im Vorderen Orient*, Heidelberg 1968.

9 Cf. H. Hendriksen, *Untersuchungen über die Bedeutung des Hethitischen für die Laryngaltheorie*, Copenhagen 1941, 52.

10 On the reflection of Proto-Indo-European "laryngeals" in Hittite in the form of the consonant *ḫ*, see Th. V. Gamkrelidze, *Khettski yazyk i laringal'naya teoria. Trudy Instituta yazykoznania, Seria vostočnykh yazykov* 3, Tbilisi 1960, 15 sqq.

11 Cf. H. Hendriksen, *Untersuchungen....*, 53.

12 See H. Pedersen, *Hittitisch und die andere indoeuropäischen Sprachen*, Copenhagen 1938, 36.

13 J. Kuryłowicz, *Études indo-européennes*, Kraków 1935, 46 sqq.

14 The existence of aspirated phonemes in the Hittite phonological system can be demonstrated by the correspondence in several cases of Hittite *ḫ* in initial position with the Proto-Indo-European plosive: Hitt. *ḫarš(a)n* "head": Old Ind. *śīrṣán-*, Genitive *śīrṣnáḥ*, as well as the alternation of *k*/*ḫ* observable in Hittite words themselves: cf. *ḫilammi*/*kilammi* (Dat.-Loc.) "portico"; *ḫamešḫanza*/*ḫameškanza* "spring", "harvest-time", and others. These alternations can be explained by supposing that /*kh*/ in Hittite was a strongly aspirated sound, which in initial position or after a consonant was indicated by the signs for /*k*/, sometimes replaced by those for the fricative /*ḫ*/ which stressed the aspiration of the phoneme /*kh*/.

15 Cf. Th. V. Gamkrelidze, *Peredviženie soglasnykh v klinopisnom khettskom nesitskom yazyke* (*Peredneaziatski Sbornik* 1, Moscow 1961, 211 sqq.).

16 See Th. V. Gamkrelidze & V.V. Ivanov, *Lingvističeskaya tipologia i rekonstrukcia sistemy smyčnykh v indoyevropeiskom*, in *Materialy konferentsi po sravnitel'no-istoričeskoi grammatike indoyevropeiskikh yazykov*, Moscow 1972, and *Sprachtypologie und die Rekonstruktion der indoeuropäischen Verschlüsse* (*Phonetica* 27, 1972).

17 On "aspiration" and "tenseness" as variants of a common distinctive feature, see R. Jakobson & M. Halle, *Fundamentals of Language*, 'S-Gravenhage 1956, 27 sqq.; cf. F. Falc'hun, *La langue bretonne et la linguistique moderne: Problèmes de phonétique indo-européenne*, in *Conférences Universitaires de Bretagne*, Paris 1943, 24 sqq.; B. Malmberg, *Acta Linguistica* 3, 1942-43, 131 sqq.

18 See Th. V. Gamkrelidze, *The "Akkado-Hittite" Syllabary* (quoted above), 411 s

TERMS FOR SLAVES IN ANCIENT MESOPOTAMIA *

I. J. Gelb (Chicago)

1. Introductory Remarks

The early Mesopotamian terms for chattel slaves are a r á d and i r 11 (also ì r) for "male slave" and g e m é for "female slave" or "slave woman". Occasionally, the neutral s a g "head" is used for both male and female slaves, or, with gender differentiation, s a g - n i t a for "male slave" and s a g-SAL for "female slave". Very little is known about the term š u b u r for slave. In certain situations, all these terms have meanings quite different from those denoting chattel slavery.

The two main signs for slaves are written as NITA+KUR, that is, MALE+MOUNTAIN for the male slave, and as SAL+KUR, that is, FEMALE+MOUNTAIN for the female slave. The interpretation of the components of the signs for slaves as male or female, plus mountain is self-evident from their pictures. Ever since Thureau-Dangin's study in ArOr I [1929] pp. 271f. (but cf. already SAKI p. 152 n. f), it has been generally assumed (as, for example, by A. Falkenstein, *Gerichtsurkunden* I p. 83) that the sign KUR stood for mountain, as well as foreign country, leading to the conclusion that the ancient Sumerians derived their slaves from foreign, mountainous areas. Not acceptable seems to be the explanation offered by M. Lambert in *Sumer* IX p. 200, X p. 154, RA LI p. 213, LVII p. 169, and *Syria* XLV p. 410 that KUR in SAL+KUR (and in other terms) serves as a "terme graphiquement plus noble que SAL" or that it was employed "de façon noble" and that é - g e m é (SAL+KUR), which I interpret as a women's establishment, *gynoikeia*, serving as an *ergasterion* (see Gelb, JNES XXIV [1965] p. 242 and below p. 92), is to be translated as "le palais de la princesse".

The conclusion that the terms NITA+KUR and SAL+KUR stood originally for slaves from foreign mountainous areas clashes, at first glance, with another conclusion, namely, that NITA+KUR means only "slave", while SAL+KUR = g e m é means not only "slave woman", but also generally "woman" of dependent classes, from the qualified dependency of wives of free peasants, to serfs and full chattel slaves (see below section 5). However, this difficulty is more apparent than real, provided that we do not insist that the original meaning of SAL+KUR "woman of the mountain" was "*slave* girl" or "*slave* woman", with the stress on "slave", rather than on "*girl*" or "*woman*". This difference in stress is evident when we recall that in "primitive", pre-urban societies, the abducted foreigners were not utilized for full chattel slavery, but for a household, patriarchal, family-like type of slavery, which in the case of women often ended up in marriage. Note that *gune*, the standard word for "woman" in Greek, is the most common word for slave woman in Homer (Ja. A. Lencman, *Die Sklaverei im mykenischen und homerischen Griechenland* [Wiesbaden, 1966] p. 263, cited below p. 92) and the description of the lowly position of women in India: "In many passages from ancient Indian texts women and *śudra* [the lowest caste] are lumped together in the same category" (Ras Sharan Sharma, *Light on Early Indian Society and Economy* [Bombay, 1966] p. 29).

In contrast to the conclusion that KUR means "mountain", the pictographic texts from Uruk yield clear evidence that KUR means "male", in parallelism to SAL "female", as applied to sheep, as well as humans. See Green, JNES XXXIX

[1980] p. 6, Vaiman, VDI 1974 pp. 138-148, especially p. 148, and Vaiman in Harmatta and Komoróczy, editors, *Wirtschaft und Gesellschaft im Alten Vorderasien* [Budapest, 1976] pp. 15-27, especially p. 24.

2. N i t a "*male*", a r á d "*slave*" and i r $_{11}$ "*slave*"

The forms of the signs NITA and NITA+KUR are shown on Chart I in their paleographic development from pictographic to cuneiform.

Three basic shapes of the signs NITA and NITA+KUR are distinguished, forms *a*, *b*, and *c*. As best recognizable from later stages, the three forms are characterized by the presence or absence of two final wedges, the first normally oblique, the second normally vertical. As can immediately be recognized from the chart, the standard forms and values are attested mainly in the form *a*, that is, the form with two final wedges.

Each of the three forms (*a*, *b*, and *c*) has two subdivisions, the first with the logographic value n i t a "male" and syllabic values uš and îr, and the second with the logographic values a r â d and i r $_{11}$ "slave" and the rare syllabic value i r $_{11}$.

The most common forms with logographic and syllabic values in each period are underscored.

The two slightly divergent forms ( and 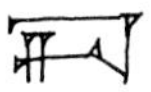) of the sign NITA (in NITA and NITA+KUR) are used interchangeably from the earliest periods down to Sargonic. The two forms begin occasionally to be differentiated in their functions in the Sargonic period, leading to a standard differentiation of n i t a and u š in later periods.

One of the most surprising results of the investigation of the early forms of the NITA and NITA+KUR signs is the form of the sign which is used with the syllabic value î r. The î r value is written regularly without the final vertical in the Fara, Pre-Sargonic, and Sargonic periods, in contrast to the n i t a and u š values, which are regularly written with both final wedges. In the Ur III period, the earlier form of the î r value continues sporadically, but the standard form is that of n i t a, with two final wedges. Thus the Fara, Pre-Sargonic, and Sargonic î r is different from n i t a, while Ur III î r is identical with n i t a.

The form *a* of the signs NITA and NITA+KUR exhibits a further characteristic, which ought to be pointed out. In contrast to the NITA sign which retained two vertical wedges after the first horizontal wedge, the NITA+KUR sign has two wedges from the earliest periods to the Sargonic period, but the form with one vertical wedge begins to appear in the Sargonic period (no. 34) and becomes normal in the Ur III period.

In the following pages are reproduced the logographic values of the sign NITA and NITA+KUR, as given in the main lexical series. Most of the readings are found in Deimel, ŠL I p. 14 nos. 89 (NITÂ) and 90 (NITÂ+KUR) and in the CAD and AHW under the respective Akkadian entries. Please note that in conformity with the development of signs, I transliterated as NITA and ARÂD what is symbolized as NITÂ and NITA in lexical series. In some cases I have added translations for guidance.

As reconstructed in the Proto-Ea series, we find the following entries in MSL XIV pp. 52 and 61:

517.	m i - e š	UŠ	Variant m e - e š (from g i š)
518.	ú š	UŠ	Cf. also ú - u š UŠ on p. 120:15-19

518a.		UŠ	
789.	n i - i n - t [a	NITA]	Cf. also p. 102:789
790.	u r - d u	⌜NITA+KUR⌝	Cf. also p. 102:790

Note that the Proto-Ea series has UŠ and NITA signs in two different places, conforming to the differentiation of the two variants of one sign which took place in the Ur III period. See above p. 82.

Portions of a lexical text published in RA XXI p. 178 iii 14-16 were entered in MSL II p. 149:14-16 and re-edited in MSL XIV p. 134:14-16 under the type of "Secondary Branches of Proto-Ea and Proto-Aa series":

14.	i r	NITA	*te-el-tu[m]*
15.	e - r a	NITA-r a	*e-ra* "(god) Era"
16.	u r - d u	NITA	*wa-ar-du-um* "slave"

The new reading *te-el-tu[m]*, given in MSL XIV for *te-ru-um* "Höfling" of MSL II, will be discussed below p. 87.

The most extensive information on the NITA and ARÂD signs is found in a text copied in CT XII 13 iii 44-45 + 30, 38744:1-10 and edited as part of the Aa series in MSL XIV p. 502 (and pp. 480f.):

205.	i r	NITA	*gít-ma-[lum]*	"perfect"
206.	(i r	NITA)	*eṭ-[lum]*	"man"
207.	[...	NITA	*x]-su-⌜u⌝*	"..."
208.	[...	NITA	*x]-⌜du-u⌝*	"..."
209.	[x-y]-⌜k i ?]	NITA	*[nap-ṭi?⌝-rum*	"..."
210.	([x-y]-⌜k i ?]	NITA)	*ma-[(x)]-rum*	"..."
211.	[n i - i] n ? - t a	NITA	*zi-ka-rum*	"male"
212.	([n i]- i n ? - t a	NITA)	*ri-⌜e-šum⌝*	"head", "slave"
213.	[á] r - d a	NITA	*ar-du*	"slave"
214.	⌜e⌝ - r u m	NITA	MIN (=*ar-du*)	"slave"
215.	s u - b a r - r u m	NITA	MIN (=*ar-du*)	"slave"
216.	a - r a d	NITA	MIN (=*ar-du*)	"slave"
217.	MIN (= a - r a d)	ARÂD+KUR	MIN (=*ar-du*)	"slave"
218.	u r - d a	ARÂD+KUR	MIN (=*ar-du*)	"slave"

The reading of the individual signs has undergone several stages. I first utilized Landsberger's old manuscript of the series, then Civil's readings, and photos of the tablet. The MSL XIV edition of this text is the result of Civil's collation of the tablet in the British Museum. There are great variations in the readings of the signs in the different versions of the series, the most important of which is the reading s u - b a r - r u m in line 215 instead of e - r a d of previous versions. Since the sign e of e - r a d is clearly different on the photo from e in g i - e in line 219, I originally preferred to read line 215 as ⌜ú⌝ - r a d. If correct, the new reading s u - b a r - r u m, proposed by Civil on the basis of a collation, is too good to be true, since it would tend to confirm my idea expressed long ago that s u b a r, š u b u r, etc., meant originally "slave" and that the word for "slave" was derived from the ethnic designation for Subarians. See below, p. 90.

In the Emesal Vocabulary edited in MSL IV p. 16 on the basis of an unpublished text we read:

66.	l a - b a r	N[ITA	*ar-du]*	"slave"
67.	e ! - r i	N[ITA	*ar-du]*	"slave"

I suspect that instead of N[ITA] (transliterated a [r a d]), we should read ARÀD (=NITA+KUR). The information on l a b a r, here given, is supported by l a - b a r *ar-du* "slave" in the series Antagal III 230 (=CT XVIII 35 iii 64 = CAD/A II p. 243b) and by the identification of the personal names L a - b a r - ᵈ N u - d î m - m u d with ARÀD-ᵈÊ-*a* in V R 44 ii 15 (cited courtesy Miguel Civil). The reading e ! - r i of the Emesal Vocabulary is supported by several examples of e - r i ARÁD *ar-du* "slave" cited in CAD A/II p. 244a.

Two more spellings should be added to the occurrences listed above. One is from a completely unreliable lexical text published in UET VII 93 rev., which has:

35.	e - r i - d a	*wa-ar-du-um*	"slave"
36.	e - r i - d a	*am-tum*	"slave woman"

The other spelling came to light recently, with the publication of an Old Babylonian bilingual inscription by Edzard, MDP LVII pp. 18-34, in which the name ARÀD- m u, well-known in the Ur III period, is spelled syllabically U r - d u - u m - g u in lines i 43 and ii 32. This gives the reading u r d u or u r d u m to the sign ARÀD.

Not treated above are the syllabic values e - e r and e - r i, which were discussed in H. Limet, *Sceaux cassites*, pp. 41 and 105, with past bibliography. The spelling e - e r, occurring in E - i r -ᵈEN.LÎL(.LÀ) was explained as Akkadian *erum* in MAD III p. 59 on the basis of a number of parallels that can now be identified with Akkadian *erum* "headband" (see CAD E p. 320); while the reading e - r i on a Kassite seal published in O.E. Ravn, *A Catalogue of Oriental Cylinder Seals and Seal Impressions in the Danish National Museum* [København, 1960] no. 86 is too doubtful for discussion. I do not know how seriously to evaluate the Sumerian spellings a - r i and a - r i - a for Akkadian *a-rad* (=*ardu*) "slave" occurring in late Assyrian and Babylonian copies of a literary composition (Sjöberg, JCS XXIV [1972] p. 127:17, plus the notes on pp. 127a and 129b, where a - r i (- a) is taken to be a mistake for e - r i).

The justification for discussing here the sign NITA, which generally is used for *zikarum* "male", together with the sign NITA+KUR, which generally is used for *wardum* "slave" in the early Mesopotamian sources, lies in the fact that the two signs have several analogous readings and meanings in lexical texts, as well as, occasionally, in early sources. Thus the sign NITA+KUR, used occasionally with the syllabic value î r in the Sargonic and Ur III periods (see pl. I nos. 39, 50, and 52), is quite frequently confused with the sign NITA from the Ur III period on. The best evidence comes from the spellings of many Ur III personal names composed of ARÀD, as listed in Limet, *L'anthroponymie sumérienne* [Paris, 1968] pp. 438-441. Cf. also n a m -NITA (UET III 1077) for n a m - a r â d "slavery" and g é m e -NITA (UET III 1364 rev.) for g e m é - a r â d "female and male slaves" (see p. 93). On the other hand, we find NITA+KUR where n i t a is expected, as in a l a m NITA+KUR and SAL (UET III 770) "statuettes of male and female", a n š e -NITA+KUR (UET III 1253, 1254, 1255, and 1257) for a n š e - n i t a (UET III 1256) "male donkey", and s a g -NITA+KUR (TMH n.F. I/II 258) for s a g - n i t a "male slave".

Listing all forms given above, we have:

a) [á] r - d a, a - r a d
b) e - r i - d a, apparently no e - r a d
c) u r - d u, u r - d u (- u m), u r - d a, apparently no ú - r a d

d) a - r i, a - r i - a
e) e - r i, e - e r, é - r u m
f) i r
g) l a - b a r
h) s u - b a r - r u m

We can classify these forms in three groups: that ending in *-d* or *-d* plus a vowel (a-c), that ending in *-r* or *-r* plus a vowel (d-f), and two still different forms, l a - b a r and s u - b a r - r u m (g-h).

The spellings with *d* obviously reflect the borrowing of the Sumerian word from the Akkadian (or pre-Akkadian) *ward* + *um* "slave", with the following phonetic changes: the elision of the initial *w* (as in the Babylonian dialect) in [á] r - d a and a - r a d; and the change of *wa* to *u* (as in the Assyrian dialect) in u r - d u, u r - d u (- u m), and u r - d a. The Akkadian word is reflected in Sumerian spellings in a nominative case, as in u r - d u and u r - d u (- u m), accusative case, as in [á] r - d a, e - r i - d a, and u r - d a, and absolute case, as in a - r a d. For these three kinds of borrowings, from Akkadian to Sumerian, see MAD II^2 pp. 5 and 11.

With the exception of Jacobsen, JNES VII [1953] p. 37 n. 8, who separates the forms with *d*, as in a r á d, from those with *r*, as in î r, scholars derive the forms with *r* from those with *d*. Thus Falkenstein, *Gerichtsurkunden* I p. 82, operates with the change u r d - a > i r d > î r, referring in fn. 7 to evidence in Oppenheim, *Eames* p. 207 n. 90 (which cannot be checked by a copy), and in Jacobsen, JNES VII p. 37 n. 8 (which is not pertinent). Similarly, Edzard, *Zwischenzeit* p. 155 n. 823 and *9e Rencontre Assyriologique Internationale* [Genève, 1960] p. 247 n. 41, operates with the phonetic change from Akkadian *ward/urd* to Sumerian e r (d), i r (d). Limet, *L'anthroponymie sumérienne* pp. 68f. and 438-441, recognizes the values î r, i r $_{11}$, î r d, and i r (d) $_{11}$, deriving them all from the Akkadian *wardum*, and Sollberger, TCS I p. 137 no. 362 cites the values î r, i r $_x$, i r (i) $_x$, deriving them from i r (i d). Krecher, ZA LXIII [1974] pp. 223f., transliterates NITA+KUR as i r $_{11}$ even though he considers the transliteration u r d u or u r d a as more appropriate. Bauer, *Lagasch* pp. 52f., has shown conclusively that there can be no connection between the Sumerian term(s) for "slave" and the word u r, since the latter, when applied to divinities, both male and female, cannot mean "slave".

As attested in early Mesopotamian sources, the main logographic values of the sign NITA+KUR end in *-r* or *-d*.

Six occurrences of NITA+KUR- r a - n i "his slave" and NITA+KUR- r a - n i - m e "their slaves" in the main text (*Dok.* I 19 = Or. XXVI p. 31 no. 1) are equated with 6(sic) NITA+KUR l ú "6 personal slaves" in the colophon. Similarly, five occurrences of g e m é "slave woman" and g e m é - n i "his/her slave woman" in the main text are equated with 5 g e m é l ú "5 personal slave women" in the colophon. These eleven slaves and slave women are neatly distinguished from 1 n i t a a m a - t u - d a "1 male houseborn slave child" and 1 SAL a m a - t u - d a "1 female houseborn slave child". Furthermore, the summations in the colophon lump the male houseborn slave child with 10 d u m u - n i t a "10 (freeborn) boys" under the class of 11 š à - d ù g - n i t a "11 male children" and, similarly, the female houseborn slave child with 10 d u m u -SAL "10 (freeborn) girls" under the class of 11 š à - d ù g - SAL "11 female children". The term š à - d ù g, translated here as "child", means originally "sweetheart". This text alone is sufficient to prove that a m a - t u - d a, literally "born of (slave) mother", means "houseborn slave", and not "Diener" (Wilcke, *19e Rencontre Assyriologique Internationale* pp. 193f.) or "serviteur" (Edzard, MDP LVII p. 28).

The above observations can be better visualized by presenting them in the form of a chart:

Main text			*Colophon*	
10 d u m u - n i t a	"10 (freeborn) boys"	=	11 š à - d ù g - n i t a	"11 male children"
1 n i t a a m a - t u - d a	"1 male houseborn slave child"			
10 d u m u -SAL	"10 (freeborn) girls"	=	11 š à - d ù g - SAL	"11 female children"
1 SAL a m a - t u - d a	"1 female houseborn slave child"			
6 i r $_{11}$	"6 slaves"	=	6 i r $_{11}$ l ú	"6 personal slaves"
5 g e m é	"5 slave women"	=	5 g e m é l ú	"5 personal slave women"

Since the best meaning of l ú is "person" (of both genders), and not simply "man", the meaning of i r $_{11}$ l ú and g e m é l ú should be "personal slave", either male or female. The two terms appear very rarely in Mesopotamian sources, all occurrences coming from the Ur III administrative texts. Cf., e.g., 4(b á n) š e - b a i r $_{11}$ l ú PN l ú - š u k u - r a "40 silà of barley rations for the personal slave of PN, the prebendary" (AnOr VII 219:1); and i r $_{11}$ l ú - m e "personal slaves" in a broken passage (*ᶜAtiqot* IV 12 ii). In two related texts listing seized g e m é - g u r u š "women and men", one text has (10) i r $_{11}$ l ú - m e (Barton HLC I 29 v), and the other lists one person as g e m é l ú (HLC III 141b iii 4, collated, the scribe incorrectly writing g e m é l ú - m e in plural), separately from one person as g e m é é - g a l "woman of the palace" (line 1, not g e m é é - g a l - m e), while the colophon apparently lumps them together in the summation as 2 g e m é l ú (iv 4), just as the 2 i m - e t a g $_{4}$ - g a - m e "2 supernumeraries" plus 3 a r á d é - g a l - m e "3 palace slaves" (i 1-13) are lumped together as 5 g u r u š i m - e t a g $_{4}$ - g a in the summation (iv 1).

Entemena, the ensi of Lagaš, calls Dudu, the high priest of Ningirsu, NITA+KUR- r a - n i "his slave" (YOS I 4 iii 1 = Sollberger, *Corpus* Ent. 16).*

The sign NITA+KUR is used with the syllabic value i r $_{11}$ once in the Sargonic period and twice in the Ur III period (see Chart I nos. 39, 50, and 52).* The syllabic value i r $_{11}$ is obviously derived from the logographic value IR$_{11}$.

In the Old Assyrian (Cappadocian) texts, the sign NITA+KUR has regularly the logographic value IR$_{11}$ and the syllabic value *ir*$_{11}$. Cf., e.g., IR$_{11}$-*dim*, in genitive, interchanging with IR (CCT IV 6d 3 and 5); IR-*dí-e-ma* in accusative plural (TCL IV 25:14); IR *ša* PN (*Gol.* 18:19); and PN *Ir*$_{11}$*-ra-a* (CCT II 41a 8 and 10). The meaning of the logogram IR$_{11}$ or IR is clearly "slave".

Generally, the form ending in *-d* is younger than the form ending in *-r*. It is attested in NITA+KUR- d a - n i "his 'slave'" of the Sargonic seals (UE II Pl. 198, U 9844; ITT I 1094; ZA IV pp. 222ff.) and NITA+KUR- d a - n i -

i r "to his 'slave'" of the Ur III "office" seals (UET I 88, 96, 97; PBS XIII 5; etc.). The *-d* ending also appears in such genitival compounds as é NITA+KUR- d a "house of a slave" (RTC 84, Sargonic) and á NITA+KUR- d a "wages of a slave", a m a NITA+KUR- d a "mother of a slave", d a m NITA+KUR- d a "wife of a slave", d u m u NITA+KUR- d a "son of a slave", g e m é NITA+KUR- d a - n i "his slave women and slaves", and š á m NITA+KUR- d a "price of a slave", all in the Ur III period (Falkenstein, *Gerichtsurkunden*, III p. 124).

Since I am not convinced by the arguments brought forth in favor of the derivation of the forms with *r* from those with *d* (p. 85), I prefer to keep them separate. Thus, I distinguish two words for "slave" in Sumerian: 1) i r_{11} the older and native word, and 2) a r á d, the younger word, certainly borrowed from a Semitic language. However, throughout this study, I also symbolize as arád all the occurrences in which the reading of NITA+KUR either as i r_{11} or a r á d cannot be ascertained.

Although there is no evidence that ì r, written NITA, means "slave", except in the Ur III period when NITA interchanges with NITA+KUR, there seems to be no way of escaping the conclusion that the syllabic value ì r must have developed from a corresponding logographic value of the NITA sign, just as the logographic value a r á d of NITA+KUR led, occasionally, to a syllabic value i r_{11}.

The strongest evidence in support of separating the words ì r and a r á d results from the observation made at the beginning of this section, in connection with the discussion of Chart I, that the syllabic value ì r is generally differentiated from the logographic value a r á d in that the former is written in the form *b* of NITA and the latter as NITA+KUR. What that means, *a priori*, is that ì r (NITA) is one kind of slave and a r á d (NITA+KUR) is another.

It might be suggested that the Sumerian terms a r á d and i r_{11} (and i r) may have served to express two different kinds of dependence. This was actually the idea of Jacobsen, JNES VII [1953] p. 37 n. 8, when he proposed that the Sumerian term u r d a (or my a r á d) and the Akkadian *wardum* meant "slave", while the Sumerian ì r and the Akkadian *tîrum* may have meant "courtier" or "palace-servant".

Jacobsen's equation of ì r with *te-ru-um* was based on the Proto-Ea syllabary that has been corrected recently to ì r = *te-el-tu[m]*. See p. 83. The use of the term *têltum* (KA.KA.SI.GA) in lexical texts implies that the value ì r is purely phonetic and that the corresponding logographic value was unknown, at least to the composer of the particular lexical series. Ever since the momentous discovery of Antal David, "Le terme Ka.Ka-siga", *Oriens Antiquus* nos. 5-12 [Budapest, 1945] pp. 5-19, we assume that such phonetic values go back to the corresponding logographic values that must have existed way back in protohistorical times.

Against the interpretation of ì r, *têrum* as "courtier" or "palace-servant", we note that it does not fit the meaning of ì r in the sources collected above on p. 85f, nor the meaning of *têrum* in the pre-Old Babylonian sources, discussed briefly below.

In summary of the data collected on p. 85f., we learn from *Dok.* I 19 that the term i r_{11}, equated with i r_{11} l ú, denotes personal, chattel slaves and is to be contrasted with a m a - t u - d a, houseborn slave children. The meaning "chattel slave" is also apparent in the Old Assyrian texts. Even in the case where Dudu is called i r_{11} of Entemena, i r_{11} does not mean "courtier", but it has exactly the same meaning as a r á d when used in the same type of construction. In innumerable cases in which the structure a r á d PN or a r á d DN occurs (and the same applies to the few cases of g e m é), it denotes a socio-economic dependence of a lower-ranking individual and his household on a higher-ranking individual or his household. In a similar sense, all kings' dependents, from slaves to the highest officials, are called slaves, just as the ruler himself is said to be slave of his god or goddess. See also p. 93f. and the discussion of Gelb in *Bibliotheca Mesopotamica* VI [Malibu, 1977] pp. 113f.

The Akkadian term *têrum* is identified in the lexical texts with the Akkadian *manzâz panî*, which is generally translated as a courtier or court attendant. Cf. LÚ.GAL.TE = t e - i - r u m = *man-za-az pa-ni* (MSL XII p. 226:146, as based on 2 R 51 no. 2), and t i - i r = *man-za-az pa-an* (RA XVII 120 iii 8).

The reading of Sumerian GAL.TE as t i - r u or t i - r u - u m is proved by GAL t i - r u TE = [t i] - i - r u m (MSL XII p. 100:149). The reading t i - r u - u m GAL.TE *ma-ri* É.GAL-*im* (MSL II p. 148:17 = XIV p. 134:17) shows that the Sumerian term was borrowed from the Akkadian, and that the term t i - r u - u m was equated with the Akkadian *mari' ekallim*, which, like *manzâz panî*, also is used for palace courtiers (MSL XII p. 226:146). The existence of the Sumerian word t i - r u as far back as the Fara period can be proved by the occurrence of l ú - t i - r u in a list of professions (Deimel, *Fara* II 48:3 = MSL XII p. 15), while GAL.TE is attested in a similar list dated to Uruk III (MSL XII p. 10:17 = pl. I ii 1).

The Akkadian term *tîrum* or *têrum* appears only in three Sargonic texts, all of them from Susa in Elam. Especially important is MDP XIV 24, whose colophon, reading ŠU.NIGÍN 30-LÁ-3 t i - r u IGI.GAR *um-ma-nim* "total of 27 t i - r u, inspection of the troops", shows that the term is not necessarily a collective, but can refer to individuals. The two other Susa texts, MDP XIV 6 ii and 25 colophon, have simply t i - r u. The men to whom the term t i - r u is applied in the three texts are, e.g., DUB.SAR "scribes", A.(A)ZU "physicians", *šu-ut* GIŠGIGIR "charioteers", SILÀ.ŠU.DU$_8$ "cupbearers", MU "bakers", s a b r a "temple stewards", and š u - i "barbers. All these professions are found under the standard personnel of all public households, and they cannot denote chattel slaves.

In résumé, we can say the following: Leaving aside the meaning of *têrum* as irrelevant for our purpose, there are two terms for slaves in historical times and they are i r $_{11}$ and a r á d. Both are written as NITA+KUR and they are synonymous. In protohistorical periods we should also reckon with two terms within the broad range of "slave": 1) The apparently older and native term i r $_{11}$ with the meaning of "qualified slave", and 2) the apparently younger and Semitic-borrowed term a r á d with the meaning of "(chattel) slave". This brings us to the consideration of the possibility that the term i r $_{11}$ was used first by the Sumerians for native-born individuals representing a domestic, patriarchal type of slavery, in contrast to the full chattel slavery ery, which they derived from foreign areas. This difference between the type of primitive household slavery and the type of the more developed, full chattel slavery was fully discussed elsewhere. It is interesting to note that Limet, *L'anthroponymie sumérienne*, p. 68, suggested that the Sumerians borrowed their main word for "slave" from the Akkadians, adding that "la notion même (d'esclavage) était étrangère au type de leur société".

3. S a g *"head"*, *"slave"*

Of the various words for "slave" the easiest one to interpret is s a g, because its meaning, "head", while rather general, is usually quite obvious in its application to slaves. The word, less common than the other terms for slaves discussed above, is attested in the Pre-Sargonic, Sargonic, and Ur III periods, mainly in legal, not administrative, texts.

The term s a g, without any qualifications, is used for male and female individuals, as in 17 s a g (= s a g -SAL, referring to manumitted female slaves, Reisner, TUT 164[12], Ur III) and 172 s a g - ḫ i - a (referring to women and children taken as booty, YOS IV 67, Ur III, discussed in Gelb, JNES XXXII [1973] pp. 75ff.). With the qualification n i t a "male" and SAL "female", we have s a g - n i t a "male slave", s a g -SAL "female slave", and s a g - n i t a - t u r - t u r "(2) slave boys" (DP 513, Pre-Sargonic), also *passim* in the Ur III period contracts and court orders (e.g., Falkenstein, *Gerichtsurkunden*, III p. 154). According to MCS VIII pp. 84-87, Ur III, a certain *Lu-šalim*, called a r á d "slave", is listed among the 18 s a g - n i t a - m e "18 male slaves" belonging to Gubbani. The spelling s a g - a r á d (that is, s a g -NITA+KUR, instead of s a g - n i t a), together with s a g - g e m é, occurs in the Old Babylonian period. [The reading g ì r - s è - g a ^{d}AMAR-^{d}EN.ZU s a g - m e of Oppenheim, *Eames*, pp. 29f. and pl. IV, should most probably be corrected to g ì r - s è - g a ^{d}AMAR-^{d}EN.ZU- k a ! - m e "personnel of Bûr-Sin".]

4. Š u b u r *"slave"*

Strangely, while the word š u b u r never appears, to my knowledge, in the administrative and legal texts of the third millennium B.C., the name Šubur and its compounds are attested quite frequently in Fara texts, as in Deimel, *Fara* III pp. 47f. The term š u b u r occurs also in the Sumerian literary texts copied from the Old Babylonian period on. Cf., for instance, Kramer *Enmerkar* line 233, where š u b u r - a - n i - i m is said of the king in relation to the goddess (similarly, in Wilcke, *Lugalbandaepos* p. 45 n. 11') and the epic "Gilgameš, Enkidu, and the Netherworld" lines 241 and 243 (cf., e.g., Shaffer, *Sumerian Sources of Tablet XII of the Epic of Gilgameš* [Diss., Univ. of Pennsylvania, 1963, pp. 85f.]), where š u b u r - a - n i is said of Enkidu in relation to Gilgameš. In two other sources of the same epic, Gilgameš speaks of Enkidu as his a r á d "slave" (lines 177 and 222). The same alternation of š u b u r with a r á d can be proved for the Kassite period, where the phrase š u b u r n í - t u k u - n a (Buchanan, *Catalogue of Ancient Near-Eastern Seals in the Ashmolean Museum* I [Oxford, 1966] no. 558), translated as "l'esclave qui te révère" by Limet, *Sceaux cassites*, p. 76, interchanges in the same context with a r á d (Limet, *op. cit.*, *passim*). Cf. Gelb in *Bibliotheca Mesopotamica* VI [Malibu, 1977] p. 124 no. XXVII.

The readings and interpretations of the sign ŠUBUR (= SUBUR) can be reconstructed from several lexical texts.

In the Proto-Ea series edited in MSL XIV p. 62 we read from an unpublished fragment:

869. [š] u - b u r ŠUBUR

Portions of a lexical text published in RA XXI p. 178 iii 18f. were entered in MSL II p. 147:18f. and re-edited in MSL XIV p. 133:18f. under the type of "Secondary Branches of Proto-Ea and Proto-Aa series":

18.	[....	ŠUBU]R	^{d}*Nin-šubur*	"(God) Nin-šubur"
19.	([....	ŠUBU]R)	*wa-ar-du-um*	"slave"

Excerpted from two unpublished fragments, we read in the S^{a} series edited in MSL III pp. 80f.:

11'.	[s u - b a r	ŠUBUR	*ar]-du*	"slave"
15'.	s u - b a r	⸢ŠUBUR⸣	*ar-du*	"slave"

In the three fragments of the S^{b} II series edited in MSL III p. 149:319 we have:

	š u - [b u r	BE+ŠUBUR	*ar-du]*	"slave" (I = CT XI 22 K 6016 rev. 23')
or	š u - [b u r	B]E+ŠUBUR	*[ar-du]*	"slave" (L = CT XI 43 K 15034:2')
or	s u - b u r	BE+[ŠUBUR	*ar-du]*	"slave" (Q = Weissbach, *Bab. Misc.* pl. 11 rev. i 24)

The readings and Akkadian correspondences of the sign ŠUBUR can be reconstructed from sources listed in the CAD A/II p. 243b, Deimel, ŠL II 53:5, and discussed in Gelb, *Hurrians and Subarians* 23f., 32, and 88.

Conclusions which can be drawn from these lexical occurrences are that the sign ŠUBUR has the Sumerian readings s u - b a r, š u - b u r, and s u - b u r and corresponds to the Akkadian *wardum* "slave".

These readings of the logogram š u b u r should be compared with the interpretation of NITA as s u - b a r - r u m = *ar-du* "slave" in a lexical text discussed above p. 83.

The readings s u b u r, s u b a r (or š u b u r, š u b a r) for the logograms ŠUBUR and ARÂD are connected with the readings s u b u r, s u b a r, s u b i r (or š u b u r, š u b a r, š u b i r) used for the ethnolinguistic term Subarian and the country Subartu (and all their consonantal and vocalic variations), leading to the conclusion that the term for "slave" was derived from an ethnolinguistic designation. These questions were discussed in Gelb, *Hurrians and Subarians* 23-31 and *passim* throughout that monograph. For the purpose of the present study, it is important to note that this conclusion lends important support to the proposition that full chattel slavery was derived from alien elements, in this case the Subarians (as in later, Old Babylonian times).

Occurrences in earlier lexical texts are few and all are found in lists of occupations. These are MSL XII p. 10:7 (= pl. I 7, Uruk III and Fara periods); MSL XII p. 13:37 (= *Fara* II no. 70 v 4); and OIP XCIX p. 65:83 (Fara period). Of these references the most important is MSL XII p. 10:7, which has (according to p. 12) two Fara variants, one reading g a l - š u b u r (= *Fara* II 75 i 7) and the other reading g a l -SU (= *Fara* II 76 i 7 and Pl. 8). The case is very important because, if all readings are correct, it confirms my long-standing position that the SU or SU.A people, like the ŠUBUR people, are Subarians. See Gelb, op. cit.

5. g e m é *"woman"*, *"slave woman"*

In parallelism to the sign ARÁD which is composed of NITA "male" and KUR "mountain", the sign GEMÉ is composed of SAL "female" and KUR "mountain". See section 1. The shapes of the sign GEMÉ are shown on Chart II. In contrast to the lengthy discussion of the much differentiated NITA and NITA+KUR signs, the discussion of the SAL+KUR sign can be held to a few lines. Three basic forms are recognizable on the chart. The form *a*, showing the clear compound of SAL+KUR; the form *b*, in which the horizontal wedge moves from the center of the triangle to the front, with KUR occupying the center of the triangle; and the form *c*, in which KUR is placed at the three corners of the triangle.

Since the form *b* of the GEMÉ sign may appear to be similar to, and therefore may be confused with certain forms of the ARÁD sign, it may be useful to point out here two general features of the GEMÉ sign: the forms *b* and *c* have regularly only one vertical wedge after the initial horizontal and they have never the final (oblique and vertical) wedges after the triangle.

A Pre-Sargonic text from Lagaš, VAS XIV 55, has the standard form *c* in the name written

- ^{d}N a n š e (- k a - k a m) in i 3, besides what appears as the form *a* in the name

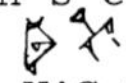

\- r a (d a m - g à r) in line 8. The second name occurs also in VAS XIV 145:2. While the first name is obviously Gemé-^{d}Nanše, the second name cannot be read as Gemé-ra, because the form *a* is unknown at Pre-Sargonic Lagaš. Thus, against the reading Gemé-ra of M. Lambert, RSO XXXVIII p. 130 no. 38 and p. 132 no. 41, I prefer to read the name as SAL- k u r - r a, in agreement with M í(SAL)- k u r - r a of Bauer, *Lagasch*, 291 and 296 and parallelism with PN N i(!) - k u r - r a of Deimel, Or. XX p.8.

The lexical readings of SAL+KUR as cited in Deimel, ŠL p. 179 no. 923 are: g e m é, g î m, g e $_{12}$, and a m a t. There are no problems with the reading of the sign SAL+KUR. The forms g î m and g e $_{12}$ are phonetic developments from g e m é and the sign name a m a t, obviously derived from the Akkadian word *amtum* "slave woman", is not used as a Sumerian word.

Similar readings, g i and g i $_{4}$, are found in a Sumerian literary text (R. Kutscher, *Oh Angry Sea [*New Haven, Conn., 1975*]* pp. 82 and 99), and g i and g i - i in a Middle Assyrian medical text (W.G. Lambert, *Iraq* XXXI p. 38).

MSL XIV p. 502:219-221 (also p. 481) lists the readings g e - e, g e - m e, and k i - r a - a š under SAL+KUR (miscopied as ARÁD+KUR) equated with *am-tum* "slave woman", p. 525:86 reads SAL+KUR as g i - i m, equated with *am-t[um]* and p. 396c' has SAL+KUR read as g e - m e and equated with *ar-da-tu* "slave woman". * As in the cases cited above, all these readings derive from g e m é, with the exception of k i - r a - a š. The Akkadian *ardatu* is a quasi-synonym of *amtu*.

Only as a curiosity we shall cite Sumerian e - r i - d a equated with Akkadian *am-tum*, found in the completely unreliable text, UET VII 93, cited above p. 84.

I do not know of a single word in the broad field of Sumerian lexicography that has been mistranslated more consistently than the word g e m é. Since g e m é is the female counterpart of the masculine a r á d "slave" in legal texts, it has been taken for granted that g e m é means "female slave", "slave woman" wherever else it occurs, and that includes masses of administrative texts pertaining to large public households. Note, for instance, that Deimel,

Or. XLIII p. 85, translated g e m é in Pre-Sargonic texts from Lagaš as "Sklavin", not worried in the least by the fact that male slaves occur in only two of the 1,800 known Pre-Sargonic texts from Lagaš.

Probably the main reason for the consistent mistranslation of g e m é arises from the Sumerian lexicon. It so happens that while Sumerian has two main terms to distinguish male slaves (a r á d) from male serfs (g u r u š), it has only one term g e m é for both female slaves and serfs.

The meaning of g e m é as a slave woman is assured only in contracts dealing with the sale or purchase of individuals, court records (*ditillas*) dealing with litigations concerning the uncertain status, free or unfree, of certain individuals, and administrative texts referring to bought or manumitted slaves.

While I have no statistics to substantiate it, it is my feeling that the translation of g e m é as slave woman fits no more than about two per cent of all texts and that the word g e m é occurs much more frequently than g u r u š, e r í n, a r á d, or any other term pertaining to dependent labor.

In innumerable cases, g e m é is simply the counterpart of g u r u š. As g u r u š means "man" (in the sense of *vir*, *Mann*, not *homo*, *Mensch*), so g e m é means "woman". The classical examples are texts that deal with rations of the dependent personnel. As discussed in Gelb, JNES XXIV [1965] pp. 238ff., the main terms used in these texts for individuals of four ages are:

Old persons:	š u - g i 4	"old"
Mature persons:	g u r u š	"man"
	g e m é	"woman"
Children:	d u m u - n i t a	"boy"
	d u m u -SAL	"girl"
Infants:	DUMU.GA	"nursing baby"

The term g e m é denotes not women, generally, but women of dependent classes, specifically, as g e m é is usually sharply distinguished from the term SAL used for women of independent classes. Note especially the crucial difference between é -SAL, the household of free, independent women, such as the household of the wife of the ruler of Lagaš, on the one hand, and é - g e m é, "women's quarters", frequently serving as an *ergasterion*, a workshop of dependent labor. In my reconstruction, the Sumerian term g e m é "woman" came to be used, probably already in protohistorical times, for all sorts of women of dependent classes, from the qualified dependency of wives of free peasants, to serfdom, to chattel slavery.

The change of meaning of g e m é from "woman" to a dependent woman of a certain status, unfree or semi-free, may be matched by good parallels in outside sources. For the change from woman to slave woman, cf.: *gune*, the standard Greek term for "woman", is by far the most common term for slave woman in Homer (Ja. A. Lencman, *Die Sklaverei im mykenischen und homerischen Griechenland* [Wiesbaden, 1966] p. 263, cited above p. 81); among the Egyptian Arabs, female slaves were never designated by the Arabic term having this meaning, but by the terms "girl" or "servant" (S.D. Goitein, "Slaves and Slave-girls in the Cairo Geniza Records", *Arabica* IX [1962] p. 3; idem, *A Mediterranean Society* ... I [Berkeley and Los Angeles, 1967] p. 131); the Chinese term *nü* means both "woman" and "slave" (F. Tökei, "Die Formen der chinesischen patriarchalischen Sklaverei in der Chou-Zeit", *Opuscula Ethnolo-*

gica Memoriae Ludovici Biró Sacra [Budapest, 1959] p. 297).

For parallels to g e m é denoting women of both the slave and serf classes, cf. medieval Latin *servus* meaning both "slave" and "serf". In medieval England, the term *servi* denotes first chattel slaves, as in classical Latin, later, native-born slaves, and ends up to cover all sorts of dependent labor, including sometimes the "free" tenant farmers. The medieval term *servus*, meaning "native-born slave", contrasts with the term *sclavus* meaning "foreign-born slave". The ethnic term *Sklábos* (*Sklabēnós*), first used for Slavs in the 6th century in Byzantine territory, in the 12th century developed the meaning "slave", whence it spread in the forms *slavus*, etc., over the rest of Europe (see H. Köpstein, *Zur Sklaverei im ausgehenden Byzanz*, *Berliner Byzantinische Arbeiten* Bd. 34 [Berlin, 1966] pp. 42ff.).

This is no place to discuss the term g e m é when it is related in function and status to that of g u r u š, e r í n, and many others who were employed in productive labor in large public households. This kind of semi-free labor will be discussed in a separate article.

6. Abstracts and Collectives

The collective term for male slaves is n a m - a r á d, as in š e - b a n a m - a r á d (wr. NITA) "barley rations for the slaves", besides š e - b a š à é - g a l - k a "barley rations for the (personnel of the) palace" and š e - b a g e m é î - s u r "barley rations for the women oil-pressers" (UET III 1077, Ur III from Ur), and in é n a m - a r á d - k a in the occurrence 3 PN's d u m u PN_x- m e é n a m - a r á d - k a î - s i g $_7$ - à m "3 PN's sons of PN_x live in slave quarters" (MCL 1262, Sargonic, unpublished). The corresponding feminine term n a m - g e m é does not seem to occur as a collective, but is used in an abstract sense, "Sklavinneneigenschaft", parallel to n a m - a r á d "Sklaveneigenschaft", in Ur III court records (Falkenstein, *Gerichtsurkunden* III p. 146). For the meaning "slavery" for n a m - a r á d - d a, as applied to the captives of Šimanum, see Gelb, JNES XXXII [1973] p. 76.

The collective term for slaves, both female and male, is g e m é - a r á d, which occurs in the Ur III period only, and there predominantly at Ur (see references in Legrain, UET III B p. 86), occasionally elsewhere (Falkenstein, *Gerichtsurkunden* I no. 206; Oppenheim, *Eames* P 2; Grégoire, AAS XXXV (81); CT X 48b 11; YOS IV 215). With the exception of g e m é -NITA in UET III 1364 rev. (see p. 84), the writing everywhere else is g e m é - a r á d (NITA+KUR). The meaning of g e m é - a r á d as female and male chattel slaves is clear in YOS IV 215, which concerns three individuals and their prices: one male at ten shekels of silver and two females at seven shekels each. This meaning is supported by the court record no. 206, which deals with g u d "oxen" and g e m é - a r á d of an individual. Conclusions that can be drawn from the texts from Ur are different. Two similar texts, UET III 1047 and 1049, are ration lists for large numbers of g e m é - a r á d in the household of Karzida (part of Ur), including g u r u š "men", g e m é "women", and d u m u "children"; some of the men are qualified as š á - g u d "oxen-driver", u k u - u š "gendarme", and NUN.ME.TAG "artisan", some of the women appear as g e m é š u - g i $_4$ "old woman", g e m é s a g - d u b - b a "head women", g e m é á - ½ "woman working half-time", g e m é ḪAR.ḪAR "woman miller". All these qualifications are never used with chattel slaves, but are normal for serfs. The only conclusions possible for the use of g e m é - a r á d at Ur are therefore: 1) That the g e m é - a r á d of Ur are not chattel slaves, but serfs, and 2) that the serfs of Ur were called slaves because they were under the controlling agency of the crown. See also p. 88 and Gelb, *Kramer Anni-*

versary Volume, AOAT XXV p. 196.

We are obliged to stress here the special position of the a r á d and g e m é of é - g a l and l u g a l, that is, the dependent personnel of the palace and the king, who were called "slave" whenever employed in the crown or royal households, irrespective of their true social status. In support of the foregoing, we could also cite the conclusions of Jacobsen in AJA LVII [1953] pp. 126f. and in *Studia Orientalia Ioanni Pedersen ... dicata* [Copenhagen, 1953] pp. 173f. and 178. According to Jacobsen, two Ur texts (UET III 1504 and 1505) deal with the preparation and distribution of wool under crown control, including issues of wool rations to several thousands of g e m é - a r á d. Such high numbers are possible only in establishments under crown, and no other, control. An important Ur III text from Umma, published in Grégoire, AAS XXXV (81), gives us information about the number of g e m é - a r á d in the household of Ur-Lisi, the governor of Umma, and in the household of Ur-Lisi's TUR.TUR- l a "children". It totalled about 200 g e m é - a r á d, to judge from the amount of barley rations for the g e m é - a r á d given in the text. It can easily be assumed that the governor's establishment, like that of other high officials, was under the indirect control of the state/crown. The Sumerian collective term s a g - g̃ e m é - a r á d for chattel slaves, which corresponds to the Akkadian *aštapīrum*, is known only from the post-Ur III periods. See the current Akkadian dictionaries.

The collective term for serfs is GURUŠ.GEMÉ "men and women", known to me only from the Sargonic text from Kish, reading GÚ.AN.ŠÈ 40 LAL 1 GURUŠ.GEMÉ ARÀD ᵈE n - k i "total of 39 men and women, slaves of Enki" (MAD V 56 end), or g e m é - g u r u š "women and men", known from the Sumerian Ur III texts. The pertinent examples for the latter are Barton, HLC I 26 and III pl. 141, 374, and BM 15804 (unpublished). In all three Ur III texts, the totals of g e m é - g u r u š GIŠt u k u l - e d a b$_5$ - b a (or g i š - e d a b$_5$ - b a) "women and men seized by force" in the colophons correspond to the numbers of g u r u š and g e m é in the texts, with the g u r u š numerically dominating the g e m é in as high a proportion as 3:1. The Sumerian principle of expressing compound words, from less "important" to more "important" ("Steigerungsprinzip"), exemplified in g e m é - a r á d and g e m é - g u r u š, is further supported by the cases of u g u l a - n u - b a n d a "foremen and supervisors", s a b r a - s a n g a "chief temple stewards and 'priests'", e n g a r - n u - b a n d a - g u d "chiefs of plow teams and overseers of field sections", and l ú - t u r - m a ḫ "small and great", actually, "young and old". See also Gelb in E. Lipiński (ed.), *Orientalia Lovaniensa Analecta* V [1979] p. 16.

ASS	=	J.-P. Grégoire, *Archives administratives sumériennes* [Paris, 1970].
AV	=	M. Lurker (ed.), *In memoriam Eckhard Unger* [Baden-Baden, 1971].
Dok.	=	M.V. Nikolsky, *Dokumenty khoziaistvennoi otčetnosti.....* [St. Petersburg/Moscow, 1908/1915].
EK I	=	S. Langdon, *Excavations at Kish*, I [Paris, 1924].
FT	=	H. de Genouillac, *Fouilles de Tello* [Paris, 1934-36].
HLC	=	G.A. Barton, *Haverford Library Collection .....* [Philadelphia & London, 1905-14].
MO	=	Man-ištušu Obelisk (MDP II).
NCT	=	N.W. Forde, *Nebraska cuneiform texts of the Sumerian Ur III dynasty* [Lawrence, Kansas, 1967].

* The following additions came to light after the manuscript was completed: asterisks in the text indicate the passages referred to.

p. 86: Similarly, Enanatum, his predecessor, calls his official, *Šu-ni-al-dugud*, NITA+KUR-*ra-ni* (Biggs, *Bibl. Mes.* III pp. 3 and 18, no. 2).

p. 86: The syllabic value ir_{11} of NITA+KUR possibly occurs already in the Fara period at Abu Salabikh. See n. 15.

p. 91: The value *ge*($\acute{n}_x$) or *gi*(n_x) is recognizable in the Pre-Sargonic occurrence of ugula GEMÉ-*ne*-ke_4-*ne* from **ge*(*n-e*)*ne*-(*a*)*k-ene*, in *Dok.* I 97 v (= *Or.* V p. 7 no. 74 and XXXII p. 59).

p. 96: The same form of ARÁD, with two vertical wedges after the first horizontal wedge, occurs also in 59 iii (collated) = *MSL* XII p. 19:177.

p. 96: Also in *OA* XV p. 176 no. 54 = pl. III rev. iii 4, Ebla.

p. 98: The form *a* occurs also at Ebla, as in *OA* XV p. 176 no. 53 and 55 = pl. III rev. 3 and 5.

p. 98: In addition to the form *b* cited on Chart II, there are four examples of the form *b* plus a horizontal wedge in an administrative text from Abu Salabikh, published in *Iraq* XL pp. 110 and 114 and pl. XVIII *d* and *e*. This form is in disagreement with any known forms of the GEMÉ or ÁRAD signs.

The research for this article was done as part of a grant from the National Endowment for the Humanities.

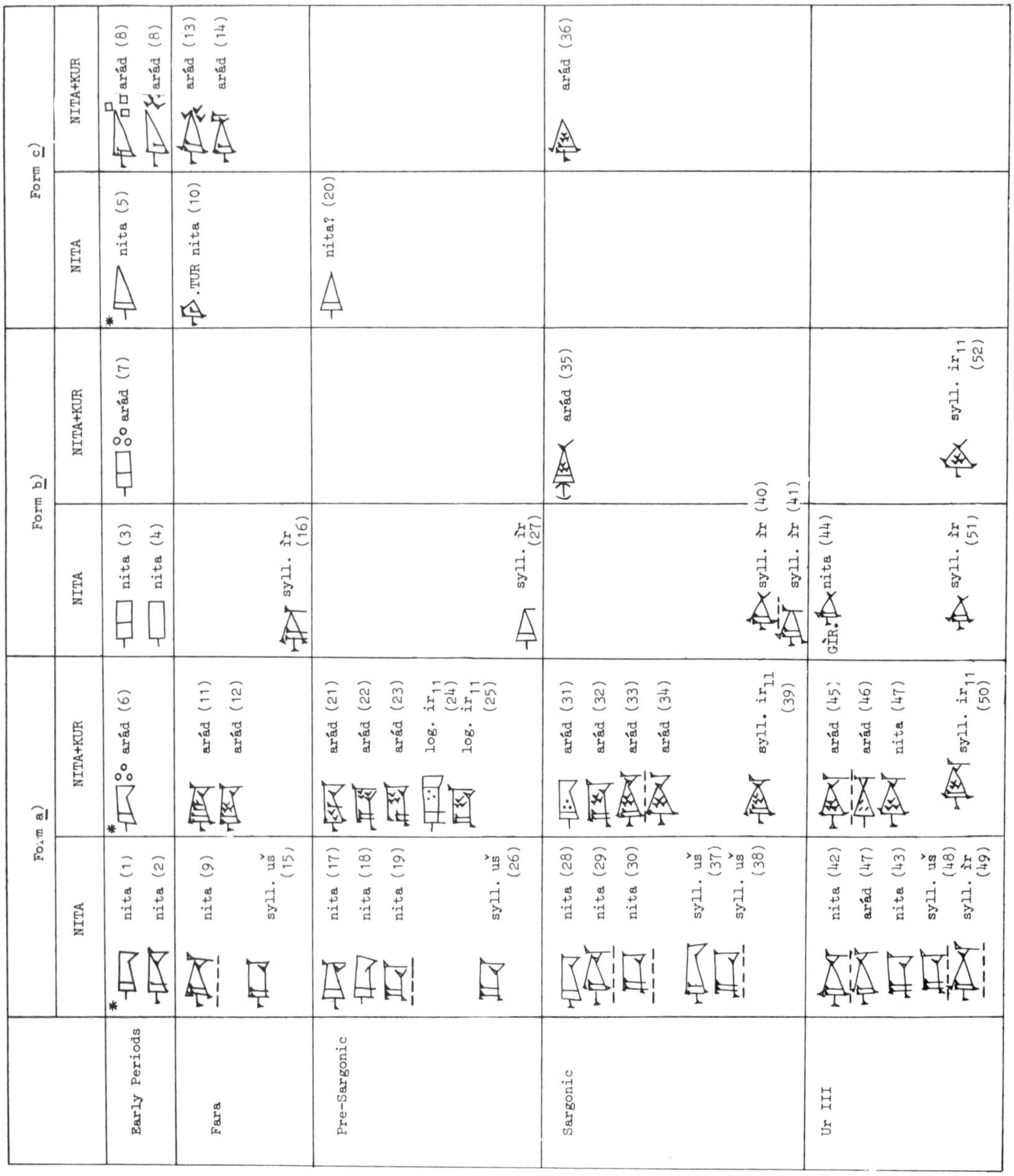
Form a)
Form b)
Form c)
NITA
NITA+KUR
Early Periods
Fara
Pre-Sargonic
Sargonic
Ur III
nita (1)
nita (2)
aråd (6)
nita (3)
nita (4)
aråd (7)
nita (5)
aråd (8)
nita (9)
syll. ùs (15)
aråd (11)
aråd (12)
syll. ìr (16)
.TUR nita (10)
aråd (13)
aråd (14)
nita (17)
nita (18)
nita (19)
syll. ùs (26)
aråd (21)
aråd (22)
aråd (23)
log. ir11 (24)
log. ìr11 (25)
syll. ìr (27)
nita? (20)
nita (28)
nita (29)
nita (30)
syll. ùs (37)
syll. ùs (38)
aråd (31)
aråd (32)
aråd (33)
aråd (34)
syll. ir11 (39)
syll. ìr (40)
syll. ìr (41)
aråd (35)
aråd (36)
nita (42)
aråd (47)
nita (43)
syll. ùs (48)
syll. ìr (49)
aråd (45)
aråd (46)
nita (47)
syll. ir11 (50)
GÌR. nita (44)
syll. ìr (51)
syll. ir11 (52)

Chart I: Forms of the Signs NITA and NITA+KUR.

NOTES TO CHART I

Early Periods

1 Unattested.

2 UET II pl. 5, 53 *passim*, Pre-Fara.

3 Kudurru 10 Blau Tablet a), stone; Falkenstein, ATU nos. 255f.

4 Kudurru 3 Philadelphia Tablet, stone, EK I pl. XXXI/1, stone; Falkenstein, ATU nos. 255f.

5 Unattested.

6 Unattested.

7 Kudurru 7 Leiden Tablet, stone; Kudurru 10 Blau Tablet a), stone.

8 UET II 259 colophon and 128 iv, Pre-Fara.

Fara Period

9 *Fara* I 41 vi 6, and *passim*; OIP XCIX 54 i, ii and *passim*, Abu Salabikh; *Oriens Antiquus* XVIII [1979] 133-4, No. 1 vi 21, vii 8, and *passim*, Ebla. The same form is used *passim* in the writing of UŠ.DÚR at Fara and Abu Salabikh, where the interpretation of the sign as u š or n i t a is uncertain.

10 NITA.TUR with NITA written in form *c)* in Unger AV p. 29 iii 10, Fara, to be equated with NITA.TUR, with NITA in form *a)* in Matouš, ArOr XXXIX 14 i 7. Cf. also UŠ.TUR in TMH V p. 24, Sargonic, and ARÁD.TUR in 6 NT 685, Ur III. All occurrences stand for a PN.

11 *Fara* III 65 viii.

12 OIP XCIX 54 iii and 55 iii, Abu Salabikh.*

13 OIP XCIX 494 ii and rev. ii, Abu Salabikh.

14 Photograph in *Nat. Geog. Mag.* 1978 p. 730 col. iv and vi, Ebla.*

15 In PN's *Uš-mi-Il*, OIP XCIX 34 rev., and *Uš-bi-a-ḫa*, ibid. 283 rev., both Abu Salabikh. Photograph of OIP XCIX 23 viii reads clearly PN NITA+KUR-*mi-Il*, with the same NITA+KUR sign as in note 14, and not *Uš-mi-Il*, as read ibid. p. 35. Should the name be read *Ir₁₁-mi-Il*, with the sign NITA+KUR having the syllabic value *ir₁₁*, which is not attested until the Sargonic Period (no. 39)?

16 In PN *Ìr-i-ba* on photograph in *Nat. Geog. Mag.* 1978 p. 790 col. vii, Ebla.

Pre-Sargonic Period

17 PBS IX 2 v 8, early Pre-Sargonic, stone.

18 Sollberger, *Corpus*, Ur-Nanše 26 iv ii, early Pre-Sargonic, stone.

19 *Dok.* I 15, 19, and *passim*.

20 In NITA-*a-su(d)* "his ...," Dossin in Parrot, *Mission archéologique de Mari* III p. 323, stone, Mari.

21 RTC 1 rev. v, early Pre-Sargonic.

22 OIP XIV 58, 60.

23 ITT V 9232 rev. i.

24 YOS I 4 iii 1, stone.

25 *Dok.* I 19 *passim*.

26 PN *Uš-ni-tum* HSS III 20 iv 7.

27 PN *Ìr-i-bum* OIP XIV 48 ii, stone.

Sargonic Period

28 MO C ix 4 etc., stone.

29 This form, appearing in HSS X 103, 183, MAD I 207, and *passim*, interchanges regularly with the form 30, appearing in HSS X 187, 190, MAD I 288, 311, and *passim*.

30 This form interchanges freely with form 29, q. v.

31 MO A vi 20, stone, and *passim*.

32 TMH V 20:2, 4, 5, etc.; *Dok.* II 1, 5, 13, late Sargonic; but form 33 in *Dok.* II 9, late Sargonic.

33 MAD V 26:6; JCS X 26 vi 2, and *passim*. See also form 32.

34 TMH V 215:3, collated.

35 BIN VIII pl. CLX, stone.

36 PBS IX 72, collated.

37 BE I 5, stone.

38 MDP XIV 90:3, 10, and *passim*.

39 Only in ITT I 1103 rev.

40 PN's *Ìr-ē-um* etc. in HSS X p. xxxiii, and *passim*.

41 Variant of form 40 appears in MAD V 54:4; PBS IX 30; and *passim*. Note especially PN *Ìr*(form 41)-*uš*(form 38)-DINGIR in FT II pl. 137, 1, seal.

Ur III Period

42 CT I 7 ii 5, 12, etc; CT V 28 i, ii, etc.; and *passim*.

43 Occasionally at Nippur: BE III 15:1; TMH n.F. I/2 51:1, etc.

44 GÌR.NITA(form *b*) in Gudea Cyl. B vii 22 and viii 7 interchanging with GÌR.NITA(form *a*) in vii 20.

45 TCL V 5666:2, 13, etc; UDT 59:19; CT V 27 ii 4; and *passim*.

46 *Passim* on seals.

47 The ARÁD sign is used frequently for NITA in the Ur III texts from Ur. See documentation on p. 84.

48 MDP IV pl. 2 ii, stone; CT XXXII 20 i 24; and *passim*.

49 UET III 33:5; Legrain, TRU 266 rev.; and *passim*.

50 Rare, as in Or. VI 59 no. 10; NCT 39:25.

51 Rare, as in BE III 66:7; YOS IV 264 ii.

52 Only in Or. XLVII-XLIX 172:6.

	Form a) 	Form b) 	Form c) 
Early Periods	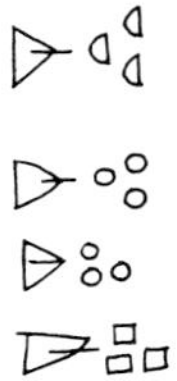 Falkenstein, ATU no. 189 Kudurru 7 Leiden Tablet UET II 50 ii, 93 ii UET II 259 col.		
Fara	 OIP XIV 56 ii (sic, collated) *	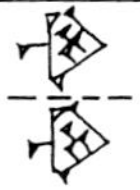 Fara Abu Salabikh (OIP XCIX 54 iii,59 iii, 256 iii 5 etc.)	
Pre-Sargonic		 ITT V 9230 iii (unique? at Lagash)	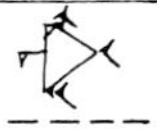 passim at Lagash
Sargonic	 passim everywhere; exceptionally at Nippur: TMH V 50:6; CBS 6136	 passim at Nippur	
Ur III	 passim		

Chart II: Forms of the Sign GEMÉ.

DIAKONOFF ON WRITING, WITH AN APPENDIX BY DARIUS

Ilya Gershevitch (Cambridge)

When I last saw Diakonoff, in Edinburgh in August 1978, I was about to finish at last my 'Alloglottography',[1] with little space left to spare for insertion of further addenda. I was anxious to learn how it fitted his view of scribal evolution in Mesopotamia. What I gave him as the upshot of my article was that the Achaemenian Elamite inscriptions and Persepolis tablets are *Persian* texts, written in Elamite language much as Aramaic was next to become a vehicle language for writing Persian, and their Elamite was well on its way towards ideography; and that if the phonetic writing of Persian in Old Persian cuneiform script is found only in a few prestige inscriptions, this is because scribal schools had since long been committed to maintaining and refining alloglottographic traditions.

Diakonoff's reaction was so helpfully instructive, and rich in details beyond my competence to report reliably, that I begged him to let me have for inclusion in my article a statement summing up the essential in words of his own choosing. Two days later I received from him the letter to be quoted below. In my article I could not have published it without drastic indulgence in what at its end Diakonoff himself suggested: 'Cut the letter and edit it as you want'. To me this would have seemed sheer vandalism. Never before had I received so well-conceived an extempore treatise thrown off in a hotel room in spare moments from an exhausting congress. I now, therefore, take this opportunity to present Diakonoff's letter to a wider audience.

Admittedly in a volume all other contributors to which flocked together to honour Diakonoff with quills of their own, my appearing in plumes borrowed from the honorand himself verges on impudence. But I rely for extenuation on the fact that the plumes nevertheless redound to *his* honour.

As regards the leave which he gave me to edit his wording, I have made only minimal use of it, determined to reproduce not only the international scholar's wisdom and vision, but also the lively English style of the extemporizing Russian letter-writer.

[Diakonoff]. "It has always been something of a difficulty both for Iranian and for Semitic scholars to understand why and how such a cumbersome and intricate writing system as the heterographic came into being, a system using whole words, phrases and even sentences of a language *A*, pronounced as words, phrases and sentences of a language *B*. The Aramaic heterograms in Iranian languages seemed enigmatic, and it was also uncertain at what moments the scribes ceased to treat their writing as Aramaic and began to treat heterograms as sophisticated spellings of Iranian words, like *viz.*, *i.e.*, *e.g.*, *etc.* in English.

"However, the Aramaic-Iranian system is not unique in grammatological history, cf. Akkadian with its Sumerograms *and* Akkadograms, or Korean and Japanese with their Chinese pictographic spellings.

"The case of Akkadian is especially interesting. Already Ebeling showed that its system influenced the Aramaic-Iranian heterography.[2] The influence may or may not have made itself felt fully before the Parthian conquest of Babylonia.

"The pictographic writing which by the middle of the third millennium B.C. was transformed into the well-known and well-understood cuneiform system was apparently invented at the beginning of that millennium *by* the Sumerians and *for* the Sumerians. I have discussed its specific features elsewhere,[3] and I need not return here to the problem of its functioning. The point is, how did the Akkadians start to use it. The original reason was of course simply that the Akkadians, although living more or less a common life with the Sumerians, had not invented a writing of their own. However, an ideographic system does not, in principle, represent any particular language, and what the own language of the scribes was, transpires from rebus writings (especially when the writing is syllabic, e.g. d u for the sign LEG, used phonetically to render a suffix in *-u* of a stem in *-d-* for the reason that one of the words for 'going' sounds d u), and partly from the syntax, although the early scribes did not bother too much about reproducing the word order of the spoken language precisely. They were even quite negligent in reproducing the morphology, once they were certain that the reader of their accountancy text, or whatever it was, would be sure to understand and reproduce it correctly in its oral version. Anyway, in principle a short text written in Sumerian ideographic signs could also be read in Akkadian (or Eblaite), and sometimes was, as again transpires from phonetic complements. A sign WOMAN + BENCH would mean Sum. d a m 'wife' *or* Akk. *'aṯṯatum* 'wife'. But a *single* occurrence of the combination WOMAN + BENCH-(ANIMAL)SKIN instead of the usual WOMAN + BENCH-VESSEL(FOR OIL) for 'his wife' would at once tell us that the text is to be read in Akkadian: one of the readings of SKIN being s u , and one of the readings for VESSEL being n i , we have to read the first combination in Akkadian, as *'aṯṯat-su*, instead of the Sum. d a m - a n i (in the second combination). Or an Akkadian reading may be required because of the obviously Semitic word order, or because of the use of conjunctions that were foreign to correct Sumerian, etc.

"Both under Sumerian and Akkadian kings, down to the late 18th century B.C. it was more usual to write Sumerian. Writing Akkadian was easier (Sumerograms were used only to economize space on the small cuneiform tablets), but not prestigious; letters were texts that more often than others were written in syllabic signs used in their Akkadian sense, although many letters, and virtually all administrative, legal and literary texts, with very few exceptions, were written in Sumerian. This is true, on the whole, even for the time after the fall of the last 'Sumerian' kingdom, the IIIrd Dynasty of Ur (note, however, that of the five kings of this dynasty only the first two bore really Sumerian names). By then Sumerian had definitely become a dead language; some scholars think it was dead even long before.

"Thanks to S.N. Kramer, and Benno Landsberger and his pupils and successors, we know quite a lot about the school (é - d u b - [b] a) of the Old Babylonian period up to 1732 B.C. We know even the curriculum and the examination requirements, which were impressive, including, among other things, oral and written Sumerian, translation from Sumerian into Akkadian and vice versa, etc. Only mathematics was, for some reason, taught in Akkadian, although it also continued the tradition of the Sumerian achievements. Most of the reasonably well-to-do Babylonians sent their sons and even, sometimes, their daughters to school. A shepherd who was chief of four to five cow-boys would be able to account for the cattle entrusted to him, in writing. This of course does not mean that he could compile a legal document or copy a religious text.

"All teaching was based on learning different *Frahang*-type lists by rote:

there were hundreds of tablets listing the Sumerian spelling of all kinds of objects, utensils, plants, legal terms, typical proper names and what not. The teachers saw to their pupils' memorizing such lists well; thus, a proper name which was included in a school list was hardly ever misspelled, although outlandish or unusual names very often were. There is no doubt at all that the scribes understood perfectly well what they were doing when they were using Sumerian heterograms in their Akkadian texts. In fact, if a graduate scribe bore the honorific title 'scribe' (d u b - s a r , *tupšarru*), the really good scribe who could use his Sumerian actively, i.e. write it (and speak it?), would be called a 'Sumerian scribe' or, for short, a 'Sumerian', while the one who did not get much beyond the three hundred or so syllabic and the most commonly used ideographic values of the more common signs was called a 'Hurrian scribe' (a 'Highlander' as it were). However, judging by their names, all of them were Babylonians, with the qualification that a few of the students, apparently destined for a priestly career, had Sumerian names, sometimes rather quaint.

"By about 1800 B.C. most scribes tended anyway to use, often erroneously, only the most common Sumerian administrative and legal formulae, and whenever they did not remember the Sumerian equivalent, they wrote the less standard parts of the text, and sometimes even the whole of it, in Akkadian. Increasingly they used phonetic complements, like KI^{tim} 'earth, land' for Akk. *erṣetim* (Gen.), since Sum. k i had a number of other 'values' as well. There is hardly any doubt that the scribes *read* their legal and administrative (but not the purely Sumerian literary) texts in Akkadian. This is clear from the obvious calques and the atrocious Sumerian grammar in the non-standard Sumerian parts of the texts, as well as from phonetic complements. However, there are some very rare cases when a scribe wrote down a Sumerian formula in syllabic signs used exclusively for Akkadian, probably as a result of writing from dictation. So the texts *were* dictated in a mixed Sumerian-Akkadian gibberish!

"Troubled by the tendency which the use of KI^{tim} for *erṣetim* exemplifies, some scribes representing the older Sumerian tradition tried to stop it. A special handbook called *Ana ittišu*, was compiled, which contained a number of non-standard sentences alongside of standard formulae, and such sentences were sometimes even arranged in little stories with some 'human interest'. The handbook is written in two columns, Sumerian and Akkadian. But it was too late, the book was little used, and has come down to us only by sheer chance.

"This largely secular school system lasted until the great rebellion of Southern Babylonia in 1732 B.C., when the main cities and their schools were destroyed. Thereafter would-be scribes studied cuneiform with private tutors, who mostly seem to have been incantation priests not connected with any particular temple or chancellery.

"I think something of the same kind happened when the illiterate Medes and Persians began to feel the need for a system of administration with written accounts. The Nisa documents, some of the earliest known texts in alphabetic heterographic script,[4] show that the scribes obviously read their texts in Parthian, as proved by (1) phonetic spellings alternating with heterograms (*PḤT'*/ *ḥštrp* 'satrap'), (2) the phonetic spelling of word-compounds due to the reverse word-order of the components being required by Aramaic syntax (*KRM'* = *raz*, but *rzkr* = *razkar* is usual; *'ḤYBRY* for 'nephew' is quite unique, and thoroughly non-Aramaic),[5] and (3) phonetic complements, admittedly rare. But at school the Parthian scribes studied, apart from the alphabet, mostly or more probably only, the Aramaic formulae, as appears from actual school ostraca found in Nisa. When a scribe knew the official Aramaic formula he used it; which in administrative practice is what happened in 99% of the cases; when his Aramaic failed him, and a text equivalent to the one to be rendered had not been used in his school curriculum, the scribe wrote in his own language, using the Aramaic script. This may mean that the writers still thought of themselves as 'Aramaic scribes', just as their Old Babylonian counterparts thought of themselves as 'Sumerian scribes', although in both cases the scribes bore native names, Parthian and Babylonian respectively, and most texts, though not all, were practically read in the native language of the scribes.

"As regards the situation in ancient Western Iran, when I tabulated all the peculiar grammatological (graphemic) features of the so-called 'Old Persian' cuneiform syllabic script and looked for typological analogies in other scripts with which the 6th century Iranians could possibly have been acquainted,[6] I found analogies with Assyrian-Babylonian, Aramaic, and - most important - with Urartian which was certainly extinct by about 590 B.C., but none with Elamite. The Persians would not have had *any* contact with Urartian scribes, the Medes certainly did have contacts with them. The Persians lived together with Elamites in one country, Anšan, due in time to be renamed Parsa.[7] Both the Medes and the Persians had contact with Assyrian and Babylonian scribes, and with Aramaic scribes who existed in Babylonia as well as in Assyria. We know for certain that the Assyrian kings used officially and simultaneously two types of scribes (obviously checking in this way their accounts), one scribe writing in cuneiform on clay tablets, the other in Aramaic on parchment. Whether or not the Aramaic scribes were officially used by the kings of Babylonia before Cyrus we do not know, although this is probable; but it is highly *im*probable that Aramaic scribes were used in Elam before its fall.

"After the division of the Assyrian Empire between Media and Babylonia the frontier ran from a point south-east of Assyria proper to the south of Ḫarrān, and apparently crossed the Euphrates below Carchemish. This means that the royal Assyrian scribes fell into the hands of the Medes.

"To my mind all this can mean only (1) that the 'Old Persian' script was invented before 590 B.C. and therefore in Media;[8] (2) that it had little practical application because the higher officials, who like most officials were Iranian, did not bother to learn to read and write; and (3) that the Persians, at least beginning with the first Achaemenians, employed scribes with a knowledge of the Elamite language and script, which practice lingered on locally until Xerxes' time and perhaps a little longer, while the Medes took over the Assyrian Aramaic scribes and tried to imitate the Assyrian bilingualism by inventing a cuneiform script of their own.

"The practice of using Aramaic scribes had great international importance and was, in its turn, taken over by Cyrus and Darius I for the whole empire, young Iranians being trained in Aramaic schools for office work. Already under Artaxerxes I at the latest the practice of inserting Iranian words and phrases when the scribe's Aramaic failed, is known to have existed. At what moment Aramaic with Iranian insertions became Iranian with Aramaic heterograms, is a question which the Iranian scribes themselves would hardly have been able to answer. However, everyone who knows cuneiform knows that ideographic writings may often be a help, and not a hindrance, to the reader."

This is what I have from Diakonoff on writing.

But Darius, too, made a statement on the subject, in §70, originally the last, of his Behistun inscription in the two Persian versions of it, the elamographically written, and the phonetically written (henceforward referred to for short in usual manner as the 'El.' and the 'OP' version). The statement differs slightly in the two versions. We shall first quote the El. variant, with the translation which Diakonoff offered of it in 1969.[9] He would be the first to urge reconsideration of it, since at the time of writing he was not yet in a position to take into account Hallock's *opus magnum*, which also appeared in 1969.[10]

zaumin d.*Uramasda.na* v.*ú* h.*tuppime da'e ikki hutta harriya.ma appa šašša inni* ŠA*ri kudda* h.*halat.ukku kudda* KUŠ.lg.*ukku kudda* h.*hiš kudda eppi hutta kudda tallik kudda* v.*ú.tibba bepraka meni* h.*tuppime amminnu* v.*dāyawiš marrida hatima* v.*ú tinkeya* v.*taššupe sapiš*

'By the aid of Oromazdes I made (= put) the text on to other (copies) in Aryan, which before did not happen (lit. 'be, exist'; or '[such a text] as did not exist before'): both on clay tablets and on leather; both the name and the ... I made, and (it) was written, and before me (it) was read. Thereafter the aforementioned (?) text, which I sent into all provinces, the people studied (?).'

From Hallock's treatment, in his Glossary, of each word of §70, one gathers that his translation of it might not differ from Diakonoff's except at '...', where for *eppi* he gives 'lineage (?)', at 'aforementioned (?)' = *amminnu*, for which he gives 'this (same)', and at the final word, 'studied (?)' = *sapiš*, which according to him meant 'copied'.

Hinz takes it for granted[11] that *eppi* meant 'lineage', but differs from Hallock, as well as from Diakonoff, in taking *tuppime* to mean not 'text' but 'script', and in translating the last word, *sapiš*, by 'sie erlernten'. That *tuppime* meant 'text', however, can scarcely be doubted, after the spirited defence which Diakonoff put up of this view.[12]

We now turn to the OP variant of Darius' statement, in which unhappily many signs have perished. Cameron reproduced what he saw on the rock as follows:[13]

*va-ša-na-a : a-u-ra-[ma]-za-da-a-ha : i-ma : di-i-pa-i-⌜ma?⌝-i-[+ - + - + - + :]a-da-ma : a-ku-u-na-va-ma : pa-ta-i-ša-ma : a-ra-i-ya-a : a-ha : u-ta-a : pa-va-sa-ta-a-y[a-a :]u-ta-a : ca-ra-ma : ga-ra-[+ - + - + - + - + - +] : [+ - +]-i-ša-ma-i-[+]-ya : [+ - + - + - +]-fa?-ma : a-ku-u-na-va-ma : ⌜pa-ta⌝-i-ša-[ma : +]-va-a-da-a-[*space for 7 or 8 signs*] : u-ta-a : ⌜di-i-pa-i⌝-[+ - + - + - + :]ma-a-ma : [+ - + - + - + - + - +]-ya : pa-i-[ša?⌝-i-ya-a : ma-a-[ma]: pa-sa-a-[va]: i-ma : di-i-pa-i-[+ : a]-da-ma : [+ - + - +]-sa-ta-a-ya-ma : [+ - + - + - +]-da-a : a-ta-ra : da-ha-ya-a-[va] ◯ : ka-a-ra : ha-ma-a-[ta]-xa-⌜ša]-ta-a*

The latest restoration and normalization of the text is Hinz's, who partly included and partly amended the earlier results of Kent. His translation reads: 'Nach dem Willen Ahuramazdās ist dies meine Schrift, die ich gemacht habe (the 'die' is restored); überdies (*patišam*) war (*āha*) sie iranisch. Und sie ist auf Tontafeln und auf Pergament angebracht worden (by restoring *gr[ftam āha]* after *čarma* 'leather'). Überdies habe ich [in ihr] meinen [Vor- und Familien-]Namen gemacht, und überdies habe ich [in ihr] die Genealogie gemacht. Und sie wurde geschrieben und mir vorgelesen. Dann habe ich diese Schrift in alle Lande gesandt. Die Leute erlernten sie.'[14]

Here the last three sentences, apart from the doubtful final verb, agree with consensus and, above all, with the Elamograph. But in the fourth but last sentence the Persian original is illegible at the point where Hinz has 'Namen' (let alone 'Vor- und Familien-'), and his pressurizing the signs *]va-a-da-a[* into forming part of a nowhere attested word for 'lineage' seems a risky procedure. All one can confidently say is that the OP sentence contains one *akunavam* corresponding to El. *hutta* 'I made' (Hinz's second *akunavam* is wholly restored), and that to express whatever may have been meant by El. *hiš kudda eppi hutta* 'I made *hiš* ("name") and *eppi*' the OP used considerably more than four words. But one may readily grant Hinz that for 'I made *hiš* and *eppi*' the OP said 'I made *hiš* and I made *eppi*'; and assume that the remaining excess of OP words was due to each or either of the Persian notions represented by El. *hiš* and *eppi* having been expressed in the phonetic variant by more than one word.

This said it will be clear that, to understand what Darius meant at the point where Hinz's fourth but last German sentence occurs, we depend exclusively on El. *hiš kudda eppi*.

I had often been wondering what 'to make name' might conceivably mean. When I mentioned the nonplus to Nicholas Postgate, his prompt reaction was "but in Akkadian, *šumu(m)* means not only 'name' (and 'son') but also 'line of a text';[15] could it be that by h.*hiš kudda eppi* 'lines and columns' were meant??"

This did feel like a breath of fresh air. For I had been troubled by yet another oddity, that the sentence 'and (it) was written and read out before me' should follow immediately upon a statement supposedly amounting to saying 'I wrote my name and genealogy'. Moreover, once the fresh air is let in, one realizes that no punctuation mark should be inserted between the Elamogram for 'parchment' and the noun *hiš*, not if *hiš* here means 'line'. Of the six *kudda*s the first, fifth and sixth will then be seen to connect sentences, the second substantives, and only the third and fourth will combine to express 'both .. and ..'.[16] The resulting translation will be: 'And on clay and parchment I made (= ordered to be drawn) lines and *columns(?), and (it, viz. the text) was written and read out before me'. Of course a doubt must remain in respect of *eppi* (by which I do not mean that no doubt whatsoever any longer attaches to *hiš*), since unlike *hiš* it lacks the horizontal determinative.

The need for Hinz's 'ist angebracht worden', surmised by him for the OP despite its absence from the El., now seems so much less cogent that one is led to ask if even his 'überdies' in the preceding sentence is a correct translation. It certainly takes no notice of Harmatta's reasonable plea that OP *patišam* should not without good reason be treated as a word distinct from Avestan *patišam*.[17] The latter, in conformity with its being a derivative of the preposition and preverb *pati* discussed at length in my 'Alloglottography', occurs with two opposite meanings. As an adverb it has a directional function close in meaning to that of the preposition and adverb *abi* 'towards', though it is used also for 'forward, in front'; as an adjective it means 'contrarius, widrig, abweichend, ungleichartig'. Choosing the latter alternative, Harmatta took the OP word to correspond to El. *da'e* 'other', and translated 'these inscriptions, which I caused to be made, were otherwise, in Āryan (language)'.

This interpretation does import into the OP version the notion conveyed by El. *da'e*, of which, however, it may be thought that the OP version stood in no need, as the bringing into existence of a text that was 'other', i.e. phonetic, required mention not in that 'other' text itself, but only in the text written in usual, elamographic fashion. What on the other hand even Harmatta's 'other*wise*' leaves unsolved as a serious problem, is the *ikki* sandwiched between *da'e* and *hutta*. In genuine El. usage *ikki* is a directional postposition governing the word to which it is attached, or, if that word is an adjective, it and a preceding noun which it qualifies. 'Another text' would make excellent sense, but *tuppime* cannot depend on *ikki* if it is, as it surely must be, the direct object of *hutta* 'I made'. This is why Hallock, s.v. *da'e*, reached the conclusion that the adjective here acts as a substantive. He did not, however, unlike Diakonoff, offer a translation of the phrase, while Diakonoff's proposal that a noun with the crucial meaning 'copies' is *implied*, can never be expected to set at rest doubts.

But if, in search of a solution, one considers relating *ikki* to *patišam*, whose directional function in Avestan is similar to that of *abi*, there immediately comes to mind that in the Elamography of Persian, postposed El. *ikki* normally corresponds to preposed OP *abi*, cf. 'Alloglottography', 170. But as noted *ibid.*, 174f., the Elamite language had very much fewer postpositions than OP had prepositions and postpositions, so that occasionally one of the former was pressed into being employed for more than a single one of the latter. In principle, therefore, *patišam*, being synonymous with *abi*, stands as good a chance of corresponding to the inexplicable *ikki*, as to the *da'e* whose only inexplicability resides in its apparent dependence on *ikki*.

We have said, in n.16, that Darius must have dictated his statement twice without troubling to use in every respect identical wording. If one applies to *ikki hutta* an ideographic scrutiny strictly adhering to rules of Persian word order, one obtains an OP verb **abi-kr-* corresponding to the Vedic verb *abhi-kr-*. The latter means 'to produce, procure', 'producing' here being derived from 'making towards' or from 'making face', namely the onlooker. When Darius dictated the El. variant of §70, he will have used, for 'I produced', the imperfect of **abi-kr-*, namely **abi(y)-akunavam*, which form his elamographist scribe recorded by writing *ikki* for *abi* and *hutta* for *akunavam*. When Darius dictated the OP variant he will have used, instead, the adjective *patišam* agreeing as a predicate with the neuter noun *dipi-* 'text'. The OP of §70 will then be saying 'this my text (which) I produced (lit. "(which) I made *patišam*") ...', with the deictic 'this' pointing, as it were, to the preceding sixty-nine paragraphs of phonetically written Persian narrative. The elamographed version will simply say 'I produced (*ikki hutta*) another text', meaning the text which in the OP variant is referred to as 'this'.

The El. version then continues 'in Iranian, as previously WAS not', while the OP, being the very proof that by now it WAS in Iranian, simply adds 'was in Iranian'. The reason for 'was' in the OP version, instead of 'is' as *we* might expect, will be that Darius was viewing the act of reading in its temporal dimension: by the time the reader has reached §70, his reading of the sixty-nine previous paragraphs belongs to the past; and what he has been reading, he is now told, 'was in Iranian'.

Of course after 'in Iranian' Harmatta was quite right in supplying in parenthesis a noun implied. But the noun implied is not 'language' (since the language of the elamographed version was also Iranian), it is 'script'. Here, in the implication only, lies the notion of the OP script which Hinz was seeking; and because it lies here, the preceding El. *tuppime* = OP *dipi-* remains free to mean 'text' as it *must* mean at its second appearance in the paragraph.

Having dealt with the middle and with the beginning of §70, we must turn to its very end, the preterite 3rd plural El. *sapiš*, which corresponds to the OP 3rd singular imperfect restored by Cameron as *ham-a-[ta]xšata* (the subject, 'people', is plur. in El., sing. in OP). Diakonoff's 'studied(?)' and Hinz's 'erlernten' impose an *ad hoc* meaning on *han-taxš-*, since elsewhere this OP verb occurs solely in the sense of 'to strive'.[18] Needless to say, the *ad hoc* imposed on *han-taxš-* would be even harsher if Hallock were right with his 'they copied' for El. *sapiš*.

Hallock applies the same prescription to the sentence v.*puhu* v.*paršipe* v.*tuppime sapimanpa* which occurs on two Persepolis tablets in identical context, by translating it 'Persian boys (who) are copying texts'. He evidently interprets the verb *sapi-* in the light of the reduplicated noun *sapsap* which he takes for the El. equivalent of *battiziknuš* = **pati-čaγna-*, the OP word for 'a copy'.[19]

Supposing Hallock's premise to be correct, our own formulation of it would be as follows: if *sapsap* is the Elamograph of Persian **pati-čaγ-na-*, reduplicated because copies amount to duplication, then the verb *sapi-* might be the Elamograph of a Persian verb whose SOUND was **pati-čaγ-*, but whose meaning would not have to be 'to copy' seeing that *sapi-* displays no reduplication.

Such reasoning at once brings to mind the Sogdian verb for 'to take, hold, receive' whose present stem is *pat-čaxš-* and past stem *pat-čaγd-*. If it were its OP counterpart (in the imperfect tense) **pati(y)-a-čaxšata* 'took/received' which the unreduplicated *sapiš* elamographs, and the latter's meaning 'to copy' were assured, we should say that the homonymity of 'copying' and 'taking/receiving' was here due to the multivalence of the preverb *pati*,[20] semantically corresponding in one case to German 'wieder', in the other to 'entgegen'. And we should hasten to add that the Elamographer's reliance (regardless of whether or not it was well-founded) on the gamma of **patičaγna-* would prove the base of the Sogdian verb to have been **čag-* (and not **čak-* or **čax-*), a precious survival of IE **kagh-*, *kogh-*.[21] But just as promptly would follow the rider that a copy is not a 'Wieder-nahme', but a 'Wieder-gabe' as Benveniste justly wrote, invoking the *čag-* of Avestan *čagvah-* etc.[22] To keep the latter distinct from IE **kagh-*, *kogh-*, one may entertain, in the wake of Bartholomae,[23] the possibility that we have here a *gh*-extension of IE **ken-*.[24]

We are at last ready for the kill. Our reconstruction of the OP underlying the Elamogram *sapiš* was **patiy-a-čaxšata*. But in fact the phonetic version of §70 has *ham-a-[.]xšata*. For us, therefore, to be bound to restore the missing sign as *[ča]* instead of Cameron's *[ta]* only one condition needs to be fulfilled: the meaning of **han-čaxš-* must emerge as sufficiently close to **pati-čaxš-* for *sapi-* to appear employable as Elamogram of either.

Corresponding to an OP **han-čaxš-* one would expect to find in Sogdian a present stem **ančaxš-*, with *ančaγd-* as its past stem. Such a past stem actually occurs, in an unpublished text:[25] *pr 'pt'yn'kw cšmy L[' w]yt βwt rtγw 'pt'yn'k γwš L' ptγwšt pr 'pt'yn'k δstw L' 'nc'γt L' ZY ms pr ['pt'y]n'k 'z-β'k 'spt'kw prβ'yr't βwt* '(the soul is such as) cannot be seen by the bodily eye, the bodily ear does not hear (it), (it) cannot be *grasped by the bodily hand, nor can (it) be wholly defined by the bodily tongue'. The meaning 'grasped' of the hapax *ančaγd* results from the context, and is supported by the meaning of the obviously cognate *patčaγd* 'taken'. The latter, in its turn, establishes the unattested present stem as **ančaxš-*.[26]

If in Sogdian **ančaxš-* was a grasping with hands, then OP **han[ča]xš-* in §70 will have referred to mental grasping. And what is more probable even on merely contextual grounds, than that Darius sent the text to all his subjects with the preoccupation uppermost in his mind not that they study or copy it, but that, regardless of language barrier they should all *understand* it?

No doubt, however, most of the king's subjects were illiterate. If they understood the text, they can only have done so while listening to scribes reading it out to them, in each country in its inhabitants' native language. But what the scribes were reading out to them from the clay tablets and parchment which Darius had sent them, was what in the first place Darius had listened to for approval, who would understand it only if the reading was done in Persian language.

Hence different scribes, looking at one and the same text, read it out some in Persian, some in Egyptian, some in Greek, some in Lydian, and so forth. What they were looking at, was therefore inevitably written in Aramaic language used for recording Darius' original Persian dictation alloglottographically, except that in Persis itself and in Elam, but only in these two countries, an elamographed text would fulfil the same purpose. It has of course always been assumed that the 'parchment' Darius mentions was inscribed in Aramaic. That also the 'clay' which the king mentions, bore the text in Aramaic will now seem extremely likely.[27]

As to the 'Persian boys' receiving payment at Persepolis because they *tupp-ime sapimanpa*, they become rather more deserving of it and of our esteem if they understood the texts, than if all they did was to copy them.

---

1 I. Gershevitch, 'The Alloglottography of Old Persian', *Transactions of the Philological Society*, 1979, 114-190, where the following misprints and oversights need correction: p.135 line -11, read 'but' for 'by'; p.136 top line, read 'that' for 'the'; p.154 n.66 end of first line, insert 'of'; p.163 top line, insert 'and' between 'versa' and comma; p.166 second line, 'seems to have fallen out of use' should be in roman, not italics; p.177 sect. II.23, read in both parentheses 'end of II.21' for 'end of II.22'; p.180 last line and p.181 lines 9 and 10, read one final (righthand) vertical for two in the sign *taš*; p.182 line -13, read '145f.' for '1454'.

2 Erich Ebeling, *Das Aramäisch-Mittelpersische Glossar Frahang-i Pahlavik im Lichte der assyriologischen Forschung*, 1941.

3 I.M. Diakonoff, 'Ancient Writing and Ancient Written Language: Pitfalls and Peculiarities in the study of Sumerian', *Sumerological Studies in honor of Thorkild Jacobsen*, 1975, 99-121.

4 First century B.C. See their edition, still in progress, by I.M. Diakonoff and V.A. Livshits, *Parthian Economic Documents from Nisa*, 1976-9 (Corpus Inscriptionum Iranicarum).

5 On *'ḤYBRY* see I. Gershevitch, 'Genealogical Descent in Iranian', *Bulletin of the Iranian Culture Foundation*, vol. I, part 2 (1973), 74f.

6 I.M. Diakonoff, 'The Origin of the "Old Persian" Writing System and the Ancient Oriental Epigraphic and Annalistic Traditions', *W.B. Henning Memorial Volume*, 1970, 98-124.

7 'Anšan, due in time to be renamed Parsa' is a gloss of mine representing a current view which I imagine Diakonoff shares, but to which I must not presume to represent him as committed.

8 I have omitted above, because I cannot accept (see 'Alloglottography', 148, n. 37, first paragraph) what Diakonoff adds at this point: "... and therefore in Media, and is *not* Old Persian but, loosely, Western 'Aryan' (= Iranian; even Darius did not claim that he wrote in Persian!), with local dialect features creeping to a greater or lesser degree into the text, depending on the place and time, and on the scribal school which compiled the inscription. Thus all Assyrian inscriptions, although struggling to use the correct literary 'Young Babylonian', are full of Assyrian dialect forms, and some may even be regarded as written, for all

practical purposes, in the Assyrian dialect!"

9 I.M. Diakonoff, 'On the interpretation of §70 of the Bisutun Inscription (Elamite version)', *Acta antiqua Academiae scientiarum Hungaricae*, tomus XVII, fasc. 1-2, 1969, p. 107.

10 Richard T. Hallock, *Persepolis Fortification Tablets*, 1969, referred to, in what follows, simply as 'Hallock', and mostly in respect of the Glossary of this book.

11 Walther Hinz, 'Die Zusätze zur Darius-Inschrift von Behistan', *Archaeologische Mitteilungen aus Iran*, NF, 5, 1972, 244.

12 *Art. cit.* (n.9 above), 106.

13 George G. Cameron, 'The Old Persian text of the Bisitun Inscription', *Journal of Cuneiform Studies*, 5, 1951, 52.

14 *Art. cit.* (n.11 above), 244f.

15 Cf. W. von Soden, *Akkadisches Handwörterbuch*, 1275b.

16 If this analysis is correct, it will allay the alarm I raised in 'Alloglottography' 158, sect. I.10. Darius necessarily dictated twice what he had to say about writing, since his initial words, destined to be written phonetically, were inapplicable to what was to go on show in elamographed form exclusively. It would be unreasonable to expect the king to make sure of uttering each time the same number of 'and'.

17 J. Harmatta, 'The Bisitun Inscription and the introduction of the Old Persian cuneiform script', *Acta antiqua Academiae scientiarum Hungaricae*, XIV, 1966, 274f.

18 More exactly, 'sich anstrengen'. I have no faith in the current etymology of *taxš-*: contamination of *taš-* 'to fashion, build' and *θwaxš-* 'to be busy'. To my mind OP *han-taxš-* has its unattested past participle **han-taxta-* actually represented by Ossetic **ændaγd*, of which only the comparative is quoted as being in use, *ændaγddær*, in the sense of 'more intensively, to a greater extent'. This points to **han-taxta-* having meant, intransitively, 'intent, assiduous'. The base will be the **tak-* seen in Avestan *taxma-* 'strong'. Cf. the semantic relation between Engl. *strength* and German *anstrengen*.

19 On OP **patičaγna-* see Benveniste, JAs. 225, 1934, 180ff. On El. *sapi-* and *sapsap* see Hallock, JNES, IX, 1950, 244 and his Glossary s. vv.; on the 'Persian boys' in question see 'Alloglottography' 144 n.7.

20 Discussed in my 'Alloglottography', 118, 182, and passim.

21 On which see J. Pokorny, *Indogermanisches etymologisches Wörterbuch*, 1959-69, 518.

22 *Art. cit.* 184. A further cognate, recognized by W.B. Henning in *Ein manichäisches Bet- und Beichtbuch*, 1937, 108, is Middle Persian *ʾw(y)zxt-* 'graced, favoured', from **abi-čaγda-*; cf. the Persepolis name elamographed *Appizaknuš* (Gershevitch, *Studia .. Antonino Pagliaro*, ii, 1969, 182).

23 C. Bartholomae, *Altiranisches Wörterbuch*, 1904, 576 s.v. *čagvah-*.

24 On which see Pokorny, *op. cit.*, 515.

25 TM 389 *a* R 20-24, in Sogdian script.

26 This 'grasping' base I would recognize also in Ossetic *ærcaxs-* 'to seize',

which in W. Miller and A. Freiman's Dictionary is unconvincingly analyzed as from *ær-s-axs-*. I have a note of the existence in Ossetic also of *niccaxs-* with the same meaning, but unfortunately no reference to my source for it.

27 The likelihood stems not only from Darius' making no distinction between what was written on clay and on parchment, and from Elamography being useless outside Persis and Elam, but also from the 'hundreds of Fortification texts in Aramaic on clay' mentioned by Hallock in my 'Alloglottography', 154 n.66.

EINIGE BEMERKUNGEN ZUM HETHITISCHEN TEXT KUB 48, 105

G. Giorgadze (Tbilisi)

Die ziemlich grosse Anzahl hethitischer Keilschrifttexte, in denen NAM.RA "Zivilgefangene, Deportierte" (heth. *arnuwala-*) erwähnt werden, ist noch durch ein umfangreiches Dokument bereichert worden, das über Wirtschaftsstiftungen mit Zivilgefangenen (aber auch von Hornvieh, Dreschplätzen, Saatgetreide und verschiedener Geräte) an die Gottheiten verschiedener Städte Ḫattis berichtet. Dieser hethitische Text wurde in einer Keilschriftkopie 1977 von H. Klengel im KUB 48 unter der Nummer 105 veröffentlicht.[1] Neben anderen heth. Texten, die einzelne Seiten der hethitischen Tempelwirtschaft darlegen, ist das uns interessierende Dokument eine wichtige Quelle nicht nur für das Studium von Deportiertenproblem in der heth. Gesellschaft überhaupt, deren Schicksal I.M. Diakonoff unentwegt interessierte,[2] sondern auch für das Studium zu Fragen der Tempelwirtschaft Ḫattis, insbesondere ihres Arbeitspersonals.

Der Abfassung des Textes KUB 48,105 lag wahrscheinlich die Absicht zugrunde, die Königsstiftungen schriftlich zu fixieren und die Festsetzung einer bestimmten Norm dieser Stiftungen für jede Gottheit dieses oder jenes bevölkerten Punktes zu dokumentieren. Unter denen gab es auch Stiftungen in Form von lebender Arbeitskraft, die sich "ehemalig" (heth. *annalliš*, *annaleš*, *annallaš*)[3] im Besitz von Privatleuten (verständlicherweise von Königspersonen) oder auf irgendwelchen Staatswirtschaften befanden. Folgedessen hielt es der König für nötig, bei Stiftungen nicht nur neue Fonds, sondern auch ehemalige Grundbestände zu benutzen und somit zu einer Neuverteilung seines alten Besitztums in Form von Deportierten, Vieh usw. zu verwirklichen.

Von dem uns interessierenden, im Moment seiner Abfassung wahrscheinlich mehr als 32 Paragraphen umfassenden, grossen einkolumnigen Text, sind nur einige Stellen fast völlig unversehrt. Vollständig oder Teilweise sind 12 Paragraphen auf der Vorderseite und 20 Paragraphen auf der Rückseite, im Ganzen 91 Zeilen umfassend, erhalten geblieben. Der Anfang der Vorderseite und das Ende der Rückseite des Dokuments sind nicht bewahrt. Nach der Meinung des Textherausgebers H. Klengel sind nur zwei Drittel der Keilschrifttafel geblieben.[4] Ungeachtet dessen, geben uns die erhaltenen Teile die Möglichkeit, über das Prinzip der Textzusammenstellung, das sich folgendermassen äussert, zu urteilen.

Den Anfangszeilen der unversehrt oder nur teilweise erhalten gebliebenen Paragraphen nach (es sind mehr als 20), fing jeder Abschnitt mit den Worten an: "In der Stadt *x* stiftete die Sonne für die Gottheit *y* (oder für Götter) folgendes".[5] Diese Worte wiederholten sich stereotyp wahrscheinlich am Anfang jedes Paragraphen, danach folgte die Aufzählung der gestifteten "Häuser" (Wirtschaften) mit ihren Deportierten (mit Angabe ihrer Anzahl und ihres Berufes), der Menge des Viehes, der Gerätschaften usw.

Wie aus dieser stereotypen Formel hervorgeht, wurde am Anfang jedes Abschnittes auf die Stadt mit ihrer Gottheit (Götter) hingewiesen. Sieben Städtenamen sind unversehrt erhalten geblieben. Das sind: Nenašša (Vs. 29′), Uwalma (Vs. 31′), Wizidaša (Vs. 36′), Pattanijaša (Vs. 38′), Kalašmitta (Rs. 14), Tamettaja (Rs. 16) und Durmitta (Rs. 20). Weiterhin haben sich Endungen einiger Siedlungsbezeichnungen erhalten: -šina (Vs. 19′), -taškurija (Vs. 42′), -ratta (Rs. 12). Nach dem Prinzip der Zusammenstellung urteilend (jeder

Abschnitt war einer Stadt gewidmet), waren im Text wahrscheinlich mehr als 32 Städte aufgezählt, die, wie aus den obengenannten Aufzeichnungen hervorgeht, in den verschiedenen Gegenden des Hethiterreiches lagen. In allen diesen Städten befanden sich Filialen der Tempelwirtschaften, für deren Wohlergehen der König - oberster Priester selbst - sorgte und, den Umständen entsprechend, verschiedene Stiftungen an die Tempel machte (was aus anderen hethitischen Quellen auch zu ersehen ist).

Die Stiftungen wurden einer bestimmten Gottheit oder Göttern gewidmet (in einigen Fällen ist der genaue Name des Gottes nicht angegeben). Im Text sind der Wettergott (in den Städten -šina, Tamettaja; Vs. 19′ und Rs. 16), Pirwa (in Wizidaša, Pattanijaša,-ratta: Vs. 36′, 38′, Rs. 12), Nanaja (in -taškurija: Vs. 42′), DLama (=Innara), Ala (beide in Kalašmitta: Rs. 14), Anzili (in Tamettaja: Rs. 16) und "Gottheiten" (in Uwalma, Durmitta: Vs. 31′, Rs. 20; sowie in 2 anderen Städten, deren Namen nicht erhalten geblieben sind: Rs. 6,9) erwähnt.[6]

Nach dem uns interessierenden Text wurde das Ausmass der Stiftungen von der "Sonne" (dem König), dessen Namen nicht genannt wird, bestimmt. Zweifellos war es ein Herrscher des Neuhethitischen Reiches (wahrscheinlich Muršili II., der im Laufe der ersten Zehn Jahre seiner Herrschaft aus den verschiedensten Gebieten Kleinasiens 88 Tausend Deportierte vertrieb,[7] oder Ḫattušili III., während dessen Regierungsperiode verschiedene Stiftungen und Schenkungen gemacht wurden[8]. Vielleicht war es auch Tutḫalija IV.[9]

Zu dieser Schlussfolgerung lässt uns auch der sprachliche Charakter des Textes kommen, in dem jegliche Merkmale der althethitischen Sprache fehlen. Ausserdem wurden Dokumente mit analogen Inhalten üblicherweise im Neuhethitischen Reich abgefasst (siehe, z.B. KBo 52,53 und andere).[10]

Nach den obengenannten stereotypen Formeln, folgen im Dokument Aufzeichnungen mit der Anzahl gestifteter "Häuser" mit Deportierten. Die auf die erhaltenen Textzeilen basierende Rechnung zeigt, dass für die Gottheiten (Tempel) ungefähr 130 "Häuser" mit NAM.RA bestimmt wurden. Ebenfalls wie auch in anderen hethitischen Dokumenten wurde hier bei der Aufteilung der Deportierten das Dezimalsystem angewandt.[11] (Wie bekannt, wurden im späten Sparta die Heloten ebenfalls zu 10 oder 15 Personen verteilt). Auf diese Weise befanden sich in den genannten "Häusern" ungefähr 1300 Deportierte. Die Anzahl der Gestifteten musste jedoch weit grösser gewesen sein, da von mehr als 130 Wirtschaften in den nicht erhaltenen Teilen die Rede gewesen sein müsste (nach H. Klengel erreichte die Zahl der gestifteten "Häuser" ungefähr 150, die der Deportierten - 1500).[12]

In dem uns interessierenden Dokument wurden verschiedenen Stellen auf die Herkunft der Deportierten hingewiesen. Es waren Menschen aus Azzi, Kazaḫa, Šarmanzana, Šuluppašija, Aḫariwaša, womöglich aus Ḫappala, Arzawa und aus anderen Nachbargebieten Ḫattis,[13] in welche die Hethiter Kriegszüge unternahmen. (Nur Anfangsteile einiger geographischer Benennungen sind geblieben: Zip-, Ḫatta-, Daḫa- und andere).[14] Zweifellos stammten die Vertriebenen, die in der Folge den hethitischen Göttern in Form von Arbeitskräften zur Verfügung standen aus ebendiesen Siedlungen.

Im Text finden wir Angaben bezüglich der Beschäftigung dieser NAM.RA Menschen. Einige von Ihnen waren Rinderhirten (LÚ^{MEŠ} SIPAD.GUD),[15] andere - Weber des Königs (LÚ^{MEŠ} UŠ.BAR *ŠA* LUGAL),[16] dritte - "Speerleute" (LÚ^{MEŠ} ^{GIŠ}ŠUKUR),[17] noch andere fertigten "lange Waffen" an (NAM.RA^{MEŠ} ^{GIŠ}TUKUL GÍD.DA).[18] Der Text nennt Pferdehirten (LÚ^{MEŠ} SIPAD.ANŠE.KUR.RA)[19] usw. Das alles bestätigt die Meinung der Fachleute, die sich darauf berufen, dass in Ḫatti die "Häuser" mit Deportierten gewöhnlich nach deren Tätigkeit aufgestellt wurden.

In dem betrachteten Text werden öfter "*upati*-Leute" (LÚ^MEŠ *upatijaš*)[20] erwähnt. An einigen Stellen des Dokumentes (Vs. 26', Rs. 7) stehen vor diesem Ausdruck die zweifellos kleinasiatischen Personennamen - Daduili und Gašgaili (Kaškaili), auf der Vs. 23' aber war wahrscheinlich ebenfalls irgendein Name geschrieben, der auf -zina endete. Es ist nicht ausgeschlossen, dass diese Namen gerade die "*upati*-Leute" oder deren Oberhäupter trugen. Wer jedoch diese Leute waren und welche Tätigkeit sie ausführten, geht aus dem Text nicht hervor, da es seine Beschädigung unmöglich macht, über die Bedeutung des Terminus "*upati*-Leute" genauer zu urteilen. (In anderen hethit. Quellen wird dieser Terminus ebenfalls in einem unverständlichen Kontext gebraucht).[21] Von den Angaben KUB 48,105 ausgehend, kann man nur schlussfolgern, dass die "*upati*-Leute" aus den Reihen der Deportierten stammten und irgendeiner (Berufs?) Gruppe von Leuten angehörten.

Die Erläuterung der Bedeutung des uns interessierenden Terminus wird noch dadurch erschwert, dass es bisher nicht gelang die genaue Bedeutung des Wortes *upati-* (Genitiv *upatijaš*) zu finden. Man nimmt an, dass es "Lehen, Lehensgut (?)" und mit dem ebenfalls unbekannte Bedeutung habenden Wort *uppa-* (irgendeine Art der Leistung?) zusammenhängt.[22] Möglich wäre auch, dass *upati-* mit dem ugaritischen *ubdy* (*'bdj*) "Lehensgemeinschaft; Dauerpacht; Dauerpächter" im Zusammenhang steht[23] (*ubdy* wird manchmal als "Lehensland" übersetzt, das in Ugarit den Königsangestellten zugeteilt wurde).[24] Jedoch wahrscheinlicher ist die Annahme, dass das hethitische *upati-*, sich dem Wort *upatinnum* der "kappadokischen" Tontafeln nähert und das irgendeine Organisation von Lehensträgern,[25] oder aber eine Gruppe Einheimischer (kleinasiatischer) Herkunft bezeichnete, die auf dem Gemeindeland lebten und arbeiteten. (Nach I.M. Diakonoff ist *upatinnum*/*ubadinnum* ein akkadisiertes Wort hurrischer Herkunft **ubadinne* "service" oder "obligation connected with the holding of communal land"[27]). Es ist auch nicht ausgeschlossen, dass die "*upati*-Leute" Eigentümer irgendeiner Landkategorie waren.

Die im Text aufgezählten Stiftungen wurden nicht nur vom König sondern auch von ihm untertänigen Personen gemacht. Im Text sind folgende, den Gottheiten stiftende, Personen aufgezählt: eine Person, deren Namen auf -uwa endete (Vs. 5'), Innarawa (Vs. 11'), Piḫananaja (Vs. 14', siehe auch KBo XII 53, Vs. 13', 15') und viele andere stark beschädigte Namen. Auf Befehl der "Majestät" ("Sonne") sollte ein uns dem Namen nach unbekannter König vom Land Tumma(n)na, das im Norden oder Nordosten Kleinasiens lag und mindestens seit den Kriegszügen Muršiliš II. (AM, 152 ff.) zu Ḫatti gehörte, grosse Viehbestände stiften. Den Stiftungen des Königs Tumma(n)na an die verschiedenen Gottheiten Ḫattis sind 13 Abschnitte im Text gewidmet, an deren Ende jedesmal beigefügt wurde, dass die bestimmte Menge von Vieh "der König des Landes Tumma(n)na gibt" (der Gottheit einer Stadt) - LUGAL KUR ^URU*Tumma(n)na pāi*.[28] Dieser König stellte den Göttern über 50 Rinder, 400 Schafe und 20 Kühe zur Verfügung. Weshalb so grosse Stiftungen an Vieh von dem König Tumma(n)na, das wahrscheinlich reiche Viehbestände hatte, gefordert wurde, geht aus den Aufzeichnungen des Textes nicht hervor. Ausserdem ist ungeklärt, wie es praktisch möglich war, die Stiftungen des Königs Tumman(n)a an Vieh den Gottheiten der verschiedenen Städte des Landes, insbesondere, der im Süden des Hethiterlandes gelegenen, zu verwirklichen.

In einer ganzen Reihe von Fällen ist im Text die ehemalige Abhängigkeit der Deportierten vor ihrer Übergabe an die Gottheiten unterstrichen. Einige gehörten den Wirtschaften verschiedener Institutionen oder Privatpersonen, wie auch dem König persönlich an. So sind im Text genannt: Deportierte, die dem "Hause

Gazzimarija" angehörten,[29] "3 Häuser, darin 30 Deportierte des Palastes",[30] "1 Haus, darin 10 Deportierte [des] GIŠTUKUL GÍD.DA",[31] "1 Haus, darin 16 Deportierte der Bergbewohner",[32] "1 Haus, darin 10 Deportierte - Sklaven (Diener) des Innara",[33] "1 Haus, darin 4 Deportierte des Priesters",[34] "1 Haus, darin 10 Deportierte - Weber des Königs"[35] usw. Somit wird klar, dass bis zur Stiftung an die Götter diese Leute nicht unter das Tempelpersonal fielen, sie befanden sich unter der Herrschaft des Palastes oder von Privatpersonen, die wiederum dem Herrscher des Landes untertan waren.

Besonders werden im Text die den Gottheiten gestifteten Wirtschaften unterstrichen, die sich schon früher im Besitz der Tempelwirtschaften befanden. Es sind erwähnt: "140 (?) Deportierte, die früher einer Gottheit angehörten",[36] "2 Häuser [darin 20 Deportierte] - ehemalige Sklaven Gottes"[37] usw. (das Wort "ehemalig" war auch an anderen Stellen fixiert, die jedoch beschädigt sind - Vs. 20′, 34′).

Auf diese Weise wurde ein Teil der Deportierten, früher den Wirtschaften einzelner Königsangestellten oder verschiedener Königswirtschaften angehörend, auf Entschluss des Königs zum Tempelpersonal gezählt. Nur darin bestand der Wechsel ihrer persönlichen Abhängigkeit. In anderer Hinsicht gab es keine Veränderungen, da die soziale- und ökonomische Stellung sowie die Ausbeutungsform die alte geblieben war. Anstelle für ihre ehemaligen Herrn zu schaffen, arbeiteten sie von nun an zugunsten des Tempels.

Einige Angaben des Textes KUB 48, 105 lenken unser Augenmerk auf die soziale Stellung der Deportierten. Wie schon oben konstantiert, wurde in Bezug auf die Zivilgefangenen in einer Reihe von Fällen festgestellt, dass sie "Sklaven (Diener) des Innara" (ÌR^{MEŠ} *ŠA* ^{I}Innarā), "Sklaven (Diener) des Gottes" (ÌR^{MEŠ} DINGIR^{LIM}) usw. waren. Vom rechtlichen Standpunkt aus, waren diese sowie auch andere, die im Text nicht als "Sklaven" genannten, im gegebenen Fall tatsächlich staatliche Sklaven, die letzten Endes als Königseigentum anerkannt werden konnten. Gerade deshalb hatte er das Recht der Aufteilung von staatlichen Deportierten, die nicht selten in verwüsteten Gegenden ($URU.DU_6$ - im Text sind 3 solche Siedlungen erwähnt, Vs. 20′) angesiedelt wurden. Beispiele in KUB 48, 105 zeugen dafür, dass der König manchmal eine Aufteilung der Arbeitskräfte vornehmen konnte.

Obgleich vom rechtlichen Standpunkt aus als Sklaven angesehen, kann man Deportierte vom ökonom. Gesichtspunkt aus kaum als solche anerkennen, da sie im Produktionsprozess einer unsklavischen Ausbeutung unterworfen waren. Nach den Angaben anderer hethitischen Texte zu urteilen, bekamen die auf dem Land angesiedelten Deportierte Grundstücke ("Felder"). Gleichzeitig gab man ihnen Saatgut und Rinder sowie Kleinhornvieh, verschiedene Gerätschaften usw. Anfangs bekamen diese Deportierte Milchprodukte und Wolle.[38] Das alles hatte eine selbstständige Wirtschaftsführung zum Ziel und schuf die Bedingungen für einen bestimmten materiellen Anreiz und für wirtschaftliche Initiative von Seiten der Deportierten. Die aus den eroberten Gebieten vertriebenen Leute waren jedes Eigentumrechtes, auf die ihnen von der zentralen Macht zur Verfügung gestellten Produktionsmittel, entzogen, da sie nicht frei über diese verfügen konnten und nur Benutzungsbefugnisse hatten. Nach Erhaltung des Landes waren die Deportierten zu Naturalleistungen (*saḫḫan-*), wahrscheinlich auch zu Arbeitsleistungen (*luzzi-*) verpflichtet. Sie brauchten allerdings nicht gleich vom Moment der Erhaltung der Grundstücke die Leistungen erfüllen, sondern erst nach Verlauf einer bestimmten Frist - 3 Jahre (wenn die restaurierten Wörter [NAM.RA$^{HI.A}$] am Anfang des Paragraphen 112 der hethitischen Gesetze richtig sind).[39] Erst vom 4. Jahr an waren sie verpflichtet, die Naturalleistungen zu den Bedingungen zu erfullen, die von den "Leuten ^{GIŠ}TUKUL" gefordert wurden. Von diesem Moment an wurden sie wohl kaum als Sklaven, im eigentlichen Sinne des Wortes, angesehen. Sklaven blieben die Deportierte, die kein Land erhielten und nur als Hilfsarbeitskräfte auf Wirtschaften lebten.

In einigen Textabschnitten KUB 48, 105 (Vs. 13´, 27´, 28´, 37´, 41´; Rs. 1, 22, 23), standen gewöhnlich nach den Aufzählungen der Stiftungen (entweder am Anfang oder in der Mitte der Abschnitte) folgende Sätze: ^{GIŠ}TUKUL DÙ-*(an)zi x parisu* NUMUN KISLAH DÙ-*(an)zi* "sie werden ^{GIŠ}TUKUL machen, sie werden einen Dreschplatz (für) *x Parisu* (Saat) Getreide machen" (manchmal war nur der erste Satz geschrieben - Rs. 22,23, manchmal nur der zweite- Vs. 37´, 41´; Rs. 1). Der Sinn des ersten Satzes ist nicht ganz verständlich, weil erstens, ^{GIŠ}TUKUL nicht im eigentlichen Sinne des Wortes gebraucht wird, nämlich im Sinne von "Waffe (Gerät)", zweitens ist unklar, wer mit "sie" gemeint ist. Von Angaben einiger hethitischen Texte ausgehend, in denen dem Wort ^{GIŠ}TUKUL die Bedeutung "Dienst (Dienstleistung)" beigegeben wird,[40] kann man jedoch annehmen, dass im gegebenen Fall ^{GIŠ}TUKUL eben die Bedeutung "Dienst" hat, dessen Erfüllung wahrscheinlich nur den gestifteten Deportierten (im Text im Plural angegeben) zur Pflicht gemacht wurde. Deshalb übersetzen wir den obenzitierten ersten Satz folgendermassen: "Sie (d.h. die Deportierte) werden den Dienst leisten" (buchstäblich "machen"). Wahrscheinlich sollte damit die Verpflichtung zur Erfüllung der Arbeiten in "Häusern", einschliesslich der Pflege des Viehs, der Zubereitung von Milchprodukten und die Teilnahme an landwirtschaftlichen Arbeiten usw. unterstrichen werden. Die Richtigkeit dieser Vermutung muss jedoch noch durch weiteres Studium des von uns betrachteten Textes, mit dessen Hilfe wir unser Wissen bezüglich des Deportiertenproblems vertiefen konnten, bewiesen werden.

AM = A. Götze, *Die Annalen des Mursilis* (MVAG 38 [1933]).

HG = J. Friedrich, *Die hethitische Gesetze* [1959].

HW[1] = J. Friedrich, *Hethitisches Wörterbuch* [1952].

SMEA = *Studi micenei ed egeo-anatolici* [Roma].

StBoT = *Studien zu den Boğazköy-Texten*, herausg. von H. Otten.

---

1 Der Text wurde von H. Freydank nach dem Original kopiert.

2 S.z.B., I.M. Diakonoff, MIO XIII [1967] 363 f.

3 Vs. 20´, 29´, 34´, 40´; Rs. 15, 20.
Betreffs dieses Wortes siehe J. Friedrich & A. Kammenhuber, *Hethitisches Wörterbuch*, Lief. 1 [Heidelberg, 1975] 74 ff.

4 H. Klengel, SMEA XVI [1975] 195. Bezüglich des Textes KUB 48, 105 s. auch H. Otten & Vl. Souček, StBoT 1 [1965] 43 u. 48.

5 *INA* ^{URU}*x ANA* ^{D}*y*(*ANA* DINGIR$^{\text{(MEŠ)}}$) UTU$^{\textit{ŠI}}$ *ki* ME-*iš* (*dāiš*). Vs. 6´, 9´, 10´, 16´, 19´, 29´, 31´, 36´, 38´, 42´. Rs. 3, 6, 9, 12, 14, 16, 20, 23, 25, 27 31, 34, 37, 43. Diese Formel wird im Text mit analogem Inhalt angeführt - KBo XII 53.

6 Auf der Vs. 29´, wo die Stadt Nenašša erwähnt wird, ist wahrscheinlich vom Schreiber vergessen worden, die Gottheit anzugeben.

7 A. Götze, AM, 56f., 64f., 70f., 76f., 78f., 136f.

8 H. Otten & Vl. Souček, StBoT 1.

9 Bezüglich der Zugehörigkeit des Textes in die Regierungszeit des Tutḫalia IV. siehe S. Heinhold-Krahmer - I. Hoffmann - A. Kammenhuber - G. Mauer, *Probleme der Textdatierung in der Hethitologie* [Heidelberg 1979] 233.

10 Ibid., 233.

11 G.G. Giorgadze, *Očerki po sotsial'no-ekonomičeskoi istorii khettskovo gosudarstva* [Tbilisi 1973] 77 ff.; H. Klengel, SMEA XVI [1975] 195; Vl. Souček, ArOr 47 [1979] 79f.

12 H. Klengel, SMEA XVI [1975] 195.

13 Vs. 21', 25', 39'; Rs. 5, 15, 38-39.

14 Vs. 22', 39'; Rs. 6 und andere. Eventuell könnte Daḫa- so rekonstruiert werden wie Daḫarijatta im Text KBo XII 52 II 6, in dem ebenfalls Königsstiftungen aufgezählt wurden.

15 Vs. 24': "3 Häuser, darin 30 Deportierte - Rinderhirten".

16 Vs. 34': ". . .1 Haus, darin 10 Deportierte - Weber des Königs".

17 Rs. 4 : "1 Haus, darin 10 Deportierte - Speerleute".

18 Vs. 32': ". . . 1 Haus, darin 10 Deportierte - (Hersteller) der langen Waffen"; Rs. 3: "2 Häuser, darin 20 Deportierte - (Hersteller) der langen Waffen".

19 Vs. 37': ". . . 4 Häuser, [darin 40] Deportierte - Pferdehirten".

20 Vs. 23', 26'; Rs. 7, 28, 29.

21 Dem Text KUB XIII 4 I 44 zufolge, wurden "Feste der *upati*-Leute" veranstaltet - EZEN x ŠE^{MEŠ} LÚ^{MEŠ} *upatijaš*. Im KUB XIII 9 I 11 sind sie (in Form von *upati*$^{\text{HI.A}}$) gleichzeitig mit den "leuten *šarikuwaš*" erwähnt. Bezüglich des Wortes *upati*- siehe ebenfalls KBo IV 10 I 30; KUB XXXII 87 II 20.

22 HW^{1}, 235.

23 HW^{1}, 235; J. Aistleitner, *Wörterbuch der ugaritischen Sprache*, B. [1967] 3.

24 M. Heltzer, *Orientalia Lovaniensia Periodica* 8 [1977] 49f. u. Anm. 15.

25 HW^{1}, 235.

26 L. Matouš, ArOr 47 [1979] 38 f. u. Anm. 14-17.

27 I.M. Diakonoff, ArOr 47 [1979] 40 f.

28 Vs. 30', 35', 37', 41'; Rs. 2, 5, 10, 13, 19, 21, 24, 26, 29. "Der König des Landes Tumman(n)a" ist auch im Zusammenhang mit Vieh im KBo XII 53 Rs. 9 erwähnt.

29 Vs. 7': NAM.RA^{MEŠ} *ŠA* É *Gazzimarija*

30 Vs. 9': 3 É$^{\textit{TU}_4}$ ŠÀ 30 NAM.RA^{MEŠ} É.GAL.

31 Vs. 31' f.: 1 É$^{\textit{TU}_4}$ ŠÀ 10 NAM.RA^{MEŠ} [*ŠA*] ^{GIŠ}TUKUL GÍD.DA.

32 Vs. 32': 1 É$^{\textit{TU}_4}$ ŠÀ 16 NAM.RA^{MEŠ} *ŠA* LÚ^{MEŠ} ḪUR.SAG.

33 Vs. 32' f.: 1 É$^{\textit{TU}_4}$ ŠÀ 10 NAM.RA^{MEŠ} ÌR^{MEŠ} *ŠA* ^{I}Innarā.

34 Vs. 33': 1 É$^{\textit{TU}_4}$ ŠÀ 4 NAM.RA^{MEŠ} *ŠA* ^{LÚ}SANGA.

35 Vs. 33′ f.: 1 É^{TU_4} ŠÀ 10 NAM.RA^{MEŠ} LÚ^{MEŠ} UŠ.BAR *ŠA* LUGAL.

36 Vs. 29′: 1 *ME* 40 (?) NAM.RA^{MEŠ} *annalliš* *ŠA* DINGIR^{LIM}.

37 Rs. 14f.: 2 É [ŠÀ 20 NAM.RA] *annalliš* ÌR^{MEŠ} DINGIR^{LIM}.

38 Giorgadze, *Očerki* . . ., 81 ff.

39 J. Friedrich, HG [Leiden 1959] 64f.; F. Imparati, *Le leggi ittite* [Roma 1964] 124 f.

40 H. Otten & Vl. Souček, StBoT 1, 29 f.; Giorgadze, *Očerki*. . ., 123 f.

TWO POINTS ON HURRIAN-ARMENIAN LEXICAL RELATIONSHIPS

John A.C. Greppin (Cleveland, Ohio)

It has been known for some time that words resembling forms from both Hurrian and Urartian have been absorbed into the lexicon of Proto-Armenian. The first solid etymologies were presented in 1902 by Msériantz[1] at the Thirteenth International Congress of Orientalists in Hamburg. Msériantz pointed out the accord between Urart. *ṣar* 'orchard', Arm. *caṙ [tsaṙ]* 'tree', and Urart. *ṣue* 'sea', Arm. *cov [tsov]* 'id'. Numerous additional contributions have been made. Of note are Urart. *ulṭu* 'camel', Arm. *ułt* 'id'[2]; Hurr. *pala*, Urart. *pili* 'canal', Arm. *peł-em* 'dig'[3], and Urart. *harharšu-* 'destroy', Arm. *xarxar-em* 'id'[4].

In this paper, in honor of Igor Mikhailovich Diakonoff, I would like to propose another Hurrian-Armenian correspondence, and make a further comment on a second word that has already been discussed elsewhere.

V. Haas and M.J. Thier, in a paper in *Ugarit-Forschungen*,[5] have made some lexicographical comments on Hurrian botanical terms. From the second tablet of the series *itkaḫi* 1230/v, they give a transliteration of lines 24-32, which appears to be a list of botanical terms. Some of the terms are already known (*tabrana* 'juniper', *šerminḫi* 'cypress', *kišipsuwaa* 'reed', *ḫinzuri* '[apple] tree', *taškarḫi* 'beech tree'). From what can immediately be translated, it would seem that this section deals principally with arboreal terms. One of the words, *ḫinzuri*, is already known to appear in Armenian as *xnjor [khəndzor]* 'apple',[6] and we might wonder if another of these Hurrian terms would have an Armenian correspondent with the value of 'tree name'.

There is only one clear instance, from the dozen or so unidentified Hurrian botanical terms listed, where we have an exact phonetic accord between a Hurrian and Armenian term: Hurr. *māḫri* (*ma-a-aḫ-ri*), Arm. *maxr*.[7] It is difficult to give an exact definition to the Armenian term. The *Haybusak*[8] calls it, impossibly, a *Pinus picea*; elsewhere it gives reference to the *Abies cephalonica*, the Silver Spruce. Various modern Armenian lexicons describe the *maxr* as a 'spruce', a 'pine', and a 'fir'. It seems likely that we cannot give a precise definition for this Armenian word.[9] However, we do know a few things about the *maxr*. In an ancient *Bžškaran* (medical handbook) quoted in the *Haybusak*, the *maxr* (there identified as a type of cedar *[mayr]*!) is said to have an oil helpful in treating wounds and disorders of the skin. In the *Book of Merits* (7th C.),[10] the *maxr* is noted for its production of a flammable pitch. And in Step῾annos Lehac῾i, a seventeenth century lexicographer, we read that the *maxr* and the willow are trees that bear no fruit.[11] Thus from our Armenian texts, ancient and medieval, we find support for a gloss of 'resinous conifer'.

And there are other interesting aspects, for *maxr* appears commonly in the form *marx*. The following are the modern dialects in which the word, in either form, is recorded: Svedia *muxr*[12]; Hamšēn, both *maxr* and *marx*[13]; Šamaxi *marx*[14]; and Sebastia (Sivas) *marx*, Hačin *mōxrə* and Zēyt῾un *mŏxrə*.[15] The standard literary form is usually given by modern lexicographers as *marx*. The basis for this twofold pronunciation might be found in Iranian, seeing that (North) Kurdish has *mərx* with the meaning of 'resinous fir'. The Western Iranian form probably contaminated the Armenian pronunciation, as have so many other Iranian words, a point well documented.[16] We can thus tentatively posit that Hurr. *māḫri* is continued in Armenian as *maxr* and, through later interference, as *marx*.

My second point deals with the exact source of the Hurro-Urartian intrusions into the Armenian lexicon. Did the loans come into Armenian from both Hurrian and Urartian, or from just one of these languages? For the most part, these two languages have very similar root structure, and it is difficult, given a single word, to diagnose it as of one origin and not the other. Archaeological evidence would tend to hint that the loan vocabulary would be of Hurrian origin. This position, admittedly not a strong one, is formed by acknowledging that the proto-Armenians would not have entered the Urartian area before 635 BC,[17] from the South, during the chaotic period following the Scythian invasion and the collapse of Assyrian and Urartian power in the Lake Van area, and before the establishment of Median power. It is more likely that the proto-Armenians would have earlier picked up their loan vocabulary from the more southern Hurrians, while they were still in power, rather than from a dissolved Urartian people. There is one piece of linguistic evidence that tends to confirm this.

Hurr. *awari* 'field' is a well known word, appearing over twenty times in literature; its meaning is made secure by its correspondence in a Hurrian/Ugaritic text[18] where Hurr. *awari* is paralleled by Ugaritic *šadu* 'field'. Another confirmation of this lexical value comes from a Hurrian text from the archives at Ugarit,[19] in the parallel MAL//GAN : *e]q[(?)-lu]* : *a-wa-ar-ri*, where the Sumerian and the Akkadian equivalents are fairly clear. The Armenian correspondent to Hurr. *awari* would be Arm. *agarak* 'field',[20] which shows the standard shift of Proto-Armenian prevocalic **w* to Arm. *g*.[21] The final *-ak* is an Iranian noun formant which is highly productive in Armenian, and is found on words of various origins.[22] Thus Hurrian *awari* > Arm. *agar* (with regular loss of final syllable) + Ir. *-ak*. The particularly interesting point about Hurr. *awari* is that this word could not have appeared in the same shape in Urartian, for in Urartian, non-prefinal intervocalic *w* drops; note Hurr. *šawala* 'year', Urart. *šāle* 'year'.[23] Thus Hurr. *awari* would appear in Urartian as **āre*, and Urart. **āre* could never have produced Arm. *agarak*. Thus Arm. *agarak*, if it indeed comes from the Hurro-Urartian substratum, must come from Hurrian, not Urartian. This observation, of course, does not preclude the possibility that both Hurrian and Urartian left residue in proto-Armenian. However, it does tend to support theories that our slim archaeological evidence would suggest.

---

1 "Les éléments ourartiques dans la langue arménienne", in *Verhandlungen des XIII. Internationalen Orientalisten-Kongresses*, Brill, Leiden 1904, 128-129.

2 Igor Diakonoff, "Materialy k fonetike urartskovo yazyka", in *Voprosy grammatiki i istorii vostočnykh yazykov*, M-L 1958, 27-53, esp. 43.

3 Grigor Kapancyan, *Xayasa -Kolybel' Armyan*, Yerevan 1948, 216, and "khurritskoe slova armyanskovo yazyka", *Teghekagir* 1951/5, 35-50, esp. 39-40 (also reprinted in *Archiv Orientální* 19, 1951, 579-605).

4 Norayr Vrouyr, *Répertoire étymologique de l'arménien*, Antwerp 1948, 88.

5 "Ein Beitrag zum hurritischen Wörterbuch", *Ugarit-Forschungen 11*, 1979, 337-352.

6 Kapancyan, *op. cit.* 1951, 39. The listing is further found in Diakonoff, *Hurrisch und Urartäisch*, Munich 1971, 85.

7 A correlative form, *meḫru* 'a type of pine', appears in Akkadian, but that

vocalism could not produce Arm. *a*. Further, it is likely that all Armenian words that have been said to be of Akkadian origin are more likely from Aramaic, a language with a substantial substratum in Armenian. A paper to this effect will eventually be published by Diakonoff in *Patma-banasirakan handes*.

8 *Haybusak, kam haykakan busabařutᶜiwn*, Venice 1895, 411, a study of 3400 Armenian botanical terms.

9 Plant names vary greatly from place to place, and are particularly subject to loose usage. In English there is also a frequent lack of precision in identifying conifers, and they are often loosely called 'pine trees'. In cultures which existed before there were any standardized classifications, precise identification is frequently impossible.

10 *Girkᶜ vastakocᶜ*, Venice 1877, 41, 132; a text from the so-called Hellenizing School, a representative of a stylistic genre well known for its usage of obscure vocabulary and unpredictable spellings.

11 "sterǰ cařkᶜ en uři, marx" (*NHB*).

12 *Svediayi barbařə*, Tigran Andreasyan, Yerevan 1967, 374 [*HAB*^{2}.3.284 *miwxər*].

13 H. Ačaŕyan, *Kᶜnnutᶜyun Hamšeni barbaři*, Yerevan 1947, 244 [*HAB*^{2}.3.284 *maxrə*].

14 Ṙ.H. Bałramyan, *Šamaxii barbařə*, Yerevan 1964,213.

15 All from *HAB*^{2}.3.284.

16 The Iranian intrusion into Armenian began in Parthian times; during the Middle Armenian period numerous other Iranian forms entered. The Iranian form that influenced Arm. *maxr* must have done so during the later period since at an early stage a foreign *marx* would have become **mařx* in Armenian, with a trilled *ř*, not the *marx* we have. Note that in Persian the metathesis of *xr* is late, to judge from NPers. *surx* 'red' (Pahl. *suxr*, Av. *suxra-*); cf. also NPers. *čarx* 'wheel' (Av. *čaxra-*). (North) Kurdish, though its word for 'red' is *sor*, has at least *čərx* 'wheel' to parallel what we are proposing as origin of its *mərx*.

17 I. Diakonoff, *Predistoria armyanskovo naroda*, Yerevan 1968, 207ff, with discussion. An English translation of this book should be available from Caravan Books, Delmar NY in late 1981.

18 E. Laroche, "Documents en langue hourrite provenant de Ras Shamra", *Ugaritica V*, 1968, 447-544, esp. 450.

19 J. Nougayrol, "Textes suméro-accadiens des archives et bibliothèques privées d'Ugarit", *Ugaritica V*, 1-371, esp. 234.

20 The first statement of this can be found in Greppin, "Two Hurrian Words in Armenian", in *Classical Armenian Culture: Influences and Creativity, Proceedings of the Conference Held at The University of Pennsylvania, November 4-6, 1979*, forthcoming.

21 Parallels are abundant. Note Arm. *aganim* 'spend the night', Gk. ἄϝεσα (νύκτα) 'spent (the night)'; Arm. *gorc* 'work', Gk. ϝέργον 'id'.

22 A fine example is Arm. *aregaknak* 'balcony', from *areg-akn* 'sun' (< IE **(A)rew- + *okʷ-*). The same suffix of course appears on words of Iranian origin in Armenian; Arm. *bun* 'nature' (< Parth. *bwn* 'true'), *bnak* 'native'. See J. Greppin, "Middle Persian Nominal Suffixes in Classical Armenian, *REArm* 10, 1973-1974:1-10.

23 I. Diakonoff, *Hurrisch und Urartäisch*, Munich 1971, 56.

THREE CONTRACTS FROM BABYLON

O.R. Gurney (Oxford)

Two of the three documents here published, dated in Babylon in the reigns of Shamash-shum-ukin and Darius I respectively, were formerly - and one is still - in private possession. In neither case is the history of acquisition known. The third tablet, dated in the first year of Xerxes, also at Babylon, was received by the Ashmolean Museum in 1924 as one of the tablets excavated at Kish. It is hoped that this small contribution to the social history of Babylon may be of some interest to Professor Diakonoff.

1. Purchase of an Orchard of Date Palms

This tablet, in almost perfect condition on the obverse, but damaged in the upper part of the reverse, is part of a small private collection.[1] It is dated in the fifth year of Shamash-shum-ukin (665 B.C.) and may be added to the list of tablets from this reign published by E. Weidner in AfO XVI [1952-3] 36 f.[2] As far as preserved, it contains no unusual features and conforms to the usual scheme for warranty deeds of this period.

^{1}*1* GUR *2* (PI) *3* (BÁN) ŠE.NUMUN GIŠ.SAR GIŠ.GIŠIMMAR *zaq-pu* ^{2}A.GÀR ^{uru}*A-bal-li* GÚ ^{íd}*Pu-rat-ti*

^{3}UŠ AN.TA ÚS.SA.DU $^{I.d}$EN-DIN-*iṭ* A ^{I}*Mi-ṣir-a-a* ^{4}UŠ KI.TA ÚS.SA.DU A.ŠÀ *šá* DUMU.MEŠ ^{lú}GÍR.LAL ^{5}SAG AN.TA GÚ ^{íd}*Pu-rat-ti* ^{6}SAG KI.TA ÚS.SA.DU $^{I.d}$EN-DIN-*iṭ* A ^{I}*Mi-ṣir-a-a*

^{7}KI ^{I}*Bi-bi-e-a* DUMU ^{lú}ŠID ^{d}*Na-na-a* ^{8} $^{I.d}$AG-MU-SUM-*na* DUMU ^{I}*Da-bi-bi* ^{9}*ki-i 8* MA.NA *15* GÍN KÙ.BABBAR KÙ.PAD.DU ^{10}KI.LAM *im-bi-e-ma i-šam* ^{11}*a-na ši-me-šú gam-ru-tu*

^{12}PAP *8* MA.NA *15* GÍN KÙ.BABBAR BABBAR-*ú* ^{13}*ina* ŠU^{II} $^{I.d}$AG-MU-SUM-*na* DUMU ^{I}*Da-bi-bi* ^{14} ^{I}*Bi-bi-e-a* DUMU ^{lú}ŠID ^{d}*Na-na-a* ^{15}ŠÁM *1* GUR *2* (PI) *3* (BÁN) ŠE.NUMUN GIŠ.SAR GIŠ.GIŠIMMAR ^{16}*zaq-pu ki-i* KÙ.BABBAR *ga-mir-ti* ^{17}*ma-ḫir a-pil za-ku ru-gúm-ma-a* ^{18}*ul i-ši ul i-tur-ru-ma* ^{19}*a-na a-ḫa-meš ul i-rag-gu-mu* ^{20}*ma-ti-ma ina* EGIR.ME U$_4$-*me ina* ŠEŠ.ME ^{21}[DUM]U.ME IM.RI.A *ni-su-tú u sa-lat* ^{22}[*šá* É] ^{lú}ŠID ^{d}*Na-na-a šá* E$_{11}$-*ma*

Rev. . . . . . .

1′ [KÙ.BABBAR *im-ḫu-ru a-di 12*$^{ta.àm}$ *i-t*]*a-nap-pal*

2′ [*i-na ka-nak kan-gi*] *šu-a-ti*

1.

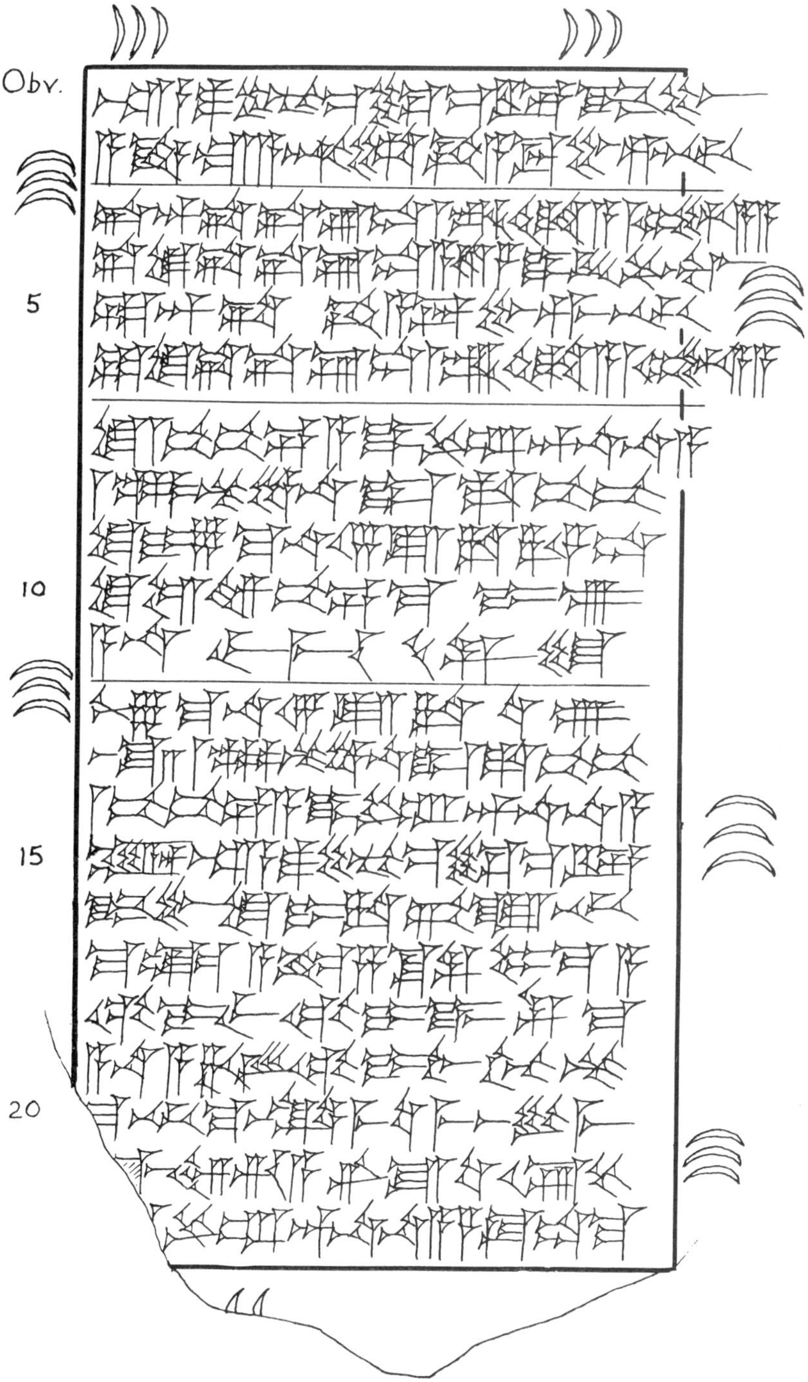

3′ [IGI . . . . DUMU] ^{I}*Da-bi-bi*

4′ [IGI . . . . .]x x [. . DUMU] ^{I}LÚ-*a-a*

5′ [IGI . . . . .]x-*a*-[. . . DUMU] ^{I}*Da-bi-bi*

6′ [IGI . . . . .]x-DIN-*i*[*ṭ* DUMU] ^{I}LÚ-*a-a*

7′ [IGI ^{I} x]-*gi-i* DUMU ^{lú}ŠID ^{d}*Na-na-a*

8′ [IGI] $^{I.d}$UTU-ZALÁG-*ir* DUMU ^{I}*E-gi-bi*

9′ [IGI] $^{I.d}$EN-*ib-ni* DUMU ^{I}*In-gal-li-e-a*

10′ IGI ^{I}*La-qí-pi* DUMU ^{lú}ŠID ^{d}*Na-na-a*

11′ IGI $^{I.d}$AG-ŠEŠ.MEŠ-SUM-*na* DUMU $^{I.d}$EN-*e-ṭe-ru*

12′ IGI ^{I}*Du-um-mu-qu* DUMU ^{lú}BAḪÂR

13′ IGI ^{I}*Ba-la-ṭu* DUMU ^{lú}BAḪÂR

14′ IGI ^{I}ZALAG-*e-a* DUMU $^{I.d}$30-*i-mit-ti*

15′ IGI $^{I.d}$EN-*re-man-ni* DUMU ^{I}*Da-bi-bi*

16′ *ù* ^{lú}ŠID *šá-ṭir kan-gi* $^{I.d}$AG-SIG$_{5}$-*iq* 17′ DUMU ^{lú}*šar-rap-tu-u* DIN.TIR^{ki} ^{iti}IZI 18′ U$_{4}$ *21*^{kam} MU *5*^{kam} ^{d}GIŠ.ŠIR-MU-GI.NA

19′ LUGAL DIN.TIR^{ki} *ṣu-pur* ^{I}*Bi-bi-e-a* 20′ DUMU ^{lú}ŠID ^{d}*Na-na-a* GIM *kan-gi-šú*

Translation

[1]An orchard (of an acreage requiring) 1 *kor* 2 *pān* 3 *seah* of seed, planted with date palms, in the commons of the township Aballu, on the bank of the Euphrates: [3]the upper long side adjoining (the estate of) Bēl-uballiṭ son of Miṣirai, [4]the lower long side adjoining the field of the sons of the butcher, [5]the upper end on the bank of the Euphrates, [6]the lower end adjoining (the estate of) Bēl-uballiṭ son of Miṣirai: [7]from Bibiea, son of the priest of Nanā, [8]Nabû-shum-iddina son of Dābibu, [9-10]after stating the value, bought for 8 minas 15 shekels in cash, [11]at its full price. [12]The total of 8 minas 15 shekels of white silver, [13]from the hand of Nabû-shum-iddina son of Dābibu, [14]Bibiea son of the priest of Nanā [15-16]as full price for the orchard (of an acreage requiring) 1 *kor* 2 *pān* 3 *seah* of seed planted with date palms [17]has received. He is paid, he is satisfied, [18]he has no (further) claim. They will not come back and [19]raise claims against each other. [20]If in future days among the brothers, [21]sons, family, household or kinsmen [22]of the house of the priest of Nanā anyone should arise and ... [rev.].. [make a claim concerning that orchard . . . saying "The orchard was not given, (or) the silver was not received",] 1′ [the silver that he received] he shall repay [twelvefold]. 2′ [At the sealing] of this [document] the witnesses were: 3′ [. . . . son of] Dābibu, 4′ [. . . . son of] Amēlai, 5′ [. . . . son of] Dābibu, 6′ [. . .]-uballiṭ [son of] Amēlai, 7′ [. . .]gî son of the priest of Nanā, 8′ Shamash-unammir

1.

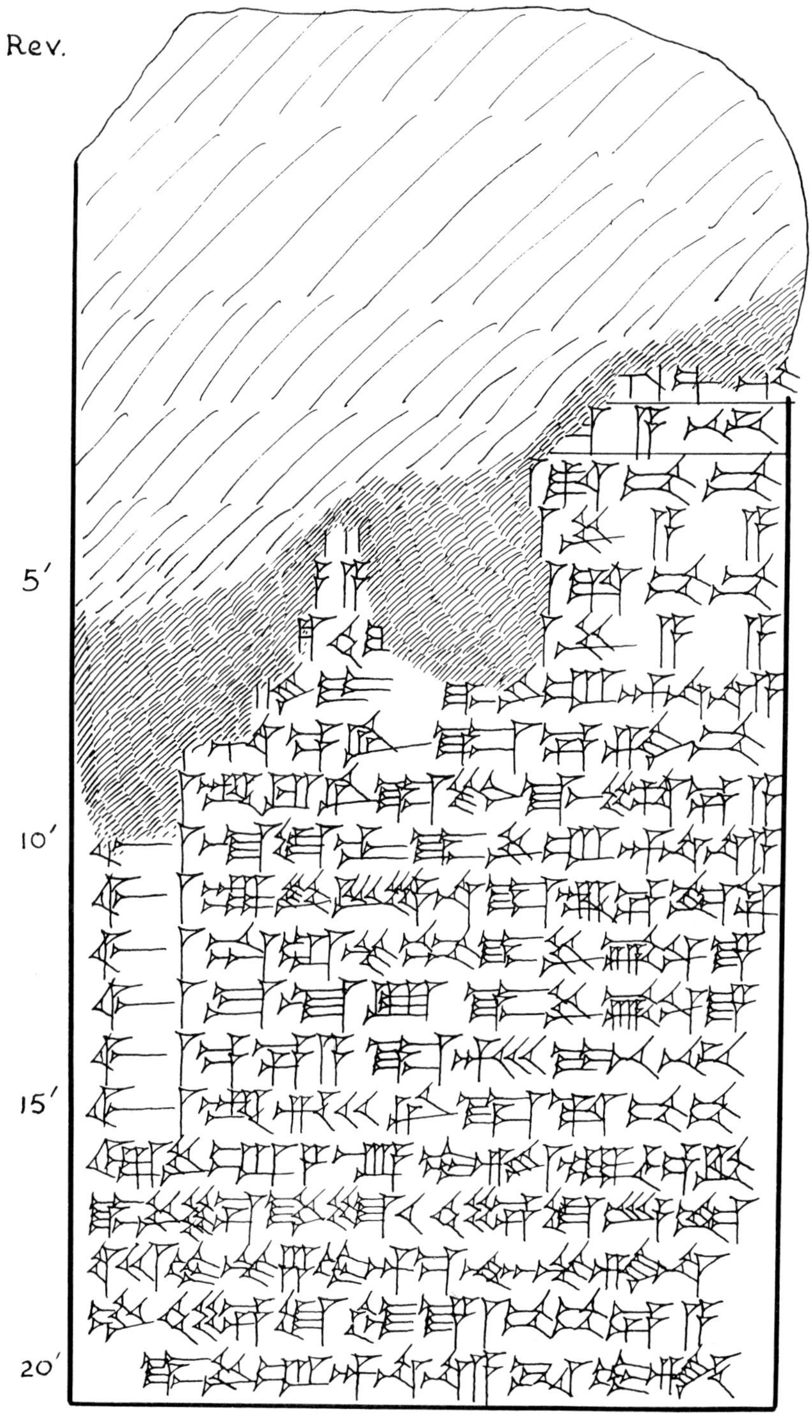

son of Egibi, $^{9'}$Bēl-ibni son of Ingallēa, $^{10'}$Lāqīpu son of the priest of Nanā, $^{11'}$Nabû-ahhī-iddina son of Bēl-eṭēru, $^{12'}$Dummuqu son of the potter, $^{13'}$Balāṭu son of the potter, $^{14'}$Nūrea son of Sīn-imitti, $^{15'}$Bēl-rēmanni son of Dābibu, $^{16'}$and the scribe who wrote the document, Nabû-udammiq, $^{17'}$son of the *šarraptû*-official. Babylon, month Abu, day 21, $^{18'}$year 5 of Shamash-shum-ukīn, $^{19'}$king of Babylon. Finger-nail of Bibiea $^{20'}$son of the priest of Nanā, instead of his seal.

2. Hire of a Boat

This tablet was copied by me many years ago when it was in the possession of Rugby School. It has since been presented to the Ashmolean Museum, Oxford, where it bears the accession number 1963-1469, and a new copy has been made. It is dated in the 35th year of Darius I (487 B.C.) It is completely preserved, but the whole surface is worn and at the thickest point of the reverse the signs have disappeared. Contracts for the hire of boats are not common and this one contains some unusual features.

^{1}GIŠ.MÁ *šá* ^{I}*A-du-ra-a-ta ku-ut-tu-m[u]* ^{2}*šur-su-ud-du šá* ŠU^{II} ^{I}*Du-ub-ba-a-'a a-n[a]* ^{3}*man-da-at-tu*$_{4}$ *ina* IGI $^{I.d}$EN-*it-tan-nu* A-*šú šá [ ]* ^{4} $^{I.d}$EN-*ke-šèr a-ki-i ú-ìl-tì šá* ^{I}*Du-ub-ba-a-'a* ^{5} $^{I.d}$EN-*it-tan-nu a-na man-da-at-tu*$_{4}$ *a-na a-ḫi* ^{6}*a-na* MU.AN.NA *13* GÍN KÙ.BABBAR BABBAR-*ú* ^{7}*a-na* $^{I.d}$EN-MU A-*šú šá* $^{I.d}$AG-*it-tan-nu id-din* ^{8}*ul-tu* U$_{4}$ *20*^{kam} *šá* ^{iti}ZÍZ GIŠ.MÁ *ina* IGI-*šú* ^{9}*ina* MU.AN.NA *2* ITI.MEŠ *na-áš-pa!-tu*$_{4}$ $^{I.d}$EN-MU ^{10}*u* $^{I.d}$EN-*it-tan-nu ina* GIŠ.MÁ *il-lak-ku-'u* ^{11}*[K]Ù*.BABBAR-*àm 1/3* MA.NA *6* GÍN x x ^{12}*it-ti a-ḫa-meš a!-na* ^{I}*Du-ub-ba-a-'a* ^{13}*iṭ-ṭir-ru-'u* GIŠ.MÁ *ina ka-ri-šú-nu* ^{14}*ú-kát-tam-'u ú-šur-su-du-'u* ^{iti}KIN ^{15}KÙ.BABBAR *i-nam-din-nu-'u ina* MU.AN.NA ^{16}*3-šú* ⸢*šu*- «*a*» -*gar-ru-ú i*⸣-*nam-din-nu-'u*

^{17} ^{lú}*mu-kin-nu* $^{I.d}$AG - x - x A-*šú šá* $^{I.d}$UTU-MU ^{18} $^{I.d}$AG-*it-tan-nu [*A-*šú šá]* $^{I.d}$AG-*i(?)-qiš-šú* ^{19}ÌR-*ia* A-*šú šá [*$^{I.d}$U*]*TU-ŠEŠ-MU ^{20} $^{I.d}$AG-*ku-ṣur-šú* A-*šú [šá* ^{I}. . .*]-a* ^{21} $^{I.d}$AG-*ta-at-tan-nu* ^{lú}DUB.SAR A-*šú šá* ^{I}*Ka-* . .

^{22}DIN.TIR^{ki} ^{iti}ZÍZ U$_{4}$ *20.1*.LAL^{kam} ^{23}MU *35*^{kam} ^{I}*Da-ri-ia-a-mu-šú* ^{24}LUGAL DIN.TIR^{ki} *u* LUGAL KUR.KUR.MEŠ

^{25}⸢*I-en*⸣$^{ta.àm}$ *il*-TI-*ú*

^{26} *šá i-ša-nu-ú 10* GÍN KÙ.BABBAR S*[UM?]*

Translation

^{1}A boat belonging to Adurata, covered (and) ^{2}...... , which is in the hands of Dubbā (but) is ^{3}at the disposal of Bēl-ittannu, son of ^{4}Bēl-kesher for rent, according to the contract of Dubbā, ^{5}Bēl-ittannu for rent, a half share ^{6}for a year, (namely) 13 shekels of white silver, ^{7}has given to Bēl-iddin, son of Nabû-ittannu. ^{8}From the 20th day of Shabāṭu the boat is at his disposal. ^{9}In the year, for 2 months (each in turn), Bēl-iddin ^{10}and Bēl-ittannu will do

2.

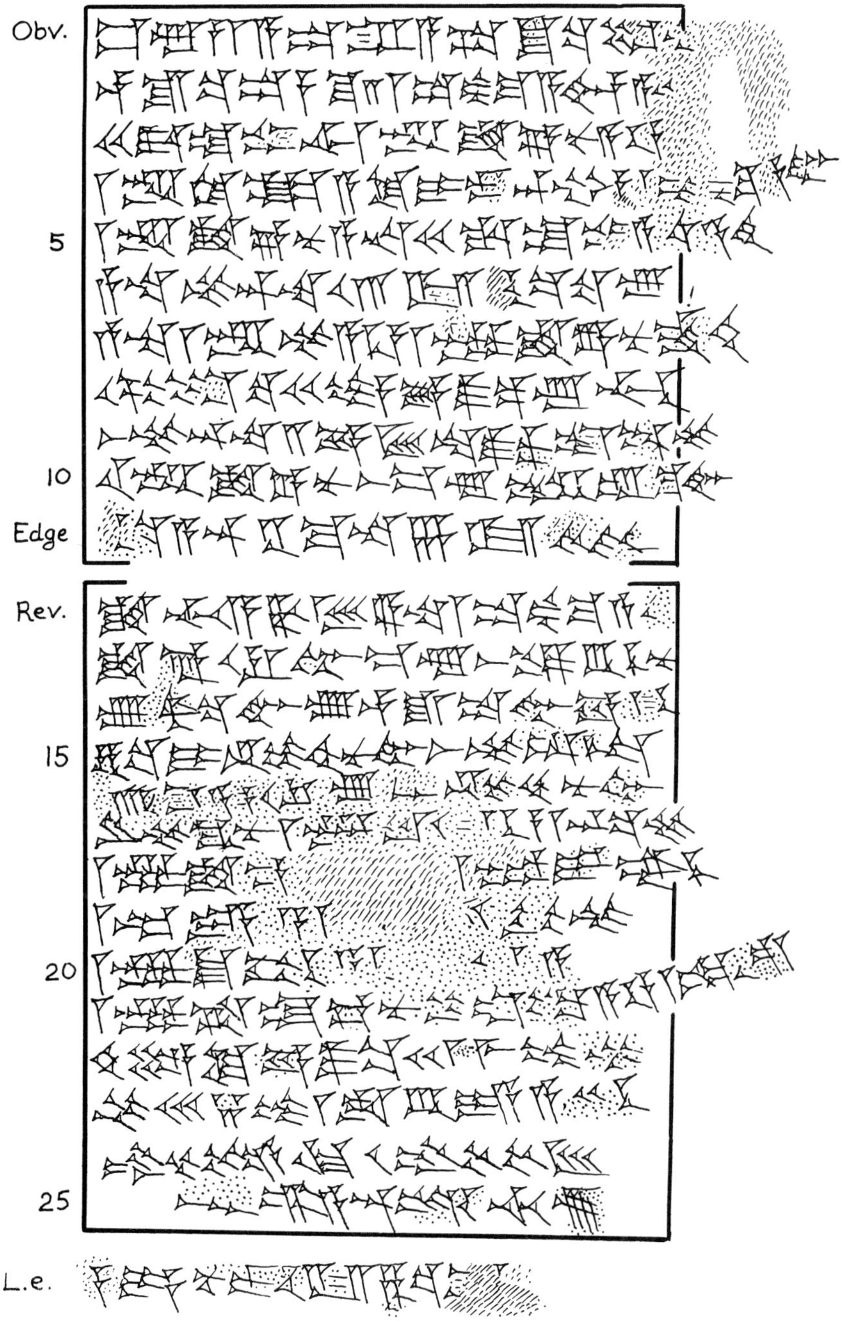

business in the boat. [11]The silver, 1/3 mina and 6 shekels ...... [12]together to Dubbā [13]they will pay. At their (own) quay [14]they will cover and ...... the boat. In the month Ulūlu [15]they will pay the money. During the year [16]they will give "presents" three times.

[17]Witnesses: Nabû-..... son of Shamash-iddin, [18]Nabû-ittannu *[son of]* Nabû-iqīshshu(?), [19]Ardiya son of Shamash-aha-iddin, [20]Nabû-kuṣurshu son *[of . . . . . .]*, [21]Nabû-tattannu the scribe, son of Ka......

[22](At) Babylon, month Shabāṭu, day 19, [23]year 35 of Darius, [24]king of Babylon, king of the lands.

[25]One (copy) each they have taken.

[26]Whoever changes (the terms) *[shall pay]* 10 shekels of silver.

Commentary

Contracts for hire made by the owner of a boat exist (e.g. YOS VI, 195, 215, VII 80, 148, CT IV 44a) but are less well attested than secondary contracts by which the hirer lets out the boat to a third party (cf. A.L. Oppenheim, *Untersuchungen zum babylonischen Mietrecht*, 49 and A. Salonen, *Nautica Babylonica*, 56 ff.). Here a contract of the latter kind has evidently been made by Dubba with Bel-ittannu (line 4), but the present contract is concerned with a further arrangement between Bēl-ittannu and Bēl-iddin by which the boat and the rent for it are shared between them for the period of hire.

1-2: *kuttumu* "covered" is attested in YOS VII 173, 1, and *kuttumu šursud-(d)u*, as here, in CT IV 44a; for the latter word cf. von Soden, AHw 1286 ("unklar"). Line 14 of the present text contributes verbal forms (*ukattamu, ušursudu*) indicating that the operation of giving the boat these two characteristics would be carried out by the hirers at their own quay. There is still insufficient information to determine the exact meaning of either word.

11: I cannot read the signs at the end of this line. The word *mandattu* would be in place here, but that does not seem to be what is written.

It was much cheaper to hire a boat for a longer period (cf. Salonen, op. cit., 53f.). This rent for the half year, 13 shekels, was a normal rent for a month (e.g. YOS VII 147, 148, VS IV 145). In CT IV 44a the rent for a whole year is only 20 shekels.

14-15: The rent is paid at mid-term. Normally it is paid at the beginning of the year or in two instalments (Oppenheim, op. cit., 16 ff.).

16: A clause about supplementary payments termed *nūptu, kīnaiātu* or *šugarrû* is not uncommon at this point in contracts for house-letting, but it has not been found before in connexion with the hire of boats. See Oppenheim, op. cit., 84-88. Thus there can be little doubt that the traces must be read *šu-gar-ru-ú* here, though there seems to be an extra sign. These payments are made once, twice or three times in the year (Oppenheim, p. 85). The closest parallel is in the Seleucid text BRM II no. 1: *ina* MU.AN.NA *3 šu-gar-ru-ú ina-an-din*. Other references to *šugarrû* payments: BRM I 43, 9; 74, 10; 85, 10; VS IV 146 (= NRV no. 131), V 117, 16; Dar. 378, 7-8; CT 44, 76, 16; UET IV, 37, 10. For the original meaning of the word see AHw 1260 and references *ad loc*.

25: The first two signs must be the lower part of the ligature *I-en*, though nothing is visible above these three wedges on the worn corner of the tablet. *il*-TI-*ú* is a strange mixture of phonetic and logographic writing.

26: Presumably a variant for the curse formula for which references are given by von Soden, *AHw* 1167a (top, under 8), but I do not know of any exact parallel.

3. Hire of a Boat

This tablet is published as a companion to no. 2. It is part of the Kish collection in the Ashmolean Museum, where it bears the number 1924-1607, but like some twenty other tablets in the collection it was written at Babylon and may have been purchased by the Kish expedition. It is dated in year 1 of Xerxes (485 B.C.).

^{1}GIŠ.MÁ *šá* $^{\mathrm{I.d}}$EN.A.MU DUMU *šá* $^{\mathrm{I.d}}$UT[U- . . . .] ^{2}*šá a-na* ^{lú}MÁ.LAḪ$_4$-*ú-tu ina* IGI ^{I}[*Ri-mut*] ^{3} ^{I}*Si-lim*-^{d}EN *u* ^{I}*A-na*-^{d}EN-*ú-pa-q*[*a* . .] ^{4} ^{I}*Ri-mut* ^{I}MU-^{d}EN *u* ^{I}*A-na*-^{d}EN-[*ú-pa-qa*] ^{5}GIŠ.MÁ *a-na i-di-šu a-na* U$_4$-*mu 1* [GÍN KÙ.BABBAR] ^{6}*a*$^{!}$-*na* $^{\mathrm{I.d}}$EN-*it-tan-nu* DUMU *šá* ^{I}*Li-ši*[*r* . .] ^{7}*id-din-nu-'u ul-tu* U$_4$ *3*^{kam} *šá* [^{iti}. . .] ^{8}[GIŠ.MÁ *ina* IGI-*šú* . . . .]

Rev. $^{1'}$ ^{lú}[*mu-kin-nu* . . . .] $^{2'}$ *Šá*-^{d}EN(?)-[. . . . .] $^{3'}$ $^{\mathrm{I.d}}$EN-DIN-*iṭ* DUMU *šá* ^{I}UD -*d*[*i*-. . . .] $^{4'}$ $^{\mathrm{I.d}}$EN-*it-tan-nu* DUMU *šá* ^{I}SUM-[. . . . .] $^{5'}$ $^{\mathrm{I.d}}$EN-DÙ-*uš* ^{lú}ŠID DUMU ^{I}[. . . . .] $^{6'}$ DUMU $^{\mathrm{I.d}}$*30*-NÍG.DU-PAP(?) DIN.TIR^{ki} [^{iti}. . . .] $^{7'}$ U$_4$ *2*^{kam} MU *1*^{kam} ^{I}*Aḫ-š*[*i-ia-ar-šú*] $^{8'}$ LUGAL DIN.TIR^{ki} LUGAL KUR.KU[R.MEŠ]

Translation

^{1}A boat belonging to Bēl-apla-iddin son of Shamash-[. . . . . .] ^{2}which is at the disposal of [Rimut], Silim-Bēl and Ana-Bēl-upaqa for plying the boatman's trade, ^{4}Rimut, Silim-Bēl and Ana-Bēl-upaqa ^{5}have given the boat for hire at 1 [shekel] per day ^{6}to Bēl-ittannu son of Lishir[-. .] ^{7}From the third day of [the month ....] ^{8}[the boat is at his disposal. . . . .]

Rev. ^{1}[Witnesses: . . . .], ^{2}Sha-Bēl-[.... son of ......], ^{3}Bēl-uballiṭ son of Tamdi(?)[-. . .], ^{4}Bēl-ittannu son of Iddin-[. . .], ^{5}Bēl-īpush the priest, son of [. . . . . and . . . . . .] ^{6}son of Sin-kudurru-uṣur. Babylon, [month . . .], ^{7}day 2, year 1 of X[erxes] ^{8}king of Babylon, king of the lands.

Commentary

This is a secondary contract, closely parallel to VS V 98, the owner having let his boat in the first instance *ana malāḫūti*; but here the hirer is a syndicate of three men, and the contract is between them and a fifth man. Even the price, 1 shekel a day, is the same as in VS V 98.

4 . MU as a logogram for *silim* is unknown: possibly a mistake.

Rev. 8'. Xerxes did not drop the title "King of Babylon" till his eighth year (Weissbach, ZDMG LXII, 644).

3'. On the element UD-*di*- cf. K. Balkan, *Kassitenstudien*, 213.

3.

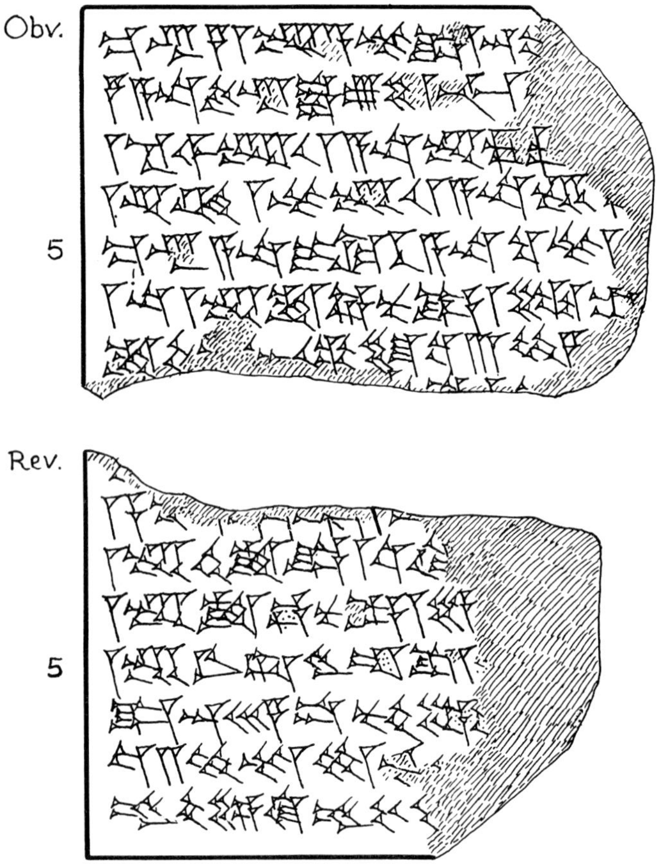

---

1 I gratefully acknowledge the owner's permission to copy and publish this tablet. The same gentleman is also the owner of the Pazuzu plaque published by H.W.F. Saggs as BE 33683 in AfO XIX [1960] 124. Both objects were acquired by his father and were on loan to me for many years. Since the plaque is known to have been excavated by the German expedition (Weidner, AfO XVI [1952-3] 73), it seems possible that the tablet may have had the same history.

2 The following tablets in the Ashmolean collection are also dated in the reign of Shamash-shum-ukin: 1924.528, 578, 942, 2372(?); 1929.22, 825; 1930.366a.

ORAL TO WRITTEN

Thorkild Jacobsen (Harvard)

Professor Albert Lord has called attention to the basic incompatibility of oral poetry with writing as techniques that are "contradictory and mutually exclusive".[1] For the oral poet every performance is a free creation out of stock formulaic materials, dependent on a free flow of ideas and associations, there is no one authoritative text, only the essentials of the story told have stability. In contrast, written poetry - and recordings of performances of oral poetry as well - establish a standard text not to be deviated from.

Transition from one of these two forms to the other, from oral to written, is difficult and refractive. If a singer of oral poetry is persuaded to dictate rather than sing his song so that it can be written down, the change of pace to a slow dictation speed is apt to throw him off and interfere with his normal processes of composition; in consequence the written version - even apart from other factors that may play in - will be different from those of his regular performances, for better, perhaps, or for worse. Moreover, with the writing down, a norm has been established, a standard text. As Lord says: "The change has been from stability of essential story, which is the goal of oral tradition, to stability of text, of the exact words of the story".[2]

It follows that the many prized literatures we have that go back to oral tradition are all at a decisive remove from true oral works. They are "dictated texts" and from the outset conditioned by that fact. How their original fixation in writing took place, the incentives for it, the specific way in which it was done, and the various factors that might have played in and affected the result are usually matters not easily come by. Mostly one has to depend almost totally on Lord's careful study of the process as it could be observed in modern Yugoslavia. It may accordingly be of interest to call attention to a few passages in Sumerian literature which bear on such writing down of oral poetry, for comparison with it.

Spontaneous Oral Composition

Extensive knowledge of oral poetry, appreciation of it, and ability to compose in its modes would seem to have been widespread among the upper classes of Sumerian society. Professional singers, such as the "elegist" (g a l a) and the "bard" (n a r) were originally almost certainly performers in the oral tradition but by the time of Ur III they may well have become dependent on a fixed written repertoire.[3] Among nonprofessionals however, the oral tradition persisted and at least two examples of nonprofessionals spontaneous breaking into song under pressure of strong emotion, happy or unhappy, can be quoted.

In the story called "The Myth of Inanna and Bilulu" a messenger brings news of the killing of Ama-ushumgal-anna to his young bride Inanna. She responds by breaking into a song in praise of her slain husband giving vent to a rush of feelings of tenderness and pride in him for his devotion to his charges:

⌜nin⌝-e nitalam-ni-ir sîr mu-un-ši-ib-ù-dú
    ⌜sîr⌝ mu-un-ši-ib-dím-e

[kug ^{d}Inan]na-ke$_4$ ^{d}Dumu-zi-ra ⟨sîr mu-un-ši-íb-ù-d
    sîr mu-un-ši-ib-dîm-e⟩

[mu-l]u ná su$_8$-ba mu-lu ⌜ná⌝ en-nu-un-ba me-⌜gub⌝

^{d}Dumu-zid mu-lu ná en-⟨nu-un-ba me-gub⟩

^{d}Ama-ušum.gal-an-na mu-⟨lu ná en-nu-un-ba me-gub⟩

^{d}Utu-da gub-ba si$_8$-mà en-⟨nu-un-ba me-gub⟩

mé-da ná-ná si$_8$-mà en-nu-un-ba me-gub

(My) lady gave birth to a song to her young husband,
    was fashioning a song to him
"The chief herdsman who lies at rest, the shepherd, the chief
    herdsman who lies at rest stood guard over them,
Dumuzi, the chief herdsman who lies at rest
    stood guard over them
Ama-ushumgal-anna, the chief herdsman who lies at rest
    stood guard over them
At the getting up with the sun, he stood guard
    over my sheep.
At the lying down by night, he stood guard
    over my sheep.[4]

Not only the surge of feelings of love, tenderness and pride called up at the word of sudden loss, will serve as occasion for song, also the joyous reunion with a husband and lover may be the inspiration. A Shulgi hymn tells how the king travelled by boat to Uruk and entered Eanna dressed to best advantage, with sacrificial animals as gifts. The goddess Inanna, greatly taken with his looks, and remembering his prowess as a lover in the rite of the sacred marriage, breaks into enthusiastic song, keeping it up, incidentally, for no less than sixty-two lines or perhaps more. We are told that:

sipad-zid Šul-gi-re šag$_4$-ki-ag̃ TÚG-ma$_6$ túg mu-mu$_4$

hi-li men-šè sag̃-g̃á mi-ni-g̃ál

^{d}Inanna-ke$_4$ u$_6$ mu-ni-dug$_4$

ní-te-ni-šè sîr ba-ši-ni-ra

èn-du-šè im-e$_{11}$

a m - r a u m u n - r a

a m u - n a - a - t u_5 - a - d í m

etc.

The good shepherd Shulgi had dressed in cloak
and robe a loving heart,
had put a periwig as diadem upon the head.
Inanna looked at him in admiration,
and by herself she wove a song about him,
gave it out as a lay:
"In as much as I bathed
for the shepherd, for the lord ... etc.[5]

Recording in Writing

In these examples of spontaneous oral composition, nothing is said about recording them in writing. For that we must turn to other passages. One such is the introduction to the "Keš Temple Hymn" one of the oldest Sumerian literary works known to us. We are told there that on a certain occasion the god Enlil in his capacity of king brought out the emblem of the office of prince from the house, that is, from storage, presumably intending to confer it on a worthy candidate. Looking out over Sumer he was impressed by the proud bearing of Kesh and broke into praise of it. His eulogy, which went on for all of one hundred and twelve lines, was recorded by the goddess of the scribal art, Nidaba. We hear that:

^{d}E n - l í l - l e K e š$^{k i}$ z a g - m í à m - m a - a b - b é

^{d}N i d a b a n u - i n i m - d e l e - b i - i m

i n i m - b i - t a s a - g i m i m - d a - a n - s u r

d u b - b a - s a r - s a r š u - š è a l - g̃ á - g̃ á

Enlil was giving praise unto Kesh,
Nidaba was its (i.e. of the praise) "spinner
of single statement"
and from its words she entwined a netlike (word structure)
it was being written on its tablet
and was being laid to hand.[6]

The statement, if we understand it correctly, is remarkably informative. The praisehymn was spoken by Enlil. It was listened to and committed to memory by the goddess of writing, Nidaba, who wrote her version down as the authoritative text. She was its "spinner of single statement" which presumably means that as one spins a single thread out of the many fibers of wool, so she created a single version out of the many potential oral versions of Enlil's speech. And

she did more, she twisted these words into a structure of cross-references of
meanings, a poem, which would seem to imply either that Enlil spoke in prose or
that she improved and tightened up his oral poetry.   Having done so she committed it to writing, thereby making it generally available for present and
future reference.

The recording of an oral poem or formal statement in writing seems thus
here to imply (1) establishing of a single authoritative text (2) editing for
poetic form - or perhaps even rendering it in poetic form - and (3) writing it
down for ready reference.

Somewhat similar, in so far as it too deals with the recording of an oral
poetic statement in writing, is a later passage, Shulgi Hymn B lines 311-315
which reads:

š u d u   É - k u r - r a   k i   ḫ é - ú s - s a - m u - u š

d u b - s a r   ḫ é - d u   š u - n i   ḫ é - i b - d a b₅ - b é

n a r   ḫ é - d u   g ù   ḫ u - m u - u n - n i - r e - d é

é - d u b - b a - a   d a - r í   u r₅   n u - k ú r - r u - d a m

k i - u m ú n   d a - r í   u r₅   n u - š i l i g - g e - d a m

> To my salutations, when I may stride into Ekur,
>
> let the scribe go, so he may capture them,
>
> let the bard go, so he may hum them,
>
> thus they will not be replaced in the schools ever,
>
> thus they will not be discontinued in the academies ever.[7]

Here the purpose of recording in writing is clearly stated: pride in author-
ship and desire for lasting fame.   The evanescent nature of all oral performance has to be overcome by the magic of writing and by making both words and
tune part of the school and academy curricula.

Scribal Editing

The examples just quoted appear to rely on scribal memory, rather than on
dictation, to bridge the gap between oral and written.   That was probably as
good a way to do it as any; for it will clearly have been difficult, and often
impossible, to have had the author of a spontaneous outburst recall it slowly
and in a different mood altogether.   Moreover, the Ancient Mesopotamian
scribes were trained in memorizing from school and could undoubtedly reproduce
long spoken sequences correctly to a degree astounding to us moderns.[8]   Relying
thus completely on scribal memory could not, however, but introduce the possibility of control by the scribe, conscious or unconscious, over the text, for
the scribes were trained in oral poetic forms and would be likely to adjust a
remembered wording to conform with what they considered right.[9]

That such editing was not unusual seems clear from protestations by Shulgi
in his Hymn E.   He says:

n í ĝ - n a r   è n - d u - ĝ á   l ú   b a - r a - m a - n i - i n - ĝ a r

š u d u - ĝ á   n í ĝ - n u - m u - ù - s ì - s ì - g a   m í - e š   b a - r a - n i - d u₁₁

Š u l - g i - m e   s á - ĝ a r   á - d i r i - g a   s ì r - r a   b a - r a - b a - ĝ a l

kug-sa$_6$-ga-gim zalag-zalag-g̃u$_{10}$-um
g̃eštú-ga-sîr-zu inim-zu-g̃u$_{10}$-um
sipad-me níg̃-nam-e zag-til-til-la-g̃u$_{10}$-um

> No man ever put the bardic artistry into my lays for me
> nor ever went over carefully my salutory hymns, things inimitable,
> I being Shulgi, there never is boasting and
> exaggerating of power in the songs,
> it is *my* refining (they show), as of fine silver
> it is *my* knowing songs by ear and
> skill with words,
> It is *my* encompassing anything, I being the shepherd.[10]

Shulgi's insistence on having done everything himself may not have been typical. As an instance where editing and perfection by professionals seems to be taken for granted as natural and desirable one may quote a hymn celebrating the goddess Inanna's wedding to Dumuzi. On her way to the bridal chamber, accompanied by girlfriends and her retinue of servants she sings the praise of her bodily charms.

šà-ab-mu a-ra-zu-a mu-ni-[ib-kúš]
kug-a-ra-zu-a mi-⌜rí⌝-p[à-dè-en]
⌜šutur⌝ (⌜TÚG⌝-⌜MAḪ⌝)-túg-kalag-ga-ša-an-an-na-me [-en]
gala-e sîr-ra mu-ni-íb-[a$_5$-ke$_4$]
nar-e èn-du-⌜a⌝ mu-ni-íb-[tag-tag]
mu-ut-na-mu mu-da-an-[ḫúl-le]
am-^{d}Dumu-zid mu-da-an-[ḫúl-le]
ka-an-tuku-e ka-ka-na(!?)-⌜a⌝ [mi-ni-mà-mà]
mu-⌜ba⌝-⌜an⌝-⌜tuku⌝ ⌜lú⌝-tur še-⌜er⌝-⌜ra⌝ [mi-ni-zu-zu]
⌜ù⌝-⌜ul⌝-zi-zi Nibru$^{k[i]}$ [ezen-àm]
ù-[ul-ma]r-mar tur an-d[u$_{11}$-du$_{11}$]
⌜in⌝-nin$_9$-e ⌜sal⌝-[l]a-⌜ni⌝ de-e-e[š ba-ab-bé]
gala-e sîr-ra m[u-ni-íb-a$_5$-ke$_4$]
<nar-e èn-du-a mu-ni-íb-tag-tag>
^{d}Inanna-ke$_4$ de-e-eš [ba-ab-bé]
sal-la-ni sîr-ra mi-ni-[íb-i-i]

> My heart has pondered what I am about to let you know,
> and what I advisedly let you know I will have you disclose
> - I, Inanna of the grand dress, the two-ply dress -
> The elegist will make it into a song,

the bard will weave it into a lay,
my bridegroom will thereby rejoice in me
the shepherd, Dumuzi, will thereby rejoice in me;
whoever has a mouth will take the words into his mouth,
whoever hears it will teach the song to a youngster;
when it is soaring (to full chorus)
    it will be (like) Nippur (celebrating) a festival,
when it is settling down it will be hummed softly.
The damsel was praising her parts,
and the elegist was making it into a song,
the bard weaving it into a lay,
Inanna was glorying in them,
was praising her parts in song.[11]

Her praisehymn which follows, is eleven lines long. Exactly how one is to imagine the interplay of Inanna and the two singers here is unfortunately not clear. We have assumed that she improvises the song and that the two singers help out with suggested minor improvements, but it is, of course, also possible that Inanna merely threw out key words or images, which they then, as trained improvisators, elaborated and gave form on the spur of the moment. They may also have been expected to edit and perhaps write out the resulting popular ditty with which she hoped to publicize her intimate charms countrywide.

Written Composition

As a last passage to be considered we may quote a few lines from Shulgi's Hymn E in which he insists on the reliability and truthfulness of anything the bards have said in his hymns. After listing a variety of possible achievements to which he does not lay claim he asserts that such things:

sìr(?)-me-ša(?) mu-gub-du$_{11}$-ga(?) x [- x]
a-a-ar-ra-na a-na aka-[a-bi ḫé-a]
inim-ma-na a-na ki-šu-tag-ga-[bi hé-a]
nar-re èn-du-ni-šè [ba-ra-ba-ši-g̃ar]

into a dictated draft which was
    to become a song,
or into any statement of praise of his whatever,
or into any ornate passage of his text whatever,
no bard ever put them into his lay.[12]

To judge from this, it would seem that a written poem might go through a preliminary version, a draft, before reaching its final form.

Conclusion

The passages here considered would seem to indicate that oral composition was still alive and practiced by ordinary people, although perhaps not by professionals, as late as the Third Dynasty of Ur when writing and written literature had been well established for centuries.

Incentives to write down oral literature may well have been many. In the case of the hymn to Kesh the importance to Kesh of preserving Enlil's favorable judgment on it would seem to have been a factor, in the case of Shulgi desire to perpetuate his fame is clearly central.

In the process of recording oral poetry in writing, reliance on the scribe's memory rather than on direct dictation seems to have been the preferred way, but things may have differed from case to case.

In establishing the final written form the scribes who were well versed in poetics are likely to have done a good deal of editing. Here recording and written composition tend to overlap and we seem to have at least one testimonial to use of draft versions as a step on the way.

1 Albert B. Lord, *The Singer of Tales* [Cambridge, Mass. 1964] p. 129. For the following see generally his chapter 6 "Writing and Oral Tradition" *op. cit.* pp. 124-138.

2 *op. cit.* p. 138.

3 In the myth about gu$_4$-dam (PBS V no. 26) the song with which the bard reproves his master: î-gu$_8$-a-zu î-gu$_8$-a-zu / ninda nu-e-gu$_8$ uzu-zu-um î-gu$_8$ / î-nag̃-a-zu î-nag̃-a-zu / kaš nu-e-nag̃ úš-zu-um î-nag̃ "As you ate, as you ate, you ate not bread, you ate but your (own) flesh! / As you drank, as you drank / you drank not beer, you drank but your (own) blood!" is surely an improvisation. Also the fact that in the myth of "Enki and Ninmah" Enki determines bardship as fate for the blind man suggests its independence from written texts.

By the time of Ur III, Shulgi's concern with finding and reviving old literary works, and his determined efforts to have all songs about himself written down and made part of the school curriculum, makes it possible, perhaps even plausible, that the professionals by then would have been performing from a body of standardized written texts. The age undoubtedly was one of extensive copying and editing of literary texts as shown by internal evidence in many of the works we have, indicating that they were given their present form at that time.

4 JNES XII [1953] p. 174-175 lines 80-87 (=Th. Jacobsen, *Toward the Image of Tammuz*, p. 64-67) and pl. LXVI ii.11'-18'. However, the endingless intransitive punctualis forms militate against the translation as 2 p. sgs there given and indicate 3 p. sgs. In line 83 me-gub, contracted from mu-e-gub (see note 51 to the passage) contains the infix -e- with 3rd. p. non-personal reference: discussed AS XVI p. 85 section C. It resumes the inessive -a of the preceding en-nun.b(i).a. In lines 86 and 87 we assume that an inessive -a "in", "at" has been contracted with gub.a and ná.ná. Construction with -da, which after vowel would become -d and remain unexpressed in writing is also a possibility.

5 J. van Dijk, *Tabulae cuneiformes a F.M. Th. de Liagre Böhl* II [Leiden, 1957]

no. 2 i.9-15. The verb e$_{11}$ in line 13 which we have translated "gave out" literally means "brought up". What goes on in the mind is "deep down", what is communicated to others is "up high". Cf. Akkadian *eliš ina šapte.šu itammâ ṭubbati šaplanu libba.šu kaṣir nirtu* "above with his lips he speaks pleasantries, deep down his heart plots murder" Streck *Assurbanipal* (VAB VII) 28 iii.81.

6 Gene B. Gragg "The Keš Temple Hymn" in Sjöberg and Bergmann, *The Collection of the Sumerian Temple Hymns* [TCS III, Locust Valley, N.Y. 1969] p. 167 9-13. In line 10 the phrase KA d e l e "one mouth", "single statement" is familiar from i n i m (KA) d e l e: *purussû* "decision" lit. single statement as against several conflicting ones. Cf. also (with variant d è š for d e l e) KA- d è š - a s î - g a: *tašmêtum* "unanimity" lit. "making the mouths/statements like unto one" (ŠL 15.34). Here, where the term is applied to the writing down of an oral hymn of praise, it can hardly refer but to the establishing of a single authoritative text.

The sign NU which precedes is not without its problems. The lexical texts list for it only the reading n u (Proto e a 450 MSL II p. 67 =MSL XIV p. 49, Proto A a MSL II p. 139 = MSL XIV p. 99. 450. 1-4; RA IX, 77f = MSL II p. 142 i.4 = MSL XIV p. 125-126: 723-726, Sb. I 277 (= MSL III p. 120) e a IV. 107 (= MSL XIV p. 359) A a IV/2 217' (= MSL XIV p. 377). A proposed reading s i r$_5$ seems to be based solely on the fact that NU alternates with the sign s i r$_4$ (ŠIR) (Deimel ŠL I 2d. ed. [Rome 1930] p. 122 no. 75.3). However, since it is now known that ŠIR has the value n u$_{11}$ obviously no value s i r$_5$ for NU can be deduced from their alternation. The sign, when denoting "to spin" Akkadian *ṭamû* (ŠL 75.8 cf. 75.23) is therefore in all probability to be read n u, and that would also be the form of the transitive active participle n u: "spinner", "spinster".

That the sign was read as n u in the line under discussion is clear from the fact that MS. D (= TCL XVI 55) has the variant n u n, and MS. LL (= ISET 1 p. 117 [= 59] Ni 4465) has l û. For the alternation n u / n u n see Gragg's *op.cit.* p. 178 note to line 10, for the variant l û note MSL XIV p. 126. 726 (n u = *a-[wi-lum]*), MSL II p. 142 AO 5400 i.4. Both variants are probably due to copyists who did not understand the metaphorical use of n u "spinner" in the context. In line 12 it seems likely that d u b - b a - s a r - s a r is Sandhi for d u b . b(i).a a. s a r - s a r. The variant D (= TCL XVI. 55) and B(= BL. 197) have the prefix a - followed by mark of propinquity - l -. See AS XVI p. 78.

7 Castellino, *Two Šulgi Hymns* [Rome, 1972] p. 62, Hymn B 11. 311-315. See Falkenstein in WO I 185 and Sjöberg AS XX p. 174. For š u - d a b : *kamû* see A n t a g a l E a 1f., CAD K p. 128 *kamû* lex. sect. For k û r "replace" in line 14 note its use to indicate replacing of one dynasty by another in some versions of the Sumerian Kinglist. See AS XI p. 37.

8 Cf. Sjöberg AS XX p. 163f. The quotations indicate extensive learning by rote. Cf. also Lord, *The Singer of Tales* p. 27f. on the ability of the unlettered singers to pick up and reproduce long songs after a single hearing of them.

9 Cf. Lord, *The Singer of Tales* p. 127 on the editing done by "a well trained and intelligent scribe like Nikole Vujnović".

10 de Genouillac TCL XV 14 ii 2-7. For á - d i r i - g a "exceeding/excessive strength" see Gudea Cyl. A XI 22 n i t a ḫ á - d i r i - k e_4 "the man of exceeding power" describing the northwind. The entry á - d i r i: *la ma-tar* in the group vocabulary ZA 9. 161. ii. 18 (Cf. CAD M, p. 405 s.v. *matar*, lex. sect.) must be due to textual corruption.

11 S.N. Kramer, PAPS 107 [1963] p. 519 ii. 3-13 cf. p. 505 f. See also our *Treasures of Darkness* [New Haven, 1976] p. 45. The restorations m u - n i - í b - [a_4 - k e_4] and m u - n i - í b. [t a g̃. t a g] in lines 6 and 7 are based on Çığ,Kızılyay,Salonen, *Die Puzriš-Dagan Texte* no. 270. 4-5 1 g u d - š e B a - l a - l a n a r/u d s î r - ^{d}E n - k i - k a i n - n a - a k "one grainfed ox (to) Balala, the bard, on the day he made the song of Enki for him" and RA VIII [1911] p. 192, Delaporte, *Tablettes de Drehem* no. 14 (p. 192f) 1-5 2 ḪAR k u g - b a b b a r 9 g é n - t a/Ḫ é - d u - u t - ^{d}A m a r - ^{d}S u. e n/d u m u D a - d a g a l a / m u è n - d u i n - t a g̃ - t a g - a - š è i n - b a" 2 silver rings of 9 shekel each to Ḫedût-Amar-Suen, daughter of Baba, the elegist/because she composed (lit. "wove") a lay/ he gave". These restorations can of course be conjectural only, but terms for composing seem clearly indicated. After line 15 a line corresponding to line 5 above seems to have been accidentally omitted by the scribe.

12 Šulgi E 187-190 quoted from the MS of a forthcoming edition of this important text by J. Klein. We are grateful to Professor Klein for placing his MS. at our disposal. For the term m u - g u b in line 187 see CAD I p. 135 *immugubbû*. It denotes a kind of exercise text that was used in the schools. It is listed in Hh. X 443 (MSL VII p. 102) and is explained in Hg 115 (*ibid* p. 112) as *šipirtum* "message", "letter", a translation also given (*ibid* 116) for im ù - m u - u n - n e - d u g_4 "letter". The point of contact, in view of the qualification d u_{11} - g a (?) "dictated" in Šulgi E may well be that both are renderings of oral statements. In the context of Šulgi E 187f. such a rendering can hardly represent other than a first draft.

THE MITANNIAN ŠATTIWASA IN ARRAPḪE

N.B. Jankowska (Leningrad)

The treaty between Šattiwasa[1] of Mitanni and Suppiluliuma, King of Hatti, had, as is well known, two versions, published by E.F. Weidner.[2] The shorter is formulated from the point of view of Šattiwasa, the longer from that of Suppiluliuma.

Suppiluliuma's version contains a history of that king's military achievements during the delimitation of the spheres of influence between him and the kings of Mitanni. While supporting Šattiwasa, who was opposed to an alliance between Mitanni and Aššur, Suppiluliuma did his best to strengthen his own influence in Mitannian affairs. With this in view, he gave his daughter in marriage to Šattiwasa, demanding that she be recognized as MÍ.LUGAL, a title both political and priestly, and probably similar in the Hurrian sphere to the *tawanannas* in the Hittite Empire. The future children of the Hittite princess should have the rights due to them both as Hittite and as Hurrian princes.

Šattiwasa's shorter version describes events in Mitanni. Šattiwasa denounces Šuttarna for wasting the ancestral palace treasures in the Mitannian capital Waššuganni, after the death of Dušratta: having allied himself with Aššur and Alzi (on the lower reaches of the Arsanias-Muradsu[3]), he sent them rich presents, among other things returning to Aššur the doors ornamented with gold which had been taken from there by Saussadattar. Together with these presents Šuttarna sent, probably as hostages, a number of Mitannian dignitaries who had fallen from his favour. The allies however refused to receive them and sent them back, whereupon Šuttarna impaled them around the fortress-walls of Taidi. After that, fearing a similar fate, one of the Mitannian dignitaries, a military commander by the name of AgitTešub, fled to Babylonia with 200 chariots. Contrary to his expectation, the king of Babylon seized the chariots and property of AgitTešub and treated him as equal to[4] a simple charioteer. The king attempted to murder Šattiwasa (who was apparently in AgitTešub's detachment), but the latter escaped from him and fled to the Hittites. He reached Suppiluliuma with three chariots, two Hurrians and two *ālik arki*, without so much as a change of clothes. But the Hittite king rejoiced at his coming, gave him royal presents and his daughter in marriage (under the conditions mentioned above), and swore to support Šattiwasa even should Šuttarna win. After questioning Šattiwasa about Mitannian affairs and customs, which probably involved learning about the future position in the country of his daughter, the future queen of Mitanni, Suppiluliuma achieved a victory over Šuttarna and, after several battles, managed to take Waššuganni. At the beginning of the text Šattiwasa states that he did not ask to be made king, proposing that Artadama, the father of Šuttarna, should be left as king, with himself, Šattiwasa, to become "the next" (*ana terdennūti-šu luzziz*). He must have had doubts about the possible reaction in Mitanni to his being put on the throne by the Hittites, and he did not fear Artadama personally, since the latter had "miraculously risen from the dead", and was probably practically incapacitated by a serious illness.

The actions of the Babylonian king, who was probably Burnaburiaš II, are to be explained by his impending alliance with Suppiluliuma by marriage.

There is no mention of Arrapḫe in either of the versions of the treaty and in their stories of the internecine strife in Mitanni. If it was involved in the conflict, it was only unintentionally and indirectly, as a buffer state. Note that the alliance between the Mitannian prince Šuttarna and Aššur, an old natural enemy of Arrapḫe, destroyed the latter's own alliance with the Mitannian kingdom, which was formerly so strong. For Arrapḫe this alliance had been an important defence against its neighbours. Therefore it was but natural that Arrapḫe would be willing to aid and abet the enemies of Šuttarna, if this could be done without attracting too much attention.

The administrative and economic archives of the citadel of Nuzi, which we are now about to cite, date almost exclusively from the fifth and sixth generation of the Arrapḫeans known from the excavated documents. The reason is, that while the legal documents were kept for future use and reference, the running administrative documentation was periodically destroyed,[5] and only the latest of the tablets were kept a short while for the sake of control. This can easily be seen from the prosopographic data. We shall base our argument on four groups of documents, each group a small archive in itself: two of them were found in the inner rooms of the citadel, sector R (Room 79) and sector N (Room 120), and two in the outer parts, sector C (Rooms 19 and 28) and sector D (Rooms 3 and 6).

The mobilization rolls of Nuzi, listing the names of charioteers of the fifth generation, including Tešurḫe, the great-grandson of the well-known TeḫibTilla,[6] mention about a hundred charioteers. The general mobilization of all men capable of bearing arms involved about a thousand warriors for a military district (*ḫalṣu*). The rations for the men of the palace, according to the document HSS XIV 596 (including a secretary, scribes, merchants, smiths, carpenters, potters, weavers, herdsmen, etc.) was the wartime minimum of 20 *qa*, or 15 litres. The grain was acquired through the Lullubi mountain people, the eastern neighbours of Arrapḫe, at the price of 10 minas (5 kg) of bronze for 1 *imēru* (100 *qa*, or about 75 litres).[7]

Arrapḫe seems to have been blockaded: people journeying to the "community of the merchants" (*dimtu tamkarḫe*) to buy barley sometimes disappeared (HSS XIV 20-21, letters of TadibTešub, Šeḫramušni and Agibtašenni); there was an edict forbidding travel to the Lullubī without a document, and another ordering the ransoming of Arrapḫeans who had become slaves of the Lullubī; a doubled price was being demanded for the ransom of a private slave (viz. 60 shekels instead of 30 - JEN 195). All this points to a critical situation in the country.

The documents of the citadel reveal two directions from which arrivals came to Arrapḫe: there are Arrapḫeans returning from Mitanni, where they may have lived as hostages, and others from Kassite Babylonia. The first return individually or in groups of men or women separately; the second flee with their families, their wives being Arrapḫean or Kassite. On the Assyrian border a different situation prevailed. Here servants and slaves, obviously of Assyrian origin, fled home to Aššur: the city's status had changed for the better, and it was no longer less privileged than Arrapḫe in its relations with Mitanni.

It seems that there was pressure on Arrapḫe from both sides simultaneously, but since the Babylonian king was opposed to Assyria, and Assyria was allied to Mitanni, AgitTešub, fleeing from there, naturally sought refuge in Babylonia.

Hildegard Lewy thought that the Assyrian invasion took place in the time of

Takku, grandson of TeḫibTilla, while the Babylonian one happened in the next generation, that of Tešurḫe. However, in the documents it is impossible to keep the adjoining generations apart: representatives of two generations constantly meet, and sometimes this is even true for representatives of three generations.[8] This, among other reasons, is why we think that Arrapḫe experienced pressure from both sides more or less simultaneously, now one and now the other being the stronger.

Seeing that the documents show a picture of food shortage, and having a good idea of the military potentialities of Arrapḫe, one must concede that it is rather remarkable that the document HSS XIV 171, found in sector D, attests to the expenditure of 910 *imēru* of barley for the maintenance of Mitannian charioteers (10 *qa* daily being spent on each chariot). The document lists the expenditures for a month and a half, which is also unusual, the normal accounts of this type being for one month. The chariots were stationed in two big villages, Ari and ArnAbu. Dividing the total amount of the grain by the 10 *qa* ration for each chariot, we find that the number of chariots was 200. This was well above the military potential of such villages as Ari or ArnAbu. From the document HSS XVI 205, registering the income of 57½ *imēru* of barley, we learn that seven villages were listed in the district of Ari. The big *dimtu* Kissuk is known to have acted similarly as the centre of a group of nine villages;[9] the head of Kissuk, KelTešub, commanded 50 chariots (JEN 612). But even two major villages could hardly support 200 extra chariots for a long time: the case was out of the ordinary.

The ration of 10 *qa* (1/10 *imēru*) for one chariot means that there were more than one horse to each chariot: there is evidence that a charioteer received 2 *qa* of barley per day for one horse (HSS XIV 58). From the text HSS XIV 171 we learn that the ration for the horse included meal-and-water (*billu*) and crushed grain (*ḫišiltu*). It is possible that the total of 10 *qa* was calculated for two harness horses and two spare horses, a charioteer, and an archer. A detachment of 200 chariots would thus mean a minimum of 800 horses and 400 men.

The military rolls from Nuzi include up to 230 cavalrymen in one list, but with the reservation that they do not have horses of their own. Not only was the fodder of the horses a problem, but they were themselves expensive. They were acquired by 10 cavalrymen jointly, with the horses passing in turn from one man to another while on active service.[10] The horses were acquired through the same "(community) of the merchants" (AASOR XVI 100). It seems that no horse-studs existed locally.

With all this in mind, it seems evident that the appearance of such a considerable Mitannian military detachment as is attested by the expenditures in HSS XIV 171 must have been connected with some extraordinary event. Might not the 200 Mitannian chariots stationed in Ari and ArnAbu be the identical chariots with which AgitTešub fled from Mitanni?

In the temple archive of Nuzi (sector G, Room 29) there was found a list of Mitannian charioteers which originally included 60 names (HSS XV 32). The text is much damaged, but of the preserved names most are uncommon for Arrapḫe. Some are Aryan,[11] whereas no Aryan names are known among the original Arrapḫeans. The chief of this detachment of charioteers dwelt in Abena; the *dimtu* ArnAbu, one of the communities mentioned in the account of expenditures for the 200 Mitannian chariots, also belonged to the district of Abena ("the town of the donkeys"). The lands of the second community, Ari, adjoined those of Nuzi (JEN 662), which may be the reason for the royal visits there, of which more below. In the list HSS XV 72 there are mentioned, among others, the communities of Ari and ArnAbu as well as that of Kabra, in whose district the "merchant community" of Arrapḫe was situated. All these villages and towns may have lain along the road passing through Kabra, a town of importance for the international trade of Arrapḫe. It was already important under ŠamšiAdad I, perhaps because the trade-route had to by-pass the empire which blocked or heavily taxed caravans on the more direct route.[12] It was probably after the triumph of the pro-Assyrian party in Mitanni that Kabra passed into Assyrian hands (HSS XVI 328), which means that the town must have lain close to the border. Kabra is no longer mentioned by the text HSS XV 124, and the villages of Ari and ArnAbu are also marked as captured by the enemy. That the Mitannian chariots should have been stationed just there is a relevant fact, as we shall try to show below.

A direct mention of military operations is to be found in the text HSS XIV 523: two battles seem to have occurred nearly simultaneously, at Ṣillia and at Lubdi. The document concerns the delivery of valuable garments to prince ḪudTešub and to Ḫudaurḫe, son of prince ḪudibUraššе. Both persons concerned belong to the fifth generation. They were not at the moment present in Nuzi, and the garments were received from the treasury by Tirwenari; one garment was then taken for the prince by the runner Ennamadi, and was delivered from the treasury to Kulbenari. Two officers' garments were given to one ḪeldiAbu for the chiefs of the Mitannian chariots "when they fought at Lubdi".[13] The document is dated in the month of Ḫuri (the second month of the year).[14] This means that the battles of Ṣillia and Lubdi took place either in Ḫuri or earlier; below, we shall try to establish the date more precisely, but in any case they happened at the beginning of the year, in the spring.

Another important chain of events is attested by the document HSS XIV 643: the delivery of garments to Agibtašenni is dated in the period "when a statue was erected to Ištar of Nuzi in the month of Šeḫli". Now there were three *šeḫli*-months: the eighth, the ninth and the twelfth, which means that the event occurred in the second part of the year. The garments were received from the treasury by Tirwenari; another delivery according to the same document was received by ḪeldiAbu. Then, after a delivery of garments to the prince ḪudTešub, there are mentioned deliveries of garments to representatives of the communities of Teliberra and Irḫaḫḫe "when the enemies were expelled(?) and he came for (his) present".

It can easily be seen that the same circle of persons is concerned in both documents, which must have been separated by a short interval of time. The last deliveries in HSS XIV 643 (that of a garment and "good, light oil" for Ḫašimaru, received by Tirwenari during the feast in Al-ilāni, and simultaneously of a purple garment received by one Kulbenari for Karmiše) are dated in Kinūnu, the first month of the year (i.e. the next year after the erection of the statue of Ištar). All these persons we shall have occasion to mention again below. Also the deliveries to the villages of Irḫaḫḫe and Teliberra can be dated at about this time.

Thus the chain of events can be reconstructed to give the following outline: two battles, those of Ṣillia and Lubdi, happened before or in the second month of a certain year. The erection of the statue of Ištar, a warrior-goddess, may have taken place by way of celebration of the victories, most probably in the Šeḫli-month of Tešub (the 8th), during the most important feast of the autumn-and-winter half-year. The deliveries to the communities of Irḫaḫḫe and Teliberra were most probably also connected with some kind of feast. Ḫašimaru received the garment and the oil in the first month of the next year. The delivery in question may be connected with the data on the organization of military protection for an embassy to the Lullubians: the head of the embassy was the above-mentioned Ḫašimaru, while the *šakin māti* (representative of the local self-governing communities), Agibtašenni, son of Ennamadi, was ordered by the king, on pain of death, to safeguard Ḫašimaru on his way there and back (HSS XIII 30). The present given to Ḫašimaru in the month of Kinūnu probably means that his mission went off favourably.[15] The fact that the villages of Irḫaḫḫe and Teliberra are mentioned in the same document allows us to connect the activities of the man with the events in which the two villages were involved (see below).

We can of course learn more details of the course of events from the other texts of the archives in sector D (Rooms 3+6), where the document about the 200 Mitannian chariots was found. The text HSS XVI 163, dated in Ḫuri (second month), is a report of barley deliveries during that month and the preceding one (Kinūnu). Among others, there was a delivery of 5 *imēru* 40 *qa* to 10 servants of Mitannian officers, getting 30 *qa* each, and to two groups of Kassite women who received different rations: 30 women received 6 *imēru*, or 20 *qa* each, and 21 women 5 *imēru* 25 *qa* (probably here the rations varied within the group). Nowhere else in the documents do we encounter so many Kassite women at once, and the rations delivered according to this document are not the usual monthly ones: one of the two months in question must have been incomplete, probably the first one, Kinūnu, which must then have been the month when the Kassite women arrived at Nuzi. The document HSS XVI 117 is also dated in the months of Kinūnu and Ḫuri: it records the delivery of 60 *imēru* of grain to Lubdi, where the battle was fought.[16] The grain was delivered through Arnuia (ArnAbu ?), son of Agabtukke.

In Mitirunni (also a month of feasts - JEN 388:21-22), the month following Ḫuri, the arrival of the king was expected in Nuzi (HSS XV 240). He was to come from Ansukkallu, a town known to have lain near to the estates of the decendants of the queen Amminaia.[17] It was supposed that the king would stop on his way in Zizza, the headquarters of the *šakin māti*. The royal escort actually reached Nuzi in Mitirunni and stayed there for eight days, perhaps for the duration of the festival (HSS XIV 60). Note, however, that contrary to usual procedures the expenditure of barley for these eight days was only recorded two months later, in the month Ḫiyari. Perhaps this means that a certain sequence of events came to an end in Ḫiyari.

The interval between Mitirunni and Ḫiyari was full of troubles, as can be seen from the following evidence. In the fifth month (Imburdanni) there arrived 13 refugees from Ḫanigalbat, i.e. Mitanni. They were all handed over to the *sukkallu* Agia, who will reappear later more than once. In HSS XVI 392 these refugees are registered as Arrapḫeans, residents of the towns of Zizza, Turšenni, Ansukallu and Nuzi. In the same month the above-mentioned Tirwenari delivered garments from the treasury at Nuzi ....

^{5}*šum-ma awēlūti*^{MEŠ} *ša* ^{māt}*Ak-ka*$_4$*-di* ^{6}*i-na arḫi*^{ḫi} *im-bur-dà-an-nu* ^{7}*i-na* ^{māt}*Na-ás-be* ^{8}*i-duk-ku-uš-šu-nu-ti* .... ^{13}*šum-ma amēlūti*^{MEŠ} ^{14}*ša* ^{māt}*A-šur* ^{15}*i-na* ^{āl}*Ta-ri-ba-du-gur* ^{16}*i-na arḫi*^{ḫi} *im-bur-dà-an-nu* ^{17}*i-du-uk-ku-uš-šu-nu*

(HSS XIII 63). Another sign of troubles on both frontiers of Arrapḫe simultaneously! In the month of Imburdanni the king again arrived in Nuzi and stayed there for eight days (HSS XV 271). His coming was unexpected, so that the barley for the maintenance of his escort had to be borrowed from UrḫiTešub, the *ḫazannu* of Ansukkallu (cf. HSS XV 125).

The most interesting for us are the documents dated in the sixth month (Ḫiyari). During this month garments were delivered for the guests of Agit-Tešub the Mitannian (HSS XIII 112). This is noteworthy first because of the presence of AgitTešub, called the Mitannian to distinguish him from his local namesake, and secondly because the garments are brought to him through an *ubāru* (more or less equivalent to the Greek *xenos*, i.e. a foreigner in the land), which shows that AgitTešub, although himself a foreigner, was a person of some importance. The fact that he had to be contacted through intermediaries shows that he was not present in Nuzi itself; perhaps he needed the garments because his own had been taken by the Babylonian king together with the chariots and all the rest of his property.

In the same month of Ḫiyari one Šattiwasa appears in the escort of the king of Arrapḫe. The name Šattiwasa is mentioned in nine Nuzi texts (HSS XIV 48, 49, 52, 55-58, 72, 135). Among the men listed in these documents AgitTešub is absent, and the Mitannian officers and charioteers are no longer mentioned either - evidently they have departed after having been robbed by the Babylonian king. Where to may be guessed from the evidence of the following documents.

The archives of sector C contain documents concerning the activities of the military commanders of the last period at Nuzi. Among them are four texts (HSS XV 264; HSS XVI 89, 92 and 103) relating to the maintenance of prisoners-of-war in the two villages Irḫaḫḫe and Teliberra. The grain was usually brought by the two heralds, Arnia and Kiptalili, and it was therefore a state matter. The detention of the prisoners for a lengthy period, in spite of difficulties with good supply, must have been the consequence of certain events out of the ordinary. The biggest delivery (100 *imēru* at a time) was through Tešurḫe, the great-grandson of TeḫibTilla. More than 174 *imēru* of grain was sent from Nuzi alone, according to the surviving documents. Of these HSS XVI 103 refers to expenditures in the month of Ululu (1 *imēru*) and HSS XVI 89 for seven days in the month of Šeḫli of Tešub (3 *imēru*). The month Ulūlu may have been the intercalary one in the middle of the year.[18] We suppose that the documents record the expenditures for the last days of Ulūlu, for the entire seventh month (Ḫinzuri, the month of apples), and the first seven days of the eighth month (Šeḫli of Tešub). If every man received 1 *qa* a day, like the Mitannians, this means there were about 400 prisoners. Note that the documents are dated in the second half of the year: if it is the same year, this means that the time of the battles was long since past. Where did the prisoners come from, why were they fed from public funds, and that at a time when the rations of the residents of Arrapḫe themselves were very scarce? Prisoners-of-war in the ancient Orient were usually assigned as soon as possible to some kind of work, and from then on no longer listed as prisoners, or they were sold to private persons.

Let us remind the reader that the month Šeḫli (of Tešub ?) was that in which a statue of Ištar was erected, and gifts presented to the towns of Irḫaḫḫe and Teliberra in connection with their liberation. From whom? Perhaps from those unwanted persons feeding on the bread of the land? We are dealing here not with the apocryphal truths of royal military relations, but with the documents which tell of things as they really were. The charioteers of Mitanni were detained in Babylonia and robbed of their chariots and property, but nothing is said of the Babylonians' seizing the men themselves, so evidently they were let free without their chariots. Might not these ca. 400 prisoners have been hostages kept by the Arrapḫeans in order to get back the men of Mitanni? This seems very plausible since the Mitannians, fleeing from Babylonia, had nowhere to turn to except Arrapḫe: the way to the north was cut off by the Assyrians, that to the west by their hostile homeland, and to the south by the Kassites who had robbed them. Nevertheless, they could not stay in hungry Arrapḫe either. The mission of Ḫašimaru, who was sent to the Lullubians and returned with a favourable answer early in the (next) year, may have been designed to get a *laissez-aller* for the Mitannian warriors from Arrapḫe; in any case, they all disappeared except for Šattiwasa.

The identification of Šattiwasa in the Nuzi documents with Šattiwasa, son of King Dušratta of Mitanni, is based on the context in which his name is mentioned.[19] He was a person of some importance, because no menials are mentioned by name in the lists of the royal escort; grooms, chariot-drivers, water-carriers, dragomans, runners etc. are all nameless. Half of the 42 men whose names appear in the lists with Šattiwasa are mentioned together with him constantly. These are: (1) Agibtašenni, son of Sisatna; two *sukkallus*: (2) Agibtašenni II or Agia and (3) TildAššura; five princes: (4) TadibTešub, (5) ḪudTešub, (6) ḪudibUrašše, (7) Wiraḫḫe and (8) TubkiTešub; a certain lady, (9) AlašsiḪurri; and also (10) AmarSīn, (11) Alwišuḫ, (12) Adrakkama, (13) Purniḫu, (14) PaiTilla, or Paia, (15) EḫliTešub, (16) ḪeldiTešub, (17) Kulbenari, (18) Šadenšuḫ, (19) Tirwenari; (20) Uiratti, and (21) Utḫabtae. Among the constantly recurring names there are ten that are preserved only once, but may also have recurred as they may have been in the lacunae of the other lists. These are: (22) Agavadil, (23) Ennamadi, (24) Kardiberwi, (25) Šimigari, (26) Ḫura, (27) IririTilla, (28) TeḫibAbu, (29) TeḫibTilla, (30) the *sukkallu* WurTešub, (31) the *šakin māti* Wantia.

Let us begin with a document which is nearly unique, HSS XIV 72. It is a list which contains only five of the recurring names, those of prince ḪudibUrašše, prince TadibTešub, Kulbenari, Šadenšuḫ and Šattiwasa: the other ten names are never mentioned elsewhere. The text concerns deliveries of sesame for sowing and for oil. The month of the biggest deliveries of ready oil is Ḫiyari (ASSOR XVI 46 sq.). Counting the time necessary for the growing of the sesame, this means that it was probably sown in the third month, Mitirunni, which is accordingly the probable date of our document. Among the recipients we encounter a high priestess (*entu*), which should mean that the delivery was connected with some cultic ceremony or ritual. As the sequence of the names and the amounts are important, we cite the document in full. At the head of the list is the prince ḪudibUrašše - 60 *qa*, then follow: the *entu*-priestess of Abena - 40 *qa*, Tamartae - 20 *qa*, Kulbenari - 30 *qa*, the village of Temtena - 1 *imēru*, a man of Lubdi - 20 *qa*, Šadenšuḫ - 10 *qa*, TarmiTešub, son of Ḫudia - 10 *qa*, Paienni - 4 *qa*, TeḫitTešub - 4 *qa*, Ardimalu - 12 *qa*, NulTešub - 12 *qa*, WaḫarTešub, son of Tagia - 10 *qa*, Šattiwasa - 5 *qa*, Kulaḫubi - 34 *qa*, "in all, 2 *imēru* 74 *qa*". Separately there follow: Ḫutta - 50 *qa*, Zigaia - 50 *qa*, TadibTešub - 7 *imēru*, the oil-manufacturer - 10 *imēru*. All in all "let the men of the *sakenu* bring" 21 *imēru* 74 *qa* of the town of Ulamme. The *sakenu* may be the same as the *šakin bīti*, the head of the palace economy (a West Semitic form?). Note that among the persons listed in this document no less than five had to give women hostages to the city officials of Nuzi, according to the documents HSS XV 120 and 207B: these were the *entu* of Abena, the prince ḪudibUrašše, Kulbenari, TadibTešub and WaḫarTešub, son of Tagia. There is a certain probability that the hostages were taken in connection with the events which led to the appearance of Šattiwasa. We do know, at least, that the women from Temtena, the village mentioned in our document, were given as hostages to the Lullubians, although later they were exchanged for women from Azuḫina. One of the two documents referring to this action (HSS XVI 387) has a seal of Agibtašenni, the *šakin māti* to whom the royal order about the safeguarding of Ḫašimaru's mission to the Lullubi was addressed. The *entu* of Abena might also have had something to do with the appearance of Šattiwasa.

Šattiwasa was in the king's escort when the latter visited Abena (HSS XIV 56), and the 200 chariots from Mitanni were partly quartered in the district of Abena (see above). In the list, the horses of Šattiwasa are mentioned directly after those of the king's bodyguard. After them follow the horses of the princes TadibTešub, ḪudibUrašše and ḪudTešub, of Šadensuḫ, Agibtašenni, Tirwenari and of three more persons, names destroyed. The document concerns the delivery of barley for two days to the escort "when the king dwelt in the City of Donkeys (Abena)". The minimum delivery there is 10 *qa*; the royal horses get 1 *imēru* 30 *qa*, those of the prince ḪudibUrašše get 30 *qa*, those of Šattiwasa 24 *qa*. Usually the royal horses were given about seven times as much as those of the princes.

Only one of the texts mentioning Šattiwasa is dated to the month. This is HSS XIV 48, dated to Ḫiyari, the same month in which AgitTešub the Mitannian received the garments, the man who, as we suggest, is to be identified with the military commander who fled from Šuttarna to Babylonia and there was robbed by the Kassite king. We suggest that AgitTešub with his warriors now continued his flight to the Lullubians, while Šattiwasa stayed with the King of Arrapḫe.

The names listed in HSS XIV 48, all but two, recur in the other documents: they are Nos. (16), (17), (14), (7), (3), (20), (1) and (10) of the list above, then Šattiwasa, then Nos. (18), (4), (29), (2), (19), (11), (21) and (28). Five names are destroyed; but the importance of the document lies mainly in the persons not mentioned by name and not belonging to the usual group of royal menials. At the beginning of the list is registered the expenditure of barley for six days for "the horses of the king's feet" - 7 *imēru* 20 *qa*; then came the horses of the MÍ.LUGAL - 90 *qa*; the horses of the substitutes of the princes (*kīma pūḫi-šunu šinaḫiluḫli*, i.e. *terdennu* "crown princes") get as much. Guests from Akkad (Kassite Babylonia) received barley (amount broken off) for five days, i.e. they arrived a day later than the king or departed a day earlier. Then 17 Kassite women and 3 Lullubian women received 8 *imēru* of barley for the two months Imburdanni and Ḫiyari: this means 20 *qa* for a full month each, which was the ration for the male palace personnel at Nuzi.

It seems that the negotiations with both the Kassites and the Lullubians took place during these two months, and this is why women hostages from both countries were maintained by the Arrapḫeans. This interpretation seems more plausible because of the presence of guests from Babylonia. The appearance of substitutes for princes may be explained by the absence of one or more of them on some diplomatic mission. We may even guess that this was ḪudTešub, a constant member of the royal escort, listed as one of the first and who took part in current events, who is actually absent in this document.

It is known that the negotiations with the Kassites were carried on with considerable display in the capital of Arrapḫe, Al-ilāni. This is attested by the document HSS XIV 136 which concerns the delivery, under the responsibility of Alwišuḫ (No. 11), of 30 gold and silver cups, with ornaments and molten figures. These cups were issued from the treasury of Nuzi "when prince Ḫud-Tešub arrived with the men of Akkad", through ElḫibTešub, the head of the palace economy. This must have had a connection with the negotiations with the guests from Akkad in the month of Ḫiyari. Of course, we cannot be sure that it was then that AgitTešub lost all his property in an attempt to use the Kassite king as an ally against the new leaders of Mitanni, but it can hardly be doubted that the negotiations with Kassites must have had something to do with the presence in Arrapḫe of the Mitannian refugees with AgitTešub at their head, and with his attempt to get help from Babylonia. The result of his activities is known to us from the Boghazköy documents.

The document HSS XIV 49 is dated "in the days of Ištar", i.e. probably in the days of the erection of her statue in Nuzi. Here the name of Šattiwasa is mentioned among the 25 names of the list, which is complete. Fifteen of the names coincide with those in the document HSS XIV 48 (the exceptions are PaiTilla, TeḫibTilla and TeḫibAbu, Nos. (14), (2) and (28) of the list on p.144). The ten names which do not occur in HSS XIV 48 do so in other documents mentioning Šattiwasa: these are the lady AlaššiḪurri (No. 9) and Nos. (2), (13), (23), (5), (26), (24), (25), (15), and (8) of the same list above. This document is distinguished by the mention of the high priest, who received 20 *qa* of barley, and his deputy, who received 1 *imēru* 30 *qa*; probably one of them was going away. We may compare the situation with that in the royal letter to the decurion of the cavalrymen, ŠarTešub, son of Utḫabtae (HSS XIV 14). The king orders ŠarTešub[20] to safeguard, on pain of death, the entry of the high priest and the *sukkallu* into Abena; in Zizza he is to secure the help of ḪudiAbu, the *šakin māti*.

Another interesting character in HSS XIV 49 is the lady AlaššiḪurri, whose name means "Hurri(ans) are the lordship/ladyship". She is mentioned together with Šattiwasa four times (HSS XIV 49, 55, 58, 135); two of these documents are very short lists of the royal retinue. In HSS XIV 55 Šattiwasa is named at the head of the list after the "horses of the king's feet", before prince Wiraḫḫe, AlaššiḪurri, Uiratti, TildAššura, Agibtašenni, TadibTešub and AmarSīn. Wiraḫḫe is named twice in the list, each time receiving a different amount of barley. Perhaps he was absent, and then returned. HSS XIV 58 is the shortest: only six people are mentioned - Agibtašenni, Uiratti, Šattiwasa, AlaššiḪurri, and the princes Wiraḫḫe and ḪudibUrašše. All of them receive barley for one day. One charioteer received 2 *qa* of barley for one horse; the horses "of the king's feet" received 80 *qa*, so it is probable that the king had 40 horses for his needs.

The most interesting text of the four in which Šattiwasa and AlaššiḪurri are mentioned together is HSS XIV 135, referring to issues of beer. The list is headed by the MÍ.LUGAL, she is followed by the ladies of the harem, and a nameless "daughter-in-law"; by AlaššiḪurri; the wet-nurse of ŠasuTešub; young ladies from Mari; ḪudibUrašše; TadibTešub; Tirwenari; certain "substitutes of the king", Agibtašenni; the *sukkallu* Agia; TildAššura; AmarSīn; runners; dragomans; Šattiwasa; wet-nurses again; ladies of the harem; and people of uncertain professions. At the end of the text are named the sons of ŠilwiTešub (the well-known prince; or possibly, at that time already the king), and Purniḫu (No. 13 of the list on p.144). The document bears the seals of the prince Wiraḫḫe, of the *šakin māti* Wandia, and of (the *sukkallu*) Agia. The mention of the sons of ŠilwiTešub (unfortunately not named) proves that we are indeed here in the times of the fifth generation, and the appearance of Wandia in the role of *šakin māti* shows that Agibtašenni the son of Ennamadi was no longer serving in that capacity, while Tešurḫe, who was last in that office, had not yet been appointed.

Very important is the mention of the girls from Mari. They are, of course, the usual woman hostages in Nuzi, which proves that certain negotiations with Mari were afoot. What the negotiations were is clear from the document HSS XV 84, in which the guests from Mari are given two chariot teams for the occasion "when Ša[ttiwasa ?] goes away to his womenfolk". All this looks very much like a preparation for the escape of Šattiwasa. After having pushed AgitTešub and his men away to the mountains, the Arrapḫeans were now preparing the journey of Šattiwasa to the neutral territory of Mari. It was near Mari that the Hittite frontier crossed the Euphrates at that period, and where the Hittite Empire could be reached by-passing Mitanni. It seems that Šattiwasa started with one chariot in the company of two Arrapḫeans (the "Hurrians" of the Boghazköy text); the other two chariots accompanied him through Mari with two *ālik arki*.

Who AlaššiḪurri was, and her subsequent fate, can be learnt from the following three documents, where she is named without Šattiwasa. In the list of the royal escort HSS XVI 111 she is mentioned among the usual retinue: here we find Agibtašenni, the princes ḪudTešub and ḪudibUrašše, two *sukkallus*: TildAššura and the other Agibtašenni, Uiratti, Utḫabtae; the head of the palace economy at Nuzi, ElḫibTilla,[21] and five new persons, of whom Ḫudibtašenni is mentioned among the men of the royal escort which visited Nuzi in the month Šeḫli of Tešub (HSS XIV 53). In the month of Arkabinni, when the cold set in, AlaššiḪurri received her ration of wheat together with the ladies of the harem and a singer (*nāru*). There was a feast in this month, and AlaššiḪurri may have taken part in it (hence the wheat), on hearing of the safe arrival of Šattiwasa in Hatti (HSS XVI 115). The last document (HSS XVI 331) is curious. It was written in connection with the "leading into the palace" of 26 persons. At the head of the list we find the two princes, TadibTešub[22] and Urḫatadi, with AlaššiḪurri named between them; then follow 20 men, all of them with patronymics, among them Tešurḫe, son of Takku, the great-grandson of the well-known TeḫibTilla. The list bears the seal of the *sukkallu* Agia (Agibtašenni). After his seal are named two more citizens, the scribe Nannaigidu and one Ḫuttirwe, who are "led" not into Nuzi but into Purulluwe. The persons led into the palace of Nuzi are identified as *ša pišanna* - unfortunately the Hurrian term (plural) is unknown, but "leading into a house" is a *terminus technicus* for taking as hostage. If all these persons, and among them AlaššiḪurri, were detained, then it was probably done in the expectation that the political situation would clear up. We know that it ended with the installation of Šattiwasa in the Mitannian capital with the help of the Hittites, but the venture was a risky one. AlaššiḪurri must have been Šattiwasa's mother, and he would have to ransom her or recover her in exchange for some valuables or hostages. This was probably the end of the episode connected with the sojourn of Šattiwasa in Arrapḫe.

We have not yet touched on two documents mentioning the name of Šattiwasa, HSS XIV 57 and 52. The first is remarkable for the fact that the horses "of the king's feet" are mentioned not at the beginning but at the end of the list. Judging from the rations, the text records a one day visit of the king. This is the only time when a third *sukkallu* is mentioned along with TildAššura and Agibtašenni (or Agia) - namely, WurTešub. Their function is not quite clear, but they seem to have had something to do with international conflicts, each at his own frontier: Agibtašenni was concerned with Mitanni and TildAššura with Aššur. WurTešub must therefore have been concerned with the Kassites, or with the new ally, the Lullubians.

The document HSS XIV 52 is interesting because the horses of Šattiwasa are rationed separately from those of his chariot-drivers - the first get 20 *qa*, the second 50 *qa*. Also a man of Aššur receives separate rations for his own horses, and, separately, for the horses of his charioteer (20 *qa* and 10 *qa*). Thus at that time Šattiwasa had a retinue of his own, five times as big as that of the Assyrian. To judge from the figures, this was also a one day visit of the king. Hildegard Lewy once observed that Assyrians never appear in the Nuzi economic texts at the same time as the Kassites; her inference was that there was an interval between the Assyrian and the Kassite offensives against Arrapḫe. From our point of view, it proves only that the negotiations with the two countries were conducted strictly separately. This is a natural result of the opposition in which Arrapḫe's two neighbours found themselves in respect to each other.

It is well known that Mitanni did not regain her status as great power, but gradually declined. Consequently the royal house of Arrapḫe, originally connected with the great king Saussadattar of Mitanni, also lost much of its original authority and power. The centralized economy of the palace falling into decay, the documentation of its operations was discontinued, while the traditional economy of the extended family communes does not require documentation.

---

1 For the pronunciation Šattiwasa for KUR-*ti-wa-az-za* see I.M. Diakonoff, *Nochmals Mattiwazza-Kurtiwazza-Šattiwazza*, AOF III [1975] 167-8.

2 E.F. Weidner, *Politische Dokumente aus Kleinasien* [Leipzig 1923].

3 On the localization see I.M. Diakonoff, *Predistoria armyanskovo naroda* [Erevan 1968], 87 etc.; on Alzi as an important political entity see L.M. Golovleva, *Tsarstvo Alzi....*, in *Hin Aravelk' /Drevni Vostok* 3 [Erevan 1978], 71-87.

4 This interpretation of the verb *uštemḫir* in the text was suggested by I.M. Diakonoff.

5 The same is true of the administrative archives of Knossos, Pylos and Ugarit, where the last years of the existence of these cities are well documented, while the earlier years are represented by stray texts only.

6 M.P. Maidman, *The Teḫip-Tilla Family of Nuzi: A Genealogical Reconstruction*, JCS 28 [1976] 127-155.

7 The operations of sale of "copper with its tin" for barley are documented in HSS XIII 493; cf. HSS XIV 593; XV 162; XVI 37; XIII 172; XIV 535; etc.

8 N.B. Jankovskaja, *Tsarskie brat'ya v rodoslovnoi khurritskikh dinastov Arrapkhi* [N.B. Jankowska, *The Royal Brothers in the Genealogy of the Hurrian Dynasts of Arrapḫe*] [Leningrad 1978], 33, especially HSS XIII 410 and footnotes 6, 23; and p. 47.

9 N.B. Jankowska, *Communal Self-Government and the King of the State of Arrapḫa*, JESHO XII [1969], 264ff.

10 The documents HSS XIV 37-38 (sector C) record the contribution of silver from 10 cavalry-men to acquire horses. The decurion, ŠarTešub, son of Utḫabtae, and his companion, pay 12 shekels from 40. The note HSS XIV 12 registers the fact that one horse was bought for the price of 10 minas of bronze. In the same archive there are records of transfer of horses (HSS XIV 40, etc.) and a record of an exchange of a slave-girl for a horse (HSS XIV 119).

11 This text has been specially discussed by Hildegard Lewy and Manfred Mayrhofer, *A propos of the text HSS XV 32*, *Orientalia* NS 34 [1965], 30-31.

12 See also the situation of Tyre and Muṣaṣir later (N.B. Jankowska, *Some*

Problems of the Economy of the Assyrian Empire, in *Ancient Mesopotamia* [Moscow 1969], 255ff.).

13 It is probable that the battle of Lubdi (on the Kassite border) was the occasion when the Mitannian chariots, heading for a refuge in Babylonia, were seized by the Kassites.

14 N.B. Jankovskaja, *Kalendar' khurritskoi Arrapkhi* [The Calendar of Hurrian Arrapḫe], VDI 1978/1, 105.

15 Note that the month Kinūnu was the time of the greatest spring festival.

16 If the ration was 30 *qa*, like that of the servants of the Mitannian officers, the amount would be sufficient for 200 men.

17 According to our reconstruction she was the wife of ItḫiTešub, son of KibiTešub (N.B. Jankovskaja, in "*Kultura Vostoka....*", 36-40, 43; cf. note 8 above).

18 In the calendar of Arrapḫe the month Ulūlu is never encountered in texts mentioning series of months, therefore it is probably either intercalary, or identical to some other month bearing a Hurrian name; in any event, it belongs to the middle of the year, before Ḫinzuri.

19 Note also that Šattiwasa is not only a name entirely unknown to the onomasticon of Arrapḫe, but an Aryan name, and in the archives of Arrapḫe these are borne exclusively by Mitannians.

20 ŠarTešub is known from several documents of sector C as an active participant in the events preceding the fall of Nuzi (HSS XV 28, 99; XVI 90, 91, 93, 95, 106-108 etc.). In the military lists he is recorded on the same flank as KelTešub, the lord of the *dimtu* of Kissuk and its military district, and appears as a witness in the litigation about that *dimtu* (JEN 321:70).

21 The letter of ḪeldibAbu (cf. HSS XIV 523) about the delivery of two talents of copper to Tešurḫe, the great-grandson of TeḫibTilla, was addressed to him (HSS XIV 587). It was he who took the gold and silver cups from the treasury of Nuzi for the reception of the Kassite envoys in the capital, Al-ilāni (HSS XIV 136). And it was he who received at the palace the grain of the Lullubians brought by the scribe Aḫajamši and Ninuari who had bartered for the bronze from Nuzi (HSS XIII 172). Thus the different threads from the events of the period are brought together in the person of ElḫibTilla, which proves once again that they were roughly simultaneous.

22 In the text there is a scribal mistake: read TadibTešub for ḪudibTešub. The list is nearly identical with one in HSS XVI 332, where 14 names recur, and in six cases the names of the sons are substituted for the fathers'. At the head of this second list are the princes TadibTešub and Urḫatadi again, but AlaššiḪurri is absent.

DAS ENDE DES TYPISCH ALTEN DUKTUS IM HETHITISCHEN

Annelies Kammenhuber (München)

§0. Dieser Beitrag hat zwar eine gewisse exemplarische Bedeutung, insofern er unter anderem die Grenze mechanischer Textdatierungen aufzeigt; jedoch ist er des verehrten Jubilars und Freundes mit seinen grossen, bewunderungswürdigen Leistungen eigentlich nicht würdig. Es geht dabei nämlich nur um eine der von Zeit zu Zeit fälligen Bereinigungen in der Hethitologie, die eine für Hypothesen besonders anfällige Wissenschaft ist.

§1. Von den beiden Komplexen, an denen die Hethitologen hauptsächlich von 1969 bis 1979 mechanische Datierungen nach Graphie und/oder Duktus bzw. Zeichenformen versucht haben, war bis vor einiger Zeit der der Unterscheidung zwischen althethitischen "Originalen" und Althethitisch in Abschrift ziemlich sicher, während der Komplex "Mittelhethitisch" umstritten und selbst für Eingeweihte kaum mehr durchschaubar war.

Während das *Hethitische Wörterbuch* (HW^2, S. 9 und passim) mit der Unterscheidung von Aheth. (ca. 1650/1600 bis 15. Jh.) und Jheth. (ca. 1420-1200) ebenso verfährt wie die Assyriologie, die neue Sprachstufen dort ansetzt, wo ein Texthiat vorausging, wollen andere die Zeit von Tutḫaliya II. (mit Nikalmati = 2 Texte!), Arnuwanda I. und neuerdings auch von Šuppiluliuma I. als sogenanntes "Mheth." vom Jheth. (ab Muršili II., Mitte des 14. Jh.) als eigene Sprachstufe abheben. Dabei bilden die Grundlage des "Mheth." aber nicht datierte Königstexte, sondern wenige aus sprachlichen Gründen um 1400 datierte Texte und hauptsächlich zu Recht oder zu Unrecht vom 13. Jh. in das ausgehende 15. Jh. umdatierte Texte.

Wir können uns hier auf das Aheth. beschränken, dessen "Originale" weniger als 1% des heth. Gesamtmaterials ausmachen, weil eine Münchener Gemeinschaftarbeit in THeth 9 [1979] von S. Heinhold-Krahmer - I. Hoffmann - A. Kammenhuber - G. Mauer, *Probleme der Textdatierung in der Hethitologie* (*Beiträge zu umstrittenen Datierungskriterien des 15. und 13. Jh. v. Chr.*) jetzt umfassend informiert über die Geschichte der Forschung (I : S. 1ff. von S. Heinhold-Krahmer), die Texte (II : S. 63ff.), und zwar die unumstrittener Datierung von Tutḫaliya II. - Šuppiluliuma I. und Tutḫaliya IV. - Šuppiluliuma II. (Gruppe II.1, von I. Hoffmann), die in der folgenden Untersuchung scharf getrennt werden von den Texten umstrittener Datierung (II.2 [Teil des sogenannten Mheth.], von S. Heinhold-Krahmer).

Wie die Texte II.1 und II.2 werden auch die verschiedenen Datierungsmethoden in der Untersuchung scharf getrennt. I. Hoffmann bietet die bisher umfassendste und systematischste Untersuchung nach Zeichenformen (III : S. 86ff.), unter anderem mit einer Auswahl relevanter Zeichen gegenüber nur handschriftlichen Varianten (S. 98) und mit der Erkenntnis, dass ganz neue Zeichenformen wie das jüngere *li* aus Mitanni übernommen worden sind. G. Mauer überprüft die bisher aufgestellten graphischen und grammatischen Kriterien (IV : S. 150ff.) mit dem Ergebnis, dass von 37 [39] aufgestellten Kriterien 35 [37] entfallen, weil sie nicht die ausnahmslose Gültigkeit haben, die bei mechanischen Kriterien zu fordern ist, sondern auch im 13. Jh. begegnen können. A. Kammenhuber bietet (V : S. 206ff.) ergänzendes Material zu Kap. IV aus HW^2, neue an HW^2 gewonnene sichere Datierungen wie z.B. der Beginn von neuen Ideogrammen mit Applikation auf die Texte II.1 und II.2;

dabei zeigt sich unter anderem immer wieder, dass der Madduwatta-Text KUB XIV, 1+, der nach H. Ottens Schule und anderen sicher aus dem 13. Jh. ins "Mheth." umdatiert sein soll, Schreibungen hat, die erst mit Muršili II. beginnen. Aus den bisherigen Untersuchungsergebnissen (VI : S. 244ff.) und dem Zitatindex (S. 276ff.) kann man unter vielem anderen ersehen, dass bei den drei Datierungen nach Zeichenformen, Graphie und lexikalischen Monographien unterschiedliche Datierungen herauskommen können. Mechanische Kriterien ersetzen demnach nicht die philologische und sachbezogene Bewertung von Texten. Eine gesonderte Untersuchung nach historischen Gesichtspunkten wird Frau Heinhold-Krahmer in einem späteren Band vorlegen.[1]

§2. Im Anschluss an die 1952 erfolgte Entdeckung der ersten aheth. "Originaltafel" in dem sogenannten schweren (womöglich durch einen anderen Griffeltyp verursachten) Duktus, der sofort in die Augen springt und dessen Kenntnis ich H.G. Güterbock verdanke, war eine Unterscheidung zwischen Aheth. in "Originalen" und Aheth. in Abschriften möglich geworden (THeth 9, 2ff.). Obgleich nie ermittelt wurde, wie lange dieser schwere Duktus gebraucht wurde (vgl. §8), erzielte man mit obiger Unterscheidung zunächst einige hoffnungsvolle Ergebnisse. So ermittelten 1961 unabhängig von einander H.G. Güterbock an Hand des Duktus und Vf. an Hand von aheth. philologischen Kriterien die aheth. "Originale" A, K, M, q aus J. Friedrich, HG [1959]. Grössere "Originale" wurden veröffentlicht von H. Otten & V. Souček, StBoT 8 [1969]; E. Neu, StBoT 12 [1970, hier aber Hauptexemplar eine gute Abschrift (des 14. Jh.)]; H. Otten, StBoT 17 [1973; Text A = KBo XXII, 2]; und E. Neu, StBoT 18 [1974; Anitta-Text A]. Datierung nach der Sprache und dem Duktus bildeten damals eine Einheit.

§3. Ohne nachteilige Wirkung auf die philologische, chronologisch orientierte Erforschung des heth Wortschatzes blieben zwei neuere Erkenntnisse:

1971 veröffentlichte H.G. Güterbock in KBo XVIII, 151 ein Orakel, das nicht den schweren Duktus zeigt, aber sprachlich zum Aheth. (der Texte §2) gehört (A. Ünal & A. Kammenhuber, KZ 88 [1974] 157-80; cf. THeth 9, 91f.; 223; 233; §6 mit Anm. 2).

H.G. Güterbock wies 1978 (Güterbock 1978, S. 126 mit Anm. 2) in einem Vortrag nach, dass sich unter den aheth. "Originalen" im schweren Duktus auch Abschriften von Texten finden. Das bewies der Schreibfehler *la-a-* im aheth. "Original" KBo VI, 2 (+) I, 8 (HG Text A) für *kar-* in B = KBo VI, 3 (+) I, 15 (das um 1400 geschrieben ist [§7]).

In Anführungsstriche gesetzt, liess sich nach der bisher geschilderten Forschung weiterhin zwischen aheth. "Originalen" und Aheth. in Abschriften unterscheiden.

§4. Bei der Edition von z.T. kleinen und kleinsten Festfragmenten und Ähnlichem in KBo XVII [1969] benützte H. Otten für Fragmente in dem schweren Duktus die in KBo XVI [1968] begonnene Unterscheidung "typisch alter Duktus". Texte in typisch altem Duktus beinhalteten damals "Originaltexte" in (meist) aheth. Sprache, während "alter Duktus", "ältlicher Duktus", "älterer Duktus" usw. keine aheth. Sprache zu implizieren brauchten.

Eine Überprüfung von KBo XVII seitens der Vf. in MSS 29 [1971] 75-109 (*Das Verhältnis von Schriftduktus zu Sprachstufe im Heth.*) wies erneut - ebenso wie Or. NS 39 [1970] 561ff. zu KBo XVI, 67ff. - nach, dass Graphie, Duktus bzw. Zeichenformen und textinterne Datierungen kein einheitliches Ergebnis zu zeitigen brauchen; S. 103 stärkste Bedenken gegen den (typisch) alten Duktus aus StBoT 8, 42f.

H. Ottens Konsequenz bestand nun nicht etwa in Skepsis gegen mechanische Datierungen von Fragmenten, die sprachlich nichts aussagen, sondern darin, dass er in den folgenden Editionen meistens zu dem bei ihm verwässerten Begriff "alter Duktus" zurückkehrte. Zum vollendeten Chaos führte dies Wechseln der Terminologie dann bei der nächsten Edition von kleinen und kleinsten Bruchstücken, die irgendwie aheth. sein sollen, in KBo XXV [1979] (und schon in KBo XX [1971]). In KBo XXV gibt es kaum Texte mit ganzen Sätzen. Man kann von Glück sagen, wenn ein Fragment ganze Wörter enthält. Ohne Literaturangaben werden als Nr. 1 und 2 ein Stückchen Leberomen (4½ Zeilen) und ein anderes Omen-Stücklein (12 frgm. Zeilen) vorangestellt (deren grundsätzliche Datierung man THeth 7 [1976] Kap. IV entnehmen kann); ein weiteres Omen-Frgm. (8 Zeilen mit 1-2 Wörtern, aber "aheth." genannt) ist vielleicht noch Nr. 108. Photos oder Beweise fehlen. Ob E. Neu, der noch eine Transkription der "aheth." Texte aus KBo XXV in StBoT 25 vorlegen soll, ausreichende Beweis (Photos!) nachliefert, bleibt abzuwarten.

§5. Da H. Otten immer häufiger gezwungen ist, Zusatzstücklein zu einem ein Band oder wenige Bände vorher veröffentlichten Fragment nachzuedieren, lässt sich an Hand einiger solcher Joins mühelos nachweisen, dass das, was er seit 1969 (KBo XVII) als aheth. "Original" in dem schweren Duktus zu erkennen vermeint, zum Teil unzuverlässig ist. Damit ist spätestens ab 1969 nun auch dieses mechanische Datierungssystem entwertet. Es ist zu bedauern, dass H.G. Güterbock mit seiner reichen Erfahrung und systematischen Erfassung von Textgattungen nicht mehr an dieser Forschung beteiligt worden ist.

Beispiele (Ausrufezeichen, wenn in der wechselnden Terminologie H. Ottens bei der Edition nicht aheth. "Original" in schweren Duktus gemeint war):

1) KBo XXV, 12 (alt) + KBo XVII, 20 (-!) + KBo XX, 5 (typ. alt) + KBo XVII, 9 (typ. alt) + ABoT 5 (-): frgm. Festritual (=EZEN) mit einem sehr häufigen Typus (A. Archi, *Mat. heth. Thes.*, Lfg. 3-7 [1976-78], Nr. 5 *eku*-Kap. V, VI); sprachlich wohl aheth.; "Original" oder gute Abschrift wie StBoT 12, B (§2).

2) KBo XXV, 19 (alt) + KBo XX, 33 (ältlicher Duktus!) + KBo XVII, 21 (-!) + KBo XVII 46 (ähnlich altem Duktus!): atypisches EZEN-Frgm. (wie Nr. 1), sprachlich uncharakteristisch; lässt sich m.E. nur datieren, wenn untersucht wird, ob nur aheth. Götternamen vorkommen.

3) KBo XXV, 52 (alt) + KBo XVII, 19 (Schrift wirkt ältlich, doch könnte der einfache Kolumnentrenner auch auf eine flüchtigere Abschrift deuten[?]): EZEN-Frgm. ohne sprachliche Charakteristika.

4) KBo XXV, 54 (alt) + KBo XX, 17 (älterer Duktus!): EZEN-Frgm., sprachlich nicht datierbar.

5) KBo XXV, 56 (alt) + KBo XVII, 33 (-!) + KBo XX, 6 (typ. alt) + KBo XX, 22 (alt); und Duplikat KBo XVII, 36 (alt!) + ABoT 35 (-) + KBo XX, 20 (alt); noch immer ohne ganze Sätze: sprachlich merkwürdig, aber nicht aheth. (MSS 29 [1971] 101f. worauf H. Ottens ganze Antwort daraus zu bestehen scheint, dass er bei KBo XX, 6 wieder *expressis verbis* von typ. altem Duktus spricht, während das sonst in KBo XX oft "alter Duktus" heisst! Leider führt H. Otten damit auch seine Duktusangaben in KBo XX [1971] *ad absurdum*).

6) KBo XXV, 68 (alt) + KBo XVII, 13 (-!): EZEN-Frgm., zu wenig Sprache um zu datieren.

7) KBo XXV, 129 (alt) + KBo XVII, 50 (alt!): EZEN-Frgm., zu wenig Sprache um zu datieren. Wer H. Ottens Datierung "glaubt", müsste nach KBo XVII,

50 Rs.! (Edition: Vs.?) + KBo XXV, 129 Rs.? III:14 mit hatt. *]x te-e ma-al-ḫi-ip-wa$_a$-aḫ-ga-al-li[* schlussfolgern, dass man schon in aheth. Zeit hatt. Wörter nicht mehr zu trennen vermochte; *malḫip* "gut".

8) KBo XXV, 142 (alt) + KBo XX, 69 (ältlicher Duktus!): EZEN-Frgm. mit Hattisch (Vs. 3 *]x lu-ú-wa-a-i[*); zu wenig Text, um sprachlich zu datieren.

9) Für die Diskrepanz zwischen (brauchbaren Texten in) aheth. Sprache und Duktusbezeichnungen sowie für verschiedenartige Duktusbezeichnungen bei Stücken ein und derselben Tafel vgl. noch KBo XVII. Aheth. Sprache zeigen 1-7 (StBoT 8), 9 (oben Nr. 1), 10, 11 (StBoT 12 "Original" = A), 15 (trotz älterem Duktus), 18, 22, 23, 25, 28, 43, 74 (StBoT 12, Abschrift = B). F. Starke, StBoT 23 *[1977]* 10f. (s. §6) nimmt als aheth. "Originale" Nr. 15 (s. oben!), 18 mit 43, 44+.

10) Textzuwachs zu StBoT 8 (Ritual für das Königspaar) mit den Duplikaten KBo XVII, 1-6, 7+? IBoT III, 135 in altem Duktus = typisch alter Duktus in KBo XVII:

1 + KBo XXV, 3 (-);
3 + 4 + KBo XX, 15 (älterer Duktus!) + KUB XLIII, 32 (ed. K.K. Riemschneider mit "alter Duktus" nach StBoT 8, 42f.; s. unten Nr. 14);
7 +? IBoT III, 135 (-) + KBo XXV, 7 (ohne Angaben).

11) Textzuwachs zum EZEN(!) StBoT 12:

A "Original" KBo XVII, 11 (typ. alt) + KBo XX, 12 (alt);
B Abschrift KBo XVII, 74 (-) + KBo XXI, 25 (-) + KUB XLIII, 26 (s. Nr. 14!) + ABoT 9 (-). Vgl. E.Neu & Ch. Rüster, *Festschrift Otten [1973]* 235-42. (Für IV:7-18 s. nun *Mat. heth. Thes.* Nr. 5 *eku-* S. 123f.).

Dies wäre so weit in Ordnung bis auf die Frage, nach welchen Gesichtspunkten H. Otten in KBo XX *[1971]*, von dem nach S. V etwa die ersten 50 kleinen und kleinsten EZEN- Nummern "aheth. Duktus" haben sollen (etwas anders S. VIf.), seinen "typisch alten Duktus" und seinen "alten Duktus" v e r t e i l t. Für eine gewisse Bevorzugung von "typisch alt" bei nicht-aheth. Fragmenten könnten oben Nr. 5 und z.B. KBo XX, 11 sprechen.

12) Schon die *MELQĒT*-Listen (zum Teil Bestandteil von EZEN) aus KBo XVI *[1968]* zeigen, dass bei H. Ottens Edition nach (vermeintlichem) Duktus meistens für die Spracherforschung wertlose Fragmente als "aheth." übrig bleiben. S. schon Vf., Or NS 39 *[1970]* 561ff.: "Bei den *MELQĒT*-Listen KBo XVI, 67-84 zeigt sich erneut, dass eine Datierung nach dem Schriftduktus ein notwendiges Experiment ist, aber keine verlässlichen Kriterien bietet. Laut Vorw. zeigen Nr. 71-73, 76, 80, 84 typisch alten Duktus (schmaler Kolumnentrenner); Nr. 67 wirke - wie auch die folgenden Stücke - etwas alt, und Nr. 74 zeige anscheinend älteren Duktus. - Vom Sprachlichen und Inhaltlichen her ergibt sich demgegenüber, dass alle *MELQĒT*-Listen altheth. bzw. in altheth. Zeit entstanden sind, vergleichbar den EZEN KBo XVI, 49 mit 78". Loc. cit. 563: Sprachstufe unklar bei Frgm. 82; 84 (dessen 3½ halbe Zeilen ausgerechnet typisch alten Duktus zeigen sollten).

Mit nachträglich veröffentlichten Zusatzstücken (und Korrekturen) ergibt sich für die beiden einzig brauchbaren, da nicht allzu zerstörten aheth. *MELQĒT*-Listen KBo XVI, 68 + KBo XX, 55 + KUB XXXIV, 86 und KBo XVI, 69 + KBo XX, 54 kein typisch alter Duktus, wie H. Otten *expressis verbis* bei KBo XX, 54f. feststellt.

EZEN KBo XVI, 71 (entgegen früheren Textzusammenschlüssen StBoT 23, 10 [CTH 627.17], wo auch als aheth. "Original" anerkannt) in typisch altem Duktus + KBo XX, 24 (alter Duktus) + KBo XXV, 13 (hier nur noch "aheth. Festritual" genannt)!

13) Erwähnt werden muss im Rahmen dieser Bereinigung leider noch, dass H. Ottens Autographien fehlerhaft sein können. S. H.A. Hoffners Kollation von KBo XXII, 222 an Hand des Photos in BiOr 33 [1976-77] 237a.

14) Was herauskommt, wenn ein Editor aheth. "Originale" nach den von H. Otten, StBoT 8, 42f. aufgestellten Kriterien edieren wollte, zeigt K.K. Riemschneiders Edition KUB XLIII [1972] S. V mit Anm. 2, die H. Otten zu Recht nie anerkannt hat.

Unter "Alt- und mittelheth. Texte" Nr. 23-59 (mit 13. Jh. z.B. in Nr. 40-47) sollten Nr. 23-33, 35, 39 "alten Duktus" gemäss StBoT 8, 42f. [= typ. alter Duktus in KBo XVII, 1-7] zeigen und davon Nr. 24-28, 39 den "typisch alten Duktus"!

Aheth. Sprache kann man bei den in der eigenwilligen Handschrift K.K. Riemschneiders edierten Fragmenten fast nur bei den Zusatzstücken zu oben Nr. 10, 11 anerkennen. Dabei hätte das "Original" KUB XLIII, 32 (+KBo XVII, 3+) dann "alten Duktus" und die Abschrift KUB XLIII, 26 (+KBo XVII, 74+) dann "typisch alten Duktus" gehabt!

Das *MELQĒT*-Frgm. XLIII, 24 mag nach oben Nr. 12 aheth. Sprache haben; ein ähnliches Frgm. KBo XX, 66 ist dafür von H. Otten dann als "älterer Duktus" ediert (CTH 523 und RHA XXXI).

F. Starke, StBoT 23, 10f. mit H. Ottens augenblicklicher Datierung (§6) akzeptiert als aheth. "Originale" die atypischen EZEN-Frgm. (die wegen der zum Teil langen Tradition im heth. Staatskult besonders subtile Datierungskriterien erfordern):

XLIII, 28 (nicht beweisbar! vgl. HW^2 357a);
XLIII, 30 (jheth.! wie z.B. noch XLIII, 23 [wohl 13. Jh.], 29, 33).

§6. Wir schliessen in §7 mit einem Überblick über die zur Zeit verbleibenden aheth. Texte, die sogenannte "Originale" (in dem schweren Duktus) sind, nach Vf., KZ 83 [1969] 257ff. (nach der Autopsie von H.G. Güterbock und H. Otten) und nach der von H. Otten betreuten, überarbeiteten Dissertation von F. Starke, StBoT 23 [1977] 8ff. (besonders 10f.). §8 behandelt gesondert das infolge nicht ausreichenden Materials auch hier nicht lösbare Problem der Landschenkungsurkunden.

Es geht um die Frage, ob die Ermittlung von aheth. "Originalen" nur durch menschliche Unzulänglichkeit *ad absurdum* geführt worden ist (§§4f.) oder ob sie überhaupt sinnlos ist, weil in älterer Zeit womöglich - wie das aheth. "Original" KBo XVIII, 151 nahe legt - nebeneinander mit verschiedenen Griffeln (so wie früher bei uns mit dickeren und dünneren Federn) geschrieben worden ist (§§ 2, 3!).[2] Ich überlasse es dem Leser, sich selbst ein Urteil zu bilden. Betonen möchte ich nur, dass die Unterscheidung zwischen aheth. Sprache in "Originalen" und in Abschriften nahezu, wenn nicht ganz, irrelevant geworden ist, weil sich Abschriften wie KBo XVII, 74+ (§5 Nr. 11) und wie z.B. KBo III, 27, 40 und 60 nach F. Starke, StBoT 23, 9[28] in der Sprache und sogar in der (erheblichen unwichtigeren) Graphie überhaupt nicht von "Originalen" zu unterscheiden brauchen, dafür aber besser erhaltene Texte liefern. Mechanische Datierungsmethoden, appliziert auf EZEN-Bruchstücklein ohne sprachlichen und inhaltlichen Aussagewert (wie z.T. KBo XVI, XVII, überwiegend XX, XXV), sind darüber hinaus Versuche am untauglichen Objekt. Philologie in dem ganzen umfassenden Sinn des Wortes lässt sich nicht durch Mechanismen ersetzen.

Mit dem hier auf umständlichstem Wege Ermittelten deckt sich im wesentlichen das, was E. Laroche (Anm. 1) feststellt.

§7. Aheth. "Originale" in historischen Texten im weiteren Sinne des Wortes nach CTH [1971] angeordnet, Rest nach Editionen:

CTH 1/Cat 5 Anitta: KBo III, 22, StBoT 18, A.

[CTH 2.2 Anumḫerwa$_a$: KUB XXXVI, 99? (StBoT 23, 10). 16 frgm. Zeilen in aheth. Sprache; in H. Ottens Edition ohne Merkmale des typischen alten Duktus; habe ich nicht kollationiert.]

Zu CTH 3 Zalpa: KBo XXII, 2 (alter Duktus) = StBoT 17, A.

CTH 8/Cat 24 Palastchronik: D = KUB XXXVI, 104.

CTH 9.5/Cat 25 dasselbe ? Nennt einen Ḫuzziya: KBo VIII, 42. (Wirklich "Original"?)

CTH 15/Cat 7 Zukraši von Aleppo: A = KUB XXXVI, 100 + KBo VII, 14 (zuerst entdecktes aheth. "Original").

[CTH 5/Cat 9 Ḫattušili I.: bei Vf., loc. cit., der damals H. Otten, MDOG 86 [1953] 60[2] gefolgt ist, was nach StBoT 23, 10[30] (9[28] !) ein Fehler war, entfallen KBo III, 27 (BoTU 10 ß) als gute Abschrift des 13. Jh. und KBo III, 28 (BoTU 10γ) = CTH 9.6/Cat 25 als gute Abschrift, wohl 14. Jh.; beides durch Kollation A. Archis in Ostberlin bestätigt. Vermutlich nach §6 nun nicht mehr relevant, ausserdem völlig uninteressant, ob eine gute Abschrift ins 13. oder 14. Jh. datiert.]

CTH 25/Cat 17 Vertragsfrgm. von Zidanza (wohl = Zidanta, 3. König vor Telipinu): KUB XXXVI, 108. (Bedenken von O.R. Gurney; O. Carruba bei J.J.S. Weitenberg [s. Anm. 1], 291[7].)

CTH 27/Cat 122.6 Ḫabiru-Vertrag, soweit erhalten, ohne Namen: KUB XXXVI, 106 + KBo IX, 73.

CTH 291f./Cat 181-5, HG-Texte in schwerem aheth. Duktus mit den Siegeln aus J. Friedrich, HG, I. Tafel:
A (kein "Original"! §3) = KBo VI, 2 + KBo XIX, 1 (alter Duktus) + KBo XXII, 61 + 62 (ohne Angaben).
M = KUB XXIX,16 + KBo XIX, 2 (älterer Duktus!).
K(?) = Frgm. KUB XXIX, 13.
[B = KBo VI, 3 + KBo XXII, 63 entgegen Vf., loc. cit. 261 nicht aus der Zeit Telipinus, sondern "mheth." nach HW^2 152f.]
Tafel II, q = KUB XXIX, 25 (+) 28 (+) 29 + 30 (+) 32 (+) 35 + 36 (+) 38, neu ediert von H.G. Güterbock, JCS 16 [1962] 18ff. (StBoT 23, 10 ungenau).

Was bezweckt H. Otten mit der Angabe "älterer Duktus" bei M+ ? Will er H.G. Güterbocks und meine Untersuchungsergebnisse in Frage stellen, denen er selbst AfO 21 [1966] 8f. gefolgt ist? (Damals hatten M und Zusatzstück "typisch althethitischen Duktus".) Oder soll man daraus ebenso wie aus §§4f. schliessen, dass der schwere aheth. Duktus überhaupt nicht mehr oder für H. Otten nicht mehr erkennbar ist?

Sonstiges (zum Teil auch in StBoT 23, 10f. als CTH 414ff. passim):

KUB XXVIII, 24 Hattisch (Vf. loc. cit. nach H.G. Güterbock).
KUB XXIX, 3 Baurit. der hatt.-heth. Schicht, CTH 414/Cat 308.
KUB XXXI: CTH 733/Cat 365 mit den von E. Laroche, JCS 1 [1947] 187ff.

erkannten und bearbeiteten hatt.-heth. Bilinguen mit Anrufung der Götter mit ihren unter den Göttern und unter den Menschen gebräuchlichen Namen: aheth. "Originale" KUB XXXI, 143; 143a + VBoT 124(? - nicht kollationiert) und KBo XXV, 112 (205/s+, StBoT 23, 11, wo aber KUB VIII, 41 als jheth. Redaktion und

428/t + = KBo XXV, 122 als nicht zugehörig entfallen). Aheth. KBo XXV, 112 läuft, soweit erhalten, parallel zu KUB XXVIII, 75, einer jheth. Abschrift des hattischen Textes, und bestätigt, dass man im 14./13. Jh. nicht mehr in der Lage war, den hatt. Text zu ändern. Auch von H.S. Schuster, *Die hattisch-hethitischen Bilinguen*, Teil 1 [1974] 29f. erkannt; vgl. dort auch zu anderen hatt. Texten. Bei einer Bearbeitung dieses wohl interessantesten Textes aus KBo XXV (weitere, zum Teil aheth. genannte Frgm. Nr. 113-120; KUB XLIII, 27, die sich auf Anhieb nicht sprachlich fixieren lassen; XLVIII, 12) wäre von Interesse, ob KUB VIII, 41 im Rahmen der bewussten Kultkontamination Ḫattušilis III. abgeändert sein könnte. Ich wollte hier mit einer diesbezüglichen Untersuchung E. Laroche nicht vorgreifen.

KUB XXXV, 165 Palaisch (Vf., loc. cit).

[Falsch StBoT 23, 11: KBo XVII, 25 (in ziemlich alter Schrift) mit aheth. Sprache (+) KUB XXXV, 164 (jheth.-palaisch). S. jetzt KBo XXV, 139 (*expressis verbis* als jheth.) + KUB XXXV, 164.]

KUB XXXVI, 110, CTH 820/Cat. 538, hatt.-heth. Schicht, erst nachträglich als aheth. "Original" erkannt (StBoT 23, 11; bestätigt durch Kollation von A. Archi als typisch alter Duktus). Damit wird H. Ottens Kritik IF 81 [1976] 306f. gegen schon aheth. Pl. N.A.n. *-at* neben *-e* beim Pronomen *-a-* bedenklich. Seine Interpretation des par. Passus *Mat. heth. Thes.*, Lfg. 3, Nr. 4 S. 22 ist willkürlich.

[KUB XXXVII, 223 Leber- (oder Gallenblasen-)Modell mit Akkad. und fehlerhaftem Heth.; Photo MDOG 73 [1935] 31; vgl. §4 zu KBo XXV, 1, 2. Hoffentlich gelangen nicht auch noch Texte, die womöglich ausserhalb von Hattuša geschrieben worden sind, in das Sammelbecken aheth. "Originale".]

[KUB XXXIX, 64 als Totenritual, 10 frgm. Zeilen; 1963 nach H. Otten in altem Duktus; nicht bei Vf. und StBoT 23.]

KUB XLIII [1972] s. §5 Nr. 14!

KUB XLVIII [1977] hält H. Berman Nr. 54 (Hattisch) für alten Duktus, was möglich ist. (Aheth. Sprache ausser in den Zusatzstücken Nr. 77, 79 [H. Klengel, a.a.O.] und in 101-103 [ganz oder zum Teil] = Landschenkungsurkunden (LS) 25-27 in Nr. 81 und Nr. 89 [HW² 318a sub III] historisch mit aheth. *šu* [cf. *Mat. heth. Thes.* 1, Nr. 2].)

KBo XVI s. §5, Nr. 12; XVII s. §5, Nr. 9-11; XVIII nur ein aheth. Text, sc. "Original" in nicht-schwerem Duktus Nr. 151 (§§3, 6). KBo XIX [1970]: unter dem Heth. nur aheth. Zusatzfragmente Nr. 1-2, 90f., 96f. KBo XX [1971] s. §§4-5 passim; einige aheth. Fragmente z.B. unter den ersten Nummern. KBo XXI [1973]: z.B. geht das brauchbare EZEN Nr. 90 auf aheth. Vorlage zurück; winzige Schrift nach Autopsie. KBo XXII [1974]: aheth. Sprache haben die "Originale" Nr. 1 (bearbeitet von A. Archi, *Festschrift Laroche* [1979] 45ff.) und Nr. 2 (StBoT 17, A, CTH 3), beide "alter Duktus" genannt; aheth. wohl noch Nr. 81 und 170 (Dupl. zu KUB XLI, 23 = Bo 2544, Vf. loc. cit. 260). KBo XXV [1979] s. §§4-5, 7 passim.

§8. Für die zeitliche Dauer des schweren Duktus hat man die gesiegelten und daher zeitgenössischen Landschenkungsurkunden (LS) bemüht; = CTH 221f. (und RHA XXXI)/Cat 154, 156 nach K.K. Riemschneider, MIO 6 [1958] 321-81 (mit LS 1 = CTH 223; LS 2-28 [29]), davon jetzt LS 25-27 ediert in KUB XLVIII, 101-103, wobei sich für LS 26 Korrekturen ergeben. Nicht sicher, ob man die akkad. LS aus İnandık (K. Balkan, 1973, mit Photos) und vielleicht (?) LS 3-6 und 1312/u (H. Otten, MDOG 103 [1971] 59ff., 62) als Texte in schwerem (altem) Duktus anerkennen darf; Zeichenformen nicht einheitlich nach K. Balkan, 1973, 90ff. Die vielfach diskutierte Problematik der LS (s. in der unten genannten Literatur) ist auch hier nicht lösbar, weil die LS sprachlich nicht viel aussagen, viele sehr fragmentarisch (und ohne erhaltenes Siegel) sind und das vergleichbare Namensmaterial zu dürftig ist.

H.G. Güterbock, SBo I (1940) 47ff., 74ff., mit Autographie von:

LS 2 ([wie LS 19 = KBo VIII, 26] mit Ḫuzziya-Siegel SBo Nr. 85 [CTH 221]);
LS 3-16 mit für anonym gehaltenen Tabarna-Siegeln;
Nr. 87 - negativ - in LS 3-6 [1312/u, MDOG 103 [1971] 61];
Nr. 88 B, C LS 7; ferner auf LS 28 aus Tarsus;
Nr. 89 auf frgm. LS 8, bzw.
mit verloren gegangenem Siegel bei LS 9-16 [17ff. aus MIO 6 = CTH 222].

H.G. Güterbock konstatierte S. 53 ausdrücklich, dass sich die Schrift von LS 2-16 in keiner Weise von der Schrift der übrigen Boğazköy-Tafeln unterscheide. S. 53ff. Datierung vor den Beginn des Neuen Reiches; jüngste LS Nr. 1 = KBo V, 7 von Arnuwanda I. und Schwester Ašmunikal mit dem Siegel Nr. 60, wo erstmalig der Königsname in heth. Hieroglyphen geschrieben wird.

K.K. Riemschneider (loc. cit., MIO 6 [1958]) datierte LS 2ff. in das "Mittlere Reich", einen [m.E. nicht wahrscheinlichen] Ḫuzziya II. nach Telipinu ansetzend.

Neuere schriftgeschichtliche Diskussion von LS 2ff.: Vf. KZ 83 [1969] 258 bei der Frage nach dem Ende des schweren (alten) Duktus: H.G. Güterbock hielt JAOS 84 [1964] 109 mit Anm. 20 LS 3 und 4 für die ältesten, aber nicht nach der Schrift. [Gleiches Ergebnis für aheth. Sprache von LS 3, 4 und 1312/u HW² s.v. *alaleššar*.] - Mir schienen nach Autopsie LS 2, 19 (Ḫuzziya) nicht den schweren Duktus zu zeigen.

H. Otten, MDOG 103 [1971] 59ff. (ohne Kenntnis der LS aus İnandık; mit Autographie aller unten unter Museumsnummern zitierten LS) anlässlich des Neufunds Bo 69/200 mit dem bisher unbekannten König *ta-ba-ar-na Ta-ḫa/ur-wa-i-li*, der nach Siegel und Schrift den LS von Ḫuzziya am nächsten stehe. Er bietet S. 62ff. versuchsweise erneut eine Entwicklung nach Siegeln und Schrift:

a) LS 3-6, 1312/u mit Siegel Nr. 87 hätten die "Charakteristika der alten Schrift", aber mit einigen Unterschieden.

b) LS 7 mit dem typologisch entwickelteren Siegel Nr. 88: Schrift sei alt, aber nicht so schwer wie bei LS 4,5.

c) LS 2, 19 (Ḫuzziya) mit Siegel Nr. 85 und dazu vielleicht [m.E. sicher] noch LS 22 = KBo IX, 72: Das Siegel wirke typologisch entwickelter, Schrift wirke graziler und erweise insofern deutlich einen zeitlichen Abstand von dem alten, schweren Duktus von LS 3-7. Daraus ergäbe sich aber keine eindeutige Datierung von Ḫuzziya vor oder nach Telipinu; jedoch Tabarna-Urkunden älter als die von Ḫuzziya und als Taḫa/urwaili und Alluwamana (SBo I Nr. 86).

d) Über Ḫapuwaššu GAL DUMU.É.GAL, den Grossen der Palastjunker, verknüpft H. Otten an Texten mit verlorenem Siegel: LS 11, 12 (Duktus ziemlich alt, aber nicht so schwer wie bei LS 5, 6); LS 18+20 (=162/k + 38/l, Siegel fast ganz zerstört) in "ziemlich altem Duktus" und 301/z (ohne Autographie), und 518/z in "ältlichem Duktus".

e) Abschliessend fragt sich H. Otten, ob die anonymen Tabarna-Urkunden jünger seien als die aheth. "Originale" HG, A [von ihm und Vf. auf Ḫattušili I. datiert; nun aber als Abschrift jünger (§3!)], StBoT 8 und Zidanza-Vertrag CTH 25.

Grundlegend jetzt K. Balkan, 1973, mit der Veröffentlichung der akkad. LS aus İnandık. Hier so viel:

a) Er verknüpft diese S. 53f. einerseits durch den Namen ^{m}*Tandamei* UGULA 1 *LI* $^{LÚ.MEŠ}$IŠ mit LS 3 Vs. 13(!) und 1312/u Vs. 16f. und datiert sie andererseits S. 72 durch einen Vergleich mit Namen aus der Palastchronik CTH 8 mit hoher Wahrscheinlichkeit in die Zeit Ḫattušilis I. Wahrscheinlich ist auch die schrittweise S. 75ff. vorgenommene Datierung von LS 4 (5*[?]*, 6*[?]*) mit demselben Siegel wie LS 3, 1312/u und von LS 11, 12, 18+20 usw. (oben bei H. Otten sub d)) in dieselbe Zeit. *[*Zu LS 11, 12 mit Obermundschenk Zidanni gehört dann m.E. noch LS 26; KUB XLVIII, 102 Vs. 7 lies *]*Ẹ *Iš-pu-i-ši-me-i.]*

b) K. Balkans weiterer Versuch, loc. cit. 76f., alle bisher für anonym gehaltenen Tabarna-Siegel in Siegel Ḫattušilis I. mit dessen Namen Tabarna umzudeuten, bleibt dagegen unsicher wegen der dürftigen Überlieferung der LS mit und ohne erhaltenem Siegel und - nach bisherigem Wissen - auch wegen LS 28 aus Tarsus in dem in aheth. Zeit selbständigen Staat Kizzuwatna.

c) Schwere Bedenken gegen unsere Ermittlung von aheth. "Originalen" an sich und erst recht gegen solche Ermittlungen an sprachlich nicht aussagekräftigen Bruchstücklein erweckt K. Balkans sauberer, hochinteressanter Vergleich der Zeichenformen aus der LS İnandık (Spalte I) mit LS 2 (Ḫuzziya), LS 3-16, 1312/u, 162/k + 38/l = LS 18+20, 518/z (II), Zukraši-Text CTH 15 (III), StBoT 8 (IV) und den normalen Zeichenformen nach E.O. Forrer, 1 BoTU (V) auf S. 90ff. Interesse erheischen die handschriftlichen Varianten ein und derselben LS und das - mit H.G. Güterbock, SBo I *[*1940*]* 53 übereinstimmende (?) - Ergebnis, dass man nach den Zeichenformen die LS 2 von Ḫuzziya nicht von den älteren LS İnandık, LS 3, 4, 1312/u usw. unterscheiden kann.

Balkan, 1973	=	K. Balkan, *Eine Schenkungsurkunde aus der althethitischen Zeit, gefunden in Inandık 1966* *[*Ankara 1973*]*.
Cat	=	E. Laroche, *Catalogue des textes hittites* (RHA XIV/58-59, XV/60, XVI/62 *[*1956-58*]*).
CTH	=	E. Laroche, *Catalogue des textes hittites* *[*1971*]*; *Addenda* RHA XXXI *[*1972 (1974)*]*.
Festschrift Laroche	=	*Florilegium Anatolicum, Mélanges offerts à Emmanuel Laroche* *[*1979*]*.
Festschrift Otten	=	*Festschrift Heinrich Otten* *[*1973*]*.
Güterbock, 1978	=	*Some aspects of Hittite Prayers*, in *The Frontiers of Human Knowledge* (Skrifter rörande Uppsala universitet, C: 38, Acta Universitatis Upsaliensis *[*Uppsala 1978*]* 125ff.).
HG	=	(J. Friedrich), *Die hethitischen Gesetze* *[*1959*]*.
HW^{2}	=	J. Friedrich & A. Kammenhuber, *Hethitisches Wörterbuch*, Zweite, völlig neubearbeitete Auflage auf der Grundlage der edierten hethitischen Texte *[*1975ff.*]*.
IF	=	*Indogermanische Forschungen*.
KZ	=	*Zeitschrift für Vergleichende Sprachforschung*.
Mat. heth. Thes.	=	*Materialien zu einem hethitischen Thesaurus*, herausg. von A. Kammenhuber *[*1974ff.*]*.

MSS = *Münchener Studien zur Sprachwissenschaft.*

SBo = H.G. Güterbock, *Siegel aus Boğazköy I* [AfO Beiheft 5, 1940], *II* [AfO Beiheft 7, 1942].

StBoT = *Studien zu den Boğazköy-Texten*, herausg. von H. Otten.

THeth = *Texte der Hethiter*, herausg. von A. Kammenhuber.

---

1 Zusätzliche schriftgeschichtliche Lit. zu THeth 9 [1979] und unten §§3ff. passim: E. Laroche, *Problèmes de l'écriture cunéiforme hittite*, in *Annali della Scuola Superiore di Pisa*, Serie III, Vol. VIII/3 [Pisa 1978] 739ff. (sehr reserviert gegen die Paläographie der Schule H. Ottens). J.J.S. Weitenberg, *Einige Bemerkungen zu den heth. Diphtong-Stämmen*, in *Hethitisch und Indogermanisch*, Innsbrucker Beiträge zur Sprachwissenschaft 25 [1979] 289ff. (mit genauesten Datierungen der Einzelbelege nach der bisherigen Lit.). H. Otten und seine Schule: H. Otten, *Original oder Abschrift - Zur Datierung von CTH 258 [KUB XIII 9+]*, in *Festschrift Laroche*, 274ff. (ohne Beweis für einen früheren Tutḫaliya; erinnert sei nochmals, wie schon KZ 83 [1969] 278[64], daran, dass H. Otten, MDOG 91 [1958] 73-5 das Dupl. 99/p[+] mitbenützt hat, um die Schicht Ḫattuša-Unterstadt 1a auf Tutḫaliya IV. bzw. nach Muwatalli zu datieren). E. Neu, *Zum sprachlichen Alter des Ḫukkana-Vertrages [Šuppiluliumas I.]*, in KZ 93 [1979] 64-84 (versucht mit denselben graphischen Kriterien, die THeth 9, 150ff. als nicht relevant abgelehnt wurden, das Original Ḫuqq B als mheth. und eine nähere Beziehung des Mheth. zur "älteren Sprache" als zum Jheth. zu beweisen. Dafür fügt er als neuen Beweis das Pronomen *a-ši* [belegt ab Aheth. in Abschriften] und *i-ni* [erst nach-aheth.!] ein. Da nach HW[2] s.v. *aši*(Etymologie) aber sein Sohn Muršili II. ebenso schreibt (neben *e-ni*), müsste logischerweise nach E. Neu auch das "klassische" Jheth. Muršilis II. mittelhethitisch werden). N. Oettinger übernimmt in seiner überarbeiteten, von Karl Hoffmann und H. Eichner betreuten Dissertation "*Die Stammbildung des heth. Verbums*" [Erlangen 1979] 573ff. (7ff. passim) mit dem Material aus H. Ottens Thesaurus auch dessen Datierungen. Beim Aheth. unterscheidet er - im Gegensatz zu F. Starke, StBoT 23 [1977] 10f. (hier §§5-6) - aber nicht zwischen den von ihm Texte in "althethitischem" und "typisch althethitischem Duktus" Genanntem.

2 KBo XVIII, 151 wird von H. Otten zur Zeit zum Mheth. gerechnet! Vgl. E. Neu, KZ 93 [1979] 68 und N. Oettinger, *Dissertation*, 576ff. mit einer ziemlich heterogenen, "Tafeln in mittelhethitischem Duktus" genannten Liste.

NOTES ON SUMERIAN GRAMMAR

Irina T. Kaneva (Leningrad)

In continuation of her studies on Sumerian grammar,[1] the author of the present paper now makes an attempt to explain the presence of the dimensional prefix[2] of the comitative case in a series of finite verbal forms which do not have appropriate correlation in the sentence, i.e. a noun in the comitative case.

Dimensional relations could be expressed in Sumerian in structures of finite forms of the verb as dimensional prefixes composed of a pronominal element (denoting the person of the indirect object) and of the appropriate dimensional demonstrative element. In cases where the indirect object is represented by a pronoun, it is not as a rule lexically realized in the sentence, its presence being shown only by the appropriate dimensional prefix of the finite verbal form.

The comitative case in Sumerian, along with other meanings, could stand for the means of the action (including means expressed by nouns of the socially-passive class)[3]: d u m u K i š^{ki}- k e$_4$- n e ^{giš}a l - g a r - s u r$_{10}$- d a e - n e i m - d i - n e "citizens of Kish are playing on the 'algarsur'-instrument" (FA 33-4), š è m - a - n i r - r a - d a X ḫ é - e m - m i - s i - i g "you had led (somebody) into silence with the drum of weeping" (EWO 441). The comitative case appearing in the same meaning with nouns of the socially-active class[3] stood for the personal object, the mediator, for example: k i - g a - a g u r u š - e a m a - u g u - n i - i r k i n m u - u n - d a - r a - š i - i n - g i$_4$ "the young man has sent a message by a messenger to his mother, to his life-giving mother" (VS X 123:iii.17), where k i - g a - a derives from *k i - g a - a - d a. Judging from the context and pattern of the sentences (analogous to that quoted above), the comitative case expresses the same relations in the three following instances: e n s í - d a L a g a š^{ki}- e ḫ é - g á l - l a š u m u - d a - p e š - e "Lagash through its ensi enlarges prosperity" (Gudea Cyl. B XIX 14-15), ^{d}E n - l í l - d a u n - e ḫ é - g á l - l a š u m u - u n - d a - a n - p e š - e "the people through Enlil enlarges prosperity" (TCL XV 36:19), and ^{d}E n - k i - d a k a l a m - e ḫ é - g á l - l a š u m u - u n - d i - n i - i b - m ú - m ú (variant: š u m u - u n - d a - a n - p e š - e) "the land gets prosperity by prayer through Enki" (EWO 328).

In the examples quoted there are sentences expressing some kind of action. The Sumerian verbal base does not by itself express either action or state, therefore it could be used in a dual way. The meaning of the verbal base appears formally through the structure of the sentence, i.e. a) through its morphological setting: the finite verbal forms expressing action are conjugated in a different way from those expressing state; b) through its syntactical setting: structures with verbal forms expressing action have quite a different construction from those sentences with verbal forms expressing state. In sentences with verbal forms expressing state two components have to be present: the subject of the state (the noun in the absolute case) and the predicate. In sentences with verbal forms expressing action three components are present: the subject of the action (the noun in the ergative case), the subject of the state (a noun in the absolute case) and the predicate. For example: IM- a n - n a ḫ é - d a - a - g i_4 "let the rain stop for him" (lit.: "let it turn away from him", Gudea Stat. B IX 19); [d u] m u - ù a m a - n i - r a g ù - d ù - d a n u - m a - n a - d u g_4 "the son did not oppose his mother" (lit.: "the son did not utter (his) opposition...", Gudea Cyl. A XIII 4-5).

Judging from the formal criteria - that is, from the verbal forms and the sentence structure - as well as the usual types of sentence (e.g. ì - g u b - e n "I stand", ì - n à d - e n "you lie", é r e n - b i a l - t u r "their army is small", etc.) we should include in the group of sentences expressing state a) sentences which are semantically close to constructions expressing action, but differing from them in not having the subject of the state (= the direct object), for example: ù s a n l a - b a - s ì g ^{kuš}á - s i l a - b a - s ì g "the whip did not beat, the lash did not beat" (i.e. they were in the state of not-beating, Gudea Stat. B IV 10-11); u š u m g a l e d e n - n a b a - k i n - g á - g i m "as a big snake which is burrowing (searching) in the steppe" (ELA 351) [a type of sentence which is rare in Sumerian texts]; b) sentences semantically close to a passive, but not expressing the subject of the action, for example: m u k u - l i b a - g a z - <š è> "because Kuli was killed" (NSGU 41:5); e g e r - a - n i ù d a m - d u m u - n i d u m u - B a - b a - m e - k e_4-n e b a - n e - s u m - m u "his inheritance and his wife and children were given away to the sons of Babame" (NSGU 41:6'-8'); m u - z u - š è t ù r ḫ é - e m - š i - d ù - d ù "let sheep-pens be built for you" (Gudea Cyl. B XXII 17); u d - 7 - à m š e l a - b a - à r a "the grain was not being ground for 7 days" (Gudea Stat. B VII 30); [m] u ? - n a m - l ú - u_{18}- l u b a - g a r - r a - a - b a "after the name of the people has been established" (GH 9); i m - b i ..... k u r - ḫ a - š u - ú r - r a - t a i m - k í d - a "this clay .... is being brought from the hills of the *ḫašur*-tree" (LE 415-6); š a g_4 b a - s î g "the heart is broken" (GLL 23).

This type of sentence is often represented in the Sumerian texts. We may assume that the expression *čelovek ubit* "the man (is) killed" (and the examples similar to this quoted above) was assumed - in similar contexts - by the Sumerians as the state of the person himself and was regarded as close to the type of expression *čelovek umer/mërtv* "the man died/is dead", and hence there was no need to refer to the source or cause of this state.

We have succeeded in finding only two examples with a lexically-indicated source or cause of the state. In one of them (which belongs to the Neo-Sumerian period, when Sumerian was probably still alive, a spoken language, though already subject to strong influences from the other spoken language of the country, Akkadian: the document is dated to 2032 B.C.) there is a phrase composed of š u "hand" + name of the person + the postposition -t a: ^{d}U r- ^{d}L a m a a b - b a Š e š - k a l - l a - k e_4 .... š e - b a s í g - b a š u - A l - l a d u b - s a r - t a n a m - ì r - š è b a - n a - s u m - [m a] "(they had confirmed) that the grain-ration (and) wool-ration were given by the scribe Alla (lit.: from the hand of the scribe Alla) to Ur-Lama, father of Šeškala, because of his being a slave (lit.: owing to slavery)" (NSGU 32:5-9). In the other example (from the Late Sumerian period, beginning of the 2nd millennium B.C.), the cause of the state is expressed by nouns in the comitative case: u r u n u - d ù [é] n u - d ù ^{d}E n - k i - d a MAR.DÚ m a š - a n š e s a g - e - e š m u - n i - r [i g_7] "to him who is not building cities, to him who is not building houses (for the citizens of the land) Mardu, wild animals are granted through the god Enki" (EWO 246-7). Therefore, with nouns of the socially-active class, the comitative case could express the mediator of the action and the cause or reason of the state in question.

It is quite possible that among the finite verbal forms having the inexplicable dimensional infix - d a - cases could occur where this - d a - stands for the same meaning. Let us first examine sentences with verbal forms expressing action. Here, first of all, a group of examples could be set apart with one common feature: they all begin with applying to a person (mostly a god) who, to judge from the context, appears afterwards as mediator: e n - dN i n - g í r - s u š a g4- b i n u - m u - ù - d a - z u "Lord Ningirsu, you did not let me know the meaning (of the prophecy)" (lit.: I do not know its meaning because of you; Gudea Cyl. A XIII 21-2); e n-dN i n - g í r - s u m à a n - n a m u - ù - d a - z u "Lord Ningirsu, what you had given me to know" (lit.: what do I know because of you?; Gudea Cyl. A IX 4); l u g a l - m u t u k u m - b i k u r - r a i - i n - t u r5- t u r5 - d è - e n dU t u ḫ é - m e - d a - a n - z u "My Lord, if you wish to go to the mountain, let Utu know (this) through you" (GLL 9-10, 12); u d - d a u d - u g5 - g e - m u n u - u n - z u e d e n a m a - u g u - m u i n i m m u - e - d è - z u - u n "if she did not know the day of my death, steppe, you let my mother know through your means" (DD 13); dE n - l í l ḫ é - g á l - z u a -GABA g u b - b a - à m s u m - m a - d a - a b (var.: dE n - l í l s u m - m a - d a - a b) l a - z u s u m - m a - d a - a b U r íki - š è g a - g i n í d - d a a - e š t u b s u m - m a - d a - a b U r íki - š è g a - g i n "Enlil your abundance ..... bestow it upon me (i.e. Su'en) through you; your craft bestow upon me through you, and I shall go to Ur; many carp in the rivers bestow upon me through you, and I shall go to Ur" (MNS 151:57-9 = NSJN 330-2); a - a dM u - u l - l í l ṭ u - m u - z u m u - l u k u r - r a n a m - b a - d a - a n - g ú r - e k u g - š a g5- g a - z u s a ḫ a r - k u r - r a - k a n a m - b a - a n - d a - š á r - e z a - g ì n - š a g5- g a - z u z a - z a d i m - m a - k a n a m - b a - d a - a n - s i - í l - l e gišt a š k a r i n - z u g i š - n a g a r - r a - k a n a m - b a - d a - d a r - d a r - r e k i - s i k i l -dG a - š a - a n - n a k u r - r a n a m - b a - d a - a n - g ú r - e "Father Enlil, through you(r favour) let nobody kill your daughter in the nether world; through you(r favour) let nobody cover your wonderful silver with the dust of the nether world; through you(r favour) let nobody crush your wonderful lapis lazuli for the stone of the jeweller; through you(r favour) let nobody split your box-tree up for carpenter's beams; through you(r favour) let nobody kill the girl Inanna in the nether world" (IDNW 43-7).

To the second group belong examples constructed after a similar pattern: the man (or: the god) is realizing some action and the people (or: the land, the city) because of (- d a -) him get or do something. The sentence-pattern k a l a m - e ḫ é - g á l - l a š u ḫ é - a - d a - p e š - e "the land because of you increases abundance" (Gudea Cyl. A XI 9) has served as the basis for selecting this group of examples. This differs from the other example quoted above (dE n - k i - d a k a l a m - e ḫ é - g á l - l a š u m u - u n - d i - n i - i b - m ú - m ú [var.: š u m u - u n - d a - a n - p e š - e] "the land gets prosperity by prayer by Enki") in that it lacks the noun in the comitative case. The context of the passage which interests us at present is the following: "Ningirsu says to Gudea: Gudea, when *you* will build up my temple, *I* shall call rain into the sky, from the sky abundance will fall upon you, the country through you will indeed increase its abundance".

We shall now quote examples which seem to us to belong in the same category: G ù - d é - a i m ù - š u b - b a ì - g a r n í g - d u7 p a b í - é d é - a s i g$_4$-b i p a - é d m u - n i - g á - g á k u r - k u r - r e i à m u - d a - s u d - e e r e n m u - d a - s u d - e u r u - n é k i - L a g a š^{ki}- e SIG- n i - a u d m u - d ì - n i - í b - z a l - e "Gudea has put the clay into the brick-mould, has done everything necessary, has favourably *formed* bricks for the temple, all the countries offer oil because of him, offer cedar because of him, his city, the land of Lagash, because of him spend the days ......" (Gudea Cyl. A XVIII 24-XIX 2); g á n - g a l - g a l - e s u m a - r a - a b - í l - e e p a$_5$ g ú - b i m a - r a - a b - z ì g - z ì g d u l - d u l k i a n u - è d^2- d a a m a - r a - è d - d è KI.EN.GI- r e$_6$ i à - d i r i g m u - d a - d é s í g - d i r i g m u - d a - l a l "I shall put into order spacious fields for you, I shall lift water into canals for you, to the mounds where the water does not reach the water will be lifted up for you, Sumer shall offer much oil because of me, there will be weighed much wool because of me" (Gudea Cyl. A XI 12-17).

Having surveyed verbal forms expressing action, we may, we believe, separate from among verbal forms expressing state instances with the dimensional infix - d a - reflecting the cause or source of the state in question: ^{im}š u - r i n - n a - t a è d - d a - z u - d è b a - e - d a - g a z "when you take (this) out of the kiln, you break (it)" (lit.: the tablet will be broken because of you; D.1 179-80); s i n u - m u - e - d a - í l - i? a - b a - à m s i - í l - i - d è - n a m m à - e n u - m u - e - d a - g a z i - n i - d u - d u - d è - *e n* "you will not toss me (lit.: I shall not *be* in the state of tossing by you), who shall toss me? I shall not be killed by you, I shall go away" (SP I 112).

Hence, 1) the dimensional infix of the comitative case did not have an appropriate correlation (i.e. a noun in the comitative case) in those sentences in which the indirect object was represented by a pronoun without lexical expression; 2) nouns of the socially-active class in the comitative case could express the mediator in the action and the cause or source of the state, and the dimensional infix of the comitative case could be used with this meaning.

D.1 = Edubba Dialogue No. 1 (quoted from G.B. Gragg, *Sumerian Dimensional Infixes*, Kevelaer/Neukirchen-Vluyn, 1973, 53)

DD = B. Alster, *Dumuzi's Dream. Aspects of Oral Poetry in a Sumerian Myth*, Copenhagen 1972.

ELA = S.N. Kramer, *Enmerkar and the Lord of Aratta*, Philadelphia 1952

EWO = S.N. Kramer, *Enki und die Weltordnung*, *Wissenschaftliche Zeitschrift der Fr.-Schiller-Universität Jena* 9 (1959-60) 231-56; A. Falkenstein, ZA 56 (NF 22) (1964) 44-113.

FA = A. Falkenstein, *Fluch über Akkade*, ZA 57 (NF 23) (1965) 43-124

GH = S.N. Kramer, *Gilgamesh and the ḫuluppu-Tree*, Chicago 1938

GLL = S.N. Kramer, *Gilgamesh and the Land of the Living*, JCS 1 (1947) 3-46

Gudea Cyl. A and B quoted from F. Thureau-Dangin, *Les cylindres de Goudéa* ...., Paris 1925; Stat., quoted from E. de Sarzec, *Découvertes en Chaldée*...., Paris 1884-1912

IDNW = S.N. Kramer, *Inanna's Descent to the Netherworld*, JCS 5 (1951) 1-17

LE = C. Wilcke, *Das Lugalbandaepos*, Wiesbaden 1969

MNS = Å. Sjöberg, *Der Mondgott Nanna-Suen in der sumerischen Überlieferung*, I, Stockholm 1960

NSJN = A.J. Ferrara, *Nanna-Suen's Journey to Nippur*, Rome 1973

NSGU = A. Falkenstein, *Die neusumerischen Gerichtsurkunden*, Munich 1956-57

SP = E.I. Gordon, *Sumerian Proverbs*, Philadelphia 1959

---

1 So far published: *Šumerski geroičeski epos. Grammatičeski očerk* [The Sumerian Heroic Epic. A grammatical study] VDI 1964/3, 252-60; *Glagoly dviženia (na materiale šumerskovo geroičeskovo eposa)* [Verbs of Motion (on the material of the Sumerian Heroic Epic)], *Assiriologia i egiptologia. Sbornik statei*, Leningrad 1964, 51-9; *Spryaženie šumerskovo glagola (na materiale šumerskikh geroiko-epičeskikh tekstov)* [Conjugation of the Sumerian Verb (on the material of the Sumerian Heroic-Epic texts)], *Peredneaziatski Sbornik* 2, Moscow 1966, 16-96, 165-8; Review of Th. Jacobsen, *"About the Sumerian Verb"*, VDI 1968/2, 176-80; *Participles in Sumerian*, MIO 16, 1970, 541-65; *Iz istori šumerskoi padežnoi sistemy (Funktsi orudino-otložitel'novo padeža)* [From the history of the Case System in Sumerian (Function of the Instrumental-Ablative)], *Drevni Vostok* 3, Erevan 1978, 47-54, 261-2; *Napravitel'ny (allativny) padež v šumerskom yazyke* [Directive (Allative) Case in the Sumerian language], *Peredneaziatski Sbornik* 3, Moscow 1979, 113-21, 271.

2 For the use of the term "prefix" instead of the more commonly used "infix" see I.M. Diakonoff, *Yazyki drevnei Perednei Azi*, Moscow 1967, p. 66 tab. 2; id., *Yazyki Azi i Afriki*, III, Moscow 1979, p. 26 tab. 2; id., in *Sumerological Studies in Honor of Th. Jacobsen* (AS 20), 116[34].

3 For the terms "socially-active" and "socially-passive" see I.M. Diakonoff, *Yazyki drevnei Perednei Azi*, Moscow 1967, 54 para. 5:
sotsial'no-aktivni = Personenklasse, animate, and
sotsial'no-passivni = Sachklasse, inanimate.

ON THE TYPOLOGY OF THE HURRO-URARTIAN VERB

M.L. Khačikjan (Yerevan)

The Hurro-Urartian language is of ergative type, with several features characteristic of languages of active typology, following the terminology of G.A. Klimov.

These features are especially apparent in the material of the "Babylonian" dialect (the language of the incantations from Mari and those published by Van Dijk) in the so-called "participial" or I conjugation, which is formed by adding the following pronominal endings: *-tta* (1 p.sg.); *-di-lla* (1 p.pl.); *-b*, *-n*, *-Ø* (3 p.sg.), *-lla* (3 p.pl.) - to the so-called "participial" form, composed of the verbal root + vowels *-i*, *-a*, *-o* (markers of transitivity, intransitivity and state respectively). It is worth noting that *-b* (in Urartian *-bə*) is not known in all Hurrian dialects: it is present in the "Babylonian" dialect, in the dialect of Urkiš, in Urartian and in personal names, where it is to be considered as an archaism; for examples see Appendix, §1.

One further remark: the subject of the transitive verb in the I conjugation needs no ergative marker; cf. §2.

Characteristic of the "Babylonian" dialect is the opposition of the I conjugation forms expressing action (transitive (marker: *-i*) or intransitive (marker: *-a*)) to those expressing state: the 3 p.sg. of the verbs of action is formed by adding the element *-b* to the verb of action, while the 3 p.sg. forms expressing state take the zero marker or *-n*; see §3. Later on, the disappearance of this opposition causes the disappearance of *-b* in later Hurrian dialects.

The development of the Urartian verb was somewhat different. As a result of the replacement of the opposition action:state by the opposition transitivity:intransitivity a new, II conjugation (see below) came into being, and the transitive verbs were no longer conjugated in the old way (I conjugation), the formant *-bə* thus becoming the marker of intransitive action only; see §1(c).

On the other hand, the forms expressing state lost their marker *-o* and were given that of intransitive action, *-a*. Thus the formant *-a* became the marker of intransitivity in general. The only verb in *-o* in Urartian - *man-o* "to be" - is to be considered as a relic of the active past of the Hurro-Urartian language. It is probable that the suffix *-m* of the form *pahaštum* of the TišaRI-inscription ("Urkiš"-dialect) corresponds to the *-b* of other dialects, and not to *-n*, as was once supposed, cf. I.M. Diakonoff, *Hurrisch und Urartäisch* (München 1971) 111.

Besides the conjugational system described above, there is in Hurro-Urartian another, reflecting the later, ergative state of the language (the so-called II conjugation). This system covers only the transitive verb, while the intransitive verb is conjugated in the old way. In this case, unlike that of the I conjugation, the subject takes the ergative marker *-š̄* (positionally voiced *[z̄]*) in Hurrian and *-šə* in Urartian, going back to the suffix *-š̄š̄e* (Hur.), *-šə* (Ur.); see below. The verbal form of the II conjugation contains the verbal basis + personal endings, which go back to the possessive pronouns, see §4. In Hurrian the II conjugation is completely subjective (i.e. the verbal form contains only the subject marker, which is obligatory, while the object marker is optional), see §5(a). In Urartian the conjugation is mixed:

the verbal form may contain the marker of the subject, as well as that of the object, both of them being often optional; see §5(b). The subject markers, as was already shown, go back to the possessive pronouns, while the object markers are taken from the I conjugation (see above, p.), and are given a new, objective function. Unlike Urartian, where the transitive verbs are conjugated in the new (II) conjugation only, in Hurrian the I conjugation is preserved for transitive as well as intransitive verbs; see §6.

Somewhat isolated from all the other Hurrian dialects is the "Ugaritic I" dialect (the language of the Sumero-Hurrian vocabulary), where the 3 p.sg. verb conjugated in the I type has, instead of the expected subject markers *-b* or *-n*, the ending *-z̄* known in other dialects as a gerundive element; see §7.

Before we try to explain the meaning of this element, we shall examine the attributive construction in Hurro-Urartian. Characteristic of the attributive construction with the attribute in the Genitive is the phenomenon called *Suffixübertragung*, a kind of agreement in which the inflection of the determined noun is repeated in the attribute, being added to it by means of the coordinative particle *-ne*; see §8(a). In cases where the determined noun is not inflected (i.e., stands in abs. sg.), the coordinative particle is no longer needed; see §8(b).

The situation is similar with the attributive clause, which is virtually a variety of attribute. There are two types of attributive clause in Hurrian: that with the relative pronoun *je-*, and that without it; see §9. In the attributive clause the inflection of the determined noun is added to the kernel of the attributive clause (the verb), by means of the coordinative particle *-s̄s̄e* (not *-ne*, as in the case of the attribute in the Genitive). When the attributive clause is not introduced by *ije-* the particle *-s̄s̄e* is necessary, regardless of whether the determined word is inflected or not, for in that case *-s̄s̄e* is the only marker of the attributive clause; see §9(b). Thus the function of *-s̄s̄e* in the attributive clause introduced by *ije-* is the same as that of *-ne* in the nominal attribute, whereas in the attributive clause without *ije-* the function of *-s̄s̄e* may be compared with that of the Genitive marker *-we* in the nominal attribute. The typologically earlier type of the attributive clause with the coordinative suffix *-šə* is not attested in Urartian. It is entirely superseded by another type, introduced by the relative pronoun *alə*; see §10.

Now briefly about the so-called Hurrian copula *-n* (sg.). Genetically as well as semantically it goes back to the subject of state *-n(na)*, its plural form being *-lla*, just like the 3 p. pl. of the subject marker; see §11. On the other hand, it is connected with the coordinative particle *-ne* (the second, later, function of this particle being definitive), for it actually coordinates the subject with the predicate. Consequently, the subject of state *-n(na)*, as well as all the pronouns of that set (*-tta*, *-dilla*, etc.), perform a coordinative function.

The second conjugation, as was mentioned above, is possessive, which means that here too we have to deal with the coordinative function. That is a good reason to conclude that there is a connection between the coordinative particle *-s̄s̄e* and the ergative marker.

We may now return to the I conjugation in the "Ugaritic I" dialect. What has been said above elucidates the nature of the particle *-z̄*: it has a coordinative function and goes back to the suffix *-s̄s̄e*. The difference between the element *-z* and the subject markers *-b*, *-n*, etc. perhaps lies in the following distinction: the former performs a coordinative function without any concretization, while the function of the latter is, besides the coordinative function, to demonstrate the person and number of the subject. That is why the plural forms in the "Ugaritic I" dialect require, apart from -*z̄*, an additional -*lla*; see §12.

As was mentioned above, the markers of transitivity, intransivity and state are -*i*, -*a* and -*o* respectively. The situation is somewhat different in the "Urkiš"-dialect of Hurrian and in Urartian, where, besides the usual transitive marker -*i* (in non-predicative(?) participle), there appears another one, -*u*; see §13.

To sum up: originally the Hurro-Urartian language was a language of active typology with the opposition of action to state expressed by the opposition of the subject of action (marker -*b*) to the subject of state (marker -*n* or -*∅*), and, perhaps, the opposition of the action marker to the state marker as well. There is no possibility of reconstructing the action marker, for three different formants are attested: -*i* and -*u*, expressing transitive, and -*a*, expressing intransitive action. As to the marker of state, it was perhaps -*o*. The next period, which may be called the transition period from active to ergative typology, was associated with the following changes: within the verbs of action two groups came into being: a group of verbs expressing transitive action (marker -*i*, -*u*), and a group expressing intransitive action (-*a*). In the next stage a new type of conjugation (the II conjugation) came into being. This marked the establishment of the ergative system, with its opposition of transitivity to intransitivity.

As the opposition transitive action (-*i*): intransitive action (-*a*): state (-*o*), and, later on, the II conjugation appeared, the need to oppose the subject of action (-*b*) to the subject of state (-*n*) no longer arose. As a result, -*b* disappeared in most of the Hurrian dialects, while -*n* lost its function as subject of state and became a copula. The presence of the opposition -*i* : -*a* : -*o* is exactly the reason for the use of the element -*z̄* with all verbs, without any differentiation, in the "Ugaritic I" dialect.

In Urartian we have the following situation: unlike Hurrian, where the transitive verb may be conjugated in both I and II types, the Urartian transitive verb is conjugated in the new II type only. The next peculiarity of the Urartian verb is that the element -*bə* has not disappeared. Formerly a marker of action, this element was here transformed into the marker of the subject of the intransitive action exclusively. Later on, when the I conjugation type completely absorbed the verbs of state, the element -*bə* became the marker of the subject of both intransitive action and state. These peculiarities, as well as the disappearance of special forms expressing state in Urartian, unlike Hurrian, testify that the Urartian language is further developed and is more consistently ergative than Hurrian.

IH = E.A. Speiser, *Introduction to Hurrian*, New Haven 1941.

Mari = F. Thureau-Dangin, *Tablettes hurrites provenant de Mâri*, RA 36, 1939, 1-28.

Mit. = J. Friedrich, *Kleinasiatische Sprachdenkmäler*, Berlin 1932, 8-32 (Der Mitanni-Brief).

UKN = G.A. Melikišvili, *Urartskie klinoobraznye nadpisi*, Moscow 1960.

Urkiš = A. Parrot & J. Nougayrol, *Un document de fondation hourrite*, RA 42, 1948, 1-20.

Voc. = F. Thureau-Dangin, *Vocabulaires de Ras-Shamra*, *Syria* 12, 1931, 225-266 (RŠ 8) and *Nouveaux fragments de vocabulaires de Ras-Shamra*,

Appendix

1 (a) "Babylonian" dialect: *pašš-i-b* Mari 1:3, 2:9; *šiw-a-b* VS 17 *[=NF 1]* 5:3,5.

(b) "Urkiš"-dialect: *pahašt-u-m* Urk. 6.

(c) Urartian: *nun-a-bə*, *ušt-a-bə* UKN, passim.

(d) *Un-a-b-*, *Ag-a-b-*, *Ḫaž-i-b-* cf. IH p. 85.

2 *šeniffu* ..... *šudaman paššoži* "and my brother sent to me" Mit. I:50

3 *pašš-i-b* Mari 1:3, 2:9; *ḫir-i-b* Mari 1:4, 2:11; *šiw-a-b* VS 17 *[=NF 1]* 5:3,5; *šatt/d-o-n* Mari 1:6.

4

	II conjugation	*Possessive pronouns*
1 sg.	*-aw*, *-affu*	*-iff(u)*
2 sg.	*-u*, *-o*	*-w/v*
3 sg.	*-a*, *-ja*	*-(i)je*, *-ja*
1 pl.	*-aw-ža*	*-iff-až*
3 pl.	*-(j)a-ža*	*-(i)ja-ž*

Only the forms of the "Mitannian" dialect of Hurrian are cited here.

5 (a) *ḫažož-aw* "I heard" Mit. II:7; *ḫažož-affu-n* "I heard him (listened to him)" Mit. IV:9.

(b) *ḫau-və* "I took" UKN, passim (*-və* is the subject marker of the 1 p. sg.). *ḫau-nə* "he took" UKN, passim (*-nə* is the object marker of the 3 p. sg.; the subject marker is not expressed here).

6 *šeniffu* .... *šudaman paššoži* "and my brother sent to me" Mit. I:50 (the subject *šeniffu* has no ergative marker), but *šeniffu-z paššož-a* "my brother (erg. sg.) sent" Mit. II:107-8.

7 *ḫil-i-žə* "he said" Voc. I:15; *tin-i-žə* "he built, made" Voc. I:20, etc.

8 (a) *Mizirre-we-ne-ž ewri-ž* "The lord (erg. sg.) of Egypt" Mit. I:85

(b) *tiža-man šeniffuwe* "and the heart (abs. sg.) of my brother" Mit. IV:32

9 (a) *ijallenin tiwena* .... *kadožaššena* "the words that he said" Mit. IV:30

(b) *aštin* .... *šeniffuwenen tižanna širašše* "the woman that suits the heart of my brother" Mit. IV:34.

10 *alu-šə* (erg. sg.) *inə*DUB-*te tuli/e* "whoever destroys this inscription" UKN, passim.

11 *Mane-n-an šeniffuwe paššitḫe* "and Mane is my brother's messenger" Mit. IV:35.

12 *kib-a-žə* "he placed" Voc. I:31; *kib-a-ža-lla* "they placed" Voc. I:32.

13 *pahašt-u-m* "he built" Urk. 6: *(j)emeni tašp-i halle* *ᵈLubadagaž tašpuin* "Whoever destroys ("destroying"), him let Lubadag destroy" Urk. 11-14.

DIE ÖSTLICHE NEUSTADT BABYLONS IN TEXTEN ALTBABYLONISCHER ZEIT

Horst Klengel (Berlin/DDR)

Die Wiederaufnahme archäologischer Forschungen im Stadtgebiet Babylons sowie die 1978 und 1979 seitens der State Organisation of Antiquities and Heritage des Iraq durchgeführten internationalen Symposien haben zu neuen Erkenntnissen auch im Hinblick auf die Topographie dieser ausgedehnten Stadtanlage geführt. Insbesondere handelt es sich dabei um Präzisierungen oder auch Korrekturen des neubabylonischen Stadtbildes, wie es auf Grund der Grabungen R. Koldeweys entworfen werden konnte.[1] Die für die altbabylonische Periode verfügbaren, vor allem in den Jahresdaten enthaltenen topographischen Angaben sind kürzlich von J. Renger zusammengestellt und ausgewertet worden (*Sumer* 35 [1979] 204-209). Wegen des hohen Grundwasserstandes hat die archäologische Forschung bislang nur während der Jahre 1907 bis 1912 in die altbabylonische Schicht vordringen können, als sich nach dem Bruch des Hindīje-Dammes das Grundwasser zeitweilig absenkte. Die Grabungen in dem von den Arabern "Merkes" ("Zentrum") genannten Teil des Stadtgebietes Babylons, etwa in der Mitte der neubabylonischen Innenstadt gelegen und zur Zeit des Grabungsbeginns den höchsten Punkt des Stadtgebietes darstellend,[2] haben hier ab etwa 12 Meter unter der Hügeloberfläche Wohnbauten zutage gebracht, die durch Funde datierter Tafeln eindeutig der altbabylonischen Zeit zugewiesen werden können, insbesondere den Regierungen der Nachfolger Ḫammurapis. Diese altbabylonischen Tafeln, die in größerer Zahl vor allem an zwei Stellen entdeckt wurden,[3] sind zum Teil in das Vorderasiatische Museum in Berlin gelangt.[4] Es handelt sich um Rechtsurkunden, Wirtschaftsnotizen und Briefe, die demnächst in VS 22 ediert werden sollen. Das große Interesse, das I.M. Diakonoff gerade der altbabylonischen Zeit entgegengebracht hat, läßt es rechtfertigen, einige Mitteilungen aus diesem Material in dieser Festschrift vorzulegen.

Bei der Arbeit an den altbabylonischen Texten aus Babylon fanden sich Hinweise auf die Existenz einer östlichen Neustadt Babylons, wie sie außerhalb dieses Materials bislang noch nicht festgestellt werden konnten. Bereits die in MDOG 38 [1908] 8 Abb.2 im Foto gezeigte Vorderseite einer Tafel aus der Zeit des Ammīditana erwähnt diesen Teil Babylons, ohne daß dieser Beleg bisher Beachtung gefunden hat. Die Tafel ist im Planquadrat 25 p 2, der wichtigsten Fundstelle altbabylonischer Texte, in einer Tiefe von -1,20 Meter gefunden worden. Soweit nach dem Foto, das den Tafelrand nicht erkennen läßt, erkennbar ist, handelt es sich um den Kauf von 1/3 sar (12 m^2) "Grundstück" (é - k i s l a ḫ), dessen Lage in Z.2 präzisiert wird: š à u r u - g i b i l - d u t u - è (- a ?), "in der Neustadt des Sonnenaufgangs". Es befand sich zwischen dem Hausgrundstück des Nakārum, Sohn des Ibni-Marduk, und dem des Ilumaluši; seine Vorderseite grenzte an eine Straße (s i l a), seine Rückseite an ein weiteres Hausgrundstück. Vom Vater des Nakārum, Ibni-Marduk, war es zur Zeit des Samsuiluna (Datum Z.9 f. wohl das des Jahres 30?) gekauft worden; durch vorliegende Urkunde wurde es von Nakārum, dem Grundstücksbesitzer (*bēl bītim*), an seinen Nachbarn Ilumaluši sowie einen weiteren Käufer *a-na ip-ṭe$_4$-er*, "zur Auslösung", für 5½ Sekel Silber gegeben. Nakārum, dessen Siegel auf der Vorderseite links oben zweimal erkennbar ist (über dem Siegel des Schreibers), ist auch durch VS 22:15 (s. dazu unten) als Grundstücksbesitzer in der östlichen Neustadt Babylons bezeugt.

Unter den im "Merkes" gefundenen Tafeln enthalten noch mehrere den Hinweis auf die östliche Neustadt, u r u$^{(ki)}$-g i b i l$^{(ki)}$- ^{d} u t u - è (- a) / *ālum eššum ṣīt ^{d}Šamši*:

VS 22:8 (VAT 13126, Hüllenfragment: VAT 19456). Kauf von 1/3 s a r (12 m^2) é - d ù - a, "Haus in vollständigem Bauzustand",[5] š à u r u ! - g i b i l - ^{d} u t u - è (Z.1). Verkäufer sind Šamuḫtum und ihr Sohn Marduk-nīšu; Käuferin ist die *nadītum* (l u k u r) des Marduk Iltani, der Kaufpreis beträgt 16½ Sekel Silber. Datum: Samsuiluna 30. Das Hausgrundstück wird seitlich von Besitztum des Ilum-bulliṭ und der Belītum n u - g i g (*qadištum*, "Geweihte"), vorn durch die Straße (e - s í r), hinten wiederum durch ein Grundstück der Belītum begrenzt.

VS 22:4 (VAT 13439). Auslösung von 1 2/3 s a r 1 g í n (= etwa 60,6 m^2) é - d ù - a š à u r u ^{ki} - g i b i l ^{ki} - ^{d} u t u - è g ú ^{i} 7 t u - t u (Z.1-3) von Muḫadditum l u k u r ^{d} M a r d u k sowie Ummī-abumuša durch Bēl-zērim-Marduk, dessen Vater Warad-ilišu das Grundstück vormals erworben hatte. Es handelt sich demnach um den Rückkauf väterlichen Gutes für 1/3 Mine 3¼ (Sekel) Silber. Datum: Samsuiluna 31.[6] Von Interesse ist hier vor allem die Positionsangabe "Ufer des Tutu-Kanals"; vielleicht darf auf den von Sîn-muballiṭ in seinem 13. Jahr angelegten Kanal ^{d} t u - t u - ḫ é - g á l, "Tutu ist Überfluß", verwiesen werden.[7] Als Nachbargrundstücke werden die des Ikšud-appašu und Ipqu-Tašmētum genannt; die Vorderseite grenzte an die "breite Straße" (s i l a - d a g a l) der östlichen Neustadt, die durch den Zusatz k i r i $_6$ - ḫ é - g á l, "Überfluß-Garten", näher bezeichnet ist. Offenbar besaß die Neustadt mehrere solche "breite Straßen"? Die Rückseite stieß gleichfalls an ein Grundstück des Ipqu-Tašmētum.

VS 22:14 (VAT 13441, Hüllenfragment: VAT 13431). Der in 25 p 2 in einer Tiefe von -1,30 m gefundene Text (Grabungsnummer 34817 - einer der wenigen Texte mit einer solchen Bezifferung) handelt vom Erwerb einer Fläche (Zahl nicht erhalten) Bauland (é - k i - š u b - b a)[8] mit Teilen einer Lehmziegelmauer (é - s i g $_4$ $^{ḫ i . a}$) š à u r u ^{ki} - g i b i l ^{ki} - ^{d} u t u - è - a (Z.4). Das Land wird von Ipqu-Tašmētum (nach der Filiation nicht identisch mit dem I. in VS 22:4) abgegeben an Sîn-iddinam, nach dem Siegel ein Schreiber. In Z.13 erscheint in teilweise zerstörtem Kontext ein é - k i s l a ḫ š à u r u ^{ki} - g i b i l - ^{d} u t u - è - a als Besitz des Sîn-iddinam, der offenbar dafür vergeben wurde. Datum: Ammīditana 4. Wie es scheint, rundete Sîn-iddinam seinen Grundbesitz in der östlichen Neustadt Babylons ab; der genauere Vorgang ist wegen Unklarheiten und Lücken in der Textüberlieferung nicht ganz klar.

VS 22:16 (VAT 13204, Hüllenfragmente: VAT 13368 und 13403a). Kauf von 2/3 s a r (24 m^2) Haus an einer Kanalmündung(?)[9] š à u r u ^{ki} - g i b i l - ^{d} u t u - [è - a]. Verkäuferin ist Ṭāb-Esagil, eine *nadītum* des Marduk von Babylon, Tochter des Marduk-mušallim; Käuferin ist Bēltani, ebenfalls l u k u r ^{d} M a r d u k k á - d i n g i r - r a ^{ki}. Der Kaufpreis beträgt 10 Sekel Silber. Datum Ammīditanas. Die Verkäuferin hatte das Grundstück als Mitgift (*nudunnû*) erhalten. Es wurde seitlich von Besitztum des Tarībum und Rīš-Nabium (wohl identisch mit dem Zeugen in VS 22:15 Z.24, s.unten) begrenzt, an der Vorderseite von der Straße (e - s í r), an der Rückseite vom Grundstück des Ilī'ēraḫ. Eng mit diesem Text gehört VS 22:15 zusammen, wo die gleichen Zeugen und der Schreiber Gimil-Gula (vgl. den Sippar-Text CT 33:33 Z.20) erscheinen:

VS 22:15 (VAT 13143). Kauf von 1/3 s a r 2 g í n (13,2 m^2) é - k i s l a ḫ š à u r u ^{ki} - g i b i l - ^{d} u t u - è - a. Verkäufer ist der aus MDOG 38, 8 bereits bekannte Nakārum, Sohn des Ibni-Marduk; Käufer ist

Šamaš-muballiṭ. Kaufpreis 8 Sekel Silber, Datum Ammiditana 20. Nachbarn sind Ipqu-Araḫtum und Gurrudum; an der Vorderseite lag die Straße (e - s í r), an der Rückseite ein Hausgrundstück des Ili'eraḫ (gewiß identisch mit dem I. in VS 22:16).

VS 22:12 (VAT 13369). Gleicher Schreiber wie in VS 22:15 und 16 (Gimil-Gula), Datum: Ammiditana 18. Kauf von 1 s a r (36 m^2) é - k i s l a ḫ . . . š à u r u ^{ki} - g i b i l - ^{d} u t u - è - a. Verkäuferin ist Iltani l u k u r ^{d} M a r d u k k á - d i n g i r - r a ^{ki}, Tochter des Baši-ilum,[10] die das Grundstück von zwei anderen Personen erworben hatte (diese Angabe fehlt im Text der Hülle). Käufer ist Abī'ēšuḫ-muštal, Sohn des Ja(ḫa)mmu,[11] der Kaufpreis 8 Sekel Silber. Nachbarn zur Seite sind Azzanitum, ebenfalls *nadītum* des Marduk von Babylon, Schwester der einstigen Besitzer, sowie die Straße (e - s í r), während an der Vorderseite die "breite Straße" (s i l a - d a g a l) verlief und an der Rückseite das Hausgrundstück eines Ibbi-Ninšubur lag.

VS 22:17 (VAT 13442), bislang jüngster Beleg (Ammīṣaduqa 11). Der Text ist nur bruchstückhaft erhalten, nennt jedoch die gleichen Grundstücksnachbarn wie VAT 13369 (VS 22:12) und dürfte demnach von demselben Besitztum [š à u r u ^{ki} - g i b i l] - ^{d} u t u - è - a handeln.

Die Flächen der in den hier notierten Texten bezeugten Grundstücke liegen zwischen 12 und 60 m^2 und bewegen sich damit innerhalb der auch sonst aus altbabylonischer Zeit bekannten Größen.[12] Auch die Preise halten sich etwa im Durchschnitt, wenngleich der Preis für ein "Haus in vollkommenem Bauzustand" (é - d ù - a) etwas höher als der zu sein scheint, wie er aus dem spätaltbabylonischen Sippar überliefert ist.[13]

Als Besitzer von Grundstücken in der östlichen Neustadt Babylons werden mindestens dreißig Personen bezeugt, wobei das mehrfache Auftreten von *nadīatum* des Marduk (von Babylon) auffällt: Iltani und Muḫadditum zur Zeit des Samsuiluna, Ṭāb-Esagil,[14] Bēltani, Iltani und Azzanitum zur Zeit des Ammīditana (bzw. noch des Ammīṣaduqa).[15] Ist vielleicht anzunehmen, daß es vorrangig die Familien solcher Priesterinnen des Stadtgottes waren, die in der östlichen Neustadt Grundstücke besaßen? Seine Gesetze belegen für Ḫammurapi das Bemühen um eine Besserstellung der *nadīatum* des Marduk von Babylon: Sollten etwa Grundstückszuweisungen dann auch eine ökonomische Besserstellung bewirken? Fragen, auf die die hier notierten wenigen Zeugnisse noch keine schlüssige Antwort erlauben.

Die bisher verfügbaren Belege stammen aus den Regierungszeiten des Samsuiluna, Ammīditana und Ammīṣaduqa, während sich in den Samsuditana-Texten bislang keine Erwähnung der östlichen Neustadt Babylons findet. In VS 13:24 (= HG 1662) wird unter dem Jahr Ḫammurapi 41 der Tausch von 1 / 3 s a r é - k i s l a ḫ š à u r u - g i b i l - u t u - è behandelt (vgl. CAD Ṣ 216 b). Die Herkunft der Tafel ist jedoch unklar, und auch die Personennamen lassen eine Zuweisung an Babylon nicht vornehmen. Somit bleiben als sichere Belege für die östliche Neustadt Babylons nur jene, die in den späten Regierungsjahren des Samsuiluna einsetzen. Ob die Gründung dementsprechend Samsuiluna anzurechnen ist, der die Stadt Babylon nach allen Richtungen hin erweitert haben will,[16] bleibt unklar.

Die Lage der östlichen Neustadt altbabylonischer Zeit ist nicht zu präzisieren; sie dürfte aber wohl innerhalb des neubabylonischen Stadtbereiches zu suchen sein. Wenn als ein altes Zentrum das Gebiet um den Marduk-Tempel angenommen werden darf,[17] dann wird die östliche Neustadt im Hinblick auf die noch geringe Ausdehnung der altbabylonischen Siedlung gewiß nicht allzu weit davon entfernt gelegen haben und vielleicht nahe dem "Merkes" vermutet werden dürfen? Tiefergehende Grabungen nach Absenken des Grundwasserspiegels könnten auch hierüber einmal Aufschluß geben.

---

1 Vgl. dazu R. Koldewey, *Das wieder erstehende Babylon* [Leipzig ^{4}1925]; E. Unger, *Babylon die heilige Stadt* [Berlin -Leipzig 1931]; ders., *Babylon*, in RlA I [1928] 330-369; zuletzt G. Bergamini, *Levels of Babylon Reconsidered*, in *Mesopotamia* XII [1977] 111ff.

2 B. Kienast, *The Name of the City of Babylon*, in *Sumer* 35 [1979] 246ff., nimmt für Babylon auf Grund seines Namens ein hohes Alter an (älter als altakkadisch, Name "protoeuphratisch"). Der "Merkes" dürfte wohl eines der ältesten Besiedlungsareale bezeichnen.

3 O. Reuther, *Die Innenstadt von Babylon (Merkes)* [Leipzig 1926] 6ff., 46, 48f.; vgl. R. Koldewey, *Das wieder erstehende Babylon*, 233ff.

4 Die Zahl der im Grabungsjournal ausgewiesenen altbabylonischen Tafelfunde übersteigt die der Stücke, die im Vorderasiatischen Museum identifiziert werden konnten. Die auf Fotos (MDOG 38, 8 Abb.2 und R. Koldewey, op. cit. 238 Abb.157) abgebildeten Tafeln lassen sich nur zum Teil im Vorderasiatischen Museum nachweisen. Ein größerer Teil der Tafelfragmente aus Babylon ist durch die Lage im Grundwasser weitgehend zerstört; die besser erhaltenen werden in VS 22 herausgegeben.

5 Vgl. zuletzt D.O. Edzard, "Haus", in RlA IV [1972-75] 221.

6 Das Datum nennt das 4.Jahr mit dem Namen á g - g á ^{d}e n - l í l - l á (Samsuiluna 28). In dieser Form m.W. bislang nicht bezeugt, wohl Variante zu 31.

7 m u ^{i}7 ^{d}t u - t u - ḫ é - g á l m u - u n - b a - a l, "Jahr, in dem er (d.i. Sîn-muballiṭ) den Tutu-ḫegal-Kanal grub".

8 Nach D.O. Edzard, "Haus", in RlA IV [1972-75] 221: "verfallener Ort".

9 Unsicher, da die Lesung von Z.1 é *pî* (k a) *pa-al- gi* unklar. Vgl. etwa den Tutu-Kanal? Die Hülle VAT 13368 bietet Z.2' wohl den Hinweis auf ein vorhandenes/fehlendes Dachgeschoß (*r] u-ug-gu-bu*).

10 Der Name Iltani war unter den l u k u r verbreitet; vgl. J. Renger, *Untersuchungen zum Priestertum in der altbabylonischen Zeit*, in ZA 58 [1967] 164ff. Die hier genannte Tochter des Baši-ilum ist nicht identisch mit der Iltani l u k u r ^{d}M a r d u k in VS 22:8. In VS 22:12 Z.31 wird ein Ilušubani, Sohn des Aḫīlumur, als Ehemann der Iltani erwähnt.

11 Zum Namen Abī'ēšuḫ-muštal in diesem Text vgl. schon H. Klengel, *Ḫammurapi und seine Nachfolger im altbabylonischen Onomastikon*, in JCS 28 [1976] 158. Inzwischen können noch weitere PN mit dem Königsnamen Abī'ēšuḫ nachgewiesen werden: Für Abī'ēšuḫ-muštal s. noch VAT 13287: 16.19.26 (= VS 22:29, Ammīditana 19, wohl gleiche Person wie in VS 22:12), ebendort Z.35 Abī'ēšuḫ-ili und Z.41 Abī'ēšuḫ-šemi. CT 45:55 bietet in Z.11 den PN Abī'ēšuḫ-lidiš. In VAT 13369 (VS 22:12) wird Z.18 der Name des Vaters des Abī'ēšuḫ-muštal *Ja-am-mu* geschrieben, auf der Hülle Vs.15 *Ja-ḫa-am-mu*.

12 D.O. Edzard, "Haus", in RlA IV [1972-75] 221f.

13 R. Harris, *Ancient Sippar* [Istanbul 1975] 26f.

14 Die in VS 22:16 Z.7 und 11 genannte Ṭāb-Esagil, auf ihrem Siegel als Dienerin des Marduk und der Ṣarpanītum ausgewiesen, war Tochter des Marduk-musallim. Sie ist nicht identisch mit der in YOS XIII 91:24 erwähnten Ṭ. l u k u r ᵈM a r d u k k á - d i n g i r - r a ᵏⁱ, Tochter des Marduk-muballiṭ.

15 Vgl. dazu J. Renger, *Untersuchungen zum Priestertum in der altbabylonischen Zeit*, in ZA 58 [1967] 149ff.; insbesondere zu Marduk von Babylon S.174f. Die erwähnten l u k u r/*nadītum* sind bisher nicht belegt.

16 VS 1:33 III 19ff., vgl. schon den Hinweis bei E. Unger, "*Babylon*", in RlA I [1928] 331. Sumer. Duplikat bei L.W. King, *The Letters and Inscriptions of Ḫammurabi, King of Babylon*, III [London 1900] 199ff.

17 G. Bergamini, *Levels of Babylon Reconsidered*, in *Mesopotamia* XII [1977] 111f., hält es für nicht ausgeschlossen (S.141ff.), daß die von R. Koldewey freigelegten Reste von Etemenanki bis in die altbabylonische Zeit zurückdatieren.

ZUR GESELLSCHAFTLICHEN RELEVANZ DER HAMMURAPISCHEN GESETZE

Josef Klíma (Praha)

Ursprünglich war es meine Absicht, die schwere und lange Genesis der Forschungen über die mesopotamische Gesellschaft vorzulegen. Der Raummangel erlaubt mir jedoch nur kurz von dem ernst gemeinten Postulat dieser Forschungen von Hrozný bereits aus dem Jahre 1914, über den geflügelten Ausspruch von Gelb aus dem Jahre 1965 "we never shall know what was the nectar of the gods until we learn the daily bread of the people" bis zur rührenden Feststellung der Redaktion des RLA rasch zu kommen, die in der Einführung zum Rölligs Beitrag "Gesellschaft" noch erklären konnte: "Die Sozialstruktur Mesopotamiens ist bisher nur in wenigen Einzelpunkten Gegenstand der Forschung gewesen". Hiemit enden jedoch die allgemeinen Beschwerden auf diesen Mangel und beginnt ein echter Strom von Fachbehandlungen der sozialwirtschaftlichen Probleme Mesopotamiens.[1]

Jetzt möchte ich also *in medias res* unserer Erörterungen eintreten, in der Hoffnung, dass ich bei einer künftigen Gelegenheit die übrigen Haupt- und Teilprobleme unseres Themas berühren werde. Die mit ihm verbundene Bipolarität ist bereits aus seinem kargen Titel erkennbar. Einerseits ist die Gesellschaft der hammurapischen Epoche erfassbar, soweit sie sich einer legislativen Regelung oder wenigstens einer Erwähnung bedürftig zeigt. Andererseits muss man sich mit jenen Faktoren auseinandersetzen, welche ihre Gewalt über die konkreten Gesellschaftsklassen - und innerhalb dieser über die einzelnen Berufskategorien unmittelbar oder kraft beauftragter Bevollmächtiger ausüben und dadurch ihren Willen zur Gestaltung dieser Gesellschaft den erstrebten Ausdruck geben sollen.[2]

Ebenso wie bei der Darstellung der Gesellschaft kann man auch bei der heutigen Beurteilung des richtigen Umfangs des Wesens dieser Faktoren in ähnliche Verzweiflung geraten, die neuerlich beim F.R. Kraus vorkommen.[3] Wir können, um die Problematik unseres Themas zu vereinfachen, die mit exekutiver Gewalt ausgestatteten Faktoren mit dem Begriff *ekallum*, "Palast"[4] bezeichnen. Dieser kann nicht nur als Abbild der Regierungshoheit, als Darsteller einer staatlichen[5] Souveränität dienen, sondern auch den Fiscus schlechthin bedeuten, d.h. die gesamte materielle Grundlage, Immobilien wie Mobilien, die Einkünfte des Palastkassa (Abgaben, Steuer, Pfründe, Geschenke, Kriegsbeuten, usw.) umfassen, also alles, dessen das Haus - É/*bitum* - bzw. die Kammer des Herrschers und dadurch sein Land für die Festigung und Erweiterung ihres wirtschaftlichen und auch des politischen Machtbereichs bedürfen.

In der Gegenüberstellung der beiden Faktoren, also einerseits der Bewohner des Landes, andererseits des Landesherrschers, liegt der Hauptkern unseres Themas. Innerhalb dieser Gegenüberstellung beabsichtigen wir, die Frage des Verhaltens des Herrschers als Gesetzgebers, bzw. auch derjenigen zu berühren, die als vom Herrscher beauftragte Schöpfer, also die von ihm berufenen Praktiker, das lebendige Werk geschaffen haben. Den letztgenannten war die wirkliche sozialökonomische Lage des Reiches aus der täglichen Ausübung ihrer Kompetenz oder wenigstens aus dem Kontakt mit jenen Richtern bekannt, die die praktischen Fälle zu entscheiden hatten, so dass es ihnen nicht unmöglich war, jene Fragen zu beantworten, die uns - wie es richtig, wenn auch mit etwas überflüssigem Verzicht F.R. Kraus[6] anführt - heute noch kaum restlos beantwortbar erscheinen. Jedenfalls ist es nicht schwer einzusehen, dass alle Fragen, die sich aus dem Text des CH ergeben, um dortselbst eine mehr oder weniger befriedigende Lösung zu treffen, auf jene Eigenschaft dieser Gesetze abzielen, die man kurz als ihren "Sitz im Leben"[7] der mesopotamischen Gesellschaft zu bezeichnen pflegt.

Es ist also begreiflich, dass sich die Regierungsmassnahmen jedes Herrschers im Rahmen seiner Innenpolitik vor allem auf die normative Regelung und zugleich auf die Förderung jener Gebiete der Tätigkeit und des Unternehmungsgeistes seiner Untertanen richteten. Dem Herrscher bzw. seinen durch die Fachschulung und Rechtspraxis erzogenen Beratern war es genug klar, dass nur die fachmännisch geleitete Tätigkeit der Bewohner des Reiches zur erwünschten Einteilung der Produktion, zur Erhöhung der Arbeitsproduktion sowie auch zum Aufschwung des ökonomischen Reichseinkommens und zur Festigung des Wohlstandes des Landes wie ein Bewegungshebel wirken könnte. Denn nur eine mit diesen ökonomischen Mitteln versehene Gesellschaft war gezwungen, auch ihr soziales und kulturelles Leben zu vertiefen und sich unter dem Zeichen eines "festen Pfluges und scharfen Schwertes" nicht nur die innerliche Ordnung zu erhalten, sondern auch dem Feind von aussen Widerstand zu leisten und eigener Expansionslust einen Durchbruch zu verleihen.[8]

Wenn wir nun nach diesen einführenden Gedanken zum eigentlichen Thema übergehen, so können wir gleich sagen, dass die gesellschaftliche Relevanz des CH eine andere war, als jene der Werke aus der vorhergehenden sumerischen Zeit, weil sich das Bild des mesopotamischen Gesellschaft im 18.Jh.v.Chr. gegenüber der Ur-III.-Zeit wesentlich entwickelt hat. Anstatt der Gemeindeneinheiten, der sg. *rural communities*,[9] wo sich das sozialökonomische Leben durch das Kollektiv der Dorfgemeinde auf gemeinsamen Boden abspielte, kommt mit dem Auftritt der nomadischen oder seminomadischen amoritischen Stämme auf der babylonischen Szene eine neue sozialökonomische Anordnung auf, wenn wir auch einige Residuen der alten Ordnung sogar in den Vorschriften des CH vermerken können.[10] Erst in der kassitischen Zeit kommt, in der Regel, die einstige Ordnung wieder zum Ausdruck.[11]

Die in theokratischer Form organisierte Gesellschaft der Ur-III.-Zeit hat also ihren Kollektivcharakter auf dem Gebiete der Wirtschaft praktisch unter der altbabylonischen Dynastie verloren, es kam relativ bald zur Bildung einer im Grundsatz verbürgerlichten Gesellschaft,[12] was wohl der sich individualisierenden Wirtschaft entsprach.[13] Die Erfassung einer solchen Gesellschaft, die Ausnutzung ihrer ökonomischen Erträge durch die amoritischen Herrscher, wenn sie erfolgreich werden sollten, verlangten jedenfalls von ihnen eine ähnliche Politik, wie sie den Herrschern der Ur-III.Dynastie eigen war[14]: wenn einerseits während der Regierung Hammurapis die Dorfgemeinschaft ihren Platz im sozialökonomischen Leben des Landes verlor, entwickelten sich andererseits auch die tiefgreifenden Eingriffe in die Sphäre der Individualität durch die Massnahmen des mit der Zentralisation und Unifikation Hand in Hand schreitenden Bürokratismus.[15]

So kommen wir dem Kern unseres Themas näher. Der Charakter jedes Regierungssystems wird vor allem nach den von ihm promulgierten Gesetzen, nach deren Wirkungsbereich und nach ihrer Anwendung beurteilt. Wir fragen bereits bei den ältesten uns bekannten Normen, ebenso wie später bei den Römern oder bei den modernen Gesetzen, nach ihrer *ratio* bzw. *occasio*[16] oder direkt nach der *voluntas legislatoris*, d.h. nach dem Willen des Gesetzgebers bzw. derjenigen, die sich in seinem Auftrage mit der Ausarbeitung der konkreten Norm befassten. Wenn wir dabei nach der Relevanz der Gesellschaft fragen, nach ihrer Stellung und Bedeutung forschen, dann suchen wir vor allem die Antwort, inwieweit der

Gesetzgeber sein Interesse der ihm untergeordneten Gesellschaft, d.h. seinen Untertanen, widmete und ihr seine Fürsorge und Pflege gewährte; auch fragen wir, ob dieses Interesse und diese Fürsorge für alle Mitglieder dieser Gesellschaft – wohl unter Ausschluss der Unfreien (Sklaven) - gleichwertig war oder ob gewisse Kategorien der Bevölkerung bzw. Stände der freien oder beschränkt freien Bürger eine grössere oder weniger bedeutsame gesellschaftliche Relevanz innehatten.

Zur Beantwortung dieser Grundfrage gemäss dem CH ist es nicht ohne Wichtigkeit, wenigstens kurz den Standpunkt zu beurteilen, den auf diesem Gebiete der Gesetzgeber selbst einnimmt. Wir müssen dabei zweierlei unterscheiden: 1. Was bedeutet für ihn die Masse seiner Untertanen, als deren Herrscher - wohl "deorum gratia" - er sich proklamiert? Darauf kann man die Antwort am ehesten im Prolog oder im Epilog des CH finden.[17] 2. Wie kommt die gesellschaftliche Relevanz in den eigentlichen Gesetzen Hammurapis und teilweise auch in seiner amtlichen Korrespondenz zum Ausdruck? Die Antwort auf die erste Frage kann nur in glatten Worten, immerhin aber in charakteristischen Zügen jener Texte des Prologes bzw. Epiloges entnommen werden, aus welchen die Adressaten dieser Rahmentexte hervortreten, die mit den Entscheidungen im weiteren Sinne des Wortes seitens ihres Urhebers in einer sehr oft metaphorischen Form betroffen oder begünstigt werden. Dieser Umstand verrät ganz deutlich, dass bei der Auswahl der sg. legislativen Kommission der Stele, die Hammurapi ebenso wie nach mehr als zweitausend Jahren der byzantinische Kaiser Justinian aus seinen besten Spezialisten, Lehrern der Schreiberschulen, zusammengestellt hat, der Herrscher besonderen Nachdruck auch auf die psychologische Gewandheit der Redaktoren dieser Gesetzestexte, gelegt hat.

Es sei von vornherein nur kurz auf die bekannte und öfters diskutierte Spaltung der Herkunft der legislativen Gewalt ḫingewiesen. Einerseits stellt sich Hammurapi als Bevollmächtiger des Gottes Šamaš und Vollstrecker seiner Gerechtigkeitsanweisung[18] vor (CH XXIV 84 und XXV 95f.),[19] womit also die herkunft seiner Gesetzgebung *in iure divino* besteht, andererseits - und zwar bereits im Prolog (CH V 20ff.) - lässt er keinen Zweifel übrig, dass er sich selbst als Gesetzgeber betrachtet. Damit ist auch gesagt, dass er die Regelung der ihm unterstellten Gesellschaft für seine Aufgabe und seine Berechtigung hält. Für die primäre, allgemeine Bezeichnung dieser Gesellschaft benutzen die Redaktoren der Rahmentexte entweder den einfachen Ausdruck *nišû̂m* (*forma pluralis*),[20] "die Massen, Menschen, Einwohner" - und zwar einmal in der Wendung *kiššat niši* (CH I 12), "die Gesamtheit der Menschen"[21] oder in der Kombination *šir niši*, "das Wohlergehen (wörtl. das Fleisch) der Menschen".[22] Eine andere Bezeichnung der Menschenmassen, ebenfalls nur in den Rahmentexten benutzt, ist die Wendung *ṣalmat qaqqadim*, "die Schwarzköpfigen",[23] also die Masse der Menschen, die wohl der Herrscher von seinem erhöhten Standpunkt, vom Throne, als Personen mit gebeugten Häuptern tief unter sich erblickt.[24]

Manchmal wird für den Begriff des Volkes als Landbewohner im abstrakten Sinne der Ausdruck *matum*, "das Land" benutzt (wie z.B. im CH I 6f: *ša'im šimat matim*, "der die Geschicke des Landes bestimmt", d.h. der Bevölkerung des Landes) oder im CH V 17f.: *matim uṣim šuḫuzim*, "dem Land - also seinen Bewohnern - die Führung einzuordnen".[25] Auch benutzt der Prolog für die Kollektivbezeichnung aller Bewohner des Landes das Wort *ammum*[26] und zwar in der Mehrzahl *ammi*.[27]

Bei allen diesen Termini wird ausschliesslich an die gesamte Bevölkerung des Reiches als an ein Ganzes gedacht, ohne ihre soziale (nach Klassenunterschieden), sprachliche[28] oder standesmässige Zugehörigkeit besonders herauszustellen: es handelt sich um die Fälle, in denen die Erfassung aller Kategorien der

Untertanen ausgedrückt werden sollte, in solchen Fällen spricht man nie über die *awilu*, *muškenu*, u.ä.

Dadurch wird zugleich seine absolute Macht sowie auch die alle seine Untertanen umfassende Rechtspflege klargestellt. Man könnte bei diesen Ausdrücken, mit denen der Herrscher seine Untertanen bedachte, die Geburt jener Herrschergesinnung feststellen, die bei den Monarchen "von Gottesgnaden" aus erst unlängst abgelaufener Zeit in ihren selbstbewussten Manifesten, die sich an "Meine Völker" adressierten, eine äquivalente Formulierung finden. Auch der Zentralisation und der Unifikation des Reiches wird dadurch ein klarsprechender Ausdruck verliehen.[29] An dieser Stelle ist die Bemerkung nicht zu unterlassen, dass diesem Reichsgedanken auch die Stellung des Klerus entsprechen sollte, dessen sakrale Bedeutung und auch ökonomische Grundlage (durch den Schutz des Tempelvermögens) von Hammurapi anerkannt und geregelt wurde; sein Einfluss auf die Reichspolitik und seine politische Autorität wurde jedoch schlechthin unterbunden.[30]

Andererseits finden wir in den Rahmentexten des CH nie die Bezeichnung der Reichbevölkerung in der Art, wie sie z.B. im Prolog zum CL vorkommt, d.h. wo die Redaktoren die Untertanen entweder als "Söhne und Töchter" der *nominatim* aufgezählten Städte[31] oder allgemein des ganzen Landes Sumer und Akkad (s.oben N.28) angesprochen haben.[32] Man könnte nur noch erwähnen, dass bereits Entemena[33] in seinem Edikt die Bevölkerung seines Landes als Einwohner von einzeln genannten Städten[34] anführt.

Demgegenüber kommt im CH die Bezeichnung *mar(u) mati*, "Söhne des Landes" nicht mehr im Sinne der Bevölkerung des Reiches schlechthin vor - wir treffen sie also nie im Rahmentext, sondern in einer konkreten Vorschrift, wo sie bereits die Bedeutung eines vollfreien Bürgers des Reiches[35] hat. Diese Bezeichnung kommt im CH nämlich nur im §280 vor, wo mit ihr ein einheimischer, d.h. ein babylonischer Sklave[36] gemeint ist, der im Ausland von einem babylonischen *tamkarum* (siche §281) gekauft wurde und mit ihm nach Babylonien zurückkommt; hier wird er von seinem ursprünglichen Herrn erlammt; das Gesetz gewährt ihm eine unentgeltliche Freilassung.[37] Dieser Fall, den der §280 regelt und dessen Interpretation sich als zu verwickelt zeigte,[38] bietet zugleich eine gediegene Gelegenheit zum näheren Nachdenken im Rahmen unseres Themas. Es handelt sich hier nämlich um die Würdigung des Standpunktes, welchen der Gesetzgeber zur Klasse der Unfreien eingenommen hat und dessen Regelung im ganzen CH nur selten vorkommt.[39]

Wir müssen uns vor allem klarmachen, welche soziale Eigenschaft diesen *maru matim* zugebilligt werden kann. Man kann sie sich kaum anders als Schuldknechte eines Babyloniers vorstellen, die entweder ins Ausland (*mat nukurtim*, eigentlich "Land des Feindes") gekommen oder in feindliche Kriegsgefangenschaft geraten sind. Diese Umstände konnte der babylonische *tamkarum* im Ausland entweder durch ihre eigene Aussage oder mittels Bestätigungen dritter Personen in seiner Stellung als Sklavenhändler feststellen.[40] - Für den Fall eines in feindliche Gefangenschaft geratenen *redum* oder *ba'irum*, also der am meisten erwähnten Soldaten im CH, ist die Verpflichtung der Palastkasse zur Regelung des Loskaufpreises im §32 vorgesehen: der Palast muss den *tamkarum*, der einen solchen Gefangenen losgekauft hat,[41] entschädigen, jedenfalls subsidiär, d.h. nur dann, wenn - *primo loco* - der Losgekaufte selbst oder - *secundo loco* - der Tempel seines Heimatsortes sich als insolvent erwiesen hatten.[42] Im Falle der Lösung eines babylonischen Sklaven nach dem §280 wird diese subsidiäre Entschädigung des *tamkarum* nicht erwähnt. Es bleibt zu vermuten, dass dieser als Sklavenhändler im Auftrage des Palastes auf Grund entsprechender kommerzieller Vertragsabmachungen handelte. Diese privilegierte Regelung galt nicht im

Falle, wenn es sich um die Lösung der *maru matim šanitim* handelt, wo ihr Käufer berechtigt war, das für sie erstattete Lösegeld von ihren Herren nach dem §281 zu verlangen.

Dieser Fall bietet eine gute Basis für unser Thema: der Staat, repräsentiert hier durch den Palast (*ekallum*)[43] als Arbeitsgeber des *tamkarum*,[44] hatte ein besonderes Interesse an der Rückgewinnung seines Staatsangehörigen sei es aus der Sklavenschaft im Ausland (§280), sei es aus der Kriegsgefangenschaft (§32). Im ersten Falle spielte es sogar keine Rolle, dass dieser Mensch augenblicklich kein *awilum* war: für das Ausland (*mat nukurtim*) galt er als ein Babylonier, der zwar in Babylonien die Zugehörigkeit zur Klasse der *awilu* verloren hat, aber ausserhalb Babyloniens ist er als Freigeborener zu beurteilen. Man neigt in diesem Falle zur Vermutung, dass es sich hier seitens des Palastes, d.h. der Staatsführung, um eine gewisse Art des "Prestige-Komplexes" handelte, von dem neuerlich Renger in einem zwar anderen, aber doch nicht so entfernten Sinne spricht.[45]

Die soeben besprochenen gesetzlichen Massnahmen haben zweierlei Ziele erreicht: Sie zeugen nicht nur von der Gewandheit des Herrschers, ein günstiges "business" durch die Rückgewinnung seiner Staatsbürger zu realisieren, aber zugleich, was wohl vom Standpunkt der hammurapischen Reichspolitik noch viel wichtiger war, von einem Beweis der eigenen Gewalt im sozialökonomischen Bereich gegenüber den Nachbarländern, also von einer politischen Geste, die jenen zuzuordnen ist, die aus dem CH vor allem ein politisches Denkmal machen.

Zu solchem Zwecke eignete sich überhaupt nicht der Begriff *mar ali(m)*, "Stadtangehöriger",[46] denn er wäre eine starke Andeutung des lokalen Partikularismus, gegen den sich der Herrscher mit allen Mitteln seines Strebens um Zentralismus und Unifikation abheben musste. Deshalb spricht er, wenn es sich um die Erfassung seiner Untertanen handelte, vom Volk, der Masse oder den Menschen schlechthin,[47] im konkreten Falle dann von den Staats (Reichs) bürgern, bereits als von Personen mit dem sozialen Status Freigeborener.

Doch finden wir noch eine konkrete Bezeichnung jener Personen, die vorher als Mitglieder der grundlegenden sozialen und wirtschaftlichen Einheit, der sg. Dorfgemeinschaft (*rural community*, *communauté rurale*) gelebt hatten,[48] und die sich während der hammurapischen Periode nur noch im Absterben befanden. Im CH können wir die Bezeichnung der Mitglieder dieser Gemeinschaft unter dem Terminus *maru ugarim* erkennen (CH XV 27).[49] Ihre Erwähnung zur Zeit, wo die Dorforganisation schon unter Reichskontrolle stand, wäre wohl überflüssig, wenn sie nicht gerade in jenem Falle erfolgte (§54 CH), der zugleich die Wichtigkeit der Wasserwirtschaft bestätigt (indem die Pflicht der Mitglieder der Dorfgemeinschaft zur Aufrechterhaltung der Dämme, bzw. zur Kontrolle ihrer Zustände festgesetzt und sanktioniert wird). Die Wasserwege, ihre einwandfreie Funktion und Beherrschung und deshalb ihr ständiges Aufrechterhalten bildeten die Hauptquelle des ökonomischen und deshalb auch des politischen Lebens des Landes.[50] Der Begriff *ugarum* (ohne Verbindung mit *maru*) kommt nur noch im §58 und §259 vor, in beiden Fällen wohl in der Bedeutung der Flur der Dorfgemeinschaft.[51]

Bei allen bis jetzt besprochenen Fachausdrücken, seien es die aus den Rahmentexten, seien es die aus den wenigen einzelnen seiner Bestimmungen, wandte sich der Gesetzgeber entweder an die Masse der Bevölkerung schlechthin oder an jene einzelnen Mitglieder dieser Masse (*maru matim*) oder an ihre grösseren Einheiten (*maru ugarim*), wo immer er vor allem sein Interesse am Wohlerhaben der Untertanen einerseits (gleich ob bei allen oder bei einzelnen, die im konkreten Falle als *pars pro toto* fungieren sollten) zeigte, oder, andererseits, seinen Willen zum Aufrechterhalten der wirtschaftlichen Prosperität in jenem

Sektor bewährte, der in seinem Zentralisationsstreben eine wichtige Rolle spielte.[52]

Diese allgemeinen Proklamationen (im Rahmentexte) bzw. Massnahmen (in den konkreten Bestimmungen) bilden in ihrem öffentlichrechtlichen Charakter[53] die Vorstellung einer Gesamtheit, der der Herrscher aus entweder rein propagandistischen Absichten oder aus utilitaristischen Gründen seine allgemeine Aufmerksamkeit als "guter Hirte des Volkes"[54] oder als verantwortungsvoller Verwalter und Bewahrer des Reichstums seines Landes zuwandte. Bliebe unsere Darstellung auf diese Gegebenheiten beschränkt, so wäre das Bild der Relevanz der altbabylonischen Gesellschaft nur einseitig und fragmentarisch dargestellt.

In allen vorhergehenden Erwägungen sollte die Relevanz der mesopotamischen Bevölkerung quantitativ, d.h. der gesamten Gesellschaft als einer Einheit, dargestellt werden, wenn auch dabei gewisse Töne einer bestimmten Singularität anklangen, wie es gerade im Falle der Mitglieder der Dorfgemeinschaften, also der anfänglichen Vertreter der freien Bevölkerung des Landes, war. Doch beweist gerade das Werk Hammurapis, dass ihre einstige Sonderstellung in der Zeit der Promulgierung der Stele nicht mehr den Regierungstendenzen des Herrschers entsprach und die *maru ugarim* lange nicht den Mitgliedern des *nišu* gleichgestellt wurden; den letzteren versprach der Herrscher im Rahmentext seinen Schutz, seine Hilfe und Fürsorge, dagegen waren die *maru ugarim* nur Gegenstand seiner konkreten Bestimmung, in ähnlicher Art wie die anderen Schichten bzw. Berufskategorien der Reichsbevölkerung, aus den wir sie herausgewählt haben, um die grosse Verwandlung der mesopotamischen Gesellschaft zu betonen, die zugleich ihre nicht zu unterschätzende qualitative Abänderung bedeutete.

Wir wollen jetzt die qualitative Relevanz der mesopotamischen Bevölkerung unter staatspolitischen, sozialen und wirtschaflichen Gesichtspunkten messen, wobei nicht zu vergessen ist, dass bei keiner Gruppe die gesellschaftliche Relevanz die gleiche Intensität erreicht. - Das völlige Übergehen des babylonischen Priestertums im ganzen CH,[55] wie bereits bemerkt (Anm. 30), muss gerade nicht allzusehr überraschen und wir dürfen daraus besonders nicht auf ein Fehlen der gesellschaftlichen Relevanz der hierarchischen Kategorie schliessen. Schon deshalb nicht, weil dieser nur scheinbare Mangel in mehr als genügender Form durch die vom Herrscher in den Rahmentexten so feierlich proklamierte Ergebenheit gegenüber den babylonischen Göttern und die Sorge um die Ausstattung der babylonischen Tempel ersetzt wird.[56] Damit wird auch sein positives Verhältnis zur Hierarchie angedeutet, wenigstens überall dort, wo es sich im Einklang mit der weltlichen Reichspolitik des Herrschers befand. Diese Politik könnte wohl gewissermassen als eine Trennung des Staates von der Kirche, wenn wir uns dieser modernen Terminologie bedienen dürfen, bedeuten, wodurch natürlich die Relevanz des Priestertums auf gesellschaftlichem und wirtschaftlichem Gebiete[57] nicht unterschätzt werden konnte. Der Herrscher hat sicher in die Stellung des Priestertums durch die Laizisation eingegriffen,[58] diesen Eingriff in die bisher geltende Rechtslage hat er jedoch nicht im Rahmen der Bestimmungen seiner Stele durchgeführt. Diese Tatsache zeugt jedenfalls von den bereits erwähnten psychologischen Begabung der Redaktoren des CH, denn sonst hätte die Promulgierung eines solchen Eingriffs in den Augen der Öffentlichkeit die gesellschaftliche Relevanz des Priestertums doch berührt.[59] Es ist nicht ausgeschlossen, dass dieser Eingriff in der Form eines *ṣimdat šarrim*[60] durchgeführt werden konnte, jedenfalls haben wir aber dafür keine Unterlage. Ferner ist es nicht ausgeschlossen, dass z.B. im Wege einer ähnlichen *lex specialis* die Regelung des Status der Priesterschaft des Tempels von Marduk, dem neuen Reichsgott, stattfand.

Gegenüber dieser stillschweigenden Stellungnahme des CH zum Priestertum könnte vielleicht auffallen, dass der Gesetzgeber die Relevanz des weiblichen Tempel- und Klosterpersonals aller Stufen, der sg. Kloster- oder Tempelpriesterinnen, bzw. der sg. Stiftdamen,[61] in zahlreichen Bestimmungen, also öffentlichrechtlichen sowie privatrechtlichen, bestätigt.[62] Der §127 CH hinterlässt zwar nicht den Eindruck, dass sich nicht einmal die höchststehende Priesterin, die *ugbabtum*, einer höheren Einschätzung erfreut hat, weil sie gegen böswillige Verleumdung in derselben Weise geschützt wurde wie die Ehefrau eines beliebigen vollfreien Bürgers (*awilum*). Eine *naditum*-Priesterin ist berechtigt, ebenso wie ein Kaufmann (*tamkarum*), ihre Immobilien zu verkaufen.

Eine umfassende Gruppe von Bestimmungen (§§178-184) regelt die familien- und erbrechtlichen Verhältnisse der einzelnen Kategorien dieser Frauen.[63] Die Praxis bestätigt ihre rege Geschäfts- und Unternehmenstätigkeit.[64] Die hohe gesellschaftliche Relevanz war besonders zwei Kategorien dieser Priesterinnen vorbehalten - den *naditu* und *ugbabtu*, die ausserhalb des Klosters wohnten. Der Gesetzgeber hat nämlich ihren guten Ruf dermassen geregelt, dass er ihnen unter Todesstrafe den Eintritt in die Schenke untersagt hatte (§110). Die Gründe bzw. Motive für diese, so scharfe, Entscheidung[65] werden nicht angegeben, nur die Plazierung dieser Bestimmung unmittelbar hinter jener (§109), wo die Schankwirtin die verbrecherischen Elemente duldet und keine Anzeige macht, zur Todesstrafe verurteilt wird, sollte verhüten, dass die Priesterin in verdächtiger Gesellschaft ertappt würde: jedenfalls deutet diese Bestimmung etwas Sonderbares an, denn sie stellt die Priesterin in den Zusammenhang mit der Sorge des Herrschers um die Erhaltung der öffentlichen Ordnung und wohl auch der Staatssicherheit.

Jedenfalls ist es nicht ohne Interesse, dass der Gesetzgeber dem weiblichen Tempelpersonal relativ grosse Aufmerksamkeit widmete - besonders im Vergleich mit dem völligen Übergehen der männlichen Priesterschaft. Es sei noch kurz zugefügt, dass zwar die familien- und erbrechtlichen Bestimmungen des CH (besonders die §§178,179) ihre Anwendung in der privatrechtlichen Praxis finden,[66] für die öffentlichrechtlichen gibt es bisher kein Urkundenbeleg. Es ist nicht ausgeschlossen, dass hier weiterhin die Grundsätze des Gewohnheitsrechtes[67] ihre Geltung bewahren, indem sie der CH rezipiert hat. Man muss aber auch damit rechnen, dass die Klöster, deren Verwaltung die Priesterinnen in den Händen hielten, wichtige Zentren der Produktion auf verschiedenen Gebieten waren. Vielleicht bewog auch dieser Umstand die Redaktoren des CH dazu, die sozialwirtschaftliche Relevanz der Klosterdamen vor allem durch die oben erwähnten öffentlichrechtlichen Bestimmungen auszudrücken.[68]

Die viel diskutierten §§6 und 8 verfolgen nämlich den Diebstahl des Tempels- und Palastvermögens (*makkur* - geschrieben NÍG.GA - *ilim u ekallim*) und stellen sogar den Schutz des Tempelvermögens vor jenen des Palastvermögens, wobei die Strafsanktionen in beiden Fällen die gleichen sind. Der Schutz bezieht sich natürlich nur auf Taten verbrecherischer Elemente. Andererseits, bedeutet die Säkularisierung des Tempelsvermögens,[69] als Ausdruck der stärkeren Hand der Palastautorität, jedenfalls eine Abschwächung der Relevanz des Priestertums, die jedoch wiederum ungünstige Wirkungen für die Staatspolitik, wie wir schon bemerkt hatten (Anm.30), zeitigte.

Wenn wir nun zu einer weiteren Kategorie der altbabylonischen Gesellschaft, nämlich zum Beamtentum, also zum Bereich der Darsteller und Vollzieher des bürokratischen Apparates, übergehen, dessen Entwicklung in der hammurapischen Zeit, wie wir bereits oben mit M. Lambert vermerkt hatten, eine beinahe tausendjährige Tradition hinter sich hatte, so kommen wir zu einer nicht allzustark abweichenden Feststellung von jener, die wir beim Priestertum getroffen hatten. Man könnte sogar an das bestimmte, absichtliche Bestreben des Gesetzgebers bzw. der Redaktoren der Stele denken, die Amtsgewalt und die Kompetenz der hohen Vertreter des administrativen Apparates schlechthin für die breitere Öffentlichkeit nicht erkennbar zu machen, sondern diese eher im Wege einer Sonderverfügung (*ṣimdat šarrim*) erkennbar zu machen. Ausserdem spielte hier auch das Bewohnheitsrecht seine Rolle, das durch die neuen Massnahmen nur dann ersetzt bzw. ergänzt wurde, wo die abgeänderten Verhältnisse es verlangten.

An der Spitze dieses Apparates stand der Herrscher, was absolut klar besonders aus den Rahmentexten des CH hervorgeht. Auf seine soziale Relevanz braucht hier nicht näher eingegangen werden; wir begnügen uns, die Tatsache zu erwähnen, dass er als höchster Gesetzgeber, Richter, Verwalter des Reiches und oberster Befehlshaber galt.[70] Seine Gewalt wird im CH nirgends verfassungsrechtlich geregelt. Wenn wir eine solche Regelung in dem Titel *šar mišarim*[71] erblicken wollen, so geschieht es allenfalls unter der Voraussetzung, dass dieser Titel nicht nur eine Apotheose des Herrschers, sondern zugleich seine Verpflichtung bedeutet, die Rechtsordnung nicht nur aufzustellen, sondern sie auch selbst zu bewahren. Ansonsten sollten die übrigen Titel (bzw. Epitheta) des Herrschers vor allem seine Tendenzen zur Universalität der Machtherrschaft deutlich machen, bei Hammurapi besonders der Titel *šarrum muštešemi kibrat arba'im*, "König, der die vier Weltteile auf sich hören lässt"[72] Mit Ausnahme des §129, nach welchem der Herrscher berechtigt war, den Partner der ehebrecherischen Frau zu begnadigen,[73] enthält der CH keine Sonderregelung, die sich auf etwas bezieht, was man als Ausdruck der verfassungsrechtlichen Stellung des Herrschers bezeichnen könnte.

Mit dem Mangel der verfassungsrechtlichen Regelung des Herrscherstellung hängt auch die Lücke im CH zusammen, in der ansonsten die Kompetenz auch der weiteren Würdenträger ihre Regelung gefunden hätte, die als direkte Vollzieher der Herrschermacht fungierten und auf diese Weise zu den prominenten Darstellern des sg. Hofstaates[74] gehörten. Noch weniger findet man im CH eine Regelung bzw. den Status des Beamtentums, nicht einmal bezüglich seiner höheren Mitglieder.[75] Auf diesem Gebiete ist der CH noch ärmer als die GE[76] oder später der Edikt von Ammiṣaduqa.[77] Wenn wir den Titel *belum* (EN) aus dem Epilog (CH XXVI^{r} 41) als einen Würdenträger der priesterlichen Kategorie interpretieren, bleibt nur jener des *iššakkum* (ENSÍ)[78] im Sinne des "Statthalters, Provinzverwalters" (CH XXVI^{r} 42) übrig und ferner könnte man nur noch jenen des *mar gerseqqim*[79] *muzzaz ekallim*, "Sohn des Höflings, der beim Palast dient" erwähnen. Schliesslich bemerken wir noch, dass mit der Funktion des öffentlichen Organs in Gestalt eines Ausrufers bzw. Herolds[80] der *nagirum* betraut war (§16).

Die Relevanz der Vertreter und Vollzieher des Gerichtswesens wurde - im Unterschied zu anderen altbabylonischen Gesetzwerken - im CH stark betont, denn die Aufrechterhaltung der öffentlichen Ordnung, der Rechts- und der Staatssicherheit lag nicht zuletzt in ihren Händen. Während z.B. die GE[82] nur noch von *babtum*, "Bezirk, der zum Sprengel eines bestimmten Stadttores (=*babum*) gehorte", wo die Gerichtsverhandlungen stattfanden, sprechen (Art. 54,56,58), führt uns der CH die Person des Richters, *daianum* im Zusammenhang mit seinen obersten Dienstverpflichtungen vor (§5).[83] Auch der Begriff eines Richterkollegiums, *puḫrum*, kommt im CH vor (§§5, 202).[84] Ein anderes, ebenfalls kollektives Gerichtsorgan, das vermutlich für die Streitsachen im Sprengel eines Stadtbezirkes kompetent war, hiess *babtum*. Seine Mitglieder hiessen wohl - ausserhalb des CH - *maru babtim*.[85] Seine Bedeutung lag offenbar darin, dass gerade seine Mitglieder imstande waren, die sozialwirtschaftlichen Verhältnisse ihres

Bezirkes aus eigener Kenntnis unmittelbar zu beurteilen und zu entscheiden: nach dem §126 entscheiden sie über die unbegründete Anklage wegen des Verlustes des in Verwahrung gegebenen Vermögens, nach dem §142 über die Beschwerde der von ihrem Mann erniedrigte Ehefrau und nach dem §251 stellen sie die Stössigkeit eines Rindes fest: diese drei Fälle belegen, wie breit gefächert die Relevanz dieser Organe war, das man in gewissem Sinn als Volksgericht bezeichnen könnte.- Schliesslich sei noch auf den öffentlichen Funktionär *rabianum*, "Gemeindevorsteher" hingewiesen; seine Stellung ist in den §§23 und 24 geregelt,[86] wobei nur seine Verpflichtungen, d.h. seine (und seiner Gemeinde) Verantwortlichkeit für die im Sprengel der Gemeinde begangenen Raubüberfall bzw. Raubmord festgehalten werden.

Im Zusammenhang mit dem Beamtentum und dem Gerichtswesen kann zweifellos die Berufskategorie der Schreiber, *ṭupšarum*, angeführt werden[87] denen wohl auch die Aufgabe oft zugefallen ist, die von ihnen ausgefertigten Urkunden mit dem Abdruck des Rollsiegels zu versehen.[88] Es ist bemerkenswert, dass die Bezeichnung dieses Berufes im CH überhaupt nicht vorkommt, obwohl gerade den Schreibern - und unter ihnen sind nicht nur jene, die diesen Beruf technisch durchführen, sondern auch die gelehrten Absolventen der Schreiberschulen,[89] die bei der Redaktion des CH als Mitglieder einer legislativen Kommission tätig waren - die Entstehung des CH zu verdanken war. Doch ist die Relevanz dieser Kategorie indirekt dadurch gegeben, dass im CH[90] für eine Reihe von Rechtsakten die Errichtung einer Urkunde bzw. auch ihre Besiegelung vorgeschrieben wurde, wozu geschulte Schreiber berufen waren.[91] Die Schreiber, wenn wir nur an die öffentlichen denken, gehörten wohl zum meistbeschäftigten Zivilpersonal des Palastes, aber auch der Tempel, besonders in den Buchhaltereien dieser Institutionen. Von unserem Standpunkt aus ist die grösste Relevanz den Autoren und den Kopisten der literarischen Werke im weitesten Sinne des Wortes zuzubilligen, die uns die grössten Schätze der Kultur ihres Landes aufbewahrt haben. Wenn die Redaktoren bzw. die Kompilatoren der Gesetzeswerke nirgends von sich selbst sprechen, muss dahinter nicht gerade ihre Bescheidenheit stecken; wie bei den meisten literarischen Texten sind gegebenenfalls auch ihre Werke anonym geblieben, was wohl auch als Ausdruck ihrer Taktik (d.h. unbekannt und unverantwortlich vor der Öffentlichkeit zu bleiben) oder als eine Direktive des gesetzgeberischen Herrschers zu verstehen ist.[92]

Wenn wir uns erst jetzt den militärischen Personen zuwenden, soll damit keineswegs gesagt werden, dass ihre gesellschaftliche Bedeutung geringer war als jene der Angehörigen der "zivilen" Funktionäre, denen bis jetzt unsere Aufmerksamkeit gehörte. Es wäre wohl nicht angebracht, die beiden Komponenten gegeneinanderzustellen,[93] schon deshalb nicht, weil eine bemerkenswerte Menge des Militärs vom Palast als einen Ausgleich für die geleisteten Dienste (*ilkum*) unter gewissen Bedingungen den Boden zur Bewirtschaftung bekam. Den Redaktoren des CH ist es gelungen, die das Heer betreffenden Bestimmungen in einer zusammenhängenden Gruppe (§§26-41) zu ordnen,[94] die man gern als "Militärordnung" bezeichnet.[95] Hier werden auch die Verhältnisse der Kriegsgefangenen, d.h. der Schutz ihres Vermögens und ihrer Ehe, geregelt (§§27-28).[96] Die Intensität der sozialen Relevanz der Heeresangehörigen kann man am Umfange der Fürsorge messen, die der Staat ihnen zuteil werden liess (vgl.z.B. §§34,36,37, 38,41). Diese Fürsorge ist auch begreiflich, denn von ihrer persönlichen Einstellung her war im Falle eines bewafneten Konfliktes in nicht zu unterschätzendem Masse das Schicksal des Reiches abhängig. - Die gesellschaftliche Relevanz des Heeres wollte der Gesetzgeber auch durch Disziplinarverordnungen und die Aufforderung zur Erhaltung der Rechtsordnung erzielen, weil die Beachtung dieser Postulate den Offizieren (PA.PA und NU.BÀN.DA[97]) unter dem Todesstrafe auferlegt wurden. Einerseits wurden sie bestraft, wenn es in ihren

Mannschaften zur Desertion kam (§33), andererseits auch, wenn sie sich gegenüber ihren untergeordneten Soldaten (*redum* oder *ba'irum*) rechtswidrig benommen oder ihnen in einem Streite mit einer sozial stärkeren Person (*dannum*) keinen Schutz gewährt hatten (§34). Diese "eiserne" Diszipline war wohl der Umstand, der den letzten deutschen Kaiser angeregt hat, Hammurapi mit dem preussischen König Friedrich Wilhelm I. zu vergleichen.[98] Die soziale Relevanz der militärischen Personen wurde auch durch ihre ökonomische Sicherstellung ausgedrückt.[99] Die ihnen als Gegenwert für ihre Dienstleistungen zugeteilten Liegenschaften waren unveräusserlich (§36) und konnten weder der Ehefrau bzw. der Tochter noch den Gläubigern überlassen werden (§§38-39). So bildeten diese Personen während der Friedenszeit eine wohl umfangreiche Kategorie von Kleinbauern,[100] deren unumstrittene Relevanz wir bei nachster Gelegenheit noch näher prüfen werden.

Beim Übergang zu einer weiteren Kategorie der altbabylonischen Bevölkerung, jener der Händler (DAM.KÀR, *tamkarum*[101]), sind wir uns dessen bewusst, dass sie eine Analogie zur vorhergehenden bildet: Was das Heer für das Reich auf dem Gebiete seiner politischen Sicherheit und Expansion bedeutete, so die Kaufmannschaft als eine Komponente, die vor allem dem ökonomischen Aufschwung dienen sollte, wenn auch damit wohl ihre ganze Tätigkeit nicht erschöpft wurde. Deshalb hat auch der CH die Stellung des Händlers in zahlreichen Bestimmungen erfasst, ja sogar die Händler privilegiert: der altbabylonische *tamkarum* gehörte zur engen Schicht jener Personen, denen die freie Verfügung mit den ihnen als *ilkum* zugeteilten Liegenschaften vorbehalten blieb (§40). Es ist nicht ohne Interesse, dass ebenso wie unter den Bestimmungen über die Beamten oder über das Heer, auch bei jenen über die Händler die leitende Persönlichkeit derselben, *wakil tamkari*, bzw. ihre Gewerkschaftsorganisation, *karum*, nicht einmal im CH genannt werden.[102] Andererseits wird, und zwar ziemlich umfangreich, das Geschäftsverhältnis zwischen dem *tamkarum* und seinem Agenten, *šamallum*, geregelt (§§100-107),[103] was eben die Relevanz der beiden Darsteller des Handels vom Standpunkt des Handelsunternehmens aus bestätigt. Als Vertreter des Kleinhandels wird die Schankwirtin, *sabitum*, im CH genannt,[104] die wir bereits bei der Behandlung der Klosterpriesterinnenordnung kennen gelernt haben. Andererseits bleibt vom CH völlig unbeachtet ein anderer Kleinhändler, *saḫiru*, der am meisten mit einem wandernden Krämmer verglichen werden kann.[105]

Zuletzt wollen wir noch kurz die soziale Relevanz der Angehörigen der Handwerkschaft und auch die derjenigen Standeskategorien berühren, die wir im römischrechtlichen Sinn als "*artes liberales*" zu bezeichnen gewöhnt sind. Dem Interesse der Redaktoren an der verhältnismässig breiten Regelung der öffentlich- sowie privatrechtlichen Stellung der Handwerker kann man ihre grosse gesellschaftliche Relevanz und ihre tiefgehende Bedeutung für die nationale Wirtschaft schlechthin entnehmen. Dies beruht auf der (zur Zeit Hammurapis) bereits mehrhundertjährigen Tradition und dadurch auch auf der ausserordentlichen Reife des altbabylonischen Handwerkes.[106] Es ist deshalb nich zu wundern, dass der CH[107] bereits zum Anlernen der Handwerkerlehrlinge Stellung genommen hat,[108] ohne die Länge der Ausbildung zu fixieren. Ebenso wie die Kaufmannschaft, waren auch die Handwerker in Gewerkschaften organisiert, deren Vorstand *wakil ummanim* hiess. In §274 wurde auch der Lohn für 10 verschiedene Kategorien von Handwerkern festgesetzt.[109] Doch war die Bedeutung der Handwerker nicht so gross wie jene der Händler, weil sie nicht auch die politischen Pläne des Herrschers zu erfüllen vermochten. Nach altbabylonischer Auffassung war es nicht immer leicht, eine feste Trennung zwischen Handwerk und "freien Berufen" zu ziehen.[110] Dies ergibt sich aus der Tatsache, dass die Handwerker seit längerer Zeit in einem Dienstverhältnis zum Palast (bzw. zu den Tempeln) standen.[111]

Zu den Vertretern der "freien Berufe" gehörten jene Personen, die sich verpflichteten, eine Leistung gegen Honorar (*qištum*) oder gegen Lohn durchzuführen. Es ist Beweis der besonderen sozialen und kulturellen Auffassung der Redaktoren des CH, dass sie die höchste Relevanz dem Arzt (§215ff), mindestens aber nur dem Chirurgen (*asu*) zuerkannt haben.[112] Einerseits werden ihm für verschiedenartige, erfolgreich durchgeführte Behandlungen fixe Beträge zuerkannt, die weder als Honorar noch als Lohn bezeichnet werden.[113] Aber auch die schwere Strafe für eine wegen Fahrlässigkeit des Arztes misslungene Behandlung beweist, dass der Arzt mittels dieser Sanktion zu höchster Erweiterung seiner Kenntnisse und Konzentration seiner Aufmerksamkeit angehalten wurde; dadurch hat er hohes gesellschaftliches Ansehen erhalten und die seinem Stande zugebilligte Relevanz sichergestellt. - Es ist bemerkenswert, dass der CH sich nicht mit jenen Ärzten befasste, die sich mit der Behandlung anderer als der einen chirurgischen Eingriff erfordernden Krankheiten beschäftigten. Dieser Sektor der Medizin lag nämlich in den Händen der verschiedenen Kategorien von Priestern (Beschwörer, Exorzisten, Wahrsager, u.a.) und diese fanden im CH, wie wir bereits bemerkt hatten, keinen Platz. - Auch der "Stomatologe" war bekannt; mit Zahnextraktionen befasste sich der *gallabum* (ŠU.I),[114] der sonst nach den §§226-227 als Scherer, der die Sklavenmarke schert, verstanden wird; es ist deshalb fraglich, ob seine Tätigkeit zum Kreis der "*ars liberalis*" gehörte; eher war er ein Handwerker, der Zahnextraktionen nur handwerklich und nicht auf Grund einer Fachschulung vornahm.- Zu den freien Berufen konnte eher die Hebamme gehört haben. Wie bereits ihr akkadischer Name *s/tabsutum* (ŠÀ.ZU), "das Weib, das des Mutterleibes kundig ist", andeutet, war sie in der Geburtshilfe[115] geschult; in den altbabylonischen Gesetzen kommt sie jedenfalls nicht vor, im Unterschied zur Amme, *mušeniqtum* (UM.ME.GA.LÁ), deren Verantwortung für den ihr anvertrauten Säugling der §194 regelt, während die GE (Art.32) das Entgelt für die Amme in Naturalien bzw. in Geld festsetzten. Es scheint, dass der Gesetzgeber bei diesen Frauen eine Ausbildung und fachliche Qualifikation voraussetzte und dementsprechend nicht nur ihre Ansprüche, sondern auch ihre Verantwortung regelte.

Die besondere Bedeutung der Landwirtschaft und der Viehzucht ergibt sich auch aus der Tatsache, dass in §§224f. auch die Stellung des Veterinärs[116] berücksichtigt wird, der jedoch für seine Behandlung der Tiere bereits seinen Lohn (*idu*) in tarifierter Höhe (=1/6 Sekel) vom Inhaber des Tieres bekommt. Andererseits muss er ein Fünftel des Tieres bezahlen, das er infolge seiner Fahrlässigkeit umgebracht hat (§225). Im Vergleich zum Entgelt des Arztes ist der Lohn des Veterinärs unvergleichbar niedriger, aber auch sein Risiko für den Fall eines verursachten Misserfolges war entsprechend geringer. Die gesellschaftliche Relevanz des Arztes und des Veterinärs kann also nicht viel differieren.[117]

Vom freien Beruf des Baumeisters, *itinnum* (ŠITIM), kann man nur dann sprechen, wenn er nicht im Dienste des Palastes oder der Tempel stand (vgl. Anm. 111). Wenn er sein Privatunternehmen leitete, galten für ihn die §§228-233, wobei im §228 sein Honorar (*qištum*) festgesetzt wird,[118] während die übrigen Bestimmungen seine Verantwortung und den Umfang seiner Ersatzpflicht regeln. - Ähnlich wird in den folgenden Bestimmungen (§234) die Stellung eines Schiffbauers, *malaḫum*(MÁ.LAḪ$_4$), festgelegt: das Honorar (*qištum*) richtet sich nach der Tonnage (2 Sekel Silber pro 60 gur=180hl); ferner wird seine Haftung für die Sachmängel geregelt, die binnen einem Jahr auf dem Schiff erscheinen (§235). - Schliesslich kann in diese Kategorie auch der Schiffer (ebenfalls *malaḫum*) einbezogen werden, der zugleich mit dem Schiff gemietet wird (§236); auch hier werden zusätzlich die Bestimmungen bezüglich seiner Haftung (§§237, 238) und seines Lohns (§239)[119] angeführt.

Bei der heutigen Gelegenheit, die uns leider nicht erlaubt, das im Titel angegebene Thema zu erschöpfen, sind wir uns völlig vor allem der grossen Schuld bewusst, in der wir gegenüber den Darstellern der Landwirtschaft, der Viehzucht, der Fischerei und anderer wirtschaftlichen Faktoren,[120] also den Hauptquellen der sozialökonomischen Lebens Mesopotamiens, in der Erörterung ihrer Relevanz im CH noch weiterhin stehen. Wir haben bereits beobachtet, dass der CH auf mehrere Fragen, die sich auf das gegebene Thema beziehen, keine oder nur eine sehr lückenhafte Antwort gibt. Unsere Erörterungen müssen deshalb auch die Dokumente aus der juristischen und wirtschaftlichen Praxis, die Briefe, aber auch die literarischen und besonders die religiösen Texte[121] in Betracht ziehen, wenn das Bild der differenzierten Relevanz einzelner Kategorien unter verschiedenen Gesichtspunkten geprüft werden soll.

Es bleibt noch ein wichtiges Teilgebiet unseres Themas für die zukünftige Analyse übrig, nämlich jenes, das sich mit dem Verhältnis des Gesetzgebers zu vollfreien Bürgern in allen Fällen befasst, wo diese ohne Rücksicht auf ihren Beruf oder ihren Stand schlechthin vorkommen. Ferner unterliegt einer eingehender Prüfung die Kategorie der *muškenu*, die immer noch das Finkelsteinsche "evervexing problem" bilden.[122] Allerdings verdienen auch noch die Sklaven, die sonst in der Regel nur Rechtsobjekte waren, im Rahmen des gegenwärtigen Themas eine gewisse Aufmerksamkeit. Ihre Bedeutung, wenn auch unvergleichbar geringer als jene der meisten freigeborenen Personen, lässt sich im CH doch nicht verheimlichen: den Fall des Loskaufes des babylonischen Sklaven (*maru matim*) im Ausland durch den *tamkarum* und den §280 haben wir schon erwähnt (vgl. oben S.177). Eine Berücksichtigung der Familienangehörigen, deren Schuldknechtschaft §117 auf drei Jahre festgesetzt hat, ist begreiflich, weil sie die soziale Einheit und die wirtschaftliche Kraft der Familie - der grundlegenden Einheit des Reiches - zu bewahren suchte; wir treffen aber im CH auch Fälle, die die Relevanz der Sklaven *in radice* bezeugen, wie z.B. den §146, nach dem die Herrin einer Sklavin, die ihr Kinder geboren hat, diese Sklavin nicht aus dem Hause in die Sklaverei verkaufen darf, wenn die Sklavin gegen sie revoltiert. Aus §223 erfahren wir, dass der Herr eines erkrankten Sklaven dem Arzt das Honorar in Höhe von 2/5 dessen bezahlt, was für die Behandlung eines *awilum* vorgeschrieben ist.[123] Die altbabylonischen keilschriftlichen Quellen haben bis jetzt keinen Beleg über Sklavenaufstände bzw. Rebellionen gebracht,[124] was von einer noch mässigen Zahl der Sklaven und vom erträglichen Verhältnis zu ihren Herren zeugt.[125] Dies machte die Sklaven zu notwendigen Gliedern im nationalen Arbeitsprozess und hat auch zu ihrer ihnen vom Gesetzgeber zugestandenen Relevanz beigetragen.[126] Es ist wohl anzunehmen, dass einerseits auch der Fatalismus der mesopotamischen Bevölkerung, der freien sowie der unfreien, ihre fast bedingungslose Unterordnung unter die zeitgenössischen herrschen den religiösen Vorstellungen und die unzählbare Menge von abergläubischen Ansichten,[127] andererseits aber der Mangel einer Persönlichkeit, welche fähig wäre, die Massen für einen revolutionären Kampf zu gewinnen und zu organisieren, hier die bedeutende Rolle spielte.

Um unsere bisherigen Erwägungen zu schliessen, kann man, m.E., mit vollem Recht dem Herrscher und seinen vernünftigen und gebildeten Beratern ein angemessenes Bemühen um den Wohlstand der Bevölkerung des Reiches zugestehen. Die Motiv dafür lagen nicht, wenigstens nicht vor allem, in der Sorge des Herrschers um seinen Thron wegen einer Revolte seitens der Massen,[128] sondern in der Überzeugung, dass sein Land nur dann zu einem wirklichen Weltreich ausgebaut werden kann, wenn die Bevölkerung nicht bloss unter einem, wenn auch gesetzlichen und gut erwogenen Zwang, sondern sich aus eigener Überzeugung von dem grossen Wert der Ordnung und der inneren Sicherheit wohl fühlt, ihre Kräfte zur Aufrechterhaltung und Vergrösserung des Wohlstandes sammelt und gegen den äusseren Feind zu kämpfen entschlossen ist.

Zum Schluss sei noch ein Gedanke[129] angefügt, dessen Richtigkeit sich im Laufe der langen Vergangenheit bewährt hat: "Es soll uns weniger darauf ankommen, nachzuzeichnen, wie die Einrichtungen im geschichtlichen Ablauf tatsächlich funktioniert haben, als vielmehr zu zeigen, wie sie nach dem Willen ihrer Schöpfer funktionieren sollten". Diese Kasersche Devise hilft uns, nicht nur im Bereiche des jetzigen Themas, sondern auch sonst, das heikle Problem der Anwendung und dadurch auch des wirklichen Charakters des hammurapischen Werkes zu berühren: Hammurapi hatte wie kein Gesetzgeber vor ihm und nach ihm, immerhin nicht soviel Macht und Kraft, seinen Willen auf dem Gebiete der Gesetzgebung in allen, ja nicht einmal in allen wichtigen Richtungen, durchzusetzen. Dazu müsste er tatsächlich ein so allmächtiger Herrscher gewesen sein, wie er in der Geschichte der Menschheit, ohne Zweifel zu ihrem Glück, nie erschienen ist. Einen solchen könnten wir nur in der metaphysischen Sphäre suchen. Und unter diesem Gesichtspunkt ist auch das hammurapische Werk zu beurteilen: als ein politisches und propagandistisches Denkmal, dessen Lebenskraft sich dort durchzusetzen vermochte, wo das Leben es brauchte. Sonst ist es nur als stummer Text und als pompöse Worte auf dem Steine der Stele geblieben, der nur vorübergehend *ad maiorem imperatoris gloriam* dienen sollte.

AOF = *Altorientalische Forschungen* [Berlin]

CH = *Codex Hammurapi*

Finet, CH = A. Finet, *Le Code de Hammurapi* [1973]

Klengel, CH = H. Klengel, *Hammurapi von Babylon und seiner Zeit* [1976]

Schmökel, CH = H. Schmökel, *Hammurabi von Babylon* [1958]

Szlechter, CH = E. Szlechter, *Codex Hammurapi* [1977]

CL = *Codex Lipit-Ištar*

GE = Gesetze Eschnunnas

JURA = *Jura: Rivista internazionale di Diritto Romano e Antico* [Napoli]

Korošec, *Keilschriftrecht* = *Handbuch der Orientalistik*, Erg.bd. III : *Orientalisches Recht* [1964]

NO = *Nový Orient* [Praha]

RHDF = *Revue historique de droit français et étranger* [Paris]

RIDA = *Revue internationale des Droits de l'Antiquité* [Brussel]

RSJB = *Recueil de la Société Jean Bodin* [Brussel]

RSt. = P. Koschaker, *Rechtsvergleichende Studien zum Gesetzbuch Hammurapis, Königs von Babylon* [Leipzig 1917]

SATE = E. Lipiński, ed., *State and Temple Economy in the Ancient Near East* [Leuven 1979]

ZfVRW = *Zeitschrift für Vergleichende Rechtswissenschaft*

1 Zur Entwicklung des Interesses um die mesopotamische sozial-ökonomische Problematik und zur grundlegenden Fachliteratur auf diesem Gebiete vgl. übersichtlich bei Klíma, JVRA 24[1973]23ff. Die meisten sowjetischen Beiträge zu diesem Thema hat I.M. Diakonoff in dem Sammelband *Ancient Mesopotamia* [Moskau 1969] herausgegeben.

2 Hier dürfte jedenfalls noch die Rolle der öffentlichen Meinung in die Betrachtung einbezogen werden. Zu ihrer Bedeutung vgl. besonders die Akten der Internazionalen Konferenz in Brussel, 1973: "*La voix de l'opposition en Mésopotamie*" (ed. A. Finet). Siehe auch Klíma, JEOL 19[1967]492ff.

3 Vgl. F.R. Kraus, SATE II, 424ff.

4 Kraus lehnt hier (l.c., S.425) den Ausdruck "Krone" ab, den Yoffee (in seinem Werk *The Economic Role of the Crown in the Old Babylonian Period*) benützt.

5 Zum jetzt häufig gebrauchten Begriff des Hofstaates vgl. besonders Renger, RLA 4,435 (vor allem S.445b).

6 Vgl. Kraus, SATE II, 424: "...wie gross war die Bevölkerung? Wie war sie (im Königreich Babylon) auf Dienstleute des Königs, Tempelpersonal, Freie, Sklaven verteilt? Wieviel wurde wovon seitens wessen produziert? Wer zahlte wieviel Steuern wovon?". - Diese verfänglichen Fragen könnten wir *ad libitum* vermehren (besonders um jene, die sich auf die verschiedenen Kategorien der Freien und ihre ungleiche rechtliche Behandlung beziehen).

7 Vgl. bereits Klengel, OLZ 77[1977]367; Gelb, SATE I, 3.

8 Zur politischen Entwicklung Babyloniens während der vor- und hammurapischen Zeit vgl. Schmökel, *Hammurabi von Babylon* (=CH) [1958]34ff. und Klengel, *Hammurapi von Babylon und seine Zeit* (=CH) [1976]34ff.

9 Vgl. Klíma, ArOr 46 [1978]23ff.; siehe jetzt Komoróczy, SATE II, 411ff. (mit der entsprechenden Literatur).

10 Unter dem Begriff *ugarum* versteht man die Dorfgemeinschaft wohl in §§53,54, 58,259 (zum letzten Diakonoff, VDI 1952/2,256[8], nach dem zwar das gestohlene landwirtschaftliche Gerät, *epinnu*, einem Privaten gehörte, jedoch dem Bedarf der ganzen Gemeinschaft diente; zum Wesen des *epinnu* vgl. noch Cardascia, RA 60 [1966]153ff.) - Sonst kommt noch der Ausdruck *alum* vor (§§23,24), den Diakonoff, l.c., 230 ebenfalls mit "obščina" (=Dorfgemeinschaft) wiedergibt. Sonst wird er als "die Stadt" übersetzt (siehe CAD A/i,382b); vgl. auch D.S. Baret, *La Parola del passato* CXXXVIII [1971]201ff. - Im §32 übersetzt auch Diakonoff *alum* als "poselenie" Gemeinde, und nicht als "Dorfgemeinschaft", weil es sich hier um militärische Personen handelt, die unmittelbar mit dem Palastboden - und nicht jenem der Dorfgemeinschaft - verbunden waren (siehe Diakonoff, l.c.,231[5]).

11 Siehe z.B. F.X. Steinmetzer, *Über den Grundbesitz in Babylonien zur Kassitenzeit* [1919]; Matouš NO 19/3 [1964]68ff.; idem, *Das Altertum* 15 [1969]3ff.

12 Vgl. Klengel, CH, 57.

13 Vgl. Komoróczy, SATE II,414.

14 Klengel, l.c., vermutet, dass der Zusammenbruch des Reiches von Ur die Zentralisation beseitigt hat, was dem selbstbewussten Sumerer besonders

willkommen war. Jedenfalls hat Hammurapi dieselbe zentralisierende Politik ganz skrupellos weitergeführt.

15 Zu den ersten Anzeichen von Bürokratismus noch in der sumerischen Zeit vgl. M. Lambert, *La naissance de la bureaucratie*, Revue Hist. CCXXIV/1 [1960] 1ff.; idem, *Le premier triomphe de la bureaucratie*, l.c., 457 [1961] 21ff.

16 Bezüglich dieser Terminologie vgl. zur ersten Information R. Monier, *Petit vocabulaire de Droit Romain* [1930] 225.

17 Dazu vgl. Klíma, RHDF LIII [1975] 575ff. (mit der entsprechenden Literatur); idem, *Festschrift L. Matouš* [Budapest, im Druck].

18 Vgl. Szlechter, RIDA 4 [1957] 83f.; W. Preiser, *Festschrift K. Engisch* [1969] 32f.; Klíma, *Festschrift M.A. Beek* [1974] 151f.

19 Während am Ende des Prologes (CH V 15ff.) die Rolle des bevollmächtigenden Gottes dem Marduk zugewiesen war (in der Version von Wiseman, JSS 7 [1962] 161f., wird als solcher der Gott Enlil angeführt).

20 Vgl. CH I 12; II 41,50; IV 12,30,38,45; V 16; XXIV^{r} 35,50; XXV^{r} 23, 35; XXVI^{r} 16,74,92; XXVII^{r} 12; XXVIII^{r} 33,47,80. Nach Gelb, SATE I, 93, wird *nišu* verstanden als "people" who were released (from debt slavery) : jedenfalls ist an solche konkrete Interpretation in den besprochenen kaum zu denken. Mann kann allenfalls die weitere Deutung von *nišu* annehmen (siehe Gelb, l.c.), nach der *nišu* dem sumerischen u k ù gleichgestellt wird, im allgemeinen Sinne des "people - especially people of a nation".

21 Finet, *Le Code de Hammurapi* (=CH) S.31, übersetzt: "la totalité des gens"; Szlechter, *Codex Hammurapi* (=CH) S.14: "tous les peuples". Vgl. bereits Madeleine David, ArOr 15 [1946] 341 ff.

22 Vgl. CH I 47; XXV^{r} 93. Sonst wird auch die Wendung *šir matim*, "Wohlergehen des Landes (d.h. der Bevölkerung)" benutzt (CH XXIV^{r} 33).

23 Vgl. CH I 41; XXIV^{r} 11; XXV^{r} 86.

24 Vgl. Seux, *Hymnes et prières aux dieux de Babylonie et d'Assyrie* [1976] 103[3], der diese Wendung interpretiert als "Expression poétique pour désigner l'humanité dont il est difficile de dire à quoi elle fait illusion". Siehe noch CAD Ṣ 76a: "The expression (*niši*) *ṣalmat qaqqadi* is a poetic term referring to mankind as a totality, created by the gods and kept in safe pastures by the kings". Wenn auch eine poetische Färbung der Rahmentexte unbestritten bleibt, so war es immer die Absicht der Redaktoren, gerade in Form einer Metaphor den echten Tatbestand anzudeuten, wenn nicht sogar direkt verständlich zu machen. Vgl. noch AHw 1077b: "Schwarzköpfige, Menschen" (ohne nähere Erklärung, nur mit Hinweis auf Landsberger-Gurney, AfO 18 [1957] 83,Nr.179).

25 Vgl. ebenfalls CH I 43: *matim nuwurim*, "das Land (d.h. die Bewohner) zu erfreuen"; vgl. Finet, CH, S.30: "pour ... illuminer le Pays"; Szlechter, CH, S.14: "que je réjouisse le pays".

26 Vgl. CH IV 54f.: *mušušer ammi*, "der die Völker ordnet"; cf. Finet, CH, S.42: "celui qui dirige les peuples"; Szlechter, CH, S.17: "qui rendit justice au peuple". Siehe AHw 44b: *mušušer am-mi*, "der in Ordnung bringt die Völker"; CAD A/ii, 77a: "who provides justice for the people". Siehe auch AHw 255a: "Menschen ... (ge)recht leiten (von *ešeru*) und CAD E 352b: "to be put in order, to be fitted out correctly".

27 Die Louvre-Tafel des Prologes (vgl. Nougayrol, RA 45 [1951] 75 IV 10) hat die Variante *ḫa-am-mi*; vgl. Finet, CH, S.42.

28 Wenn auch sonst die Wendung *mat Šumerim u Akkadim*, "das Land von S. und A." benutzt wird (vgl. CH V 8f., XXIV^{r} 50f.).

29 Dazu vgl. C.H. Gordon, Stratification of Society in HC, *The Joshua Starr Memorial Volume* [1953] 17f.; Schmökel, CH, 49ff.; Cardascia, *La monocratie*, RSJB 20 [1970] 349; Klengel, CH 42ff.; siehe auch Harris, JAOS 88 [1969] 727ff. (mit den entsprechenden Textbelegen).

30 Man spricht in dieser Richtung von der Säkularisierung der hammurapischen Priesterschaft, in dem Sinne, dass die Kontrolle der Reichsangelegenheiten vom Tempel auf den Herrscher überging (vgl. C.H. Gordon, l.c., 19; Harris, JCS 15 [1961] 117ff.). Es scheint jedoch, dass diese "Laizisation der Staatsverwaltung nicht die erwartete Wirkungen hatte und dass gerade sie sogar zu einem der Gründe der politischen und wirtschaftlichen Schwächung des Reiches bereits am Ende der hammurapischen Regierung führte" (so Renger, SATE I,252); vgl. neustens Limet, *Akkadica* 21 [1981] 56.

31 Vgl. CL III 57 f. (Prolog): d u m u - n i t á d u m u - m í N i b - r u^{ki} ... U r i m^{ki} . . . I s i n^{ki} .

32 Vgl. CL III 63f. (Prolog): d u m u - n i t á d u m u - m í k i - e n - g i k i - u r i und CL III 17′ (Epilog ex UM 29-16-218): s u - k i - e n - g i k i - u r i ḫ u - m u - d ù g (nach Steele, CL, S.23[105]: "Literally: made well the bodies of the Sumerians and Akkadians").

33 Vgl. M. Lambert, *La Revue du Louvre* 21 [1971] Nr. 4/5, S.3f.; Edzard, *Acta Antiqua* 22 [1974] 145f.

34 D.h. Lagaš/Girsu, Uruk, Larsa und Badtibira.

35 Vgl. Finet, CH, S.134: "originaires du Pays"; Szlechter, CH, S.174: "originaires (litt. enfants) du pays". Siehe AHw 616a: "Landeskind"; CAD M/i, 315b: "citizen, native (of a city, a country)".

36 Im §281 wird der Fall geregelt, dass es sich um einen fremden, d.h. nicht-babylonischen, Sklaven handelt, der als *maru matim šanitim* gekennzeichnet wird. Für diesen Sklaven muss sein ehemaliger Herr dem Käufer den Loskaufpreis, den er für ihn bezahlt hat, ersetzen.

37 Die Versuche um die sinngerechte Interpretation dieser Bestimmung sind bereits seit der Studie von M. Schorr, WZKM 22 [1908] 385f., zu verfolgen. Vgl. Koschaker, RSt., 101ff. und neuerlich Haase, ZfVRW 67/2 [1965] 150ff.

38 Korošec, *Keilschriftrecht*, 115f., spricht sogar von einer "wahrhaften *crux interpretum*".

39 Nur beispielsweise könnte man den Fall des §117 anführen (Beschränkung der Schuldknechtschaft auf drei Jahre) oder jenen des §146 (Schutz der Sklavin, die ihrem Herrn, der mit einer *naditum* verheiratet war, ein Kind geboren hat, gegen den Verkauf seitens der *naditum* aus dem Hause) bzw. den Fall der milden Bestrafung des revoltierenden Sklaven gemäss dem §282 u.a.

40 Vgl. Leemans, RLA IV [1973] 85 (mit der entsprechenden Literatur).

41 Vgl. Jakobson, VDI 1963-2, 130; Szlechter, RA 58 [1964] 27ff.; idem, CH, S.66f.

42 Es sei noch bemerkt, dass gemäss dem Schlusssatz des §32 die Immobilien des

gefangenen Kriegers für seine Lösung nicht verwendet werden dürfen (sie bilden nämlich das ihm aus dem Titel seines Dienstverhältnisses vom Palast zugeteilte Gut).

43 Zu diesem Begriff vgl. jetzt Kraus, SATE II, 425f.; Gelb, SATE I, 4f.; Renger, SATE I, 251f., Bogaert, SATE II, 746f.

44 Vgl. Klengel, AOF IV [1976] 97.

45 Vgl. Renger, SATE I., 253f.

46 Siehe AHw 616a (sub 10a): "Bürger".

47 Mit Ausnahme von Fällen, in denen, die Redaktoren der Rahmentexte als gute Psychologen und fast mit einer getarnten Demagogie entweder die Verdienste des Herrschers um die Konsolidation, Entfaltung und sogar um die Üppigkeit der bereits seit früherer Zeit zum babylonischen Reich gehörenden Städte (z.B. Nippur, Uruk, Kiš, Kutha, Borsippa) oder sein diplomatisches Benehmen gegenüber den eroberten Städten (Larsa, Malgûm, Mari, Tuttul, Ešnunna) betonen. Vgl. Finet, AIPHOS 20 [1968-72 (publ.1973)] 240f.; Klíma, *Festschrift M.A. Beek*, 163[82] und 164[83].

48 Die Erforschung dieser Organisation in allen Richtungen ist Gegenstand von zahlreichen Studien (in erster Reihe jener von I.M. Diakonoff) und war auch Thema von internationalen Sessionen; vgl. dazu Klíma, ArOr 46 [1978] 23ff.

49 Cf. Finet, CH, S.62: "les occupants de la terre à limon"; Szlechter, CH, S.85: "les gens de la plaine"; ganz deutlich Diakonoff, l.c., 234: "ljudi vozdelanoj zemli obščiny" (=Menschen am Kultivierten Boden der Dorfgemeinschaft) und neuerdings Haase, *Die keilschr. Rechtssammlungen* [1979²] 37: "die 'Söhne' der Flur" mit der Note 37[4]: "d.h. die Dorfgenossen".

50 Dazu neuerdings Renger, *Encycl. Britt.* [15.Edit.,1974] 599; idem, AfO 23 [1970] 73ff.

51 Zum §58 CH, wo die zeitliche Regelung der Weide von Kleinvieh (die sg. Sömmerung) auf gemeinsamem Gelände (*ugaru*) in schwer interpretierbarer Weise dargestellt wird, vgl. aus der umfassenden Literatur bes. Dossin, RA 66 [1972] 77ff.; F.R. Kraus, RA 70 [1976] 173ff. und neuerdings K. Butz, SATE I, 349ff.- Zum *ugarum* im §259 vgl. bereits Anm.10 oben.

52 Vielleicht hat diese Tatsache d.h. die unbedingte Nötigkeit, die ordentliche Bewirtschaftung der bei den Wasserwegen liegenden Geländen zur Aufrechterhaltung der Dorfgemeinschaftsorganisation beigetragen - natürlich unter der Leitung der staatlichen (Palast) Aufsichtsorgane.

53 Vgl. Szlechter, RIDA 4 [1957] 77f.

54 Vgl. CH IV 45 (*re'um niši*); siehe im allgem. I. Seibert, *Hirt, Herde, König* [1969]; Limet, *La voix de l'opposition*, 2, mit Rücksicht auf W.G. Lambert, BWL 229,232.

55 Die einzige Ausnahme könnte wohl der Ausdruck *belum* (geschrieben mit dem Zeichen EN) im CH XXVI[r] 41 bilden, was wohl auch den Pontifiken bedeuten könnte, wie Szlechter in der analogen Passage des Epiloges von CL (cf. RA 51 [1957] 81) diesen Ausdruck als "un pontife-EN" überführt. Im Sinne dieser Analogie sollte in der obigen Stelle des CH eher *enum* als *belum* unter dem Zeichen EN verstanden werden.

56 Vgl. Klengel, CH, S.149ff.

57 Vgl. z. B. Renger, ZA 59 [1969] 121f. und bereits ZA 58 [1967] 114ff.

58 Vgl. z. B. Schmökel, CH, S.59; Klengel, CH, S.112.

59 Aus diesen Gründen ist gerade bei jenen Akten, zu deren Vollzug die Anwesenheit der Öffentlichkeit gegeben war (wie z.B. beim Ordal, bei der Vereidigung der Zeugen oder der Parteien) die Kompetenz der Priester als Gerichtsorgane nicht geändert. Man kann wohl schwer den altbabylonischen Klerus gegen den laikalen Teil der Bevölkerung in Opposition stellen, wie wir es beim C.H. Gordon, l.c., 19, finden (vgl. seinen Titel "Clergy vs.Laity").

60 F.R. Kraus, RA 73 [1979] 62, übersetzt diesen Ausdruck in der älteren (primären) Form als "königliche Massregel", die "eine bestimmte Art von Eingriff des Königs in das herrschende Recht" bezeichnet; zum *ṣimdatum* vgl. ebenfalls M. deJ. Ellis, JCS 24 [1972] 74ff.

61 So nach der bevorzugten Bezeichnung dieser Frauenkategorien von Klengel, CH, S.75 u.ö.

62 In den Fragmenten des CL kommen diese Frauen (und nur einige ihrer Kategorien - *ugbabtum*, *naditum* und *qadištum*) in der erbrechtlichen Bestimmung des Art. 27(22) vor.

63 Zu den ersten Assyriologen, die sich mit diesen Frauen beschäftigten, gehörte der tschechische Orientalist V. Hazuka, der in seiner Studie "Beiträge aus den altbabylonischen Rechtsurkunden zur Erklärung des Hammurabi-Kodex" [1907] eine Sektion der "Vermietung von Feldern der Priesterinnen" (S.22-30) widmete. Die Literatur über die sg. Klosterpriesterinnen ist heute sehr umfassend: aus der älteren B. Landsberger, ZA 30 [1915-16] 72ff.; Klíma, *Untersuchungen zum altbabylonischen Erbrecht* [1940] 39ff., und die schon oben zitierten, neuen und grundlegenden Darstellungen von R. Harris und J. Renger.

64 Vgl. V. Hazuka, l.c., 22ff.; R. Harris, *Ancient Sippar* [1975] 142ff., 209ff., 302ff.

65 Die Ausübung dieser Kapitalstrafe geschah durch den Feuertod, also in der Form, die einerseits abschreckend wirkte, andererseits eine grosse Schau für das breit Publikum darstellte.

66 Vgl. vor allem R. Harris, Or NS 30 [1961] 163ff.

67 C.H. Gordon, l.c., kommt zur Überzeugung, dass der Status der männlichen Priesterschaft durch Gewohnheitsrecht geregelt wurde. Zum Gewohnheitsrecht im allgemeinen vgl. Haase, RLA III, 322f.

68 Vgl. Gelb, RA 66 [1972] 4f. (bei der Behandlung der sg. *arua*-Institution).

69 Vgl. Harris, JCS 15 [1961] 117ff.

70 Vgl. Edzard, RLA IV [1975] 335ff. (Art. "Herrscher"), dazu Hirsch, WZKM 68 [1976] 97; Renger, RLA IV, 445f. und WdO 8 [1976] 228ff.; siehe auch Leemans, *Symbolae David* II [1968] 207ff.

71 Siehe bereits bei A. Walter, *Das altbabyl.Gerichtswesen* [1915] 80 (besonders für die Tätigkeit, die der Herrscher unter der Bezeichnung *mišaram šakanu* ausübte); vgl. ferner zu diesem Titel Van Proosdij, *Symb.Van Oven* [1946] 29ff.; Szlechter, RIDA 4 [1967] 83; Seux, *Epithètes* [1967] 316f.; Renger, WdO 8 [1976] 228ff.

72 Vgl. Hallo, *Royal Titles*, 49ff.; Seux, l.c., 305ff., und bereits RA 59 [1965] 11ff.

73 Wohl aber erst dann, wenn der Ehegatte seiner Frau verziehen hat; vgl. bereits San Nicolò, RLA I, 467f.; Szlechter, CH, S.116.

74 Zum Begriff des Hofstaates während der altbabyl.Zeit vgl. jetzt Renger, RLA IV [1975] 445f.

75 Zu altbabyl. Beamten vgl. Krückmann, RLA I, 444ff. (Beitrag "Beamter" sub b die Beamten der ersten Dynastie von Babylon); vgl. jetzt Renger, l.c. 445 (§34:Liste von Angehörigen des königlichen Hofstaates).

76 Diese kennen z.B. den Titel *šakkanakkum*, "Verwalter einer Stadt", *šapir narim*, "Obervorsteher der Navigation und Irrigation" (nach AHw 1172: "Flusskommandant") und *bel tertim*, "Beauftragter" (vgl. AHw 120b u.1350b): alle kommen im Art. 50 GE vor.

77 EA:GÌR.ARAD *matim*, "der Vorstand einer Provinz" (Art. 22); *ra'ibanu*, "Stellvertreter" (Art. 22); vgl. F.R. Kraus, *Edikt*, 180; Stol, *Studies in Old Babylonian History* [1976] 73ff. - In keinem von den altbabyl. Gesetzen kommt *šandabakku* (sumer.: š a_{13}-d u b - b a) vor, den jetzt Souček, *Dějiny pravěku a starověku* (=Geschichte der Vorzeit und des Altertums) I, 224 für den Finanzbeauftragten in der hammurapischen Zeit hält. Nach einer brieflichen Mitteilung (ex 7.4.80) von J. Krecher, kann man in š. einen "mit Rechnungen betrauten Funkzionär" erblicken - wohl keinen "Finanzminister".

78 Zum ÉNSI-*išš(i)akku(m)* vgl. Hirsch, ZDMG 68 [1976] 97; F.R. Kraus, SATE II, 429ff.

79 Zum *girseqqum* vgl. jetzt Renger, l.c., 442,445f.; bereits Gelb, *Festschrift A. Salonen*, 54f.

80 Der Herold konnte sowohl ein untergeordneter Funktionär als auch ein hoher Würdenträger werden; vgl. Kienast, RLA IV, 333f.; Renger, l.c., 446a. Siehe schon Ebeling, RLA I, 332 (Beitrag "Ausrufer").

81 Vom Beamtentum der hammurapischen Epoche sind wir am besten durch die amtliche Korrespondenz des Herrschers mit seinen Statthaltern sowie auch durch mehrere Privaturkunden unterrichtet; zur ersteren vgl. besonders Thureau-Dangin, RA 21 und F.R. Kraus, ABb 4 sowie Ungnad, *Babylonische Briefe*, a.a.O.; zu anderen vgl. neuerlich Klengel, AOF IV, 97ff.

82 Im Art. 35(30) CL kommt der Ausdruck d i - k u_5, "Richter" vor; vgl. zu ihm z.B. Falkenstein, NG, I, 32.

83 Vgl. zu ihm jetzt ausführlich Szlechter, CH, S.29ff. Ausserdem kommt der Ausdruck *daianum* noch in den §§9,16,131,172 (als Richter in den Strafsachen), 168,171 (als Richter im Arbitrageverfahren) vor. Im Epilog wird Šamaš mit dem Epitheton *daianum* versehen (XXIV^r 85, XXVII^r 14).

84 Im §5 wird der unkorrekte Richter aus dem Richterkollegium entfernt und des Amtes enthoben; im §202 wird der Mensch, der eine Realinjurie gegenüber einer dem Range nach höher stehenden Person begeht, vor dem *puḫrum* bestraft.

85 Vgl. F.R. Kraus, *Vom mesop. Menschen*, 76.

86 Vgl. D.S. Barett, l.c., 203; Klíma, ArOr 46 [1978] 34; Klengel, AOF IV [1976] 98 und bereits OrNS 29 [1960] 372ff.; Harris, JAOS 88 [1968] 730; Szlechter, CH, S.56f. und 57[157].

87 Vgl. besonders F.R. Kraus, *Vom mesop. Menschen*, 18ff. (mit der entsprechenden Literatur).

88 Vgl. Cassin, *Annales* 1960, n° 4, S.742ff.; Renger in *Seals and Sealing in the Ancient Near East* [1977] 75ff.

89 Vgl. bereits Falkenstein, WdO 1 [1948] 172ff.; Gadd, *Teachers and Students in the Oldest Schools* [1956] u.a.

90 Bereits auch in GE (Art. 27).

91 Vgl. die §§7,Q,104,122,151,165,171,177,178,179,182.

92 Völlig *a contrario* z.B. der justinianischen Konstitution "*Omnem*", die vom Kaiser allen Mitgliedern der kompilatorischen Kommission des *Corpus Iuris* namentlich adressiert wurde.

93 Vgl. C.H. Gordon, l.c., 19f. ("Military vs. Civilian").

94 Vgl. zu ihr Petschow, RLA III, 258; E. Salonen, RLA IV 1975 246; Klengel, CH,S.146ff.,169ff.

95 "Veterans Bill of Rights" nach C.H. Gordon, l.c.

96 Zur Stellung der Kriegsgefangenen vgl. besonders Szlechter, RA 58 [1964] 23ff.

97 Zu diesen militärischen Funktionären vgl. neuerlich Harris, JAOS 88 [1968] 730f.; Szlechter, CH,S.67[192],68f.; es ist nicht ohne interesse, dass im CH der Oberkommandant, *wakil amurim*, UGULA MAR.TU, nicht genannt wird; vgl. zu ihm E. Salonen, l.c.,245a; Harris, l.c.,730.

98 Siehe Wilhelm II., *Das Königtum im alten Mesopotamien* [1938] 27.

99 Vgl. C.H. Gordon, l.c.,20.

100 Vgl. Komoróczy, SATE II, 417f.

101 Zur Namenetymologie vgl. Landsberger, *Festschrift Baumgartner* [1967] 178; A. Salonen, *Fussbekleidung*, [1969] 109; E. Salonen, *Erwerbsleben* [1970] 7; Leemans, *The Merchant*, 4[24]; F.R. Kraus, *Vom mesop. Menschen*, 111; Garelli, *Revue Historique* 260/2 [1978] 284f. Siehe auch die Beiträge in den Akten der XXIII RAI: "Trade in the Ancient Near East".

102 Vgl. F.R. Kraus, SATE II, 428ff.

103 Zur Interpretation dieser Bestimmungen vgl. Szlechter, CH, S.104ff.

104 Vgl. die §§108-111 (und später auch die Art. 16′, 17′, 18′ des EA); siehe Bottéro, ZA 23 [1965] 156ff.; Klengel, CH,148ff.

105 Vgl. Landsberger, l.c., 179ff.

106 Vgl. E. Salonen, *Erwerbsleben*, 28ff.; dazu Diakonoff, BiOr 32 [1975] 225f.; für die neubabylonische Periode vgl. Weisberg, *Guild Structure and Political Allegiance in Early Achaemenid Mesopotamia* [1967] (siehe das Register dortselbst); Cocquerillat, RLA IV [1973] 98ff.

107 Vgl. §§188,189 (der ausgelernte Lehrling gehörte schon der Gewerkschaft und durfte nicht von den Eltern revindiziert werden).

108 Der Handwerker heisst *mar ummanim*, DUMU.UM.MI.A, was also als "Mitglied der Handwerkergewerkschaft" übertragen werden kann. Vgl. jetzt Szlechter, CH,S.147. Andererseits, Kraus, *Vom mesop. Menschen*, 71, übersetzt *m.u.* als "geborener Handwerker", woraus er auf die Vererbung des Handwerkerunternehmens schliesst. Es ist wohl angebrachter, nach der Analogie etwa zum "*mar tamkarim*=Mitglied der Kaufmannschaft" die Szlechtersche Interpretation des *m.u.* zu wählen.

109 Leider ist gerade der Text dieser Bestimmung ziemlich stark beschädigt; so erfahren wir wenigstens, dass die Löhne des Steinschneiders, des Schmiedes, des Zimmermanns, des Schusters, des Rohrarbeiters und des Maurers festgesetzt wurden (immer pro 1 Tag).

110 Zu *artes liberales* vgl. neuerlich Hengstl, ZS 93 [1976] 553f.

111 Davon scheint der Ausdruck *arad ekalli* zu zeugen (siehe A.L. Oppenheim, ArOr 17/2[1949] 227ff.), der "Baumeister" bedeutet; dies entspricht der Verbindung zwischen dem konkreten Handwerk und seiner Ausübung im Dienste des Palastes bzw. der Tempel, d.h. der einzigen Unternehmer, die die Mittel für die Besorgung des entsprechenden Materials hatten.

112 Vgl. Von Soden, WZKM 55 [1959] 49ff. Der Ausdruck *asu* wurde früher als "Kenner des Wassers" (oder in der Form *iazu* als "Kenner des Öls") interpretiert; nach CAD A/II, 347b, wird diese Interpretation verworfen: "not to be interpreted as one who knows the water "; Biggs, RA 60 [1966] 176[4], interpretiert den *asu* als einen Schreiber, der in der Medizin eine fachliche Ausbildung erhalten hat und als solcher in die Kategorie der Handwerker gehört. Gegen diese letztere Vermutung scheint jedoch der Umstand zu sprechen, dass der *asu* nach dem CH keinen Lohn erhielt, sondern ein nicht bezeichnetes Entgelt, was bestätigen könnte, dass der *asu* ein in der Schreiberschule (d.h. in einer Lehranstalt vom breiteren Sinn) Fachmann in der Heilkunde geworden ist, der dann als Zugehöriger zur Reihe der die *artes liberales* Ausübenden angesehen werden kann.

113 Die Höhe dieser Beträge ist verschieden, nicht nur nach der Art des chirurgischen Eingriffes, sondern auch nach der sozialen Stellung des Patienten (z.B. für den Sklaven bezahlt sein Herr ein Fünftel des Betrages, den für denselben Eingriff der *awilum* zu zahlen hat). Vgl. R. Biggs, *History of Science* 8 [1969] 94ff.; A.L. Oppenheim, *Bull. of the Hist. of Medic.* 36 [1962] 97ff.; Von Soden, WZKM 55 [1959] 53ff.; Haase, *Deutsches Ärzteblatt* 67 [1970] 856ff.

114 Vgl. Contenau, *La médicine en Assyrie et Babylonie*, [1938] 33.

115 Vgl. Von Soden, AfO 18 [1957] 119ff.

116 Siehe die Wendungen: *asu alpim* (Rinderveterinär) und *asu imerim* (Eselveterinär).

117 Zu dem Veterinär gebührenden Ersatz vgl. Szlechter, CH, S.155f.

118 Die Grösse des Honorars richtet sich nach der Fläche des Baugrundstückes (pro Sar=ca 35m^2 gehören ihm 2 Sekel Silber).

119 Im Text wird nur gesagt, dass der gemietete Schiffer pro Jahr 6 *gur* (=18 hl) Getreide erhält.

120 Dafür findet man ausgezeichnete Anregungen nicht nur in den älteren Werken von Koschaker (besonders ZA 47 [1942] 135ff.), sondern auch in der neuen Literatur, z.B. bei Diakonoff, Gelb, Kraus und neuestens bei Klengel, Ellis, Yoffee, in dem Sammelwerk "Essays on the Ancient Near East" (=*Memorial for J.J. Finkelstein* [1977] ed. Ellis) in SATE I,II.

121 Einen dringenden Anstoss zur Berücksichtigung dieser Texte liefert neuerlich der Beitrag "*Inuma Ilu awilum*" von T. Jacobsen in *Memorial for J.J. Finkelstein*, 113ff.

122 Vgl. Klíma, Acta Antiqua 22 [1974] 268.

123 Der Herr ist natürlich nicht verpflichtet, seinen erkrankten Sklaven durch den Arzt behandeln zu lassen. Dass Honorar bildete eigentlich das Zehntel des durchschnittlichen Preises eines Sklaven, so dass es für den Herrn vorteilhafter werden konnte, das Honorar zu bezahlen, besonders wenn es sich um einen bewährten und mit Fachkenntnissen versehenen Sklaven gehandelt hat.

124 Der einzige bemerkenswerte Aufstand der Massen ist aus der Zeit Sargons von Akkad belegt (vgl. Garelli in *Histoire générale de travail* [1960] 100ff.).

125 Sogar der Sklave, der seinen Herrn verleugnet hat, wurde nur durch das Abschneiden des Ohres bestraft (§282), damit seine Arbeitskraft nicht gefährdet wäre (vgl. jedoch §173 der hethit. Ges., wo in solchem Falle dem Sklaven die Todesstrafe droht). Dagegen dem Sohn eines *awīlum*, der seinen Vater geschlagen hat, wurde die Hand abgehaut (§195).

126 Vgl. Gelb, *Kramer Anniversary Volume* [1976] 200.

127 Vgl. Bottéro, JESHO IV [1961] 162ff.

128 Eher wegen eines durch individuelle Personen geplanten Komplottes (deshalb die vorsichtige Massnahme im §109).

129 Vgl. Kaser, *Jahrbuch der AdW in Göttingen* [1966] 32; dazu Poláček, *System und Strukturen* [1976] 29 u.55.

ZUR FRAGE DER PERIODIZITÄT DER ALTBABYLONISCHEN *MĪŠARUM*-ERLÄSSE

G. Komoróczy (Budapest)

Seit F.R. Kraus den Text des *mīšarum*-Erlasses des Königs Ammī-ṣaduqa (1646-1626) in einer umfassenden Bearbeitung vorgelegt hat,[1] gelten dieser Text und seine - weniger bekannten - Parallelen als erstrangige Dokumente der Wirtschaftspolitik des altbabylonischen Staates.[2] Trotzdem ist der "Sitz im Leben" der altbabylonischen *mīšarum*-Akte noch nicht in allen seiner Aspekte hinreichend geklärt worden.[3] In den folgenden Ausführungen, die der Quellenlage entsprechend bloss spekulativen Charakter haben können, möchte ich zu den Diskussionen um ihre eventuelle Periodizität, und dadurch auch zum Problem ihres wirtschaftsgeschichtlichen Hintergrunds, Stellung nehmen. Seien diese Gedanken Igor' Mikhailovič gewidmet, dem Gelehrten, der unsere Vorstellungen über die Gesellschaftsstruktur Mesopotamiens gründlich umgestaltet hat,[4] und von dem auch ich, ohne dass ich wirklich sein Schüler gewesen wäre, in zahlreichen, stets anregenden Gesprächen sehr viel Wesentliches lernen durfte.

Dem Text nach kennen wir lediglich einen *mīšarum*-Erlass beinahe vollständig, den Ammī-ṣaduqas.[5] Ausserdem ist noch ein Fragment des Erlasses von Samsu-iluna (1749-1712) bekannt.[6] Die zahlreichen Belege für verschiedene *mīšarum*-Akte in den Quellen der altbabylonischen Zeit[7] erlauben uns dennoch, den *mīšarum*-Akt als eine, während der altbabylonischen Zeit mehrmals praktizierte Massnahme zu postulieren.

Das Wesen des *mīšarum*-Aktes ist bereits von M. Schorr richtig erkannt worden.[8] Gleich nach der Erstveröffentlichung des kleinen Londoner Fragments BM 78259,[9] welches später von F.R. Kraus als ein Exemplar des Erlasses von Ammī-saduqa ("Exemplar B") erkannt worden ist,[10] hat er den Akt "Seisachthie" genannt. In diesem Wortgebrauch schloss sich ihm später auch C.J. Gadd an.[11] Seisachtheia (σεισάχθεια) heisst im Griechischen "Abschüttlung einer Last" (vgl. ὡς ἀποσεισάμενον τὸ βάρος).[12] Das Wort wird von den Alten als Euphemismus für "Nachlass von Schulden" (ἡ τῶν χρεῶν ἀποκοπή) betrachtet.[13] Mit diesem Wort wurde im alten Athen der Schulderlass Solons (594 v. u. Z.) bezeichnet, d. h. jene einmalige Massnahme des Ersten Archonten, durch die er "alle bestehenden hypothekarischen Schulden für hinfällig und die Verpfändung eines Atheners für ungesetzlich" erklärte.[14] Tatsächlich beweist der von F.R. Kraus vorgelegte Text die Richtigkeit der frühen Benennung,[15] wie es schon aus der nachstehenden Übersicht klar hervorgeht.

Der *mīšarum*-Erlass des Königs Ammī-ṣaduqa enthält u. a. die folgenden Bestimmungen.[16] "Weil der König dem Land gerechte Ordnung geschaffen hat",[17] werden die verzinslichen Schulden der Landesbürger (lú *ak-ka-di-i ù* lú *a-mu-ur-ri-i*) an Gerste und Silber getilgt (§ 4), die Abgaben verschiedener Hirten, die sie dem Staat ("Palast") zu liefern hatten, sofern diese im Rückstand sind, erlassen (§ 12), bestimmte Abgaben von dem Ernteertrag nicht zugeteilt (§ 15),[18] die Rückstände der Schenkin dem Staat gegenüber bzw. die Schulden (sc. der Landesbürger) einer Schenkin gegenüber erlassen (§ 16[19] bzw. § 17), die in Schulddienst gegebenen freien Personen freigelassen (§ 20) usw. Der Erlass erstreckt sich nicht auf normale Handelsbeziehungen, wie etwa Vorschuss auf Kaufpreis (§ 8), Einlage in einer Geschäftsreise oder einer Gesellschaft (vgl. § 9), Sklavenverkauf (§ 21[20]). Die eventuelle Nichtbeachtung der Bestimmungen wird streng bestraft (vgl. §5, 6, 7, 18, 22). Der König rechnet auch damit, dass das verzinsliche Darlehen, damit die Bestimmung umgangen wird, später betrügerisch als Kaufpreis oder Einlage hingestellt werden kann; für Versuche dieser Art sind ebenfalls strenge Strafen in Aussicht gestellt (§ 6, 7).[21]

Denn der *mīšarum*-Akt war, wie später auch die Seisachtheia Solons, ein Korrektiv im alltäglichen Ablauf des Wirtschaftslebens, das zur Aufhebung gewisser ungünstiger Entwicklungen bestimmt war.

Bei der historischen Interpretation einer solchen Massnahme ist vor allem ihr Inhalt von Belang; jedoch braucht man für die richtige Einschätzung chronologische Koordinaten. Damit sind wir schon bei dem Problem der Periodizität selbst.

F.R. Kraus hat in seinem Buch alle Textstellen gesammelt und chronologisch geordnet behandelt, die in den schriftlichen Quellen der ersten Hälfte des 2. Jahrtausends v. u. Z. einen *mīšarum*-Akt bezeugen können.[22] Seine Sammlung umfasst über 60 Belege. Manche davon beziehen sich auf den Anfang dieser Epoche, auf das 20. Jahrhundert v. u. Z.,[23] manche auf das 19. Jahrhundert v. u. Z.,[24] die meisten aber auf die Regierungszeit des Königs Rīm-Sîn von Larsa (1822-1763)[25] und auf die Regierung der Dynastie von Babylon, von Sîn-muballit (1812-1793) an.[26] Aus diesen Belegen, die wir hier nicht ausführlich zu zitieren brauchen, sieht man genau, dass sich die *mīšarum*-Belege etwa seit Rīm-Sîn, dem ausgehenden 19. Jahrhundert v. u. Z., stark vermehren. Der *mīšarum*-Akt scheint gerade in dieser Zeit zu einer recht oft praktizierten Massnahme zu werden. Auf die meisten Herrscher fallen nun mehrere *mīšarum*-Akte.

Auf Grund der von F.R. Kraus angeführten Unterlagen hat später er selbst,[27] und auch J.J. Finkelstein[28] eine ausführliche chronologische Liste der aus Babylon bekannten *mīšarum*-Akte zusammengestellt. Dem letzteren diente die Liste als Ausgangspunkt für die Behandlung der Periodizität dieser Erlässe.[29]

J.J. Finkelstein sah klar, dass "it is not yet possible to establish any fixed interval of recurrence of *misharum* enactments",[30] trotzdem versuchte er, dieses "not yet" zu eliminieren.[31] Auf Grund der Analogie mit den bekannten alttestamentlichen Forderungen auf Schulderlass u. ä. (*d^e^rōr*, *š^e^miṭṭā*),[32] zugleich auch "the inner logic of the situation" gelten lassend, wollte er den *mīšarum*-Akt als eine regulär-periodisch - d. h. mit gleichen Zeitabständen - wiederkehrende Massnahme darstellen. Das Modell, das er für die Erklärung des altbabylonischen Wirtschaftslebens um die *mīšarum*-Akte konstruierte, scheint mir jedoch in sehr starkem Masse "amerikanisch" zu sein.[33]

Aus der Zeit zwischen Rīm-Sîn von Larsa und Samsu-ditana von Babylon (1625-1595), d. h. aus dem 18./17. Jahrhundert v. u. Z., haben wir Kenntnis von etwa 20 *mīšarum*-Akten. Davon fallen 4 oder 5 sicher in das 1. Jahr des jeweiligen Königs.[34] Nach Ḫammurapi (1792-1750) hat wohl jeder König gleich nach seiner Thronbesteigung bzw. in seinem 1. Regierungsjahr einen *mīšarum*-Akt erlassen.[35] Die übrigen Erlässe zu datieren ist meistens sehr schwierig. Bei Rīm-Sîn fallen die uns bekannten *mīšarum*-Akte in die Jahre 26, 35 und 41.[36] Es ist gut möglich, dass Ḫammurapi nach seinem 1. Regierungsjahr auch in den Jahren 12, 21/22 und 30+x je einen *mīšarum*-Akt erlassen hat.[37] Bei seinem Nachfolger Samsu-iluna sind *mīšarum*-Erlässe aus den Jahren 1 und 8 bekannt,[38] bei Ammīṣaduqa aus den Jahren 1 und 9.[39]

Um die Frage, ob die *mīšarum*-Erlässe regulär-periodisch sind oder nicht, beantworten zu können, brauchen wir eine nähere Analyse der Zeitabstände zwischen den einzelnen *mīšarum*-Akten. Von den *mīšarum*-Akten der späten Larsa- und der altbabylonischen Zeit sind uns sicherlich nicht alle bekannt. Und was bekannt ist, lässt sich nicht immer einwandfrei datieren. Infolgedessen sind die Aussichten für sichere Ergebnisse recht bescheiden. Trotzdem scheint mir ein Umstand des Nachdenkens wert zu sein.

Bei einer solchen Massnahme kann man von vornherein annehmen, dass sie nicht in jedem Jahr getroffen wurde. Es ist also als wahrscheinlich anzunehmen, dass die kleinsten uns bekannten Zeitabstände zwischen den sicher datierbaren *mīšarum*-Erlässen die historische Realität widerspiegeln, dass es also zwischen ihnen keine weiteren *mīšarum*-Akte gegeben hat.

Was an solchen Mindestabständen uns bekannt ist, ist wiederum nicht besonders viel. Bei Rīm-Sîn betragen die Abstände zwischen den belegbaren *mīšarum*-Akten 9 bzw. 5 Jahre, bei Ḫammurapi 11, 9 (oder 10) bzw. 8+x Jahre, bei Samsuiluna 7 Jahre, bei Ammī-ṣaduqa 8 Jahre. Bei diesen Zahlen ist offensichtlich keine Gesetzmässigkeit festzustellen. Die Zahlen 9, 5, 11 und 7 sind alle ungerade, die 5, 11 und 7 sogar Primzahlen, das heisst, sie sind nicht durch 2 oder (von der 9 abgesehen) durch grössere Zahlen teilbar, sie haben keinen gemeinsamen Faktor folglich bezeichnen sie wirkliche Mindestabstände oder mindestens lassen sie sich nicht in gleiche Abstände unterteilen. Schon allein durch diesen Gedankengang wird m. E. unwiderlegbar bewiesen, dass die Auffassung J.J.Finkelsteins, der *mīšarum*-Akt sei eine regulär-periodische Massnahme, nicht zutrifft und nicht zutreffen kann.

Es liegt die Folgerung auf der Hand: Die *mīšarum*-Erlässe wurden recht oft, jedoch stets in unregelmässigen, nicht voraussehbaren Zeitabständen veröffentlicht. Diese Irregularität scheint mir gerade ihr wesentlichstes Merkmal zu sein. Durch den Umstand, dass der König in der Regel gleich nach seiner Thronbesteigung bzw. in seinem 1. Regierungsjahr den ersten *mīšarum*-Akt erliess, wird diese Folgerung nur unterstützt: Der Tod des Königs ist eben nicht vorauszusehen.

Sind die *mīšarum*-Akte nicht in regelmässigen Abständen erlassen worden, so sind sie in jedem einzelnen Fall von den augenblicklichen Umständen erzwungen, und zwar vom Bedarf, der natürlich einen ökonomischen Bedarf bedeutet. Die *mīšarum*-Erlässe sind, wie gesagt, ein Korrektiv, durch welches der König in seiner Eigenschaft als höchster Dignitar des Staates das wirtschaftliche Leben seines Landes zu regulieren -- wieder in gesunden Gang zu bringen -- versuchte.

mīšarum heisst, um die wohlbekannte Bedeutung des Wortes in Erinnerung zu bringen, "Gerechtigkeit", "redress";[40] *mīšaram šakānum* ist also "gerechte Ordnung schaffen".[41]

Von diesen Bedeutungen des Wortes bzw. der Wendung ausgehend, kann man sich, unter Berücksichtigung der oben Festgestellten, einige Vorstellungen von dem hinter den *mīšarum*-Erlässen stehenden Wirtschaftsleben gewinnen.

Durch die *mīšarum*-Akte versucht der König, d. h. eigentlich der Staat, die übermässige Verschuldung der produzierenden Bevölkerung zu verhindern und zwar sowohl die seiner eigenen Leute, als auch die der ausserhalb der königlichen Wirtschaft Lebenden. In den letzteren möchte ich einfach Bauern sehen, den Privatsektor[42] der altbabylonischen Wirtschaftsstruktur.[43] Die Verschuldung dieser Leute entsteht dadurch, dies geht selbst aus dem *mīšarum*-Erlass Ammī-ṣaduqas klar hervor,[44] dass die kleineren und kleinsten Wirtschaftseinheiten auf Darlehen aller Art angewiesen sind. Für Ankäufe brauchen sie etwas Geld, für den eigenen Unterhalt gegebenenfalls - bes. vor der Ernte - Gerste u. ä. Sie können dann und wann auch die Steuern nicht entrichten. Die Mehrheit der Bevölkerung des altbabylonischen Staates gehörte wohl dieser Schicht an. Sie lebte von einem Jahr auf das andere, und wenn es zu einer übermässig schlechten Ernte kam, mussten sie sich, um existieren zu können, bei dem *tamkārum* verschulden.[45] Die wirtschaftliche Kapazität der Bauern dieser Schicht war zur Bewahrung der Stabilität zu klein. Die Verschuldung war dann meistens der erste Schritt zur totalen Ruinierung. Die vermutlich massenhafte Verschuldung der ärmsten Schichten der freien Bevölkerung führte von Zeit zu Zeit zu einer "ökonomischen Unordnung" (*désordre économique*), wie sie von J. Bottéro trefflich genannt wurde.[46] Die Unordnung wieder "in gerechte Ordnung" zu bringen, war die Aufgabe der Wirtschaftspolitik des Staates bzw. des Königs, und zwar im Interesse des ganzen Systems, d. h. nicht nur der kleinen Produzenten, sondern auch des Staates selbst. Durch einen *mīšarum*-Akt ist nicht das System, die Wirtschaftsordnung, verändert worden, sondern er korrigierte nur die unerwünschten Auswüchse, vor allem die massenhafte Ruinierung der Bevölkerung durch Verschuldung. Die Notwendigkeit solcher Massnahmen beweist übrigens, dass die freien Produzenten, die Bauern, einen prozentual wohl bedeutenden Teil der Bevölkerung ausmachten, so dass es im Interesse des Staates lag, ihre Wirtschaftsführung "in gerechter Ordnung" zu halten.[47]

Auf Grund dieser Überlegungen scheint mir die Annahme der regelmässigen Periodizität der *mīšarum*-Erlässe eben irreführend zu sein. Regelmässig-periodische Schulderlässe, die voraussehbar und berechenbar waren, hätten das normale Wirtschaftsleben gehemmt, weil sie die Gläubigen davon abgehalten hätten, ihre Gelder zu jeder Zeit zu verleihen. Das System der *mīšarum*-Akte konnte nur funktionieren, wenn die Erlässe unerwartet angekündigt wurden.

Die *mīšarum*-Erlässe sind in der Form, wie ich sie hier gedeutet habe, eine Äusserung der altbabylonischen Zeit. Ihre eigentliche Geschichte möchte ich von der Zeit Rīm-Sîns von Larsa an rechnen; sie würde dann über die Zeit der späten Larsa- und der altbabylonischen Dynastie dauern. Was die letztere betrifft gibt es in den Quellen Anspielungen auf einen *mīšarum*-Akt auch zur Zeit Sîn-muballiṭs;[48] da seine Regierung in die Zeit Rîm-Sîns von Larsa fällt, verändert sich die allgemeine Beurteilung durch diese Tatsache kaum.

Es gibt jedoch eine Reihe weiterer Angaben, die auf *mīšarum*-Akte aus den dem späten 19. Jahrhundert v. u. Z. vorangehenden Jahrhunderten hinweisen. Manche Könige der Dynastie von Isin[49] berufen sich etwa in ihren Jahresnamen auf einen *mīšarum*-Akt, auf die Art und Weise, die die betreffende Formel bereits in ihrer ausgeprägten Form zeigt. Und noch mehr: Die Wendung "gerechte Ordnung schaffen" u. ä. ist eigentlich seit der Zeit Enmetenas und Uruinimginas, dem 25./24. Jahrhundert v. u. Z., belegt.[50] Die altbabylonischen *mīšarum*-Akte haben gewiss sehr vieles mit diesen sozialen Massnahmen der früheren Herrscher gemeinsam. Ich möchte die klaren Zusammenhänge in dem Sinn interpretieren, dass die - und es sei hier betont - gelegentlichen sozialen Massnahmen der früheren Herrscher das Beispiel zeigten, wie eine drohende Wirtschaftskrise, die katastrophale Verschuldung der freien Bauern, gelöst werden kann. Die Kontinuität der Praxis wird durch die Kontinuität der Terminologie betont. Die Unterschiede sind m. E. Merkmale der veränderten Zeit: Je öfter die Verschuldungskrisen das normale Wirtschaftsleben gefährdeten, desto öfter fühlten sich die Könige gezwungen, dem traditionellen Beispiel der Schulderlässe zu folgen. Der altbabylonische König, der sich in seinen Inschriften *šar mīšarim*, "König der Gerechtigkeit" nannte, hielt sich wohl für einen würdigen Nachfolger der früheren Herrscher mit dem ähnlichen Titel. So sind die Unterschiede in der Häufigkeit und im Inhalt der *mīšarum*-Akte mit den Unterschieden in der wirtschaftlichen Lage des Landes zu erklären. Ohne in die Details einzugehen, möchte ich sagen, diese Entwicklung steht in einer unverkennbaren Parallelität mit der Entfaltung des privaten Grundbesitzes, wie sie sich in den Urkunden widerspiegelt.[51]

J.J. Finkelstein deutete seinerzeit die Vermutung an, den *mīšarum*-Akten könnte man eventuell in den Quellen zu den alltäglichen Wirtschaftsoperationen auf die Spur kommen.[52] Die Anhäufung bestimmter Geschäfte, die Erhöhung bzw. Senkung der Preise u. a. sollen die Notwendigkeit eines *mīšarum*-Aktes andeuten. Diese Vermutung hängt m. E. mit dem von J.J. Finkelstein entworfenen Wirtschaftsmodell zusammen; seine Beschreibung erinnert im Grunde an die heutigen Börsengeschäfte. Trotzdem halte ich es für nicht ausgeschlossen, dass die Urkunden, die ja den Realitäten entsprechen könnten, eine Relevanz für die Beurteilung der *mīšarum*-Akte haben, sofern sie bestimmte Wirtschaftskrisen widerspiegeln. Das Problem ist aber viel komplizierter, als man es sich vorerst vorstellt. Die Wirtschaftskrise der Kleinproduzenten in der Landwirtschaft, die vorwiegend für sich selbst, und nur bis zu einem gewissen, sicher kleinen, Grad für Verkauf produzieren, besteht in der Geschichte erfahrungsgemäss darin, dass diese für die Anschaffung einiger, für die normale Wirtschaftsführung -- für die Reproduktion -- notwendigen Produkte und Leistungen immer mehr von ihren eigenen Produkten verkaufen müssen. Durch diesen Prozess wird dann letzten Endes die Wirtschaftsführung der Bauern, selbst ihr Unterhalt, gefährdet. So gesehen, bedeuten etwa die niedrigen Getreidepreise, die man im allgemeinen als Merkmal des Wohlstands zu betrachten pflegt, eine bedrohende Gefahr für die Bauern, die vom Verkauf einer bestimmten Menge Gerste ihre Ankäufe decken sollen. Sofern sich die Landwirtschaft der altbabylonischen Zeit auf den Markt orientiert, sind für sie die Gesetzmässigkeiten der auf die Marktwirtschaft bezogenen politischen Ökonomie gültig.

Der Entwicklung der Preise und Löhne während der altbabylonischen Zeit hat H.M. Farber eine ausgewogene, umfassende Arbeit gewidmet.[53] In seiner Darstellung hat er das Problem der *mīšarum*-Akte nicht einbezogen. Vorläufig mit Recht, wie ich meine. Es ist nämlich z. Z. nicht möglich, sich von den Veränderungen der Preise ein so detailliertes Bild zu verschaffen, dass es unser Modell der altbabylonischen Wirtschaft entscheidend beeinflussen könnte. Auf diese Weise bleiben unsere hier dargelegten Gedanken reine Spekulationen, solange weitere Detailkenntnisse eine Entscheidung erlauben werden. Jedenfalls möchten wir betonen, dass die Schwankungen der Getreidepreise während eines landwirtschaftlichen Jahres, d. h. von einer Ernte bis zur nächsten, im allgemeinen wohl nicht genügen, eine tiefere Krise auszulösen. Diese Schwankungen sind gewissermassen selbstverständlich. Erst wenn sie sich in einer erweiterten Form wiederholten, konnten sie durch Summierung der nicht ausgeglichenen Verschuldungen zum Zusammenbruch einzelner Wirtschaftseinheiten, gegebenenfalls zu einer allgemeineren Krise führen. Die Verschuldung der Bevölkerung war von den sich ständig verändernden Umständen abhängig, und so haben sich die Verhältnisse, unter denen ein Schulderlass schon unbedingt nötig wurde, nicht immer gleichmässig entwickelt, bald schneller, bald langsamer, was eigentlich die Schwankung in den Zeitabständen zwischen den einzelnen *mīšarum*-Akten begründet. Diese Schwankung ist das einzig sichere Moment, das ich hier, hoffentlich überzeugend, aufzeigen konnte.

Eben an diesem Punkt unterscheiden sich die altbabylonischen *mīšarum*-Akte von den eventuellen späteren sozialen Massnahmen bzw. deren Forderungen.[54] Nach der altbabylonischen Zeit haben wir keinen sicheren Beleg für einen *mīšarum*-Akt alten Stils, obwohl selbst das Wort *mīšarum* auch später in den Königstitulaturen vorkommt.[55] Der mit ihm gebildete Titel *šar mīšarim*, "König der Gerechtigkeit", lebt weiter, nur jetzt schon ohne irgendwelche juridische Konnotation. Es gibt keinen Grund anzunehmen, wie es kürzlich auch von N.P. Lemche betont wurde, dass die alttestamentlichen Vorschriften für *d^erōr* und *yōbēl* (mit *š^emiṭṭā*), das Schabbat- und Jubiläumsjahr (mit Schulderlass), mit der altbabylonischen wirtschaftspolitischen Praxis unmittelbar zusammenhängen würden.[56] Was das Alte Testament dazu sagt, ist nicht mehr und nichts anderes, als auf ethische Überlegungen gebaute Forderung einer gerechten sozialen Ordnung. Die Regelmässigkeit der Schabbatjahre, deren Forderung also in rein theoretischen Überlegungen wurzelt, hätte - ins Leben umgesetzt - die normale Wirtschaftsordnung sicher nur gestört.[57]

---

1 F.R. Kraus, *Ein Edikt des Königs Ammi-ṣaduqa von Babylon* (Studia et Documenta... 5), Leiden 1958. (Im weiteren: Kraus, Edikt.)

2 Von der neueren Literatur zur Wirtschaftspolitik des altbabylonischen Staates s. etwa M. de J.Ellis *Agriculture and the State in Ancient Mesopotamia* (Occasional Publications of the Babylonian Fund 1), Philadelphia 1976; N. Yoffee, *The Economic Role of the Crown in the Old Babylonian Period* (Bibliotheca Mesopotamica 5), Malibu 1977; J. Renger, "*Interaction of Temple, Palace, and 'Private Enterprise' in the Old Babylonian Economy*", in E. Lipiński (Hrsg.), *State and Temple Economy in the Ancient Near East* (Orientalia Lovaniensia Analecta 5-6), Leuven 1979, 249-256; F.R. Kraus, "*Der 'Palast', Produzent und Unternehmer im Königreiche Babylon nach Hammurabi (ca. 1750-1600 v. Chr.)*", in E. Lipiński (Hrsg.), op. cit., 423-434; s. noch unten, Anm. 4. - Zu *ṣimdatum*, dem - wie es scheint - Oberbegriff von *mīšarum*, s. etwa A. Walther, *Das altbabylonische Gerichtswesen* (LSS 6, IV-VI), Leipzig 1917, 83 ff., 96 ff.; M. San Nicolò, *Die Schlussklauseln der altbabylonischen Kauf- und Tauschverträge* (Münchener Beiträge zur Papyrusforschung... 4), München 1922, 218 ff.; und kürzlich M. de J.Ellis "*ṣimdatu in the Old Babylonian Sources*", JCS 24, 1972, 74-82 (mit der früheren Literatur).

3 Von der neueren Literatur zu den *mīšarum*-Akten s. F.R. Kraus, "*Ein Edikt des Königs Ammi-ṣaduqa von Babylon*", BiOr 16, 1959, 96 f.; L. Matouš, "*Erlasse altbabylonischer Könige*", BiOr 16, 1959, 94-96; J. Bottéro, "*Désordre économique et annulation des dettes en Mésopotamie à l'époque paléo-babylonienne*", JESHO 4, 1961, 113-164; J.J. Finkelstein, "*Ammi-ṣaduqa's Edict and the Babylonian 'Law Codes'*", JCS 15, 1961, 91-104; F.R. Kraus, "*Ein Edikt des Königs Samsu-iluna von Babylon*", in *Studies in Honor of B. Landsberger...* (AS 16), Chicago 1965, 225-231; J.J. Finkelstein, "*Some New misharum Material and Its Implications*", in AS 16, 233-246; ders., "*The Edict of Ammiṣaduqa: A New Text*", RA 63, 1969, 45-64; H. Petschow, "*Gesetze. A. Babylonien: § 3. 7: Altbabylonische mīšarum-Akte...*", in RLA 3, IV, 1966, 269-276; N.P. Lemche, "*andurārum and mīšarum: Comments on the Problem of Social Edicts and Their Application in the Ancient Near East*", JNES 38, 1979, 11-22.

4 Siehe vor allem I.M. Diakonoff, VDI Nr. 102, 1967/IV, 13-35; Nr. 105, 1968/III, 3-27; Nr. 106, 1968/IV, 3-40; dieser Aufsatz wird bald auf englisch unter dem Titel "*The Structure of Near Eastern Society before the Middle of the 2nd Millennium B.C.*" in *Oikumene* 3, Budapest 1980, erscheinen. Siehe ferner "*Main Features of the Economy in the Monarchies of Ancient Western Asia*", in *Troisième Conférence Internationale d'Histoire Économique*, Munich 1965, Paris, etc. 1969, 13-32; *Economy of the Ancient Oriental City* (V International Congress of Economic History, Leningrad 1970), Moscow 1970; "*On the Structure of Old Babylonian Society*", in H. Klengel (Hrsg.), *Beiträge zur sozialen Struktur des alten Vorderasien* (Schriften zur Geschichte und Kultur des alten Orients 1), Berlin 1971, 15-31; "*Socio-Economic Classes in Babylonia and the Babylonian Concept of Social Stratification*", in D.O. Edzard (Hrsg.), *Gesellschaftsklassen im Alten Zweistromland...*, XVIII. Rencontre assyriologique internationale, München 1970 (BAW, Phil.-hist. Kl., Abh. NF

75), München 1972, 41-52; "*Slaves, Helots and Serfs in Early Antiquity*", Acta Ant. Hung. 22, 1974, = J. Harmatta - G. Komoróczy (Hrsg.), *Wirtschaft und Gesellschaft im alten Vorderasien*, Budapest 1976, 45-78; u. a.

5 Vgl. Kraus, Edikt; J.J. Finkelstein, RA 63, 1969, 45 ff.; ders., in ANET Suppl., 1969, 526-528; R. Haase, *Die keilschriftlichen Rechtssammlungen in deutscher Fassung*, Wiesbaden 1979, 62 ff.

6 F.R. Kraus, in AS 16, 225 ff.

7 Kraus, *Edikt*, 224 ff.

8 Vgl. M. Schorr, *Eine babylonische Seisachthie aus dem Anfang der Kassitenzeit* (SHAW, Phil.-hist. Kl. 1915, Nr. 4), Heidelberg 1915.

9 S. Langdon, "*A Fragment of the Hammurapi Code*", PSBA 36, 1914, 100-106.

10 Kraus, *Edikt*, 1 f., 4 f. Siehe bereits B. Landsberger, in J. Friedrich et al. (Hrsg.), *Symbolae ... P. Koschaker ...* (Studia et Documenta... 2), Leiden 1939, 230 f., Anm. 44. - Für neuere Zweifel an dessen Zugehörigkeit s. etwa F.R. Kraus, in AS 16, 228 f.; H. Petschow, in RLA 3, IV, 1966, 275b.

11 C.J. Gadd, "*Text of the 'Babylonian Seisachtheia'*", in *Symbolae ... P. Koschaker*, Leiden 1939, 102-105; vgl. auch G.R. Driver & J.C. Miles, *The Babylonian Laws*, II, Oxford 1955, 319 ff.

12 Vgl. Aristoteles, *Ath. polit.*, VI, 1.

13 Vgl. Aristoteles, *Ath. polit.*, VI, 1; vgl. X, 1; XII; Plutarchos, *Bioi: Solon*, 15 (hier ausdrücklich zum euphemistischen Sprachgebrauch) f.

14 Vgl. *[M.]* Fluss, "*Seisachtheia*", in Pauly-Wissowa, RE, Zweite Reihe, Bd. 2, Stuttgart 1923, 1118-1120.

15 Für Einwände gegen diesen Wortgebrauch s. Kraus, *Edikt*, 192 f.

16 Paragraphenzählung nach J.J. Finkelstein, RA 63, 1969, 47.

17 *inūma/aššum šarrum mīšaram ana mātim iškunu*, § 1 (Einl.) bzw. § 3 u. a.

18 Siehe dazu M. de J. Ellis, *Taxation and Land Revenues in the Old Babylonian Period* (Diss., Yale Univ.) New Haven 1969 (Univ. Microfilms No. 70-16, 262), 124 ff.; dies., *Agriculture and the State* (s. oben, Anm. 2), 148 ff.

19 Vgl. F.R. Kraus, in AS 16, 227 (Samsu-iluna).

20 Vgl. F.R. Kraus, in AS 16, 226 (Samsu-iluna).

21 Zum historischen Hintergrund s. etwa Kraus, *Edikt*, 238 ff.; D.O. Edzard, in E. Cassin et al. (Hrsg.), *Fischer Weltgeschichte* 2: *Die Altorientalischen Reihe* I, Frankfurt a. M. 1965, 204 f.; H. Klengel, *Hammurapi von Babylon und seine Zeit*, Berlin 1976, 216 ff.; und bes. ders., "*Einige Bemerkungen zur sozialökonomischen Entwicklung in der altbabylonischen Zeit*", Acta Ant. Hung. 22 (1974) = *Wirtschaft und Gesellschaft* (s. oben, Anm. 4), Budapest 1976, 249-257.

22 Vgl. Kraus, *Edikt*, 182 ff.

23 Kraus, *Edikt*, 196 ff., Nrr. 1-6: Išmē-Dagan, Lipit-Ištar, Ur-Ninurta von Isin; vgl. D.O. Edzard, *Die "zweite Zwischenzeit" Babyloniens*, Wiesbaden 1957, 80 ff., 95 ff. u. a.

24 Kraus, *Edikt*, 200 f., Nrr. 7-8: Erra-imitti, Enlil-bāni von Isin; ebd.,

224 f., Nrr. 27-31: Sumu-la-El von Babylon.

25 Kraus, *Edikt*, 201 ff., Nr. 10-26a; vgl. ebd., 210 ff.; s. noch J.J. Finkelstein, in AS 16, 243, Anm. 39.

26 Kraus, *Edikt*, 225 ff., Nrr. 32 ff.; vgl. J.J. Finkelstein, in AS 16, 243 ff.

27 F.R. Kraus, in AS 16, 229 f.

28 J.J. Finkelstein, in AS 16, 243 ff.

29 Ebd., 243 ff.: "*The Periodicity of the misharum-Act.*"

30 Ebd., 245a.

31 Ebd., 245 f.

32 Vgl. Lev. 25:1-22; Deut. 15:1-18; u. a. Zu den hebräischen Termini und deren eventuellen Zusammenhang mit den mesopotamischen *mīšarum*-Akten s. übrigens J. Lewy, "*The Biblical Institution of derôr in the Light of Akkadian Documents*", *Eretz-Israel* 5, 1958, 21*-31*; und kürzlich N.P. Lemche, JNES 38, 1979, 21 f., mit historisch sehr realistischen Schlussfolgerungen.

33 Vgl. AS 16, 245: "... enactments of this type had to recur *at fairly regular or predictable intervals*. Were this not the case, and had the kings been free to announce the *misharum* without warning and at widely disparate intervals, there would have occurred a drying-up of the sources of credit and a virtual paralysis of economic activity every few years - after a reasonable lapse of time from the previous enactment. At worst, arbitrariness in such activity on the part of the crown would have served only to encourage subterfuges on the part of creditors and debtors, buyers and sellers, etc. to avoid being affected by the *misharum*, so that the very purpose of the act would have been frustrated."

34 So bei Ḫammurapi (Kraus, *Edikt*, 225, Nr. 33); Samsu-iluna (Kraus, *Edikt*, 227, Nr. 36); Abī-ešuḫ (1711-1684) (Kraus, *Edikt*, 228, Nr. 38, s. auch D.O. Edzard, *Altbabylonische Rechts- und Wirtschaftsurkunden aus Tell ed-Dēr*... (BAW, Phil.-hist. Kl., Abh. NF 72), München 1970, Nr. 234); Ammī-ditana (1683-1647) (Kraus, *Edikt*, 228, Nr. 41); Ammī-ṣaduqa (Kraus, *Edikt*, 229, Nrr. 43-45).

35 Nur bei Samsu-ditana, dem letzten König der altbabylonischen Dynastie, ist (vorläufig?) kein *mīšarum*-Akt aus seinem 1. Regierungsjahr belegt; für den *mīšarum*-Akt seines 2./3. Jahres s. S. I. Feigin & B. Landsberger, JNES 14, 1955, 149 f.; F.R. Kraus, in AS 16, 229b: F (13); J.J. Finkelstein, ebd., 245.

36 Siehe Kraus, *Edikt*, 201 ff.; vgl. J.J. Finkelstein, in AS 16, 243.

37 Siehe Kraus, *Edikt*, 225; ders., in AS 16, 229a: A (1); J.J. Finkelstein, ebd., 243 f.

38 Siehe Kraus, *Edikt*, 225 ff.; ders., in AS 16, 229a: B (3) f.(?); J.J. Finkelstein, ebd., 244.

39 Siehe Kraus, *Edikt*, 229; ders., in AS 16, 229b: E (11); J.J. Finkelstein, ebd., 245.

40 Vgl. W. v. Soden, AHw 659 f.; und kürzlich CAD M/II, 116 ff.

41 Siehe CAD M/II, 117: meaning 1.

42 Vgl. I.J. Gelb, "*On the Alleged Temple and State Economies in Ancient Mesopotamia*", in *Studi in onore di E. Volterra*, VI, Milano 1969, 139-154.

43 Siehe dazu ausführlicher G. Komoróczy, "*Zu den Eigentumsverhältnissen in der altbabylonischen Zeit: Das Problem der Privatwirtschaft*", in E. Lipiński (Hrsg.), *State and Temple Economy* (s. oben, Anm. 2), 411-422.

44 Vgl. § 4 u. a.

45 *tamkārum* hier selbstverständlich nur *cum grano salis*; s. übrigens etwa W. Schwenzner, *Zum altbabylonischen Wirtschaftsleben* (MVAG 19, IV), Leipzig 1915, 32 ff.; W.F. Leemans, *The Old-Babylonian Merchant...* (Studia et Documenta... 3) Leiden 1950; N.B. Jankowska, *Private Credit in the Commerce of Ancient Western Asia...* (V International Congress of Economic History, Leningrad 1970), Moscow 1970.

46 J. Bottéro, JESHO 4, 1961, 113 ff., bes. 152 ff.

47 Vgl. G. Komoróczy, "*Landed Property in Ancient Mesopotamia and the Theory of the So-Called Asiatic Mode of Production*", *Oikumene* 2, 1978, 9-26, bes. 17 f.

48 Kraus, *Edikt*, 225, Nr. 32.

49 Vgl. oben, Anm. 23 f.

50 Siehe dazu ausführlich und mit Quellenangaben D.O. Edzard, "*'Soziale Reformen' im Zweistromland bis ca. 1600 v. Chr.: Realität oder literarischer Topos?*" Acta Ant. Hung. 22 (1974) = *Wirtschaft und Gesellschaft* (s. oben, Anm. 4), Budapest 1976, 145-156.

51 Vgl. L. Matouš, "*Les contrats de partage de Larsa...*", ArOr 17/II, 1949, 142-173; ders., "*Les contrats de vente d'immeubles...*", ArOr 18/IV, 1950, 11-67; D.O. Edzard, *Die "zweite Zwischenzeit" Babyloniens*, Wiesbaden 1957, 4 f., Anm. 20; H. Klengel, Acta Ant. Hung. 22 (1974) = *Wirtschaft und Gesellschaft* (s. oben, Anm. 4), Budapest 1976, 252 ff.; ders., *Hammurapi von Babylon* (s. oben, Anm. 21), 57 ff.

52 J.J. Finkelstein, in AS 16, 245 f.: "... We might then detect a series of regular fluctuations in prices, interest rates (at least marginal ones), etc. and simple frequency fluctuations. If our hypothesis proves valid, the years immediately preceding a *misharum* should show a low rate of frequency in transactions in general, higher interest rates, lower sales prices for real estate, etc. (the risk to the potential buyer and creditor being then much greater). Additional *misharum*-acts might even be postulated where none are known if suggested by the emergent pattern. The period immediately after a *misharum* would be expected to show a pattern that would be the reverse image of that of the years before such an enactment."

53 H.M. Farber, *An Examination of Long Term Fluctuations in Prices and Wages for North Babylonia during the Old Babylonian Period* (Thesis, Northern Illinois Univ.), DeKalb, Ill. 1974; vgl. ders., "*A Price and Wage Study for Northern Babylonia during the Old Babylonian Period*", JESHO 21, 1978, 1-51.

54 Siehe dazu kürzlich N.P. Lemche, JNES 38, 1979, 13 ff., 15 ff.

55 Vgl. B.A. van Proosdij, "*Šar mēšarim*, titre des rois babyloniens comme législateurs", in M. David et al. (Hrsg.), *Symbolae ... J.C. van Oven ...*, Leiden 1946, 29-35; M.-J. Seux, *Épithètes royales akkadiennes et sumé-*

riennes, Paris 1967, 316 f.; N.P. Lemche, JNES 38, 1979, 15, mit Anm. 24 ff.

56 N.P. Lemche, JNES 38, 1979, 21 f.

57 Eine hebräische Urkunde aus dem Bar-Kochba-Aufstand (P. Benoit et al., *Discoveries in the Judaean Desert*, II, Oxford 1961, Nr. 24B) zeigt uns, wie das neu eingeführte Erlassjahr, das ja im voraus gewusst war, bei den Verträgen, um die nachteiligen Folgen zu umgehen, in Kauf genommen werden konnte. - Für neuassyrische Belege, nach denen der Gläubiger dem schon erwarteten, für ihn natürlich ungünstigen Schulderlass (*durāru* = *andurāru*) vorzubeugen versucht, s. etwa C.H.W. Johns, ADD, Nr. 629, Rs. 13 f. (s. dazu J. Lewy, *Eretz-Israel* 5, 1958, 30*; N.P. Lemche, JNES 38, 1979, 21, mit Anm. 69); J.N. Postgate, *The Governor's Palace Archive* (CTN 2), London 1973, Nr. 248, Rs. 13' ff. (s. dazu wiederum N.P. Lemche, JNES 38, 1979, 21, mit Anm. 68); vgl. auch CAD A/II, 115 ff. s. v. *andurāru*.

THREE OLD BABYLONIAN balag-CATALOGUES FROM THE BRITISH MUSEUM

Samuel Noah Kramer (Philadelphia)

The nature and scope of the Sumerian literary works current in the Old Babylonian period can be assessed, evaluated, and appreciated from two sources. First and primary are the hundreds of Sumerian compositions of diverse genre and type that can be restored wholly or in part from the more than five thousand tablets and fragments scattered throughout the museums and tablet collections the world over.[1] A secondary and supplemental source consists of the catalogues prepared by the Old Babylonian men of letters, that is, lists of incipits compiled by them for one reason or another, and arranged in accordance with a varied assortment of scribal procedures.[2] To date fifteen such Old Babylonian catalogues are known,[3] and one of them, the Clark Cylinder, is noteworthy as a catalogue listing seventeen incipits designated by the ancient scribe as balag-dingir-re-e-ne, "balag-compositions of the gods".[4] This paper presents an edition of three small Old Babylonian Cylinders recently identified in the tablet collection of the British Museum which, like the Clark Cylinder, are inscribed with lists of balag-compositions - between them they list more than thirty incipits, quite a number of which are altogether new.[5] It is a pleasure and a privilege to dedicate this article to the savant who virtually single-handed introduced the study of Sumerian literature to Soviet scholarship, to my colleague and friend of many years, Igor Diakonoff.

The three small British Museum catalogue cylinders edited in this paper are: BM 23612, 85564, and 23249. BM 23612, the smallest and best preserved of the three, is inscribed with six incipits, four of which are new, preceded by the designation dub-balag-me-eš and followed by the designation balag-^{d}inanna - all six incipits are therefore the initial complexes of balag-compositions in which the goddess Inanna is the major protagonist.[6] The text also includes two significant scribal notations, one of which is known from the Clark Cylinder while the other is altogether new. The incipits (and notations) of BM 23612 read as follows:

(1) 6[7] egí-re a-še-ir-re	The princess by sighing
(2) 1 ur-ra na-mu-un-u$_5$ šà-egí-re-a-še-ir-re	She rode upon the dog - the middle of egí-re a-še-ir-re
(3) 1 ù-u$_8$ ur$_5$-re im-me	"Woe!" she says
(4) 1 um-ma-ra ta KA-ká-dingir-ra^{ki}	To the umma, what--the cry(?) of Babylon
(5) 1 a-uru-mu im-me	"Woe, my city!" she says
(6) 4 áb-gim tùr-mu-a KA-ká-dingir-ra^{ki}	Like a cow in my stall--the cry(?) of Babylon

Commentary. The initial line of the balag-composition that began with the first incipit on this cylinder may have read: egí-re a-še-ir-re ba-an-ku$_4$-ku$_4$ [8] which may perhaps be rendered as "The princess is overcome by sighing". Or it may have read: egí-re a-še-ir-re àm-ma-ni-ma-al with a meaning approximating "The princess has given herself over to sighing".[9]

The rendering of the second incipit assumes that the n a- of the verbal form is the now well-known positive thematic particle, but it may of course be the negative optative particle, and if so, the rendering would be "Let her not ride upon the dogs",[10] though this is hardly likely. Quite interesting is the phrase š à - e g í - r e - a - š e - i r - r e that follows the incipit, and which is probably a notation by the scribe intended to indicate that u r - r a n a - m u - u n - u $_5$ is the incipit of a section in the middle of the composition whose incipit is e g í - r e a - š e - i r - r e --if so, this is the only known example of this scribal practice.[11]

The third incipit is virtually identical with that of the Ninšubur i r š e-m m a listed in *Cat. A* 46=*Cat. B* 69, which reads ù - u $_8$ u r $_5$ - r e g ù i m - m e. The reading and rendering of the fourth incipit are tentative attempts that may prove to be quite erroneous[12] --note that it might turn out to be identical with the incipit 4R 49 which ends in m a - r a t a. The complex of rather uncertain meaning and significance that follows the incipit, KA- k á - d i n g i r - r a ^{ki} (cf. also the sixth incipit of our cylinder) is identical with that which follows the eighth incipit of the Clark Cylinder which reads š à (!) - z u (!) t a - à m - m e - i r (!).[13]

The fifth incipit is identical with that listed in 4R 48; the complete first line of the composition no doubt read: a - u r u - m u i m - m e a - é - m u i m - m e.[14] The rendering of the second complex of the sixth incipit is somewhat uncertain since it might have been expected to read t ù r - m à instead of t ù r - m u - a; the second half of the line beginning with á b - g i m t ù r - m u - a might have read g ù b í - d é "I cried out" or g ù i m - m e (e n) "I cry out".[15] For the KA- k á - d i n g i r - r a ^{ki} notation following this incipit, cf. comment to the fourth incipit.

BM 85564 is a small cylinder inscribed with eleven incipits preceded by the designation d u b - b a l a g - m e - e š and followed by the designation b a l a g - d i n g i r - r e - e - n e.[16] Seven of these incipits are identical with those known from other catalogues, and four are altogether new. The eleven BM 85564 incipits are as follows:

(1)	2 e - l u m g u d - s u n	Honored one, fierce bull
(2)	2 z i - b u - ú - u m	
(3)	2 é - s a g - a š - a	The house of the lone one
(4)	1 u $_4$ - r i - a	In those days
(5)	1 ^{d}u t u - g i m è - i m - t a	Come forth like the sun
(6)	1 u $_4$- d a m k i à m - u š	It (Enlil's word) being a storm, has pressed down upon the earth
(7)	3 a - a b - b a - ḫ u - l u ḫ - ḫ a	The raging sea
(8)	1 u $_4$ - d a l - l e - n e i m - m a - a n -..	
(9)	3 a - g i $_6$ - ^{id}b u r a n u n - n a e b u r	The flood-water of the Euphrates--the crop
(10)	1 a m - e a m a š - a - n a	The wild ox in his sheepfold

(11) 1 t ù r - á b - s á g - d u g $_4$ - g a	The stall (from which) the cows have been scattered

Commentary. The first incipit is virtually identical with that listed in 4R 13; the b a l a g-composition of which it is the incipit is preserved in large part, and its first line reads e - l u m g u d - s u n m u - z u k u r - k u r - š è "Honored one, fierce bull, your name (reaches?) all the lands".[17] The second incipit that consists of the obscure word z i - b u - ú - u m which seems to be an Akkadian loan-word, is no doubt identical with that listed in 4R 17 that can be restored to read [z i - b u - ù - u m] z i - b u - ù - u m and is there designated as a b a l a g of Enlil;[18] the composition itself is preserved in large part, cf. SK 8 and its duplicate SK 9 with its obscure first line that reads: z i - b u - ù z i - b u - ù s u d - DU - á m z i - b u - ù.

The third incipit é - s a g - a š - a is altogether new; its rendering as "The house of the lone one" seems reasonably assured, but it is not clear who the deity described as "the lone one" might be--it hardly seems to be suitable for Enlil, for example. The fourth incipit, u$_4$ - r i - a, is the initial complex of several compositions,[19] none of which are of the b a l a g genre, however, except perhaps that listed in the *Jena catalogue HS 1504* No. 6 (see note 2). The fifth incipit is identical with that listed in 4R 5 and Clark Cylinder 8[20]; a fragment of the Old Babylonian version of this composition has been published in PBS I/1 No.8-- cf. PBS X/4 pp. 309-310,[21] and note that the part of the first line following the incipit is unfortunately destroyed. The sixth incipit is identical with that listed in 4R 6 and Clark Cylinder 7.[22] The seventh incipit is identical with that listed in 4R 18 and the *Jena Catalogue HS 1477* No. 22 (see note 2); for a valuable tentative attempt at reconstructing the text of the composition from Old Babylonian, Middle Assyrian, New Assyrian, and Seleucid tablets and fragments, cf. Raphael Kutscher, *Oh Angry Sea* (YNER 6 [1975]).[23]

The meaning of the eighth incipit, hitherto unknown, is altogether uncertain and obscure. The ninth incipit, also hitherto unknown, is probably the initial complex of a b a l a g-composition in which Enki is the major protagonist; the first line probably read in full: a - g i $_6$ - ^{íd}b u r a n u n - n a e b u r i s i n $_x$ (PA.ŠE)- b a s ù - s ù "The flood-waters of the Euphrates that drown the crop on its stalk".[24] The tenth incipit is identical with that listed in 4R 7 and 37;[25] the initial line of the composition read: a m - e a m a š - a - n a š e g i g - b i b í - i b - š a $_4$ "The wild ox mourned bitterly in his sheepfold".[26] The eleventh incipit, hitherto unknown, may be the initial complex of a b a l a g in which either Nanna or Dumuzi is the major protagonist.

BM 23249 is a rather poorly preserved small cylinder that was originally inscribed with approximately fifteen incipits preceded by the designation d u b - b a l a g - m e - e š and followed no doubt by the designation b a l a g - d i n g i r - r e - e - n e (now destroyed). To judge from the nature of the incipits, a number of which begin with the word e d i n,[27] it is probably such deities as Inanna, Geštinanna, and Ninḫursag-Aruru who are the major protagonists of the relevant b a l a g-compositions. One of the incipits, it is worth noting (No. 8) duplicates one on the Clark Cylinder (No. 13). Moreover, the two cylinders resemble each other in another respect: both list i m - g í d - d a's (extracts) of compositions - two on the BM cylinder and three on the Clark Cylinder. The incipits listed on BM 23249 read as follows:

Nos. 1 and 2 are destroyed

(3)	2(?) edin-na í [r]	In the steppe, te[ars] .....
(4)	2(?) edin-líl-a šà-mu-líl-a	Desolate the steppe, desolate my heart
(5)	3 ma-ma-al-e	
(6)	1 a-lu-lu šà-mu ír-re	Woe, my heart to tears
(7)	3 é-mà mu-lu-e	In my house the man
(8)	2 é-^{d}a-ru-ru	The house of Aruru
(9)	1 edin-na na-mu-un-di	She wandered about in the steppe
(10)	1 edin-?-? ír na-mu-un-ma-al	In(?) the ...steppe she wept
(11)	6 im-gíd-da edin	
(12)	? im-gíd-da a-.....	
(13)	? edin(?)-na(?)	

Nos. 14 and 15 are destroyed

Commentary. The first two incipits are destroyed. The third incipit may perhaps be restored to read: edin-na ír-gig mu-un-ma-al "She wept bitterly in the steppe". The fourth incipit may be that of the balag-^{d}maḫ published by Scheil in RA 17 [1920] 50, whose third kirugu begins with edin-líl-lá šà-mu-líl-lá,[28] on the assumption that its missing first kirugu began with the same two complexes, and that the líl-a of our BM cylinder is but a variant of líl-lá.[29] The meaning of the fifth incipit is ambiguous and obscure.[30] The sixth incipit probably began a line reading: a-lu-lu šà-mu ír-re ba-an-da-ni-ib-mar "Woe, my heart has been given over to tears".[31] The seventh incipit is new, and it is difficult to surmise what the entire first line may have read. The eighth incipit is identical with the first é-^{d}a-ru-ru of the thirteenth incipit of the Clark Cylinder, and no doubt designates the same composition.[32] The ninth incipit is new; the entire line may have read: edin-na na-mu-un-di edin-na še àm-ša₄ "She wandered about in the steppe, she mourned in the steppe".[33] The tenth incipit which is only partly legible is also new. The remainder of the text is too fragmentary for comment.

Cat. A and *B* Cf. *Studia Orientalia* 46 (Festschrift A. Salonen) 141ff.

Cohen Mark E. Cohen, *An Analysis of the balag-compositions to the God Enlil* (Dissertation of the Graduate School of Arts and Sciences, U. of Pa. [1972])

FPS S.N. Kramer, *From the Poetry of Sumer* [1979]

4R H.C. Rawlinson, *The Cuneiform Inscriptions of Western Asia*, Vol. 4 (all references in this paper to 4R are to Col. i of the *Assyrian Catalogue*, 4R 53, unless otherwise specified).

SK H. Zimmern, *Sumerische Kultlieder aus altbabylonischer Zeit* (VS 2 and 10)

SKly J. Krecher, *Sumerische Kultlyrik* [1966]

WZJ *Wissenschaftliche Zeitschrift der Friedrich-Schiller Universität Jena*

1 For full details, cf. the first chapter of FPS and note especially the reference on p. 12 to Miguel Civil's forthcoming catalogue of virtually all the known Sumerian literary works, that will mark a milestone in the recovery and restoration of Sumerian literature.

2 For tentative attempts to understand and explain some of these procedures, cf. the relevant introductory comment to the *Nippur and Louvre catalogues* in BASOR 88 [1942] 10 ff.; to the *Ur catalogue* in RA 55 [1961] 169 ff.: to *Cat. A* and *B* in *Studia Orientalia 46* p. 141 ff.; to the *Jena catalogues* in WZJ 6 [1956-7] 389 ff.

3 For eleven of the Old Babylonian catalogues, cf. *Studia Orientalia 46* p. 147, note 1; the twelfth was identified by Hallo in *Studia Orientalia 46* p. 47 ff.; the thirteenth is the Clark Cylinder published by Luckenbill in AJSL 26 [1909-10] 28 (for a photograph cf. *Atiqot* 4 plate 44). Luckenbill dated it to the Neo-Babylonian period, and so did several scholars who followed him (Krecher in SKly p. 19 and Hallo in JAOS 83 [1963] 169), but in my opinion it is Old Babylonian. Mark Cohen treated two more from Andrews University in RA LXX [1976] 130-33 (Old Babylonian).

4 The Clark Cylinder which is now in the Museum Haaretz in Tel Aviv, is to be published by Aaron Shaffer, who has provided me with a tentative transliteration. For the nature of the contents of the lamentful compositions designated as b a l a g by the ancient scribes, and for their stylistic features and cultic significance, cf. SKly p. 19 ff. and *Cohen* p. 40 ff.

5 The numerical uncertainty is due to the rather fragmentary condition of one of the cylinders, BM 23249.

6 As noted in the commentary, it may turn out that the second incipit is that of one of the sections from the middle of the composition identified by the preceding first incipit, and if so, only five b a l a g-compositions are listed in this cylinder.

7 The numerals immediately preceding the incipits indicate the number of copies of the composition that the scribe had in his possession.

8 Cf. No. 26 of *Cat. A*.

9 Cf. SK 25 i 16-17. Note that the incipit 4R 50 may now be restored to read: e g í - r e a - š e - i r - r a, and that the entire line may have read: e g í - r e a - š e - i r - r a u_4 m u - n i - i b - z a l "The princess spent the days in sighing", cf. e.g. *Cat. A* 21= *Cat. B* 37.

10 For Inanna riding on seven big dogs, cf. line 105 of the Inanna hymn i n - n i n š à - g u r $_4$ - r a published by Sjöberg in ZA 65 [1975] 161 ff. Note that the incipit may be read u r - r a - n a m u - u n - u_5 "She rode upon her dogs", although this seems rather unlikely.

11 It is not clear why the scribe found it necessary to include the incipit of a section from the middle of the composition. Most likely the latter was inscribed on two tablets, the second of which began with u r - r a n a - m u - u n - u_5.

12 Note that there seems to be an erased sign following the first sign.

13 š à - z u t a - à m - m e - i r is the incipit of the b a l a g- composition BM 29616, the contents of which are sketched in FPS pp. 91-92, and which I plan to publish in the near future.

14 Cf. e.g. lines 248-249 of the *Lamentation Over the Destruction of Ur* (AS 12).

15 Cf. CAD sub *littum* (lexical section).

16 Most of the compositions listed in this cylinder are, however, b a l a g's of Enlil, cf. commentary for details.

17 Cf. PBS X/4 p. 29 ff. for the text and bibliographical references; for the ritual use of the composition cf. SKly p. 27 and *Cohen* p. 54; note that e - l u m g u d - s u n is also the incipit of an i r š e m m a (cf. 4R ii 15).

18 z i - b u - u m z i - b u - u m is also the incipit of an Aššur b a l a g according to 4R ii 15.

19 Cf. Nos. 28, 29 and 30 of the *Ur Catalogue* (see note 2) where the other examples are noted.

20 Cf. also SKly p. 30 note 9 (*sub* 5).

21 Cf. also SKly note 65 and *Cohen* pp. 53-54.

22 Cf. also SKly note 9 (*sub* 6) and *Cohen* pp. 52-53. For an edition of the composition based almost entirely on first millennium bilinguals cf. *Cohen* pp. 57-93.

23 For the cultic use of the composition as well as its place in the catalogues cf. *Oh Angry Sea* pp. 16-18.

24 Cf. e.g. CAD sub *isinnu* (lexical section).

25 Cf. also SKly note 9 (*sub* 7) and note 31; *Cohen* p. 55.

26 Cf. CAD sub *damāmu* (lexical section), and note that the Akkadian rendering there cited seems unjustified.

27 There are only few extant incipits beginning with e d i n even if we include those which begin a section of the composition rather than its beginning; those I could collect are: e d i n i - l u g̃ a r - ù. *Louvre Catalogue* 12 and *Nippur Catalogue* '10 (cf. note 2); e d i n - e i - l u - e u$_4$ m u - n i - i b - z a l - e, SK 25 ii 44; e d i n - n a - NE š e š - t a e d i n - n a - NE, SK 1 iii 9; e d i n - n a i - i b - s u e d i n - n a i - i b - s u PRAK b 471 obv. (beginning of third section); e d i n - l í l - l á š à - m u - l í l - l á, (cf. comment to the fourth incipit); also e d i n - n a d i - d i e d i n - n a š e - à m - š a$_4$ PBS X/4 No. 13 rev. 13, if this line can be assumed to be the beginning of a new section. None of these e d i n incipits can be identified with the e d i n-incipits of BM 23249, except perhaps the fourth.

28 The entire line reads: e d i n - l í l - l á š à - m u - l í l - l á l ú - é - ḫ u l à m - m e l ú - u r u - ḫ u l à m - m e "Desolate the steppe, desolate my heart, says he whose house has been destroyed, says he whose city has been destroyed".

29 BM 94411 is a small tablet in the British Museum which I plan to publish in the near future, that is inscribed with k i r u g u 9 and 10 of this

composition, it thus duplicates k i r u g u 9 of the Scheil text and in addition provides us with the text of k i r u g u 10 which the scribe of that text omitted altogether except for its first line, presumably for lack of space--a scribal practice that might help to explain such one line k i r u g u's as CT 36 plate 43 obv. ii 15 ff.

30 The initial m a may have one of several unrelated meanings such as "house", "I", "where"; m a - a l may be the Emesal for g á l; the final - e may be the beginning of a new complex.

31 Cf. e.g. line 77 of the *Lamentation Over the Destruction of Ur*. The first complex a - l u - l u is probably another variant of the exclamatory expressions for mourning and lamenting, cf. CAD *sub lallarātu*.

32 It is not impossible that the b a l a g-composition which began with é - [d] a - r u - r u is the one published in PRAK b 471, a fragmentary text that involves the goddess Aruru and her "house", note, too, that PBS X/2 No. 2 seems to be part of a composition in which the lament of Aruru for her house is the predominant theme.

33 Cf. e.g. PBS X/4 No. 13 rev. 13.

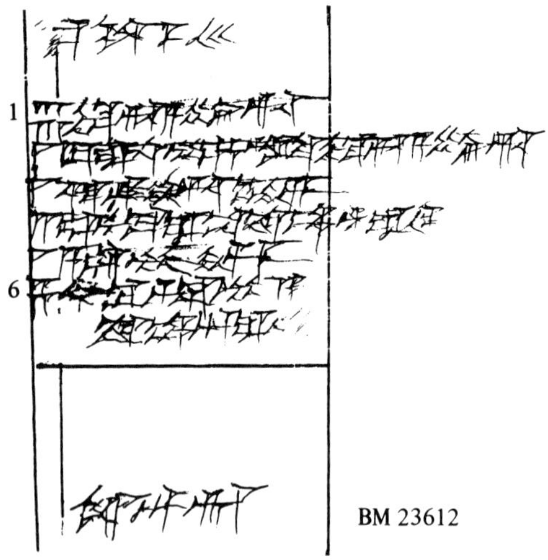

BM 23612

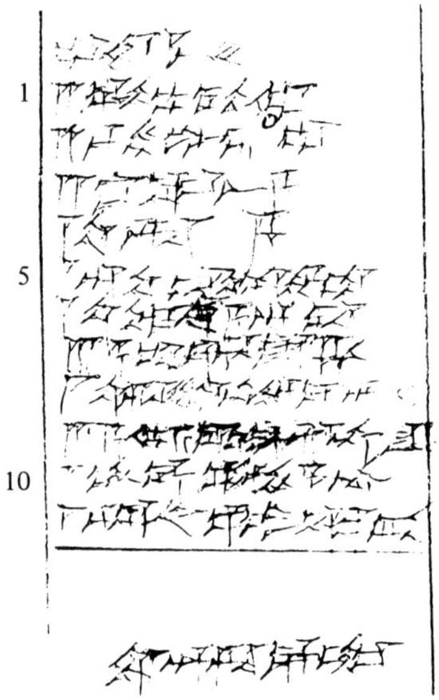

BM 85564

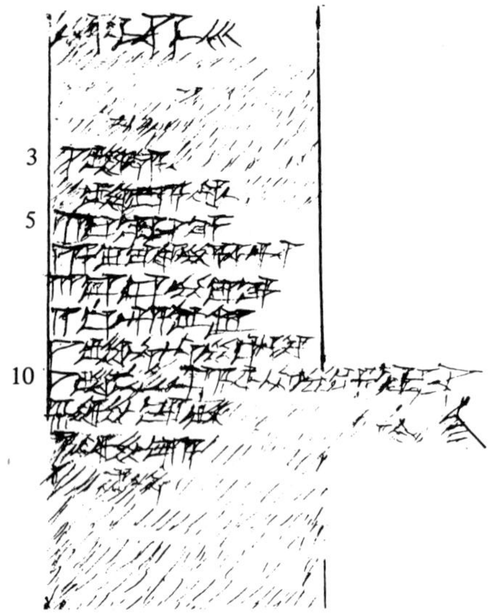

BM 23612 — 5 cm — BM 23249

(85% life size)

BM 85564

YOUR MONEY OR YOUR LIFE! A PORTRAIT OF AN ASSYRIAN BUSINESSMAN

Mogens Trolle Larsen (Copenhagen)

The phrase which inspired the title of this paper is found in a letter which was written at the request of two Old Assyrian ladies, called Tarām-Kūbī and Šimat-Aššur, and addressed to the Assyrian trader Imdi-ilum. The two women spent their lives in the city of Assur during the nineteenth century B.C., and the letter was obviously sent from there to the Assyrian commercial colony attached to the city of Kanesh in central Anatolia. The letter ran:

> Here we ask the women who interpret oracles, the women who interpret omens from entrails, and the ancestral spirits - and (divine) Assur gives you a serious warning: You love money! You hate your life! Can't you satisfy Assur (here) in the City? Please, when you have heard the letter then come, see Assur's eye and save your life! As to the proceeds from my textiles, why don't you send that to me?[1]

The recipient of this letter, Imdi-ilum, will be the subject of this paper. It is not possible to provide a detailed portrait of him as a man, a clearly defined individual, for his own letters are stubbornly concerned with the multitude of practical matters which were relevant for the unceasing pursuit of profit. It is an intriguing fact that the unusual and deeply personal, strongly emotional outbursts and references to matters of religion and daily family concerns must be sought nearly exclusively in letters from women.

My preoccupation here will therefore not be a real portrait, but rather a description of a typical Old Assyrian businessman, his family relations and his economic and social world. For this purpose Imdi-ilum is well suited; the main reason is that we have a considerable number of textual references to him which make it possible to provide a fairly detailed analysis. Furthermore, we do possess at least some fragmentary evidence of an archaeological nature concerning his house in the Kanesh harbour, enough to allow us to reconstruct part of his archive. Finally, Imdi-ilum appears to have had a unique name, which is extraordinarily helpful for any analysis of the textual corpus. I know of only one patronymic, Šu-Laban, and I assume that all references to Imdi-ilum concern this man, Imdi-ilum son of Šu-Laban.

Imdi-ilum's archive.

It is practically impossible to carry out satisfactory archival studies in the textual material from Kanesh at the present time, since the majority of the available texts stem from illicit diggings and since, moreover, the excavations carried out during one field season in 1925 by Hrozný appear to have been rather confused. The competent Turkish excavations, which have so far resulted in the finding of more than 15,000 texts, have provided us with some excellent reports dealing with the architectural and artifactual findings, but practically none of the texts have been made available for study. Since the basic socio-economic unit in the Old Assyrian society was the family firm, whose structure and functions were directly reflected in the individual private archives, we are in a very difficult situation when trying to analyse institutions, procedures, families etc. We must attempt to piece together again the scattered and obviously quite incomplete remains of these archives, and in this task we are faced with formidable and indeed often insurmountable difficulties which seriously limit the power of our conclusions.[2]

The archive which I propose to study here is represented both in the published collections of European and American museums and in the corpus found by Hrozný. Of course, when he finally persuaded the villagers to tell him where they had been finding the tablets which had then been fed into the antiquities market for forty years, they showed him precisely those locations where they had been digging. Accordingly, he discovered what remained there of archives which had already been partly "excavated", and he tells us that he found "dans un endroit où les villageois avaient auparavant beaucoup creusé" part of Pūšu-kēn's archive; in two rooms he discovered ca. 250 tablets which had formed part of the archive of Imdi-ilum and his father Šu-Laban.[3]

In the volume ICK 1, where Hrozný published nearly 200 texts found by him, he also provided a plan of his excavations of the field called "la prairie de Hadji Mehmed", and on this plan he indicated by numbers 12 locations where tablets had been found; the list of texts in the volume contains references to these loci so that it is possible to determine which texts had been found together.[4] Hrozný himself pointed out that "les tablettes les plus nombreuses, où est nommé *Imdilum*, proviennent de l'emplacement 4, et sont presque toutes noircies par le voisinage d'une source".[5] Regrettably, Hrozný's notes on his excavation had disappeared when Matouš in 1962 brought out the second volume of texts from the excavations at Kültepe, so it is not possible to determine where the large majority of Hrozný's finds came from. It must also be admitted that the plan given in ICK 1 is rather unclear so that it is impossible to combine the walls shown on it so as to form intelligible house-plans. Hrozný was aware that he was digging in an area where previous trenches had caused disturbances, and a further complicating factor - of which he was not aware - was the existence of more than one building-level.

The Turkish excavator Professor Tahsin Özgüç started his own activity at the site in an area which was immediately adjacent to Hrozný's old trenches. It appears that Imdi-ilum's house must have been entirely within Hrozný's area, but Özgüç found at least one house which had been partly excavated by Hrozný, one which had belonged to an Assyrian merchant called Laqēpum. Texts from his archive had been discovered by Hrozný at locus 12 on his plan, and Özgüç reported finding further tablets from this archive. The rooms dug by Hrozný must be located in squares G 10-11 on the plan published by Özgüç.[6] We know from the further excavations that Laqēpum and another Assyrian called Adad-ṣulūlī were neighbours of Imdi-ilum, and it is interesting to see that these persons do not play any role in Imdi-ilum's archive.

It must be kept in mind that only fifteen out of the total of 163 letters which are known to me, where Imdi-ilum appears as either sender or recipient, were discovered by Hrozný. On the other hand, practically all of Imdi-ilum's loan-documents have been found by Hrozný.[7] It therefore seems virtually certain that letters were kept separate from texts of other types in Imdi-ilum's house, and it is indeed possible that they were stored in a different house.

The two lots of tablets mentioned by Hrozný as found in adjoining rooms and belonging to the archive of Imdi-ilum and his father Šu-Laban must correspond to loci 3 and 4. The plan indicates that another lot was found at locus 5 which appears to be in the same room as locus 4; however, only two texts are known to have been found at locus 5, ICK 1:31 and 33, letters which have no relation to Imdi-ilum's archive. I assume that they should be assigned to level 1b and thus came from a later building which stood at the same spot.[8]

Of the texts published in ICK 1, 67 were discovered at locus 4, and 5 were

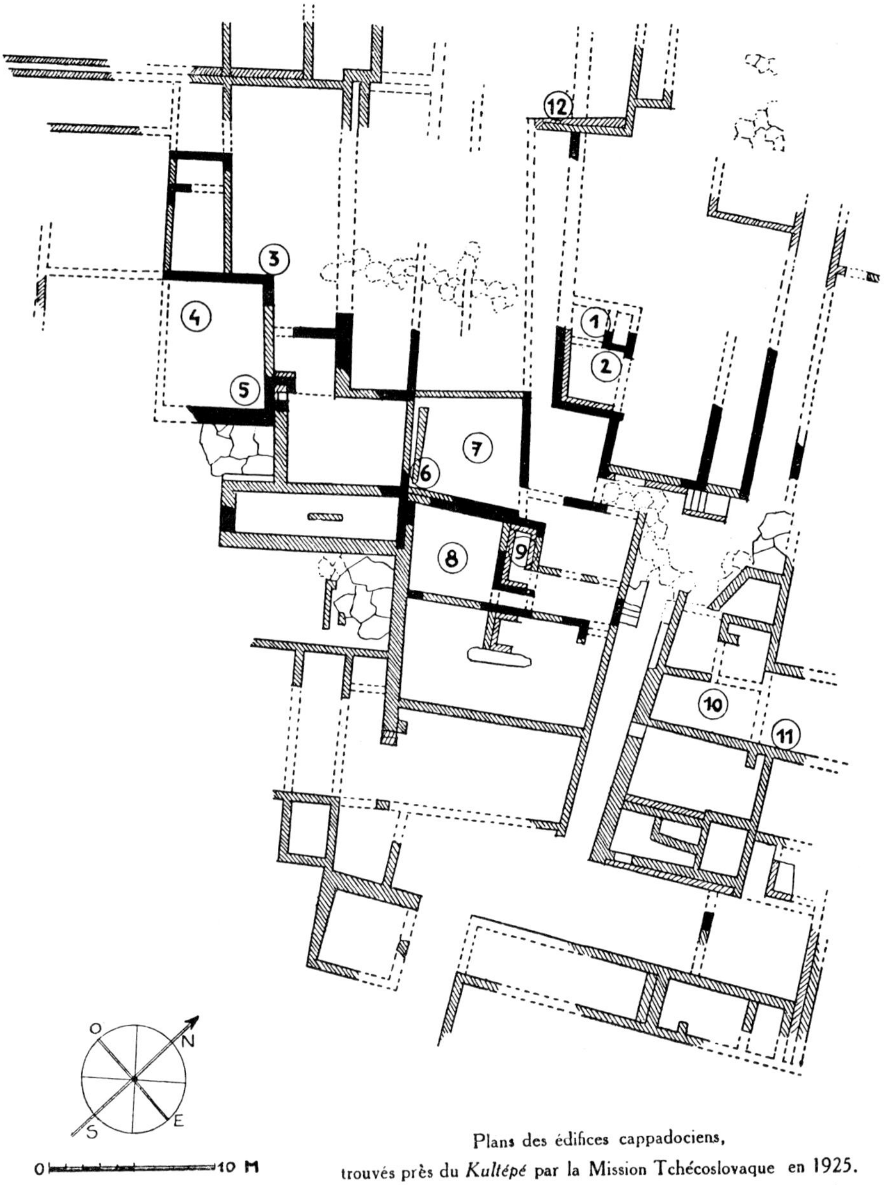

Plans des édifices cappadociens,
trouvés près du *Kultépé* par la Mission Tchécoslovaque en 1925.
Les chiffres indiquent les places où les archives cappadociennes ont été trouvées.

found at locus 3. These 72 texts thus constitute only a fraction of the 250 documents which Hrozný said that he found here; some of the remaining ones have of course been published in ICK 2, others probably still await publication. It is hardly possible to determine which of the texts in ICK 2 came from Imdi-ilum's archive; 25 texts directly mention this person and may therefore be included with certainty, and at least ten or twenty more may be added because they mention persons who are known to have been members of Imdi-ilum's close family. However, no more than half of the tablets found by Hrozný at these loci may confidently be grouped as belonging to Imdi-ilum's archive.

In spite of these restrictions the group of 72 texts in ICK 1 constitute an invaluable tool which may provide us with clues about the nature of the archive as a whole. The first basic observation then is that Imdi-ilum himself is mentioned in only 26 of these documents, i.e. about forty per cent. 14 texts are written out in the first person or mention no names at all and are consequently not amenable to any analysis,[9] so we are left with 32 texts out of 72 whose presence in the archive must be explained on the basis of a study of the persons who appear in them.

In nine of these remaining texts we find one or more of Imdi-ilum's brothers, Ennam-Bēlum, Aššur-ṣulūlī and Puzur-Aššur (28, 72, 95, 99, 161, 176, 183, 186 and 190). Šu-Laban, presumably in all cases Imdi-ilum's father, is found in four of the texts (7, 105, 140 and 156). Finally, Imdi-ilum's son Puzur-Ištar is the recipient of one letter (54), which means that 14 of the 32 texts can fairly easily be explained as indeed belonging to Imdi-ilum's archive. This leaves us with no less than 18 texts which need some further explanation.

Five of these texts refer to one Idī-Ištar (64, 83, 142, 175 and 178), and three to a man named Uṣur-ša-Aššur (70, 110 and 151); these men, sons of Aššur-malik, had close relations with Imdi-ilum's sons, but it is obvious that the documents in question could not have been attributed to Imdi-ilum's archive without Hrozný's notes concerning their findspot. Two other texts (36 and 152) concern a man by the name Amur-Ištar who was probably identical with Imdi-ilum's uncle of this name.

For the remaining eight texts no really satisfactory explanation can in fact be given here. Two of them may be intrusive and belong to different archives altogether,[10] and the six which remain are:

94 : a quittance involving Ilī-nādā, Alāhum son of Zukuhum, and Alāhum son of Ibezua,
132: a letter to Annali and Ilabrat-bāni from Abum-ilī,[11]
143: a loan: Aššur-bēl-awātim son of Šu-Hubur owes an amount of copper to Ennu-Dagān,
160: a loan: Puzur-Anna son of Šu-Ilabrat owes an amount of gold to Idī-Aššur
166: a loan: Maṣi-ilī owes an amount of silver to Sukallija,
189: a letter, names of sender and recipients missing.[12]

These texts could perhaps give support to the doubts expressed by Hrozný himself in the introduction to ICK 1, where he said that the previous extensive diggings in the area could well have disturbed the archaeological context to such an extent that most of the tablets were in fact not found *in situ*. However, these remarks stand somewhat opposed to Hrozný's first report from 1927 where he noted that tablets were regularly found associated with remains of large pots in which they had originally been stored; in fact, some tablets were discovered lying in such a pot.[13] It seems probable that the two lots of Imdi-ilum texts discovered by Hrozný were relatively undisturbed, but it remains likely that they fell from an upper storey when the house was burnt down.

The incomplete and somewhat uncertain evidence available does make it clear that Hrozný found part of the archive which had been used by the *family and firm* of which Imdi-ilum was a leading member. Whether such an important man as his uncle Amur-Ištar also had his own archive must remain uncertain, although highly likely, and the evidence available does not make it possible to even begin to speculate about the reasons for the presence of individual texts in the Imdi-ilum archive.

The letters found by Hrozný show that Imdi-ilum's archive contained messages sent to him as well as from him, and some of the letters have Imdi-ilum appearing in the company of a number of other persons, some of them clearly not members of his family. The list of letters provided at the end of the article indicates the difficulties involved in a reconstruction of the archive on the basis of the scattered material from illicit diggings, for it is obviously impossible to decide whether for instance a letter addressed to Imdi-ilum and Pūšu-kēn should be allocated to one or the other archive. In fact, one might suspect that in at least some instances more than one copy of such letters would exist, but duplicate texts are exceedingly rare in the Old Assyrian material. The list of letters must therefore not be regarded as a kind of inventory of Imdi-ilum's archive.

Imdi-ilum's family.[14]

Since patronymics are used sparingly in the Old Assyrian texts and are nearly always absent from the letters, it is necessary for any study of a family group to build the analyses primarily on an evaluation of context and content. This is naturally a perilous procedure where we run the risk of becoming involved in elaborate circular arguments. Moreover, homonymy quickly becomes a barrier to our reconstructions, which means that our analysis must be conducted and evaluated on different levels in consonance with the distance from the central figure. Imdi-ilum's closest relatives, father, brothers, children, occur so often together with him in intimate relationships that their place is fairly easy to ascertain. Women are always more poorly represented, and on the level of uncles, grandparents, grandchildren and in-laws we must accept an unpleasantly high degree of uncertainty. The reconstruction which follows must be understood in the light of these observations.

The name of Imdi-ilum's father was as already stated Šu-Laban. Perhaps the clearest evidence for this conclusion is found in the letter ICK 1:182, found at locus 4 in Imdi-ilum's house; this is a message from the king of Assur to the Kanesh colony which explains the background for the sending out to Kanesh of the attorney appointed by the city assembly to assist Imdi-ilum son of Šu-Laban in a lawsuit.[15]

This patronymic is found associated with a few other names, and a glance at the list of Imdi-ilum's correspondents will show that some of these names do indeed refer to Imdi-ilum's brothers. Ennum-Bēlum, Puzur-Aššur and Aššur-ṣulūlī occur as some of the most frequent correspondents and are often found together. Puzur-Aššur is twice in letters to Imdi-ilum described as "your brother",[16] and his death is discussed in another letter in the correspondence.[17]

I do not know the name of Imdi-ilum's mother. We do know, however, his children, two boys called Puzur-Ištar and Amur-ilī,[18] and a girl called Ištar-baštī. As shown by J. Lewy, she moved from Assur to Kanesh at a certain point in her life; in her letter KTS 1b to her brother Puzur-Ištar she urges him to come to Assur and fetch her, "so that in Kanesh I can watch over your father's house and you". Ištar-baštī married twice; her first marriage was to an Assyrian called Al-ṭāb, and after his death she married an Anatolian by the name of Anuwa. It is not known whether she had any children in her first marriage, but a letter refers to a daughter of hers from her second marriage.[19]

The two sons unfortunately have very common names and it is therefore very difficult to determine what their own family-ties were. Puzur-Ištar may have been married to a girl called Ištar-lamassī, the daughter of a certain Aššur-nādā and the sister of Aššur-nēmedī and Annina. A marriage-contract concerning a Puzur-Ištar - unfortunately without patronymic - and this girl is known,[20] and Garelli has argued convincingly for the existence of close ties between Ištar-lamassī and Puzur-Ištar's family.[21] We also have two letters exchanged between these two persons, but only one name occurs in them: Enna-Suen, and that again is a very common personal name.[22] It must certainly be kept in mind that none of Ištar-lamassī's brothers seem to have had close connections with Puzur-Ištar; her father Aššur-nādā was dead when she was given in marriage, and it is quite uncertain whether he was identical with the person of this name who appears in Imdi-ilum's correspondence.

I have not been able to establish whether Amur-ilī was married and had children.

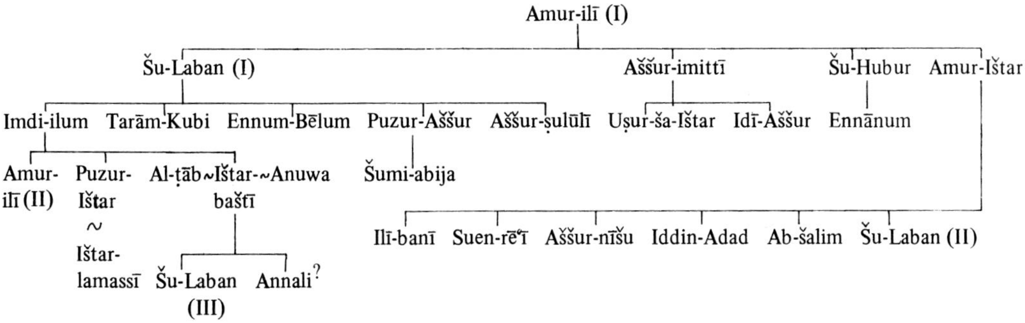

Even though we do have some letters exchanged between Imdi-ilum and certain women, it is not possible to establish the identity of his wife with certainty. Other traders of his generation corresponded fairly regularly with their wives who spent their lives in Assur, and an obvious example is of course Imdi-ilum's close associate Pūšu-kēn whose correspondence with his wife Lamassī is quite substantial and varied in nature.[23] The letter quoted at the beginning of this article was obviously despatched by women who had very close relations with Imdi-ilum, and it is my suggestion that Šīmat-Aššur, who appears together with (and after) Tarām-Kūbī there and in one further letter, was most probably Imdi-ilum's wife. It was hardly Tarām-Kūbī, even though she had a higher status than Šīmat-Aššur, for Tarām-Kūbī was presumably identical with the wife of another well-known Assyrian trader in Kanesh: Innaja.[24] I suggest therefore that she was Imdi-ilum's sister; it should be noted that also Pūšu-kēn's sister, Tarīš-mātum, is known to have retained extremely close connections with her brother and his family affairs in Assur, in spite of the fact that she was herself married - namely to Aššur-malik son of Šu-Kūbum.[25] This pattern has a number of parallels in societies where males are absent from their homes for long periods of time, often in connection with long-distance trading; we find an added emphasis on women as carriers of titles and the guardians of male interests, and of particular relevance is the observation made by Marvin Harris that absentee males tend to "turn over the care of jointly owned houses, lands and property to their sisters. Absentee males rely on their sisters rather than their wives because wives are drawn from someone else's paternal interest group".[26] It is further interesting to note that neither Imdi-ilum nor Pūšu-kēn appear to have had very close contacts or extensive commercial dealings with their brothers-in-law.

Šīmat-Aššur's position is reflected by a group of letters which are concerned with the question of the purchase of houses for Imdi-ilum in Assur. In ICK 1:192 he writes to his representatives that Pūšu-kēn is on his way to the capital with 20 minas of silver which is to be given to "the women" who have lent an amount against interest to the representatives, money which have been used to pay for houses. He urges that the women should be made to accept that no interest is to be paid, but that he will take care of their business in Anatolia *in lieu* of interest, "doing my utmost over every single shekel of silver". The unpublished letter from Tarām-Kūbī and Šīmat-Aššur, to be edited by Sally Moren, refers directly to this affair; we hear that one of the women has given the 20 minas of silver and she complains that the representatives in Assur have not yet paid her back. In a further unpublished text from Imdi-ilum to these ladies (to be edited by Matouš as no. 50a) the writer promises that Pūšu-kēn will bring the money, and he asks them to send textiles which he can sell for them. Finally, the letter MET 10 (also unpublished) is from the recipients of ICK 1:192 and contains the following passage:

> For 10 minas of silver we bought the house belonging to Bēlānum son of Nūr-Ištar; for 3 minas 5 shekels of silver we bought the house of Šu-Bēlum for you. We borrowed the money from Šīmat-Aššur and paid. We shall give her 5 minas of silver out of this shipment of goods.[27]

It was thus presumably Šīmat-Aššur who advanced the money mentioned in the other texts, and one may well ask whether it is in fact likely that Imdi-ilum's wife would lend her husband money against interest. This must remain uncertain, but the very close ties existing between these two persons - also reflected in the references to small consignments sent to her from Imdi-ilum[28] - make it at least possible. It is worth noting that these women were able to dispose over such very large funds which clearly constituted their private, personal property; I would guess that such sums had their origin in a system of dowry, but that again is speculative.

Moving to the problem of Imdi-ilum's grandfather and uncles we step further into the realm of speculation and uncertainty. The name Šu-Laban is associaed with no less than eight different patronymics: Amur-ilī,[29] Al-ṭāb,[30] Amur-Ištar,[31] Bazi,[32] Dannu-ilī,[33] Kurub-Ištar,[34] Šu-Aššur,[35] and Šumi-abija.[36] Only Bazi occurs as a patronymic in one of the texts from Imdi-ilum's archive, and he was hardly Imdi-ilum's grandfather since the text records a loan extended by Imdi-ilum to Šu-Laban son of Bazi. The patronymics Al-ṭāb, Amur-Ištar and Šu-Aššur must all refer to persons too late to belong in this context. Šu-Laban son of Al-ṭāb could in fact be Imdi-ilum's grandson, from the first marriage of Ištar-baštī. And Šu-Laban son of Amur-Ištar was probably Imdi-ilum's cousin.

The only likely candidate as Imdi-ilum's grandfather is in fact Amur-ilī, attested once in the letter KTS 34a, where a certain Elāli writes about his purchase of a garden in Assur:

Šu-Laban son of Amur-ilī agreed (on a price) for the garden, but Aššur-imittī said: "If you buy you must send 10 minas..."[37]

Aššur-imittī was in fact the name of one of Imdi-ilum's paternal uncles, i.e. a brother of Šu-Laban,[38] which nicely explains why he appears in the passage quoted above. We have a number of references to one Aššur-imittī son of Amur-ilī, a very influential man in Assur who is known to have entertained close relations with the king.[39] I suggest that it was this man who figured so prominently in Imdi-ilum's correspondence and was indeed his direct boss in Assur.

If it is thus correct that Amur-ilī was the name of Imdi-ilum's grandfather, we can go one step further and identify the man Amur-Ištar who also figures so often in Imdi-ilum's letters as the son of Amur-ilī, and thus another paternal uncle of Imdi-ilum. This Amur-Ištar is known to have been a close partner of Pūšu-kēn,[40] and his very active role in the trade as a contemporary of Imdi-ilum and Pūšu-kēn could be easily explained if he was the youngest son of Amur-ilī.

Just as it seems likely that the name Šu-Laban recurs in other generations and branches of Imdi-ilum's family, as suggested above, it is thus probable that Imdi-ilum's son Amur-ilī was named after his great-grandfather.

In my reconstruction of Imdi-ilum's family-tree I have placed one further son of Amur-ilī: Šu-Hubur. The letter BIN 4:33, to Aššur-imittī and Šu-Hubur from Pūšu-kēn, shows that the two recipients were brothers,[41] but it must be admitted that there is no attestation known to me of a Šu-Hubur son of Amur-ilī. On the other hand both this name and Aššur-imittī occur as sons of one Elāli, and it has therefore usually been assumed that it was this Šu-Hubur - known also to have held the year-eponymy - who wrote a great many letters to Pūšu-kēn. My suggestion is naturally quite tentative, but it should be remembered that especially those men who lived in the capital, and who therefore never appear in lists of witnesses, are only very rarely attested with patronymics. A Šu-Hubur can certainly be seen to have had close connections with Imdi-ilum, and his son Ennānum was Imdi-ilum's trusted man in Assur.[42]

Attempts to ascertain whether Imdi-ilum's brothers were married and had children run into serious difficulties because of their names which are all very common.[43]

Imdi-ilum's main business-contacts.

The basic premise upon which much of the following discussion is built may be formulated as follows: in the introductory formula of any letter the sequence of the names is determined by the status of the individuals involved; when we have only one sender and one recipient the situation is simple: "From A to B" shows that A has the higher status. When we have more than one sender and/or recipient the status relations of some of the persons must necessarily become obscured: when A and B send a letter to C and D we can conclude that A outranks all the others, and that C outranks D; but it remains unclear whether B has a higher or lower status than C and D.[44]

The three tables presented here show that the principle outlined is valid for the vast majority of the persons, and in fact the rigidity of the system is a powerful indication of the importance of social status in the Old Assyrian society. A restricted group of persons can be found in introductory formulae which place them both higher and lower than Imdi-ilum; obviously, some persons must have been regarded as equals, in which case other considerations may determine the relative position of these men: courtesy, anger or pure chance.

Correspondents with a higher status than Imdi-ilum:

name	location	attestations	
Adad-bānī	Assur	2x	
Alili	Assur	1x	
Amur-Aššur	Assur	1x	
Aššur-imittī	Assur	19x	+ 2 unclear att.
Aššur-rēṣī	Anatolia?	1x	
Buzutaja	Kanesh	2x	
Ikuppī-Aššur	Assur	2x	
Išma-Aššur	Assur	1x	
Ištar-pilah	Anatolia?	1x	
Puzur-Ištar (I)	Assur	2x	
Šalim-ahum	Assur	1x	
Šu-Hubur	Assur	4x	+ 3 unclear att.
Šu-Laban	Assur?	2x	

Correspondents with a lower status than Imdi-ilum:

Adu	Anatolia	3x	
Ah-šalim	Anatolia	4x	
Ahu-waqar	Anatolia	6x	
Al-ṭāb	Anatolia	2x	
Amur-ilī	Kanesh, Anat.	13x	
Amur-Šamaš	Kanesh	1x	
Anah-ilī	Kanesh	1x	
Annali	Anatolia	5x	
Asu	Anatolia	1x	
Aššur-damiq	Anatolia	1x	
Aššur-idī	Anatolia	1x	
Aššur-malik	Anat., Assur	1x	+ 1 unclear att.
Aššur-nādā	Anatolia?	2x	
Aššur-ṣulūlī	Kanesh, Anat.	13x	+ 1 unclear att.
Aššur-ṭāb	Kanesh, Anat.	8x	
Bazu[..]	Kanesh	1x	
Bēlija	Assur	1x	
Buburānum	Assur	1x	+ 12 unclear att.
Buzia	Anatolia	4x	
Ennānum	Assur	2x	+ 12 unclear att.
Ennum-Aššur	Kanesh, Anat.	8x	
Ennum-Bēlum	Anat., Assur, Kanesh	21x	+ 5 unclear att.
Hadaja	Kanesh?	1x	
Huraṣānum	Anat., Kanesh	3x	
Idī-abum	Kanesh?	1x	
Idī-Adad	Anatolia	10x	
Idnaja	?	2x	
Ikūnum	Kanesh?	1x	
Ikuppīja	Assur, Anat.	6x	+ 1 unclear att.
Ilī-ašrannī	Anatolia	3x	
Ilī-bānī	?	2x	
Inah-ilī	Kanesh	1x	
Innaja	Kanesh	1x	+ 2 unclear att.
Ištar-baštī	Kanesh	4x	
Itūr-ilī	Anatolia	3x	
Kurara	Anatolia	3x	
Kurub-Ištar	Kanesh, Assur?	3x	

name	location	attestations	
Kutallānum	?	1x	
Lalija	Kanesh	2x	
Laqēpum	?	1x	
Lulu	Anatolia?	1x	
Luzina	Anatolia	1x	
Pilah-Ištar	Assur, Anat.	2x	+ 2 unclear att.
Puzur-Adad	Anatolia	1x	
Puzur-Anna	Assur	1x	
Puzur-Aššur	Kanesh, Anat., Assur	14x	
Puzur-ilī	Anatolia	2x	
Puzur-Ištar (II)	Kanesh, Anat.	11x	
Šamaš-abī	Kanesh?	1x	
Šu-Bēlum	Kanesh	2x	
Šu-Ištar	Anat., Assur	1x	+ 11 unclear att.
Šu-Kubum	Kanesh?	1x	
Šumi-abija	Kanesh	1x	
Tarām-Kūbī	Assur	3x	
Usānum	Anatolia	1x	
Uṣur-ša-Aššur	Anatolia	3x	+ 1 unclear att.
Uṣur-ša-Ištar	Kanesh, Anat.	6x	+ 1 unclear att.
Uzua	Anatolia	5x	
Zuba	Kanesh	1x	+ 1 unclear att.

Correspondents with unclear or mixed attestations:

		higher	lower	unclear
Alāhum	Assur, Kanesh	3x	3x	
Amur-Ištar	Anatolia	9x	8x	2x
Aššur-taklāku	?	1x	2x	
Dadija	Assur			1x
Idī-Aššur	Assur, Kanesh	2x	2x	
Kuzizia	Anatolia			1x
Pūšu-kēn	Assur, Kanesh	5x	11x	4x
Puzur-Ti'amtim	Kanesh			1x
Šalim-Aššur	Kanesh, Assur?	2x	1x	
Šīmat-Aššur	Assur	1x	3x	

The pattern which emerges from the three tables is quite clear and indicates the importance of the basic bipartition of the Old Assyrian society into two branches of unequal status: the capital city Assur and the many colonies in Northern Syria and Anatolia.

In the capital we find Imdi-ilum's superiors, led by his uncle Aššur-imittī who appears in 21 of the letters in the correspondence. He is surrounded by a small group of men who write and receive letters together with him: Ennānum and Buburānum (each 12 times), and Šu-Ištar (11 times). Twice he appears together with Šu-Hubur, which is particularly interesting in view of the fact that the latter has written two letters addressed to Buzutaja, Pūšu-kēn and Imdi-ilum in which he acts as a protector of the interests of Aššur-imittī's heirs.

Both Aššur-imittī and Šu-Hubur have been tentatively described as Imdi-ilum's paternal uncles. It seems that his father Šu-Laban died relatively early, for it was obviously his brothers, and especially Aššur-imittī, who took care of the interests of the family and directed the activities in the colonies. We have only two letters from Šu-Laban to Imdi-ilum; one of them, written together with an otherwise unknown Dādija to Imdi-ilum and Bazu*[..]* is a caravan-account referring to purchases of a small number of textiles in Assur;[45] in the other letter Šu-Laban says that he will build a house and explains that he is alone; he goes on with a good deal of advice concerning the proper way to handle certain affairs, and asks Imdi-ilum to act in such a way that he will not become unhappy but may hear good tidings from him instead: "Please take care and let me see you act like a man!"[46]

Whereas for instance Pūšu-kēn's father Su'ejja, who must have been roughly contemporary with Šu-Laban, is never found alive in our documentation, Imdi-ilum's father did live to see his sons in full action in Kanesh. This is confirmed by a passage from the letter VAT 9247 to Ennum-Bēlum and Aššur-ṣulūlī from Puzur-Aššur,[47] in which the latter says that he gave a consignment of tin and textiles to Uṣur-ša-*[Aššur]* "while our father was still living".

Of the persons who occur together with Aššur-imittī only one can be confidently identified as a member of Imdi-ilum's family: Ennānum was undoubtedly a son of Šu-Hubur.[48] Buburānum who nearly always appears together with Ennānum must surely have been another close relative, but I do not know of any patronymic for him. These two, who are of lower rank than Imdi-ilum, appear to have had special relations to him. Ennānum writes in one letter how he takes care of all of Imdi-ilum's wishes in Assur,[49] and of particular interest is the letter CCT 3:46b in which both warn him of Aššur-imittī's attempts to pass on the responsibility for some losses to Imdi-ilum:

> Concerning the silver which you entrusted to Idī-Aššur for (?) Aššur-imittī, your father's brother, he will sue you for the losses. He says: "It is not my affair! " - Confirm your witnesses there that you did entrust the silver to Idī-Aššur ! Further, concerning the tin which was lost in ... Aššur-imittī says: "That is not my affair! The tin belonged to Imdi-ilum!" Aššur-imittī will sue you in these matters. Take care and be prepared!

Aššur-imittī's letters are concerned with many different subjects but some are of special interest; I have already referred to the purchase of houses in Assur on behalf of Imdi-ilum, and to the large amounts of silver which he received in that connection. We also have some texts which show how Aššur-imittī and his associates in Assur took care of the purchase of very substantial shipments of tin and textiles for Imdi-ilum. Both in MET 10 and VAT 9218 the men in Assur acknowledge receipt of no less than 1 talent of silver, for which money they have bought large quantities of tin and textiles. MET 10 is of quite special interest since it seems that the caravan referred to here, containing a shipment of 8 talents 40 minas of tin under seal, 50 minas of tin for expenses, 100 *kutānum*-textiles, plus seven donkeys, is also mentioned in the account ICK 1:124; this latter document makes it clear that the shipment belongs to three partners, namely Imdi-ilum, Pūšu-kēn and Šalim-Aššur.[50] The damaged text Bursa 3376 presumably contained a quotation from another such caravan-account. The letter TC 3:54 refers to a shipment brought by a certain Pilah-Ištar, probably the son of Uzua, one of Imdi-ilum's trusted agents in Anatolia, and Aššur-imittī and his associates are asked to assist the transporter with the purchases and in particular see to it that the *nishātum*-due is levied "with us". They must also represent Imdi-ilum when Pilah-Ištar's *naruqqum*-tablet is written so that Imdi-ilum invests 2 minas of gold.[51] Such negotiations, where Aššur-imittī acts for Imdi-ilum in connection with investments to be made in other traders' *naruqqum*-capital, are also reflected in the letter VAT 9253.[52]

The two letters TC 3:44 and MAH 10823, where we find a different group of people surrounding Aššur-imittī, two of them, Idī-Aššur and Adad-bānī being his superiors, deal with the complex business of transferring the assets of the dead trader Šu-Aššur, son of Alāhum, to his brother Aššur-malik. The same affair is briefly mentioned in a letter from Aššur-imittī to Pūšu-kēn, CCT 2:41a. In these letters we find Imdi-ilum among the men in Assur, and very significantly he is the lowest ranking member of the group.

The letter CCT 2:35, addressed to Aššur-imittī, Ennum-Bēlum, Ennānum and Burānum from Imdi-ilum, Pūšu-kēn, Aššur-ṣulūlī and Uṣur-ša-Ištar, is concerned with the financial difficulties connected with the death of Puzur-Aššur. The men in Kanesh have assembled all of the deceased man's assets, from Kanesh, Wašhania, Wahšušana and Purušhaddum, but it all amounts to no more than about 1 talent of silver, which is said to be too little. What emerges from the text is first of all the complexity of the relations between the capital and the colonies, where the major decisions clearly belong to the men in Assur. The dead merchant's money and tablets must be sent there, and it is in Assur that the final accounting will take place.

Pūšu-kēn appears together with Imdi-ilum in five of the Aššur-imittī letters, and we furthermore have a number of letters exchanged between these men without any mention of Imdi-ilum.[53] It is uncertain, however, whether we are in all cases dealing with the same Aššur-imittī, and it should be pointed out that in a number of letters Pūšu-kēn is placed before Aššur-imittī.[54] Also Šu-Hubur writes letters to Pūšu-kēn, sometimes in company with Pūšu-kēn's boss Šalim-ahum. I cannot find the proper basis for the very close contacts which clearly existed between Pūšu-kēn and his family on the one side and Imdi-ilum and his family on the other. The correspondence indicates that the two men were of equal status, and the 20 letters involving Pūšu-kēn show the constant and diversified contacts that existed between them. Three documents, ICK 1:124, 2:97, and BIN 4:33, all outside the Imdi-ilum correspondence, provide examples of their partnership involving joint investments in the overland trade, and the same pattern is revealed by our letters. According to CCT 3:21a they are jointly representatives for Šu-Hubur, a role which Pūšu-kēn has alone in TC 2:72.

A completely similar pattern is found in the correspondence which involved Amur-Ištar, identified here as Imdi-ilum's uncle. It is interesting that this man had a formalised partnership with Pūšu-kēn, a contractual relationship which was terminated by the two merchants' heirs according to ATHE 24. It is accordingly not surprising that we have a number of letters exchanged between these two men.

Amur-Ištar was a very active man who functioned in various capacities. We have a considerable number of references to his activities concerning the trade in copper and wool, and he is known to have travelled a great deal in Anatolia in connection with these transactions: we find him of course in the copper-producing centers in Eastern Anatolia in such places as Tišmurna, Durhumit and Kunanamit,[55] but also in Purušhaddum where he had dealings with the local palace administration.[56] He also acted as caravan-leader on the long overland haul between Assur and Kanesh. The texts Gelb 62 and ICK 2:145 show how Imdi-ilum represented his interests in court, and we hear once that he was entrusted with Puzur-Aššur's seal.[57] He is mentioned frequently in the letters exchanged between the other members of the group, and his position is shown for instance in the letter CCT 4:27a from Uzua to Imdi-ilum, where the former complains that he has written repeatedly to Amur-Ištar and Pūšu-kēn to be allowed to go to Durhumit to do business in copper, but Amur-Ištar has denied him that permission.

The impression one gets from all these texts is of a man whose position in the daily routine of the firm was quite different from the one held by Imdi-ilum. Amur-Ištar travelled much, and although we do find Imdi-ilum engaging both in travel in Anatolia and in leading a caravan to Assur, it is obvious that he was usually stationed in Kanesh where he directed the affairs of the numerous agents. Amur-Ištar was apparently the most highly placed such agent.

Imdi-ilum's brothers, and especially Ennum-Bēlum, played a very conspicuous role in the running of the affairs of the family. They were the trusted agents who could deal with all aspects of the commercial and legal transactions. Ennum-Bēlum was apparently in Assur quite a number of times, and he writes letters back to Imdi-ilum in Kanesh together with Aššur-imittī and the other representatives there. We find him collecting debts and negotiating with customers; in the letter KUG 36 he recounts how he intervened in an affair because he found that Imdi-ilum's agent acted irresponsibly. His position is also reflected in a letter from Imdi-ilum to the son Amur-ilī where the latter is commanded to assist Ennum-Bēlum, obviously with the daily routine of the business.[58]

Ennum-Bēlum had his own affairs as shown by the fact that he had a *naruqqum*-capital; interestingly, Pūšu-kēn was one of the investors with an amount of 2 minas of gold; one of the witnesses to the document was his brother Puzur-Aššur.[59] We have references to shipments owned jointly by Imdi-ilum and Ennum-Bēlum: the extremely complex legal affair reflected by the documents TC 3:130 and ICK 1:188 involved the transportation of a consignment of tin and textiles to Ennum-Bēlum and Imdi-ilum's representatives, whose names were Enna-Suen and Huraṣānum; the consignment was owned by the two brothers and the transporter was Imdi-ilum's son Amur-ilī. The very close relations between these men did not prevent occasional litigation, as shown by for instance ICK 1:185 dealing with a shipment of a large amount of silver.

It seems that Imdi-ilum went to Assur and stayed there, maybe enjoying his otium after a number of years in the colony at Kanesh;[60] Ennum-Bēlum probably took over the business in Anatolia together with Imdi-ilum's sons. We have an intriguing letter from Ennum-Bēlum to his other brother Aššur-ṣulūlī which could refer to this period and which gives us a picture of conflict and strife in the family:

> To Aššur-ṣulūlī: Please sell your goods for cash and be ready and cleared before I arrive so that we may go to the City together and (see to it that)

our father's house does not get destroyed. Let us clear ourselves! Don't you know how our brother is wicked? All the silver that I send from here, our brother indeed keeps it! He did not make any accounting with our father![61]

The brother referred to here could be either Imdi-ilum or Puzur-Aššur, of course, but I do not know of any references which indicate that the latter spent any long period of time in the capital. Another possibility is that the kinship terms here - as in so many Old Assyrian contexts - cover other relations, so that the "brother" could have been one of their associates. It seems obvious at least that the "father" in this letter was not their real father who must have been dead by then.

Puzur-Aššur, whose status, and thus presumably his age, was lower than Ennum-Bēlum's, did not ordinarily stay in Kanesh. He corresponded with his three brothers in a few letters, and even though it is impossible to determine his usual home-city, these letters make it clear that it was somewhere to the southeast of Kanesh, i.e. most probably in one of the major caravan-cities on the road to Assur. He is involved in smuggling a number of times and can be seen to have had particularly close ties with Hahhum and Timelkia.[62] When we hear that he has handed over fairly substantial consignments of goods to other people who bring them to Kanesh and further on to Purušhaddum or Wahšušana, it is possible that he is referring to re-loading procedures along the overland caravan trail rather than to purchase transactions which took place in Assur. He was certainly in the capital now and then,[63] and it remains possible that he was not in fact stationed permanently anywhere but that he functioned as a transporter. However, the information which we possess does point to a colony in Syria or southern Anatolia as his base.

About the last of the brothers, Aššur-ṣulūlī, there is little to say. He does not seem to travel as much as Ennum-Belum or Puzur-Aššur, but normally functioned in Kanesh together with Imdi-ilum, presumably as a junior associate dealing with the daily business there. A couple of letters show him in Wahšušana on his way to Durhumit; he became entangled in a lawsuit there and asked Imdi-ilum for help, and according to KTB 6 a letter from the latter proved effective. This is a very clear indication of his relatively modest place in the hierarchy.

The sons Puzur-Ištar and Amur-ilī are found in all the roles described for the other members of the family. Puzur-Ištar is especially interesting because of his role as Imdi-ilum's caretaker in Kanesh at a time when he himself was in Assur; the letters TC 1:24 and VAT 9241 refer to a lawsuit involving "attorneys" sent out from Assur, and the same matter is dealt with in BIN 6: 219.[64] But also such letters as ATHE 59 and KTS 19b (related to CCT 2:11a and LB 1202) show Puzur-Ištar in action in Kanesh, collecting debts and handling the sale of shipments arriving from Assur. On the other hand, TC 3:50 shows that he was in Assur, and refers to a complex legal conflict with Ennānum.

Puzur-Ištar's business is further illuminated by a memorandum which enumerates a number of loan documents where he is the creditor. In all this document, Gelb 56, refers to an outstanding credit of 12 minas 31 shekels of silver and 55 minas of copper, and his activities are thus - according to this one text - on a quite modest scale. None of the loans extended by him amount to more than about 3 minas of silver.

Amur-ilī is especially well known as a transporter, both on the overland haul to and from Assur and within Anatolia.[65] One letter makes it clear that he is supposed to assist Ennum-Bēlum, apparently in Kanesh, and we do in fact find him in a number of letters together with this man. Otherwise, it is difficult to gain a clear impression of Amur-ilī's functions within the family-firm.

Amur-ilī was apparently not a very reliable person, or at least his father seems to have thought so. Imdi-ilum writes once to Ištar-baštī and Amur-ilī and enjoins upon the daughter to keep an eye on her brother:

> Let him know how to obey! He must not interest himself (only) in bread and beer! Let him be a man![66]

Ištar-baštī herself held a rather dim view of both of her brothers according to her letter TC 3:112; it was addressed to Puzur-Ištar and must have been sent from Assur to Kanesh, i.e. from before the time when she moved to Anatolia. She is extremely worried and asks Puzur-Ištar why the brothers keep quarrelling with each other:

> Who began the quarrel? As for me, and you both, why doesn't one listen to what the other says, but (like) an evildoer does harm to your father's house? On top of my illness and you who quarrel, I also heard about the revolt in the land and became extremely worried about you. ... When the land is again peaceful, then act in accordance with your father's instructions, set out and come here. Your father must not worry. And do be at peace with your brother and do not quarrel!

Amur-ilī himself has written a long letter to his father in which he presents a very elaborate defence against a whole series of accusations:

> Why is it that you keep writing to me, saying: "You constantly send off your money in deceit[67] so that other people's firms may levy the *nishātum*-due! So, your transgressions are many and concern for you has eaten me up!" What silver of mine is it that you don't know about? Give me an opportunity[68] to go anywhere to take anything and place it before you in order to satisfy you! (It is true) that I observe others take away from their fathers' money some 10 minas of silver for themselves, and send it off for purchases under their fathers' noses, so that when their fathers hear about it they become angry - but when have I done such things? You say[69] that they keep doing such things and make their fathers angry, so that their fathers utter a curse before their gods - let that be *their* concern! And (divine) Assur and Massāt must not make such matters my business. When I was small ... did I not stand at your side? I never made trouble or wickedness. Today it is I who have in truth become your small brother.

Amur-ilī crowns these protestations of unflinching loyalty with saying that if he has done anything wrong "then may the palsy seize me! You are unique, my god, my trust, my guardian angel!"[70]

Apart from these members of Imdi-ilum's immediate family we find a handful of men who repeatedly take care of the interests of Imdi-ilum's firm. All of them seem to have higher rank than Imdi-ilum's sons, but I am unable to establish their own family-relations and thus to determine whether they belonged to another branch of the family. The best attested are Adu, Annali, Idī-Adad and Uzua, and they are often in direct relation with each other and with one or more of the close relatives of Imdi-ilum.

Adu seems to have been based more or less permanently in Purušhaddum, where he was involved in the sale of tin and textiles; he goes on some trips, of course, to Uššа, Ulama and certainly occasionally to Kanesh.[71] Idī-Adad and Annali are often found together, writing joint letters and acting as transporters of letters and shipments. Idī-Adad was clearly the more important of the two, and we find him alone in a group of letters, CCT 4:30b and 50a, ATHE 27 and BIN 6:74, which all deal with his action on behalf of Imdi-ilum against Ennum-Aššur who owes a large amount of silver. The first of these letters is from Idī-Adad to Imdi-ilum and it recounts in detail the negotiations between Ennum-Aššur and himself; he ends with a plea to Imdi-ilum to write an angry letter directly to his debtor who has concluded his talks with Idī-Adad in disagreement and harsh words.

This same Idī-Adad, who acts so virtuously in the letter just discussed, became involved in a brawl with Amur-Ištar, Imdi-ilum's uncle, and is accused both by him and by Uzua of having spread slander and false accusations against Amur-Ištar. The letter KTS 17 from Uzua gives a very precise picture of the difficulties that could arise so easily in the competitive and tense life of these roving merchants:

> There Idī-Adad must not say: "Amur-Ištar has wasted a lot of money", and you must not become worried! Do not worry at all! And do not pay attention to Idī-Adad's slander!

Uzua was quite clearly often in a position to know about Amur-Ištar's affairs, for he was also involved primarily in the trade in copper with Anatolia. He has written a letter together with Amur-Ištar, and he refers to him in his own writings. He has left us a very unhappy letter, the unpublished VAT 9301, which shows him in deep trouble in the town Kunanamet in the copper-region in Eastern Anatolia. This very long letter of 67 lines gives us a sad picture of a once trusted employee in Imdi-ilum's firm who had been abandoned and forgotten:

> Since I arrived at Kunanamet I have been moved far away from your breast. May Aššur and Massat be my witnesses that I have never heard a letter from you! Because I have heard no letter from you, my face became heavy (with longing) to go to you. ..... Because I have not heard any orders from you whatsoever my foot has been barred from entering the colony. I have been afraid for your sake.... As for me, I sweat and toil over every single shekel of silver that I make. My dear father and lord, why must your faithful servant, namely me, be destroyed for want of a protector?[72]

Imdi-ilum's correspondence thus shows us what we must call a "family firm" in action. The men in Assur who directed the affairs of the firm in a general way, and who controlled the essential purchase procedures of tin and textiles which were the economic foundation for the existence of the colonial system, were his father's brothers. It seems that Imdi-ilum himself belonged to the first generation of Assyrian traders who stayed permanently in the Kanesh harbour of the level 2 period; like the other men of his generation he had left his wife in Assur, hundreds of kilometers away, but his sons moved to the colonies and their generation appears to have had wives in Anatolia.

In Kanesh itself Imdi-ilum had at least one house, and we find several members of his close family there with him: his brothers Ennum-Bēlum and Aššur-ṣulūlī, his daughter, and his sons Amur-ilī and Puzur-Ištar. One brother appears to have been stationed in a colony on the road to Assur, and his uncle Amur-Ištar clearly spent a great deal of his time in the copper region of Eastern Anatolia together with some employees,[73] first of all Uzua. In Western Anatolia and the Konya plain, where we must find the major metallurgical center Purušhaddum, Imdi-ilum seems to have relied on agents like Adu, Annali and Idī-Adad.

Imdi-ilum's death is not directly referred to in any text known to me. We do have a number of letters exchanged between his sons, and they indicate that a partially different cast of persons took over the firm in the following generation, men such as Ilabrat-bānī and his brothers. However, an investigation of this period is outside the scope of this study.

Imdi-ilum's business and status.

The preceding analysis of Imdi-ilum's family and firm has shown that we are dealing with a man who had considerable influence in the Kanesh harbour and in the colonial system as a whole. The disastrous situation where only a fraction of the excavated textual material is available for study makes it impossible to determine more precisely what position he held in the community of the Kanesh harbour, and we must certainly be wary of conclusions concerning the importance of this particular family as compared to other families whose archives have not been published. Nevertheless, it seems entirely justified to characterise Imdi-ilum as an important man, presumably a very wealthy man, and most probably involved in the running of the affairs of the Assyrian community. We know that he functioned as week-eponym in Kanesh a number of times:

text	*year-eponym*	*month*[74]	*together with*
b/k 114	Elāli	IX	Garwaja
a/k 1304	*ša qati* Idī-abum	II	Garwaja
El 93	*ša qāti* Idī-abum, son of Narbutum	IV	Šamaš-bānī
KTH 20	Aššur-idī	VII	Pilah-Ištar
TMH 1:13b	Ṭāb-Aššur	IV	Aninum
b/k 687	Ilšu-rabi, son of Bazia	VII	Aninum
ICK 1:117	?	?	Ilī-ālum
BIN 4:153	?	?	Aššur-ṣulūlī

All these dates place him squarely in the first half of the chronological chart of year-eponymies which I have attempted to reconstruct, the period when the week-eponymy was usually held by two men, rather than one.[75] His partners as week-eponyms cannot all be said to have had any close relations to him or his family: the brother Aššur-ṣulūlī appears once, and Pilah-Ištar in the list is probably identical with the man of this name who appears repeatedly in the correspondence.

We are in the unusually lucky situation that a couple of texts provide us with detailed information about Imdi-ilum's current business at two different moments, and this gives us a unique chance to evaluate the scope of the economic activities of his family in Anatolia. Otherwise, it is obviously extremely hazardous to attempt to establish figures for the volume of the Old Assyrian trade; Veenhof has collected all the references known to him concerning shipments of tin and textiles from Assur to Kanesh, and on the basis of the information contained in 188 texts he could conclude that we possess direct documentation for shipments of in all some 14.500 textiles and some 27.000 minas of tin (450 talents, or ca. 13.500 kgs).[76] Now one single unpublished text from Berlin, VAT 9210, practically doubles the figure for tin by mentioning a shipment of no less than 410 talents of tin. Moreover, this is described as "the consignment in Imdi-ilum's caravan".[77] This truly enormous shipment is not mentioned anywhere else. The text makes it clear that the total was composed of a large number of individual shipments, probably 35, which belonged to different persons, so we cannot conclude that Imdi-ilum by himself could control such vast amounts of tin. In fact, his own share seems to have been the largest single part, amounting to no less than 57 talents of tin, but even this figure may not represent his private investment but could describe the common fund of a partnership of which he was only a member.

The two texts referred to above are CCT 2:8 and ICK 1:191+; the former is a letter sent by Imdi-ilum to Ennum-Bēlum, Huraṣānum and Amur-ilī; the other text is a memorandum, *tahsistum*, a note which gives in abbreviated form the text of a great number of loan-documents where Imdi-ilum appears as creditor. It seems reasonable to assume that both texts refer to affairs which were current at the time when they were written, and this is virtually certain with regard to the letter. We have a few other fragmentary memoranda and a number of loan-documents,[78] but the two texts by themselves cover several times more transactions than we find recorded in all the other texts taken together. This indicates once again that we do not possess the whole of Imdi-ilum's archive; part of the explanation is undoubtedly to be sought in the practice which is recorded at the end of some memoranda, where we are informed that the original tablets which have been summarised and repeated on the memorandum have been sent to Assur.[79]

CCT 2:8 enumerates some 32 loans,[80] referred to laconically as follows: "x minas of silver with PN". We are not given any dates or conditions of the loan, but occasionally we are told that an amount was given *ana be'ālim*, "to dispose over", or that part of the debt has been paid, etc. The text also informs about transactions in the office of the colony at Purušhaddum where certain persons have deposited textiles on accounts, and the money for these must be transferred to Imdi-ilum. Finally, some people have borrowed tin and textiles for which they must pay. The end of the text is unfortunately damaged at exactly the point where Imdi-ilum's instructions to the recipients were given, but tentatively I suggest the following translation:

> My dear brothers, to ... and make the customers pay, and Amur-ilī must not delay! ... Place this *[letter]* among my own tablets![81]

The text contains reference to debts outstanding amounting to a little over 3 talents, 7 1/2 minas and 9 3/4 shekels of silver, 21 shekels of gold, and 60 *kutānum*-textiles. A number of these amounts were owed by members of the family, and some others are directly related to caravan-procedures. Since the memorandum CCT 6:9a partly duplicates our text, giving the complete text of some of the original loan-documents, we can suggest a date in the first half of level 2 (Puzur-Nirah is no. 4 and Alāhum is no. 13 in my preliminary ordering of the year-eponymies); the fact that some of the transactions are referred to in letters from Imdi-ilum to Ištar-baštī and Amur-ilī (CCT 4:28a and TC 3:57) makes it probable that the text refers to a period when Imdi-ilum was living in Assur.

The memorandum called by me ICK 1:191+ is a composite text which is reconstructed in the following way:

1:191	covers lines 1-62
2:132	covers lines 63-106
2:129	covers lines 1-10, 37-40, 45-47, 87-93, 135-141
2:130	covers lines 10-37, 41-44, 47-72, 142-3'
2:131	covers lines 72-86, 94-134

This very long text does not overlap at any point with CCT 2:8, even though a few of the debtors appear in both documents. We can therefore assume that they describe two different moments in the life of Imdi-ilum. ICK 1:191+ cannot be connected with other texts from his archive except the unpublished Matouš-text called K.536 (37a). It contains no clear year-datings, but all the week-eponymies mentioned are of the double type, which again indicates that

Imdi-ilum's activities must be placed in the first half of level 2.

ICK 1:191+ refers to more than 3 2/3 talents of silver as debts outstanding to Imdi-ilum. Because of breaks in the text we cannot ascertain the precise figure, but it is interesting to see that we reach a total which is quite close to the one found in CCT 2:8. Since both documents comprise both very large and very small amounts it is reasonable to assume that they are meant to cover the total outstanding debts at a certain time. This leads to the further conclusion that between 3 and 4 talents of silver, or some 100-120 kgs, constituted the total liquid assets of Imdi-ilum at any given time. That is certainly a very considerable sum of money, but it is actually a reasonable figure in view of the scattered information which can be gleaned from our sources. For instance, when Puzur-Aššur, Imdi-ilum's younger brother, died in Anatolia, his total assets there were estimated at over 1 talent of silver, and this was obviously not enough to cover his obligations.[82] That the boss of the Anatolian branch of the firm should be able to count on 3-4 times as much as Puzur-Aššur seems convincing. Another point to make is the fact that Imdi-ilum at least twice could send a shipment of 1 talent of silver to his representatives in Assur for purchases. We also know that Imdi-ilum was able to buy up a number of houses in Assur and paid enormous sums, more than 20 minas of silver, for some of them. Another indication of the general correctness of the figures in our texts may be found in TC 3:187, a document which enumerates a number of amounts in silver related in an unclear way to persons, and which sums up: "In all: 4 talents, 28 1/3 minas minus 1/2 shekel: the lot of Pūšu-kēn". Even though the background to this text remains unknown, it does not seem too far-fetched to compare it with the two documents which enumerated Imdi-ilum's current assets.[83]

Finally, the previously mentioned text VAT 9210 connects Imdi-ilum with a shipment of 57 talents of tin: the purchase price for this shipment alone would amount to nearly 4 talents of silver, and its value on the market in Anatolia would be in the neighbourhood of 8 talents of silver. We are here dealing with such huge amounts that we would be justified to describe these Old Assyrian merchants as millionaires. Imdi-ilum's assets as described by our texts would correspond to between 60 and 70,000 dollars, using the current exchange-rate for silver. It is obvious that such a comparison is only to be regarded as a vague pointer, but the scale cannot be totally wrong.

We are not in any doubt, then, that the women writing to Imdi-ilum had a quite accurate impression of his priorities. Imdi-ilum comes through to us in his correspondence as a tough but rather dull and uninspiring man, rich and successful and undoubtedly a highly competent manager of the family's business. He stands as a typical Old Assyrian merchant, but we have to admit that in spite of the extensive documentation available we cannot say very much about his person. Let us be charitable and assume that he was also an amusing and lively man with many friends, a keen intellect and an open and searching mind - some of the qualities which we all admire and appreciate in the master in whose honour this was written.

CCT 2:8

debtor	*amount*	*note*
Ennum Bēlum	17 minas of silver	
Enlil-bānī, son of Ili-banī	10 minas of silver	Cf. CCT 6:9a, 1-10, dated to week of Aššur-bēl-awātim, son of Panaka, and Aššur-ṭāb son of Karria, II, year Puzur-^{d}Nirah
Uṣur-ša-Aššur, son of Aššur-malik	30 minas of silver	
Idī-Aššur, son of Pappilum	25 1/2 minas of silver	
Aššur-ṣulūlī, son of Šu-Laban	5 minas of silver	
Uṣur-ša-Ištar, son of Aššur-imittī	2 minas of silver	
Uṣur-ša-Ištar	10 1/2 minas 5 1/2 shekels of silver	Cf. CCT 4:28a, 33-37
Ištar-pilah, son of Aninum	1 1/3 minas 3 3/4 shekels of silver	5 minas paid already; cf. CCT 6:9a 6'-9', and TC 3:57, 16-17
Kuzizia	21 shekels of gold	cf. CCT 6:9a, 11-18, dated to week of Pūšu-kēn and Kurub-Ištar, XI, year Alāhum, son of Enah-ilum
Idī-Aššur, son of Aššur-imittī	1 mina of silver	cf. CCT 6:9a, 19-22
Ennum-Aššur, son of Šalim-ahum	1/2 mina of silver	*ana be'ālim*; cf. CCT 6:9a, 22-23
Amur-ilī, son of Ibezua	3 minas of silver	
Susaja and Ṭāb-pī-Aššur, sons of Šu-Ištar	1 mina of silver	
Amur-Ištar, son of Dada	1 mina 7 shekels of silver	
same	3 minas of silver	
Kurara, son of Abu-šalim	1 1/3 mina 4 shekels of silver	cf. TC 3:57, 14-15
Aššur-ṭāb, son of Karria	12 minas of silver	
Uzua, son of Abia	2 1/2 minas 1 1/2 shekel of silver	
Aššur-ṭāb, son of Alāhum	20 minas of silver	cf. CCT 2:6, 22ff.
Ennum-Aššur, son of Usaria	5 minas of silver	
Pilah-Aššur, son of Al-ṭāb	36 shekels of silver	
Daja, son of Mannua	1/2 mina of silver	his working-capital
Suen-pilah	x mina of silver	
Uṣur-Anum	x mina of silver	

CCT 2:8, continued

debtor	*amount*	*note*
Susaja and Ṭāb-pī-Aššur	1/2 mina of silver	"if Šu-Ištar does not pay 4 minas of tin from my caravan to my representatives in the City"
Ennānum, son of Abu-šalim	15 shekels of silver	Susaja will pay when he comes from Assur
Aššur-damiq, son of Aššur-rēṣī	2 minas of silver	"Ennum-Bēlum will pay the money"
Puzur-Adad, son of Šu-Hubur	28 *kutānum*-textiles	
Aššur-ṣulūlī	5/6 mina of silver	price of 2 donkeys
Ennum-Bēlum	32 *kutānum*-textiles	sold to the palace at Purušhaddum for 40 minas (of copper) a piece
Irraja's son	10 shekels of silver	
Nab-Suen	1 mina 5 shekels of silver	
Šu-Bēlum, son of Šalim-Aššur	10 shekels of silver	
Idī-abum, son of Idī-Ištar	22 1/2 minas of silver	creditors I. and Aššur-imittī; cf. CCT 6:9a, 10-16, dated to week of Aššur-taklāku and Itūr-ilī, VII
Uṣur-ša-Aššur, son of Aššur-malik	1 5/6 mina of silver	
Idī-Suen, son of Alāhum	5 minas of silver	
[Babar]šimala	2/3 mina of silver	

ICK 1:191+

debtor	*amount*	*date*	*note*
Šalim-A[ššur]	8 minas of silver	week: Ennānum, s. Enaki, and Šalim-Aššur	
Šudaja	10 m. silver	week: Ilī-bānī and Amurrum-bānī	var.: debtor Uṣur-ša-[..]
Rabi-Aššur	5 m. 15 s. + 1/2 m. silver	week: Aššur-im[ittī and Amur-Ištar]	
Aššur-ṭāb, s. Karria	15 m. silver	week: Ennānum and Šalim-Aššur	
Idnaja, s. Laqēp	10 m. silver	week: Aššur-rē'ī and Ennam-Anum	

ICK 1:191+, continued

debtor	*amount*	*date*	*note*
Kuzizia and Šumi-abija, s. Puzur-Aššur	22 m. silver	week: Karria and Laqēpum	
Kuzizia	2 m. silver		price of donkeys; further textiles and tin
Šumi-abija, s. Puzur-Aššur	1 1/3 m. 4 s. silver		
Puzur-Adad, s. Idī-Ištar	12 m. silver	week: Amurrum-bānī and Ikūnum	cf. ICK 2:13?
same	12 m. silver	week: Elāli and Šamaš-bānī	cf. Mat. K.536 (37a)
Ikuppī-Enlil	2 m. + 1 m. silver	week: Kura and Sukallija	
Al-ṭāb, s. Annali	15 m. 15 s. silver	week: Aššur-bēl-awātim and Akuza	
Lulu, s. Azua	1 2/3 m. silver	week: Ilī-ālum and Laqēpum	var.: debtor Kura
Pappilum	4 m. 17 s. silver	week: Ilī-bānī and Amurrum-bānī	
Suen-nādā, s. Šu-Suen	10 m. silver	week: Ennānum and Šalim-Aššur	
same	4 m. tin		var.: 3 1/3 m.
Zikur-ilī	4 m. silver		
Ennam-Aššur, s. Aššur-nādā	2 m. silver		
Kasia, s. Amria	4 m. 8 s. silver	week: Kabria and Aššur-malik	
Pilah-Ištar, s. Aššur-malik	10 m. silver	week: Ennam-Anum and Aššur-rē'ī	
Idī-abum, s. Idī-Ištar	3 m. silver	week: Alāhum and Buzia	
Uṣur-ša-Aššur	4 m. silver		*ana be'ālim*
Buzia, s. Šu-Anum	30 m. silver	week: Laqēpum and Ilī-alum	cf. Mat.K.536 (37a), CCT 6:28d, 1–11
Idnaja	1 m. 3 s. silver		Alāhum gets 25 s., Imdi-ilum gets 38 s.
Šu-Laban	x m. silver		
Šu-Anum and [..]-Ištar	1/2 m. silver		
Puzur-Aššur, the scribe	10 s. silver		
Adad-rabi, s. Aššur-bānī	x m. silver		
Dan-Aššur, s. Nabi-Suen	10 s. silver		
Alāhum	21 s. silver		

ICK 1:191+, continued

debtor	*amount*	*date*	*note*
Abu-qar	8 m. silver	week: *[...]* and Dadānum	
Atata, Kukua, and "his brother's son"	5 m. silver		
Zuḫa, s. Ištar-pālil	2 m. silver		*ana be'ālim*
Aššur-ṣulūlī	1/3 m. silver and 5 m. tin		
Amurrum-bānī	13 1/4 s. silver		
Amur-Ištar	10 1/3 s. 10 grains silver		
Abia	4 1/3 s. 15 grains silver		
Pilah-Ištar, s. Ibezua	10 s. silver		
Amur-Ištar	20 s. silver		
Aššur-imittī, s. Agua	2/3 m. 5 s. silver		
Puzur-šadue	1/2 m. silver		
Ikūnum, s. Ilī-bānī	1/2 m. silver and 5 m. tin		
Elamma	2/3 m. silver		

Imdi-ilum's correspondence

	sender	*recipient*
Adana 237-S[84]	*Imdi-ilum	[Luz]ina and Puzur-Ištar
AnOr 6:2	*Aššur-imittī, Šu-Ištar, Šu-Hubur, Ennanum and Buburānum	Imdi-ilum
AnOr 6:6	*Imdi-ilum	Idī-Adad, Annali and Puzur-Ištar
ATHE 27	*(Imdi-ilum) - second page of letter.[85]	(Ennum-Aššur and Idī-Adad)
ATHE 28	*Šalim-Aššur, Imdi-ilum, Pūšu-kēn and Ilī-bānī	Kuzizija
ATHE 46	Idī-Aššur	*Imdi-ilum
ATHE 59	*Imdi-ilum	Inah-ilī and Puzur-Ištar
ATHE 60	*Imdi-ilum	Ennum-Bēlum, Huraṣānum, Idī-Adad and Amur-ilī
ATHE 61	*Imdi-ilum and Idī-Aššur	Uṣur-ša-Ištar
ATHE 62	*Imdi-ilum, Ennum-Bēlum and Aššur-ṣulūlī	Puzur-Aššur
ATHE 63	Puzur-Aššur	*Imdi-ilum
BIN 4:5[86]	Idī-Adad, Annali and Puzur-Ištar	*Imdi-ilum
BIN 4:27	Alāhum, Imdi-ilum and Puzur-Aššur	*Šalim-ahum and Pūšu-kēn
BIN 4:30	Pūšu-kēn	*Imdi-ilum, [...]a and *tamkārum*
BIN 4:56	Ennum-Bēlum	*Imdi-ilum
BIN 4:84	*Imdi-ilum	Puzur-Aššur
BIN 6:12[87]	Idnaja	*Imdi-ilum
BIN 6:27	Amur-ilī	*Imdi-ilum
BIN 6:29	*Aššur-imittī, Šu-Ištar, Ennānum and Buburānum	Imdi-ilum
BIN 6:34	*[Aššur-i]mittī	Pūšu-kēn, Imdi-ilum, Šu-Bēlum, Šalim-Aššur, Uṣur-ša-Ištar and Anah-ilī
BIN 6:39	Amur-Ištar	*Imdi-ilum
BIN 6:48	Imdi-ilum	*Aššur-[...]
BIN 6:74[88]	*Imdi-ilum	Ennum-Aššur and Idī-Adad
BIN 6:76	*Amur-Ištar	Imdi-ilum
BIN 6:79	Imdi-ilum and Pūšu-kēn	*Šu-Hubur
BIN 6:133[89]	Imdi-ilum	*Amur-Ištar, I[m...], Uṣur-ša-Aššur and Uṣur-ša-Ištar
Bursa 3776	Imdi-ilum	*Aššur-imittī, [(...)], Šu-Ištar Ennānum and Buburānum
CCT 2:5	*Imdi-ilum	Pūšu-kēn
CCT 2:6[90]	*Imdi-ilum	Lulu, Alāhum, Aššur-ṭāb and Idī-Adad
CCT 2:7	Imdi-ilum	*Aššur-imittī, Šu-Ištar, Šu-Hubur, Ennānum and Buburānum
CCT 2:8	*Imdi-ilum	Ennum-Bēlum, Huraṣānum and Amur-ilī
CCT 2:11a	*Imdi-ilum	Ikuppīja, Ahu-waqar and Puzur-Ištar
CCT 2:12a	*Imdi-ilum	Puzur-ilī

	sender	*recipient*
CCT 2:23[91]	Amur-Ištar, Uṣur-ša-[Aššur] and Uṣur-ša-Ištar	*Imdi-ilum
CCT 2:35	Imdi-ilum, Pūšu-kēn, Aššur-ṣulūlī and Uṣur-ša-Ištar	*Aššur-imittī, Ennum-Bēlum, Ennānum and Buburānum
CCT 2:42	*[Aššur]-imittī and Ennum-Bēlum	Imdi-ilum and Aššur-ṣulūlī
CCT 2:44a	*Aššur-imittī	Pūšu-kēn and Imdi-ilum
CCT 2:49a	Amur-Ištar	*Imdi-ilum
CCT 2:50	Puzur-ilī	*Imdi-ilum
CCT 3:1	Amur-Ištar	*[Aššur-tak]lāku and Imdi-ilum
CCT 3:2a	*Alāhum and Amur-Ištar	Imdi-ilum and Aššur-ṭāb
CCT 3:11	Ennānum and Bēlija	*Imdi-ilum and Ennum-Bēlum
CCT 3:15	Ennum-Bēlum	*Imdi-ilum
CCT 3:16a	Buzia	*Imdi-ilum
CCT 3:21a	*Šu-Hubur	Imdi-ilum, Pūšu-kēn, Amur-Šamaš and Zuba
CCT 3:22b	*Šu-Hubur and Aššur-imittī's sons	Buzutaja, Pūšu-kēn and Imdi-ilum
CCT 3:34a	*Šu-Laban	Imdi-ilum
CCT 3:40a	Kurara	*Imdi-ilum
CCT 3:45b	*Alāhum	Imdi-ilum
CCT 3:46b	Ennānum and Buburānum	*Imdi-ilum
CCT 4:8b	Al-ṭāb	*Imdi-ilum and Šum-abija
CCT 4:10b	*Aššur-rēṣī and Amur-Ištar	Imdi-ilum and Buzia
CCT 4:18a	*Imdi-ilum	Puzur-Aššur
CCT 4:18b	Ennum-Bēlum	*Imdi-ilum
CCT 4:22b	*Imdi-ilum	Ennum-Bēlum, Itūr-ilī, Ahu-waqar and A[mur-ilī]
CCT 4:26b	Ennum-Aššur	*Imdi-ilum
CCT 4:27a	Uzua	*Imdi-ilum
CCT 4:27b	Ennum-[...]	*Imdi-ilum and Šu-Bēlum
CCT 4:28a	*Imdi-ilum	Ištar-baštī and Amur-ilī
CCT 4:30b[92]	Idī-Adad	*Imdi-ilum
CCT 4:44a	Usānum and Adu	*Imdi-ilum
CCT 4:47a[93]	Imdi-ilum	*Amur-Ištar
CCT 4:50a[92]	*Imdi-ilum	[Ennum-Aššur] and Idī-Adad
CCT 5:49c	*Šu-Laban and Dādija	Imdi-ilum and Bazu[...]
CCT 6:12a	*Amur-Ištar	Imdi-ilum
CCT 6:18c	Ikuppīja	*Imdi-ilum, Laqēpum and Innaja
CCT 6:19b[94]	*Amur-Ištar and Puzur-[...]	Imdi-ilum
CCT 6:37a	Imdi-ilum	*Amur-Ištar
CCT 6:43b	*Aššur-imittī, Šu-Ištar, Ennānum and Buburānum	Imdi-ilum
Cole 4	*Imdi-ilum	Amur-ilī
Cont. 18	*Išma-Aššur	Imdi-ilum
Cont. 27	*Imdi-ilum	Aššur-nādā
Cont. 30	Puzur-Aššur	*Imdi-ilum, Ennum-Aššur and Aššur-ṣulūlī
Gelb 62	Amur-Ištar	*Imdi-ilum, Pūšu-kēn, Ikūnum, Idī-abum and Hadaja
Herring	*Imdi-ilum	Amur-ilī
I 693	*Imdi-ilum, son of Šu-Laban	Enna-Suen, son of Šu-Ištar, and Puzur-Ištar, son of Imdi-ilum

	sender	*recipient*
ICK 1:51[95]	*Imdi-ilum, Ennam-Bēlum and Aššur-ṣulūlī	Puzur-Aššur
ICK 1:52	Puzur-Aššur	*Imdi-ilum, Ennum-Bēlum and Aššur-ṣulūlī
ICK 1:82	Puzur-Aššur and Puzur-Anna	*Imdi-ilum and *tamkārum*
ICK 1:84	Aššur-taklāku	*Imdi-ilum, Pūšu-kēn, Buzia, Šu-Kubum and Ennum-Aššur
ICK 1:85	Aššur-ṣulūlī	*Imdi-ilum
ICK 1:135	*Imdi-ilum	Puzur-Aššur and Ah-šalim
ICK 1:184	*Imdi-ilum and Aššur-ṣulūlī	Ennum-Bēlum
ICK 1:189	*[Imdi-ilum]	[...]
ICK 1:192[96]	Imdi-ilum	*Aššur-imittī, Šu-Ištar, Buburānum and Ennānum
KTB 6	Aššur-ṣulūlī	*Imdi-ilum
KTH 11	Aššur-malik, Azu and Idī-Adad	*Imdi-ilum, Pūšu-kēn and Aššur-ṣulūlī
KTS 14c[97]	Idnaja	*Imdi-ilum
KTS 15	Amur-ilī	*Imdi-ilum
KTS 16	Šu-Ištar	*Imdi-ilum
KTS 17[98]	Uzua	*Imdi-ilum
KTS 18	Amur-Ištar and Uzua	*Imdi-ilum
KTS 19a	Aššur-damiq and Ilī-ašrannī	*Imdi-ilum
KTS 19b[99]	*Imdi-ilum	Puzur-Ištar
KTS 20	*Imdi-ilum	Amur-ilī
KTS 21a	*Alili, Ikuppīja and Šu-Hubur	Pūšu-kēn, Imdi-ilum and Kurub-Ištar
KTS 21b	*Šu-Hubur and Aššur-imittī's sons	Buzutaja, Pūšu-kēn and Imdi-ilum
KUG 36	Ennum-Bēlum	*Imdi-ilum
KUG 45	Imdi-ilum	*[A and B]
KUG 49	Kurara	*Imdi-ilum
L 29-571	Imdi-ilum	*Amur-Ištar
L 29-579	*Imdi-ilum	Aššur-ṭāb
MAH 10823[100]	*Idī-Aššur, Adad-bānī, Aššur-imittī, Ikuppī-Aššur, Puzur-Ištar and Imdi-ilum	Pūšu-kēn, Zuba, Aššur-ṣulūlī, Innaja and Pilah-Ištar
MAH 19609	Uṣur-ši-Ištar	*Imdi-ilum
Matouš K 536	*Imdi-ilum	Pilah-Ištar, Kurub-Ištar, Ennum-Bēlum and Aššur-ṣulūlī
K 581	*Imdi-ilum	Ennum-Bēlum, Itūr-ilī, Pilah-Ištar, Ahu-qar and Amur-ilī
K 671+696	Huraṣānum and Ilī-bānī	*Imdi-ilum
K 888	Imdi-ilum	*Amur-Aššur
K 926	*Imdi-ilum	Tarām-Kūbī and Šīmat-Aššur
MET 1[101]	Puzur-Aššur	*Imdi-ilum, Ennum-Bēlum and Aššur-ṣulūlī
MET 4	Aššur-ṭāb	*Imdi-ilum
MET 10[102]	*Aššur-imittī, Šu-Ištar, Ennānum and Buburānum	Imdi-ilum
MET 11	*Imdi-ilum, Ennam-Aššur and Aššur-ṣulūlī	Puzur-Aššur
Moren 2	Tarām-Kūbī and Šīmat-Aššur	*Imdi-ilum
TC 1:5	Tarām-Kūbī and Šīmat-Aššur	*Imdi-ilum
TC 1:16	*Imdi-ilum	Annali, Aššur-idī and Amur-ilī

	sender	*recipient*
TC 1:24	*Imdi-ilum	Puzur-Ištar, Aššur-ṭāb and Lalija
TC 1:53	Ah-šalim	*Imdi-ilum
TC 2:22	Kurub-Ištar	*Imdi-ilum and Pūšu-kēn
TC 2:35	Uṣur-ša-Aššur	*Šalim-Aššur and Imdi-ilum
TC 2:36	Uzua	*Imdi-ilum
TC 2:37	Ah-šalim	*Imdi-ilum
TC 2:38	Buzia	*Aššur-imittī and Imdi-ilum
TC 2:45	*I[mdi-ilum]	Aššur-taklāku and [...]
TC 3:44	Pūšu-kēn, Puzur-Tiamtim and Innaja	*Idī-Aššur, Adad-bānī, Aššur-imittī, Ikuppī-Aššur, Puzur-Ištar and Imdi-ilum
TC 3:45	Kutallānum	*Imdi-ilum
TC 3:46	Aššur-ṭāb	*Imdi-ilum
TC 3:47	Al-ṭāb	*Imdi-ilum
TC 3:48	Amur-Ištar	*Imdi-ilum
TC 3:49	Adu	*Imdi-ilum
TC 3:50	Puzur-Ištar	*Imdi-ilum
TC 3:51	Ennum-Bēlum	*Imdi-ilum
TC 3:52	Ennum-Bēlum	*Imdi-ilum
TC 3:53[103]	Ennum-Bēlum	*Imdi-ilum
TC 3:54	Imdi-ilum	*[Aššur-imittī], Ennum-Bēlum and Pilah-Ištar
TC 3:55	*Imdi-ilum	Ennum-Bēlum, Itūr-ilī, Ahu-waqar and Amur-ilī
TC 3:56	*Imdi-ilum	Ištar-bāštī
TC 3:57[104]	*Imdi-ilum	Ištar-bāštī and Amur-ilī
TC 3:58	*Imdi-ilum	Uṣur-ša-Aššur
TC 3:104	Adu and Ikuppija	*[Imdi-ilum]
VAT 9218	*Aššur-imittī, Šu-Ištar, Ennānum, Buburānum and Ennum-Bēlum	Imdi-ilum
VAT 9229[105]	Alāhum and Kurara	*Imdi-ilum
VAT 9233	*Imdi-ilum	Ištar-bāštī
VAT 9301	Uzua	*Imdi-ilum
VAT 9241	*Imdi-ilum	Šamaš-abī, Lalija and Puzur-Ištar
VAT 9253	Imdi-ilum	*Aššur-imittī and Aššur-malik son of Laqēp
VAT 9271	*Imdi-ilum	Ennum-Bēlum
VAT 9273	*Imdi-ilum	Puzur-Aššur
VAT 13471	*Imdi-ilum	Ikuppija
LB 1202	*Imdi-ilum	Ilī-ašrannī, Ikuppija, Ahu-waqar, Idī-Adad, Aššur-ṭāb, Annali and Puzur-Ištar
CCT 6:46a	Ennum-Aššur	*[Imdi-il]um and [...]
AO 22505[106]	*Aššur-imittī, Š[u-Iš]tar, Buburānum and [Ennān]um	Imdi-ilum
LB 1208[107]	*Imdi-ilum	Ilī-ašrannī, Ikuppija, Ahu-waqar, Idī-Adad, Aššur-ṭāb, Annali and Puzur-Ištar
LB 1295	Puzur-Adad	*Imdi-ilum
LB 1296	*Šīmat-Aššur	Imdi-ilum
LB 1313	*Imdi-ilum	Uṣur-ša-Ištar

	sender	*recipient*
LB 1290	Imdi-ilum and Alāhum	*Amur-Ištar
C 20[108]	Amur-Ištar	*Imdi-ilum, Pūšu-kēn and Ennum-Bēlum
C 16	Ah-šalim and Ikuppija	*Imdi-ilum
C 29	*Aššur-imittī, Šu-Ištar, Ennānum and Buburānum	Imdi-ilum
C 31	*[Amur-]Ištar	Pūšu-kēn, Imdi-ilum and Puzur-Aššur
Ank. 2804	*Aššur-imittī, Šu-Ištar, Ennum-Bēlum, Ennānum and Buburānum	Imdi-ilum
Cont. 29	[Imdi-ilum]	*Aššur-imittī, Šu-Ištar, Ennānum and Buburānum

---

* When the present manuscript was completed and in press I learned that Dr. Metin Ichisar had concluded a "These de Doctorat" at the Sorbonne under the direction of Professor Garelli, which was a comprehensive study of all texts relating to Imdi-ilum's family. This work includes an introduction which contains a reconstruction of this family and there is accordingly a considerable overlapping. It has been agreed that both studies will nevertheless be published since this can happen more or less simultaneously. It is a pleasure to see that the two investigations reach nearly identical results. I have not been able to incorporate any of Dr. Ichisar's conclusions in this article, even where he has clearly reached more convincing results than I.

---

1 TC 1:5; cf. Hirsch, *UAR*, p. 14.

2 It is instructive to compare with the studies which can be conducted on for instance the Nuzi-material where full archaeological data are available. See M.P. Maidman, "A Nuzi Private Archive: Morphological Considerations", in *Assur* 1/9, 1979, pp. 179-186.

3 *Syria* 1927, p. 8; see also photograph, Pl. III, no. 2.

4 List on pp. 3-7; one text, ICK 1:3, is said to come from an unmarked locus "13". It is the marriage-contract of Laqēpum and Hatala and probably belongs to locus 12.

5 Preface to ICK 1.

6 See map 1 and pp. 128ff. in Özgüç, *Ausgrabungen in Kültepe 1948*, [Ankara 1950].

7 The only exceptions appear to be CCT 6:9a, a partly broken memorandum, and BIN 6:228, a note regulating the sale of goods for silver. Also CCT6:28d.

8 They are dated to the year-eponymy Dādija son of Šu-Ilabrat.

9 Including 181, a list of deliveries of bread and beer to a large number of persons.

10 121 probably belongs to Laqēpum's archive which was found at locus 12; Hrozný himself was apparently not sure that 158 was discovered at locus 4 since he adds a questionmark.

11 For Annali see perhaps below, pp. 228-229.

12 The style of this letter (cf. J. Lewy, *OrNS* 29, p. 31) indicates that it

could well have been written by Imdi-ilum.

13 Cf. *Syria* 1927, p. 7, and Pl. III, no. 4.

14 Cf. J. Lewy, *ArOr* 18/3, p. 374 and 421; *JAOS* 78, p. 92f.; *OrNS* 29, p. 31; *OACP*, pp. 30-31; Veenhof, *Aspects*, pp. 321-322; *OACC*, pp. 184-186; Garelli, *ArOr* 47, pp. 45-48.

15 Cf. OACC, pp. 177-178. The list of names in ICK 2 refers to a woman with the name Imdi-ilum who is supposed to have been a daughter of Suen-namir, but this interpretation is based on a misunderstanding of ICK 2: 152.

16 CCT 3:45b; BIN 6:29, 35.

17 CCT 2:35. Cf. also CCT 5:43, 26 (Puzur-Aššur son of Šu-Laban), CCT 2:8, 8 (Aššur-ṣulūlī son of Šu-Laban), and CCT 5:43, 24 (Ennum-Bēlum son of Šu-Laban).

18 BIN 6:219, 1, and CCT 5:41a, 27; cf. *OACP*, p. 30, n. 42, for references to Amur-ilī's seal.

19 Cf. Hecker, *OrNS* 47, p. 415, with references to texts and to previous discussions; see especially the unpublished text Leiden 4, communicated by H. Lewy, *AS* 16, p. 273, n. 8. Veenhof informs me that the correct number of this text is LB 1217.

20 Cf. J. Lewy, *HUCA* 27, pp. 6-8.

21 See *ArOr* 47, pp. 45-48.

22 The letters are BIN 6:111 and VAT 13547. A man called Enna-Suen is known to have functioned as Imdi-ilum's representative together with Huraṣānum (ICK 1:188, 21-22), and he received letters and goods together with Inarawa from Puzur-Ištar (CCT 3:40b and VAT 9258).

23 Cf. Veenhof, *Aspects*, p. 103-123.

24 Cf. Hecker, op.cit., p. 408.

25 Cf. Veenhof, *Aspects*, p. 121, and Garelli, loc.cit.

26 Marvin Harris, *Cannibals and Kings*, Fontana, 1978, pp. 70-71.

27 (40) *a-na 10 ma-na* KUG.BABBAR (41) É *Bi-lá-nim* DUMU *Nu-ur-Ištar ni-eš-a-ma-kum* (42) *a-na 3 ma-na 5* GÍN KUG.BABBAR É (43) *Šu-Be-lim ni-eš-a-ma-kum* KUG.BABBAR *iš-tí* (44) *Ší-ma-at-A-šùr ni-il₅-qé-ma* (45) *[ni-iš-]qul 5 ma-na* KUG.BABBAR *i-na lu-qú-tim a-ni-tim* (46) *[ni-da-]ší-im*

28 Cf. Veenhof, *Aspects*, p. 119. Veenhof kindly refers me to the unpublished letter LB 1296, in which she appears to address Imdi-ilum as "my brother". Was she in fact his sister?

29 KTS 34a, 24.

30 TC 1:79, 2; he is a witness to a settlement among the heirs of Pūšu-kēn.

31 ATHE 24, 4-5; the text deals with the dissolution of the partnership between Pūšu-kēn and Amur-Ištar, after the death of these men.

32 ICK 1:87, 25.

33 ICK 1:4, 11.

34 ICK 2:345, 8.

35 CCT 6:15a, 14; the text deals with the legal fight over the inheritance

left by Pūšu-kēn's associate Puzur-Aššur son of Išar-kitti-Aššur. Cf. Matouš, *ArOr* 37, 156-180.

36 ICK 1:23A, 2.

37 (24) *Šu-Lá-ba-an* DUMU *A-mur*-DINGIR (25) *ki-ri-am im-gu$_5$-ur-ma* (26) *um?-ma A-šur-i-mì-tí-ma* (27) *šu-ma ta-ša-am 10 ma-na* (28) KÙG.BABBAR *gám-ra-am! ša! ki- [ri-im]* (29) *[šé-]bi$_4$-il$_5$*.

38 Cf. CCT 3:46b, quoted below, p. 224.

39 Cf. *OACC*, p. 142, n. 102.

40 Cf. ATHE 24.

41 Cf. especially lines 20-27.

42 Cf. CCT 3:11.

43 My suggestion concerning Šumi-abija son of Puzur-Aššur is merely a guess; cf. CCT 4:8b, BIN 4:66, VAT 9271, and ICK 1:191+, 18 and 29.

44 Cf. *OACC*, pp. 125-126. For references to individual letters see the list of Imdi-ilum's correspondence at the end of the article.

45 CCT 5:49c.

46 CCT 3:34a.

47 Unpublished. Copy J. Lewy.

48 Cf. TC 3:50, 11-12.

49 CCT 3:11.

50 Cf. my discussion of this text in *Iraq* 39, pp. 135-136. Cf. for this shipment also Ank. 2804 (translit. Landsberger).

51 Cf. *OACP*, p. 74, n. 28.

52 The text refers to Aššur-malik son of Laqēp as the recipient of *naruqqum*-investments; for these procedures see *Iraq* 39, pp. 119-145.

53 For instance BIN 6:24, CCT 2:41a, 44a, 44b, KTS 22a, TC 2:15, BIN 4:24, 29, CCT 2:36b, TC 3:44.

54 Cf. also TC 2:40, a letter from Ennum-Bēlum to Aššur-imittī, Aššur-ṣulūlī, Aššur-ṭāb and Usānum.

55 Cf. BIN 6:76, L 29571, CCT 6:12a, BIN 6:133, CCT 2:23, 3:1.

56 Cf. CCT 4:47a and the connected text CCT 6:19b.

57 KUG 49.

58 Herring, *JCS* 15, p. 127.

59 CCT 5:43.

60 Cf. J. Lewy, *ArOr* 18/3, p. 373, n. 44.

61 TC 2:40, 21-33.

62 Cf. MET 1, 11, ATHE 62, CCT 4:18a, VAT 9273. See Veenhof, *Aspects*, p. 320.

63 Cf. ICK 1:82.

64 See *OACC*, p. 184-186.

65 CCT 2:7, 4:22b, 28a, 50a, Cont. 30, TC 3:56.

66 CCT 4:28a, 31-32.

67 *i-sà-al-e*; according to *AHw*, p. 1017, this noun should mean something like "Unkenntniss". However, the OA examples do convey the concept of cheating, presumably by way of the withholding of information.

68 *lu ú-šu-ra-ku*.

69 The suggestion in *AHw*, p. 1087, is to interpret the form *tù-ZA-wa* as the only attested Akkadian example of a verb *ṣawwûm* with the meaning "reden".

70 KTS 15; cf. *UAR*, p. 15.

71 Cf. TC 3:49 and 104.

72 (2) *iš-tù a-na Ku-na-na-me-et* (3) *e-ru-bu-ni a-na ir-tí-kà* (4) *a-ru-qú A-šùr ù Ištar*.ZA.AT *li-tù-lá* (5) *ma-tí-ma* DUB-*pí-kà lá áš-me-ú ki-ma* (6) DUB-*pí-kà lá áš-me-ú pá-nu-a a-ṣé-ri-kà* (7) *a-na a-lá-ki-im kà-a[b]-tù* ... (13) *ki-ma tí-ir-ta-kà mì-ma-a-ša* (14) *lá áš-me-ú a-na kà-ri-im šé-pí* (15) *pá-ar-sà-at a-šu-mì-kà pá-al-ha-ku-ma* ... (19) *a-na-ku a-na-kam i-ṣé-er* (20) KUG.BABBAR 1 GÍN *ša e-pu-šu a-hu-al ù a-zu-áb* (21) *a-bi a-ta be-lí a-ta mì-šu-um* ÌR-*ad- [kà]* (22) *ke-nu-um a-na-ku i-na lá a-ší-ri* (25) *a-ha-liq*.

73 J. Lewy, *HUCA* 27, p. 64, n. 271, called him "a resident of Durhumit".

74 The sequence of the months used here is based on my suggestion that the first month in the year was Bēlat-ekallim; cf. Matouš, *ArOr* 46, 217-231.

75 Cf. *OACC*, pp. 375-382.

76 *Aspects*, pp. 69-76 with comments on pp. 79-80.

77 See already J. Lewy, *JAOS* 78, p. 92, for comments on this text. As pointed out to me by Veenhof, the figure of 410 talents must probably represent *the value* of the caravan; we would accordingly not be faced with a caravan which actually brought so much tin, but even with this modification the shipment referred to was truly huge, and its significance for our statistics is not vitally affected.

78 CCT 6:9a, ICK 1:30, 41, 93, 117 (cf. 2:36), 146, 187, 2:47, 54, and BIN 6: 228.

79 Cf. *EL* 1, pp. 215ff. It is perhaps significant that most of the loan-documents from Imdi-ilum's archive deal with loans extended to local Anatolians; perhaps such texts did not have to be sent back to Assur?

80 Cf. the table below.

81 (73) *a-hu-ú-a a-tù-nu a-na [*x x x x x*][*x*]-ma* (74) *[*x (x)*]-ma* DAM.GÀR-*re-e-a ša-áš-qí-lá-ma A-mur*-DINGIR *lá i-sà-hu-ur [*x x x DUB*][-pá-am]* (75) *[a-]*NIM *i-na li-bi₄* DUB-*pì-a-ma šu-uk-na-šu*.

82 CCT 2:35.

83 J. Lewy, *RHA* 38, 119-120, explained the text as "a balance-sheet recording property of Pūšu-kēn which had been - or still was - in the hands of partners, employees, or simply debtors of his". That would of course make it an exact parallel of the two Imdi-ilum texts discussed here.

84 Unpublished. Asterisk indicates the person named first.

85 Cf. BIN 6:74, CCT 4:50a and Cont. 27.

86 Cf. VAT 9241.

87 Cf. KTS 14c.

88 Cf. note 85.

89 Cf. CCT 2:23.

90 Cf. VAT 9229.

91 Cf. BIN 6:133.

92 Cf. note 85.

93 Cf. CCT 6:19b.

94 Cf. CCT 4:47a.

95 Cf. ICK 1:52 and TC 3:162.

96 Cf. Mat. K. 926 (50a) and MET 10.

97 Cf. BIN 6:12.

98 Cf. BIN 6:39.

99 Cf. CCT 2:11a.

100 Cf. TC 3:44.

101 Cf. TC 1:25.

102 Cf. ICK 1:192.

103 Cf. TC 3:54.

104 Cf. CCT 2:8.

105 Cf. CCT 2:6.

106 I thank P. Garelli for his reference to this text which he will publish shortly.

107 Veenhof has kindly provided me with transliterations of these unpublished texts in Leiden.

108 The next five letters are known to me in transliterations made by Landsberger.

THE PATTERN OF SETTLEMENT IN THE BABYLONIAN COUNTRYSIDE

W.F. Leemans (Warmond)

Travelling in the countryside of various countries, one can observe differences in the patterns of settlement: Here the rural population lives scattered in the countryside, in farmsteads near to their fields, elsewhere the peasants live concentrated in villages or even in fortified towns. In the Netherlands, almost everywhere peasants, having one-man farms (formerly sometimes with a servant) live scattered in the countryside near their fields; in that case villages, necessary as local supply centres, may be at a rather large distance from one another. In the upper Rhine valley the peasants, with similar farms, live in villages, which are there rather close to one another; in northern Switzerland the farms are scattered, while in the south the peasants live concentrated in villages. In the region north of Paris, one finds yet another pattern: very large farms of hundreds of acres, scattered in the countryside, but with several small houses annexed, formerly for a number of labourers. Sometimes peasants have their farmhouses inside the towns, as in Orange in the south of France in the 15th Century, and until recent times in the Dutch town of Kampen (in this latter instance because the countryside was subject to inundations).

Is it possible, on the basis of information provided by texts and by archaeological surveys, to recover a picture of the settlement of the countryside in ancient Babylonia? This is a question that belongs in the special field of interest of I.M. Diakonoff, who, by his stimulating work, has contributed much to the study and knowledge of conditions of life in ancient Mesopotamia.

As Adams and Nissen have shown for the region of Uruk,[1] the occupation of the Mesopotamian plain began, in the 4th millennium BC, with small agglomerations. Their number increased in the Late Uruk period, and was still considerable in the Jemdet Nasr period. The same evolution took place in other regions, somewhat earlier or later.[2] But, in the first half of the 3rd millennium, the population gradually concentrated into urban centres - cities and big towns - and the villages decreased in number or almost disappeared. In the south, Uruk became the largest city, in the north, Kish.[3] In this way, in the Presargonic and Old Akkadian periods, life was centred on large cities. The cultivation of the fields in the region of a city was conducted from the city, largely under the supervision of the temples. According to the texts, in cities like Girsu and Ur agriculture was a main means of subsistence: There were enormous storehouses for agricultural products and there was great activity in the production of dairy products. The land between cities like Girsu and Umma was uninhabited, and could become a bone of contention. The deeds of sale of this period concern either fields or houses, never both at the same time, i.e. farms.[4]

The settlement pattern remained the same in the Ur III period. In accordance with this statement, the number of places registered in the *Répertoire Géographique* is relatively small. Besides the towns, there were some a n z a g a r (*dimtu*), fortified buildings, around which (sometimes) a small settlement came into existence.[5] As far as cultivable land was in the possession of and worked by private persons or groups of persons, there is no evidence of the way of life of these people. Probably they lived in the towns, or perhaps sometimes in an extended *dimtu*, as long as they were not cattle-breeding nomads or semi-nomads.

In the Isin-Larsa period, the pattern remained much the same. Private ownership of land now increased: Several inhabitants of cities such as Ur and Larsa had fields outside the town, but farms, i.e. buildings with cultivable land round them, are never mentioned, whether in deeds or in divisions of property or in landlease contracts. The *dimtu* remained: A remarkable example is one in private hands, that of Sîn-nur-matim and later that of his son Balmunamḫe, during the reigns of Warad-Sîn and Rim-Sîn. Such a *dimtu* could develop into a village (*ālu*), thus *dimit*-Balmunamḫe, later *Āl*-Balmunamḫe. Around it, Balmunamḫe had wide tracts of fields and date-groves, and employed a large number of people.

Turning now to the time of king Ḫammurapi, one is inclined to look first at his Laws. In them we find a number of laws regarding the farms of soldiers and similar people. Ḫammurapi introduced on a large scale the system of allotting fields to soldiers for the maintenance of them and their families under the obligation of service (*ilkum*). These laws (30-41) always refer to the field, orchard and house of the soldiers. This suggests that they were given units, comprising a house and cultivable land, i.e. a farm, on which the obligation of service rested, and would imply that they lived scattered in the countryside.

Letters and other texts from the administration show that this image does not agree with actual facts: The correspondence in the archives of Šamaš-ḫazir, Ḫammurapi's administrator in the South, is most closely associated with the laws of the CH just mentioned.[6] Ḫammurapi settled large numbers of soldiers and civil servants in the conquered kingdom of Larsa and tried, in this way, to stimulate a revival of the South. It is remarkable that almost all of these 166 letters concern fields, and sometimes date-groves (*kirû*), allotted to various people. Only in very rare cases is a house mentioned: in No. 96 in an obscure context; in No. 161 land and a house are mentioned as separate units;[7] in No. 137 only is there a mention of house, field and orchard, just as in the CH, but the writer of the letter is complaining that the field is at a great distance from the house. In many instances the letters refer to fields in (the district of) a certain village, sometimes a town (Larsa in Nos. 1 and 27, Maškanšapir in No. 77).

It may be assumed that the cultivators of the fields did not live on their fields, in the countryside, but in the villages, and that as a rule only fields, and not houses, were provided by the government for the people to whom the letters refer. Otherwise houses would have been mentioned more often in the correspondence. This would suggest that the tenants had their own houses in the towns or villages.[8] However, the small archive of the soldier (*rēdûm*) Ubarrum in the village of Ṣupur-Šubula, probably not far from Kutha, shows that fields and houses belonged to the tenancy of this soldier: *eqlum, bītum u ilkum* had to be divided between him and his *taḫḫum* ("substitute"). Each took a part of the fields, which bordered on watercourses and the fields of other people, and of the house in the s i l a d a g a l, the main street of the village. This suggests that the house was inside the village and the fields outside.[9] The case of Ubarrum is certainly not an isolated one; it may rather be representative for a larger group in the North.

In accordance with the pattern of settlement as described, there were many villages; many more names are mentioned than in the preceding periods. The mention of fields in several villages in AbB VI 114 suggests that these villages were at no great distance from one another.

The tenure of the fields was as a rule the element creating the obligation to services: According to AbB II 55, people who possessed fields on the bank of a canal were obliged to dredge the canal. It appears from AbB II 147 that such people lived in villages (*ālu*) on the bank of the canal. The banks of the river or a canal may often have been the best places for settlement, because these are somewhat higher and consequently less wet than the land behind, as the result of the deposition of sediments by the river (thus, in the lowlands of Holland, people settled along the old river-courses). Because of the inundations and the swampiness of the countryside it may often have been unsuitable for settlement;[10] for this situation see the letter Kienast, *Kisurra* 178.

The picture given by the private contracts - deeds, exchanges, gifts, etc. - is almost the same. These contracts only refer either to houses or to fields or groves; houses bordered only on houses, fields only on fields. Fields and houses were not leased by the same contract. Some rare cases are known from Sippar, where a complex that seems to have been a farm was sold; but the building in these cases was not a *bītum* (as in the town) but a *dimtum* ("tower"): BE VI/1 70 (=HG III 412): purchase, in the time of Abi-ešuḫ, of a large complex of fields with a *dimtum* and a barn in the neighbourhood of Sippar;[11] Scheil, *Sippar* 10 (=HG III 457): a father gives to his daughter several fields with a *dimtum* on the road to Sippar, but she also receives a house and a shop in the city, where she may have lived (cf. also *Sippar* 100 = HG III 495).[12] Here we find the same phenomenon as at the end of the Larsa Dynasty in the South: A few large estates with a fortified building, whereas in general the land was exploited from the towns and villages. As in earlier times, and also later in the land of Arrapḫa, the *dimtum* seems to have been inhabited and could even lead to the emergence of a village, so it may be assumed that the *dimāti* in Northern Babylonia were also, at least on occasion, inhabited, either by the owners or by their personnel. They were, however, also used for the storage of grain (*Kisurra* 178). A *dimtum* could be sold with only a small plot of land: a *nadītum* bought a *dimtum* of 1 s a r and 9 s a r *nidūtum* ("fallow") from another *nadītum*.[13]

It is clear that the general situation was that the peasants lived inside the towns or villages. In Northern Babylonia, the *dimtum* certainly did not play an important role in the occupation of the countryside. The fields belonged to a town or a village. Several contracts refer, for example, to fields in the district of the village of Ḫalḫalla near Sippar. The picture obtained from the texts from other towns - Kish, Kisurra, Nippur, etc. - is a similar one.

At Lagaba, a small commercial and agricultural town in Northern Babylonia, the pattern is the same: A large proprietor wrote to his manager at Lagaba that he should not neglect his house (*bītum*), cattle, and servants, and he gave him instructions for the cultivation of the fields. As the house is called a *bītum* and the letter was probably found inside Lagaba, it may be assumed that the cultivation of the fields outside the town was carried on from the house (not a *dimtum*) inside the town (AbB III 11 and 12; time of Samsuiluna). The same situation is encountered in AbB II 43 (cf. also on No. 50).

The conclusion of this short examination may be that - just as in the preceding periods - in the Old Babylonian period peasants (and other people) did not live scattered in the countryside of Southern Mesopotamia, near their fields, but in the villages and towns. The latter had a predominantly agricultural character, and the former were rather numerous. The *dimtum*-system, in this period only occasional, developed in the next period, in the land of Arrapḫa and in Kassite Babylonia, where similar units were then called *bītum*. In the Old Babylonian period there did not even exist a real word for a farm, a unit of agricultural lands and buildings. It turns out that settlement patterns comparable with those mentioned in our introductory lines can be found in ancient Babylonia, dominated by and adapted to the local situation: towns like Kampen, villages like those of the upper Rhine valley, and a few large estates (*dimtum*) like those north of Paris.

---

1 R. McC. Adams & H.J. Nissen, *The Uruk Countryside* [1972], Chapter 2.

2 Ibid., p. 89, and R. McC. Adams, *Land behind Baghdad*. H.T. Wright found a somewhat different pattern in the region of Ur, where villages were less numerous (*The administration of rural production in an early Mesopotamian town* [Ann Arbor 1969]).

3 McG. Gibson, *The city and area of Kish* [1972], 48-9. See also my report for the meeting of the Société Jean Bodin in Warsaw in 1976 (publication delayed).

4 D.O. Edzard, *Sumerische Rechtsurkunden des III. Jahrtausends* [Munich 1968] (in No. 61 the seller - the merchant Enlile - was the same in several instances, but what he sold was not a farm).

5 *Rép. Géog.*, pp. 11-12 and 31.

6 F.R. Kraus, AbB IV.

7 In AbB ii 156, also field and house did not form a unit.

8 Otherwise G.R. Driver & J.C. Miles, *The Babylonian Laws*, I, 116.

9 See E. Sollberger, JCS 5 [1951] 77ff.; E. Szlechter, JCS 7 [1953] 81ff., esp. 94-5; B. Landsberger, JCS 9 [1955] 121ff.

10 Cf. AbB II 85: swamps around Larsa.

11 Cf. for big estates, R. Harris, *Ancient Sippar*, 235.

12 Cf. also CT 47 12: house in the *gagûm* and field outside. The deed TCL I 63 (=HG V 1144) of a somewhat earlier date (Apil-Sîn) records the purchase of an orchard, *dimtum* and *nidūtum* by a *nadītum* of Sippar.

13 CT 47 25. It is quite possible that the *nidūtum* and the *dimtum* in the same district (*ugārum*), referred to in CT 47 27, are the same ones. In CT 47 33, also, a *dimtum* and *nidūtum* are mentioned as adjacent. The exact nature of a *dimtum* in the Sippar region is not in discussion here; see CAD D 144ff. s.v. *dimtu*.

VILLE ET CAMPAGNE DANS LE ROYAUME D'UGARIT. ESSAI D'ANALYSE ÉCONOMIQUE

Mario Liverani (Roma)

§1. Notre évaluation des civilisations anciennes est sans doute fort influencée par le bilan (qui est loin d'être équilibré) entre ce que nous connaissons et ce que nous ignorons, entre ce que les fouilles archéologiques révèlent à notre attention et ce qui reste caché, entre ce qui est souligné en tant qu'étrange ou exceptionnel et ce qui reste inaperçu en tant que normal, enfin entre ce qui est le résultat final d'un processus (et qui nous est donc parvenu) et tout ce qui se situe dans les étapes préparatoires. En traitant d'une société presque totalement analphabète, notre attention de savants se concentre sur les archives; en traitant d'une société paysanne, de village, la recherche archéologique ce concentre sur la ville - et dans la ville sur le palais royal. On obtient un double résultat pratique: d'un côté d'ignorer presque tout des conditions de vie de la population ordinaire, d'autre côté de considérer un fait "normal" la présence d'une ville et d'un palais comme celui d'Ugarit. Mais peut-on considérer une organisation comme le palais royal d'Ugarit un fait normal pour les conditions économiques, technologiques, sociales du bronze récent? Déjà les contemporains le trouvaient assez exceptionnel.[1]

Enfin, un concentré de richesse, un effort technique (architectural, artisanal, scribal, etc.), un niveau de vie tels que le palais royal d'Ugarit nous les révèle demandent évidemment des coûts socio-économiques qui dans le cadre des possibilités du bronze récent sont loin d'être ordinaires. Il s'agit sans doute d'un effort exceptionnel. Qui est-ce qui a payé ces coûts exceptionnels? L'entretien de groupes entiers de spécialistes non-producteurs de nourriture, et la destination de ressources considérables à des buts non productifs, demandent de la part du palais une concentration de surplus économique (c'est à dire alimentaire) tiré de la population paysanne.[2] Le prélèvement du surplus est le passage déterminant de tout le processus: c'est le mécanisme qui rend possible l'accumulation et donc la vie du palais; mais c'est aussi le mécanisme qui, s'il est utilisé d'une manière trop dure et s'il va peser sur des niveaux démographiques et technologiques déjà assez bas, peut avoir des conséquences très sérieuses pour la population paysanne.

Des études récentes et encore en progrès sur la démographie et sur l'agriculture du royaume d'Ugarit permettent de poser ce problème au point de vue spécifiquement économique. Il s'agit - bien entendu - de recherches qui demandent d'être encore poursuivies; mais déjà on est en gré de proposer des hypothèses de travail et de fixer des lignes générales pour caractériser un modèle économique de la Syrie du bronze récent.

§2. Au point de vue démographique on a essayé récemment (M. Heltzer[3] et moi-même[4]) de calculer d'une manière approximative quelle pouvait être la population du royaume d'Ugarit, et les chiffres obtenues indépendemment semblent raisonnables et concordantes. On peut donc penser que la ville d'Ugarit comptait grosso modo un millier de familles (pour la plupart de dépendants du Palais, non-producteurs de nourriture), pour un total de 6.000 à 8.000 personnes: l'estimation sur base archéologique et les données des textes sont assez concordantes à ce propos. Il y avait encore 150 villages environ, pour un total de quelque 25.000 personnes (producteurs de nourriture). Les paysans des fermes agricoles du Palais étaient (comme on va voir) presque négligeables au point de vue numérique. Au total donc quelque 32.000/33.000 habitants de tout le royaume d'Ugarit, dont 1/4 ou 1/5 concentrés dans la ville capitale. Ces premières données sont déjà assez indicatives de l'effort productif nécessaire pour soutenir des réalisations architecturales et artistiques éclatantes par une base démographique aussi modeste.

Quant à la distribution de la population, on connait dans le bronze récent (et déjà à partir du bronze moyen) une tendance générale dans la plupart du Proche Orient à abandonner les régions moins favorisées, et à concentrer les établissements dans les régions mieux pourvues en eau et en terre. Les vastes plaines de l'intérieur - dans lesquelles la civilisation du bronze ancien avait connu sa floraison - sont dans une certaine mesure abandonnées, et d'ailleurs on n'a pas encore entrepris l'exploitation agricole des collines et des montagnes qui va caractériser l'âge du fer. Les établissements du bronze récent dans le territoire d'Ugarit sont en effet localisés sur la côte ou dans la vallée du Nahr el-kebir;[5] et ce cadre est confirmé par les données des archives juridiques et administratives du Palais. Sur un territoire de quelque 2.250 km^2 (une bande de 75 km sur 30) on doit penser que moins d'un tiers était soumis à culture (le reste étant occupé par bois et pâturages), d'ailleurs avec une jachère plus ou moins prolongée. La densité de la population serait donc de 15 habitants environ par km^2 sur le total du territoire, mais de 40-45 habitants sur les terres mises à culture.

Quant au type des établissements, on a l'impression (qu'on doit préciser par des recherches ultérieures) que le système des communautés de village se gardait mieux dans les parties du royaume moins proches de la capitale (plaine de Geblé, vallée du Nahr el-kebir, etc.), et que au contraire aux environs immédiats d'Ugarit le système des fermes agricoles (*gt*) l'emportait, avec concentration de la vigne et de l'horticulture (contre la céréaliculture extensive des communautés de village). Le phénomène du grand établissement urbain qui "brûle" les établissements des environs immédiats, pour les adapter à ses exigences, est bien connu à toute époque (avec des caractères et une importance différents), et peut être considéré tout à fait normal. Plus en général, on peut décrire le territoire ugaritique comme caractérisé par un double système d'établissements: à la distribution uniforme des communautés de village (héritage néolithique) un autre système s'est superposé, un système d'établissements spécialisés - dont la ville palatine n'est que le centre - différemment organisé en rapport à ses buts qui ne sont pas la production primaire (ports, établissements artisanals, cultures spéciales, etc.).[6]

Quant au niveau démographique du bronze récent dans la Méditerranée orientale, les recherches de J.L. Angel - basées surtout sur les données égéennes - donnent une durée moyenne de vie pour les adultes (qui aient passé les 15 ans) de 39,3 pour les hommes et de 32 pour les femmes.[7] Cela signifie - compte tenu de la mortalité à la naissance ou dans les premiers ans - que la population pouvait bien rester à des niveaux stables, pourvu de ne pas soustraire trop de forces au cycle reproductif. On va voir que le surplus alimentaire est obtenu en particulier par des forces de travail qui ne se reproduisent pas. Monogamie et polygamie sont aussi différemment distribuées dans la population. Somme toute, les marges que le niveau technologique et sanitaire de l'époque a accordés à une reproduction stationnaire ou même en légère croissance, sont en effet destinés plutôt à des buts de différenciation productive et sociale.

Dans son complexe, le cadre démographique se caractérise par un équilibre précaire, non loin des limites minimales. La distribution de la population est très variée, faite de pleins et de vides, de surcharges et de raréfactions, qui correspondent à une situation socio-économique complexe. Dépassé le niveau "néolithique" avec ses communautés locales isolées et semblables, toutes adonnées seulement à la reproduction physique moyennant leur propre production de nourriture, le cadre est maintenant bien différent. C'est le cadre d'un arrangement diversifié des groupes humains au fin de tirer un surplus alimentaire qui est utilisé en partie pour l'entretien des spécialistes, en partie pour des oeuvres d'intérêt collectif (temples, fortifications, bâtiments publiques), en partie enfin immobilisé dans des utilisations ostentatoires, de prestige pour la classe dirigeante. Il n'est pas sûr que l'effort des paysans néolithiques pour survivre ait été plus grand que l'effort des paysans du bronze récent pour survivre et en plus donner un "surplus" au Palais.

§3. La productivité agricole a été récemment étudiée par moi même[8] sur la base surtout de deux textes (PRU V 13 et PRU II 98) qui nous révèlent des données très concrètes sur la culture des céréales dans les fermes agricoles (*gt*) du Palais. Avant tout, la productivité du sol (rapport entre semence et recolte) varie de 1:3 à 1:5. C'est ce qu'on pouvait s'attendre pour une région à cultures non irrigables et avec la technologie du bronze récent. Mais il s'agit quand même d'une donnée remarquable si on la compare aux rendements des régions dans lesquelles le système du Palais s'est développé à l'avance et avec des résultats plus éclatants. Des rendements de l'ordre de 1:10 sont normals pour l'Egypte et aussi pour l'Assyrie, et les rendements de la basse Mésopotamie peuvent atteindre facilement le niveau de 1:20 ou même de 1:30 (suivant l'époque). Il est évident que les médiocres rendements syriens comportent de nécessité un pourcentage plus haut d'immobilisation pour les semences (justement de 1/3 à 1/5 du total de la recolte), et un effort productif plus lourd: pour obtenir une quantité donnée de céréales on doit semer et travailler bien plus. Mais on doit souligner encore que des rendements médiocres et sujets à un régime de pluies instable (et non à une régulière irrigation artificielle) comportent des oscillations saisonnières qui peuvent arriver à des années dans lesquelles le recolte reproduit à peine la semence. Dans ces conditions, tirer un surplus est une tâche bien plus incertaine et bien plus lourde. L'importation dans des régions à agriculture pluviale d'un modèle de développement (le modèle palatin) qui a été créée d'abord dans des régions à agriculture irriguée avec des rendements hauts et même très hauts, comporte des difficultés non négligeables.

Outre que la semence pour l'année suivante, sur la recolte on doit charger aussi les rations pour les paysans et pour les animaux de travail. Les paysans reçoivent 12 *dd* de blé par an; un *dd* est donc la ration standard d'un mois pour un adulte mâle. Les boeufs (il y en a presque une paire pour chaque paysan) s'entretiennent à la pâture pendant toute l'année, mais reçoivent une intégration alimentaire en céréales dans la période du labourage (10 *dd* dans l'année, probablement concentrés en quatre mois). Le rendement de ces forces productives est plutôt variable en rapport surtout à l'extension de la ferme (dans les fermes petites les rendements par paysan sont plus élevés) et aussi évidemment en rapport à la qualité du sol. Mais en général chaque paysan doit semer en moyenne de 8 à 20 *dd* de blé, et recueillir de 50 à 65 et jusqu'à 100 *dd* de blé dans l'année. Une valeur de moyenne générale est de 60 *dd* par année et par paysan.

Sur ces 60 *dd* par année la semence constitue une charge qui va (comme on a déjà vu) du 20% (rapport 1:5) au 33% (rapport 1:3); les rations (hommes et boeufs) constituent une charge qui va du 20% au 25%. Les frais d'exploitation gravent donc dans une mesure qui va des 2/3 aux 2/5 du total, en moyenne dans la mesure de la moitié du total. Cela signifie que des 60 *dd* produits chaque année par paysan, le Palais en tire 30, qui sont le soutien de 2,5 personnes à rations standard de 12 *dd* (donc adultes mâles; femmes et enfants reçoivent naturellement des rations plus petites). Chaque paysan des *gt* du Palais produit donc, sur la terre du Palais et avec l'aide de boeufs et d'outils en bronze fournis par le Palais, de la nourriture suffisante pour l'entretien de soi-même et encore de 2,5 adultes non-producteurs de nourriture. Cette valeur comme telle est très modeste. Si on transfère cette valeur aux communautés de village, où travaillent des paysans qui font partie de familles nucléaires (une femme, deux-trois fils mineurs, en moyenne), on obtient une situation de subsistance stricte: une femme à 8 *dd*, 3 fils à 3x6 = 18 *dd*, total 26 *dd* sur 30.

L'avantage économique du système des *gt* pour les Palais est donc confié à deux éléments. Le premier élément, qui est déterminant, est le fait que les paysans des *gt* palatines sont depourvus de famille. On pourrait dire tout simplement que au lieu d'entretenir femme et fils ils entretiennent des spécialistes non producteurs de nourriture. Le deuxième élément est le fait que les forces productives des *gt* palatines sont adonnées aussi à d'autres productions plus spécialisées et moins indispensables pour la subsistance, surtout à la production du vin, qui afflue au Palais en bonnes quantités. On doit encore souligner que d'autres unités productives palatines (comme l'élevage du petit bétail, et encore tout le secteur artisan) ne se caractérisent pas comme mécanismes *producteurs* de surplus, mais comme mécanismes *transformateurs* de surplus. Par exemple dans le cas de l'élevage des moutons il paraît que la valeur des céréales qui entrent dans le mécanisme (rations pour le personnel) est économiquement équivalente à la valeur de la laine qui sort du mécanisme: on a donc transformation de blé en laine, un processus de diversification du surplus.

La différente fonction économique des deux secteurs de la population paysanne est désormais claire. Le secteur des communautés de village remploie dans son intérieur presque tout le surplus produit, et avec ce remploi de surplus chaque famille nucléaire peut assurer sa propre reproduction (femme, fils). Le secteur des *gt* au contraire ne se reproduit pas par des mécanismes internes (manque de vie familiale) et destine le surplus à la réalisation directe ou indirecte d'activités spécialisées: cultures spécialisées, transformation du surplus, et surtout entretien des spécialistes non producteurs de nourriture (artisans, administrateurs, gardes, etc.). Pour le fonctionnement complet du système il est nécessaire que le Palais soit capable d'obtenir la reproduction du secteur des *gt* par moyen d'un transfèrement de forces qui somme toute ne peuvent que provenir des communautés de village (directement ou indirectement et par des histoires personnelles différentes). On pourrait dire, d'une manière simplifiée et grossière que chaque famille nucléaire du secteur des communautés de village élève deux fils qui (au point de vue statistique) vont prendre la place de leurs parents, et un troisième fils qui une fois grandi ira travailler dans les fermes du Palais jusqu'à s'y éteindre.

§4. On peut maintenant essayer d'insérer les données quantitatives sur la population (qu'on a vu au § 2) dans le mécanisme économique (qu' on a décrit au § 3), pour bâtir un petit "modèle" économique du royaume d'Ugarit. On va se limiter au problème (qui d'ailleurs est essentiel) de la constitution et de l'utilisation du surplus alimentaire au sens stricte (céréales). Dans les comptes qui suivent on devra employer évidemment des données simplifiées d'une manière très nette, de type statistique. En particulier on va calculer la semence comme 1/4 de la recolte, on va considérer comme producteur le seul adulte mâle, dans la mesure de 60 *dd* par année; on va calculer les rations comme fixées en 12 *dd* pour les adultes mâles, en 8 *dd* pour les femmes, en 6 *dd* pour les enfants. On va enfin imaginer une famille nucléaire standard constituée par un père, une mère, trois enfants. On doit tenir compte du fait que les rations standard ne correspondent pas nécessairement à autant de personnes physiques, qui doivent avoir été en nombre inférieur à cause de phénomènes de suralimentation, accumulation, gaspillage par les classes supérieures du milieu palatin.

Pour rendre l'analyse plus évidente on va proposer d'abord un modèle "réaliste", c'est à dire basé sur les données démographiques les plus vraisemblables; puis on va proposer deux modèles alternatifs, caractérisés par un différent rapport quantifatif entre *gt* et villages (à l'avantage de l'un ou de l' autre élément). On peut anticiper que la comparaison entre les trois modèles va montrer comment le modèle "réaliste" soit en effet en gré de fonctionner, tandis que les autres seraient impossibles. Naturellement ce procédé est très grossier; il serait nécessaire d'établir non seulement trois cas particuliers, mais tout un *continuum* des relations quantitatives entre *gt*, villages, Palais, pour établir l'*optimum* de fonctionnement (qui ne correspond pas nécessairement à la réalité historique). Mais notre procédé simplifié est mieux compréhensible aux non spécialistes en économetrie (en commençant par moi-même), et plus convenable à l'état occasionnel et insuffisant de la documentation.[9]

§4.1. *Modèle "réaliste"*. On calcule environ 150 villages avec 25.000 personnes (c'est à dire 5.000 familles standard); environ 40 *gt* palatines avec 300 personnes (tous producteurs) et environ 500 personnes (tous producteurs) dans des petites *gt* de fonctionnaires du Palais (avec 1-2 personnes par *gt*); enfin environ 7.000 non producteurs (c'est à dire 1.400 familles standard) dans l'organisation palatine. Les données de la production sont les suivantes:

(a) villages: 5.000 producteurs x 60 *dd* = 300.000 *dd* (produit par an)
10% = 30.000 *dd* au Palais comme "dîme"
25% = 75.000 *dd* immobilisés comme semence

rations:	5.000 adultes mâles	=	60.000
	5.000 femmes	=	40.000
	15.000 enfants	=	90.000
	total		190.000 *dd*

Total général 295.000 *dd*. Il ne reste presque rien (5.000 *dd*) comme rations des boeufs. Le système est quand même en équilibre complexif.

(b) *gt*: 800 producteurs x 60 *dd* = 48.000 *dd* (produit par an)
dont 50% = 24.000 au Palais et 50% pour semence et rations.

(c) Palais: le Palais obtient 30.000 *dd* des villages + 24.000 *dd* des *gt* = 54.000 *dd* au total. Par cette quantité de blé il peut entretenir 1.420 familles standard, donc 7.100 personnes.

Dans ce modèle (nº 1) on peut voir que le bilan entre surplus et rations est équilibré: 5.000 producteurs des villages + 800 producteurs des *gt* peuvent en effet entretenir les 20.000 non producteurs des villages (femmes, enfants) et les 7.000 non producteurs du Palais (1.400 spécialistes avec leurs familles). La reproduction des producteurs des *gt* est aussi possible: si un paysan (adulte) "dure" 15 ans, 800 paysans doivent être substitués au rythme de 53 par an. Le prélèvement de 53 personnes sur 5.000 familles (des villages) signifie que chaque famille doit livrer une personne tous les 90 ans, ce qui est acceptable sans provoquer des dommages excessifs.

§4.2. *Modèle à fermes insuffisantes*. Par rapport au modèle n° 1 on a diminué à la moitié le nombre des paysans des *gt* (400), en augmentant de la sorte les habitants des villages à 25.400, et en gardant les 7.000 non-producteurs du Palais.

(a) Villages: Le produit des villages reste presque invarié:
5.080 producteurs x 60 *dd* = 304.800 *dd* (produit par an)
10% = 30.480 *dd* au Palais comme "dîme"
25% = 76.200 *dd* immobilisés comme semence

rations:	5.080	adultes mâles	=	60.960
	5.080	femmes	=	40.640
	15.240	enfants	=	91.440
		total		193.040 *dd*

Total général 299.720 *dd*. Il ne reste que 5.080 *dd*, plus ou moins comme dans le modèle n° 1.

(b) *gt*: 400 producteurs x 60 *dd* = 24.000 *dd* (produit par an)
dont 50% (12.000) au Palais et 50% pour semence et rations.

(c) Palais: le Palais obtient 30.480 + 12.000 = 42.480 *dd* au total; par cette quantité de blé il peut entretenir seulement 1.118 familles standard, donc 5.590 personnes (environ 1.500 moins que dans le modèle n° 1).

Dans ce modèle n° 2 donc le nombre des producteurs baisse de peu (de 5.800 à 5.480), mais le nombre des entretenus baisse de 27.000 à 25.910 (20.320 des familles paysannes + 5.590 du Palais), au désavantage du secteur du Palais (1.500 personnes en moins) et avec un petit avantage pour le secteur rural (320 personnes en plus). Le Palais doit renoncer à 1/4 environ de son organique (5.590 non producteurs + 400 producteurs des *gt*, total 5.990; contre 7.100 + 800 = 7.900 du modèle n° 1).

§4.3. *Modèle à fermes surabondantes*. Par rapport au modèle n° 1 on a doublé le nombre des paysans des *gt* (1.600), en baissant de la sorte les habitants des villages à 24.200, et en gardant les 7.000 non-producteurs du Palais.

(a) Villages: le produit des villages subit une réduction modeste:
4.840 producteurs x 60 *dd* = 290.400 *dd* (produit par an)
10% = 29.040 *dd* au Palais comme "dîme"
25% = 72.600 *dd* immobilisés comme semence

rations:	4.840	adultes mâles	=	58.080
	4.840	femmes	=	38.720
	14.520	enfants	=	87.120
		total		183.920 *dd*

Total général 285.560 *dd*. Il ne reste que 4.840 *dd*, presque comme dans les cas précedents.

(b) *gt*: 1.600 producteurs x 60 *dd* = 96.000 *dd* (produit par an)
dont 50% (48.000) au Palais et 50% pour semence et rations.

(c) Palais: le Palais obtient 29.040 + 48.000 = 77.040 *dd* au total. Par cette quantité de blé il peut entretenir 2.027 familles standard, donc 10.137 personnes (3.000 environ en plus que dans le modèle n° 1).

Dans ce modèle n° 3 le nombre des producteurs monte à 6.440, le nombre des entretenus monte à 19.360 + 10.137 = 29.497. Cela se passe à l'avantage du secteur du Palais qui peut augmenter le nombre de ses membres (10.137 non producteurs + 1.600 paysans des *gt*, total 11.737), ou bien augmenter l'accumulation et la suralimentation des classes supérieures. Cela se passe pourtant à la charge des villages: non tant comme prélèvement de surplus (qu'on a vu rester au même niveau), mais comme prélèvement de forces productives. Chaque famille doit céder un adulte mâle tous les 45 ans, c'est à dire à générations alternées, ce qui pourrait être tolérable seulement si le rythme de reproduction était bien au delà du danger de l'extinction.

On peut dire la même chose pour le problème de la corvée, sur lequel malheureusement la documentation ugaritique ne donne presque rien. Mais il est autant évident que les fermes du Palais devaient recevoir des intégrations de travail forcé des villages pour des travaux saisonniers intensifs. Plus le nombre des *gt* augmente par rapport aux villages, plus le poids de la corvée devient remarquable. Dans l'hypothèse (c'est seulement une hypothèse) d'un mois de corvée de dix membres de communauté comme aide pour chaque paysan des *gt*, alors dans le modèle n° 1 la corvée signifie 50 jours par an pour chaque chef de famille des villages; dans le modèle n° 3, 100 jours par an pour chaque chef de famille.

De la comparaison entre les trois modèles on tire en général que la réduction (ou à la limite: l'absence) des *gt* signifie une réduction du surplus qui arrive au Palais, tandis qu'elle signifie une réduction du poids démographique et de travail pour les villages. Au contraire l'augmentation des *gt* fait monter le surplus pour le Palais (qui peut donc s'accroître en quantité ou en qualité), mais en gravant bien plus lourdement sur la capacité de reproduction des villages. Dans le cas pratique du modèle n° 1, la présence d'un groupe de *gt* plutôt restreint (dans lequel ne travaille que le 3% de la population paysanne) donne au Palais la possibilité de presque doubler le nombre des familles de spécialistes non producteurs de nourriture. Le rapport géometrique entre le nombre des employés des *gt* et le nombre des spécialistes entretenus est le suivant:

	n. paysans (avec familiers)	employés des *gt* n.	*[%]*	n. spécialistes (avec familiers)
sans *gt*	25.800	-	-	4.075
modèle n° 2	25.800	400	*[1,5]*	5.590
modèle n° 1	25.800	800	*[3]*	7.100
modèle n° 3	25.800	1.600	*[6]*	10.137

§5. On définit conventionnellement "ville" un village dans lequel est installé un Palais royal avec tous ses annexes: palais satellites, boutiques et entrepôts, temples, fortifications, maisons des fonctionnaires, etc. Dans la ville vivent concentrés les spécialistes non producteurs de nourriture, adonnés aux activités de transformation (artisans), d'échange (marchands), et de contrôle social (administrateurs, prêtres, gardes). Cette organisation est entretenue par la nourriture qui arrive des campagnes; des villages en mesure modeste (10% du produit), des fermes palatines en mesure proportionnellement plus importante (50% du produit). La plus grande productivité et le plus grand surplus des fermes est possible grâce à un déplacement de main d'oeuvre (soit permanente soit saisonnière) des villages. Ce mécanisme dans son complexe semble stable (et en effet peut durer quelque temps), et peut même comporter pour le Palais un bilan actif, ce qui rend possible des immobilisations ostentatoires (par exemple les ornements artistiques concentrés au Palais) et un niveau de vie aisé pour la classe dirigeante (famille royale, scribes, *maryannu*, marchands, etc.).

Toutefois ce mécanisme constitue un poids pour toute la population rurale, un poids qui ne peut être ni trop léger ni excessif. Le système peut fonctionner sous deux conditions: (a) manque forcée de vie familiale pour le personnel des *gt*; ils sont en pratique des esclaves ruraux au sens stricte, assignés déjà adultes à leur travail, entretenus au niveau de survivance stricte, jusqu'à leur épuisement (la mort survient tôt, dans l'époque). (b) Une condition assez dure pour les habitants des villages pour qu'il soit possible en faire sortir un flux de main d'oeuvre qui va remplir les vides dans les *gt*. Le mécanisme de ce remplacement est évidemment surtout celui de l'endettement contre garantie personnelle: le débiteur insolvable doit céder au Palais un fils, qui va travailler dans les *gt*. Un afflux de main d'oeuvre en provenance d'autres villes ou états syro-palestiniens (qui semble documenté de quelques textes) doit son origine au phénomène des fuites d'esclaves et de débiteurs insolvables, qui connait au bronze récent une intensification remarquable. Ce phénomène ne change pas notre modèle, car l'afflux de réfugiés étrangers à Ugarit est compensé par le flux de fuyards ugaritiques à l'extérieur; au contraire ce phénomène confirme notre modèle sur le point décisif des conditions économiques difficiles diffusées dans les villages.

Il faut à ce point avouer que la productivité possible dans les conditions démographiques et physiques du milieu syrien (moins favorables par rapport aux régions à irrigation artificielle) et dans les conditions technologiques de l'âge du bronze, productivité qui permettrait facilement une reproduction ou une croissance modérée à des communautés de village de type "néolithique", soutient au contraire avec un effort considérable le prélèvement de surplus par le Palais, en particulier lorsque l'exploitation est assez dure et rigide comme pendant le bronze récent. C'est déjà normal pendant tout l'âge du bronze que des établissements soit petits (villages) soit grands (villes) subissent des crises qui se traduisent dans des coupures des niveaux archéologiques et notamment dans des niveaux d'abandon. Il faut considérer "normal" (ou quand même fréquent) le fait qu'une communauté locale n'ait pas été capable de soutenir le poids économique et démographique, et se soit éteinte ou reduite sensiblement ou déplacée. Mais dans l'époque du bronze récent ces éléments de crise paraissent se généraliser. Le passage à l'âge du fer, la période dramatique entre XIII et XII siècle, est marquée par une crise démographique et territoriale assez profonde, qu'on doit mettre en relation (à mon sens) avec une charge excessive et prolongée pendant plusieurs siècles de la part des organismes palatins. La richesse toute particulière des palais du bronze récent de la Mediterranée orientale, avec leur concentration d'ornements et d'oeuvres d'art; et aussi le considérable déséquilibre entre une culture palatine de plus en plus raffinée et une culture ordinaire de plus en plus dégradée; tout cela a été payé par une crise de proportions épouvantables.

Dans le cas d'Ugarit la crise n'intéresse pas seulement la capitale et le port, mais aussi toute la région avoisinante, dans laquelle la diffusion des fermes palatines avait sensiblement remplacé les villages. Plus loin de la capitale, en particulier dans la plaine de Geblé, la continuité est majeure, justement à cause d'une plus grande vitalité des communautés de village. Ugarit a donc "brûlé" - pour réaliser son Palais extraordinaire - tout le territoire avoisinant. Ce territoire va rester sensiblement deserté pendant l'âge du fer, et c'est bien pour cela qu'il sera choisi pour la fondation de Lattakié - après un millénaire de vide. La ville n'est donc pas un fait "normal"; elle est au contraire le résultat d'un effort exceptionnel, qui tend à brûler le territoire avoisinant, par soustraction de ressources alimentaires et par altérations des taux de reproduction. Le fait qu'à Ugarit (comme dans bien d'autres villes célèbres du Proche Orient ancien) la période du maximum d'effort économique et politique soit suivie d'une période de crise et d'abandon du territoire, est - peut-être - un fait structurel et non occasionnel.

---

1 EA 89, 50-53; cf. W.F. Albright - W.L. Moran, dans JCS 5 [1950] 163-168.

2 Sur les rapports de production dans le Proche Orient ancien cf. mon exposé *Il modo di produzione* dans *L'alba della civiltà*, II [Torino 1976] 1-126.

3 M. Heltzer, *The Rural Community in Ancient Ugarit* [Wiesbaden 1976] 103-112.

4 Article *Ras Shamra. Histoire*, dans *Dictionnaire de la Bible, Supplément* [Paris 1979] cols. 1319-20.

5 Cf. maintenant l'exposé de G. Saadé, *Ougarit, métropole cananéenne* [Beyrouth 1979] pp. 55-61.

6 Nous préparons à ce sujet une *Topografia economica del regno di Ugarit.*

7 J.L. Angel, *Ecology and Population in the Eastern Mediterranean*, dans *World Archaeology* 4 [1972] 88-105 (pp. 94-95 et 98-99).

8 *Economia delle fattorie palatine ugaritiche*, dans *Dialoghi di Archeologia* 2 [1979] 57-72.

9 Pour un modèle plus perfectionné cf. A.G. Sharratt, *Socio-economic and Demographic Models for the Neolithic and Bronze Ages of Europe*, dans D.L. Clarke, *Models in Archaeology* [London 1972] 477-542.

HELP IN NEED

D.N. MacKenzie (Göttingen)

'The best laid schemes o' mice an' men gang aft a-gley' - in this case a not so well prepared article. After truly montane labours a mouse was born more ridiculous than that turned up by Burns' plough, and certainly no fit offering for this volume. With the deadline long past, *faryād-rasī* was urgently needed if I was to pay homage at all, however inadequately, to a much respected colleague - and *fry'd* came.

In modern Persian *faryād* is 'a cry, shout, clamour; a cry for help', combined with the verbs *kardan, bar āvurdan, zadan* 'to cry (for help)'. Its earlier meaning of 'help in need' can be seen better in the combinations *faryād xᵛāstan* 'to ask for help', *ba faryād rasīdan* 'come to the relief (of)', whence *faryād-ras* 'succourer', and in the collocation *dād u faryād*, where with *dād* 'justice, redress of grievances' it has also developed the sense 'cry for justice' and so 'clamour, uproar'. In Middle Iranian only the meaning 'help' is found.

In Middle Persian the noun (spelled *plyd'tʾ*) is only attested in Book Pahlavi:

Mēnōg ī Xrad, II, 96 f. *pad hambār kardan ī kirbag tuxšāg bāš, kū-t pad mēnōgān ō frayād rasēd* 'Be diligent in making a store of good deeds, that it may come to your aid in the spiritual world (hereafter).'

II, 166 ... *u-š az bayān ud az-iz dēwān kas ō frayād nē rasēd* 'and nobody, either from the gods or even from the demons, comes to his aid'.

XXII, 6 ... *bē pas-iz pad mēnōg ō frayād rasēd* 'but later, in the spiritual world, it (diligence) comes to (one's) aid'.

Ayādgār ī Wuzurgmihr, 189f. *ud dōst kadām weh? ān ī mad-ō-frayād-tar ud andar škaftīh ayār-tar* 'And which friend is the best? He who comes to one's aid more and is more a helper in hardship.'

There is even a legend (Greater Bundahišn, IX, 35 f.) that during the 'War of the Religion' between the newly-Zoroastrian Iranians under Wištāsp and the Chionites under Arjāsp, when the former were sorely pressed, the mountain Kōmiš (Qūmis) broke off from its fellows and fell into the middle of the plain, saving the Iranians, whence they called it *Mad-ō-frayād* 'Came to (our) aid' -- a sort of *mons ex machina*.

Clearly *frayād* is at root not simply 'aid, assistance' but rather 'succour'. In both Pahlavi and Manichaean Middle Persian there are several verbal forms from the stem *frayād-*, which has kept the intransitive sense of 'come to the aid of'. In its nominal derivatives, however, the meaning seems to have been more or less weakened to a general 'help'.

Mēnōg ī Xrad, II, 106 f. *pad āzarm ud grāmīgīh wistāx ma bāš, čē pad mēnōg āzarmīgīh nē frayādēd* 'Do not pride yourself in honour or respect, for in the spiritual world respectability is of no help.'

Gr. Bundahišn, VI c, 5 ... *jud az Harburz pad 18 sāl hamāg kōf az zamīg abar āmad hēnd, kē frayādišn ud sūd ī mardōmān aziš* 'apart from Harburz all the mountains came up from the earth in 18 years, from which (there is) help and advantage for mankind'.

Wizīdagīhā ī Zādspram, IV, 13 f. *3 brād būd hēnd ud ān ī seyom Srid ... ō Kayōs pad was dar frayādišnīg* 'there were three brothers and the third one, Thrita, (was) helpful to Kayos in many respects'.

The Manichaean examples are now conveniently collected in Boyce's *Reader in Manichaean Middle Persian and Parthian*, Acta Iranica 9, Teheran-Liège 1975:

de 1 *ny pry'dynd pd h'n rwc ʿy wdnng* 'they (various luxuries) do not help on that Day of Distress', *qnygrwšn h'n ʿy xwd pry'dyd pd h'n rwc ...* 'the Maiden of Light, she who alone helps on that Day ...'.

cr 12 *nwg pry'dyšn 'c zwr ʿy zwrmnd* 'new help from the power of the mighty one',

cu 26 *'wm'n xwd pryst'nd zwr 'wd pry'dyšn* 'and may they send us power and help',

bt 2 *pry'd'g ʿy nrm'n* 'Helper of the meek' (Jesus),

cu 15 *pry'd'g''n nyw'n* 'brave helpers',

dgb 5 *pyw'cydwm 'w w'ng 'wm bwyd fry'dg [sic]* 'Answer my call and be helper(s) to me.'

In Parthian the earliest occurrence seems to be in the text of the Paikuli inscription, line 16 = c 14.4 *pry't YBʿHd* /frayād wˣāzēnd/ 'they seek help', unfortunately out of context. Otherwise, in Manichaean Parthian, only nominal *hwfry'd* and the (intransitive) verb *hwfry'd'd* occur:

bk 1 *z'd 'yy pṭ wrc 'wṭ ʿzgd 'yy hwfryd 'w pydr mrdwhm* 'you were born in miraculous power and have gone forth as helper for the Father of mankind',

dc 10 *'wš cf'r w''d pw'g 'w mn hwfry'd 'w'st* 'he brought me the four pure winds as helpers',

bg 1 *'wn bg ... 'w mn hwfry'd'* 'O god ... help me',

cv 23 *dhwm z'wr 'wd hwfry'd pd hrwyn d'hw'n* 'give me strength and succour me with every gift',

cv 14 *'wr bg, 'w mn wyn, hwfry'dwm pd ʿyn ''g'm* 'come, god, look at me, come to my aid at this time',

ac 4 *'b'wš'n 'whrmyzd bg ny hwfry'd'd 'hyndy* 'then god Ohrmezd would not come to their aid',

br 2 *hwfry'd'd 'yy cw'gwn br'dr'n* 'thou hast come to (our) aid as brothers (would)'.

The standard etymology, from Avestan *fra-dā-*, was first presented by Horn (*Grundriss der neupersischen Etymologie*, Strassburg 1893, no. 828), *fraδāta-* supposedly 'Gedeihen, Förderung' (Bartholomae, *AiWb.*, 721, 'soll in die Höhe kommen' !). Nyberg (*Hilfsbuch des Pehlevi*, II, Uppsala 1931, 70), reading *frahāt*, preferred OIr. **fraδāti-* from *fra-dā-* 'vorwärtsbringen, fördern'. (In his *Manual of Pahlavi*, II, Wiesbaden 1974, 79, it has become *friyāt*, on account of Pāzand *friāṯ*, but no etymology is offered.) The *-y-* in Parthian, especially in the inscriptional spelling, is enough to disprove this. It is the 'coming, arriving' to help that characterizes the word, immediately reminding of the verb *y'd-* (*'w*), common to Middle Persian and Parthian, meaning 'reach, attain'. (The supposed meaning 'to stretch out', still given by Boyce, *Word-list of Man. Mid. Pers. and Parthian*, Acta Iranica 9a, 1977, 102, has been disposed of by Benveniste in an article on 'La racine *yat-* en indo-iranien', *Indo-Iranica, Mélanges ... Georg Morgenstierne*, Wiesbaden 1964, 24. Any possibility of connexion with Persian *yāzīdan* 'stretch out' thus falls away.) The noun *frayād* is then from **fra-yāta/i-*. Whether the verbal stem *frayād-* is denominative as stated by Henning (*Zeitschrift für Indologie und Iranistik*, IX, 1933, 214), or directly from **fra-yātaya-*, is less certain. The Parthian verb *hwfryʾd-* has every appearance of a denominative, but it could have been reformed on *hwfryʾd* 'helpful', which itself implies a verbal stem *fryʾd-*, being formed like MP *hwnywš* 'obedient', Parth. *hwptʾw* 'patient'. Benveniste has shown (loc. cit., 22) that Av. *frā-yataya-* is essentially 'parvenir à la place due': the causative **fra-yātaya-* would be '(s'y) présenter'.

Such a verb would help out of another difficulty. The normal Khwarezmian stem 'to help' is *ʾβyw-* < **abi-ū-*, with the verbal noun *βycyk* = *yārī* (v. Henning, *A fragment of a Khwarezmian dictionary*, London-Teheran 1971, 11; Supplement, 34). At the sole occurrence of *faryād* x^v*āstan* = *istaṣraxa* 'opem petiit', however, at *Muq*. 494.6, another word appears in the Khwarezmian gloss: *fy?cyʾk kwzyd* is clear and fully pointed, but the third letter is indistinct. Whatever the unwanted mark above it may be, we can now see it to be an *alif*, and recognize *fyʾcyʾk* = *faryād* 'help' as the normal feminine verbal noun in *-ʾk* of the stem *fyʾcy-* < **frayātaya-*; for the development cf. *fyʾny* = *dūstī*, from *ʾfy* = *dūst* < *friya-*, and *ʾnpʾcy-* 'to demolish' < **ham-pātaya-*, causative of *ʾnpd-* 'fall down, collapse'.

ZUR BESTIMMUNG DER ALTASSYRISCHEN SIEGELEIGENTÜMER

Lubor Matouš (Praha)

Ursprünglich hatte ich beabsichtigt den Jubilar und meinen Freund Igor Michailovič mit einem längeren Beitrag zu seinem 65. Geburtstag zu ehren, jedoch die kurze Frist, die mir dazu bemessen war und die Vorbereitung an der Herausgabe der Prager Sammlung kappadokischer Tafeln, zwingen mich den ursprünglichen Plan auf vorläufige Bemerkungen über altassyrische Siegelung zu beschränken.

Für die Bestimmung der Siegeleigentümer auf den kappadokischen Tafeln ist besonders wichtig - wie bereits Larsen in seinem Beitrag "Seals and Sealing in the Ancient Near East" (= *Bibliotheca Mesopotamica*, Vol. VI), S. 65 bemerkt hat - in vollem Umfang den dazugehörigen Text zu veröffentlichen, weil sich oft die Namen, die auf den Legenden genannt werden, nicht im Text wiederfinden.

Wenn sich die Legende eines Siegels auf der Hülle mit dem Namen des Siegelnden auf der Innentafel deckt, kann man im allgemeinen annehmen, dass sich hinter dem Namen des Siegelnden der Eigentümer des Siegels verbirgt. Jedoch von dieser Regel finden sich oft Ausnahmen. Gut bekannt sind die Fälle der Benutzung des Siegels durch einen Dritten, wie z.B. bei der Wiederverwendung des bekannten Ibbi-Suens Siegels, das seinerzeit irrtümlich zur zeitlichen Ansetzung der assyrischen Kolonien gegen das Ende der III. Dynastie von Ur führte. Man kann wohl mit Balkan annehmen, dass nach dem Niedergang des Reiches von Ur einige Schreiber nach Assur auswanderten und mit sich dieses Siegel nach Kaneš mitgenommen haben.

Als typisches Beispiel für die Benutzung des Rollsiegels durch einen Dritten kann man den Verpflichtungsschein ICK 2,11 anführen, wo der Zeuge Šu-Bēlum, Sohn des Zurzur das Siegel eines gewissen Šu-Bēlum, des Sohnes des Šu-Ištar verwendet, das auch auf dem Duplikat Ka 589, Siegel C = ICK 2, Pl. CXVIII und Ka 708 = ib., Pl. CXXIII abgerollt ist.

Ein besonderer Fall der Benutzung eines Siegels durch einen Dritten kann der doppelte Gebrauch des Siegels B auf der Hülle I 445 angeführt werden. Während die erste Siegelabrollung, die man als B_1 bezeichnen kann, in einem Halbkreis eingeschlossen ist, findet sich eine andere Abrollung des gleichen Siegels, hier als B_2 bezeichnet, ohne diesen Halbkreis, womit angedeutet sein soll, dass es sich um zwei verschiedene Siegelnde handelt (vgl. Beilage I).

Ziemlich oft ist gemeinsame Benutzung eines Siegels belegt, besonders bei den einheimischen Eheleuten, wie in I 428, wo statt der erwarteten fünf Siegeln sich auf der Hülle nur vier finden, weil das einheimische Ehepaar gemeinsames Siegel geführt hat. Gemeinsame Benutzung eines Siegels findet sich auch unter den Brüdern, wie z.B. in der Urkunde I 452 (s. dazu *Festschrift A. Moortgat, Bagh.Mit.* 7,119-23, anders jedoch bei Larsen, l.c. 104, Anm. 60).

Weit grössere Schwierigkeiten bietet die Identifizierung der Siegelbesitzer ohne Legenden; man kann sie nur dann bestimmen, wenn auf zwei verschiedenen Hüllen Siegel mit identischen Namen vorkommen. So trägt, um hier nur ein Beispiel anzuführen, die Hülle des Verpflichtungsscheines I 458 drei Siegelabrollungen A, B und C ohne Legenden. Als Siegelnde sind angegeben: Azuja, Bezili und Ḫalkiašu. Die Siegelabrollung A befindet sich auf der Hülle I 462, wo unter den Zeugen auch ein Azuja vorkommt. Der zweite Zeuge des Schuldscheines Bezili ist auf Grund des Siegels in TC III, Pl. CCXXX no. 99 mit *Me-zi-[li]* identisch (zum Wechsel *b/m* vgl. GKT §26 e). Deswegen gehört ihm das Siegel C und der dritte Zeuge Ḫalkiašu führt das Siegel B. So kann man also durch Vergleich der Rollsiegel ohne Legenden auf verschiedenen Tafeln untereinander oft die Siegeleigentümer identifizieren.

Dass oft eine Zuordnung der einzelnen Siegel mit den im Text genannten Personen nicht möglich ist, geht aus der Siegellegende A des Gerichtsprotokolls I 450 hervor. Der Text enthält drei Siegelabrollungen, die nach Z. 1-3 der Hülle von Aššur-ṭāb, Išim-Suin und Šu-Anum stammen. Diese drei Personen sind in Z.4 als Richter bezeichnet. Nach ihren Siegellegenden sind Aššur-ṭāb und Išim-Suin Besitzer der Siegel B und C. Siegel A bietet jedoch die Legende *Ba-la* DUMU *La*-NI, ein Name, der weder auf der Innentafel, noch auf der Hülle vorkommt. Man kann wohl vermuten, dass der *tamkārum* Bala als Richter bei diesem Prozess fungierte und mit seinem Siegel statt Šu-Anum, den er vertrat, gesiegelt hat (s. Beilage II).

Die betreffenden Zeilen der Innentafel lauten:

16 *kaspam a-ni-am i-Kà-ni-iš*	Dieses Silber hat in Kaniš
17 *A-šùr-ṭāb il$_5$-qí*	Aššur-ṭāb übernommen.
18 *I-ší-im-Sú-in*	Išīm-Suin
19 *Šu-A-nu-um*	(und) Šu-Anum
20 *da-a-nu*	(waren) Richter.

Hülle:

1 *kunuk A-šùr-ṭāb* DUMU *Ša-ba-ḫa-nim*	Siegel des Aššur-ṭāb, des Sohnes des Šabaḫanum;

(Siegelabrollung A)

2 *kunuk I-ší-im-Sú-in* DUMU *A-šur-re-ṣí*	Siegel des Išīm-Suin, des Sohnes des Aššur-reṣi;
3 *kunuk Šu-A-nim* DUMU *A-šur-rē'î*	Siegel des Šu-Anum, des Sohnes des Aššur-rē'î.

(Siegelabrollung B)

4 *a-wi-lu a-ni-ú-tum da-a-nu*	Diese Leute (waren) Richter.

Siegellegende A : *Ba-la* DUMU *La*-NI DAM.KÀR

Siegellegende B : *A-šur-ṭāb* DUMU *Ša-ba-ḫa-nim*

Siegellegende C : *Iš-me-Sú-in* DUMU *A-šur-re-ṣ[í]*

Aus diesen wenigen hier angeführten Beispielen über den Gebrauch der Siegel auf den kappadokischen Tafeln kann man ersehen, wie Larsens Forderung, Siegelabrollungen mit den zugehörigen Tafeln zusammen zu publizieren, berechtigt ist.

I 455 B_1

I 455 B_2

Beilage I

I 450 A

I 450 B

I 450 C

Beilage II

Zeichnungen: Marie Matoušová

DER ALTE UND MITTELALTERLICHE NAHE OSTEN (ZU FRAGEN DER ANALOGIE DER SOZIAL -ÖKONOMISCHEN UND STAATLICHEN ORDNUNG)

G.A. Melikischwili (Tbilisi)

Auf der internationalen Tagung der Assyriologen der sozialistischen Länder in Budapest (April, 1974) wurden im unseren Referat die sozial-ökonomischen Verhältnisse in den Ländern des Nahen Ostens zur Zeit der altorientalischen Epoche geschildert.[1] Im Vortrag, wurde unter anderem, auf die Einengung der Funktionierung des Privateigentums durch die Existenz eines allmächtigen Staates und mächtiger Gemeinden, die schwach entwickelten Waren-Geld Verhältnisse, auf die "Konsum"- und die zurückgebliebene Ökonomie hingewiesen. Eine der hauptsächlichsten Besonderheiten der alten Gesellschaft des Nahen Ostens war das Vorhandensein eines ausgebreiteten Staatssektors in der Ökonomie (grosse König- und Tempelwirtschaften). Die Königsmacht monopolisierte hier tatsächlich die landwirtschaftliche und handwerkliche Produktion, hatte die Funktion nicht nur des obersten, sondern auch des unmittelbaren Besitzers und Eigentümers eines bedeutenden Teils des bearbeiteten Landes und bedeutender Handwerksstätten inne. Beachtenswert ist ebenfalls die Abhängigkeit des Handels und der Händler von der Staatsmacht - die Metamorphose der Kaufleute zu Staatsdienern, die Unterordnung der gesamten städtischen Ökonomie dem Staatssektor. Diese staatliche Monopolvorherrschaft in der Ökonomie der Länder des Nahen Ostens führte zur Bildung einer spezifischen sozialen Struktur. Die Ausführung der verwaltenden Funktionen in der gesellschaftlichen, militärischen, wirtschaftlichen und kulturellen Tätigkeit war die Grundlage für die Vorrangstellung der herrschenden Oberschicht. Die Stellung der einzelnen Vertreter der herrschenden Klasse wurde gleichzeitig nach dem Platz bestimmt,den sie in der Staatshierarchie einnahmen, der wiederum davon abhing, in welchem Abhängigkeitsverhältnis sie zum König standen. So sehen wir eine fast vollständige Verschmelzung der herrschenden Klassen mit der Staatsmacht und dem Staatsapparat. Was die ausgebeutete Klasse, die unmittelbaren Produzenten betrifft, so bestand sie aus freien Mitglieder der Gemeinden, Sklaven und Freien, die selbständig auf Königsländern wirtschafteten und zuletzt aus einer geringen Anzahl echten Sklaven, die schwere Arbeiten verrichteten oder in Haushalten tätig waren. Führend war eine Protofeudale Exploitation (Steuern, gesellschaftliche Arbeitsleistungen und Teilnahme an der Landwehr).

Der Vergleich dieser Lage mit dem mittelalterlichen Nahen Osten zeigt, dass zwischen beiden viel Gemeinsames war.

Die Aufmerksamkeit wird besonders auf den Fakt gerichtet, dass es im Verlaufe der alten und mittelalterlichen Epochen keine sprunghafte Entwicklung der Produktivkräfte im Osten gab. Wenn auch einige technische Neuigkeiten und eine Neubelebung in der Ökonomie usw. in einzelnen Perioden vorhanden waren, so hatte das keine wesentliche Bedeutung im Aspekt der Determination sozialer Gesellschaftsstrukturen und sozial-ökonomischer Verhältnisse. Wesentlicher ist, dass im Laufe des Altertums und des Mittelalters sich hier materielle Produktionsbedingungen gleichartigen Charakters für den alten - sowie für den mittelalterlichen Osten erhielten. Insbesondere waren die Naturbedingungen, die in einigen Regionen das Vorhandensein eines entwickelten Bewässerungssystems forderten, gleichartig. Ausserdem verhinderte die vorhandene Fülle an landwirtschaftlichem Nutzboden, im Gegensatz zu Europa, den Kampf um Privatland. Gleichzeitig, ist für den alten - sowie für den mittelalterlichen Osten, im Gegensatz zu Europa, das naturbedingt geringe Ausmass notwendiger Produkte gleich charakteristisch was in bedeutendem Masse die Verzögerung des sozial-ökonomischen Entwicklungstempos beeinflusste. Dieser Umstand führte an vielen Orten zur Festigung und Erhaltung der Gemeinden was seinerseits wieder eine negative Rolle in der Vertiefung der sozial-ökonomischen Differenzierung spielte. Die Gemeinde war ebenfalls für die Erhaltung der alten Wirtschaftsformen von Bedeutung, da sie, obgleich im Grunde schon in eine Staatsfiskalzelle verwandelt, doch teilweise ihre wirtschaftliche Funktion beibehielt.

Das bedeutendste Phänomen, dass den Charakter des sozial-ökonomischen Prozesses im alten – sowie im mittelalterlichen Osten bestimmte, ist in beiden Fällen die besondere Machtstellung des Staates, das hohe Niveau der Staatzentralisation, das in der Regel von einer unentwickelten administrativen und gerichtlichen Immunität begleitet war. Daraus resultierte eine hohe Konzentration des Staatseigentums einerseits und die unbedeutende Rolle der Institution des Privateigentums anderseits, die charakteristisch für den alten – sowie für den mittelalterlichen Osten waren.

Im Kalifat - der grössten Vereinigung des frühmittelalterlichen Ostens - war der Kalif theoretisch der grösste Eigentümer aller Ländereien. Bekannt ist, dass der bedeutendste Teil des Bodenfondes und die Bewässerungsbauten in den hauptsächlichsten Gebieten des Kalifats Staatseigentum waren. Sie wurden wie Pachtland bearbeitet und in Form eines "Ikta" verliehen (Übergabe dieses Bodens unter der Bedingung der Steuerpflicht oder als Dienstauszeichnung oder Pension; später bekam das "ikta" den Begriff des "Kriegslehens"). Im Osmanischen Imperium war ebenfalls der grösste Teil der Ländereien Staatseigentum. Ausser der Sultanendomäne, wurden diese Ländereien hauptsächlich als vererbbare, bedingte Lohnabfindungen an die Kriegswürdenträger der Reiterei der Landswehr vergeben (Lehensleute-Sipachi).

Vieles gemeinsam hat der alte- und mittelalterliche Nahe Osten auch in der Ausbeutungsform. In beiden Fällen haben wir es mit den Rechtsverhältnissen der freien Produzenten zu tun, die durch viele verschiedene Verpflichtungen dem Staat gegenüber belastet waren: Steuern, gesellschaftlicher Anteil an Bau- und Bewässerungsarbeiten, Wehrpflicht in der Landswehr. Letztere wird, im Gegensatz zum Altertum, in der mittelalterlichen Epoche besonders eng mit dem staatlich bedingten Landbesitz verbunden, obgleich auch im Altertum dieser Umstand anzutreffen ist (siehe z.B. die Kriegslehenverhältnisse in Babylonien in der Epoche Hammurabis usw.)

Eine besonders verbreitete Form der Ausbeutung im alten- sowie im mittelalterlichen Osten war die staatliche Steuerpflicht. Ausserdem wurden die Bauern im Osten (insbesondere im Kalifat) zum Bau von Kanälen und deren Instandhaltung, zum Bau neuer Wege und zur Ausbesserung alter, zum Brücken-, Festungs- und Städtebau und zum Bau von Befestigungsmauern verpflichtet. Die Bauern mussten diese Arbeiten mit eigenen Arbeitsgeräten und auf Kosten eigener Verpflegung verrichten. Die Exploitation der führenden produzierenden Klasse geschah im Osten überwiegend durch den Staat.

Allerdings war dem Osten die unmittelbare Abhängigkeit des Produzenten gegenüber seinem Herrn nicht unbekannt, aber im allgemeinen ist hier eine Form vertreten, die von den Forschern als staatlicher, (bürokratischer) Feudalismus charakterisiert wird.

Obgleich wir hier hauptsächlich mit dem Fakt der juristischen Vollberechtigung der gemeinen Gessellschaftsmitglieder konfrontiert werden, ist für beide Epochen das Phänomen der "allgemeinen Sklaverei" bekannt, das seine

Auswirkung in vielen Erscheinungen des gesellschaftlichen Lebens fand. Ausdruck der grenzenlosen Staatskontrolle war, unter anderem, auch in den Ländern des Ostens, die Umsiedlungsbeschränkung, in einigen Fällen das direkte Verbot für den unmittelbaren Produzenten, das jedoch nicht mit der Leibeigenschaft verglichen werden kann. Akademiker W. Barthold stellte ganz richtig fest, dass der Osten, insbesondere die "muselmanische Welt" keine Leibeigenschaft kannte.

Meistens lebten die "Besitzer" der Bauern in der Stadt und führten keine eigenen Wirtschaften. Sie sammelten die Abgaben mit Hilfe von Verwaltern und Steuereinnehmern, nicht selten durch Steuerpächter. Diese privilegierten Personen bekamen vom Staat begrenzte Rechte auf die Produzenten. Im "Siaset Name" des berühmten Nisam u'l Mulk (11. Jahrh.) lesen wir z.B.: "Die Mukta die ein Ikta besitzen sollen wissen, dass sie dem Volk (Bauern) gegenüber keinerlei Anrechte haben, ausser der Einnahme der Steuerabgaben, wozu sie beauftragt wurden; nach den Abgaben soll das Volk in Sicherheit leben an Leib, Eigentum, Frau und Kindern, in Sicherheit sollen sein ihre Besitzungen, kein Weg soll den Mukta zu ihnen führen. Wenn jemand aus dem Volke zu Hof geht, um zu klagen, soll er unbehelligt bleiben. Jedem, der anders handelt, sollen die Hände abgehauen werden, seine Ikta soll konfisziert und er soll bestraft werden, den anderen zum Schrecken."

In einem bestimmten Abhängigkeitsverhältnis befand sich im Osten auch die Stadtbevölkerung (Kaufleute, Handwerker). Sie führten verschiedene Verpflichtungen aus und zahlten hohe Steuern. Ihnen wurde der Unterhalt einer gewaltigen Armee und eines verzweigten zentralen und örtlichen Verwaltungsapparates aufgebürdet. Auch im städtischen Leben und Handel wird eine bestimmte Parallelität des alten- und mittelalterlichen Ostens festgestellt. In beiden Fällen existierte eine strenge Kontrolle von Seiten des bürokratischen Staatsapparates über diese Tätigkeitssphäre. Die Östlichen, mittelalterlichen Städte übertrafen um einiges die Bewohneranzahl der ihr zeitgenossischen europäischen Städte (in einigen Städten des 10. Jahrh. überstieg die Einwohnerzahl Hunderttausend) und der Handel hatte, im Vergleich zu Europa, ein ungeheures Ausmass. Aus einer ganzen Reihe von Umständen heraus entbehrten diese Städte, im Gegensatz zu dem europäischen, den antifeudalen Charakter, Kraft dessen sie nicht zu einer inneren gesellschaftlichen Vorwärtsentwicklung, einer neuen sozial-ökonomischen Formation - dem Kapitalismus - gelangen konnten. Im Unterschied zu Europa, konnte sich die handelnde und handwerkstreibende Bevölkerung der östlichen Städte, nie von der Kontrolle seitens der feudal-bürokratischen Aristokratie befreien. Die östlichen Städte befanden sich in der Regel unter der Kontrolle der herrschenden Aristokratie, was ein zusätzliches Hindernis für die Entwicklung der Produktivkräfte war. Der Kontakt der regierenden Aristokratie mit den Grosskaufleuten und dem Karawanenhandel schloss eine Gegenüberstellung von Kaufleuten zur Feudalaristokratie aus. Es ist bekannt, dass die weltliche- und kirchliche Aristokratie der Länder des Nahen Ostens z.Z. der Mongolenherrschaft eng mit dem Karawanen-Transit-Handel verbunden war. Im Mongolenstaat handelten die Kaufleute oft mit Hilfe des Kapitals der Aristokratie und zahlten ihr einen Teil des Gewinns. Selbst die mongolischen Chane standen mit einer Reihe von muselmanischen Handelskampagnen in Verbindung. Die reichgewordenen Kaufleute bemühten sich, in die Aristokratie aufzusteigen, was ihnen auch nicht selten gelang. Die grossen Handelskampagnen pachteten oft vom Staat die Steuereinnahmen ganzer Gebiete, Städte usw.

Eine Parallele des alten- und mittelalterlichen Ostens kann auch in Beziehung auf den Charakter der herrschenden Schicht gezogen werden. In beiden

Fällen ist Letztere durch den staatlich-bürokratischen Apparat vertreten, in dem die Hierarchie hauptsächlich nach dem Platz der einflussreichen Beziehungen zum Obersten Regenten (König-Despot) bestimmt wird. Nach vorhandenem Material urteilend, kann festgestellt werden, dass in der mittelalterlichen Epoche des Ostens die organisatorische Funktion des Staates im wirtschaftlichen Leben der Gesellschaft erschwacht und das sie mehr und mehr ein Mittel zur Ausplünderung eigener oder fremder Bevölkerung in den Händen der Aristokratie wird und einen immer grösseren parasitären Charakter aufweist. Das bedeutet allerdings nicht, dass in der mittelalterlichen Epoche die Staatsmacht im Nahen Osten ihre führende Rolle in der Wirtschaftstätigkeit aufgibt. Bekannt ist z.B., dass während der Abbasidenherrschaft im arabischen Kalifat besondere Aufmerksamkeit dem Bau von neuen Kanälen und deren Instandhaltung geschenkt wurde.

Ausserdem muss festgestellt werden, dass in Altertum sowie im Mittelalter des Nahen Ostens die Sklaverei von grosser Bedeutung war. Entsprechende Fakten sind gut bekannt. In einigen Ländern war besonders in der frühmittelalterlichen Epoche die Sklaverei nicht weniger verbreitet als im Altertum.

Im altertümlichen Osten wurde die Sklavenarbeit im Prozess der Produktion von materiellen Gütern natürlich intensiver ausgenutzt als im mittelalterlichen Osten, wo die Sklavenarbeit hauptsächlich in der Sphäre der Bedienung und in Form einer Sklavengarde Anwendung fand. Zeitweise wurden die Sklaven allerdings auch im Mittelalter z.B. im Kalifat ausgenützt, im Bewässerungssystem, auf den Baumwollplantagen, in den Bergwerken, bei der Sumpftrockenlegung, bei der Salzgewinnung, im Handwerk und in der Wirtschaft. Die Aristokratie verfügte in dieser Zeit über Tausende von Sklaven, obgleich bekanntlich, die zahlreichen Gefangenen der Araber hauptsächlich zu Staatssklaven wurden. Es gab so viel Sklaven, dass die Forscher die Sklavenformation zur Z. der Omaiden als die herrschende Formation bezeichneten. Dasselbe ist charakteristisch für die Herrschaftsperiode der Il-Chanen im Iran. Es gab zahlreiche Sklaven-Handwerker, die in Grosswerkstätten arbeiteten und die dem Staat oder den Chanen gehörten. (Handwerkliche Staatswerkstätten existierten schon im Kalifat wärend der Abbasiden, allerdings waren dort abhängige Handwerker beschäftigt.)

Bei aller Ähnlichkeit der sozial-ökonomischen und staatlichen Ordnung im alten- und mittelalterlichen Osten, muss unterstrichen werden, dass in der mittelalterlichen Gesellschaft des Nahen Ostens der Prozess der Feudalisierung im Unterschied zum altorientalischen, einen grossen Aufschwung nahm und in einzelnen Fällen zur Bildung von ziemlich hochfeudalisierten Gesellschaften führte.

Schon im Kalifat entwickelte sich ziemlich schnell eine bedingte Feudaleigentumsform - das "Ikta" (arabisch: Bodenparzelle), das den Dienenden auf Lebensdauer oder zeitweilig verliehen wurde. Im 10. Jahrh. wuchsen in Iran auf Kosten der Staats- und Tempelländereien sehr intensiv bedingte Feudalbesitze - Ikta, die allmählich in Erbbesitze übergingen. Dieser Übergang der freien Gemeindemitglieder in Feudale, abhängige Bauern, ging durch das Patronat vonstatten. Nach der Eroberung durch die Seldschuken war die Verleihung der Ikta durch die Sultanen an die Nomadenaristokratie weit verbreitet. Es wurden nicht nur Dörfer sondern ganze Provinzen mit Städten vergeben. Obgleich das Ikta juristisch noch kein Erbbesitz war, erkämpfte die Aristokratie die Sanktion des grössten Teils der Ämter mit den dazugehörigen Ländereien in Erblehen. Im 14. Jahrh. bildete und im 15. Jhrh. entwickelte sich bemerkbar eine höhere Form des Feudaleigentums in Osten, das sogenannte "sojurgal" heraus, das die Steuer-, Administrations- und Gerichtsimmunität in sich einbeschloss, jedoch bald durch die Einfälle neuer Nomadenvölker in seiner Entwicklung aufgehalten wurde.

Mit der Schwächung des Staats macht sich nach dem 11. Jahrh. in Ägypten ein spezifisches Wachstum des Ikta, auf Kosten der Staatsländereien, bemerkbar. Sie wurden anfangs nur vorübergehend an die Militärränge verliehen, verblieben später aber praktisch als Erblehen. Ende des 13. Jahrh. eroberten die Emire einen grossen Teil des Ikta von gemeinen Kriegern. Später, während der Mameluken befanden sich die Bauern (Fellachen) faktisch in einem Sklavenverhältnis zu den Iktabesitzern.

Anderseits erreicht der Feudalstand in der mittelalterlichen Epoche des Nahen Ostens einen grösseren Aufschwung im Vergleich zum Altertum. Zurückgehalten wurde dieser Prozess der Feudalisierung durch fortwährende Einfälle der Nomadenvölker und anderer Eroberer, was zur "Erneuerung" der herrschenden Schicht führte und zu einer Neuaufteilung des Länderfonds, wodurch der Feudalstand der gegebenen Gesellschaft stark herabgesetzt wurde.

Die Herrschaft der Nomadenvölker beeinträchtigte stark den Prozess der Feudalisierung. In den grössten Oststaaten (im Sassaniden-Iran, Arabischen Kalifat, Türkenstaat der Seldschuken, Mongolenimperium und Tamerlan(Timur Lenk)-imperium, im Turkmenenstaat, im Kisilbaschenstaat und Osmanenstaat) stossen wir auf periodische Neuverteilungen des Landfondes zu Gunsten der Eroberer.

Resultat der Nomadeneinfälle und ihrer Herrschaft war die Neuverteilung der Ländereien zu Gunsten der militärischen Nomadenaristokratie. Solche Neuverteilungen waren natürlich ein Hindernis für die Entwicklung der feudalischen Eigentumsformen, da die Nomadenvölker im allgemeinen an der Erhaltung des Landstaatseigentums interessiert waren.

Während der arabischen Eroberungen gingen die Länder der Sassaniden-Königen, sowie der im Krieg gefallenen Dekchanen (begüterte Landbesitzer), in die Hände der Araber über. Der grösste Teil der Länder Iraks, Syriens und Ägyptens wurde zu Staatseigentum erklärt und die ehemalig auf diesen Ländereien anwesenden Bauern, wurden zu erblichen Pächtern und mit Landsteuern belegt. In der 2. Hälfte des 13. Jahrh. wurde im ilchanischen Iran eine Neuverteilung der Ländereien diesmal zu Gunsten der Mongolenkrieger, vorgenommen. Nach den Mongoleneroberungen fielen zahlreiche Länder, bisher der hiesigen Aristokratie angehörend, und den dazugehörenden Bauern zuerst dem Staat zu, später (Anfang d. 14. Jahrh.) in die Hände der mongolisch-türkischen Militärnomadenaristokratie die Ikta- oder Mulkaanrecht besassen und an die muselmanischen religiösen Institutionen.

Uns scheint, dass alles Obenangeführte, für die Parallelität und Nachfolge der sozial-ökonomischen und staatlichen Ordnungen im alten und mittelalterlichen Osten, spricht. Es ist nicht möglich, die Entwicklung der Gesellschaften des Ostens,ähnlich wie in Europa, in den Rahmen zwei verschiedener sozial-ökonomischer Formationen (Altertum-"Sklaverei", Mittelalter-"Feudalismus") zu zwängen. Im Grossen und Ganzen, muss die Geschichte des Ostens im Rahmen der allmählichen Entwicklung der Feudalverhältnisse, angefangen vom Protofeudalismus, charakteristisch für das Altertum, bis zum eigentlichen Frühfeudalismus des Mittelalters betrachtet werden.

---

1 Siehe G.A. Melikischwili, *Quelques aspects du régime socio-economique des sociétés anciennes du Proche-Orient*, in *Acta Antiqua Academiae Scientiarum Hungaricae* XXII [1974] 79-90; die Ausführlichere Variante des Vortrages wurde in der Zeitschrift *Vestnik Drevnei Istorii*, 1975 Nr 2, veröffentlicht: G.A. Melikischwili, *Einige Aspekte zu Fragen der sozial-ökonomischen Formen in der alten Gesellschaft des Nahen Ostens* (russisch).

GOLD, SILBER UND BLEI ALS WERTMESSER IN MESOPOTAMIEN WÄHREND DER ZWEITEN HÄLFTE DES 2. JAHRTAUSENDS v.u.Z.

Manfred Müller (Leipzig – DDR)

Im Verlauf der Geschichte Mesopotamiens während der Epoche der altorientalischen Klassengesellschaft haben nach- und zum Teil nebeneinander verschiedene Metalle die Funktion des vorherrschenden oder allgemeinen Äquivalents im Warenaustausch gespielt. Für die frühesten Perioden fehlen vorläufig sichere Anhaltspunkte. Erst die Urkunden der sog. Fāra-Zeit bezeugen, daß sich im südlichen Mesopotamien etwa um die Mitte des 26. Jahrhunderts v.u.Z.[1] als Wertmesser und vorherrschendes Zahlungsmittel ein bestimmtes Metall, das Kupfer, durchgesetzt hatte.[2] Nach der "Fāra-Zeit" wurde das Kupfer in den genannten Funktionen bald durch das Silber abgelöst,[3] das dann in der Zeit des Reiches von Akkade (etwa 2340-2198 v.u.Z.) als wohl schon allgemeines[4] und während der Zeit der 3. Dynastie von Ur (2111-2003 v.u.Z.)[5] zumindest als vorherrschendes Äquivalent fungierte. Auch in der 1. Hälfte des 2. Jahrtausends v.u.Z. war Silber die Grundlage der Wertmessung im mesopotamischen Warenaustausch. Das änderte sich um die Mitte des 2. Jahrtausends als Silber in der Funktion des allgemeinen oder vorherrschenden Äquivalents in Babylonien und Assyrien, nicht aber im Osttigrisgebiet (Arrapḫe), durch andere Metalle ersetzt wurde.

Die weitgehende Ablösung des Silbers als Wertmesser in Mesopotamien während der zweiten Hälfte des 2. Jahrtausends v.u.Z. war bedingt durch die großen Umwälzungen in Vorderasien während des "dunklen Zeitalters"[6] um 1500 v.u.Z. und die damit verbundenen ökonomischen und politischen Veränderungen und erheblichen Verschiebungen im Fernhandel. Mit dem Wiederbeginn der schriftlichen Überlieferung im 15./14. Jh. v.u.Z. gibt es in Mesopotamien mehrere lokale "Währungen" nebeneinander.

Im südlichen Mesopotamien, dem kassitischen Babylonien, diente Gold als Verrechnungsmittel im Warenaustausch.[7] So ist z.B. in Mobiliarkaufurkunden gewöhnlich der Wert der Ware zu Beginn, in der Verkaufserklärung, in Gold angegeben. Die Kaufpreiszahlung erfolgte jedoch zumeist in Naturalien (insbesondere Gerste), Vieh und Sachwerten (u.a. Textilien und Metallwerkzeuge), gelegentlich aber auch unmittelbar in Gold.[8] Wenn sich der Kaufpreis dabei aus mehreren Warenarten (z.B. verschiedenen Naturalien, Textilien usw.) zusammensetzte, ist bei jedem Posten der Wert in Gold einzeln vermerkt. Diese Wertangaben wurden anschließend addiert; die Summe entspricht dann dem in der Regel zuvor genannten Wert der verkauften Ware.[9] Auch in anderen Urkundengattungen sind Wertäquivalenzangaben in Gold geläufig.[10]

Wie vor allem neuere Textpublikationen zeigen, ist Gold allerdings nicht, wie bisher allgemein angenommen,[11] die alleinige Grundlage der Warenverrechnung im kassitischen Babylonien gewesen. Neben Gold ist auch Silber als Wertmesser verwendet worden. Teils fungiert es in Kaufurkunden und bei anderen Preisangaben in der gleichen Weise wie Gold als alleiniger Wertmesser,[12] teils ergänzend zu Wertangaben in Gold als Wertmaß für kleinere Beträge.[13] Das erlaubt, von einem gewissen "Währungsdualismus" zu sprechen: einer dominierenden, möglicherweise "offiziellen" "Goldwährung"[14] und einem in seiner Bedeutung hinter der Goldwährung deutlich zurücktretenden, aber offenbar - wie die Belege aus Ur, Nippur und Dūr-Kurigalzu zeigen - im ganzen Land verbreiteten, teils subsidiären Gebrauch von Silber als Wertmesser. Nicht zu entscheiden ist allerdings bisher die Frage, ob es sich dabei um ein eingeschränktes Weiterleben der altbabylonischen "Silberwährung" handelt oder um ein Wiedereindringen der Wertmessung in Silber erst in der späteren Kassitenzeit. Für letzteres könnte sprechen, daß Silber als Wertmesser erst in Urkunden ab Kadašman-Enlil II. (1263-1255) belegt ist.[15] In Anbetracht der relativ geringen Zahl von publizierten Rechtsurkunden aus dem Jahrhundert vor Kadašman-Enlil II. mag das Fehlen von Belegen für die Wertmessung in Silber schon für diese Zeit jedoch dem Zufall der Überlieferung geschuldet sein. Die Ablösung des Goldes als des vorherrschenden Äquivalents durch Silber vollzog sich in Babylonien während des 12. Jh. v.u.Z., vermutlich ausgelöst durch den verheerenden Einfall der Elamiter und das Ende der Kassitendynastie um die Mitte dieses Jahrhunderts. Im 11. Jh. jedenfalls hatte sich das Silber als vorherrschendes oder allgemeines Äquivalent in Babylonien wieder durchgesetzt.[16]

Beim gleichzeitigen Gebrauch der beiden Wertmesser Gold und Silber im kassitischen Babylonien ist deren Wertrelation zueinander von besonderer Bedeutung. W.F. Leemans (RLA 3 [1957-71] 512) und G. Wilhelm (Bagh. Mitt. 7 [1974] 205) neigten einer Gold-Silber-Relation von 1:3 bis 1:4 zu, hielten eine sichere Bestimmung dieses Verhältnisses damals aber für nicht nachweisbar.[17] Eine Möglichkeit, das Wertverhältnis von Gold zu Silber sicher zu bestimmen, bieten jedoch die zahlreichen, durch neuere Publikationen wesentlich vermehrten Wertangaben von Textilien in Gold bzw. in Silber, die sich insgesamt durch eine hohe Preiskonstanz über eine längere Periode und in den verschiedenen Orten, aus denen mittelbabylonische Urkunden bekanntgeworden sind, auszeichnen. Eine vergleichende Übersicht der Gold- und Silberpreise von drei verschiedenen Gewandarten mag dies verdeutlichen:

1 ^{túg}*muḫtillû* = 1 Sekel Gold (*Iraq* 11 [1949] 145, Nr. 5,9; UET VII 34, Rs. 4f.; 35, 1-3; MSKH 1, Nr. 9,9) = 4 Sekel Silber (UET VII 29,4).[18]

1 ^{túg}*naḫlaptu*(GÚ.È) = ½ Sekel Gold(PBS 2/2, 27,9; UET VII, 25, 15) = 2 Sekel Silber (TuM NF 5, 38 [= H. Petschow, MRWH 5], 12; BBSt 7 I 24 [nachkassitisch]; 27, Rs. 5′ [nachkassitisch]).

1 TÚG *kabru* = ½ Sekel Gold (PBS 2/2, 27, 10; *Iraq* 11 [1949] 144, Nr. 4, 32f.) = 2 Sekel Silber (BE 14, 128a,9).

Diese Wertangaben bezeugen für die mittelbabylonische Zeit eine Gold-Silber-Relation von 1:4.

Im Unterschied zu Babylonien ist die Situation im Bereich der Wertmessung in Nordmesopotamien während der zweiten Hälfte des 2. Jahrtausends v.u.Z. vielfältiger und bisher noch weniger eindeutig bestimmt. Die Quellenlage erlaubt es, die entsprechenden Verhältnisse in zwei Staaten dieser Region zu untersuchen, in Assyrien und im hurritischen Staat Arrapḫe im Osttigrisgebiet.

In Assyrien diente als Zahlungsmittel, wie die zeitgenössischen Immobiliar- und Sklavenkaufurkunden[19] ausweisen, das meist logographisch geschriebene Metall AN.NA = *annuku* (früher als Blei, heute allgemein als Zinn gedeutet[20]). Auch Darlehen wurden überwiegend in diesem Metall, gefolgt von Gerste, und nur gelegentlich in Silber, Vieh oder anderen Waren gewährt.[21] In den mittelassyrischen Gesetzen[22] wird zum Ausdruck von Wertangaben und -maßstäben[23] und bei der Festlegung der Höhe von "Geld"strafen[24] ausschließlich das Metall AN.NA verwendet. Das beweist, daß dieses Metall zu jener Zeit in Assyrien nicht nur das geläufige Zahlungsmittel, sondern auch der allgemeine Wertmesser war. Silber spielte dagegen nur eine untergeordnete Rolle im Zahlungsverkehr. Es begegnet, wie erwähnt, hin und wieder als Darlehensobjekt[25] und als - wohl traditionelle - Vertragsstrafe in Urkunden des Personenrechts.[26] In den mittelassyrischen Gesetzen wird es als Metall - jeweils in syllabischer Schreibung als *ṣarpu* - nur dreimal erwähnt, als möglicher Bestandteil des Brautgeschenks (*zubullû*)[27] und als (alternatives?) Zahlungsmittel neben AN.NA in zerstörtem Kontext.[28] In der logographischen Schreibung KÙ.BABBAR wird es in den Gesetzen dagegen nicht für Silber als Metall, sondern stets im Sinne von "'Geld', Wert(betrag, -gegenstände)" gebraucht.[29] Gold ist selten und nur in kleinen Mengen als Gegenstand von Schuldurkunden[30] und ausnahmsweise einmal als Vertragsstrafe[31] belegt.

Die Identität des Metalls AN.NA = *annaku* schien bisher - vor allem durch die betreffende Untersuchung von B. Landsberger[32] - generell als Zinn gesichert zu sein. Doch *the adventures of the vocable annaku* haben mit der erwähnten Studie von Landsberger noch kein Ende gefunden. Der von H. Freydank in dieser Festschrift publizierte Text VAT 18062 ermöglicht eine überraschende Neubestimmung von AN.NA für die mittelassyrische Zeit.[33] VAT 18062 ist in unserem Zusammenhang vor allem in zweierlei Hinsicht von grundlegender Bedeutung:

1. In Anmerkung 27 seines Beitrags weist H. Freydank auf den methodisch einzig erfolgversprechenden Weg zur sicheren Bestimmung von AN.NA als Zinn oder Blei in den verschiedenen Perioden der altmesopotamischen Geschichte hin: Die Bedeutung von AN.NA ist "aus dem Preisgefüge der Zeit" abzuleiten. Die Grundlage dafür bieten für die mittelassyrische Zeit jetzt die Preisangaben in dem Text VAT 18062, der zwischen AN.NA BABBAR "Zinn" und AN.NA bzw. AN.NA *a-ba-ru* "Blei" unterscheidet und die Zinn-Blei-Relation mit 1:15 angibt (Rs. 11'f., vgl. 17'). H. Freydank betont in dieser Anmerkung auch bereits die Bedeutung des aus Z. 17'f. ableitbaren Preises für einen Sklaven in Höhe von 4 Talenten und 30 Minen Blei, verweist auf den annähernd identischen vorläufigen[34] Kaufpreis einer Frau in KAJ 168 (4 Talente, 20 Minen AN.NA) und zieht daraus vorsichtig den Schluß, daß AN.NA in mittelassyrischen Texten wohl nicht mit "Zinn" zu übersetzen ist. Das läßt sich durch weitere Preisvergleiche erhärten. So schwankt der Wert von Menschen zwischen 3 Talenten und 30 Minen AN.NA (Wertäquivalent für eine verheiratete Frau)[35] und 4 Talenten AN.NA (Wert einer Sklavin)[36] in den mittelassyrischen Gesetzen und 5[37], 6[38] und 7[39] Talenten AN.NA in den Rechtsurkunden dieser Zeit. Die genannten Beträge, die sich um den Sklavenpreis von VAT 18062, Rs. 17'f. bewegen, in den Gesetzen etwas niedriger und in den Urkunden etwas höher liegen, zeigen, daß AN.NA hier nicht Zinn, sondern nur Blei bedeuten kann. Diese Feststellung gilt generell für AN.NA in der Funktion als allgemeines Äquivalent und als Zahlungsmittel in Assyrien während der zweiten Hälfte des 2. Jahrtausends v.u.Z.[40]

2. Die Angaben des Textes VAT 18062 zeigen, daß als Zahlungsmittel im Fernhandel Bronze und Zinn dienten, Blei hingegen nur Grundlage der innerassyrischen Wertverrechnung war, also eine Art "Binnenwährung" darstellte.

Darüberhinaus könnte die Formulierung der Angabe der Wertverhältnisse von Bronze bzw. Zinn zu Blei (Rs. 12' und 15': 12./15.TA.ÀM *ana* AN.NA *sasû* "(auf eine Gewichtseinheit Bronze bzw. Zinn) sind bezüglich Blei je 12 bzw. 15 (Gewichtseinheiten) 'ausgerufen'") auf eine öffentliche Proklamation,[41] also eine amtliche Festsetzung der betreffenden Wertrelationen hindeuten.

In dem hurritischen, von Mitanni abhängigen Staat von Arrapḫe (15./14. Jh. v.u.Z.), dessen wirtschaftliche Verhältnisse vor allem durch die reichen Urkundenfunde in Nuzi beleuchtet werden, diente Silber als Wertmesser und Verrechnungsmittel im Warenaustausch.[42] Zahlungsmittel waren vor allem Gerste, Klein- und Großvieh, Kupfer, Zinn, Bronze, Textilien und Silber.[43] Die Funktion des Silbers als Wertmesser spiegelt sich u.a. in Mobiliarkaufurkunden wider. Wenn in diesen der Kaufpreis aus verschiedenen Warenarten bestand, war eine ähnliche Preisaufstellung wie in den entsprechenden mittelbabylonischen Kaufverträgen üblich: Die einzelnen Warenarten wurden unter Angabe der Menge und oft auch der Qualität angeführt, anschließend wurde der Wert der Waren meist zu einem Preis in Silber summiert.[44] Im Unterschied zu den mittelbabylonischen Urkunden fehlen allerdings in der Regel die Angabe des Kaufpreises in der einleitenden Verkaufserklärung und Wertangaben bei den einzelnen Posten.[45]

Ein instruktives Dokument für den Gebrauch von Silber als Verrechnungsmittel ist der Text HSS XIV 37. Er enthält Z. 1-12 eine Aufstellung über zu leistende Zahlungen von 11 Personen in unterschiedlicher Höhe, die in Sekel Silber angegeben sind und den Gesamtbetrag von 40 Sekel Silber (Z. 13) ergeben. Dieser Betrag ist Äquivalent (Ersatzleistung?) für eine Sklavin (Z. 14). Die darauf folgende Angabe der verbindlichen Umrechnungskurse von Zinn und Bronze in Silber (Z. 15-17) zeigt, daß die zuvor genannten Silberbeträge in erster Linie die Verrechnungsgrundlage für die zu erbringenden Leistungen der einzelnen Personen darstellen, die Zahlungsweise aber offenlassen.

In der jüngeren assyriologischen Literatur ist zum Ausdruck gebracht worden, daß in den Urkunden aus Nuzi neben Silber gelegentlich auch Gold als Verrechnungsmittel fungiere.[46] Dies geschah jedoch nur ganz ausnahmsweise.[47] Die allgemeine Verrechnungsgrundlage in Arrapḫe war das Silber. Das beweisen vor allem die Fälle, wo Gold in Silber als das allgemeine Äquivalent umgerechnet wird. So sind in JEN 492, 12-14 5 Sekel Gold, 1 Talent Kupfer, 1 *allūru*-Gewand und 1 Rind zu einem Wert von 95 Sekel Silber summiert. Besonders aufschlußreich ist dafür der Kreditkaufvertrag HSS XIX 127[48], in dem angegeben ist, daß 3 Sekel Gold, der kreditierte Kaufgegenstand, auf der Verrechnungsgrundlage von 27 Sekel Silber[49] in Zinn oder Gerste zu bezahlen sind. Als Zahlungsmittel ist Gold jedoch mehrfach belegt.[50]

Neben Silber als der allgemeinsten Grundlage der Wertmessung und -verrechnung waren im Staat Arrapḫe in bestimmten Bereichen noch traditionelle Wertmessungen in Gebrauch. Dies gilt z.B. für die häufige Bemessung der Höhe des "Brautpreises" (*terḫatu*) mit 1 Rind, 1 Esel, 10 Schafe und 10 Sekel Silber, was einem Wert von 40 Sekel Silber entspricht. Daß es sich dabei um eine traditionelle Wertmessung handelt, deren Leistung auch in anderer Form erfolgen kann, belegt der Text HSS V 79: Der "Brautpreis" wird darin mit 40 Sekel Silber beziffert (Z. 6), dann aber festgelegt, daß der Vater des Bräutigams 36 Minen Zinn anstelle des Rindes, 24 Minen Zinn anstelle des Esels, 10 Schafe und 10 Sekel Silber zu zahlen habe.[51] In dieser Urkunde erfolgt die Wertangabe zwar in Silber, als Grundlage der Berechnung der für einen Teil der "Kauf"summe zu liefernden Zinnmengen dient dann aber die traditionelle Art der Bemessung des "Brautpreises". So ist Silber in Arrapḫe zwar schon allgemeines, aber noch nicht ausschließlich benutztes Äquivalent.

Die Untersuchung hat gezeigt, daß in der zweiten Hälfte des 2. Jahrtausends v.u.Z. in Mesopotamien zu gleicher Zeit drei verschiedene Metalle als vorherrschendes oder allgemeines Äquivalent im Warenaustausch innerhalb der einzelnen Staaten in Gebrauch waren: Gold (neben Silber) in Babylonien, Blei in Assyrien und Silber in Arrapḫe. Nach der Dominanz des Silbers als Wertmesser in Mesopotamien seit der präsargonischen Zeit ist diese Aufsplitterung in verschiedene "Währungen" eine Folge der Umwälzungen um die Mitte des zweiten Jahrtausends v.u.Z. in Mesopotamien: dem endgültigen Eindringen und der politischen Machtübernahme der Kassiten in Babylonien und der Hurriter in weiten Gebieten Nordmesopotamiens, dem damit verbundenen politischen und wirtschaftlichen Verfall Babyloniens und Assyriens, der Verlagerung des politischen Schwergewichts im alten Vorderasien nach dem Norden (Hethiter, Mitanni, Nordsyrien) und dem zeitweiligen weitgehenden Zusammenbruch des Fernhandels. Am auffallendsten ist die - im alten Vorderasien singuläre - Durchsetzung oder Einführung des Bleis als allgemeines Äquivalent in Assyrien. Erstaunlich ist weiterhin, daß diese

Art der Wertmessung erhalten blieb, als Assyrien wieder erstarkte und sich politisch und ökonomisch in die vorderasiatische Staatenwelt integrierte. Daß Blei auch noch zu dieser Zeit in Assyrien als allgemeines Äquivalent und dominierendes Zahlungsmittel in der Binnenwirtschaft diente und zur innerstaatlichen Verrechnung des Warenaustauschs im Fernhandel benutzt wurde, ist wohl nicht nur allgemein als Beharren an der Tradition zu erklären, sondern möglicherweise auch eine Folge staatlicher Regulierungen.

Die Rückkehr zur "Silberwährung" vollzog sich in Mesopotamien schrittweise: in Babylonien im Zusammenhang mit den Erschütterungen gegen Ende des 2. Jahrtausends v.u.Z. und dem Zusammenbruch der Kassitenherrschaft, in Assyrien wesentlich später, wohl erst gegen Ende des 8. Jh. v.u.Z.[52]

AoF = *Altorientalische Forschungen* [Berlin]

MRWH = H. Petschow, *Mittelbabylonische Rechts- und Wirtschaftsurkunden der Hilprecht-Sammlung Jena* [Berlin 1974]

MSKH = J.A. Brinkman, *Materials and Studies for Kassite History* [Chicago 1976-]

MVN = *Materiali per il vocabulario neosumerico* [Roma 1974-]

SR = D.O. Edzard, *Sumerische Rechtsurkunden des III. Jahrtausends aus der Zeit vor der III. Dynastie von Ur* [München 1968]

TSŠ = R. Jestin, *Tablettes sumériennes de Šuruppak* [Paris 1937]

---

1 Zum Problem der Datierung der "Fāra-Zeit" vgl. zuletzt W.W. Hallo, in Or. NS 42 [1973] 228-235. - Meinem Kollegen J. Oelsner bin ich für Unterstützung bei der Literaturbeschaffung und Überlassung von Transliterationen (UET VII) zu Dank verpflichtet.

2 Vgl. die Kursangaben von Gerste in Kupfer in den Urkunden A. Deimel, Fara III, 31 (=D.O. Edzard, SR 23) I 3f. und R. Jestin, TSŠ Nr. X (=SR 1), IX. In den Immobiliarurkunden aus Fāra und der En-ḫegal-Tafel (vgl. die Bearbeitungen in D.O. Edzard, SR; J. Krecher, ZA 63 [1974] 145ff. und G. und W. Farber, WO 8 [1975/76] 178-184) dominiert Kupfer gegenüber Silber als Zahlungsmittel etwa im Verhältnis 3:1 aller bezeugten Käufe. Vgl. auch H. Limet, *Métal*, 32, 46f.

3 Für die entsprechenden Verhältnisse im präsargonischen Lagaš vgl. z.B. W.F. Leemans, in RLA 4 [1972-75] 79. Der Wert von Waren wird in dieser Zeit überwiegend in Silber (vgl. DP 32 [= D.O. Edzard, SR 32] I 6′-II 1; 513 [= M. Lambert, in RA 47 [1953] 60f.]; Nikolski 230 VII [= RA 47, 116f.]; 293 [= RA 47, 66f.]; 300 [= RA 47, 114f.]), teilweise aber auch in Gerste (vgl. DP 332 [= RA 47, 66f.]; VS 14, 183 V [= RA 47, 114f.]; I.J. Gelb, MAD 4, 153 I 5 [= J. Krecher, in ZA 63 [1974] 222]) angegeben. Als Zahlungsmittel ist Silber im präsargonischen Lagaš geläufig, auch bereits bei Pachtzinszahlungen und gewissen Abgabeleistungen z.B. der Hirten. Bei Kaufpreiszahlungen in Gerste ist z.T. der jeweilige Umrechnungskurs von Gerste in Silber als Wertmesser angegeben (vgl. DP 31 [= SR 31] VI 1-3; Or. NS 42 [1973] 236 VIII 2-4).

4 Das bezeugen die in Silber ausgedrückten Kursangaben für Gerste, Datteln und Fett (vgl. G.G. Hackman, BIN 8, 39 [= SR 55], 2f. und 5; 169 [= SR 81], 9f.; 175 [= SR 54], 14f., 18-20; I.J. Gelb, MAD 4, 15, 2f. und 17f. [=

J. Krecher, in ZA 63 [1974] 247f.]; 151, 5 [= Krecher, a.a.O. 215]; D.I. Owen, MVN 3, 100, 13f.) sowie Wertangaben und Summationen in Silber bei Preiszahlungen in Form von Naturalien, Metallwerkzeugen oder Textilien (vgl. BIN 8,39 [= SR 55], 6-11.17.20; 172 [= SR 17], 2f.; 175 [= SR 54], 10f., 13b-22; 179 [= SR 18], 1f.). Vgl. auch B.R. Foster, in *Iraq* 39 [1977] 35f.

5 Vgl. M. Lambert, *L'usage de l'argent-métal à Lagash au temps de la IIIe dynastie d'Ur*, in RA 57 [1963] 79-92, 193-200; zur Rolle des Silbers als Wertäquivalent in der Ur III-Zeit zuletzt H. Neumann, in AoF 6 [1979] 39-41. Zur Funktion des Silbers als allgemeines Äquivalent in der folgenden altbabylonischen Periode vgl. W.F. Leemans, *Foreign Trade in the Old Babylonian Period* [Leiden 1960] 130f.

6 B. Landsberger, *Assyrische Königsliste und "dunkles Zeitalter"*, in JCS 8 [1954] 31-45, 47-73 und 106-133.

7 Vgl. D.O. Edzard, in JESHO 3 [1960] 39f. und 43; W.F. Leemans, in RLA 3 [1957-71] 509f.

8 Vgl. z.B. die von D.O. Edzard, in JESHO 3 [1960] 39 Anm. 1 und 40 mit Anm. 2 und 3 genannten Urkunden mit Zahlungen in Gold sowie I. Bernhardt, TuM NF V 66 (= H. Petschow, MRWH 1); O.R. Gurney, UET VII 41, 10ff.; 43 Rs. 8f.; Peiser, UDBD P117; PBS 8/2, 162.

9 Vgl. dazu z.B. die Sklavenkaufurkunden BE 14,7; UET VII 21; 22; 25.

10 Vgl. z.B. die *ṭuppi aḫuzzati Iraq* 11 [1949] 144 Nr.4; die *ṭuppi zununnê* ebd. 145 Nr.5; die Prozeßurkunde UET VII 10, 14-16.

11 Zuletzt W.F. Leemans, in RLA 4 [1972-75] 86a: "Der Wert der Waren wurde immer in Gold angegeben". S. auch oben Anm. 7.

12 Vgl. BE 14, 128a; *Iraq* 11 [1949] 148 Nr.11, 11-14; TuM NF V 71 (= H. Petschow, MRWH 3); 38 (= ebd. 5); UET VII 14; 29; 33.

13 Vgl. *Iraq* 11 [1949] 145 Nr. 5, 26f. (P[AP] 9 GÍN GUŠKIN *ù* 3 GÍN KÙ.BABBAR); UET VII 34, Rs. 6 (PAP 2 GÍN GUŠKIN 2 GÍN KÙ. [BABBAR]); 57, Rs. 4' f. (PAP 5 GÍN GUŠKIN 7 GÍ[N] KÙ.BABBAR 2 (PI) 3 (BÁN) ŠE.BAR). Nur ganz selten wird, wie in dem letztgenannten Beleg, auch Gerste als zusätzlicher oder ausnahmsweise selbständiger Wertmesser gebraucht. Vgl. dazu UDBD 95, 6f: Angabe des Wertes von zwei Gewändern in Gerste (1 ^{túg}*muḫ-til!-le-e reš!-tu*$_4$ *ki-i* 3 (GUR) ŠE.BAR, 1 ^{túg}GÚ!.È! SAL *reš-tu*$_4$ *ki-i* 3 (PI) 2 (BÁN) ŠE.BAR) und Summation dieser Wertangaben in Gerste zusammen mit einem Gersteposten (Z.5) zu einer Gerste-Gesamtsumme (Z.8). In UET VII 33 ist der Preis für eine Kuh in Höhe von 9 Sekel Silber mit zwei Gewändern im Wert von 8 Sekel Silber und - für den restlichen Sekel Silber - mit einem Tongefäß im Wert von 2 Scheffel (*pānu*) Gerste und einem ergänzenden Gerstebetrag beglichen worden.

14 Zur Frage der Herkunft des Gebrauchs von Gold als Wertmesser im kassitischen Babylonien s. D.O. Edzard, in JESHO 3 [1960] 45f.

15 TuM NF V 38 (=H. Petschow, MRWH 5): Kadašman-Enlil II., Jahr 2; 71 (=ebd. 3): Kudur-Enlil, Jahr 3. Vgl. auch D.O. Edzard, JESHO 3 [1960] 40 mit Anm. 6.

16 Wertäquivalenzangaben in Kudurrus dieser Zeit beziehen sich ausschließlich auf Silber, vgl. BBSt 7 I 15-27 (Zeit des Marduk-nādin-aḫḫī, 1099-1082 v.u.Z.); 27, Rs. 4'f. (Simbar-Šipak, 1025-1008); 9 II 35, III 11f.,

16-22, IV A 11-13, 14f. [Kursangabe von Gerste in Silber(!)] (Nabû-mukīn-apli, 978-943).

17 Vgl. auch W.F. Leemans, RA 60 [1966] 76. Der Versuch, die Wertrelationen von Gold zu Silber in mittelbabylonischer Zeit über Preisangaben für Gerste zu bestimmen (vgl. dazu H. Farber, JESHO 21 [1978] 6, Anm. 11), führt, auch bei umfassender Auswertung der vorhandenen Belege, wegen des schwankenden Gerstepreises und lokaler Preisunterschiede nur zu annähernden Ergebnissen. Die unlängst von M. Heltzer in *Iraq* 39 [1977] 205 postulierte Relation von 1:9, die sich offenbar auf RA 60 [1966] 75, 25′ gründet, beruht auf einem Irrtum: Z. 25′ enthält keine Gold-Silber-Relation, sondern die Einzelsummierungen der Gold- und der Silberspalte von Z. 22-24.

18 BBSt 7 I 23 [nachkassitisch] bietet: 2 túg*muḫ-til-lu-ú ki-i* 12 KÙ.BABBAR, also *1 muḫtillû*-Gewand für 6 Sekel Silber. Es ist jedoch nicht auszuschließen, daß der Steinmetz am Anfang der Zeile bei der Zahl der Kleider einen senkrechten Keil vergessen hat zu schreiben. In letzterem Falle würde 1 *muḫtillû*-Gewand ebenfalls 4 Sekel Silber kosten. Diese Emendation ist deshalb erwägenswert, weil bei einer anderen Gewandart (s. dazu oben im folgenden unter túg*naḫlaptu*) die kassitischen und nachkassitischen Preise exakt übereinstimmen.

19 Vgl. die von E. Ebeling, in MAOG VII 1/2 [1933] 57-85 bearbeiteten entsprechenden Urkunden aus Assur sowie TR 3004 (*Iraq* 30 [1968] Pl. LVIII).

20 Vgl. dazu die grundlegende Studie von B. Landsberger, *Tin and lead: The adventures of two vocables*, in JNES 24 [1965] 285-296. Von den Wörterbüchern verzeichnet AHw 49 [1959] "'Zinn' und wohl auch 'Blei'", CAD A/ii [1968] 127 ausschließlich "tin".

21 Vgl. z.B. die von M. David und E. Ebeling, *Assyrische Rechtsurkunden* [Stuttgart 1929] bearbeiteten Darlehensurkunden aus Assur (Nrn. 9-70). Die Verhältnisse in Tell ar-Rimāḥ (H.W.F. Saggs und D.J. Wiseman, in *Iraq* 30 [1968] 154-205) sind ähnlich; unter den Urkunden aus Tell Billa ist der Anteil der Gerste-Darlehen höher (J.J. Finkelstein, in JCS 7 [1953] 122-136, 148-168).

22 Vgl. G.R. Driver and J.C. Miles, *The Assyrian Laws* [Oxford 1935] [Texte A-J]; E. Weidner, in AfO 12 [1937-39] 46-54 mit Taf. III-VI [Texte K-O]; J.N. Postgate, in *Iraq* 35 [1973] 19-21 mit Taf. XII. Letzte zusammenfassende Einführung, Übersetzung und Kommentierung: G. Cardascia, *Les Lois assyriennes* [Paris 1969].

23 Text A §5, 59; 24, 58f.; B §7, 8′; C §1, 4′.

24 A §7, 76; 18, 81; 19, 92; 21, 102; 22, 110; 51, 86; B §9, 24′; C §8, 5′.

25 Vgl. KAJ 32; 39; 44; VAT 8878 (=David-Ebeling [Anm. 21] 14f.).

26 Vgl. z.B. KAJ 1, 26; 7, 15.

27 A §30, 37.

28 O Rs. II 4′f.

29 A §31, 46.49; 55, 34.39; 56, 46 (Zu §§55f. vgl. B. Landsberger, in *Symbolae ... Martino David* [Leiden 1968] 51f.); B §6, 2′.4′; C §§2-4 passim; F 10′; G passim; M Rs. 8′. Vgl. auch EN KÙ.BABBAR "Darlehensgeber, Gläubiger" in A §48,44.

30 KAJ 48; 49; 55.

31 KAJ 57, 18.21 (1 Talent Gold!).

32 Vgl. oben Anm. 20.

33 Herrn Dr. H. Freydank, der mir das Manuskript seines Beitrags zur Verfügung stellte, möchte ich auch an dieser Stelle meinen herzlichen Dank dafür aussprechen.

34 Ein Kaufpreisrest ist evtl. noch nachzuzahlen, vgl. Z. 14-16.

35 A §24, 58f.

36 C §1, 4′.

37 KAJ 169, 10.

38 KAJ 170, 10. Nach freundlicher Kollation der Tafel VAT 8999 durch H. Freydank sind am Ende der Zahlenangabe vor GUN AN.NA entgegen der Kopie nicht nur ein, sondern zwei Waagerechte zu erkennen. Danach ist die Zahl sicher zu 6 zu ergänzen.

39 TR 2066, 8 (= *Iraq* 30 [1968], Pl. LII), Verkauf der eigenen Tochter.

40 Das heißt nicht, daß AN.NA in mittelassyrischen Texten in anderem Zusammenhang nicht hin und wieder auch "Zinn" bedeutet. Dies trifft z.B. für KAV 205, 16 zu, wo eine Legierung von 1 Mine Kupfer und 7½ Sekel AN.NA zur Herstellung von Schermessern einem Schmied übergeben werden soll.

41 H. Freydank, a.a.O. Anm. 8. Vgl. die Vorleseklauseln am Ende der mittelassyrischen Palasterlasse (VAT 9629, Rs. 5′ = AfO 17 [1954-56], Taf. VII), des Palasterlasses AASOR 16, 51 aus Nuzi (Z. 26-29), in hethitischen Staatsverträgen (vgl. V. Korošec, *Hethitische Staatsverträge* [Leipzig 1931] 101f.) sowie die Bestimmung in Deut. 31, 10f. über die öffentliche Verlesung des Gesetzes vor dem versammelten israelitischen Volk.

42 Vgl. D. Cross, *Movable Property in the Nuzi Documents* [New Haven 1937] 41f.

43 Instruktiv dafür ist die von C. Zaccagnini, in JESHO 22 [1979] 4-6 gegebene Übersicht über die Preise und Zahlungsgegenstände in den sog. Verkaufsadoptionen, den Feldkaufurkunden aus Nuzi. Vgl. auch die Zusammenstellungen der Darlehensobjekte in den Krediturkunden mit antichretischem Personen- oder Feldpfand bei B. L. Eichler, *Indenture at Nuzi* [New Haven/London 1973] 16-18 und C. Zaccagnini, a.a.O. 8-10.

44 Vgl. z.B. die Sklavenkaufurkunden JEN 179; HSS XIX 110; 124; 128.

45 Vgl. jedoch HSS IX 25, einen Vertrag über den Kauf einer Sklavin. Hier ist der Preis in Silber (20 Sekel) bereits in der Verkaufserklärung genannt. Bei der Aufstellung der als Kaufpreis dienenden Waren sind Zwischensummierungen vorgenommen worden, wobei die Textilien einerseits (12 Sekel Silber) und alle übrigen Warenarten (Bronze, Zinn und Schweinefett) andererseits (8 Sekel Silber) zusammengefaßt wurden. Dann folgt Z. 12f. der Vermerk: ŠU.NÍGIN 20 GÍN KÙ.BABBAR^{meš} *an-nu-ú ḫa-ša-ḫu-še-en-ni* PN_1 *a-na* PN_2 *i-din*^{in} "Insgesamt diese 20 Sekel *ḫašaḫušennu*-Silber hat PN_1 (= Käufer) dem PN_2(= Verkäufer) gegeben". Der in diesem Zusammenhang relevante hurritische Terminus *ḫašaḫušenni/u* soll an anderer Stelle untersucht werden.

46 D.O. Edzard, in JESHO 3 [1960] 43; G. Wilhelm, in Bagh. Mitt. 7 [1974] 207f.

47 Vgl. JEN 86, 7f. (s. dazu C. Zaccagnini, in JESHO 22 [1979] 5).

48 Bearbeitet von G. Wilhelm, in Bagh. Mitt. 7 [1974] 206f.

49 Dieser Betrag schließt einen Zins in Höhe von 50% ein. Die Gold-Silber-Relation in Arrapḫe lag bei 1:6, s. dazu demnächst M. Müller, in *Nuziana - Studies on the Civilization and Culture of Nuzi in Honor of Ernest R. Lacheman*.

50 Vgl. JEN 492, 14; HSS IX 17, 9; XV 228; XVI 63, 17. Als alternatives Zahlungsmittel ist Gold neben Silber und Zinn in RA 32 [1926] 145 Nr. 14, 8' erwähnt; als Darlehensgegenstand begegnet es in den *tidennūtu*-Urkunden JEN 302; 303; 319; 489 und 609.

51 Vgl. z.B. die traditionelle Strafe für Diebstahl: 2 Rinder, 2 Esel, 20 Schafe, s. dazu R.E. Hayden, *Court Procedure at Nuzu* [Diss. Waltham/Mass.] 65f. In HSS V 47, 37-40 wird diese Strafe von den Richtern zwar auf 1 Mine beziffert, anschließend aber in der traditionellen Weise erläutert. - E.A. Speiser hat in Or. NS 25 [1956] 9-15 derartige Zahlungen von je 1 Rind, 1 Esel und 10 Schafen (oder des Doppelten) untersucht und als "ceremonial payment" mit sehr alter Tradition gedeutet.

52 Als hauptsächliche Zahlungsmittel dienten in Assyrien im 9. und 8. Jh. v.u.Z. Kupfer und Bronze, vom 7. Jh. an Silber, s. J.N. Postgate, in CTN II, S. 25. Welches Metall bis gegen Ende des 8. Jh. die Rolle des allgemeinen oder vorherrschenden Äquivalents in Assyrien spielte, ist vorläufig nicht sicher zu bestimmen (Kupfer oder bereits Silber?).

LANDVERGABE IM KASSITISCHEN BABYLONIEN

Joachim Oelsner (Jena – DDR)

Die Kassitenzeit gehört noch immer zu den am schlechtesten bekannten Perioden des alten Mesopotamien. Dies hat verschiedene Ursachen. Einmal ist die Quellenlage äusserst ungünstig, zum anderen hat sie aber auch in der Forschung relativ wenig Beachtung gefunden und wird nicht selten als eine Periode des Verfalls betrachtet. Im Grunde ist die Kenntnis der wirtschaftlichen und sozialen Verhältnisse dieser Zeit nicht weit über den durch die Arbeiten von Flach, Cuq und Steinmetzer[1] schon zu Beginn unseres Jahrhunderts erreichten Stand hinaus gediehen. Auch in der sowjetischen Wissenschaft hat man sich kaum mit Problemen der Entwicklung Babyloniens in der 2. Hälfte des 2. und dem Beginn des 1. Jahrtausends v.u.Z. befasst, wie der verehrte Jubilar einmal bedauernd feststellte.[2]

Die Zahl der bis jetzt für die Kassitenzeit zur Verfügung stehenden Denkmäler ist nicht sehr gross, und auch inhaltlich ist ihre Aussagekraft begrenzt, da sie jeweils nur bestimmte Bereiche des gesellschaftlichen und wirtschaftlichen Lebens widerspiegeln. Für dieses sind neben den Tontafeln (Briefen, Rechts- und Verwaltungsurkunden)[3] von besonderer Bedeutung die Kudurru-Inschriften.[4] Sie sind zugleich fast die einzigen Denkmäler, die für diese Zeit Aussagen über die Besitzverhältnisse am wichtigsten Produktionsmittel des Altertums, am Grund und Boden, erlauben. In der Forschung haben sie deshalb auch immer eine zentrale Stelle eingenommen. Inhaltlich handelt es sich meist um Schenkungen von Land durch den Herrscher an Tempel, Priester, hohe Beamte oder andere Personen, die sich Verdienste erworben haben. Es ist ziemlich allgemein anerkannt, dass es sich dabei um die Überführung von kollektivem Sippeneigentum in private Hand handelt.[5]

Es kann hier nicht beabsichtigt werden, die sozialökonomische Situation der Kassitenzeit umfassend zu untersuchen. Es sollen vielmehr nur einige Bemerkungen zu Fragen, die sich bei der Beschäftigung mit den Texten aufgedrängt haben, vorgelegt werden.

Die frühesten unter einem Kassitenherrscher datierten und hier zu nennenden Urkunden stammen nicht aus Babylonien im engeren Sinne, sondern aus dem am mittleren Euphrat gelegenen Gebiet des spätaltbabylonischen Königtums von Ḫana. Zwei Texte - einen Hauskauf bzw. einen Feldkauf betreffend[6] - sind unter einem König Kaštiliašu ausgefertigt worden. Auch wenn nicht zu bestimmen ist, um welchen Träger dieses Namens es sich handelt,[7] ist besonders der letztere Vertrag interessant, da ein relativ kleines Grundstück (14 *iku* = ca. 4,4 ha) veräussert wird. Es liegt in der gleichen Grössenordnung wie die etwa gleichzeitigen, nach einheimischen Herrschern datierten königlichen Feldschenkungen.[8]

Von Landschenkungen, wie sie für die Kudurru-Inschriften typisch sind, hören wir zum ersten Male unter Gulkišar, König des Meerlandes. Als Empfänger wird ein Tempel genannt, leider ist die Grösse des Objekts nicht erhalten. Auf uns gekommen ist auch nicht die Originalurkunde, sondern eine über Jahrhunderte später erfolgte Restitution des Tempelbesitzes auf Grund königlicher Entscheidung nach Beschwerde eines Priesters gegen den Übergriff des Provinzstatthalters.[9]

Dass es sich auch hier um ein Areal von beträchtlicher Grösse gehandelt haben dürfte, darf man aus anderen Urkunden dieser Periode schliessen. Durchweg handelt es sich bei Landschenkungen an Tempel um grössere Gebiete. Von Kurigalzu I.[10] ist ein als Königsinschrift stilisierter Bericht über eine Landschenkung an die Göttin Ištar (von Uruk) in zwei Exemplaren auf Ton erhalten.[11] Danach erhält der Tempel - neben der Festsetzung von regelmässigen Opfergaben - ein gewaltiges Gebiet von rund 525 km^2 einschliesslich der darauf befindlichen Ortschaften.[12] Im übrigen sind die Schenkungen auf den in der Regel aus Stein[13] bestehenden Kudurrus überliefert. Da sie zum grossen Teil in fragmentarischem Zustand auf uns gekommen sind, stehen nicht einmal 20 Inschriften mit verwertbaren Angaben zur Verfügung.[14] Bei dieser geringen Zahl ist es nicht ratsam, eine zeitliche Differenzierung zu versuchen. Mehrfach werden frühere Schenkungen durch spätere Herrscher bestätigt oder auch erweitert.

Das grösste Areal, das uns entgegentritt, ist die Vergabe von 700 *Kurru* in der Umgebung von Babylon (einschliesslich 5 Ortschaften) an den Marduktempel in Babylon (MDP II, 86ff. = Seidl, Bagh.Mitt. 4 [1968] Nr. 48; Nazimaruttaš[15]). Dabei wird noch einmal differenziert zwischen dem, was der Tempel direkt erhält (494 *Kurru*), und dem, was eine nicht näher bezeichnete, aber wohl als Priester zu betrachtende Person empfängt (206 *Kurru*). Mehrere Grundstücke mit einem Umfang von mindestens 230 *Kurru* (RA 66 [1972] 169ff.; Kadašman-Enlil/Kudur-Enlil) bzw. 100 *Kurru* (ibid. 194ff.; Burnaburiaš/Nazimaruttaš) erhalten Priester in Larsa. Aus den beiden zuletzt genannten Dokumenten wird die enge Verflechtung von Herrscher und Tempel besonders deutlich, da der König auch über Tempelpfründen verfügt und sie vergibt. In einem weiteren Beispiel ist die Grösse des Grundstücks nicht erhalten (BBSt. Nr. I; Kurigalzu I./Kadašman-Enlil).

Unter König Meli-Šipak erhält der Kronprinz und spätere König Marduk-apla-iddin rund 170 *Kurru* (MDP II, 99ff. = Seidl, Nr. 32), einer Tochter des Königs werden 40 *Kurru* mit 3 Ortschaften übergeben (MDP X, 87ff. = Seidl, Nr. 23). Gleichzeitig enthält das letzte Dokument noch eine zweite Urkunde, in der berichtet wird, dass der König ein Gartengrundstück von 3 *Kurru* käuflich erworben und seiner Tochter übereignet hat.[16] Mit der Schenkung an die Mitglieder des Königshauses wie auch an die Priester in Larsa sind Privilegien und die Befreiung von Abgaben und Verpflichtungen (*zakûtu*) verbunden.[17]

Neben den genannten Empfängern erscheinen vor allem Beamte bzw. Personen, deren Stellung nicht näher angegeben wird, in den Texten. Die Grösse der Grundstücke bewegt sich hier zwischen 10 *Kurru* (BBSt. II = Seidl, Nr. 1; MDP II, 95f.[18]) über 30 (MDP VI, 31ff. = AfO 23 [1970] 23ff. = Seidl, Nr. 61; Prozessurkunde) bzw. 50 (BBSt. IV = Seidl, Nr. 12) bis zu 120 *Kurru* (MDP II, 95 = Seidl, Nr. 3; Burnaburiaš/Kastiliaš; auch hier Streitigkeiten um das Grundstück); zu vergleichen ist auch der Rest einer älteren Urkunde auf dem Stein BBSt. II, wo noch [x+]30 (GUR) NUMUN zu erkennen ist (älter als Kurigalzu II.).[19] In anderen Fällen ist die Grössenangabe verloren (MDP VI, 42f. = AfO 23 [1970] 17ff. = Seidl, G 3; AfO 23 [1970] 1ff.[20]; *Sumer* 23 [1967] 45ff. = Seidl, Nr. 51). Singulär ist die Angabe der Grundstücksgrösse in den bis zur altbabylonischen Zeit gebräuchlichen Feldmassen in BBSt. V (= Seidl, Nr. 62; Marduk-apla-iddin I.; Empfänger von 18 *Bur* 12 *Iku*,[21] umgerechnet ca. 272 ha, ist ein Provinzgouverneur). Bezeugt ist auch die Angabe der Seitenlängen anstelle des Flächeninhalts (MDP VI, 39ff. = AfO 23 [1970] 11ff. = Seidl, Nr. 59; VS I, 58 = BE I, 150 = Seidl, Nr. 8[22]), wobei auffällt, dass in beiden Fällen relativ kleine Objekte Gegenstand der Urkunde sind.

Besonders interessante Angaben enthalten die Prozessurkunden MDP VI, 31ff.

(s.o.) und BBSt. III (= Seidl, Nr. 25), da sie zeigen, dass sich an die Schenkung unter Umständen langwierige Auseinandersetzungen anschliessen konnten. Im letzteren Fall zogen sich Rechtsstreitigkeiten im Zusammenhang mit der Vererbung von Grundbesitz längere Zeit hin und wurden schliesslich vom König entschieden. Obwohl infolge Beschädigung des Steines gerade entscheidende Stellen nicht voll verständlich sind, gibt es einige Aussagen, die Beachtung verdienen: der Besitz eines ohne Erben verstorbenen Priesters wird vom Herrscher seinem Bruder, vielleicht ebenfalls Priester, übergeben. Später entsteht darüber ein Streit, wahrscheinlich im Anschluss an den Verkauf von 5 *Kurru* Land aus diesem Besitz. Ob diese einen Teil der später genannten 10 *Kurru* darstellen, ist nicht klar. Offensichtlich wird der Verkauf durch königlichen Einspruch rückgängig gemacht. Die Grundstücksgrösse von 10 *Kurru* (Kol. III 3) entspricht der oben mehrfach bezeugten.[23]

Ein weiteres wichtiges Dokument ist die in einer unvollständigen Abschrift vorliegende Prozessurkunde BE XIV, 39.[24] Hier geht es um die Nutzung von 30 *Kurru* Grundbesitz, die sich seit längerer Zeit (Kurigalzu I.) im Besitz einer Familie befindet und von einer nur mit Namen genannten Person übergeben worden war. Beim Streit geht es darum, ob ein Pachtfeld oder ein "erbliches" Feld (*eqel burkī/ūtı*) vorliegt.[25] Es handelt sich vermutlich nicht um ein vom Herrscher vergebenes Grundstück, sondern um eines, über das der Kläger frei verfügen kann.

Die Kudurru-Inschriften, die unsere Hauptquelle für die Grundsitzverhältnisse in kassitischer Zeit darstellen, werfen eine Reihe von Problemen auf, die weiterer Untersuchung bedürfen. Einmal wäre hier darauf hinzuweisen, dass in der Regel nicht gesagt wird, auf welche Weise das Land vom Herrscher erworben wird und wieweit die Rechte des letzteren gehen.[26] Er scheint auch nach der Vergabe weiterhin darüber verfügen zu können,[27] wobei auch die Frage der Vererbbarkeit zu berücksichtigen ist. Aus der zuletzt genannten Urkunde dürfte sich ergeben, dass keineswegs das gesamte Land in der aus den Kudurru-Inschriften erkennbaren Art vom Herrscher aufgeteilt wurde. Es wurde unlängst darauf hingewiesen, dass die vergebenen Grundstücke sich häufig im östlichen Teil des Zweistromlandes befinden.[28] Leider besitzen wir aus den zentraler gelegenen Städten nur wenige Quellen und unter den oben (Anm. 3) genannten privaten Tontafelarchiven befinden sich kaum Grundbesitz betreffende Urkunden. Wir möchten aber annehmen, dass das Zufall der Überlieferung ist, denn bereits aus dem Beginn der folgenden 2. Dynastie von Isin ist ein privater Feldkaufvertrag erhalten (BBSt. XXX).

Die sehr unterschiedliche Grösse der vergebenen Grundstücke lässt es nicht zu, einen Durchschnittswert zu errechnen. Im Überwiegen kleinerer Areale (10 *Kurru*) dürfte sich aber eine Grösse andeuten, die von Besitzer mit seiner Familie und vielleicht einigen wenigen zusätzlichen Arbeitskräften (Sklaven?[29]) oder durch Verpachtung zu bearbeiten war. In der Urkunde BE XIV, 39 scheint ja sogar ein dreimal grösseres Gelände von einer "Grossfamilie" (Z.16: "der Bruder seines Vaters mit seinen Brüdern") bearbeitet worden zu sein. Die Urkunde enthält gleichzeitig Hinweise auf Pachtverhältnisse auch in der kassitischen Zeit. Wenn jedoch bei grösseren Objekten auch ganze Ortschaften mit vergeben wurden, so schliesst das sicher ein, dass die dort ansässige Bevölkerung in Abhängigkeits- und Ausbeutungsverhältnisse zu den neuen Besitzern geriet.[30] Das gilt in ganz besondere Masse für die Tempelwirtschaften, für die in dem einzigen bis jetzt verfügbaren Archiv, dem von Nippur, die aus dem 3. Jahrt. v.u.Z. häufig als Arbeitskräfte in Grosswirtschaften bezeugte soziale Schicht der g u r u š nachweisbar ist.

Da zwischen dem Ende der altbabylonischen Zeit und dem Wiedereinsetzen der

Quellen gegen Ende des 15. Jh.s v.u.Z. eine Überlieferungslücke besteht, ist es noch nicht möglich, die Ursachen für die Praxis der Landverleihungen, die für die kassitische und auch noch die nachfolgende Periode charakteristisch ist, zu erkennen. Sie stellt gegenüber der vorhergehenden Periode etwas Neues dar, hat aber andererseits - so sicher im Bereich der Tempelwirtschaft - die Voraussetzungen geschaffen für die Grundbesitzverhältnisse, die uns im 1. Jahrt. v.u.Z. begegnen. Vielleicht sollte man die Kassitenzeit weniger als eine Periode des wirtschaftlichen und kulturellen Niedergangs denn als eine solche des Umbruchs sehen. Doch hier liegen noch viele Probleme, die erst weitere Forschungen klären können.

---

1 Basierend auf der Auswertung der sogenannten Kudurru-Inschriften (s.u. bei und mit Anm. 4). Vgl. J. Flach, *Revue historique* 94 [1907] 272-86; 95 [1907] 309-36; E. Cuq, *Nouvelle revue historique de droit français et étranger* 30 [1906] 701-38; 32 [1908] 462-88, wieder abgedruckt in: ders., *Études sur le droit babylonien* [Paris 1929] 81ff. (erweitert); F.X. Steinmetzer, *Über den Grundbesitz in Babylonien zur Kassitenzeit* [Leipzig 1919; = AO 19, 1/2]; ders., *Die babylonischen Kudurru (Grenzsteine) als Urkundenform* [Paderborn 1922; = Studien zur Geschichte und Kultur des Altertums 11, 4/5].

2 Vgl. I.M. Diakonoff, in *Gesellschaftsklassen im Alten Zweistromland und in den angrenzenden Gebieten* [München 1972 = ABAW phil.-hist. Kl., NF 75] 48. S. auch den Hinweis auf eine sowjetische Arbeit zur Kassitenzeit in I.M. Diakonoff (ed.), *Ancient Mesopotamia* [Moskau 1969] 13, Anm. 7.

3 Zusammenstellung: ZA 65 [1975] 286f. Anm. 4-8 sowie die ebd. 285ff. besprochene Edition. Einige weitere Texte sind seitdem publiziert worden, s. vor allem J.A. Brinkman, *Materials and Studies for Kassite History*, I [Chicago 1976], mit Zusammenstellung aller datierbaren Quellen. Die für die politische Geschichte wichtigen Königsinschriften ergeben kaum etwas für die sozialökonomischen Verhältnisse.

4 Die grundlegende Untersuchung für diese Gattung, die über die Kassitenzeit hinaus bis zur Mitte des 7. Jhs. v.u.Z. (Šamaš-šum-ukin) bezeugt ist, ist noch immer Steinmetzer [1922; s.o. Anm. 1]. Die bildlichen Darstellungen auf den Kudurru wurden neu bearbeitet von U. Seidl, Bagh. Mitt. 4 [1968] 7-220. Seitdem wurden einige weitere Stücke veröffentlicht: R. Borger, AfO 23 [1970] 1-11; J.-C. Margueron & D. Arnaud, RA 66 [1972] 147-76 (2 Exemplare); aus nachkassitischer Zeit: J.A. & M.E. Brinkman, ZA 62 [1972] 91-98; F. Reschid & C. Wilcke, ZA 65 [1975] 34-62, Kopie *Sumer* 32 [1976] 109-12 (arab.); vgl. auch J.A. Brinkman, RA 61 [1967] 70-74. - Aus praktischen Gründen beschränken wir uns hier auf die Kassitenzeit (1594-1155 v.u.Z.).

5 Vgl. neben den oben Anm. 1 genannten Arbeiten z.B. noch: M. San Nicolò, *Beiträge zur Rechtsgeschichte im Bereiche der keilschriftlichen Rechtsquellen* [Oslo 1931] 120; V. Korošec, in *Orientalisches Recht* [Leiden/Köln 1964; = Handbuch der Orientalistik 1. Abt., Erg.bd. III] 144.

6 Th. Bauer, MAOG 4 [1928] 1-6; TCL 1, 238 = Kohler & Ungnad, HG 1150, mit Duplikat: M. Schorr, *Babyloniaca* 3 [1910] 266f.

7 In Frage kommt nur einer der frühen Herrscher der Kassitendynastie. Eine gesicherte Chronologie scheinen bis jetzt auch die laufenden Ausgrabungen noch nicht ermöglicht zu haben. In der Regel werden die Hana-Texte als gleichzeitig mit den späten Herrschern der 1. Dynastie

von Babylon angesehen; vgl. aber die Überlegungen von A. Goetze, JCS 11 [1957] 53ff. (allerdings erwecken die Siegel auf den Kastiliašu-Urkunden den Eindruck, dass sie älter als die einheimischen Herrscher sind). Die Datierung mit Jahresformel und das altbabylonische Formular schliessen allerdings eine relativ späte Datierung (bis zu Kaštiliaš III., zur Einordnung in die Dynastie vgl. Brinkman [oben Anm. 3], 26 mit Anm. 71) nicht aus: Jahresnamen sind mindestens bis zu Kadašman-Enlil I., wahrscheinlich aber bis zu Burnaburiaš II. bezeugt, s. Brinkman, a.a.O. 402, vgl. auch M.J.A. Horsnell, ZA 65 [1975] 28-33; das altbabylonische Kaufformular ist in Nippur bis zur Zeit Burnaburiaš' II. bezeugt.

8 TCL 1, 237 = Kohler & Ungnad, HG 458; vgl. auch F.J. Stephens, RA 34 [1937] 183ff.; J. Nougayrol, RA 41 [1947] 42-5 (beide fragmentarisch, wegen des königlichen Siegels wohl Schenkungen). S. ferner VS VII, 204 = HG 459; J. Nougayrol, *Syria* 37 [1960] 205ff. (Gartenkauf). - In altbab. Zeit rechnet man mit 1-2 *Bur* (ca. 6,5 - 13 ha) für den Lebensunterhalt einer Familie, J. Renger, in RlA 3 [1957-71] 652.

9 BE I, 83 (Enlil-nadin-apli, 4. Jahr), übersetzt von A. Ungnad, Or NS 13 [1944] 96f.; Z. 14 lies [x+]1 GUR. - Zu Gulkišar s. D.J. Wiseman, RlA 3 [1957-71] 698 s.v. (ca. 1595 v.u.Z. nach mittlerer Chronologie).

10 Zählung der Herrscher im Anschluss an Brinkman (oben Anm. 3), dort 30f. auch absolute Daten.

11 CT 36, 6f.; BIN II, 33, bearbeitet von A. Ungnad, AfK 1 [1923] 19-23.

12 Umrechnung nach A. Ungnad (a.a.O.), 22; s. auch F.H. Weissbach, WVDOG 59 [Leipzig 1938] 52f. Bei der Grösse der Grundstücke wird von einem *Kurru* mit 300 *Qû* (Sila) Inhalt ausgegangen, das nach den genannten Untersuchungen etwa 8,1 ha entspricht.

13 Der Tonkegel King, BBSt Nr. I, wird auch als Kudurru bezeichnet, (unpubliziertes Duplikat: BM 135743, s. Brinkman [oben, Anm. 3], 136 sub J. 2.19.2). Vielleicht darf man sich die im Steinkudurru MDP II, 86-92 am Ende (S. 91 u./92) erwähnte Urkunde, die der Abschrift auf Stein als Vorlage gedient hat, ähnlich vorstellen.

14 Im folgenden wird nach Publikation und Nummer bei Seidl (oben, Anm. 4) zitiert. Von den dort aufgeführten Denkmälern ist ein beträchtlicher Teil noch nicht veröffentlicht; bei anderen sind die Inschriften verloren. Zum Aufbau s. Steinmetzer (oben, Anm. 1 [1922]) 215ff. Durch den in Dur-Kurigalzu gefundenen Kudurru DK_2-33 wissen wir, dass Datum und Zeugen im Formular der Grenzsteinurkunden bereits zur Zeit des Nazimaruttaš vorkommen, vgl. Seidl (oben, Anm. 4) Taf. 1 (die ursprüngliche Publikation, Taha Baqir, *Iraq, Supplement* [1944], 15 und Abb. 21, ist mir nicht zugänglich).

15 Jüngere Abschrift aus der Zeit Marduk-apla-iddins I., s.o. Anm. 13.

16 Vgl. auch die fragmentarische Kolumne IX (MDP X, 94), deren Zusammenhang mit dem vorhergehenden Text unklar ist.

17 Dazu F.R. Kraus, *Ein mittelbabylonischer Rechtsterminus*, in *Symbolae.... Martino David* [Leiden 1968], 2, S. 9-40 (S. 10-15 Übersetzung der entsprechenden Passagen der Texte aus der Zeit Meli-Šipaks).

18 Neubearbeitet von H. Wohl, *The Tablet of Agaptaha*, in *Journal of the Ancient Near Eastern Society* 4 [1972] 85-90. Es scheint sich nicht um die rechtskräftige Urkunde, sondern eher um eine private (verkürzte) Abschrift zu handeln.

19 Vgl. L.W. King, BBSt S.5 Anm. 2.

20 Da für eine Zahl um Zeilenanfang kein Platz zu sein scheint, könnte man erwägen, ob hier die Grössenangabe überhaupt ausgelassen wurde, was allerdings singulär wäre. Auch eine Lesung 50 (GUR) NUMUN wäre denkbar. Borgers Vorschlag, S. 3 zu I 1, ist auch nicht recht überzeugend. Vgl. auch noch Seidl, Nr. 7; 33; 42; 92.

21 Zur Lesung vgl. King, BBSt S. 25 Anm. 3; zur Umrechnung vgl. auch Steinmetzer (Anm. 1 [1922]), 220, der von einer leicht abweichenden Grösse ausgeht (0,495 bzw. 0,7425 m statt 0,5 bzw. 0,75 m für die Elle).

22 Datierung nach Seidl: etwa Zeit Adad-šum-uṣur.

23 Vgl. P. Koschaker, ZA 41 [1933] 75f. Als eines der wenigen Zeugnisse der Kassitenzeit mit Erwähnung eines Grundstückskaufs besitzt dieser Text eine besondere Bedeutung.

24 Umschrift und Übersetzung von Z. 4-14: J. Aro, StOr 20 [1955] 82f. S. auch D.D. Luckenbill, AJSL 23 [1906-7] 292.

25 Zu diesem noch unklaren Ausdruck s. J. Aro, StOr 22 [1957] s.v. *burkītu*. In der Briefstelle PBS 1/2, 75 Z. 12 ist infolge Beschädigung der Zusammenhang gestört.

26 Die von Steinmetzer [oben Anm. 1, 1922] 226ff. für Ankauf durch dem Herrscher und Entschädigung angeführten Stellen scheinen mir einer philologischen Nachprüfung nicht Stand zu halten; MDP II, 86ff., I 16-19; 99ff., I 21-26 scheinen eher auf Enteignung zu weisen. Von Kauf ist dagegen die Rede MDP VI, 31ff. (Prozessurkunde) II 23.

27 So könnte man die mehrfach bezeugte Unterlassung der Siegelung und Bestätigung durch einen späteren Herrscher deuten. - Der Entzug eines Grundstücks wird erwähnt in dem von F. Reschid & C. Wilcke (oben, Anm. 4) veröffentlichten Kudurru aus der Zeit der II. Dynastie von Isin. Die dort I 8-11 genannte Verfehlung des bisherigen Besitzers (Uzib-Šiparru) dürfte darin bestanden haben, dass er sich widerrechtlich Besitz des Ula-Gimdar angeeignet hatte (vielleicht nach dem Tode wie in BBSt Nr. III ?); anders die Hrsg. a.a.O. 34-7.

28 H. Wohl (oben, Anm. 18) 88f. zu Z. 6.

29 Unter den privaten Rechtsurkunden aus Nippur und Ur Befinden sich einige Sklavenkaufverträge, aber ihr Zahl ist zu gering, um das Ausmass der Sklaverei in dieser Zeit bestimmen zu können.

30 Das ganze Problem des sozialökonomischen Wesens der Landvergabe (Belehnung oder nicht, Art der Abhängigkeitsverhältnisses usw.) bedarf der Untersuchung, dazu am ausführlichsten (unter den Voraussetzungen seiner Zeit) Steinmetzer [Anm. 1, 1922] 229ff.

REMARKS ON THE TÔD TREASURE IN EGYPT

Edith Porada (New York)

In recent years, I.M. Diakonoff has concerned himself with relations between ancient languages of Asia and Africa. It may therefore interest him that relations between the continents, indicated by some of the seals in the Tôd treasure of Egypt, point not only to origins of objects in the treasure in Mesopotamia and Syria, a fact already known to the excavators, but also to Iran and possibly Afghanistan or Turkmenistan. Because of limited time, this article was based on photographs of the seals reproduced by F. Bisson de la Roque[1] and B. Landsberger[2] and on impressions of those in the Louvre, generously furnished by Pierre Amiet. An examination of the original seal stones in the Cairo Museum and at the Louvre is a project for the future.

W.C. Hayes and G. Posener summarize the general view of the Tôd treasure in the following two paragraphs excerpted from the *Cambridge Ancient History*.[3]

Hayes writes: "In the foundations of the temple of Mont at Tôd in Upper Egypt were found four bronze caskets, inscribed with the name of Ammenemes II and containing a treasure of small objects sent either as a gift or as tribute to the king of Egypt by the ruler of some important Syrian principality.[4] Besides ingots of gold and silver there were vessels of silver, one, at least, of characteristic Aegean type,[5] Babylonian cylinder-seals and amulets of lapis lazuli which must have come originally from Mesopotamia."

Posener's paragraph reads: "This treasure includes gold, silver and lapis lazuli; each of these materials is present in its crude state (ten ingots of gold and thirteen of silver, pieces of lapis) and as objects which have been worked (for instance, more than 150 metal cups and twenty-five metal chains, amulets, beads and more than fifty stone cylinders). Most of the cups have been bent and flattened by hammering; the majority of the cylinders are broken. It is possible that the broken items, and perhaps those which are intact as well, were there only for the weight of the material from which they were made. The cylinders, some of which bear cuneiform inscriptions, are clearly oriental in origin;[6] the cups and a silver pendant are of Cretan provenance, or else Asiatic imitations of Cretan models.[7] This treasure gives an idea of the material which the pharaohs of the Twelfth Dynasty received from Syria, the hub of a vast system of exchanges which had developed in those days throughout the Near East and the Eastern Mediterranean."

Hayes calls the cylinder seals "Babylonian", Posener, "Oriental". Neither term suggests the diversity of style among these cylinders which indicates considerable variety in the region and period of origin. Both writers point to Syria as the likely source for the treasure. This view was mainly based on historical considerations and on the classification by G. Contenau of some of the early cylinder seals as Syrian, without indication of any parallels that would confirm his statements.

An accurate appraisal of the differences in time among the cylinders of Mesopotamian style contained in the treasure and of the diversity of the small objects of Mesopotamian Early Dynastic type was given by H.J. Kantor in "The Relative Chronology of Egypt and its Foreign Relations" in *Chronologies in Old World Archaeology*.[8] She states: "If this motley stock of jewelers' materials was put together in one place, the Syro-Palestinian littoral seems the most likely spot . . ." The *If* beginning the sentence implies that she had doubts concerning the assemblage of the materials in one place outside of Egypt. This is one assumption made by earlier writers which I also doubt and which I will try to disprove on the basis of a few seals and other objects, whose style is so distinctive that it can easily be recognized, even in poor photographs. My explanatory sketches are merely intended as an aid to memory for the reader; they make no claim to precision.

"Syrian" Cylinders

The cylinder (Fig. 1) said by Contenau to belong to Syrian glyptic art (*Trésor de Tôd*, p. 16, s.v. pl. XL, 15226 bis), actually has its closest parallel in a cylinder found by K. Kenyon at Jericho in tomb A 1279 (Fig. a),[9] dated by A. Ben-Tor in the beginning of the Early Bronze II period, probably contemporary with the second half of the First Egyptian Dynasty. Ben-Tor included the seal in a group that he cited as related to the Jamdat Nasr type seals of the Diyala region.[10] K. Kenyon published the cylinder as a bead, which may be correct in view of its purely ornamental character.

Two other cylinders (Fig. 2), assigned by Contenau to Syria, (*Trésor de Tôd*, p. 16 s.v. pl. XLI, 15225 and 15225 bis) are also slender seals, engraved with ornamental designs that resemble festoons accompanied by delicate hatchings. They belong to a group discussed by Georgina Herrmann in her work on lapis lazuli[11] because cylinders of this group are almost always made of that stone. There is no reason to assume that the group originated in Syria, because the largest number of such seals found at one site comes from the Royal Cemetery of Ur,[12] where six examples were discovered. Moreover, a cylinder in the Iraq Museum (Fig. b), published by Amiet,[13] shows a typical Early Dynastic banqueting scene above a row of festoons, a motif thereby tied firmly to a characteristic Mesopotamian theme.

For one cylinder, however (Fig. 3), which Contenau called "Cappadocian" (*Trésor de Tôd*, p. 17, s.v. pl. XLI, 15215), a classification in the Syrianizing Colony style of Nimet Özgüç[14] is possible, nor can one exclude an origin in Syria itself. The fragmentary cylinder shows a heroic personage holding aloft a fenestrated axe and a second weapon, perhaps a javelin. A cylinder with that figure carved in the Syrianizing Colony style, contemporary with Level II at Kültepe, dated c. 1920-1840 B.C., was found at Ras Shamra.[15] On that cylinder, however, the hero's kilt is folded over in such a way as to terminate horizontally at the bottom, as does the kilt of a similar personage in a related cylinder of unknown provenance in the Walters Art Gallery (Fig. c).[16] The hero of the cylinder from the Tôd treasure, however, has a kilt which forms an oblique line at the bottom, comparable to those worn by dignitaries carved on a limestone basin from Tell Mardikh, ancient Ebla, in North Syria (Fig. d).[17] These dignitaries also have thick hair marked by parallel striations like the hero of the Tôd cylinder, who differs from the other representations of a heroic figure holding two weapons aloft in that he lacks their plumed helmet.[18]

Another feature which may point to an origin of the Tôd cylinder in North Syria is the shape of the small table with a single vertical support, ending at the bottom in two bull's feet. A table on an ivory plaque (Fig. e) from Tell Mardikh-Ebla, thought to belong to the time of the XIIIth Egyptian Dynasty,[19] is very similar, but the two bull's feet rise to form a double vertical support, firmly tied and perhaps doweled into a rounded element below the table top. Similar tables in seal impressions of the Assyrian Colony style on tablets from Kültepe (Fig. f) and also on a basin from Ebla have a sensible pair of lateral vertical supports.[20] A single vertical support for the table top, on stands which lack the bull's feet, is only found in Syrian cylinders of a somewhat later example than the one from Tôd, which doubtless belongs chronologically to the Syrianizing Colony group. The fact that tables with a single support existed in Syria, though at a later time,[21] makes it seem possible that the delicate little table of the Tôd cylinder is from an area which at all times excelled in elegant decorative woodworking, perhaps more so than regions further north. Lastly, the use of lapis lazuli for this cylinder differs from the hematite almost universally employed for cylinders of the different styles used in the Assyrian colonies of Anatolia. Again, this indicates that a Syrian origin of the cylinder is possible, though by no means certain.

Another cylinder of great interest for which a Syrian origin is tentatively suggested (Fig. 4) shows the statue of a single large animal on a platform, its body covered by a fleece with the tufts of hair arranged in several registers. The animal's head is covered by what now seems like a flat cap with upturned brim but which was probably originally a horned miter, as convincingly suggested by Contenau (*Trésor de Tôd*, p. 18, s.v. pl. XLII, 15227). The large size of the animal and the careful, naturalistic engraving reminds one of the style of the Akkad period, the iconography of which includes a monster with heavy fleece and horned miter, carrying three females on its back (Fig. g). The females are shown once fully dressed in the flounced robes of deities, and twice nude.[22] In one of the latter representations the body of the creature which supports them is formed of stars[23] (Fig. h), from which image one may conclude that the creature represented a configuration of stars. It is all the more interesting to find the creature surviving in the carvings on a basin from Ebla[24] (Fig. i). There the stars of the body are indicated by small circles, the creature is winged and has a leonine head that spews water or venom, and the hind feet are shaped like the legs and talons of a bird and the forefeet like those of a lion, resembling the lion griffin of the weather god.[25] The monster's head in the basin from Ebla can serve as the reconstruction of the creature's head in the cylinder from Tôd, since the upper jaw and the ruff of the neck are similar in both. Yet the style of the creature suggests an inverse relation between the two representations, the cylinder being the prototype for the monster on the basin from Ebla. One may assume that partial abrasion of the Akkadian cylinder seal was intended to remove the figures surrounding the monster and create a field in which a procession of figures engraved in a contemporary style would appear on the valuable lapis lazuli stone. However, the abrasion was obviously performed incompetently by one who must have been a non-Mesopotamian seal cutter; part of the upper seal broke off and the piece became scrap lapis lazuli. On present evidence, one would like to locate this process at Ebla, especially in view of the fragments in limestone and lapis lazuli of a scene of a procession showing the garments of the figures with rows of tufts of a precision reminiscent of those of the monster in the Tôd cylinder.[25a]

Despite the stylistic relations established with Ebla for two of the cylinders of the Tôd treasure, the evidence is not sufficient to suggest that these seals actually came from Ebla. So far there are no cylinder seals of related style found at that site. While North Syria seems the most likely region for the origin of at least one of the two cylinders, their precise source remains undiscovered. It is possible that several more cylinders of the Tôd treasure, carved in a crude version of Babylonian style, also originated in that area, but this cannot be ascertained at present.

Mesopotamian Cylinder Seals

The fragment of what must have been a beautifully carved Early Dynastic cylinder (Fig. 5) retains the figure of a human-headed bull that has carefully undulated strands of hair forming the beard and turning up in little curls on the side. Small curls on top of the head are indicated by little round dots. The small figure of a gazelle-like animal beside the full-sized figure indicates a late date in the Early Dynastic III period. The closest parallel I could find for the figure of the human-headed bull is the impression of the cylinder of Ama-bara(g).si(g) from Ur.[26] But as far as the impressions permit judgment, the correspondence is not close enough to suggest the same engraver's hand, and it is entirely possible that the cylinder was engraved elsewhere.

The second cylinder of Mesopotamian style chosen for discussion (Fig. 6), now badly abraded, must have been a magnificent seal of the Ur III Dynasty. An introducing goddess leads a lady toward an enthroned king while a second goddess behind the lady raises her hands in prayer. The size and execution of the cylinder suggests that it was intended for a royal personage. In view of the extreme rarity of the representation of women as worshippers conducted into the king's presence, in cylinders of the Third Dynasty of Ur it may be suggested that the cylinder originally belonged to a princess, perhaps one of the fifty children of King Shulgi (2094-2057 B.C). The reasons for which the cylinder was abraded and available as scrap lazuli in a foreign country, a little more than a century after Shulgi's death, remain a matter for speculation in view of the fact that, in general, the seal owners took their seals with them to their graves.[27]

It seems likely that both of the fine cylinders just discussed were carved in Mesopotamia proper, but it is not impossible that they were made at Mari, where accomplished artists were at work producing some of the finest Near Eastern sculptures and paintings. With few exceptions, the cylinders published in the excavations reports are not of the same high quality as the major arts, but this may have been due to the valuable stones used which were plundered in the destruction of the city, or discovered and removed in the course of the millennia in which the site has been exposed to treasure digging. The first hypothesis is based on the discovery of the cylinder of Ana-Sin-taklāku, known from the impressions of this beautiful cylinder on tablets from Mari.[28] The original cylinder was purchased in about 1965 on the antiquities market in Iran, where it had probably been shipped by modern Syrian dealers. It was re-engraved in the Old Babylonian period with the inscription of a secondary owner, the delicate minute original signs of Ana-Sin-taklāku's inscription still visible under the second, coarser inscription.

The statement about one of the most outstanding cylinders known to have come from Mari was made to substantiate the suggestion that Mari had seal cutters whose work matched that of its sculptors. The importance of Mari in relation to the Tôd Treasure becomes obvious when the amulets and other objects of lapis lazuli are compared. Amulets in the form of a lion-headed eagle (Fig. j-1) are paralleled in shell by examples from the Temple of Ishtar in Mari (Fig. j-2).[29] In the same panel of the Mari finds appear shells into which two holes have been bored, giving the effect of eyes, with one hole at the top for suspension (Fig. k-1). A shell of this form, imitated in lapis lazuli (Fig. k-2), is seen on a necklace of the Tôd Treasure. Amulets in the form of couchant bulls with small, tightly curved and slightly raised horns (Fig. l-1) are seen in the same form at Mari (Fig. l-2).[30] Most characteristic are the snail-shell curls of hair or beard from Tôd (Fig. m-1), corresponding to those found in the Temples called Ishtarat and Ninni-Zaza (Fig. m-2).[31] Such curls, which were probably employed in inlays of representations of bearded figures in the Early Dynastic period, were also made of chlorite,[32] limestone and shell.[33]

A fragment of a relief or inlay in lapis lazuli (Fig. n-1), showing a male torso and the beginning of the lower body with a striking swayback outline of the back and obliquely descending lines for the indication of a double belt, surely represents a bull-man as shown on cylinder seals of the Second Early Dynastic period, c. 2750-2500 B.C. (Fig. n-2).[34] This relief would be earlier than most of the material discovered so far at Mari, except for cylinder seals.

Three large-faceted, date-shaped beads found in the Tôd treasure (*Trésor*, pl. XLVIII, 70726-70728) correspond to those found at Ur, said by Woolley to have been, together with the faceted double conoid beads, the favorite for the man's *brîm* head-dress of the early period.[35] The same type of bead was found engraved with a text containing the name of king Mes-ane-pada of Ur in the treasure of Mari.[36]

Iranian Seals

Perhaps the most interesting cylinder seal in the Tôd treasure is one reproduced by Benno Landsberger (Fig. 7),[37] which shows in the lower part two female figures in tailor seat posture, their flounced garments covering their legs in such a way that they appear to be a solid longitudinal form with rounded corners. This type of representation is characteristic of female figures on seals from southeast Iran, and is also found in a stamp seal of the Kaftari period published in the excavation report of Tepe Malyan – ancient Anshan[38] – located in the center of Fars province in Iran (Fig. o). On the stamp, however, the figure sits on a low platform. This was pointed out to me by Holly Pittman, who will publish the glyptic material from Malyan and who has examined the original seal. Whether or not the figures in the Tôd treasure seal also sit on platforms cannot be determined from the reproduction available. The figures are robed in draped garments with many folds, perhaps indicating that they were meant to be goddesses. A spiky trefoil plant appears beside the figure at the left, and what may be a branch beside the figure at the right. The spiky plant resembles the ears of grain which rise from a seated deity on a cylinder from Shahdad in Kerman, southeast Iran (Fig. p),[39] and the draped robe recalls the garment of the seated grain deity on a cylinder from Tepe Yahya (Fig. q),[40] also situated in Kerman province. The cylinders from Shahdad and Tepe Yahya belong to the last third of the third millennium B.C., whereas the Kaftari period of Tall-i Malyan is dated approximately 2000-1700 B.C.[41]

In the upper part of the cylinder from the Tôd treasure (Fig. 7) stand two identical pairs of figures. Such a repetition of one or two figures facing in the same direction is also found in the Proto-Elamite glyptic art of the early third millennium B.C.[42] This is a compositional device which differs fundamentally from Mesopotamian artistic conventions.

In both pairs the figure at the left seems to have the sections of its robe marked by two or more drillings, whereas the figure at the right has one large drilling in each section. These vertically sectioned garments may have indicated the tiered, flounced garments of Mesopotamian deities in the late third and early second millennium B.C. Streams of water flow down, perhaps from the figures' elbows. The figures all have one hand raised; in each pair the figure at the left seems to lay its hand over that of the right-hand figure.

There is thus some difference indicated between the figures, but one cannot make any more precise statements about them, except that the seal design was meant to portray a group of deities of water and fertility for which there are parallels in other works of Iranian art.[43]

An earlier Iranian seal in the Tôd treasure is the fragmentary stamp with band handle showing a sheep with horizontally extended horns and characteristically rounded nose (Fig. 8). This seal closely parallels an unpublished white marble stamp seal from Shahdad and the figure of the reclining sheep in the cylinder (Fig. p).[43a]

Lastly, there is a cylindrical bead amulet with fantastic monsters engraved on the flat top and bottom (Fig. 9, photograph and two drawings). The distinctive shape of the amulet resembles that of a lapis lazuli one (Fig. r) published by P. Amiet and related by him to bead amulets of the Jukhar culture of India.[44] However, the amulet of the Tôd treasure and the Iranian one differ from the Indian[45] in the elaboration and delicacy of their engraving. This relationship merely seems to indicate that India and Southeast Iran had received the shape from a source situated between them, perhaps located somewhere in Bactria, the source of lapis lazuli. It is to this region that the strange monsters with curled-up wing tips engraved on the Tôd treasure amulet must be assigned. Although there are as yet no precise parallels, the combination of animal forms to create extraordinary, fear-inspiring creatures flourished on the seals which are now known to have come from Bactria.[46]

Conclusions

The aim of this article has been to define the different areas from which the lapis lazuli objects of the Tôd treasure may have come, in order to determine the nature of this assemblage. The vessels of precious metal, mainly silver, have not been included because their stylistic analysis is beyond my expertise. However, Ellen Davis has voiced the opinion that the Cretan relations, generally taken to determine the origin of the bowls, are tenuous and that an origin elsewhere, perhaps in Anatolia, should be considered.[47]

The hypothetical Syrian prince, thought to have paid tribute or sent gifts of silver and lapis lazuli to the Egyptian king, would therefore have been a potentate with sufficient wealth to purchase silver from a site north of his country and lapis lazuli objects of a type produced so far to the east that no Mesopotamian or Syrian site has ever yielded any examples. There is no historical evidence for an exchange of gifts on that scale between the rulers of Syria and Egypt in the early reigns of the Twelfth Dynasty, and the assumption that the entire treasure was sent by the person whose name appears on one of the silver bowls[48] is an unlikely one. Some ideas may therefore be voiced on the origin of the various groups of objects recognized within the treasure.

The site which provides a substantial number of parallels for the amulets and hair curls is Mari, a fact noted early by A. Parrot and J. Vandier.[49] It is not only the type of object which is important, however, but also their association and number. These are comparable to the groups of lapis lazuli objects from the temples of Ishtarat and Ninni-Zaza.[50] Unfortunately, the indications concerning the discovery of these objects are insufficient to judge the extent to which they formed units.[51] In the report on the temple of Ishtar, however, the amulets in the shape of lion-headed eagles as well as most of the shells with three holes were discovered in the room called "*Chambre des prêtres*".[52] Despite the limited archaeological information available, there is little doubt that the lapis lazuli objects from the Tôd treasure belonged to similar assemblages, although the variety of the single items is greater than in the units from Mari. Nevertheless, one may assume that the items belonged to one or more temples that would not have divested themselves of lapis lazuli items, however fragmentary, since they could always have been reused in the temple workshops; this indicates that they were forcefully removed by a conqueror.

In general, one thinks of the Akkadian rulers, Sargon (2334-2279 B.C.) and Naram Sin (2254-2218 B.C.), when questioning the destruction and subsequent pillaging of sites in North Syria. However, according to a text from Tell Mardikh-Ebla, a military commander led a victorious campaign against Mari and became king of that town.[53] I can only guess that this alien ruler of Mari might have removed lapis lazuli and other treasure from some of the temples and sent them to Ebla,[54] and further suggest that fear of divine retribution rendered the temple loot an undesirable addition to the royal treasure. Objects of such a treasure might have been used as material for an exchange with Egypt; continuing relations seem to be indicated by the presence at Ebla of two fragments of Egyptian diorite vessels with hieroglyphic inscriptions of Chephren of Dynasty IV, and of the alabaster lid of a jar with the inscription of Pepi I of Dynasty VI.[55] Of course, the items may also have gone to Egypt at some later date, perhaps together with the abraded cylinder showing a monster (Fig. 4) and the Syrianizing cylinder (Fig. 3).

The cylinder seals of Mesopotamian styles from the Akkad to the Isin-Larsa periods are so varied that they may have been collected over many decades by agents charged with obtaining lapis lazuli for the king of Egypt.[56]

The third group, consisting of seals from east Iran and possibly Afghanistan, is unique in two respects: there is no other evidence of raw lapis lazuli in excavations of Western Asia of which I am aware [but see addendum]; nor are there seals of East Iranian type found in Mesopotamia and Syria, as mentioned before. Hence I suggest that this material travelled to Egypt not overland, as the other materials might have come, but over the age-old sea routes by which early influences from Sumer and Iran had reached Egypt in the Predynastic period.[57]

Perhaps an indication of trade goods from the ports of the Persian Gulf or the Indian Ocean to Egypt is provided by the extraordinary seal impression on jar coverings found by M. Bietak in Nubia (Fig. s)[58] and kindly communicated to me by two photographs. The following account is taken from M. Bietak's letter concerning these sealings. They were discovered in Sayala, a settlement of the C-group belonging to one of the earliest in the Nile Delta. The sealings, found on a field plateau on the western bank of the Nile, probably derive from the first settlers of the C-group, people who lived in lower Nubia about 2200 B.C. (during the period of the VIth Dynasty of Egypt). Citing the extensive expeditions of the nomarch of Elephantine *Ḥrw-ḫwjf*,[59] Bietak suggests that the inhabitants of the settlement could have obtained such a sealed jar only through contact with Egyptians who had undertaken trade expeditions to the Sudan. However, as Bietak states correctly, the main problem is the manner in which the Egyptians came into possession of a jar with a seal of foreign derivation. On the basis of recent finds in East Iran, Afghanistan, Turkmenistan and Pakistan,[60] the type of compartmental seal on the jar covering could only have come from that general region. Nothing known from Mesopotamia, Palestine, Syria or Anatolia corresponds closely to the type of impressions found by Bietak, and to the related examples of Bactrian stamp seals shown in figure t.

The different route suggested here for the seals and raw lapis lazuli from the "east" contained in the Tôd assemblage, shows that at least that part of the treasure came from a different quarter and surely by trade. This supports

W. Helck's suggestion that the treasure was a *Handelssendung*[61] although he assumes a north Syrian harbor town as the only point of departure whereas the evidence shown here indicates more diverse sources of the materials and routes of access to Egypt than have been assumed until now. Moreover, the Egyptian bureaucracy is most likely to have used the words "tribute" and "gift" for the Tôd treasure since all large scale trade was undertaken on behalf of the king.[62]

The fact that the treasure was not a foundation deposit, as is quite clear from the excavator's report[63] and as M. Eaton Krause discusses at length in an as yet unpublished paper, adds some indication concerning the purpose of the materials in the caskets. H.J. Kantor's term "motley stock of jewelers' materials"[64] accurately describes the assemblage. In the case of the temple of Montu where Sesostris I, the father of Ammenemes II, had dedicated piers and lintels, it is likely that Ammenemes, the son, had had plans for the dedication of precious objects of silver, gold and lapis lazuli, for which the contents of the caskets were to be used. Obviously, these plans were not carried out; the caskets appear to have become part of the temple inventory that remained untouched, judging by the Isin-Larsa date of the latest cylinders in the treasure and the absence of cylinders whose style would indicate a date after 1800 B.C. For example, there are no Assyrian or Babylonian cylinders of the time of Šamši-Adad of Assyria (1813-1781 B.C.), nor contemporary cylinders of Syrianizing style comparable to those of Level Ib of Kültepe.[65]

The caskets must have been buried to protect them in an emergency that proved so severe that their guardians never raised them.

It is likely that further work on the material from East Iran and ancient Bactria (Afghanistan and Turkmenistan) as well as a comprehensive analysis of the Egyptian objects in the Tôd treasure, which have not been carefully examined in recent times, will provide results of greater precision than those which could be obtained from this brief and selective survey presented to honor I.M. Diakonoff.

Corpus = E. Porada in collaboration with B. Buchanan, *Corpus of Ancient Near Eastern Seals in North American Collections* (Bollingen Series 14 [Washington 1948]).

Ebla = P. Matthiae, *Ebla, un impero ritrovato* [Turin 1977].

Trésor = F. Bisson de la Roque, G. Contenau, F. Chapouthier, *Le trésor de Tôd* (Documents de fouilles de l'Institut Français d'archéologie orientale du Caire, 11 [Cairo 1953]).

---

1 F. Bisson de la Roque, *Trésor de Tôd* (Cairo Museum, Catalogue Général du Musée du Caire, nos. 70501-754 [Cairo 1950]); id., G. Contenau, F. Chapouthier, *Le trésor de Tôd* [Cairo 1953].

2 B. Landsberger, "Assyrische Königsliste und "Dunkles Zeitalter"", in JCS 8 [1954] 118-9.

3 *The Cambridge Ancient History* I/2, *The Early History of the Middle East* [Cambridge 1971] 503 and 543-4. Both chapters XX and XXI, which contain Hayes' and Posener's references to the Tôd treasure, were written half a decade before the publication of Vol. I/2.

4 Hayes' note 7, in which he gave references to *Trésor*, J. Vandier's article about the treasure in *Syria* 18 [1937] 174-82, and H. Seyrig's article in *Syria* 31 [1954] 218-24.

5 Hayes' note 8 in which he referred to H.J. Kantor, *The Aegean and the Orient* (AJA LI [1947]) 19-20, 32.

6 Posener's note 1 on p. 544, in which he referred to Contenau's statements concerning the cylinders of Mesopotamian type, and to Landsberger's statements cited in note 2 above. Posener also cited other western Asiatic cylinders found in Egypt contemporary with the Middle Kingdom: S. Smith, "Babylonian Cylinder Seals from Egypt", in JEA 8 [1922] 207-10, pl. 23; W.F. Albright, "Palestine in the Earliest Historical Period", *Journal of the Palestine Oriental Society* 15 [1935] 217-8; and S. Smith, *Alalakh and Chronology* [London 1940] 13-14.

7 Posener's note 2 with reference to *Trésor* and H.J. Kantor, op.cit. in note 5 above. At the end of his paragraph, Posener referred in note 3 to W.S. Smith, *The Art and Architecture of Ancient Egypt* (The Pelican History of Art [Harmondsworth 1958]) 113-19.

8 *Chronologies in Old World Archaeology*, ed. R.W. Ehrich [Chicago 1965] 20.

9 K. Kenyon, *Excavations at Jericho* I [London 1960] 91, fig. 27:4.

10 A. Ben-Tor, *Cylinder Seals of Third-Millennium Palestine* (BASOR, supplement series [Cambridge 1978]) 4, s.v. 1A-2, p.14, Fig. 1:2; pp. 42, 49 and 66.

11 G. Herrmann, "Lapis Lazuli: the Early Phases of its Trade", in *Iraq* XXX [1968] 33-4.

12 C.L. Woolley, *The Royal Cemetery* (UE II [London & Philadelphia 1934]) pl. 203: 129, U. 11488; 130, U.11973; pl. 207: 202, U. 8339; 203, U. 8420; 204, U. 8681; 205, U. 9263.

13 P. Amiet, *La glyptique mésopotamienne archaïque* [Paris 1961] p. 60 and pl. 80: 1055.

14 N. Özgüç in N. & T. Özgüç, *Ausgrabungen in Kültepe, 1949* (TTKY V, No. 12 [Ankara 1953]) 234ff.

15 R. Dussaud, "La Lydie et ses voisins aux hautes époques", in *Babyloniaca* XI [1930] pl. III:1.

16 E. Porada, "The Warrior with Plumed Helmet ..." in *Berytus* VII [1942] pl. VIII:1.

17 *Ebla*, fig. 88.

18 See the reproductions in my article cited in note 16 above, *Berytus* VII [1942] pl. VIII.

19 P. Matthiae, "Two Princely Tombs at Tell Mardikh-Ebla", in *Archaeology* 33/2 [1980] 14.

20 See T. & N. Özgüç, *Ausgrabungen in Kültepe, 1949* (TTKY V, No. 12) pl. LXII: 695, 700-702, and Matthiae, *Ebla*, fig. 82.

21 Examples are H.H. von der Osten, *Ancient Oriental Seals in the Collection of E.T. Newell* (OIP 22 [Chicago 1934]) No. 308; L. Delaporte, *Catalogue des cylindres orientaux... Bibliothèque Nationale* [Paris 1910] No. 451; C.H. Gordon, "Western Asiatic Cylinder Seals in the Walters Art Gallery", in *Iraq* VI [1939] no. 42.

22 They are fully dressed in a cylinder in the Buffalo Museum of Science but nude in E. Porada, *Corpus* No. 234 and Iraq Museum 3528.

23 The cylinder in the Iraq Museum, published by P. Amiet, "Notes d'archéologie mésopotamienne à propos de quelques cylindres inédits du Musée de Baghdad", in *Sumer* XI [1955] 60, fig. 12.

24 P. Matthiae, *Missione archaeologica in Siria, campagna di scavi 1965* [Rome 1966] pl. XLVII.

25 For a good representation of the lion griffin on a cylinder of the Akkad period, see *Corpus* No. 220.

25a Madeline Noveck reminded me of the fragments from Ebla (Matthiae, *Ebla*, Fig. 35) as resembling the representation of the monster in the cylinder from Tôd.

26 For a drawing and some photographs of the impression see L. Legrain, *Archaic Seal-Impressions* (UE III [London & Philadelphia 1936] No. 517. For the name of the seal owner, see E. Sollberger, "Notes on the Early Inscriptions from Ur and El-'Obēd", *Iraq* XXII [1960] 83, s.v. 49-52.

27 It must be mentioned, however, that this practice may have been limited to southern Mesopotamia because there is evidence from Nuzi for the passing of a cylinder from father to son, from Puḫi-šenni to Teḫiptilla who used his father's cylinder seal during his own lifetime, see P.M. Purves, "The Early Scribes of Nuzi", AJSL LVII [1940] 164. Similarly there are several cases of a son's use of the father's seal cited by D. Collon, *The Seal Impressions from Tell Atchana/Alalakh* (AOAT 27 [Neukirchen-Vluyn 1975]), e.g. 169, Sealing 189, Niqmepa using the seal of his father Idrimi. Furthermore, there was the use of cylinders of earlier styles as dynastic seals. Thus the cylinder of Abban, son of Šaran, Sealing 11, carved in the Syrian style of about 1700 B.C. was used by Niqmepa in the middle of the 15th century B.C., see D. Collon, op. cit., 169-70. The enigmatic sealings of "dynastic cylinders" from Ugarit, C.F.A. Schaeffer, *Ugaritica* III [Paris 1956] p. 68 fig. 92; pp. 70-1 figs. 93, 94; p. 72 fig. 95; p. 73 fig. 96; p. 74 Fig. 97; p. 75 fig. 98; p. 76 fig. 99, must also be cited here. The style of one of the cylinders belongs to the Isin-Larsa period, c. 2000-1800 B.C., that of the other is thought to be a copy of the Kassite period. However, both seem to be inscribed with the same large signs with curvaceous wedges which characterize Syrian seal inscriptions of the 17th century B.C., but continue into the Mitannian style cylinders of the 15th century B.C. (Examples of the earlier type of inscription are D. Collon, op.cit., pls. LXI:5 and LXVII:11; of the later type, op cit., pl. LXXV: 230 or the inscription on the sealing of Šaušatar, R.F.S. Starr, *Nuzi* II [Cambridge, Mass. 1937] pl. 118:I). Both "dynastic cylinders" therefore seem to have been inscribed in Ugarit although the Isin-Larsa cylinder is of Mesopotamian style.

28 For the seal impressions see A. Parrot, *Mission archéologique de Mari II: Le Palais* [Paris 1959], pl. XLVIII: 71a, 72, 73, 81b, pp. 169-85. For a reproduction of the photograph of the impression made with the original cylinder, see A. Parrot, *Syria* 43 [1966] 335; see also the enlarged photograph by E. Porada *Ancient Art in Seals* [Princeton 1980] fig. I:14.

29 A. Parrot, *Mission archéologique de Mari I: Le Temple d'Ishtar* [Paris 1956] pl. LVIII: spread eagles of shell (210, 235, 236, 213, 211, 237, 246).

30 A. Parrot, *Le Temple d'Ishtar*, pl. LVIII: 1018.

31 A. Parrot, *Mission archéologique de Mari III: Les temples d'Ishtarat et de Ninni-Zaza* [Paris 1967], pl. LXXVII.

32 Curls of chlorite or steatite were found at Tarut, an island off the Saudi-Arabian coast in the Persian Gulf, *Artibus Asiae* XXXIII [1971] pl. VIII, no. 23.

33 I owe the oral information about limestone and shell examples from Nippur to D.P. Hansen.

34 See, e.g., H. Frankfort, *Cylinder Seals* [London 1939] pl. XI b from Fara.

35 C.L. Woolley, *The Royal Cemetery* (UE II), pl. 134, U. 8693 (the two lateral beads) and text, p. 369 fig. 78.

36 A. Parrot, *Mission archéologique de Mari IV: Le "trésor" d'Ur* [Paris 1968] pl. XXI. For a corrected reading of the inscription, see E. Sollberger, "La perle de Mari", RA LXIII [1969] 169-70.

37 See note 2 above, JCS 8 [1954] 118, 70753.

38 W. Sumner, "Excavations at Tall-i Malyān, 1971-1972", *Iran* XII [1974] 172, fig. 12:i.

39 A. Hakimi, *Catalogue de l'exposition LUT, xabis (Shahdad)* [Premier symposium annuel de la recherche archéologique en Iran, 1972] No. 324.

40 C.C. Lamberg-Karlovsky, "The Proto-Elamite Settlement at Tepe Yaḥyā", *Iran* IX [1971] pl. VI, opposite p. 95, text p. 92, s.v. Fig. 2:A.

41 Sumner in *Iran* XII, 173.

42 Examples of such repetitions are P. Amiet, *Glyptique susienne* (Mémoires de la délégation archéologique en Iran, t. XLIII [Paris 1972]), Nos. 933, 934, 1012, 1017(?) and probably many others which are only partly preserved.

43 An example of goddesses with streams of water is provided by the stele of Untash-Napirisha, P. Amiet, *Elam* [Auvers sur Oise 1966] p. 374, fig. 282 and p. 377, fig. 285. The great bronze altar from Susa, which was supported by goddesses holding vases (Amiet, *Elam*, p. 383, fig. 291) doubtless had water flowing from these vases.

43a Joan Aruz drew my attention to a marble stamp seal found in levels of the Jukhar Culture of India at Mohendjo Daro, E.H.J. Mackay, *Further Excavations at Mohenjo-daro* II [New Delhi 1937] pl. XCV:479, which is so closely related to the style of the Shahdad seals that it must have been imported from that region.

44 P. Amiet, "Antiquités du désert de Lut", RA LXVIII [1974] 102 fig. 6, and reference to the bead amulets from Chanhu Daro, ibid. 101 note 8.

45 E. Mackay, *Chanhu Daro Excavations 1935-1936* (AOS Vol. 20 [New Haven, Conn., 1943]) pl. L:1.

46 See P. Amiet, "Antiquités de la Bactriane", *La revue du Louvre* XXVIII [1978] and references given in the notes, also V.I. Sarianidi, "New Finds in Bactria and Indo-Iranian Connections", *South-Asian Archaeology, 1977* (Papers from the Fourth International Conference of South Asian Archaeologists in Western Europe [Naples 1979] 655, fig.5:10, 11; also id., "Bactrian Centre of Ancient Art", *Mesopotamia* XII [1977] fig. 59: 14, 16, 17.

47 E.N. Davis, *The Vapheio Cups and Aegean Gold and Silver Ware* [New York & London 1977] 69-79.

48 J. Vandier, "A propos d'un dépot de provenance asiatique trouvé à Tôd", *Syria* 18 [1937] 179 and note 2.

49 Vandier, op.cit., p. 180 note 3. The date given in that note, however, should be changed from the 28th to the 24th century B.C.

50 Parrot, *Les temples d'Ishtarat et de Ninni-Zaza*, pl. LXXVII.

51 Unfortunately, the reports on the location of these lapis lazuli groups, said by Parrot, op. cit. pp. 265-7, to have come from Salle 13, Cour 12 of the temple of Ninni-Zaza and Salle 5 of the temple of Ishtarat, which are found in Parrot, op. cit. pp. 23-31 and pp. 19-20, do not mention the emplacement of the small finds.

52 *Le temple d'Ishtar*, pp. 159-9.

53 See G. Pettinato, "Relations entre les royaumes d'Ebla et de Mari au troisième millénaire d'après les archives royales de Tell Mardikh-Ebla", *Akkadica* 2 [mars-avril 1977] 20-28, especially p. 24.

54 In *Akkadica* 2, p. 27, Pettinato stated that in the economic text No. 1953 the sum of the tribute paid by the city of Mari to the king of Ebla as a result of the military campaign (which ended with the defeat of Mari) was 2193 minas of silver and 134 minas and 26 shekels of gold. Of this 1100 minas of silver and 93 minas of gold are explicitly mentioned as property of the defeated king Iblul-Il whereas the rest of the sum was to be paid by the Elders of Mari. In the same text the part of the tribute which was to go to the military commander, Enna-Dagan, was given as 15% of the total tribute. There is no mention of lapis lazuli objects. But if these lapis lazuli items were temple property, as I assume, the action of removal may have been unofficial.

55 See P. Matthiae, "Tell Mardikh: Ancient Ebla", AJA 82 [1978] 542.

56 For the action of agents attempting to collect lapis lazuli for the Hittite king and for one of the Assyrian kings, see A.L. Oppenheim, *Glass and Glassmaking in Ancient Mesopotamia* [Corning, N.Y., 1970] pp. 11-12, notes 20-21.

57 For the likelihood of early direct Mesopotamian-Egyptian sea trade, see H.J. Kantor, in *Chronologies in Old World Archaeology*, p. 13. For evidence concerning extensive sea routes from Mesopotamia to the east in the third and early second millennium B.C., see A.L. Oppenheim, "The Seafaring Merchants of Ur", JAOS 74 [1954] 6-17. For a statement about extensive Harappan sea trade, see G.F. Dales, "A Search for Ancient Seaports", *Expedition* 4 [1962] 44.

58 M. Bietak, *Ausgrabungen in Sayala-Nubien, 1961-1965: Denkmäler der C-Gruppe und der Pan-Gräber-Kultur* (Österr. Akad. d. Wissenschaften, Denkschriften, phil.-hist. Kl. Bd. 92 [Wien 1966]) pp. 31-2, pl. 18:11, 12, photographic reproduction, pl. 15:2.

59 E. Edel, *Inschriften des Alten Reiches VI : Die Reiseberichte des Ḥrw-ḫwjf (Herchuf)* (Veröff. d. Deutschen Akad. d. Wissenschaften, Inst. f. Orientforschung 29 [Berlin 1955]) 51-75. I owe this reference to O. Goelet.

60 Good examples of compartmental seals with geometric patterns from East Iran, comparable to those of the sealings found in Nubia are reproduced by C.C. Lamberg-Karlovsky and M. Tosi, "Shahr-i Sokhta and Tepe Yahya: Tracks on the Earliest History of the Iranian Plateau", *East and West*,

New Series, 23 [1973], Figs. 32-49 from periods II and III at Shahr-i Sokhta; Fig. 99:L, a button-back steatite stamp seal from Tepe Yahya, Level IVB.

From Turkmenistan and Afghanistan, ancient Bactria, seals of this type were published by V.M. Masson and V.I. Sarianidi, *Central Asia* [Southampton 1972], p. 143, middle left; also by V.I. Sarianidi, *Drevnie zemledel'tsi Afganistana* [Moscow 1977], pl. I:1, 6 (the latter seal, of copper, seems to have been identical with the second impression from Nubia), 9; pl. III:1-6(*passim*); p. 85, Fig. 44:14-19; p. 87, Fig. 45, *passim*; p. 94, Fig. 48:2,3,4,7; p. 95, Fig. 49; p. 50, Fig. 50:3.

For a less closely related design of the same type of compartmental stamp seal, from Pakistani Baluchistan, see W.A. Fairservis, Jr., *The Roots of Ancient India*, 2nd ed. [Chicago 1975] 142:7. Perhaps the faience seal Mackay, *Chanhu-Daro Excavations* pl. LXXXVII:23 should also be cited among the related objects.

61 W. Helck, *Die Beziehungen Ägyptens zu Vorderasien in 3. und 2. Jahrtausend v. Chr.* [Wiesbaden 1971], 2nd ed., p. 73.

62 E. Edel in "Reiseberichte des Ḥrw-ḫwjf", p. 54 (cf. note 59 above) stated that the nomarchs of Elephantine carried out their expeditions only on order of the king. He added that trade in these areas was obviously a royal monopoly. In view of the size of the undertakings, which comprised as many as 300 donkeys (Edel, op. cit., p. 72 s.v. (1)), this seems a likely assumption not only for the trade in Nubia but also for international exchanges.

63 Bisson de la Roque, *Trésor de Tôd*, p. 8.

64 Kantor, *Chronologies in Old World Archaeology*, p. 20.

65 For examples of such Syrianizing cylinder impressions, see N. Özgüç, *Seals and Seal Impressions of Level Ib from Karum Kanish* (TTKY V, No. 25 [Ankara 1968]), pl. XI:C, XIII:B, C, XV:D.

Addendum

In the Royal Palace G of Ebla, of the third quarter of the third millennium B.C. (Mardikh IIB1: ca. 2400-2300/2250 B.C.), a large amount of raw lapis lazuli was found. There are several pieces whose weights range from a few grams to nearly 600 grams, with a total of nearly 16 kg. The largest amount is of pieces yet to be worked, and in one case a regular groove with a square section has been noted, most probably caused by a working tool. Evidence of the working of lapis lazuli at Ebla is offered by the actual finding of small objects, and also microliths that could be used as borers or scrapers. The raw lapis lazuli was found all over the building, but most came from the inner court (L. 2913 of the Administrative Quarter, where it probably fell from the upper storey, and in the southern hall with columns (L. 2866). These pieces and all fragments or parts of objects made of lapis lazuli are now being studied; as regards its provenance, Neutron Activation Analysis is planned for the pieces from Ebla and for pieces collected in Badakhshan kindly offered by Mrs G. Herrman. For an earlier period see also G. van Driel, *Akkadica* 12 [March-April 1979] 19-20 mentioning the discovery of unworked lapis lazuli at Jebel Aruda.

LIST OF ILLUSTRATIONS

Seals and a Pendant from the Tôd Treasure*

Fig. 1: Impression of cylinder seal 15226bis (Louvre), *Trésor*, pl. XL.
Fig. 2: Impression of cylinder seals 15225bis and 15225 (Louvre) *Trésor*, pl. XLI.
Fig. 3: Drawing from the impression of cylinder seal 15215 (Louvre), photograph published in *Trésor*, pl. XLI.
Fig. 4: Impression of cylinder seal 15227 (Louvre) *Trésor*, pl. XLIII.
Fig. 5: Impression of fragmentary cylinder seal (Louvre) *Trésor*, pl. XXXIX, third cylinder from the left.
Fig. 6: Impression of cylinder seal 15219 (Louvre) *Trésor*, pl. XLII
Fig. 7: Drawing from the photograph of cylinder seal 70753 (Cairo Museum) *Journal of Cuneiform Studies* 8 [1954] p. 118.
Fig. 8: Stamp seal 70664 (Cairo Museum) *Trésor*, pl. XLV.
Fig. 9: Two-sided pendant 70668 (Cairo Museum) *Trésor*, pl. XLVI.
Fig. 9a; b, Drawings from photographs of two-sided pendant 70668.

* The impressions of the cylinder seals in the Louvre and the photograph of Fig. 4 were kindly furnished to me by Pierre Amiet, to whom I want to express my sincere thanks.

Explanatory Text Figures

Fig. a: Cylinder seal from Jericho, K. Kenyon, *Excavations at Jericho* [London, 1960] p.91, Fig. 27:4.
Fig. b: Impression of cylinder seal in the Iraq Museum, P. Amiet, *Glyptique mésopotamienne archaique* [Paris, 1961] pl. 80:1055.
Fig. c: Hero with plumed helmet, detail from cylinder seal in the Walters Art Gallery, C56, C.H. Gordon, *Iraq* VI [1939] No. 36.
Fig. d: One pair of dignitaries embracing from a group of three pairs on a stone basin from Tell Mardikh-Ebla, P. Matthiae, *Ebla, un impero ritrovato* [Turin, 1977] Fig. 88.
Fig. e: A table with bull's feet, detail from an ivory plaque from Tell Mardikh-Ebla *Archaeology* 33/2 [1980] p. 14.
Fig. f: Table with lateral supports, detail from a seal impression (Özgüç, *Ausgrabungen in Kültepe, 1949*, TTKY V, No. 12, Ankara, 1953. Pl. LXII Fig. 695); Kültepe Level II.
Fig. g: Impression of cylinder seal, E. Porada, B. Buchanan, *Corpus*, No. 234.
Fig. h: Impression of cylinder seal in the Iraq Museum, P. Amiet, *Sumer* XI [1954] p. 60, Fig. 12.
Fig. i: Relief on a basin from Tell Mardikh-Ebla, P. Matthiae, *Missione Archaeologica in Siria, 1965* [Rome, 1966] pl. XLVII.
Fig. j-1: Lion-headed eagle amulets from Tôd, 15249 (Louvre), *Trésor*, pl. XLIII, and 70677-70680, 70683 (Cairo Museum), *Trésor*, pl. XLVII.
Fig. j-2: Lion-headed eagle amulets in shell from Mari, A. Parrot, *Le temple d'Ishtar* [Paris, 1956] pl. LVIII.
Fig. k-1: Shell amulets from Mari, A. Parrot, *Le Templed'Ishtar*. Paris, 1956, pl. LVIII.
Fig. k-2: Shell amulet imitated in lapis lazuli from Tôd, 706518-706519 (Cairo Museum), *Trésor*, pl. XLVIII, fifth item from the right.
Fig. l-1: Couchant bulls from Tôd, *Trésor*, 15244, pl. XLIII (Louvre)
Fig. l-2: Couchant bull from Mari, A. Parrot, *Le Temple d'Ishtar*. Paris, 1956, pl. LVIII:1018.
Fig. m-1: Selection of hair curls from Tod, *Trésor*, 15251, pl. XLIV (Louvre).
Fig. m-2: Selection of hair curls from the temples of Ishtarat and Ninni-Zaza, A. Parrot, *Les temples d'Ishtarat et de Ninni-Zaza*, Paris, 1967, pl. LXXVII.
Fig. n-1: Torso of bull-man in relief or inlay from Tôd, *Trésor*, 70665, pl. XLVI (Cairo Museum).
Fig. n-2: Detail from a cylinder seal impression of Fara style from Fara, E. Heinrich, *Fara* [Berlin, 1931] pl. 46:f.
Fig. o: Stamp seal from Tall-i Malyan, W. Sumner, *Iran* XII [1974] p. 172, fig. 12:i.
Fig. p: Impression of a cylinder seal from Shahdad, A. Hakimi, *Catalogue de l'exposition LUT*, 1972, No. 324.
Fig. q: Impression of a cylinder seal from Tepe Yahya, C.C. Lamberg-Karlovsky, *Iran* IX [1971] pl. VI, opp. p. 95.
Fig. r: Two-sided circular pendant from East Iran, P. Amiet, RA, LXVIII [1974] 102, fig. 6.
Fig. s: Jar sealings made with stamp seals from Sayala, Nubia, M. Bietak, *Ausgrabungen in Sayala...* (Denkschriften d. Österr. Akad. D. Wiss. phil. hist. Kl., Bd. 92, 1966), pl. 15:2.
Fig. t-1: A compartmental stamp seal from Dashli, Bactria, V.I. Sarianidi, *Drevnie zemledel'tsi Afganistana*. [Moscow, 1977] p. 96, Fig. 50:3.
Fig. t-2: A bronze seal "from predatory excavations of burial grounds in Bactria," V. Sarianidi, *Mesopotamia* XII [1977], Fig. 57, upper left.

Fig. 1

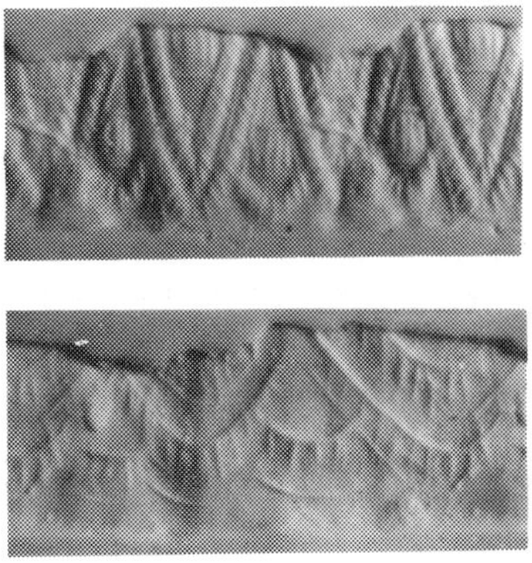

Fig. 2

Fig. a

Fig. b

Fig. 3

Fig. c

Fig. d

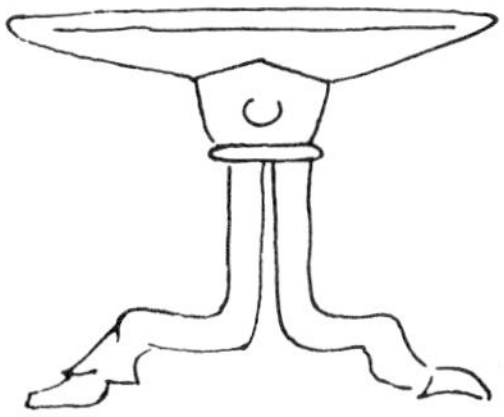

Fig. e

Fig. f

Fig. 4

Fig. g

Fig. h

Fig. i

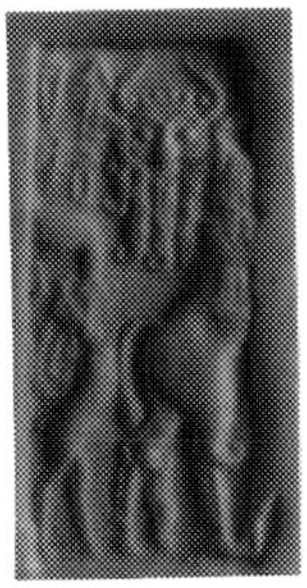

Fig. 5

Fig. 6

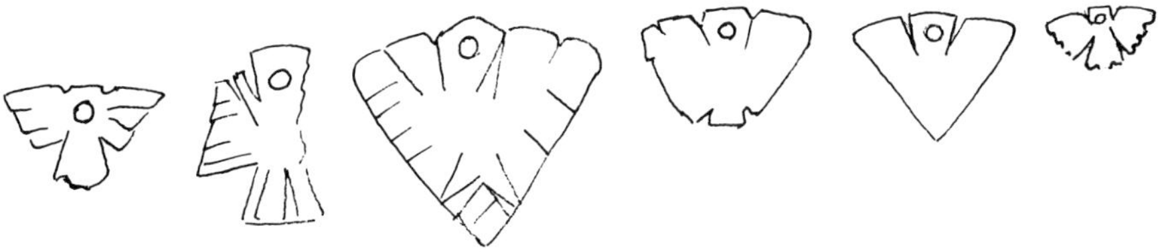

Fig. j-1

Fig. j-2

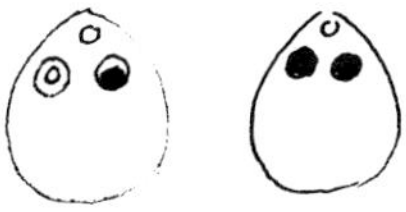

Fig. k-1

Fig. k-2

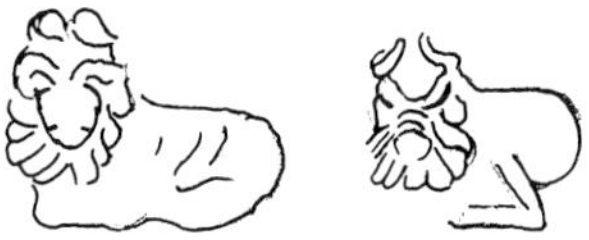

Fig. l-1

Fig. l-2

Fig. m-1

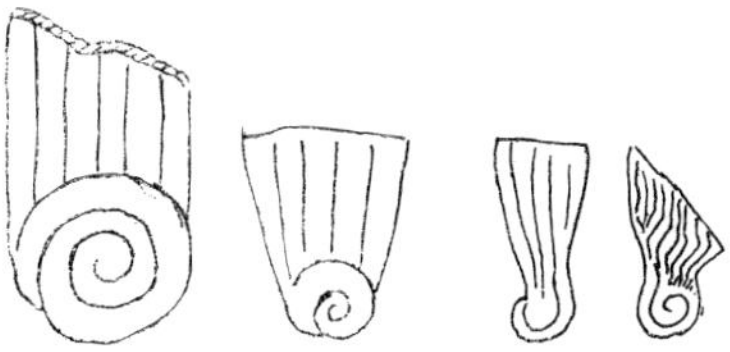

Fig. m-2

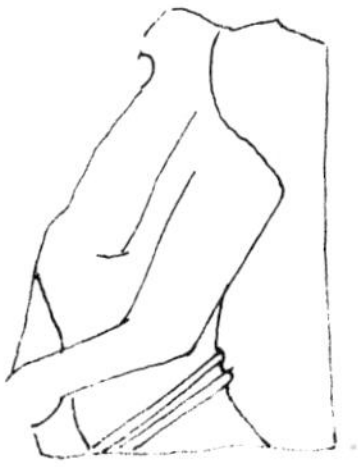

Fig. n-1

Fig. n-2

Fig. 7

Fig. o

Fig. p

Fig. q

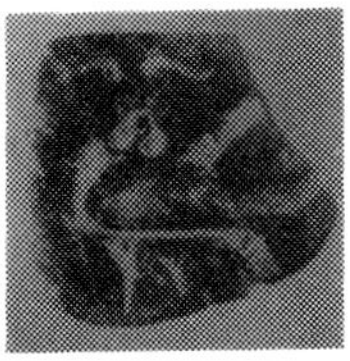

Fig. 8

Fig. 9

Fig. 9a

Fig. 9b

Fig. r

Fig. s

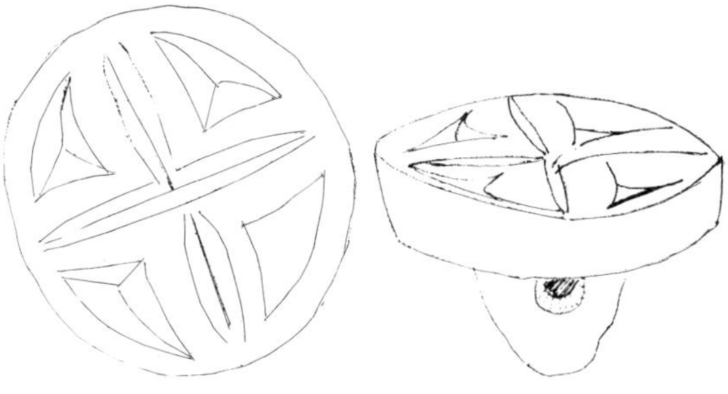

Fig. t-1

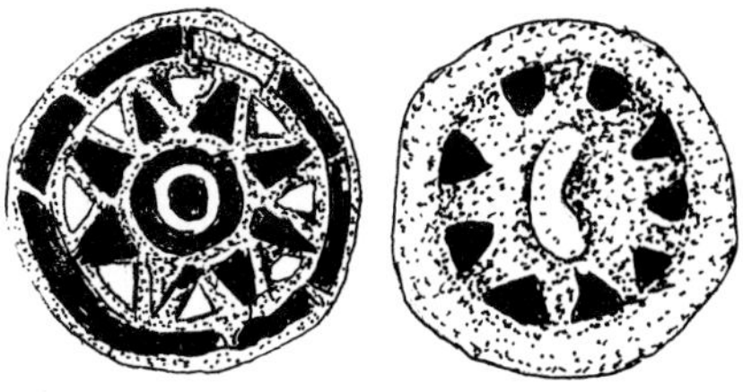

Fig. t-2

ILKU AND LAND TENURE IN THE MIDDLE ASSYRIAN KINGDOM – A SECOND ATTEMPT

J.N. Postgate (Cambridge)

Since access to and control of land was at all dates the paramount consideration in the Mesopotamian countryside, and *ilku* will usually have provided the main area of contact between the individual and the state, I hope I may be forgiven for making this second attempt at a subject which I discussed at some length less than ten years ago.[1] It seems worth doing partly because some new evidence is available, and partly in order to persuade I.M. Diakonoff that our views are perhaps not so irreconcilable as they seem at first sight. In the Middle Assyrian kingdom we would still define the *ilku* institution as a system whereby individuals owed personal service to the state for a specified length of time, as a condition of entitlement to land, and we shall now isolate some components of this definition and discuss them one by one.

The nature of ilku *service*

Was *ilku* military service? In accordance with the etymology of the word, the fundamental obligation it imposed was to "go", or serve the state, i.e. to place one's person at the disposal of the state for a period of time; even by itself the verb *alāku* retained this specific connotation, at least in Middle Assyrian times. What this personal service entailed varied: it was for the state to determine whether, having taken over a person, he should be employed on military or civilian duties, and the decision must have depended on economic and social conditions at the time, as well as on political events. Among scholars working on Old Babylonian texts there seems to be some reluctance to admit that *ilku* obligations could include military service,[2] but no such doubts seem to have afflicted Landsberger.[3] It is certainly the case at Nuzi, and under the Neo-Assyrian empire.[4] As for the Middle Assyrian system, the connection between *ilku* and military service was discussed in BSOAS 34 [1971] 496-502, but since it did not seem to a recent writer "that the evidence at present available supports his position",[5] it is necessary to review the evidence in some detail.

In certain receipts from Assur corn is issued as "rations for the *ilku* horses" (KAJ 233; 253; and now also VS 19, 44). Since even in Neo-Assyrian times horses were reserved for the army, it is a reasonable deduction that these animals were used by chariot-troops engaged on their *ilku* service. A badly preserved text from Tell al-Rimah confirms this in the closing portion of the contract:

TR 2087:10 [Š]E-*um* PAD-*at*	The corn, fodder
11 [AN]ŠE.KUR.RA.MEŠ	of the horses;
12 [(x) x]*na*? *ga ru*	the .....
13 *ša* LÚ.GIGIR *ù* A[NŠE]	of the charioteer and donkey?,
14 IN?.NU? *ša* 4 I[TI]	straw? for 4 months -
15 *i-na* UD-*me e-ri-šu-[ni]*	when he demands it
16 *i-dan*	he shall pay.

That this debt-note did refer to *ilku* obligations follows from TR 3023 (*Iraq* 30 [1968] Pl. LXIII), which also mentions corn, as horse fodder, straw (IN.NU) and oil (1 QA IÀ), received by Sikku "from the *ilku* of Abu-ṭāb" (KI *il-ki ša* A. : the same principals as in TR 3010, discussed below.

In VS 19, 72 javelins (*lištaḫu*) seem to be followed by the qualification *il-ku*; however, this is not epigraphically beyond doubt, and since one would expect *il-ki* or *ša il-ki* no argument can be based on this passage. On the other hand, we are probably entitled to take references to "goers" (*āliku*) as meaning persons performing their *ilku* service. The best examples of this usage are in VAT 18096, with the phrases ÉRIN.MEŠ BAN *a-li-ku-t[u] ša ḫu-ra-di* "archers, serving in the army" and 1 LÚ *a-li-ku ša ḫu-[ra-]di* "one man, serving in the army".[6] These passages underline the association of *ilku* with the term *ḫurādu*, first apparent from TR 3005, which mentions "the army of Nihria, who are doing *ilku* service with [their?] brothers" (cf. BSOAS 34 [1971] 49 n.9), and the meaning and importance of *ḫurādu* are supported by many new Middle Assyrian instances quoted by Freydank (AOF 4 [1976] 111-5; also KAJ 159:7 *i+na t[u-a]r ḫu-ra-di* [kindly collated for me by Dr. Freydank]). It appears beyond doubt that *ilku* service *could* lead to enrolment in the army, but the mere existence of a phrase like *āliku ša ḫurādi* tends to suggest that *ilku* duties could be performed in other, civilian, ways, and these would probably include the "king's work" (*šipar šarri*) which is threatened as a penalty in the Laws, and would correspond to the *dullu ša šarri*, known in Neo-Assyrian times to have been an alternative employment of those called up for *ilku* service.[7]

Exemption and substitution

At any period it is to be expected that those of sufficient social or administrative standing were able to avoid the performance of *ilku* service in person. The Neo-Assyrian sources offer clear instances of individuals exempted from *ilku* (among other obligations) as a personal favour from the monarch. This is probably how land came to have exempt status (*zakûtu*), which could be transferred with the land to a new purchaser, and the term rather implies that other land was normally liable to *ilku* obligations (as well as direct taxes on the crops). Quite different is the arrangement under which officials of a certain rank were entitled to commute their *ilku* service into payments in silver or in kind; we have suggested that these were the *zakkû*, a rather general term for the members of the administrative cadre (TCAE 241-3).

It is not likely that the same solution was adopted in Middle Assyrian times. Instead, there is evidence that one might engage another person to act as a substitute. As far as I know, there is no evidence for the length of time those performing *ilku* duties were needed by the state, but each individual's obligation must have been for a restricted period, and various texts prove that the time served was strictly accounted for, to the months and days. The most explicit text is TR 3010: "From day X, A and B have adjusted their accounts, and their *ilku* has been performed (*alik*) in the hand of (= by) B" (BSOAS 34 [1971] 498[10]). Although less clear, KAJ 246 obviously belongs in a similar context: "4 months 20 days in the hand of A, B has received..... of the army (*ḫurādu*) of .....". One suspects that a similar, though perhaps more complex, situation lies behind KAJ 137 too, which begins "from day X", and mentions "a month" as well as *il-ka* in l. 13; the tablet was kindly collated for me by Dr. Freydank, but it is lacking too many crucial signs to permit convincing restorations.

Although it does not contain the words *ilku* or *ḫurādu*, one of the most important documents in this context is KAJ 307 (also collated for me by Dr. Freydank).

1	KIŠIB [1]DI.KUD.[d]7.BI	Seal of Dayyan-Sibitti:
2	*iš-tu* ITI *al-la-na-te*	From 1st of Allanate,
3	UD.1.KÁM *li-me*	in the eponymate of
4	[1.d]*šùl-ma-an*-UR.SAG	Shalmaneser (I):

5	^{1}KAM.DINGIR *pa-aḫ-nu*	Erišili, the *paḫnu*,
6	NÍG.KA$_9$.MEŠ *iš-tu ma-da-te-šu*	has settled his accounts
7	*iṣ-ṣa-bat*	with his payments.
8	ANŠE.KUR.RA *i-na pi-ti*	The horse will be fed in the
9	^{1}KAM.DINGIR-*ma e-kal*	charge of Eriš-ili himself.
10	*ul-ma ù ḫa-ṣi-na*	A spear and an axe
11	*a-na pa-aḫ-ni-šu-nu*	they did not give
12	*la i-di-nu*	to their *paḫnu*,
13	*iš-tu* UD-*me an-ni-e-ma*	(but) from this day
14	*mul-te-ṣi-tu-šu-nu ša* GIŠ.GIGIR	their expenses on the chariot
15	*ki pa-ni-ti šu-nu-ma i-da-nu*	they themselves will pay, as before.

Seals and witnesses; no other date.

Notes on the text: 5: the reading *paḫnu* is secured by l. 11; it is probably to be recognized also in TR 3006, which records that "PN, LÚ *pa!-aḫ-nu* has received some tin and a horse(?)" [collated, but very worn]. 6: *maddattu* naturally does not mean "tribute" (any more than it does in VS 19, 49:4), but must bear the nuance "what *he* has to supply". 14: *multēṣītu-šunu* [-*ṣi*- and not -*šèr*- (contra CAD M/ii 289b) collated] more literally "their outlay".

This document records an agreement reached between Eriš-ili on the one hand and Dayyan-Sibitti representing an unspecified group on the other. It defines how certain expenses are to be shared between the two parties. The military connection is obvious, and it can hardly be doubted that Eriš-ili is going to the army on their behalf, with a horse and chariot, spear and axe. In these circumstances it seems probable that *paḫnu* was the technical term for a "substitute", and although it is not stated that the military service is an *ilku* obligation, this is a fair assumption, since there can hardly have been two parallel systems of this kind. Although it is conceivable that Dayyan-Sibitti represents the authorities responsible for *ilku* service, the text bears all the marks of a private transaction. Similarly in TR 3010 and KAJ 246 the phrase *ina qāt* points rather to the settling of accounts between the two parties in their private capacities, and hence to a substitution, than to a documentation of the individual's past or future *ilku* obligations to the administration.

The practice of employing a substitute to do one's *ilku* service, and the preparation of detailed accounts between the original bearer of the obligation (*qaqqad rēdîm*) and his replacement (*taḫḫum*) are attested in the Late Old Babylonian Ubarrum archive discussed by Landsberger, but neither the term *paḫnu* nor the practice of substitution in this form is found in the Neo-Assyrian sources.

Origin and transmission of ilku *liability*

Although we believe that all *ilku* obligations in the Middle Assyrian kingdom originated in theory from the tenure of land, it must be admitted that there is no proof of this connection, which is an assumption based on comparison with other regimes and on some circumstantial evidence. In Neo-Assyrian texts exemption from or liability to *ilku* is sometimes mentioned in documents concerned with land (see TCAE 81-2), showing that the *ilku* was an obligation specifically attached to particular pieces of land. Many of the Nuzi real estate adoption texts mention *ilku* duties which are obviously closely associated with the ownership or occupation of the land.[7] Both at Nuzi and in the Neo-Assyrian period it is known that *ilku* duties were inherited: a Nuzi text states "A's son is my son, with regard to my land, my house, and my *ilku*, and I have no other son"

(HSS 5, 48:28, quoted after CAD I/J 77-8), while a yet unpublished adoption text from the Nabû Temple at Kalhu includes the provision that the adopted son should share the profits and obligations of the father's house with any later sons:

10 *lū* DUMU.MEŠ-*šú ša* A, B ŠEŠ-*šunu dannu zittu issi-šunu ēkal il-ku issi-šunu illak ḫabullē-šu ušallam ḫabullē-šu ušaddana*

"Even if A (the father) has 10 sons, B is their eldest brother: he will enjoy a share (of the patrimony) with them, he will perform the *ilku* with them, he will repay his (A's) debts and recover his debts" (ND 5480, quoted by kind permission of Prof. D.J. Wiseman).

That *ilku* liabilities were inherited means that they were not imposed afresh by the authorities on individuals with regard to their own circumstances. Presumably each householder owed a measurable amount of *ilku* which was passed on from father to son, and which must have been determined by some pre-existent criterion. The mention of *ilku* in land sale documents means that the inherited *ilku* was attached to the father (and to his father, etc.) not as a person, but as a condition of the tenure of land. This appears to be the theoretical basis of the system at Nuzi and in the Neo-Assyrian period, and it may reasonably be assumed to have been current in the Middle Assyrian kingdom. However, this simple situation breaks down when the land is sold: since the original intention of the system was to secure personal service in return for land entitlement, it is obvious that the state would wish individuals to continue serving, even though landless. At Nuzi, therefore, the *ilku* obligations were not usually transferred to the new owner along with entitlement to the land, but had to be passed on to the next generation of the family selling the land, along with other debts and assets.

In the surviving Middle Assyrian land-sale texts there is no mention of *ilku*. There could be various explanations for this, but, for the same reasons as at Nuzi, it is clear that in practice the *ilku* obligation will have remained in most cases with the seller of the land. Although those land sale texts we have are only a very restricted group, as described below, we can be fairly certain that the cumbersome Nuzi real estate adoption procedure was not in use - rather they prepared explicit sale documents. Two solutions of the legal problem could be reconstructed: either the land entitlement was sold and the state officially recognized that the *ilku* obligation remained with the original title-holder - thus accepting the *de facto* separation of *ilku* from land tenure and attaching the *ilku* directly to the members of the family in question - , or, in the eyes of the state the new purchaser incurred the *ilku* along with the title to the land, but was somehow able to ensure that the actual service continued to be done by the previous owner. Whichever is right, one may guess that even after the transfer of titular ownership the same family would normally have continued to cultivate the land, although now as some kind of tenants under economic, if not legal, constraints to remain. This was probably the situation at Nuzi, where it can be proved to have happened in some cases.[8]

It was probably a relationship of this kind which lay behind the phrase *ilku ša ālāiūti* in KAJ 7. This passage was discussed at length in BSOAS 34 [1971] 496-8, where it was concluded that "a family which held land from the state in return for *ilku* service was able to have those services performed by its own dependants without losing its rights to ownership" (p. 498). The term *ālāiu*, which is found in this legal document and in the Middle Assyrian Laws, obviously had an accepted connotation precise enough to figure in legal contexts, and seems to refer to free-born persons subject to legal and economic dependence on another. This is presumably the relationship making large numbers of men dependent on wealthy families. The most explicit case of this is in VAT 15474 (see H. Hirsch, AfO 23 [1970] 79-80; H. Freydank, VS 19, 6), in which a total of 999 men (ÉRIN.MEŠ) is recorded as belonging to (*ša*) the three sons of Šamaš-aha-iddina and checked by state officials (*qīpūtu*).[9] Each son has a share (*zittu*) of men (respectively 426:230:150) and some extra men whose status is not made clear. The men are not slaves, and yet the family's hold over them is such that they can be inherited, and their dependent status is accepted by the state which employs officials to check them. Can these men all have been tenants, or at least erstwhile land-owners, whose lands have now passed into the possession of this family, leaving them to inherit only the *ilku* obligations attached to the land? It may seem improbable, but a parallel can be found in the land acquisitions of the Tehip-tilla family at Nuzi, and it is hard to know otherwise how the family could have built up so large a body of retainers.

Tenure of land – the sources

Any reconstruction of the system of land tenure in Middle Assyrian times must rely on two groups of sources: the land-sale documents and tablet B of the Laws. Since these are isolated from each other and from other sources, care must be taken to establish their exact nature and their *Sitz im Leben*, so as to avoid the danger of according them a validity wider than was in fact the case. The land-sale documents all come from a single provenance in the city of Assur, near the *Haus des Beschwörungspriesters*, and they may even belong to a single private archive: the lands in question are all in a group of villages "across the Šiššar", a river which H.J. Nissen has plausibly identified with the Wadi Tharthar.[10] The tablets are not the final deeds of sale (*ṭuppu dannutu*), but interim documents, probably made out hastily to enable the sellers to profit from the purchase price. This group of sales represents the establishment of rural estates by city families resident at Assur, a process equally attested during the 1st millennium BC for Kalhu and Nineveh. It was documents such as these which led to "a general division of society into two clearly defined strata: the more prosperous community members could now dispense with the necessity of fulfilling their obligations to the community ....., letting all these obligations rest solely on their impoverished neighbours who were dependent upon them as a result of debt or for other reasons" (I.M. Diakonoff, *Third International Conference of Economic History* [Munich 1965] 27).

The other major source for land tenure, tablet B of the Laws, as well as being much broken also has its inherent limitations. In the first place one has to bear in mind that no law can be expected to coincide precisely with currently prevailing conditions: they may either enshrine moribund traditions which have been outstripped by changes in society, or they may be freshly promulgated measures telling us more about the aspirations of their author than about the current social scene. A second point is that these are laws which apply to the city of Assur, and cannot be assumed to reflect conditions outside its immediate homeland: the land of Assur, or Assyria, was the creation of Aššur-uballiṭ I, and there is every reason to suppose that before him cities like Nineveh, Kalhu and Arbil had their own indigenous laws and traditions, probably even more strongly under Hurrian influence than Assur herself. It is therefore not surprising to find in an "interim land-sale" document from Tell Al-Rimah which includes formulae differing from those familiar from the Assur 14446 archive:

A.ŠÀ *ú-šal-ba*	"He shall delimit the field,
ki-i pi-i ri-ik-si	and according to the edict
ša LUGAL LÚ.NIMGIR *ú-sa-sa*	of the king he shall have the herald make an announcement."[11]

This use of *lawû(m)* Š is otherwise only attested at Nuzi (CAD L 76), and it here replaces the Assur phrases beginning *eqla uzakka* ..... (cf. BSOAS 34 [1971] 514[67]). Although too isolated to contribute any substantial information of its own, this outlying text serves to stress how rash it would be to consider the Assur 14446 archive as at all typical.

Land ownership – individual or communal?

All the evidence at present available suggests that the title to private land was in the name of an individual: single persons buy or sell the land in sale documents, and even if their relatives were present there is no indication that they played any legal role in the transfer of entitlement. Nor do the laws make any mention of "communal entitlement" to a piece of land, except in the case of "undivided brothers" (*aḫḫū lā zīzūte*). For obvious reasons state-controlled legal systems prefer to see the ownership of land (and any attached liabilities) registered in the name of an individual, and the property rights of the individual (even vis-à-vis his family) were of course recognized in the Old Assyrian city. *In law*, therefore, I still "see no reason to assume the existence of joint family holdings (after the death of the father) as a regular feature".[12]

This is not however to deny the importance of the extended family in the society of northern Mesopotamia. As we have stressed, laws and legal documents reflect actual social conditions only imperfectly, and *in practice* it is likely that much land was owned and tilled jointly by the consensus of extended families. This would be a normal situation for a rural society, and not implausible for families resident in the city. It was the extended family which formed the basis for Koschaker's theory of *Eigentumsgemeinschaft* (NKRA 36ff.), but we differ radically from him in that - although we admit that such joint ownership existed in practice - we cannot see how it would have achieved the legal status which would enable it *in law* to prevent a member with individual title to his land from selling it himself.

Nevertheless, there is one cogent point which shows that (whatever the legal position) land in some villages could not have been sold without the co-operation of others: "From the Law-Book (B) §5 we know that land could be delimited by a "great boundary of companions" (*taḫūmu rabi'u ša tappā'ī*) within which lay "lots" (*pūru*) divided by "small boundaries".[13] It is clear from KAV 125-129, for example, that these *pūru* were indeed pieces of land assigned to individuals by the drawing of lots, in a procedure similar to that used in the allocation of inheritance shares. This is a practice designed to achieve a fair distribution of the best land, and characteristic of villages with a regime of alternate fallow years, demanding that each cultivator's lands should be evenly disposed across the two halves of the village's land used in annual alternation. To illustrate the situation we may quote a parallel from the present century in the Hatay: "within the core and fringe villages there are anywhere from 25-30 permanent sections of the land which never change, and each head of a family has his inheritance scattered so that he has a plot in each of the permanent divisions. Within the fringe village land titles have been issued, and thus the plots are stabilized within the permanent divisions; in the core village these individual plots are changed every year according to a method whereby they draw from a hat for their position within the permanent large sections".[14]

There are two features here which need to be specially stressed: in the first place, we find a hierarchy of land-divisions - the permanent sections, evidently agreed by tradition among the heads of families, and separated by boundaries which may be taken as equivalent to the "great boundaries of companions" (implying that in this context *tappā'u* means another family-head in the same village community), and the sub-sections which may either be fixed by land-title or reassigned annually by lot. These latter correspond to the *pūru*, a term which does not apply to the larger sections, since the "small boundaries" are explicitly stated to be "of the lots" (*ša pūrāni*, MAL Tablet B §9).

The second feature of particular interest for us is the distinction between the "fringe" and "core" villages. The population on which Dr. Aswad is concentrating are "short-range herders", and she writes that "their village settlement and organization developed into a pattern of agnatic core and fringe villages. These are distinguished by the people as *merkez* (center) and *shoraba* (soup) villages respectively ..... The composition of a core or center village historically included the majority of a strong lineage plus sharecroppers, while that of a fringe village was more heterogeneous, reflecting the processes of expansion by the core into its lands and the acquisition of property by outside groups such as urban landlords to whom the core had aligned itself. Thus the agnatic core maintained its property corporately in the *merkez* village, but property in the fringe villages was owned by various groups" (pp. 24-5).

It would be naive to suggest that there is any deep-seated similarity between the 20th century Hatay and Middle Assyrian Assur, but it is still instructive to compare them. The agricultural activity of a core village is longer-established and more intensive, which would lead, even where the elder son received a double share of the patrimony, to a fragmentation of land holdings and intense competition for land, such as would call for a complex system of "lots" as described in the Middle Assyrian Laws, and militate against the assignment of stable land-titles. Such a system would make land sale a difficult procedure, to be undertaken only with the co-operation of the rest of the village, or at least of the family, but we cannot be sure whether the absence of land-sale documents referring to such villages is mere accident, or (less likely) because they were very rare or non-existent. In any case, we may guess that villages in the vicinity of Assur, to which the Laws probably were first applied, resembled the "core" villages. The Assur 14446 texts, on the other hand, slot almost too neatly into the category of a "fringe" village: probably geographically peripheral, recently established, with some evidence of provinciality in the inhabitants, and, as the documents themselves bear witness, open to the large scale encroachments of the urban landlord.[15]

In the Hatay the pattern of land tenure is inextricably entwined with factors such as historical events, ethnic origin, agricultural conditions, and the business and family connections with other villages and towns. It should serve as a warning not to try and impose a false homogeneity on Assyrian rural society, but being cuneiformists we are entitled to hope that evidence on just such factors may yet be recovered to bridge the immense hiatus between the two groups of texts on which we are forced to rely.

"Ultimate owner" – Village community or palace?

I.M. Diakonoff, and N.B. Jankowska, see the lands of villages round Assur and Nuzi as being the communal property of the "village commune".[16] While it may have been true in 3rd millennium Sumer that "The right of ultimate ownership of the land is exercised by the neighbourhood commune",[17] we seriously doubt that this can apply to Middle Assyrian Assur or to Nuzi. The disagreement is perhaps largely one of definition: it is quite true that the community, represented by a mayor and elders, was responsible for the village's territory both administratively and legally, but I can find nowhere any direct evidence that the community "owned" all this land.[18] We still believe that if there was such a thing as an "ultimate owner", it was the crown, or, in Assyrian phraseology "the palace".

Before enlarging on this point, we must first dispose of the *zitti ēkalli* "palace share", on which our previous position is in need of substantial correction. The *zitti ēkalli* texts have recently been treated by C. Saporetti, in *Egitto e Vicino Oriente* II [Pisa 1979] 151-172. Having considered the texts already known and the new VS 19, 41 (to which we shall return), he concludes that the land called *zitti ēkalli* had been conceded to individuals by the Mitannian overlords, and was forfeited to "the palace" when Assyria achieved her independence (*automaticamente considerate "eredità" del palazzo assiro*, p. 155). Without discussing his argument in detail, we must dissent from this view, but equally, we must admit that his criticisms of our own reconstruction are justified (p. 153f.). In particular, we were wrong to suggest that the *naiālu* was a childless man, and hence our idea that the entire property reverted to the palace on his death (as a *zitti ēkalli*) is invalid. Instead, I would now prefer to accept J. Nougayrol's assessment of the Ugaritic evidence and take *naiālu* as a defaulter (in his *ilku* liabilities), and the "palace share" as a part (or all) of the defaulter's property, confiscated at his death or during his lifetime, in compensation for the *ilku* he owed. That the forfeiture did not always include the entire property can be deduced from the new text VS 19, 41 (edited by Saporetti, loc. cit., 160): the crucial lines read "if he agrees to take (it) without a "divider" [LÚ *mu-zi-i-zi* - hardly = *muzzizu*, contra Saporetti], the ..... who denounced him shall take this palace-share" (ll. 8-13; in l. 12 one might collate for LÚ.A.LÁL+SAR.KI "an Assyrian"). It is entirely plausible that land which had been given to an individual in exchange for his performance of *ilku* duties, should be confiscated if he failed to perform those duties; this seems to have been the procedure at Ugarit, and the single occurrence of a *naiālu* in the Neo-Assyrian period may reflect the same situation then.[19] This sort of forfeiture does not prove that the palace was the "ultimate owner" of the land, but it makes it more likely.

But, it will be objected, if the palace "ultimately owned" *some* land, which it gave out to citizens in return for *ilku* service, this does not mean that it so controlled *all* land. My disagreement with the "village commune = ultimate owner" theory turns precisely on this point: they would see two classes of land, one controlled by the palace and conditional on *ilku* performance for the state, the other controlled by the "village commune" and conditional on performance of services for the commune.[20] I cannot see any reason to separate the two categories: admitting freely the control that in practice the commune could exercise over lands within its territory, I cannot see that in law this contradicts the claim to "ultimate ownership" of the palace.

There is as yet no proof for either opinion, but we do feel that ours has a certain historical plausibility. The military successes of the Assyrian kings could not have been accomplished without some administrative procedure for conscripting the rural population, and the *ilku* system as we describe it seems well adapted for this purpose: it is hardly likely to have excluded all those in villages with a strong traditional commune system. Hence we see the *ilku* system as imposed from above on to an existing land regime: it would not have entailed large-scale reassignment of land-ownership, merely the acknowledgement, in most cases, of the *status quo*. Nor need we envisage a Domesday Book operation, involving the issue of written land-titles by the state: clearly most existing entitlement to land would be unwritten, though fixed by custom, and the need for documentary proof probably crept in with the gradual encroachment of urban landlords.

At present the term *ilku* is unknown in Old Assyrian texts, although given their nature and provenance this is a dangerous argument *ex silentio*. Nevertheless, we cannot agree that "Die genaue Kenntniss der *ilku*-Verhältnisse in der altbab. Zeit bildet die Voraussetzung zum Verständnis der weiteren Entwicklung" (B. Kienast, RLA 5, 57-9). That is a rather Old-Babylonio-centric point of view, and if we look for parallels to the Middle Assyrian system we shall find them in Nuzi, Ugarit and Alalakh, rather than Babylonia. We believe that what we have at Assur is an adaptation of a system introduced throughout northern Mesopotamia by their Hurrian or Mitannian overlords, which may owe little more than the name to the institution of *ilku* in Hammurapi's Babylonia.[21]

AOF = *Altorientalische Forschungen* [Berlin]

MAL = *Middle Assyrian Laws* (see G.R. Driver & J.C. Miles, *The Assyrian Laws* [Oxford 1935])

TCAE = J.N. Postgate, *Taxation and Conscription in the Assyrian Empire*, Studia Pohl: Series Maior 3 [Rome 1974]

---

1 BSOAS 34 [1971] 496-520.

2 e.g. B. Kienast, RLA 5, 57-9 s.v. *ilku*; CAD I/J 80.

3 JCS 9 [1955] 128 ("*ilkum* .... purely military") with 10 [1956] 39b.

4 for Nuzi cf. JEN 327:12 *anāku ilka ina* ^{uru}X *našâk*, or 498:5 PN *ina āl ilki ašim-mi u aḫḫē-šu ana narkabāte ašbu-mi* (quoted after CAD I/J 75b); for NAss cf. TCAE 83; 218ff.; the new passages for *ilku* in CT 53, 10.r.12-13; 13.r.15-17; 87:8-14 do not necessitate any revisions.

5 M. deJ. Ellis, *Agriculture and the State in Ancient Mesopotamia*, 20[52].

6 See H. Freydank, AOF 4 [1975] 112; another new occurrence of *ḫurādu* is the *rab ḫurādāte* in VS 19, 5:1.

7 Space does not permit a discussion of the Nuzi situation, but an excellent summary of recent opinion is given in M.P. Maidman's dissertation, *A Socio-economic Analysis of a Nuzi Family Archive* [Pennsylvania 1976], 93ff. My thanks to Dr. Farouk al-Rawi for letting me consult his copy of this dissertation.

8 Cf. Maidman, op.cit., especially his comments on the views of Purves.

9 Unfortunately KAJ 306 [VAT 13623] is not directly relevant here, because the comparison with VS 19, 5:6 GAL ša É *ut-na-na-te* ("prayer-house", *utnennu* ?) shows that É UD-*na-na-*[here does not include a PN.

10 HSAO (Adam Falkenstein zum 17. September 1966), 115-6; the recent study of G. Simonet, *Irrigation de piémont et économie agricole à Assur*, is apparently unaware of Nissen's article and does not hold as much conviction (RA 71 [1977] 163-7).

11 TR 3004 (*Iraq* 30 [1968] Pl. LVIII):12′-14′; I am grateful to Dr. B.K. Ismail, head of the cuneiform section of the Iraq Museum, for permission to collate the Rimah texts quoted in this article.

12 BSOAS 34 [1971] 513[62].

13 Quoted from I.M. Diakonoff, *Ancient Mesopotamia* [Moscow 1969] 204ff., still the basic study of Middle Assyrian rural conditions. It will however be clear that we cannot accept his view that "the documents leave no doubt that these "lots" were large and comprised several smaller parcels. Hence we have the right to assume that the "great boundary" confined the entire territory of a community, *ālu*, which was divided into lots".

14 Barbara C. Aswad, *Property Control and Social Strategies in Settlers in a Middle Eastern Plain* [Ann Arbor 1971], 25. Note that R. McC. Adams also draws parallels with these conditions (see above in this Festschrift), independently but scarcely coincidentally.

15 See especially H.J. Nissen, HSAO 111-120.

16 e.g. the article in VDI 1963/1, translated in *Soviet Anthropology and Archeology* 2 No. 1 [New York 1963] 32-46; N.B. Jankowska, in *Ancient Mesopotamia* [Moscow 1969] and in JESHO 12 [1969] 233-82. But note that in everyday terms this view sees the "family community" as "collective proprietor of the means of production" (I.M. Diakonoff *Third International Conference of Economic History* [Munich 1965] 21).

17 *Soviet Anthropology and Archeology* 2 No. 1 [New York 1963] 38.

18 This does not of course exclude the possibility that some land in each village was the common property of the community - but note that land within the *ugār āli* of a village could be private property, to judge from MAL B §6.

19 For Ugarit see now M. Heltzer, *The Rural Community in Ancient Ugarit* [Wiesbaden 1976] 52-62; for the NAss reference cf. TCAE 366-7, 1.59. While on the subject of Ugarit, it should be observed that I can find no good reason for making a distinction between *ilku* and *pilku*, despite Heltzer, op. cit., 91.

20 I have yet to see any evidence at all that *ilku* could refer to services rendered to the community (as opposed to the state), despite (e.g.) I.M. Diakonoff, *Third International Conference of Economic History* [Munich 1965] 27: "obligations to the community (tax payments, partaking in community works, Ass. *ilku ša ālāiūte*)"; the most this latter phrase could be taken to prove is that *ilku* was owed in consequence of membership of the community (*ālu*) - not that it was owed to the community. For our own interpretation of the phrase see BSOAS 34 [1971] 496-8.

21 This article was completed before the writer saw the text AO 19.228 and the accompanying discussion in M.-J. Aynard and J.-M. Durand, *Assur* 3/1 [1980] 5-14. Although some of the same issues are discussed, neither text nor discussion necessitate any serious revision of my conclusions.

ON THE VERB AK IN SUMERIAN

Marvin A. Powell (Dekalb, Illinois)

The sign AK belongs to a group of fifteen Sumerian graphemes which Proto-Ea glosses with six or more readings.[1] Like all polyphonic signs, AK presents a certain amount of difficulty in its vocalization and interpretation, and this difficulty is accentuated by the (apparent) fact that all of these glosses represent verbal roots. Recent studies of AK by A. Cavigneaux,[2] D.O. Edzard,[3] and M. Yoshikawa[4] have clarified the situation somewhat, but with a small piece of additional evidence drawn from Old Babylonian mathematical texts, we may perhaps reduce the area of uncertainty a bit further.

Since it is pertinent to the arguments to be presented, let us first review the lexical evidence using M. Civil's excellent edition of the Ea-related texts in MSL 14 (1979). The nature of the textual evidence can be presented rather succinctly by means of the following table:

Evidence for AK in the surviving Mss of Proto-Ea, Ea and AA

		Text Witnesses for the Line			Witnesses for the Gloss	
PE Line	PE Gloss	Leg. MSS	Illeg. MSS	Om.	Leg. Gloss	Illeg. Gloss
524	a	4			4	
525	n a	3	1		3	
526		3	1		2	1
	š a				1	
	š a - a				1	
526a	r a	2		2	2	
527		3	1		2	1
	k e				1	
	k e - e				1	
528	a - k a	4			4	

(Based on MSL 14 XV + 17 + 53 + 78; abbreviations: Leg. = Legible, Illeg. = Illegible, Om. = Omitted; numbers refer to the number of MSS having the given characteristics.)

Ea VIII (= MSL 14 476)

21	š á - a	AK	*[ḫa-ṣa]-⌜ṣú⌝*
22	n a - a	A[K]	*[na-bu]-ǘ*
23	a	[AK]	*⌜e-pe⌝-šum*
24	k i - ⌜i⌝	[AK]	MIN
25	a - [k a]	[AK]	MIN
26	[m i - e]	[AK]	MIN

A VIII/1 (= MSL 14 490)

49	š á - a	AK	*ha-ṣa-ṣu//*
50			*hu-ṣu-ṣu*
51	n a - a	AK	*na-bu-ǔ//*
52			*e-pe-šu* 17
53	k i - i	AK	MIN
54	a k	AK	MIN
55	m i - e	AK	MIN

We may call attention to the fact that none of the glosses rests upon a single MS: a $_5$ and a k a are represented by four legible MSS, n à by three, ša$_5$, ra$_x$ and ke$_x$ (or kì) by two each. This picture is confirmed, in part, by the later lexica. Regretfully, one must observe that the state of the sources for Ea/Aa at this point still stands about where it did after R.C. Thompson's publication of CT 11 (1900) and CT 12 (1901). Only one new source has become available for this part of Ea, BM 36032, but it is described by Civil as being in poor condition,[5] and it is clear from a comparison of BM 39034 (= CT 11 42) with Civil's edition of Ea VIII 21-26 that the second source has contributed to the establishment of the texts at this point only by confirming that the Akkadian equivalents (partly damaged) and their order are essentially identical with those preserved in A VIII/1 49-55, which itself rests upon a single, but well-preserved, MS of the NB period.[6]

Departures from Proto-Ea in the MSS of Ea and Aa fall into three groups: 1) regrouping, apparently according to semantic criteria, 2) dropping or changing the vocalization of glosses, and 3) errors in the MS tradition. In Ea and Aa, ša$_5$ = *haṣāṣu* and nà = *nabû* have been shifted into first and second position, and all of the surviving *epēšu* equivalents have been shifted to the end. Only one gloss, ra$_x$, seems to have disappeared entirely from the lexical tradition. Proto-Ea's aka becomes ak in Aa, whereas Ea preserves only a-[ ]. For Proto-Ea's ke$_x$ (in one MS; only KI in the other), Aa glosses ki-i, where, in Ea, only ki-⌈x⌉ survives.[7] The gloss me$_6$ = AK = *epēšu* is clearly just an error of MS tradition,[8] and, I believe, we have to explain the loss of a$_5$ = AK = *epēšu* and the equation of nà with *epēšu* in the sole surviving MS of Aa as conflation of na-a = AK = *epēšu*. This solution is supported by the two surviving MSS of Ea, and it enables us to approach the question of whether /na/ has arisen from false sandhi split with clearer vision. Without being able to decide this question, the lexical evidence inclines me to a negative answer, but we shall return to this below.

Other Ea-related texts present a more complex picture. One text designated by Civil,[9] following Landsberger, as "an excerpt of Nippur Proto-Aa" runs the following set of equivalents:[10] a = AK = *šakānum*, a-ka = AK = *patāqum*, *kanāšum*, *zaqāpum*, ⌈*ḫuṣṣuṣum*⌉. Reciprocal Ea is rather poorly preserved, but Tablet A 129 presupposes a reading kì (Akkadian lost), line 172 is perhaps (šá-a) = A[K?] = [*ḫaṣāṣu*], and Section B 14 has the interesting entry [na]-a = AK = *na-*[*bu-ú*].[11]

All of this supports the opinion of Cavigneaux[12] and Edzard[13] that ša$_5$ must represent a different verb from ak = *epēšu*. This is also supported by the fact that ša$_5$ needed glossing in the commentary to A VIII/1 49f.[14] But that still leaves us with the readings a$_5$, aka, ke$_x$, nà, and ra$_x$. Cavigneaux is inclined to regard all of these as deriving from a root form /AK/. Edzard would tend to agree, but leaves the precise determination of ke$_x$ and the whole question of ra$_x$ open. Both would explain the gloss [na] as arising from false sandhi split in the verbal chain.

False sandhi split would appear to be a reasonable solution, until one looks more closely at the lexical evidence. In addition to the problem indicated above, namely that the lexica seem to distinguish between a verb /na/ = *nabû* and a verb /ak/ = *epēšu*, if sandhi were the correct solution, one would expect to find other examples of this in Proto-Ea where verbs of the structure VOWEL or VOWEL+CONSONANT occur. In particular, one might expect it to occur with e, è, e$_{11}$ or u$_5$, but such is not the case. Proto-Ea seems to be entirely free of the type of linguistic reasoning underlying equations like bi // bé = BI = *qabû* or logical fallacies like those underlying e = [K]A = [*qabû*][15] with which the later lexica both tantalize and deceive us. If false sandhi split is, indeed, the correct explanation (and that remains to be proven) of the readings r a$_x$ and n à, the origin of this phenomenon is most likely to be sought in verbal compounds like a - š a - a n - g à r - AK,[16] KA-ḪUR-AK,[17] and LUL-GU-AK,[18] rather than in the verbal chain itself. But the problem is rather complex. Since, as we shall presently see, the infinitive form of the verb /AK/ is, in all probability, /KE/, we must exclude the possibility of a m a ḫ - d i construction, i.e., nominal form + infinitive. This leaves us with the d u b - s a r construction,[19] but, since this construction is formed on the *ḫamṭu* root, we must expect, if indeed the root is /aK/, the final consonant to show up in morphophonemic alternation. I cannot cite a definite occurrence of this.[20]

Turning now to the question of the root paradigm of /AK/ = *epēšu*, I have presented schematically the paradigms inferable from the treatments by Edzard[21] and Yoshikawa[22] and, without repeating the evidence cited by them, have also added the paradigm which I think the evidence suggests. I have, for practical reasons, retained the terms *marû* and *ḫamṭu*, though Edzard's critique of these terms[23] is certainly, at least partly, justified.

		Finite		*Infinitive*	*Imperative*
		Sing.	*Plu.*		
Edzard:	*marû*	/aK/?	/kI/?	/aka/?	
	ḫamṭu	/aK/?	/aK/?		*/aK/
Yoshikawa:	*marû*	/ak+e/	/aK+e/		
	ḫamṭu	/aK/	/aK/	/aK+Ø/	*/aK/
Powell:	*marû*	*/aK/	/AK/	/KE/	
	ḫamṭu	/aK/	*/aK/		/aK/

By using asterisks and question marks I have tried to avoid doing violence to the opinions of these scholars, whose work is fundamental to my own hypothesis. Edzard expresses himself throughout with great reservation and nowhere explicitly posits an imperative form, nor does Yoshikawa. It will be observed that the three paradigms differ only in details. The essential difference between Edzard's paradigm and the one I am proposing concerns the infinitive, and to a lesser degree the 3rd *marû* plural. I have, with some hesitation, proposed to solve the problem by treating /AK/ as the basic morpheme, which appears as *[a]*, *[aka]*, *[age]* and *[ge]* in different morphophonemic contexts. However, there still exists a possibility that the verb is truly suppletive and that the forms /AK/ and /KE/ derive from roots as distinct as *is* and *was* in English. If such is the case, one might be faced with a root paradigm like that of e / d u g$_4$ / d i :

	Finite		*Infinitive*	*Imperative*
	Sing.	*Plu.*		
marû	/e/	/e/	/di/	
ḫamṭu	/duG/	/e/		/duG/

Here, of course, the infinitive is distinct from the finite forms, but u$_6$ - e, if it really is a form analogous to u$_6$ - d i,[24] raises the unpleasant prospect of finite "*marû*" forms which also function like an infinitive.

Unfortunately, I have no evidence for the *ḫamṭu* plural which could provide a clue to the problem. But even if we had such evidence, there is little probability of escaping from this dilemma, because a definite answer to whether one reads -AK.GÉ(.NE) and *-AK.GÉ.EŠ as -ag-gé(-ne) and *-ag-gé-eš or -AK gé(-ne) and *-AK gé-eš can only be produced by statistical analyses of the writing system, and this can only be done when thousands of lines of third millennium texts have been reduced to machine readable form. My reasons for rejecting -AK gé are purely subjective: it does not seem right in the context of third millennium orthography, but GÉ and KA, like E and GÁ are special signs and may not fit the regular patterns.

But let us return to the problem of the infinitive of /AK/. It has long been known that za-e AK-da-zu-dè occurs in Old Babylonian mathematical texts as the Sumerian equivalent for *ina epēšīka*,[25] but it is not generally recognized that this Sumerian expression occurs eight times in one text in the variant za-e gíd-da-zu-dè.[26] This, so it would seem, is rather conclusive proof that the infinitive form of /AK/ must be the /KE/ form registered in Proto-Ea.

In support of this reading, I should like to call attention to the nearly simultaneous publication of the interpretation of kar-AK//KID as kar-ke$_x$/ke$_4$ by Edzard[27] and Cavigneaux[28] and by Civil as kar-kîd/kid.[29] Proceeding from these treatments of this expression, I would suggest that kar-AK//KID//KID.AK//AK.KID should be read kar-ge$_x$//gé//géAK//AKgé and that we have here a normal maḫ-di construction, which ends, like all infinitives known up to now, in the morpheme /ED/. This is, in fact, supported by the PN with title cited by Civil from CT 10 26 i 1 (Ilú-AN-na-⌜x⌝ dumu geme$_2$-^{d}lamma kar-⌜gé⌝-da), which shows the normal /ED/ ending.

If the preceding conclusions are correct, Yoshikawa's paradigm cannot be the correct solution to the problem. That paradigm arose out of a discussion of the frustrating problem of the infixes /n/ and /b/ in preradical position, in which he classes the verb ak with a small group of verbs "which regularly or almost regularly take the *ḫamṭu*-form before the suffix -dè/-da(m) [and] have the characteristic feature in common that the -n-/-b- either denote the agentive even in the *marû*-conjugation or seldom occur in the *marû*-conjugation".[30] In fact, only two of the verbs in this group (dé, TÙM/túm, gá-gá/gar, gu$_7$, pàd, ak) are really capable of proving the point Yoshikawa wants to make, namely, that the infinitive is formed from the *ḫamṭu* root. Verb roots with vowels in final position are rarely written plene in the infinitive because it is not necessary to do this to avoid confusion, whereas, it is absolutely necessary to write plene to distinguish finite "present" from "past", and this is regularly done. The precise vocalization of TÙM is still a problem, and thus it is of little evidential value. Since /AK/ has an infinitive in /KE/, it is eliminated, and, in fact, pà-dè-dam[31] does occur, so there must be some other solution to the problematic phenomenon which Yoshikawa has described.

Finally, attention should be called to a problem which I am not in a position to resolve conclusively. Where does aka in Proto-Ea come from? After having reviewed the evidence cited by Edzard and Yoshikawa in their studies of this verb and supplementing this with a considerable amount of material from Old Babylonian literary texts and third millennium texts, I would suggest that aka is a product of the Old Babylonian script reform. Whereas third millennium texts regularly write -AK-GÉ and (-)AK-KA, to my knowledge, this never occurs in Old Babylonian literary texts, and, if it did occur, one would have to consider whether it was pre-reform or post-reform. As motives for a writing change of this type, one might consider the desire to express the voiceless character of the final consonant, which would be otherwise impossible to express, or it could have been motivated by the fact that the signs GÉ and KA are preponderantly associated with the expression of genitival relationships. Since the use of these as phonetic indicators (complements) with the verb a k would inevitably draw them to the end of the sentence or clause, it may have been perceived as confusing and, thus, by a minor script change, avoided. This may appear to be a fantastic idea, but, when one realizes that a k is the only known verb in Sumerian that ends in final /K/, it seems less unlikely.

Even though I have not reached any startling conclusions in this essay, reduction of the area of uncertainty even by a small amount can sometimes be significant as a starting point for the next scholar who attempts to deal with the problem. I have attacked the problem tree by tree while trying to remember that they are part of a forest, and I hope, perhaps, that Igor Mikhailovich, whom we seek to honor in this volume, may take some small pleasure that I have taken his wise precepts to heart.

Étude = H. Limet, *Étude de documents de la période d'Agadé* (1973; = Bibliothèque de la Faculté de Philosophie et Lettres de l'Université de Liège, Fasc. CCVI)

PUL = Patrimoine de l'Université de Liège, siglum for texts published in cuneiform copy by H. Limet in *Étude*

SGL 1 = A. Falkenstein, *Sumerische Götterlieder* I (= Abhandlungen der Heidelberger Akademie der Wissenschaften, philosophisch-historische Klasse, 1959/I)

---

1 BAD, APIN, AK, LUL: 6; NI, KA, DU, EZEN: 7; PA, NE: 8; LAGAB: 9; KAL: 10; UD, ŠID: 11; KU: 14.

2 *Die sumerisch-akkadischen Zeichenlisten: Überlieferungs-probleme* (Diss., München, 1976) 45-47.

3 ZA 66, 1976, 55-56.

4 JCS 29, 1977, 87-88.

5 MSL 14 473.

6 Cf. MSL 14 489.

7 Civil's restorations shown in my table are probably correct, but the fact remains that they are restorations.

8 So already Cavigneaux, *Zeichenlisten* p. 45.

9 MSL 14 108.

10 MSL 14 120:21-25.

11 MSL 14 526, 527, and 530. For an additional attestation of n à = *nabû*, see AHw s.v.

12 Note 2 above.

13 Note 3 above.

14 MSL 14 495.

15 Cf. MSL 14 411 (A V/1:137-160) and 306 (Ea III 71).

16 For evidence, see SGL 1 36 and TCS 3 114.

17 TCS 3 84f. and 152.

18 M. Civil, JNES 32, 1973, 60 + note 10.

19 D.O. Edzard, ZA 62, 1972, 2-6.

20 However, for a possible connection between KA-ḪUR-AK and *nabû*, cf. the form g ù - m u r ? - m u r - r a = *nubbû* cited AHw s.v.

21 Note 3 above.

22 Note 4 above.

23 ZA 66, 1976, 53-55.

24 Cf. Claus Wilcke, *Das Lugalbandaepos*, 1969, 102:124 (+ comm. to line on p. 170), 108:181, 110:198.

25 See, e.g., F. Thureau-Dangin, TMB 234 under the sign AK and 216 under *epēšu*.

26 O. Neugebauer and A. Sachs, MCT 69 + 166 + pl. 7, text H: 2, 8, 15, 21, 27, 34, rev. 3, and 15.

27 *Apud* Cavigneaux; see note 28.

28 *Zeichenlisten* 46 + note 20 on p. 163.

29 RA 70, 1976, 189f.

30 JCS 29, 1977, 88.

31 H. Limet, *Étude* no. 39 (=PUL 31) rev. 1; cf. PUL 27 and 28 for the contrast with b a - p a and Powell, *Historia Mathematica* 3, 1976, 426f. for a discussion of the context.

32 Most recently, P. Steinkeller, RA 72, 1978, 73-76 and RA 73, 1979, 91f.

Addendum

As teaching duties, prior commitments and the short deadline for contributions did not permit me to make a thorough review of the evidence, note the following oversights. On p. 316 I should have said that I have no third millennium evidence for the *ḫamṭu* pl. because 3rd pl. forms do occur in OB literature. What I had in mind as evidence was *e - AK - g é - é š. Note, in any case, e -AK- é š (with pl. subject) in Nikol'skii, *Drevnosti Vostočnya* V (=*Dokumenty*..., II) 22 r.1. Th. Jacobsen, JNES 32, 1973, 161-6, presents (very tentatively) a view of AK that is incompatible with the one I have outlined; note, in any case, that dnin-kar-ra-AK may not be a genitive. Finally, without being able to solve the dilemma they pose, note AK- g e -GIM AK-AK-d a m (*St. Sem.* 42, 64:340) and the variants p a - è b í - i n -AK- a//p a - è - a - g é (*An. Or.* 52, 98:201; cf. 90:168).

THE BABYLONIAN FÜRSTENSPIEGEL IN PRACTICE

Erica Reiner (Chicago), with an Appendix by Miguel Civil (Chicago)

Professor I.M. Diakonoff has argued, in a penetrating study in the Festschrift for Benno Landsberger,[1] that the text known as the Babylonian Fürstenspiegel (in W.G. Lambert's edition: Advice to a Prince)[2] was composed under Sennacherib, and intended as a warning to him.

A recently published text, while it does not contribute additional arguments to his dating of the text, nevertheless shows the text's *Sitz im Leben* under Sennacherib's successor, Esarhaddon, and underlines its importance "for the history of political opinion".[3] In drawing attention to this new text I do not intend to take part in the discussion about the date of the Fürstenspiegel; rather, I would like to argue that it was part of Babylonian literary heritage, and, incidentally (after more than forty years) vindicate Landsberger's insight about the literary character of such texts.

In the recently published volume of Neo-Babylonian letters CT 54, No. 212 is a letter to King Esarhaddon. In the catalogue (p. 14), M. Dietrich suggests Bēl-līšer of Nippur as sender; the traces of line 1 in the copy after the theophoric element ^{d}EN are, however, unclear.

The letter begins with a quotation from celestial omens (1-5);[4] in the next section, the writer speaks of the exemptions that have been the prerogative of the privileged cities Sippar, Nippur, and Babylon, and insists that Nippur is as privileged as Babylon ([EN.LÍL]^{ki} *kīma* DIN.TIR^{ki}-*ma* rev. 1 and 3). He then continues: *bēl šarrāni lidgul ṭup-pi šu-ú* LUGAL *ana di-i-ni la i-[qul ... i]q-ta-bi um-ma* "let the Lord of Kings (i.e., Esarhaddon) look, that tablet, '(If) the king does not heed justice' (i.e., the Fürstenspiegel) says as follows". Then, in rev. 4-6 he quotes lines 55-59 of the Fürstenspiegel:

CT 54 212	r.4	*lu-ú* LUGAL *lu-ú* LÚ.GÚ.EN.NA *lu-ú* LÚ *ak-lum lu-ú* LÚ [
Fürstensp.55		*lu* LÚ.PA-*lu lu* LÚ ŠÀ.TAM É.KUR *lu šu-ut* SAG LUGAL
	r.5	[*ša ina S*]*ippar Nippur u Bābili iš-šak-kan-ú-ma*
56		*ša ina Sippar Nippur u Bābili ana šatam* É.KUR *izzazzu*
		tup-šik-ku É.MEŠ DINGIR.MEŠ r. 6 [... *im-me-du-šú*]*-nu-tu*
57		*tup-šik-ku* É.MEŠ DINGIR.DINGIR GAL.GAL *im-me-du-šú-nu-tim*
		DINGIR.MEŠ GAL.MEŠ *ig-ga-gu-ma ul ir-ru-bu a-na ki-iṣ-ṣi-šú-nu i-né-es-su-*[*ú atmanšun*]
58-59		DINGIR.DINGIR GAL.GAL *i-gu-gu-ma ì-né-es-su-ú at-ma-an-šu-un*
59		NU *ir-ru-bu a-na ki-iṣ-ṣi-šu-un*

After the quotation, the writer goes on to assure the king that the tablet is reliable (*ṭuppi kīnumma*) and to suggest that they read it to the king (*ina pan šarri lilsû*).

The remainder of the letter is fragmentary; it seems to refer to accusations against the citizens of Nippur, Sippar, and Babylon (rev. 8f.), and invokes Bēl and Nabû, "the gods of the king"; the writer then continues: "I wrote this report to the king, my lord, [let the king, my lord,] do [as he wishes]" (rev. 12f.), and invokes blessings on the king: *Enlil Šamaš u Marduk* DINGIR.MEŠ *[Nippuri Sippari] ù* DIN.TIR[ki] *ūmē ša šarri bēlija lurr[iku ...]* "may Enlil, Šamaš, and Marduk, the gods of [Nippur, Sippar,] and Babylon give long life to the king, my lord".

The letter ends with the customary protestations of the writer's loyalty. The last fragmentary lines contain a mention of Elam.

We should note, first, that although the writer cites, as the quoted incipit shows, the Fürstenspiegel, the quote diverges somewhat from the text of the Fürstenspiegel as we know it. The difference is partly in the wording of the reference to the officials who would disregard the privileges -- both their titles and the verb denoting their appointment differ -- and partly in the sequence of the three clauses of the apodosis denoting the anger of the gods, the last two clauses being transposed.

The remaining differences in the spelling are minor; DINGIR.DINGIR GAL.GAL (an archaizing spelling) is replaced by DINGIR.MEŠ GAL.MEŠ; the playful writing NI-NI-*is-su-ú*[5] is replaced by *i-ni-is-su-[ú]*. The only grammatically significant variant is *iggagu*, a present tense form, as expected in an apodosis, as opposed to D.T. 1's use of the preterite *īgugu*. Either, then, the writer cited another copy of the Fürstenspiegel, or, as seems more likely to me, quoted it from memory, as the typically Neo-Babylonian spelling *iš-šak-kan-ú-ma* (for *iš-šak-ka-nu-ma* or the like) further indicates.

Were there other copies of the Fürstenspiegel available, in libraries or in the possession of individual scribes? Until recently, the only copy known was D.T. 1, the one from Assurbanipal's library.[6] This fact in itself would presuppose the existence of other copies. It may be no more than a coincidence that the only other known exemplar of this text that has come to light recently was found in Nippur.[7] The tablet was found together with early Neo-Babylonian texts; apart from a few variants,[8] it adds nothing else to our understanding of this composition besides the fact, not negligible in our context, that there were other copies in circulation. Perhaps Bel-līšer?, the writer of the letter to Esarhaddon, owned, or knew, this very tablet!

The first proposal that a letter contained a quotation or a paraphrase of a quotation from a "Fürstenspiegel" was made by Landsberger, in dealing with the Middle Babylonian letter 1912-5-13,2.[9] The text, in the translation of Grayson, ARI 1 § 936, runs:

> The ancient *tablets* -- the kings my forefathers *[handed them down to us]* -- with anyone let us consider the matter of *[a king who mistreats]* Nippur, Sippar, and Babylon[277] -- a nobody, a foreigner, whose sons and nobles [......] He will cause [him to see] an opponent to his sovereignty.
>
> Note 277: As Landsberger has acutely noted, this sounds very much like a reference to a kind of Fürstenspiegel ... in which a king who mistreats certain privileged cities, in this case Nippur, Sippar, and Babylon, is threatened with divine wrath.

In Landsberger's translation (AfO 10 [1935-36] 141f.):

> "Die alten [Taf]eln -- die Könige, [meine] Väter [haben sie uns überliefert(?) --] die Worte die[ser Tafeln] wollen wir bei diesem oder jenem(?) ins Gedächtnis rufen: [wenn ein König] Nippur, Sippar und Babylon [hintan-

setzt(?)] und einen Niemand, einen Fremdling seinem Sohn und seinen Grossen [befehlen lässt(?), ... dieser König] wird den Widersacher(?) seines Königtums schauen müssen(?)". So unsicher auch diese Ergänzungen der zu zwei Drittel zerstörten Zeilen sind, so ist es mir doch sicher, dass es sich hier um ein Zitat bzw. eine Paraphrase aus einem "Fürstenspiegel" nach Art von CT 15, pl. 50 handelt..."

I quote the German translation of Landsberger and his comment since from the English translation the typical formulation of the assumed quote -- in the omen form protasis-apodosis -- that led Landsberger to his assumption is missing. Also, Landsberger surmised either a direct quotation or a paraphrase, and we have seen that the quotation in the letter CT 54 212 is not quite a verbatim quote from D.T. 1; moreover, Landsberger noted that the three cities stand as representative of Babylonia[10] and the reference to Nippur, Sippar, and Babylon is not simply used "in this case".

Today, even with a much larger corpus than in 1936, and notwithstanding the help of the wording of CT 54 212, there is little that I would change in Landsberger's -- as he stressed, very uncertain -- restorations. The only suggestion that seems unlikely to me is that "the kings, [my?] forefathers" of the Middle Babylonian letter would be the subject of some such predicate as "handed down the tablets to us"; perhaps "have read them" or the like would be more suitable in view of CT 54 212. I would, moreover, suggest that *ì nuḫassisa* "let us remember (or: mind)" begins a new clause. We are then still left with the unintelligible *it-ti am-man-na-a*, for which neither the AHw. nor the CAD could offer a better suggestion than Landsberger in 1936.

It has been observed that literary texts -- those that Oppenheim classified as belonging to the "stream of tradition" -- sometimes include quotations from other literary texts: the description of the nether world in the Descent of Ištar, in the Gilgameš Epic, and in Nergal and Ereškigal, or the description of the preparation of the ark in the Atra-hasīs and the Gilgameš Epics are obvious examples.

It has not so far been observed that scribes -- to use Oppenheim's term, the intellectuals of Mesopotamian society -- used these texts not only for pedagogical purposes, and copied them not solely to enlarge their own tablet collections, but would also draw on them to influence contemporary events, just as the scholars who cited the compendia of divinatory texts in their reports to the king attempted to influence the king.[11]

Since Professor Diakonoff stressed the importance of the Fürstenspiegel for the history of political opinion, I am happy to dedicate to him this small contribution to the historical relevance of the Babylonian Fürstenspiegel.

---

1 I.M. Diakonoff, "A Babylonian Political Pamphlet from about 700 B.C.", AS 16 343-349.

2 Lambert BWL 112ff.

3 Diakonoff, p. 343.

4 For such introductory omen quotations see Oppenheim, *Centaurus* 14 [1969] 105 and 129 n. 19.

5 The verbal prefix /i/ is written with the sign NI (i.e., *ì*) also in D.T. 1:35; see also Appendix.

6 The history of the discovery of the tablet D.T. 1 and of its early trans-

lations is recounted by Franz M. Th. Böhl, *Der babylonische Fürstenspiegel* (= MAOG 11/3) 1-3; as far as I have been able to ascertain, it was Landsberger (see n. 9) who first dubbed the Babylonian poem "Fürstenspiegel". For European Fürstenspiegel see (with previous literature) Hans Hubert Anton, *Fürstenspiegel und Herrscherethos in der Karolingerzeit* [Bonn: Ludwig Röhrscheid Verlag, 1968]. See also the article "Fürstenspiegel" by P. Hadot, in *Reallexikon für Antike und Christentum*, Vol. VIII 555-632.

7 12N 110. Listed in the Catalogue of Texts, by Miguel Civil, in McGuire Gibson et al., *Excavations at Nippur: Twelfth Season* (OIC 23).

8 See Appendix.

9 Published in copy from, then, a private collection, by Pinches, JRAS 1904, 415, and in transliteration and translation by Weidner, AfO 10 [1935-36] 5f. Landsberger's discussion of the text is found ibid, p. 141f., and was cited by Böhl, MAOG 11/3 33.

10 "Auch in letzterem werden wiederholt die Städte Nippur, Sippar und Babylon als Repräsentanten Babyloniens genannt und wird (Z. 9) die Bevorzugung eines Fremden unter Strafe gestellt" (p. 142). Note also: "Sippar, Nippur et Babylone sont précisément les trois villes à propos desquelles les "Avertissements à un prince" menacent le roi de châtiments plus ou moins graves s'il porte atteinte ou laisse porter atteinte aux droits de leur citoyens. Il faudrait ... noter qu'en se conformant à ces "Avertissements", le roi ne fait que respecter ce qui a été décidé par les dieux" (Seux *Epithètes* 272 n. 37).

11 For this question see Oppenheim, *Centaurus* 14 [1969] 120f., also Oppenheim in *Propaganda and Communication in World History*, I: *The Symbolic Instrument in Early Times*, edited by Harold D. Lasswell, Daniel Lerner, and Hans Speier [Honolulu: The University Press of Hawaii, 1979] pp. 111-144, esp. p. 117.

Appendix

12 N 110 is a complete tablet in relatively good condition, except for some cracks and for the upper right quarter of the reverse where the surface is destroyed. The script is a very cursive early NB.

1	LUGAL *a-na di-ni* NU LÁ UN.MEŠ-*šú* SÙḪ-*a* KUR-*su in-nam-ma*	= D.T. 1: 1
2	*a-na di-ni* KUR-*šú* NU LÁ ^{d}*É-a* LUGAL NAM.MEŠ *šim-taš ú-šá-an-ni-*⌜*ma*?⌝	2-3
3	*a-ḫi-ti* UŠ.MEŠ-*di-šú*	
4	*a-na* NUN.MEŠ-*šú* NU LÁ UD.MEŠ-*šú* LUGÚD.DA.MEŠ	4
5	*a-na um-ma-a-nu* NU LÁ KUR-*su* BAL-*su*	5
6	*a-na is-ḫab-ba* LÁ KU KUR MAN-*ni*	6
7	*a-na ši-pi-ir* ^{d}*É-a* LÁ *a-bi-šú la*? GUR? KUR	7
8	*ina lìb-bi* DINGIR.MEŠ GAL.MEŠ *ina ši-tul-*⌜*ta*⌝ *ù* ⌜*ṭu-da-at*⌝ NÍG.SI.SÁ UŠ.MEŠ-*šú*	7-8
9	DUMU *Sip-par*^{ki} *i-da-aṣ-ma a-ḫi-am* SUM?	9
10	^{d}UTU DI.KUD AN-*e u* KI-*tim di-ni a-*⌜*ḫi-a*⌝ *ina* KUR-*šú* GAR-*ma*	9-10
11	NUN.MEŠ *u* DI.KUD.MEŠ *a-na di-ni-šú ul* NU LÁ (sic)	10
12	DUMU.MEŠ EN.LÍL^{ki} *a-na di-ni ub-lum-niš-šum-ma*	11
13	*kàt-r*[*a-a*] TI-*ma ì-da-as-su-nu-ti*	11
14	^{d}*En-líl* E[N KUR.KUR] ⌜*a*⌝-[*ḫ*]*a-a i-de-ek-ku-šum-ma* ERÍN.MEŠ-*šú a-na* LÚ.NIM *ú-saḫ-ḫar*	12-13
15	NUN *ù š*[*u-ut* SAG-*šu ina su-q*]*í* URU *x x x-ṣa-nu-du-ú-nu*	14
16	[KÙ].BABBAR LÚ.KÁ.DINGIR.RA⌜^{ki}⌝ TI-[ ] [*a*]*-na* NÍG.GA-*šú ú-še-ri-bi*	15
17	⌜*di-in*⌝ LÚ.KÁ.DINGIR.[R]A^{ki}.MEŠ [ ]-*e-ma ana qa-lim tur-ru*	16
18	^{d}⌜AMAR.UD⌝ [ ] KI-*tim a-*[*a-bi-šu e*]*-li-šú* GAR-*ma*	17
19	NÍG.ŠU-*šú* NÍG.GA-[*šú*] *a-na* KÚR-*šú* [*i-š*]*ar-rak*	18
20	DUMU *Sip-par*^{ki} EN.LÍL^{ki} *ù* KÁ.DINGIR.[RA^{ki}] *an-na e-me-di*	19

21 *a-na* É ⸢*ṣi-bit*⸣*-ti [š]u-ru-bu a-š[ar]* x x x x = D.T. 1:20-21

22 URU *ana* SUR$_7$*-[šú]* DUB-*ak a-na* É *ṣi-bit-[t]u i-ru-[* *]* 21-22

23 LÚ.KÚR (over erasure) BAR-*ú* TU-*ub*

24 *Sip-par*^{ki} E[N.LÍ]L^{ki} *ù* KÁ.DINGIR.RA$^{⸢ki⸣}$ [U]R.BI *ta[x x]* 23

25 ERÍN.MEŠ *šu-nu-[t]u tup-šik-ka e-[* *]* 24

26 [L]Ú.NIMGIR UGU-*šú-[*] 25

27 ^{d}AMAR.UD N[UN].⸢ME⸣ DINGIR.MEŠ NUN *muš-*⸢*ta*⸣*-[lum]* 26

28 ⸢KUR⸣*-su ana* LÚ.KÚR-*šú ú-saḫ-ḫar-ma* ERÍN.MEŠ KUR-⸢*šú*⸣ *tup-šik-ka* 28

29 ⸢*a-na*⸣ LÚ.KÚR-*šú i-zab-bil* 28

30 ERÍN.M[EŠ *šu]-nu-tim* ^{d}*A-num* ^{d}*En-lil ù* ^{d}*É-a* DINGIR.MEŠ GAL.MEŠ 29

31 *a-šib* AN-*e u* KI-*tim* ≪MEŠ≫ (over erasure) *ina* UNKIN *šu-ba-ri-šú-nu ú-*⸢*kin-nu*⸣ 30

32 DUMU *Sip-par*^{ki} EN.LÍL^{ki} *ù* KÁ.DINGIR.RA^{ki} 31

33 *im-ra-šú-nu a-na mur-ni-is-qi šá-ra-ki mur-ni-is-qí* 32-33

34 *[šu-ut] im-ra-a i-kul i-na ṣi-me-it-ti a-a-*⸢*bi* UŠ⸣.MEŠ 33-34

35 [ERÍN.MEŠ *šu-n]u-tu*$^{?}$ *ina di-ku-t[ú* ERÍN].MEŠ KUR IGI ERÍ[N.MEŠ] 35

rev.

36 (traces)

37 *[ṣ]i-* (traces) 38

38 A.ŠÀ.MEŠ-⸢*šú*⸣*-nu ú-šá-an-[nu-ú* ...] 39-40?

39 *ina* ⸢A.ŠÀ$^{?}$⸣ [x x] ⸢^{d}IM *i-ḫar*⸣*-[ru-up]* 40

40 ^{d}IM ⸢GÚ$^{?}$ GAL$^{?}$⸣ AN-e ⸢*ù*⸣ [ ] 42

41 EDIN *ina ḫu-šaḫ-ḫi ú-*⸢*šam*⸣*-[*]

42 *um-ma-a-an šu-ut* SAG *man-za-az [*] 45

43 ⸢*a*⸣*-mat be-lum ú-lam-man [*] 46

44 *[i]na qi-bit* ^{d}*É-a* x [ ] SAG 47-48

45 *i-na* GIŠ.TU[KUL] 48

46 *a-šar-⟨šú⟩-nu a-na na-m[e-*] 49

47 *[ár]-kàt-su-nu šá-ra [*] 50

48 *[x] ep-šet-šú-nu za-qí-⸢qí⸣ [ ]* = D.T. 1:50

49 *[r]ik-si-šú-nu ú-pat-tar* NA$_4$.[NA.RÚ.A-*šú*]-*nu ú-[ša-an-nu]-ú* 51

50 *[a-na ḫa]r-ra-a-ni ú-šé-ṣu-[šu-n]u-tu* 52

51 *[a-na] a-de-e il*$^?$*-[ ]-tu* 52

52 ⸢^{d}x.⸣-*[...]* DUB.[SAR É.SA]G.ÍL *sa-niq* NIM AN-*e* 53

53 *mu-ma-'-ir gim-ri mu-ad-du-[u]* LUGAL-*ú-tu* 53-54

54 *rik-sat* KUR-*šú ú-paṭ-ṭar-ma a-ḫi-ti [x x]* 54

55 *lu-ú* LÚ.PA *lu-ú* LÚ *šá-tam* É.KUR *lu-ú* LÚ ⸢*šu-ut*⸣ SAG LUGAL 55

56 *šá ina Sip-par*^{ki} EN.LÍL^{ki} *ù* KÁ.DINGIR.RA^{ki} *ana* LÚ.ŠÀ.TAM É.KUR DU-*su* 56

57 *tup-šik-ku* É.ME DINGIR.MEŠ *im-mi-du-šú-nu-tú* 57

58 DINGIR.MEŠ GAL.MEŠ *ig-ga-gu-ma i-ni-is-su-ú at-man-un-šú* (sic) 58

59 <u>*ul ir-ru-bu a-na ki-iṣ-ṣi-šu-un*</u> 59

---

60 ŠU^{II} ^{md}IM.DU.DU-NUMUN.SI.SÁ A *ša-mal*$^?$*-la-a*

(three or four illegible signs below subscript)
(trace of a line on left edge of reverse:) *[x]* AN *[...]*

Notes to Appendix

The horizontal rulings indicated in the transliteration are those that appear on the tablet; they do not always correspond to syntactic units.

There are added clauses in lines 7f. and 14, the first not completely legible, and 12 N 110 happens to be broken in the lines corresponding to the broken lines D.T. 1:40-41, so that it provides no restoration to these lines.

Other differences between 12 N 110 and D.T. 1 concern mostly minor spelling differences. Of these, note that *i-na* in line 34 may also be read in the corresponding D.T. 1:34 instead of the edition's *a-na*; IGI ERÍN.MEŠ in line 35 may also be read in D.T. 1:35.

Redactional differences are *ana* LÚ.NIM *usaḫḫar* in line 14 for *ušamqati* in D.T. 1:13, *a-mat be-lum* in line 43 for *a-mat* BE (to be read *bēlu* and not *-sun*?) in D.T. 1:46, and especially those in which 12 N 110 and CT 54 212 agree against D.T. 1: the listing of *aklu* among the officials (CT 54 212: LÚ *ak-lum*, 12 N 110:55 LÚ.PA), so D.T. 1:55's LÚ.PA.LU is not to be read *rē'û* but as a dittography for LÚ PA ≪*lu*≫ *lu šatam ekurri*; the expected present tense *iggaguma* for D.T. 1:58's *īguguma*.

The attractive proposal to read NUN.ME (D.T. 1:4 and 14) as *apkallu* instead of *rubû* has to be discarded since 12 N 110 has NUN.MEŠ in both lines.

Note that while 12 N 110 does not use the archaizing spellings that characterize D.T. 1, it nevertheless uses the sign NI to write the verbal prefix /i/ in line 13 (corresponding to D.T. 1:11, which writes *i* in this case).

EINE VERGESSENE FELSINSCHRIFT MIT EINEM ASSYRISCHEN OPFERTEXT

Mirjo Salvini (Roma)

Das hier vorgelegte Schriftdenkmal wurde im November 1898 von C.F. Lehmann-Haupt zur Zeit der zusammen mit W. Belck durchgeführten "Armenischen Expedition" auf der Südseite von Van Kalesi, dem Sitz der urartäischen Hauptstadt Ṭušpa, entdeckt. Von dieser Felsinschrift gab Lehmann-Haupt eine erste Notiz in den *Sitzungsberichten der Preussischen Akademie der Wissenschaften zu Berlin* im Jahre 1900.[1] Sie wurde ferner unter der Projekt-Nummer 165 in seinem *Corpus* registriert.[2] Die ausführlichste Mitteilung darüber war jedoch von Lehmann-Haupt schon 1907 in seinen *Materialien*[3] veröffentlicht worden.

Seitdem ist diese Inschrift in Vergessenheit geraten. Sie wurde meines Wissens nie transkribiert oder bearbeitet und auch nicht mehr in den späteren urartologischen Studien zitiert, mit Ausnahme von Königs *Handbuch*, wo sie einfach in der Konkordanz mit dem Vermerk "assyrisch!" aufgeführt wird.[4] Wohl deswegen ist sie auch der assyriologischen Forschung entgangen; so findet sie keine Erwähnung in Borgers *Handbuch der Keilschriftliteratur*.[5]

Da aber unsere Wissenschaft jedem auch noch so geringen Schriftzeugnis der Alten Rechnung tragen muss, scheint es mir angebracht, diese "wiedergefundene" Inschrift - ungeachtet ihres schlechten Erhaltungszustandes - zu edieren, um den Assyriologen Anlass zu sachkundigeren Überlegungen zu bieten. Mit diesem kurzen Beitrag möchte ich ferner eine von Lehmann-Haupt geleistete Pionierarbeit würdigen und weiter führen. Gleichzeitig möchte ich ihn - als bescheidener Mittler - dem Jubilar, dem grossen russischen Gelehrten Igor' Michajlovič Diakonoff, in Dankbarkeit für seine grundlegenden Beiträge zur Urartologie widmen.

Es ist zunächst notwendig - auch angesichts der Seltenheit des Werkes - die schon erwähnte Mitteilung von Lehmann-Haupt in seinen *Materialien* in ihrem vollen Wortlaut wiederzugeben:

" b) Die Opfernische auf dem Vanfelsen.

*48. Von Sardur I rührt, nach dem Schriftcharakter und der Örtlichkeit zu urteilen, höchst wahrscheinlich auch her die assyrische Inschrift in einer von mir während der Expedition auf der Südseite des Vanfelsens nahe dem Gipfelkamm entdeckten, aus dem lebenden Gestein gehauenen Nische, deren zwei erhaltene Wandungen die eine spärlichste, die andere (Fig. 41 nach Abklatsch) reichliche inschriftliche Spuren zeigten."

"Ihr Inhalt, der von Opfergaben, u.A. "8 Ochsen"; "Büffeln" spricht, rechtfertigt die Bezeichnung als Opfernische. Z. 10 und passim: *amelu ina ku-mu-(uš-)šu*."

In der Abb. 1 biete ich auch die Reproduktion der "Figur 41", welche das Photo des von Lehmann-Haupt ausgefertigten Abklatsches darstellt.

Im Vorderasiatischen Museum zu Berlin ist noch unter den vielen Papier-Abklatschen von Lehmann-Haupt das Original von diesem aufbewahrt (Inv.-Nr.: VA Abkl. 101). Ich verdanke Frau Dr. Evelyn Klengel-Brandt die Möglichkeit einer Kollation, welche, zusammen mit dem Photo, die dokumentarische Grundlage zu meiner Autographie (Abb. 2) darstellt.

Abb. 1

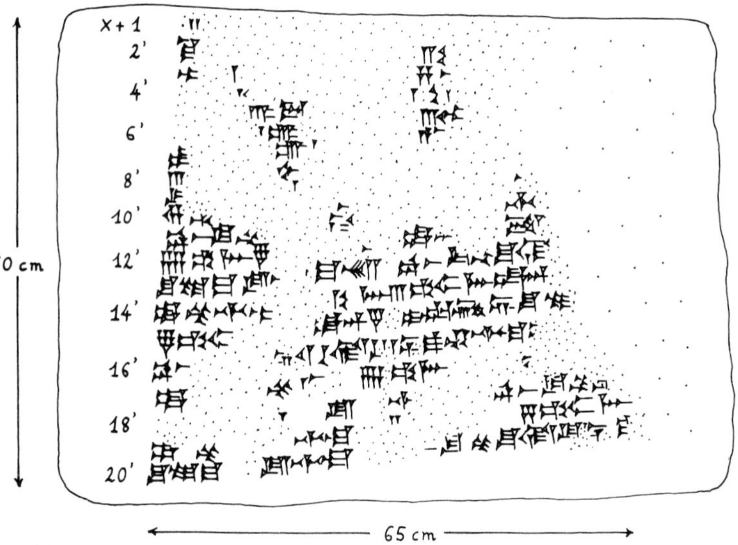

Abb. 2

Assyrische Felsinschrift auf Van Kalesi.

Die Masse der auf dem Abklatsch erhaltenen beschrifteten Fläche, und daher des Originals, sind folgende: Höhe 60 cm, Breite max. 65 cm. Auf dem Abklatsch ist noch ein von Lehmann-Haupt mit Bleistift geschriebener Vermerk zu lesen: "Inschrift der Opfernische Van-Kaleh", "Südseite", "aufgefunden 25/10 XI 98", "photographiert 10 XII (28 XI) 98". Die doppelten Daten sind offensichtlich auf die verschiedenen Kalender, den armenischen und den westlichen, zurückzuführen. Die Anmerkung "photographiert" bezieht sich sicherlich auf den Abklatsch selbst, denn ein gut gelungenes Photo des Originaltextes - wenn seine Position auf der Felswand eine Photographie überhaupt erlaubt hätte - wäre sicherlich von Lehmann-Haupt veröffentlicht worden.

Die genaue Lage der Felsnische auf der Südseite von Van Kalesi ist mir nicht bekannt. Die Steilheit der südlichen im Gegensatz zur nördlichen Seite des Vanfelsens kann eine Erklärung bieten, dass dieses Denkmal seit Lehmann-Haupts Zeiten von keinem Reisenden oder Forscher beobachtet wurde.

Aus den oben zitierten Notizen ist also zu entnehmen, dass in der Felsnische zwei beschriebene Wände erhalten waren, die eine "links" mit Spuren von insgesamt 5 Zeilen (= Projekt-Nr. 164), die andere "rechts" mit 19 Zeilen[6] (= Projekt-Nr. 165, vorliegende Inschrift). Die Nische hatte freilich neben der linken und rechten auch eine Rückwand, die aber nicht erwähnt wird, wahrscheinlich weil sie völlig abgerieben war. Est ist denkbar, dass auch diese Wand ursprünglich beschriftet war. Man darf sich fragen, ob auch die Spuren auf der linken Wandung zur selben Inschrift gehörten, die möglicherweise auf der Rückwand weiterging und auf der rechten Wand ihren letzten Teil hatte. Es ist aber auch möglich, dass auf allen drei Wänden ein und derselbe Text eingemeisselt war. Die urartäische Epigraphie bietet genügend Beispiele von nebeneinander geschriebenen Duplikattexten, sei es auf Bausteinen sei es auf Felsen. Die naheliegendste Analogie hierfür wäre dann die Felsnische von Eždaha Bulaq̄ı bei ʿAin al-Rūm in Iranisch-Azerbajdjan: auf den drei Wänden befinden sich vier Duplikate *einer* Inschrift des Menua über die Einweihung einer Brunnenanlage.[7] Aber auch die assyrische Inschrift der "Sardursburg" am Nordabhang des Vanfelsens ist sechs mal wiederholt.[8] Dies ist das unmittelbarste Beispiel vom typologischen, topographischen und chronologischen Gesichtspunkt.

Diese Überlegungen über die Anlage der Inschrift müssen aber reine Vermutungen bleiben, solange das Original - wenn überhaupt noch erhalten - nicht wiedergefunden und aufgenommen ist. Die folgende Transkription[9] kann - bedingt durch die Lage der Dokumentation und den Zustand des Textes - also nur einen vorläufigen Charakter haben.

Transkription

x+1 x[

2ʹ x[

3ʹ x x [x x x x *g*]*a*? [

4ʹ [x x G]U$_4$[x x x x] *za* x[

5ʹ [x x] *ú da*[x x x]x x[

6ʹ [x x (x)] x *ú* [x x x] 3? U[GU?

7ʹ SU[M-*an*? x (x)] *ú* x[x x x] *a* x[

8′ 3[x x x] SAL[

9′ UD[U/*l*[*u*/*k*[*u* x x x] x[

10′ 15 ^{GU_4}[ÁB^{MEŠ} SUM-*an*]x[x x x x ? x x x *šu-tu-ma* UDU.TI.LA SU]

11′ LÚ *ina ku-m*[*u-šu d*]*u*[*l-lu* DÙ-*áš* EN]TI.[LA x x ? *sum-mu* TI.LA SU$^?$ (?)]

12′ 8 GU$_4$^{MEŠ} 7[^{GU_4}ÁB^{M}]^{E}[^{Š}] SUM-*a*[*n* x]*it*/*id*/Á[ ]

13′ *šu-tu-ma* UDU.T[I].LA SU LÚ *ina k*[*u-m*]*u-šu du*[*l-lu* DÙ-*áš* EN TI.LA x x ?]

14′ *sum-mu* TI.L[A SU$^?$ x G]U$_4$^{MEŠ} 3 ^{GU_4}ÁB^{MEŠ} SUM-*an*[(ca 6 Zeichen ?)x GU$_4$^{MEŠ}]

15′ 7 ^{GU_4}ÁB[^{MEŠ} x$^?$] SUM-*an* NINDA.[x] *i-ka-sa-pu-ni šu-t*[*u-ma* UDU TI.LA SU]

16′ LÚ *ina* [*ku-mu-*]*uš-šu dul-lu* DÙ-*áš* EN TI.LA x[ ]

17′ SUM[x x]MU x [x] 8 GU$_4$^{MEŠ}[x ^{GU_4}ÁB^{MEŠ} SUM-*an*]

18′ [*šu-tu-m*]*a* UDU. TI.[LA SU] LÚ *ina ku-mu-š*[*u dul-lu* DÙ-*áš* EN TI.LA x x?]

19′ *sum-mu* TI.LA [S]U$^?$ [x GU$_4$^{MEŠ}] 5 ^{GU_4}ÁB^{MEŠ} [SUM-*an*]

20′ *šu-tu-ma* UDU.TI.LA [SU LÚ *i*]*na ku-mu-šu dul-lu* DÙ-*á*[*š* EN TI.LA x x ?]

Die Ergänzungen sind nur durch die im einigermassen lesbaren Teil des Textes zu beobachtenden Wiederholungen möglich. Ausser den angegebenen Ergänzungen füge ich hinzu, dass am Ende der Zeilen 12′, 17′ und 19′, und vielleich auch in der Mitte der Zeile 10′, höchstwahrscheinlich jeweils ein Satz mit einer Verbalform in der 3. Person Plur. Präs. G wie in Z. 15′ (Satz C, s. unten) zu erwarten ist.

Der zweite Teil des Textes von Z. 10′ bis Z. 20′ besteht also aus einigen syntaktischen Einheiten, die sich fast regelmässig wiederholen. Ich gehe davon aus, dass die Z. 20′ auch die letzte Zeile des Textes ist; so lassen sich folgende Sätze in dieser Reihenfolge isolieren:

A. *summu* TI.LA SU$^?$ [10]	"ein Täuberich des Lebens ersetzt er"
B. x *alpē* y *arḫē iddan*	"er gibt x Rinder (und) y Kühe"
C. NINDA.[X [11]] *ikasapū-ni*	"ein Brot X zerstückeln sie"
D. *šūtū-ma udutilû irīab*	"er selbst ein Schaf des Lebens ersetzt"
E. *amēlu ina kūmū-šu dullu eppaš*	"ein Mann / irgendjemand macht den (Opfer)dienst an seiner Stelle"
F. *adi balṭû* [. . . .] [12]	"solange er lebt [. . . .]"

Diese Sätze wechseln sich ab in den Z. 10′ - 20′ in dieser Abfolge: (10) B-[C$^?$]-[D] (11) E-F-[A$^?$] (12) B-X$^?$-[C$^?$] (13) D-E-[F] (14) A-B-[?] (15) B-C-D (16) E-F-[X] (17)-X-B-[C$^?$] (18) D-E-[F] (19) A-B-[C$^?$] (20) D-E-[F].

Die Terminologie der Opferanweisung, die Art der Opfergaben in diesem Text sind dem urartäischen Schrifttum fremd. Die wenigen Opfertexte, die wir in urartäischer Sprache kennen, haben eine ganz andere Struktur.[13] Sie nennen vor allem Schlachtopfer von Rindern, Schafen und jungen Böcken, welche in unterschiedlicher Menge verschiedenen Göttern des urartäischen Pantheon dargebracht werden. Im einzelnen finden wir in den urartäischen Opfertexten kaum Rinder und Kühe vereint. Vielmehr sind - wie wir aus den beschrifteten Felsnischen von Meher Kapısı[14] und Ašrut Darga[15] entnehmen können - Rinder und Kühe Gegenstand verschiedener Schlachtopfer für männliche bzw. weibliche Gottheiten.[16] Ferner ist das Brotopfer den urartäischen religiösen Texten unbekannt.

Einige Entsprechungen finden sich aber in assyrischen und babylonischen kultischen Texten. So ist die rituelle Handlung des Zerbröckeln eines Brotes im mittelassyrischen Ritual KAR 139 Vs. 5-6 zu finden.[17] Der Begriff "lebendes Schaf"[18] (UDU.TI.LA) ist aus der Beschwörungsserie *namburbi*[19] bekannt, und ist eines der Sühnemittel zur Reinigung des Palastes,[20] das auch in den Beschwörungen zur Entsühnung des Königs vorkommt.[21]

Der Text hat also anscheinend keinen Bezug zu den urartäischen Texten. Und zwar nicht allein wegen der assyrischen Sprache - denn auch die Opfergaben für Ḫaldi in der urartäisch-assyrischen Stele von Kelišin[22] sind ganz anders formuliert - sondern vielmehr wegen des Fehlens anderer Merkmale, wie Namen von Göttern oder Königen oder Wendungen, die aus den urartäischen Texten bekannt sind.

Das Denkmal hat andererseits mit dem bisher ältesten schriftlichen Zeugnis der urartäischen Dynastie, der schon zitierten[9] Gründungsinschrift der sog. "Sardursburg" (Madır Burçu) am Nordwestabhang des Vanfelsens, die Sprache und den Duktus, wie schon von Lehmann-Haupt gemerkt wurde, sowie die Lage am Vanfelsen gemeinsam. Deswegen soll dieser Text spätestens in die Regierungszeit Sarduri I. (ca. 840 - ca. 825) datiert werden. Es kann sich also um das älteste Schriftzeugnis aus dem urartäischen Raum handeln, und um ein weiteres Beispiel für die Tätigkeit jener Schreiberschule, der wir die Einführung der Keilschrift in Urarṭu zuzuschreiben haben. Diese kulturelle Abhängigkeit der ersten urartäischen Herrscher von der assyrischen Welt - wenigstens was den Gebrauch der assyrischen Sprache betrifft - dauerte, wie wir jetzt wissen,[23] mindestens bis in die Zeit von Menua (ca. 810 - ca. 785/780) an.

CICh = C.F. Lehmann-Haupt, *Corpus Inscriptionum Chaldicarum*, Textband, 1. Lieferung [Berlin & Leipzig 1928].

HchI = F.W. König, *Handbuch der chaldischen Inschriften* (=AfO Beiheft 8 [Graz 1955-7]).

TAD = *Türk Arkeoloji Dergisi*.

UKN = G.A. Melikišvili, *Urartskie klinoobraznye nadpisi* [Moscow 1960].

---

1 *Bericht über die ergebnisse der von Dr. W. Belck und Dr. C.F. Lehmann 1898/99 ausgeführten Forschungsreise in Armenien*, von Dr. C.F. Lehmann, SPAW XXX [1900] S. 619 ff. Siehe S. 626 unter den Inschriften "Unsicherer Zuweisung", Nr. 143 mit folgendem Wortlaut: "Opfernische. *Vankal'ah*. Südseite, aus dem Felsen gehauen. Assyrische fr. Inschrift, Schrifttypus wie Nr. 1-3. Königsname weggebrochen. Rechts 19 Z., links oben 1 fr. Z., unten 4 fr. Z. Opfergaben: "8 Ochsen" (Z. 19,16); "Büffel" (nicht "Wildstiere")(Z. 13.14.18).- Z. 10 und passim: LÚ *ina* [im Original von Lehmann stehen hier die Keilschriftzeichen, M.S.] *ku-mu-(uš)-šu* (vgl. [?] K 168 Lehmann, *Šamaššumukîn*, XL Rs. Z. 27)".

2 CICh, S. III unter den Inschriften unbestimmbarer Zuweisung: "*164.*165 WAN. WAN-QAL'AH. Südseite. Zwei getrennte assyrische Inschriften, deren Typus dem von Nr. 1-3 ähnelt. Königsname weggebrochen. Ber. 143."

3 *Materialien zur älteren Geschichte Armeniens und Mesopotamiens* (Abh. d. Königl. Ges. der Wiss. zu Göttingen, Phil.-Hist. Kl., NF Bd. IX/3 [Berlin 1907]) S. 63.

4 HchI, S. 31.

5 HKL I S. 304 f. und II (Supplementband) S. 181 unter Lehmann-Haupts *Materialien*.

6 Auf dem Abklatsch habe ich oben die Spuren eines Zeichen erkannt, das die Zahl der erkennbaren Zeilen um eine vermehrt. So ändert sich die Numerierung gegenüber der von Lehmann-Haupt.

7 S. meinen Beitrag *Kollation zweier urartäischer Inschriften im Iranischen Azerbajdjan* im Druck in der Fs B.B. Piotrovskij, *Drevnij Vostok i mirovaja kul'tura*, Moskau.

8 CICh 1-3 = HchI 1a-1c = UKN 1-3; E. Bilgiç, TAD 9 [1959] 45ff.

9 P. Richard Caplice, S.J., möchte ich wegen der Hilfe bei der Lesung dieses Textes meinen herzlichsten Dank ausdrücken.

10 Die Ergänzung dieses Logogramms ist nach Analogie mit Satz C wahrscheinlich; es kann ebenso eine 3. Pers. Sg. des Präsens G von *riābu* II verbergen.

11 Ich habe zwar in Erwägung gezogen, die Relativpartikel *šá*, welche das Subjunktivsuffix *ni* gerechtfertigt hätte, zu lesen; es folgen aber unlesbare Spuren eines Zeichens, die das Logogramm einer bestimmten Brotart vermuten lassen.

12 Es folgte höchstwahrscheinlich eine Wunschformel mit dem etwaigen Sinn "es soll ihm gut ergehen"; vgl. etwa CAD B 57 s.v. *balāṭu* 3c 3'.

13 S. dazu AMI NF 10 [1977] 125 ff.

14 CICh 18 = HchI 10 = UKN 27.

15 CICh 16 = HchI 8 = UKN 25.

16 S. darüber auch G.A. Melikišvili apud B.B. Piotrovskij, *Il regno di Van (Urartu)* [Roma 1966] 321.

17 Vgl. E. Ebeling, MVAG 23/II [1919] 47; s.a. CAD K 241 s.v. *kasāpu* A 1 b.

18 AHw S. 1402 b, s.v. *udutilû*.

19 BBR 43: 6 in der Bearbeitung von E. Ebeling, RA 49 [1955] 34/35.

20 BBR 26 I 20 ff.; s.a. S. 222 s.v. LU.TI.LA.

21 Ebd. Kol. V 32 ff.

22 RlA s.v.

23 Vgl. *Assur* I/8 [1978] 1-4, und *Studia Mediterranea Piero Meriggi dicata*, I, Pavia 1979, S.575ff.

ZUM PROBLEM DES HERRSCHERTITELS IN URUK DER SELEUKIDENZEIT

G. Kh. Sarkisian (Yerevan)

In einem früheren Aufsatz[1] habe ich meine Meinung zum Ausdruck gebracht, dass die Lakune der Z. 29 im Vertrag BRM II 47 aus Uruk (Jahr 157 der Seleukidenära) ^{lú}GAL ^{lú}*[...] šá bīt ilāni*^{meš} als ^{lú}*[SAG]* zu ergänzen ist. Der Text war mir damals nur in der Transliteration von C.T.T. Winckworth zugänglich.[2] Für die Ergänzung konnte ich mich jedenfalls auf die Parallele in der Bauinschrift des Herrschers von Uruk, Anu-uballiṭ-Kephalon, aus dem Jahr 201 v.u.Z., berufen,[3] wo dieser Herrscher den Titel ^{lú}GAL ^{lú}SAG URU *šá Uruk*^{ki} trägt. Die vollständige Analogie des Kontextes dieses Titels in BRM II 47 mit einer entsprechenden Stelle im Vertrag VDI Nr. 55, (1955/IV), S. 157 ff., Nr. VIII (Erm. 15544), Z. 20-22 (wo jedoch anstelle des uns interessierenden Titels ^{lú}*paq-du šá bīt ilāni*^{meš} erscheint) hat mich dann überzeugt, dass die entsprechenden Ämter identisch sein müssen. Auf Grund dieser Analogie kam ich zu dem Schluss, dass alle drei Titel ein und dasselbe Amt bezeichnen. Dieser Gedanke knüpfte sich an meine damals entstandenen Vorstellungen über die Gemeinde doppelhafter Natur der Stadt Uruk der Seleukidenzeit, nämlich die Bürger- und Tempel-Gemeinde, die einfach, wie ich bereits damals annahm, "Stadt Uruk" genannt werden kann, und die eigentlich mit dem Ausdruck *bīt ilāni*^{meš} bzw. *bītāti*^{meš} *ilāni*^{meš}, "Tempel", bezeichnet wurde. Mit dieser Bezeichnung könnte übrigens die Abweichung in der zweiten Hälfte des Titels (d. h. *šá Uruk*^{ki} bzw. *šá bīt ilāni*^{meš}) zusammenhängen.

Jetzt kann diese Vermutung bewiesen und etwas präziser formuliert werden.

Vor allem steht uns neben dem lückenhaften Text BRM II 47 eine vollständige, analoge Stelle im Vertrag Ash. 1930. 563 aus demselben Jahr (157 SÄ), die in der Arbeit von L.T. Doty angeführt wird,[4] zur Verfügung. An dieser Stelle liest man ^{lú}GAL ^{lú}SAG URU-*i' šá* É.DINGIR.MEŠ. Durch diese Stelle wird meine frühere Konjektur bestätigt und gleichzeitig auch wesentlich verbessert. Der wichtigste Beitrag von L.T. Doty besteht, selbstverständlich daneben, dass er die Stelle anführt, m. E. in der neuen Deutung des Ausdrucks ^{lú}SAG URU, der also einen selbständigen Titel *šá rēš āli* darstellt,[5] und nicht als einfaches Epitheton der ^{lú}GAL genannten Person aufzufassen ist. Bei diesem Punkt verirrten sich alle, mich mitgerechnet, die sich mit den oben angeführten Textstellen beschäftigten.

Die beiden Ausdrücke, ^{lú}*paq-du šá bīt ilāni*^{meš} und ^{lú}GAL ^{lú}SAG URU-*i' šá bīt ilāni*^{meš}, sind ohne Zweifel Benennungen für ein und dasselbe Amt. Für die Veranschaulichung möchten wir jedenfalls die entsprechenden Textstellen hier anführen. Die beiden Verträge, die voneinander nur auf 8 Jahre entfernt sind, da sie sich aus den Jahren 157 bzw. 165 SÄ datieren, stellen Pachtverträge dar. Es wird in ihnen *isiq* ^{lú}*ṭābiḫu-ú-tú*, "der Anteil der Tempelschlächter (-Pfründe)" verpachtet. Als Gegenleistung gilt die Ausführung einer bestimmten Arbeit ^{lú}*re-se-in-nu-ú-tú*, deren konkrete Bedeutung uns hier nicht interessiert. Wir möchten hier auf jene Stelle eingehen, wo die Strafe für Nachlässigkeit in der Ausführung der Arbeit beschrieben wird. Es steht im Text das folgende:

BRM II 47 (Ergänzung der Lakune auf Grund von Ash. 1930. 563): (27) *u ki-i* PN *šuāti*^{meš} *baṭ-al iš-ta-kan u si-man-[nu]* (28) *ul-tu-ti-iq* ... (29) ... *mim-ma šá* ^{lú}GAL ⌜^{lú}SAG *āli-i*[6] *šá*⌝ *bīt ilāni*^{meš} *u* ^{lú}*puḫru šá Uruk*^{ki} (30) *i-mi-du-šú i-nam-bi-il*

VDI Nr. 55, (1955/IV), S. 157 ff., Nr. VIII: (20) ... *ki-i* PN [*šuāti*^{meš}] (21) *baṭ-al iš-ta-kan u si-man-nu ul-te-ti-iq mim-ma šá* ^{lú}*puḫru šá Uruk*^{ki} *u* (22) ^{lú}*paq-du šá bīt ilāni*^{meš} *ṣe-bu-ú i-mi-du-šú i-za-ab-bil*

Die kleinen Unterschiede in der Reihenfolge der für uns wichtigen Termini und des Ausdrucks ^{lú}*puḫru* sind für die Beurteilung der allgemeinen Parallelität der beiden Texte nicht von Belang.

Ferner, nachdem ich den Vertrag *Forschungen und Berichte* 16, 1975, Nr. I veröffentlichte,[7] steht uns Information mindestens über eine Person zur Verfügung, die fast gleichzeitig (beidesmal im Jahre 91 SÄ, nur die Monate sind verschieden) in zwei Dokumenten auftritt, und zwar einmal als ^{lú}*paq-du šá bīt ilāni*^{meš} (a. a. O., Z. 16, 29, 39 und 51), anderesmal als ^{lú}GAL ^{lú}SAG *āli-a šá Uruk*^{ki} (TCL VI 1, Z. 57). Diese Person ist Anu-balāṭsu-iqbi, der Vater des oben schon erwähnten Anu-uballiṭ — Kephalon.

Wie kann nun diese Erscheinung interpretiert werden? Wegen der Gleichzeitigkeit dieser Erwähnungen hält L.T. Doty mit Recht für ausgeschlossen, dass Anu-balāṭsu-iqbi die erwähnten Ämter nacheinander erfüllt hat.[8] Von den alternativen Vermutungen, nämlich, erstens, dass er diese beiden Ämter - d. h. das Tempelamt und das bürgerliche Amt - gleichzeitig bekleidete, bzw. zweitens, dass die beiden Ausdrücke ein und dasselbe Amt bezeichnen, neigt L.T. Doty anscheinend zur ersten. Unter den Verhältnissen der damaligen Zeit, des letzten Viertels des 3. Jahrhunderts v. u. Z., gilt es wohl als Praxis, dass die Funktionen dieser beiden - ursprünglich doch unabhängigen - Ämter infolge des Zusammenwachsens der Tempelstruktur mit der Struktur der Bürger-Gemeinde nur von einer und derselben Person bekleidet werden konnten. Es dürfte gar nicht unerwartet sein, wenn in neuen Dokumenten Anu-uballiṭ — Kephalon, der Sohn des Anu-balāṭsu-iqbi, einmal als ^{lú}*paq-du šá bīt ilāni*^{meš} erwähnt würde, obwohl er z. Z. nur als ^{lú}GAL ^{lú}SAG URU *šá Uruk*^{ki} bekannt ist.

Später, nach einem halben Jahrhundert, etwa in der Mitte des 2. Jahrhunderts v. u. Z., kommt schon der hybride Name dieses Amtes vor: ^{lú}GAL ^{lú}SAG URU-*i' šá bīt ilāni*^{meš} (s. oben), in welchem die erste Hälfte aus der einen, die zweite Hälfte aus der zweiten Form stammt. Diese Entwicklung zeigt schon, dass die ehemaligen Unterschiede zwischen dieser beiden Ämtern bereits verschwunden waren, obwohl sich die Erinnerung an solche immer noch bewahrte, wie es aus dem parallelen Gebrauch der Form ^{lú}*paq-du šá bīt ilāni*^{meš} ersichtlich ist.

Auf dieselbe Entwicklung weist auch ein anderer Umstand hin, der von L.T. Doty bei seinem Versuch, ein Argument für die Existenz einer zusammengewachsenen Bürger- und Tempel-Gemeinde in Uruk der Seleukidenzeit zu widerlegen, ausser acht gelassen wird, nämlich der Umstand, dass Anu-uballiṭ — Kephalon, der Sohn und Erbe des Anu-balāṭsu-iqbi, der in seiner Bauinschrift als ^{lú}GAL ^{lú}SAG URU *šá Uruk*^{ki} auftritt, in den privatrechtlichen Urkunden[9] einfach als ^{lú}GAL ^{lú}SAG URU betitelt wird. Dies wäre unmöglich gewesen, wenn es zu dieser Zeit (Anfang des 2. Jahrhunderts v. u. Z.) in Uruk tatsächlich zwei funktionell unabhängige und verschiedene Ämter gegeben hätten, deren Namen mit den gleichen Worten angefangen (d. h. als ^{lú}GAL ^{lú}SAG URU), aber abweichend beendet worden wären (d. h. als *šá Uruk*^{ki} bzw. *šá bīt ilāni*^{meš}). Durch das Fehlen dieser beiden Endungen werden diese Titel ihrer Bedeutung nach sozusagen gleichgesetzt. Damit eröffnet sich die Möglichkeit, im Ausdruck *bīt ilāni*^{meš} bzw. *bītāti*^{meš} *ilāni*^{meš} die Benennung der gesamten Bürger- und Tempel-Gemeinde der Stadt Uruk zu sehen, obwohl dieser Ausdruck sonst - d. h. in anderen Zusammenhängen - eventuell auch in seiner ursprünglichen Bedeutung gebraucht werden konnte, nämlich in der Bedeutung "Tempel" bzw. noch enger als Name des Haupttempels der Stadt, ^{e}*Rēš*.[10]

1 G. Kh. Sarkisian, "*Samoupravlyayuščisya gorod Selevkidskoi Vavilonii*" VDI Nr. 39, 1952/I, 68-83, bes. 78 f.

2 C.T.T. Winckworth, "*A Seleucid Legal Text*", JRAS 1925, 655 ff.

3 A. Falkenstein, *Topographie von Uruk*, I, *Uruk zur Seleukidenzeit* (Ausgrabungen der DFG in Uruk-Warka, 3), Leipzig 1941, 6 (= J. Jordan, *Uruk-Warka*, 108a u. a.).

4 L.T. Doty, *Cuneiform Archives from Hellenistic Uruk* (Diss. Yale University, 1977), New Haven 1977, 22.

5 Vgl. AHw 973 ff. s. v. *rēšu(m)*.

6 In BRM II 47, Z. 29 ist auf Grund der Autographie *i* (und nicht *i'*) zu ergänzen.

7 G. Kh. Sarkisian, "*New Cuneiform Texts from Uruk of the Seleucid Period in the Staatliche Museen zu Berlin*", *Forschungen und Berichte* 16, 1975, 15-76, bes. 24 f.

8 L.T. Doty, op. cit., 22 ff.

9 G. Kh. Sarkisian, *Forschungen und Berichte* 16, 1975, 23, Z. x+13. Ein unveröffentlichter Vertrag im Museum der Chicago University, The Oriental Institute, A 3678 (der mir vom Vorstand des Instituts in Photographie zur Verfügung gestellt wurde), Rs. Z. 5 liest [lú]GAL SAG URU.

10 Vgl. L.T. Doty, op. cit., Anm. 76.

OSSETO-INDO-EUROPAEICA

Martin Schwartz (Berkeley, California)

In 1970 I proposed an Ossetic dissimilation *rærD̄* > *ræD̄* in connection with Iron *ræduvîn*, Digoran *rædovun* 'to tear off, scrape off, scratch'.[1] I took these from OIr. **fra-drauba-*, comparing Sogdian *žōβa* 'peel, husk, outer layer' < **drauba-(ka-)*, Khwarezmian **ərδumb-* 'to peel, to skin, to husk' < **drumba-*, etc., assigning them to PIr. **DRAUB*, for which I set up PIE **DREUBH*, reflected also by Gr. δρύπτω, 'to lacerate, excoriate, peel off'[2] (base ΔΡΥΦ; to my earlier examples add ἀμφίδρυφος, δρυφάδες, δρύφαξαι, αἰνοδρυφής, on which cf. P. Chantraine, *Dictionnaire étymologique de la langue grècque*). It may also be added that PIE **DREUBH* is from the root **DER* 'to flay' extended in **-W-* (cf. e.g. MPers. *drūdan* 'to harvest'); cf. also **GLEUBH*, Lat. *glubo* 'to peel', etc. Subsequently I took Sogd. *'βš'wnp-*, i.e. *əfšumb-* 'to peel' via **(ə)fžumb-* from **fra-drumba-* (cf. *βs'nt'k* 'child' **fra-zantV-*),[3] which would show the same preverb as the Oss. A vindication of my etymology of *ræduvîn* and the dissimilation it entails is in order, since it has been challenged in favor of another explanation.

D. Weber has rejected my view, writing "hier bleibt Benveniste's Erklärung (aus **fra-daub-*) auf sicherem Grund." The prestige of the late Iranist's name seems here to have induced a false sense of security in place of an independent consideration of the data, for from a semantic viewpoint there is nothing certain about the earlier etymology. Benveniste wrote: "Oss. *ræduvîn* . . . 'tirer violemment, arracher' . . . qui suppose **fra-daub-* pourrait avoir la racine **dub-* que nous connaissons seulement par sogd. *''δwβ*, *pδwβ* 'attacher' .... La relation de sens serait déterminée par la valeur spécifique de *fra-*, comme dans *ræ-mudzîn*, sogd. *βr''mc-* 'dépouiller' ou dans sogd. *βr''γrβ-* 'offrir' etc."[5]

It may be noted that the base **DAUB* (**DUB*) is also found in the Shughni Group, see G. Morgenstierne, *Etymological Vocabulary of the Shughni Group*, 1977, s.vv. *δův-*, *aδův-* 32, approving Benveniste's etym. of the Oss.; *biδafc-* 18, *niδafc-* 47, *piδafc-* 54. The latter forms are close to Sogd. *p(ə)δufs-*, Yaghnobi *budufs-* 'to be stuck, to adhere', intransitive (medio-passive) forms from **-dufsa-* (**-dub-sa-*), alongside which I reconstruct a secondary stem **-daufsa-* as etymon of Middle and New Persian *dōs* 'gum, plaster', NPers. *dōsīdan* 'to plaster, to glue, to stick together'. PIr. **DAUB*, with its basic reference to adherence, may now be explained from PIE **DHEUB(H)* 'to be deep' (OEng *dēop* 'deep', Lith. *dubùs* 'deep', *dumbù*, *dùbti* 'become hollow, sink down'; one may also compare Gr. τύφος 'wedge' (Hesychius), MHGerm. *tübel* 'peg', etc. < **DHEUBH*, perhaps < 'penetrate deeply', cf., as parallel to PIr. **DAUB* vis-à-vis 'deep' and/or 'wedge, peg', Eng. *stick*: OEng. *stician* 'to stick, pierce' and 'remain stuck', and allied Germanic forms for 'attach', etc., and prob. Latv. *stigt* 'to sink into', Lith. *stìgti* 'remain in a place'.

A development 'unglue' < 'tear off, lacerate' etc., presupposed by the development of *rædovun* from **DAUB*, is unusual, but possible. The real problem is the "valeur spécifique" of the preverb. For this B. referred to his remarks in *BSOS* 9, 1938, 508 seq. Here, however, he distinguished OIr. *fra-* "simplement 'devant, en avant'" from *frā-* "[que] repond à all. 'fort-, weg-' et marque éloignement, extraction, renoncement, selon les verbes." B. mentioned Sogd.

βr''mc- and *βr''γrβ-*, but not Oss. *ræmudzin*, which cannot be compared directly with Sogd. *βr''mc-*, i.e., *frām(V)č-* precisely because of the difference in preverbs (*ræ-* < **fra-*, but *ra-* from **frā-*). Indeed when B. actually specified the value of the Oss. preverbs, which he tried to fit into a simplistically symmetrical pattern, he stated that *ræ-* refers chiefly to movement from below to above, as seen from above (vs. *(i)s-*, as seen from below), which B's few examples fail to establish, as he himself seemed to be aware.[6] An examination of the various Oss. verbs in *ræ-* reveals a range of functions, chiefly corresponding to Germ. *vor-*, *ver-*, and *fort-*, found for **fra-* throughout Iranian.

In implying a separative function of the preverb in *ræduvin*, B. may have been misled by V. Miller's claim: "**ræ-* erscheint in manchen Verbem im Sinne von weg-, auf-, aus-, usw., z.B. *ræmodzin*, *ræmudzun* 'wegnehmen', *ræ-tīγin*, *ræ-teγun* 'verstossen, hin und her schwingen' (vgl. *tīγin* 'stossen'); *ræ-diin*, *ræ-duyun* 'sich verirren', *ræ-siin*, *ræ-suyun* 'aufschwellen', *ræ-dzæxsin*, *ræ-dzæxsun* 'ausstreuen' u.a." Here the only word with truly separative meaning is *ræmodzun*, where the idea of removal belongs to the base and not the preverb (cf. OInd. *MUC* 'to free', Ormuri *mōž-* 'to loosen', Shughni *nəməc-* 'to take out', and most importantly Oss. *nimudzin* 'to deliver up, to betray'). In fact, *ræ-* contrasts with *ra-* in continuation of the contrast of OIr. *fra-* with separative *frā-*. Thus *ræxæssin* means 'to tack on' but *raxæssin* 'to remove'. Without preverb *xæssin* is 'to draw, to pull'. Benveniste cites *ræxæssin*, glossing it only with the derived meaning 'faire des points de couture, piquer à l' aiguille', and contrasting it with *sxæssin* 'porter vers le haut'. Nor is there clear evidence for *ræ-* as 'mouvement de bas en haut vu d'en haut' in Benveniste's other examples, *rætīγin* 'soulever (le poing), brandir' vs. *stīγin* 'arracher (la peau), écorcher', and *ræxoin* 'percer, transpercer', vs. *sxion* 'frapper vers le haut'. If **DAUB* survived in Ossetic, for 'unglue' one would expect **ra-duvin*, by contrast with which *ræ-duvin* (parallel to *ræ- xæssin* vs. *ra-xæssin*) would mean 'to glue on to' and not 'to unglue', let alone 'scratch (off), lacerate'. But there is no trace of **DAUB* in Oss., so that an Ossetic formation from **ræ* plus **duv-* is eliminated; nor, it may be added, is **fra-DAUB* reflected anywhere else.

However, *ræduvin* as the only Oss. verb reflecting **DRAUB* would be paralleled by Sogdian, which also reflects *fra-DRAUB*. Semantically, this is the ideal etymon for *ræduvin*, whose medio-passive *rædivsin/ræduvsun* refers specifically to skin being lacerated. V. I. Abaev has taken up my etymology, but in modified form: **fra-draupa-* > **rældov-* > *rædov-*, *ræduv*.[7] Apart from Abaev's unjustifiable reconstruction **DRAUP* for **DRAUB* (and further his adducing semantically distant non-Iranian forms from PIE **DREP* and **DRIP*), this sequence is unlikely since **dr* gives Oss. *rd*, and Abaev's intermediary step *-Vld-* > *-Vd-* is unwarranted, since *-Vld-* remains in other words.

For another example of the (direct) change **rærD̄* > *ræD̄*, I would modify another of Abaev's etymologies: *rætaun* 'to quilt, sew, stitch' < **fra-ϑrāwa-*, cf. Gr. τιτράω 'to pierce' etc. Here Abaev posits an intermediary form **rætraw-*,[8] but since **ϑr* > *rt* is early (cf. Pontic Scythian inscr. φουρτ- 'son' < **puϑra-*, etc.) it is best to assume **fra-ϑrāwa-* > **rærtaw-* > *rætaw-*. The base **θRAW* has been posited for a form in another Saka language, Khotanese *thurs-*, which R.E. Emmerick defines as 'be oppressed' with etymon **ϑru-sa-*, medio-passive[9] (H.W. Bailey has 'to harm' with a less likely etymology).[10]

Probably we have a Saka conservation of PIE **TRE(H̯)W* 'to pierce, press through', with the Oss. having the concrete sense of Gr. τιτράω 'to pierce', τρῦμα 'hole', etc., and the Khot., if 'oppress', belonging with OEng. *đryn* 'to press', *đrēan* 'to vex, compel, threaten', or, if 'to harm', to τραῦμα 'wound', etc. (in which case Proto-Saka *θRAW would be like Gr. τρώω, both 'to pierce' and 'to wound'), cf. in any event OHGerm. *druoen*, OEng. *drōwigean* 'to suffer'.

I believe that another example of **rærD̄ > ræD̄* is *rædǽng*, for which the dictionaries furnish varied meanings: Miller-Freiman *'erectus(?): excited, passionate, bright red (of the face); without branches, dry, burning well (of wood)'; for the last meaning the sentence 'the woodsmen brought the *rædæng* wood from the forest' is given.[11]

The *Osetinsko-russki slovar'*, ed. A.M. Kasaev,[12] has three sets of definitions: 'dry, burning well (of wood)'; 'blushing, bright red, burning (of the face)'; 'full (of a man)'. The meanings which refer to the human face and body are respectively characterized as 'transferred', without further explanation; note however 'burning well': 'blushing' . . . 'burning' ? That the meaning *rædæng* as used of wood does not seem to refer to combustibility or dryness, against the indications in Miller-Freiman (which probably arise from the context of the single example) and in Kasaev (based on Miller-Freiman?), follows from Abaev's entry in *IESOY II*, where two homonymous words *rædæng* are set up: $rædæng_1$ 'slender, smooth' (of a tree), with the illustrative sentence from a literary source, 'Our white *rædæng* birch was completely charred'; $rædæng_2$ 'full of blood' (of the face), 'full, well-fed' (of a man). Abaev's etymology for $rædæng_1$ depends, as he notes, on an underlying meaning 'slender, thin', poor documentation of the word making for uncertainty. His provisional etymon is **fra-tanuka-*, cf. [and contrast] *tænæg* 'slender'. Abaev takes $rædæng_2$ from **fra-tanga-*, comparing Russ. *tugój* 'tight, stiff, slow', Lith. *tingùs* 'sluggish, flabby', ONor. *þungr* 'heavy', with PIr. **TANG* represented by Pers. *tang* (and similar forms in Pamir lgs.) 'tight, strong', *tanǰīdan* 'to pull'.

Before treating the problem of *rædæng* some difficulties with A.'s explanation of $rædæng_2$ may be pointed out. Iranian has no trace of the required **TANG*; instead it shows **θANG* throughout. Exceptional is Pers. *tanǰīdan* and *tang* (also MPers.); we may see here the early influence of **TAN* 'to stretch' (Pers. *tanīdan* 'to twist', *tana* 'web', etc.), with ϑ > *t* perhaps supported dialectally (cf. the Balochi situation); Pamir *tVng* is borrowed from Pers. With preverbs Pers. has the regular reflex of **θANG*, *-hanǰ-* (MPers. *-henǰ-*) and *-hang*. Oss. itself reflects **θANG* in *tindzin/itindzun*, *ting/iting* (**wi-θANG*); the fronted vowel of the root syllable, which arose from the old pass. stem (**ϑanǰaya-*) has spread to the noun, as also in Sogd. (Chr. *prϑync-* 'to stretch': *prϑynq* 'curtain'). Thus instead of *rædæng* one would expect **rætíng/ræting*.

It is also unlikely that homonymy would develop between words of antonymous primary meanings 'thick' and 'thin'. In Miller-Freiman the two sets of meanings are united through a hypothetical 'erectus', but this is distant from what is attested. Yet it is not necessary to reject, with Abaev, a reconciliation of different senses of *rædæng*.

The dissimilation **rærD̄ > ræd* allows for the derivation of *rædæng* via **rærdæng* from **fra-dranga-*, base **DRANG* 'to make firm, to make fast', whence Av. *drənǰaiti* 'makes firm, confirms', Wakhi *vərδɛnz-* 'to press', Kroraina *avadranga-* 'guarantee', etc. In Oss. the base is represented by *ærdong* 'herd (esp. of swine)' < **dranga-* 'that which is firmly held together against dispersal'.[13]

For the application of this PIr. base to tree trunks, it may be noted that **DRANG* also furnished the ordinary words for 'tree' in SWIr., i.e., MPers. *draxt*, Pers. *diraxt* < **draxta-* (ppp.) and Balochi *drač̌k* perh. < **dranǰaka-*. But for this conception of the tree as 'the solid, the firm' *par excellence*, one should compare the reverse situation, whereby the PIE word for 'tree', **doru-* **dru-* **dreu-*, yielded words for 'solid, firm, reliable' (etyma **drūwo-*, **drowo-*, etc.), cf. also

Lat. *robur* (older **robus*) 'oak, strength, toughness, vigor', *robustus*, etc.[14] Whereas the SWIr. words for 'tree' are based on participial forms meaning 'solid', *rædæng*, while also referring to trees, would proceed from a nominal representative of **DRANG* meaning *'compact(compressed, concentrated), of limited circumference', hence 'trim' (> 'slender'), 'smooth' (and thus also '*trimmed*, branchless', if the first gloss in Miller-Freiman is correct). It may be added that Eng. *trim* is from OEng. *trum* 'strong, solid', caus. *trymian*, *trymman* 'make strong, compact', PIE **dru-mo-*, whence also OInd. *druma-*, Gr. δρυμός 'tree', Hom. δρυμά n. pl. 'woods, forest'; thus semantically *trim* would stand to *druma-* etc. as *rædæng* would to *diraxt*. It may now be seen that Oss *rædæng*$_1$ < **DRANG* would have close correspondents in other IE languages: Prasun *ḍugó* 'stick, yoke peg', OChSlav. *drǫgŭ* 'pole', ONor. *drengr* 'thick stick' (Morgenstierne, *NTS* XV, 1949, 258).

On the basis of these forms one may reconstruct a PIE nominal derivative **dhre/ongho-* (< **DHRENGH* *'make/be solid, firm' > PIr. **DRANG*), whence one would expect **dranga-* > **ærdong* rather than **fra-dranga-* > Oss. *rædæng* (the difference in the Oss. root vowel reflects a difference in the earlier number of syllables; cf. *song*, pl. *sængtæ*, etc.). The preverb **fra-*, moreover, would seem to have a different function in *rædæng*$_2$.

From the basic notion of solidity *rædæng*$_2$, also < **fra-dranga-*, in reference to the human physique would stress robustness and substantiality, hence 'filled out, well fed', and correspondingly of the face, 'flushed with vitality' and 'full', hence 'full of blood' (as against the anemically pale and wan condition of under-nourishment). In contrast with *rædæng*$_1$ with its concentrative solidity, *rædæng*$_2$ indicates solidity as directed outwards, an orientation which would ordinarily be marked by the preverb. A solution to this difficulty will be offered after the presentation of another form in **fra-* which further confirms the dissimilation **rærD̄* > **ræD̄*.

D. *rædæxsun* (no correspondent in I.) is defined by Abaev as 'to climb' and compared with Av. *fradaxšanā* 'sling (for shooting)' (which is, however, semantically distinct), and alternatively compared with OPers. *ham-taxša-* 'to be active',[15] which is also remote in meaning, and probably a Persic modification of **ham-tuxša-* (cf. MPers. *tuxšāg* 'diligent', Av. *ϑβaxša-* 'to be industrious, to be active') due to **TAŠ* 'to hew, to fashion, to create' and perhaps **TAK* 'to run'.[cf. M. Mayrhofer, *Indo-Iranica* (*Mélanges ... Morgenstierne*), 1964, 141 seq.]

The etymology may be resolved through the definition in Miller-Freiman, where are found not only 'to climb' but also 'to cling to' (lezt' vverx, karabkat'sya, tseplyat'sya; hinaufklettern, sich an (etw.) klammern').[16] If this reflects the basic meaning, 'hold fast': 'climb' would be paralleled by Germ. *Klemme* 'a clamp', *klammern* 'to cling to': *klimmen* 'to climb', and similarly Eng. *clam*, *clamp*: *clamber*, *climb*, etc. Furthermore, Celtic has Middle Irish *drēimm* 'the act of climbing up', *dringid* 'he mounts up', Welsh *dringo* 'to mount, to climb', from PIE **DHRENGH* 'to hold fast, make firm', etc., whence PIr. **DRANG* 'id.', whose medio-passive **draxsa-* would mean 'hold oneself fast, keep oneself fastened, cling to' (cf. Parth. *draxs-* 'maintain oneself, remain'), the preverbial **fra-draxsa-* giving **rærdæxs-* and with the dissimilation, *rædæxs-*. The value of **fra-* can hardly be explained by Benveniste's 'movement from below to above as seen from above', for a "bird's eye view" is not to be expected. Instead **fra-* probably is here, as often elsewhere, '- forth, - along'; thus **fra-draxsa-* is 'to cling with reference to the length of an object', hence 'to move along by clinging; to climb'.

One may now return to the problem of **fra-* in *rædǽng*$_{1-2}$. As was already noted, a form **dranga-* as antecedent of *rædæng*$_1$ is (apart from the phonology) suggested by the Kafir, Slavic and Germanic derivatives of PIE **dhre/ongho-*; it is supported within Ossetic by *ærdong* <**dranga-* *'something held firmly together', where the sense of concentration appears again. From **dranga-*, and in distinction to it, there was formed **fra-dranga-* 'bulgingly solid, filled out' by addition of **fra-*, which, prefixed to nominal forms, means 'in front, ahead, on the exterior, facing the viewer'. Similarly from OIr. *buna-* 'base, bottom, foundation', Oss. *bīn 'id.'*, **fra-buna-* *'outward part or front of a base, a fund in advance', Oss. *ræbīn*, and from **pīwah-* 'fat' (noun; OInd. *pī́vas-*, MPers. *pīh* 'id') was formed the adj. **fra-pīwah-* *'having fat on the outside', hence MPers. *frabīh*, Parth. *frabīw*, Khwar. *šabīw* 'fat, stout'.

A counterforce to the outward (horizontal) orientation of **fra-dranga-* would have been exerted by the lengthwise (vertical) orientation of **fra-draxsa-*, both words sharing the same base (*DRANG) and both beginning with *fra-* and thus standing in the formal relationship characteristic of a verb and cognate noun (cf. MPers. *frahaxs-*: *frahang*) so that there could be a semantic attraction due to this formal relationship. In direct proportion to the resultant degree of neutralization or dilution, so to speak, of the force of the preverb, would be a weakening of the opposition in orientation, centripetal vs. centrifugal, that had existed between **dranga-* and **fra-dranga-*. An identification of **dranga-* with **fra-dranga-* could then be actualized by the circumstance that **dranga-*, describing tree trunks, shared with **fra-draxsa-* (as concerns the actual thing signified) a reference to holding firm (*DRANG) all along a surface. Furthermore, the referend *par excellence* is specifically the surface of a tree. The application of **dranga-* to *'trim(med)' trees is, as already noted, probably a pre-Iranian usage, while **fra-draxsa-* 'to climb' would be especially associated with trees through the impressions of childhood and the observation of animals; the association of climbing with trees may perhaps also have been effected by the use of simple ladders consisting of a single upright beam with crossbars. The secondary referential association of **dranga-* 'trim(med)' with a lengthwise/vertical orientation would distance it even further from the semantic field of **dranga-* as characterizing a herd. Through the mediation of **fra-draxsa-*, **dranga-* describing tree trunks would then become **fra-dranga-*, merging with **fra-dranga-* describing the human appearance. The coexistence of two virtually opposed meanings of **fra-dranga-* > *rædæng* would be permitted not only by the "neutralizing" influence of **fra-draxsa-* on the value of **fra-* in **fra-dranga-*, whereby both applications of **fra-dranga-* (i.e., in describing resp. human beings and trees) could be felt as illustrating a general sense of solidity, but also by the very difference in the respective spheres of application, whereby no confusion of meaning results, so that the two basic senses of *rædæng* were allowed to survive down to modern times.

My third example for the dissimilation **rærD̄* > *ræD̄* is I. *rædīin*, D. *ræduyun* 'to err' (ppp. *rædīd/rædud*), which has lacked a satisfactory etymology. Benveniste's comparison with OInd. *dī́yate* 'flies, soars'[17] fails phonologically and semantically. More interesting is Abaev's explanation with D. *iduyun* 'to run short, become exhausted, dry up'.[18] The latter cannot be related, as contemplated by Abaev, to OInd. *dóṣa-* 'vice', inner-Indic vṛddhi of *duṣ-*, PIE **duṣ-* 'bad-', an irreducible bound form. I take *iduyun* from OIr. **wi-dūya-*, cognate with Goth. *diwans* 'mortal', *dauþus* 'death', ONor. *deyja* 'to die', OIrish *dith* 'end, death', OEng. *dwīnan* 'to dwindle, to disappear', *dwǣscan* 'to be extinguished', Lith. *dvìsti* 'to be extinguished, to go out'. Since comparable forms in this sense are lacking elsewhere in Indo-Iranian, it is likely that *iduyun* should be added to other Ossetic examples reflecting a remarkable Saka lexical conservatism. This etymology makes it unlikely that *iduyun* and *ræduyun*, etc., are related.

In view of both form (zero grade plus *-y-* indicating an old passive) and meaning, 'to err', etc., (D.) *ræduyun* would ideally be from an earlier 'to be led astray, to be deceived'. Reconstruction **rærduy-<*fra-druya-* allows **-druya-* to be the passive of **DRAW*, pres. stem **drāwaya-*, whence I have derived Av. *drāuuaiia-* 'to lead astray', Parth. *drāw-* 'to deceive, seduce', Chr. Sogd. *ārδēw-* 'to seduce'; cf. Khwar. *ārδāw* 'demon which leads its victims far away', **ārδuc* (< **ā-druti*) 'far, seduction', etc.,[19] the base seems also to be reflected in Saka, apart from Oss., in Khotanese *drau* 'deception'.[20] Thus **DRAW* would be attested without preverb in Av. and Parth. (and Khot.?), with *ā-* in Sogd. and Khwar., and with **fra-* in Oss.

However, Oss. reflects **ā-DRAW* (stem **ā-drāwaya-*) in I. and D., *ardaun* (ppp. *ardīd/ardud*) 'to slander, stir up rumors against someone'. If the base is the same as Sogd. *ārδēw-*, etc., the underlying mg. of Oss. *ardaun* would be divergent, 'to mislead (a) person(s) with regard to (an)other person(s)'.

Benveniste compared *ardaun* with Sogd. *žāw* (*žāu*) 'rumor, reputation, noise', taking both from a base **DRAW* 'avoir une réputation'; caus. 'faire courir un bruit' > 'calomnier, exciter l'opinion contre quelqu'un'.[21] Here Benveniste separated the Oss. and Sogd. words from a grouping under **DRAW* 'to make noise' set up by H.W. Bailey. Of the remaining forms, Khot. *drro* is not 'roared' but 'such', according to R.E. Emmerick,[22] while Sogd. *žāy-* 'to speak' derives from **ǰāya-* (PIE **GEH̯₁*), as shown by the Yaghnobi and Pamir forms for 'say, recite, read' which I brought together[23] (perhaps here belong also Man. Sogd. *ptǰy'mc*, etc., 'quarrel', with **-žāy-* from weakly stressed **-žāy-*?). Theoretically Sogd. *žāw* could go therefore back to **ǰā-wa*, although it is more attractive to take *žāw* and MPers. *drāyīdan, drāyistan* 'to chatter, speak incoherently; speak (used of *daivic*, i.e., demonic beings)' from PIE **DHREW* 'to make noise', as I also remarked.

While MPers. **drāy-* can go back to **DRAW* (pres. stem **drāwaya-*), H.S. Nyberg took it from OPers. **DRĀD* < **ZRĀD* (cf. OInd. *HRĀD* 'to make noise').[24] The assumption of such a base also allowed Nyberg to read in *Dēnkird* 7.4.76 **drāhīt* 'shouted (with a voice resembling the neighing of a horse)', for which however M. Molé's reading with *grāy-* 'to slip'[25] is preferable to the otherwise unattested **drāh-*. The hypothetical OPers. base **DRĀD* also led Nyberg to read the MPers. word for 'bell' at *Ayādgār ī Zarērān* 34 as *dl'd*, i.e., *drāi* (Pers. *darā, darāy*),[26] where other scholars read *dl'g'*, i.e., *darāγ* (thus A. Pagliaro, Benveniste, and D.N. MacKenzie), which is preferable as regards the consonantism (orthographically *-g* representing /-γ/ is more likely than unmarked *-d* representing /-y/). MacKenzie designated the word as Parthian,[27] which is in keeping with the assumption of a Parthian antecedent for the Middle Persian text, and would accord with the correspondence of Parth. *-āγ* to MPers. *-āg*, Pers. *-ā(y)* < OIr. **-āka-*.

However, there is no independent indication that the word is Parthian, and the fact that *darāγ* is found in Judeo-Persian, and *darā(y)* in Classical Persian, points to its Persian provenience. A Persic variation *-āγ/-ā(y)* is also found in the word for 'lamp', MPers. (Pahl.) *cl'g'* = NPers. *čirāγ*, Psalter Pahl. *cwl'dy*, Man. MPers. *cr'h*, Judeo-Pers. *cr'*, cf. also Mazandarani *calā* and further Sogd. *cr'γ*, Oss. I. *ciraγ*, Khot. *cirau*, all of which I have traced to a base **ČUL* 'to blaze'.[28] I now take all these forms (with Aram. *šərāγā*) from early MPers. **čūrāγ/čurāw* (cf. Zor. *bāγ*/Man. *bāw* 'garden', *murγ/murw* 'bird'); from **čurāw* comes not only, in the extreme east, Khot. *čirau*, but also Shughni Group *cVrV̄v* (exc. Yazg. *carēγ*), with old *č>c*, and in the far west Hawrami *čɪráwi* (f., as Shghn.), cf. Gr. λαμπτήρ, Lat. *candela*>... Sogd. *δmt'yr, qndyl-*. MPers. *-āγ* + vb. base seems to make nouns of instrument. Like *čurāγ* is *damāγ* 'nose'<*dam-* 'to breathe'. The readi *darāγ* for *dl'g'*, if analyzed *dar-āγ*, would remain etymologically opaque. But if in place of the disyllabic interpretation (which has no independent justification) *drāγ* is read, this can be taken from earlier **drāwāγ* 'that by means of which a noi is produced' (cf. MPers. *bād<bawād*, *ār-<āwar-*, **ā-bar-*, Pahl. *'rzwk'*== NPers. *ārzō* ~ Man. MPers. *''wrzwg* < **ā-brǰ-*; see further Horn, *Grundriss der iranischen Philologie*, I/2, 24 §3).

Decisive evidence for **DRAW* 'to make noise' comes from Ossetic. I. *ærdīag*, D. *ærdewagæ* 'outcry, wailing' has hitherto lacked satisfactory explanation (Av. *driβi-* mentioned by Abaev[29] is irreconcilable in meaning, 'phlegm, slime', as well as in form, *-*b*-: -∅/*w*-). I suggest **drauyākā-*, which would be a regular antecedent of the I. and D. forms; cf. I. *niwin*, D. *newun* 'to wail' < **nauya-*, but D. *næwun* '*id.*' < **nawa-*. Thus Oss. *ærdiag*/*ærdewagæ* may be added to Sogd. *žāw*, MPers. *drāy-*, and *drāγ*, etc. < **DRAW*. PIE **DHREW* 'to make noise' is otherwise attested in Germanic (OEng. *drēam* 'jubilation', etc.), and a series of Greek forms which parallel the Iranian semantically: θρέομαι 'cry aloud, shriek', cf. Oss. *ærdiag*; θρόος 'noise, murmur, report, rumor', cf. Sogd. *žāw*; θρυλέω 'to chatter, to babble', cf. MPers. *drāy-*. For the relationship of 'bell' to these meanings, cf. Eng. *bell* (noun): *bell* (verb), Germ. *bellen* 'to bellow, bay, bark, shriek', OEng. *bellan* 'to roar', etc.

It is conceivable that **DRAW* 'to make noise' alone accounts for Oss. *ardaun*, but this is not likely: (1) the sense of calumniation is not found for any other reflexes of this base, or the extra-Iranian cognates; (2) other languages of East Iranian origin reflect **ā-drāwaya-*, formally identical to the antecedent of *ardaun*, in the sense of 'lead astray'; (3) Oss. has no reflex of **(-)drāwaya-*, the active stem of **DRAW* 'lead astray', although it does seem to reflect the passive stem **(-)druya-* (in *ræduy-*). These facts may be explained by the absorption of the two homophonous bases **DRAW* (pres. **drāwaya-*) 'lead astray' and 'make noise' in a blended **ā-drāwaya-* 'to lead astray through rumors'. It is possible that the homonymy led to the elimination of **DRAW* 'lead astray' in Southwestern Iranian, although Zor. MPers. *drāy-* as referring to the speech of demonic beings may well be due to OPers. **drāwaya-* 'to make noise' being influenced by the homonymous stem 'to lead astray'. This may even have been due to the interaction in Old Persian of everyday speech with Zoroastrian scholastic usage, which must have drawn upon the Avestan terminology.

I conclude that my supposition **ærD̄* > *ræD̄* is confirmed by *rædæng*$_{1\text{-}2}$, *rædæxsun*, *rædiin*, *rædivin*, and *rætaun*. Possibly this reflects a broader tendency **rVrC* > *rVC*. The numerous Oss. forms in *rarC-* do not provide clear counterexamples, for here the transparent construction *ra-ærC-* is made from still-living forms in *ærC-*.

The history of *rædæng*$_{1\text{-}2}$, *rædæxsun*, and *ardaun* are illustrations of phenomena which I call "syntropic" interactions (i.e. of associable features of form and meaning, taking place simultaneously between given words); this will be discussed in greater detail elsewhere.

---

1 Henceforth, after introducing Oss. words in their I. and D. forms, I shall often cite only the I., without dialect designation. Other abbreviations used here are D = any Ossetic dental stop; *H̱* = Proto-Indo-European laryngeal; IE = Indo-European; Ir. = Iranian; M = Middle; O = Old. Forms written in upper-case italics are bases ("roots").

2 *W.B. Henning Memorial Volume*, ed. M. Boyce and I. Gershevitch, 385-386.

3 *BSOAS* XXXIV/2, 1971, 310. The same etymology was independently found by I. Gershevitch, *Indogermanische Forschungen*, Bd. 70, 1970, 304.

4 *Indogermanische Forschungen*, Bd. 77, 1973, 302-303.

5 *Etudes sur la langue ossète*, 12 and 41.

6 *Op. cit.*, 93-94.

7 *Istoriko-etimologičeski slovar' osetinskovo yazyka* (henceforth *IESOY*) II, 1973, 361-362.

8 *Op. cit.*, 381-382.

9 *Saka Grammatical Studies*, 1968, *s.v.*

10 *Dictionary of Khotan Saka*, 1979, 149. Av. *ϑβarəs-* is not 'to cut' but specifically 'to carve, cut out, pierce, shape', nor is an analogical replacement of *turs-* by **ϑurs-* expected; cf. Av. *ϑβaxš-*, MPers. *tuxš-* 'be diligent', Av. **ϑβar-*, Sogd. *pəϑβār-* 'to hasten': Yaghnobi *tur-* etc. Lat. *trux* 'rough' etc. is from PIE **TREUK*, as I shall discuss further elsewhere.

11 Wsewolod Miller, *Ossetisch-Russisch-Deutsches Wörterbuch, herausgegeben und ergänzt von A. Freiman.* II, 1929 (Reprinted *Janua Linguarum*, Series Anastatica, 1/2, 1972), 995.

12 1952, 280.

13 Benveniste, *Etudes . . . oss.*, 34. [The D. form *ærγaw* 'herd' as against I. *ræγaw* < **fra-gāwa-* (Abaev, *IESOY II s.v.*) is prob. due to the influence of *ærdong* and *ærwæz* 'herd', facilitated by the relationship of the preverbs *ræ-* and *ær-*.]

14 P. Friedrich, *Proto-Indo-European Trees*, 1970, 140 seq. Note his remarks on 142 seq. against Benveniste's starting from 'solid'.

15 *IESOY* II, 361.

16 Miller-Freiman, 995.

17 *Etudes . . . oss.*, 87.

18 *IESOY* II, 362.

19 *JRAS*, 1967, 119 seq. N. Sims-Williams' subsequent establishment of *ā-* in *ārδēw-* makes it likely that the *ā-* in the Pers. borrowing of the Khwar. word for 'deceptive demon' is genuine (see the data I have assembled in *Henning. Mem. Vol.*, 388-389). *ʾrδ^{a}w* would then reflect **ārδǎw* < **ārδāw*; cf. perhaps Sogd. *ā-ǎ* < *ā-ā*, which I documented in *Memorial Jean de Menasce*, ed. Ph. Gignoux and A. Tafazzoli, 1974, 407.

20 For Khot. *drau*, see R.E. Emmerick, *Asia Major* XVI 1/2, 1971, 63-67. Differently H.W. Bailey, *Dictionary of Khotan Saka*, *s.v.*

21 *Etudes . . . oss.*, 59. Cf. and contrast Abaev, *IESOY* I, 1958, 62.

22 *Asia Major* 1971, 65 seq. Bailey now translates 'rushing', *Dict. Khot. Saka* 170.

23 *Henning Mem. Vol.* 387 fn. 10, with 385 fn. 2.

24 *A Manual of Pahlavi II*, 1971, 65.

25 *La légende de Zoroastre*, 1967, 55. [One may also read **grāyist.*]

26 *Loc. cit.* (For Pers. *darā* etc. see further J. Asmussen, *AO* (Hafn.) XXXI, 1968, 15.)

27 *A Concise Pahlavi Dictionary*, 1971, 24.

28 *Mithraic Studies*, ed. J.R. Hinnells, 1975, II, 412 fn. 7. Note now Khot. *tcūlye* 'splendid' listed with *haṃjsūl-* 'to kindle' by Bailey, *Dict. Khot. Saka* 141; these forms, with Oss. D. *idzulun* etc., are another instance of the conservatism of the Saka vocabulary.

29 *IESOY I*, 172-173, there rejecting on phonological and semantic grounds the connection with *ardaun* proposed by Miller and von Stackelberg.

A NEW INSCRIPTION OF ŠAR-KALI-ŠARRĪ

E. Sollberger (London)

Šar-kali-šarrī has left us a relatively small number of inscriptions, or, to put it perhaps more accurately, relatively few inscriptions of Šar-kali-šarrī have been published to-date. Except for one (4) which has forty lines, they are fairly short (three to twenty-four lines) and fall into two groups distinguished both by their contents and their provenance. The first one, from Nippur, concerns the E-kur; the second is from Sippar. The new text forms a third group, of uncertain provenance. The texts so far published are:

A. From Nippur: seven texts in two sub-groups:

a. Texts concerning the building of the E-kur:

1. Gate-socket A (24 lines). BE 1, 1 = Gelb 1 = Hirsch a2 = SAK 162 IX 1c.

2a. Gate-socket B (24 lines). BE 1, 2 = Gelb 2a = Hirsch a3 = SAK 164 d = IRSA 112 IIA5a. Same text as 1, with a few variations.

2b. Tablet (22 lines). Civil JCS 15 [1961] 80 (CBS 14226 + N.537) = Gelb 2c = Hirsch a3. Old-Babylonian copy of 2a with scribal errors; divine classifier before king's name as in 4, 7, and the year-name CT 50, 51.

3. Gold leaf (23 lines). Jacobsen Copenhagen 80 = Gelb 2b = Hirsch a3. Same text as 2a but obviously an impression from a lost (or as yet undiscovered) Gate-socket C.

4. Tablet (40 lines plus two-line colophon). Goetze JAOS 88 [1968] 55 f. Ur-III (or Old-Babylonian ?) copy of a monumental inscription; divine classifier (cf. 2b).

b. 'Proprietary texts' (royal name and titles) derived from sub-group a:

5a. Brick-stamp A (7 lines). BE 1, 3 = Gelb 3 = Hirsch a4 = SAK 162 IX 1a.

5b. Brick stamped with 5a. Goetze JAOS 88, 55.

6. Brick-stamp B (3 lines). YOS 9, 7 = Gelb 6 = Hirsch a5.

7. Tablet bearing impression from a stone slab or tile (5 lines), with Neo-Babylonian explanatory colophon on back; divine classifier (cf. 2b). Clay MJ 3 [1912] 23 ff. = Gelb 5 = Hirsch Bb = IRSA 112 IIA5c.

B. From Sippar: one votive inscription:

8. Mace-head (7 lines). CT 21, 1 (91146) = Gelb 4 = Hirsch a1 = SAK 162 IX 1b = IRSA 112 IIA5b.

The new inscription published here[1] (C. 9. according to the arrangement above), though only a Neo-Babylonian copy, is very important as it adds significantly to the hitherto known corpus both by its length (seventy-one lines) and its subject matter. The text does not use the divine classifier (see above ad text 2b) but, nevertheless, gives such an unexpected picture of Šar-kali-šarrī that, had his name been broken away, one would have unhesitatingly attributed it to Narām-Suen: indeed some passages seem directly borrowed from the latter's inscriptions.

The tablet, as will be readily seen from my transliteration is rather poorly preserved, but as the broken or defaced signs are fairly well identifiable and the x's are either wholly destroyed or consist of only insignificant traces, I have refrained from adding a copy to my transliteration. Needless to say, the translation is in many parts only tentative.

Obv. i
1 *šar-kà-lí-* l u g a l *-rí*
2 *da-núm*
3 l u g a l
4 *a-kà-dè*[ki]
5 b a - d ì m
6 ⸢k ù⸣ - b á r a - ⸢x (x)?⸣
7 *ʾà* [d]⸢i n a n a⸣
8 *in* INANA.AB[ki]

ii
9 ⸢*i*⸣*-nu*
10 *ki-*⸢*ib*⸣*-ra-*⸢*tum*⸣
11 *ar-ba-*⸢*um*⸣
12 *iš-ti-ni-iš*
13 *i-*⸢*ḫa*⸣*-ni-su*$_4$
14 ⸢*i-nu-mi-su*⸣
15 *[iš]-tum-ma*
16 *a-bar-ti*
17 *ti-a-am-tim*

iii
18 *sa-pil-tim*
19 *a-dì-ma*
20 *[t]i-a-am-tim*
21 ⸢*a-lí*⸣*-tim*
22 *ni-se*$_{11}$
23 *ù*
24 *sa-tu-e*
25 *kà-la-su-nu-ma*

iv
26 ⸢*a-na*⸣
27 [d]*en-líl*
28 *u-ra-iš*
29 ⸢*ù*⸣
30 u [r u - u] r u *-si-in*
31 ⸢*in*⸣ [d u$_6$]*-e*
32 *u-de-* ⸢*er-ma*⸣
33 *maḫ-rí-iš*
34 [d]*en-líl*
35 *šar-kà-lí-* l u g a l *-rí*

Rev. v
36 *da-núm*
37 *in* [n a m] - d a g *lim-*⸢*nu*⸣*-ti*
38 [d]*en-líl*
39 *in* KASKAL+x.KASKAL+x
40 *da-nu-ti*
41 *ma-na-ma*
42 *pá-ni-su*
43 *ù-la*
44 ⸢*ú*⸣*-[ba-a]l*
45 [ ]

vi
46 *ḫa-*⸢*ḫal*?⸣*-la-áš*
47 *na-gáb*
48 ⸢i d i g i n a⸣ ⸢i$_7$⸣
49 *ù*
50 NI-*u-*⸢x⸣
51 *na-gáb*
52 ⸢UD⸣.[K]IB.NUN ⸢i$_7$⸣
53 n u m u n *-sú* ⸢*ki*⸣*-ma*

54 GIŠ ⸢x x⸣
55 *in* ⸢x x⸣
⸢x⸣
vii 56 *ša ba-qí-iš*
57 ʾà ^{d}inana
58 *ib-tu-qù*
59 *ša* dub
60 *su*$_{4}$*-a*
61 *u-sa-za-ku-ni*
62 ^{d}*en-lil*
63 *ù*
64 ^{d}utu
65 *ù*
66 ^{d}inana
67 suḫuš-*su*
viii 68 *li-su-ḫu*
69 *ù*
70 še-numun-*su*
71 *li-il-qù-tu*

---

72 *a-na pí-i* na$_{4}$ na-rú-a
73 *ša* na$_{4}$ PI ḫuš-za
74 *ša ab-nam*
75 *ša-aṭ-ru*
76 ^{md}U.GUR-*šu-mi-ib-ni*
77 dumu lú *iš-šá-ak-ku*
78 *za-am-ra-am*
79 *iš-ṭú-ur*

1-9 Šar-kali-šarrī, the strong one, the king of Akkade, the builder of ..., the temple of Inana at Zabalam:-

9-13 When the Four Parts together had been subdued,

14-32 then, from beyond the Lower Sea even unto the Upper Sea, he smote for Enlil the peoples and the mountains in their totality, and he turned their cities into *heaps (of rubble)*.

33-44 Before Enlil, Šar-kali-šarrī the strong one, in *punishing* the evil (enemies) of Enlil in fierce battles, shows no mercy to anyone.

45-58 ..., the sources of the Tigris and ... the sources of the Euphrates, he ...ed like ... *the seed of him* who had *greatly* ravaged the temple of Inana.

59-71 He who should damage this tablet, let Enlil and Šamaš and Inana tear out his roots and gather his descendants!

72-75 (*Colophon*) Written according to the text of a stela of ...-stone, ...

76-79 Nergal-šumī-ibnī, of the Iššakku family, wrote it hastily.

Commentary

5-7 According to one of his year-names (SAK 226 g), Narām-Suen first built the temple of Inana at Zabalam but its name is not given. Nor is a special name for this temple given in the 'temple-hymn' Sjöberg-Bergmann TCS 3, No. 26.

6 Traces of one lower slanting wedge below two smaller ones, and faint traces of a possible further sign.

9 Erasure between *i-* and *-nu*.

9-13 For this passage, cf. the Narām-Suen texts PBS 5, 36 Rev.? ii 5′ ff.; A.H. Ayish *Sumer* 32 [1976] 63 ff. (English) = Fawzi Rashid ibid. 49 ff. (Arabic) i 5-9; IAMN 12. pl. IV, 6+7 ii.

22-25 *nišē u šadwē*, which I cannot find anywhere else, probably refers to the totality of the population of both the lowlands and the highlands.

31-32 If my restoration is correct one would have expected *a-na*.

37 Assuming that n a m - d a g is for n a m - t a g, *arnum*.

46 ⌜*ḫal*?⌝ seems written over an erased sign; there are traces of an erased sign just under it.

50 Faint traces of a few wedges.

53 One would have expected *-su*; only the outline of *ki-* can be made out.

54-55 Traces of parts of horizontal and vertical wedges

56 If correctly interpreted this would be the only occurrence of *baqāšu* before SB (cf. CAD s.v.).

57-58 As far as I am aware this example of *batāqum* occurs in OAkk only in one other text, also from the time of Šar-kali-šarrī, the year-name OIP 14, 117 where it refers to 'the [wa]ll of the temple of Enlil'.

73 For this stone-name cf. perhaps NA_4.PI in KAR 185, 4:15 (ŠL 383.11).

74 I can offer no explanation for this line.

78 The usual form is *zamar* (cf. Hunger Kolophone, 181 s.v.), but note *za-am-ra* quoted in CAD s.v. *zamar*; and in the Neo-Babylonian colophon of the fragment of copy BM 55468 (unpublished).

Gelb = *Old Akkadian Writing and Grammar*², 202f.: Šar-kali-šarrī. Original Inscriptions.

Hirsch = AfO 20 [1963] 28ff.: Die Inschriften des Šarkališarrī.

IAMN = İstanbul Asariatika Müzeleri Neşriyatı (XII = J.P. Naab & E. Unger, *Die Entdeckung der Stele des Naram-Sin in Pir Hüseyin* [Istanbul 1934]).

IRSA = E. Sollberger & J-R. Kupper, *Inscriptions royales sumériennes et akkadiennes* [Paris 1971].

SAK = F. Thureau-Dangin, *Die sumerischen und akkadischen Königsinschriften* [Leipzig 1907].

---

1 BM 38302 = 80-11-12, 184; 93 x 60 mms; inscribed parallel to the long side; registered as coming from 'Babylon', which in older registers often stands for Babylonia in general. I reported briefly on this text to the 24th Rencontre Assyriologique Internationale in Paris, 1977. I am much indebted to I.J. Gelb, who kindly read a preliminary transliteration, for the elucidation of lines 47 f. and 51 f.

ON THE SCYTHIANS IN MANNEA*

Y.B. Yusifov (Baku)

Although long the subject of scientific research, the problem of the Scythians is still not entirely resolved. The irruption of the Cimmero-Scythians into Western Asia created a new political situation which is reflected in the ancient documents. This question is not fully discussed in several works and monographs devoted to the history of Western Asia and the Caucasus.[1] The Cimmerians and Scythians appeared in this region at the end of the 8th and beginning of the 7th centuries BC, and began to intervene actively in the political events of the area. The traces of their sojourn are still preserved among the toponyms of some regions of Western Asia and Transcaucasia.[2] The intervention of the Cimmerians and Scythians in Asia was on a massive scale, but these tribes also extended to other regions, which is why in the final reckoning their political achievements remained insignificant. On the other hand, the Cimmero-Scythians became a force which for several decades troubled Assyria - then the most powerful state in Asia. This enables us to conclude that the main concentration of the Cimmerian and Scythian forces was in the region of Lakes Van and Urmia, a fact which is reflected in the inscriptions of the Assyrian kings. It is precisely from there that the Cimmero-Scythians made incursions into zones which were under the political influence of Assyria. They allied themselves with other states during their struggle against Assyrian domination, and one of these states was Mannea, where these northern tribes had also settled.

The questions of the settlement of the Scythians in the Lake Urmia area and of the formation of a Scythian state on the territory of ancient Azerbaidjan were formulated and analysed for the first time by I.M. Diakonoff.[3] Basing himself on the written sources, he suggested that the rule of the Scythians could have occupied the territory between the river Kura in the region of Kirovobad (SSR of Azerbaidjan) and the Mannean territory around Lake Urmia, south of the Araxes,[4] and he stressed that the first Scythians in the archaeological sense were pre-Scythian, and were a small component in the inhabitants of the land.[5] On the other hand, he pointed out that it was necessary to verify the correctness of this localization of the Scythian state from the archaeological evidence.[6] This is something which has been little studied, as a consequence of which several scholars deny the existence of the Scythian state on the territory of Azerbaidjan.[7] Nevertheless, Scythian artefacts and weapons have been found on Azerbaidjani territory, from Transcaucasia to Western Asia,[8] which can be taken as evidence for a wide dispersal of the Scythians. In order to confirm this we must rely on the texts.

First of all we must note that the concept of a Scythian state has its origin in Biblical sources. In the Book of Jeremiah (51:27-8) the state of Ashkenaz (Scythia) is mentioned with the states of Ararat (Urartu) and Minni (Mannea) in the events of 593 BC. This written testimony gives us the possibility of postulating the existence of a Scythian state, which appeared well before the events in question and was located in the region of Lakes Van and Urmia, where there were the states of Urartu and Mannea. The formation of the Scythian kingdom must be associated with the first interventions of the Scythians in Asia, in particular in the Mannean zone. In the inscriptions of the Assyrian king Esarhaddon (681-669 BC) they are mentioned in this area at the same time as the Cimmerians, although the lack of a date in the texts makes it difficult to arrange events chronologically. One can however be sure that these political occurrences, which were connected with the intervention of the Cimero-Scythians, took place in the 670's BC,[9] and in any case before Esarhaddon's campaign to Egypt in 671 BC.

Herodotus also gives information about the penetration of the Cimmero-Scythians into Asia in his work dealing with the events of the 7th century BC.[10] He says that "the Scythians penetrated into the land of Asia after the Cimmerians, chased from Europe. Pursuing the Cimmerians, they penetrated into the Median land".[11] This report of Herodotus belongs to the beginning of the penetration of the Cimmero-Scythians into the zone of Lakes Van and Urmia, where the Scythians traversed the Derbend pass. He was not aware of the existence of the state of Mannea in northern Iran during the Cimmero-Scythian incursions, which is why he describes the arrival of the Scythians in this area as an intervention in Media. One may consider this evidence of Herodotus as a reflection of the events of the first quarter of the 7th century BC.

The activity of the Cimmero-Scythians in the area of the kingdoms of Mannea and Urartu is also reflected in the documents of the reign of Esarhaddon. We will examine some, which can give us the most precise picture of the situation of the Scythian state at this time. Specially interesting is one text naming Partatua, which asks: "Partatua, king of Scythia (or: the king of the Scythians), who has sent his messengers to Esarhaddon, king of Assyria, for (the hand of) the king's daughter - when Esarhaddon the king of Assyria has given him his daughter in marriage, will Partatua, king of Scythia, in good faith speak faithful and true words of peace with Esarhaddon, king of Assyria, and keep the treaty of Esarhaddon, king of Assyria, and do whatever is good for Esarhaddon, king of Assyria?".[12] It appears that Partatua gave certain promises to Esarhaddon in exchange for marriage with the king's daughter.[13] Subsequent events show that the alliance between the Scythian king and Esarhaddon was indeed consolidated by a diplomatic marriage of the king's daughter, and thereafter Partatua gave up his political schemes against Assyria. This is evident from the military actions of his son Madyes in Asia Minor[14] and then in Media, when its king Cyaxares was campaigning against Assyria.[15] Where then did the realm of Partatua and Madyes lie, from which one could penetrate unimpeded into Asia Minor and Media, and even into historical Armenia?[16] It is not clear from the text where these Scythians had their dwellings, only that Partatua was the king of the land of the Scythians. But even this last expression could rather be understood as "the king of the Scythians". In any case, it gives us no evidence for the movements of the troops of Partatua, and to locate the "land of the Scythians" of the Assyrian text beyond the Caucasus[17] does not concur with the information of the written documents. There is no basis in the Assyrian text for placing the "Scythian kingdom" in the Caucasus or even in northern Azerbaidjan.

There are distorted reflections of these events in the popular legends, which were used in the "History of Armenia" of Moses of Khorene.[18] He gives the name of Skayordi (literally: son of "sak"), who was the contemporary of the Assyrian king Esarhaddon, and his son Paruyru, as taking part with the Medes in the destruction of Assyria: Paruyru has been identified with Partatua.[19] Chronology is not adhered to in the account of Moses of Khorene, which is why the actions of Madyes, who was on the same side as the Assyrians, are attributed to Paruyru. In the account of Moses of Khorene one also encounters the name of Mades Niukar, who devastated Armenia for two years. Considering these facts, one may suppose that the prototypes of Paruyru and Mades were respectively Partatua-Protothyes[20] and Madyes, whose names, associated with one another but without the chronological sequence, are reflected in popular Armenian traditions used by Moses of Khorene. The Armenian tale in which Skayordi was ruling was probably of Scythian origin, and belongs somewhere to the south of Urartu.[21]

In those days relations between Assyria and Urarṭu were peaceful,[22] but despite this Esarhaddon had established a careful watch on the northern frontiers to intercept possible contacts between Urarṭu, Hubushkia, Mannea and Media.[23] An enquiry by divination of Esarhaddon asks whether the Cimmerians and other enemies might emerge from "the place where they are dwelling" with the help of the king of Urarṭu Rusas II (685-645 BC) and attack Šupria.[24] In view of this, one can say that a part of the Scythians was on Urarṭian territory, probably on the south and south-west frontiers. Comparing the evidence, one may suggest that the king of the Scythians, Partatua, and his troops were in this area: then the alliance of Partatua with Esarhaddon would have not only assured the security of the northern frontier, but also have dissuaded the Urarṭians from attacks on the Assyrian frontiers. The available evidence therefore allows us to suggest that during the 670's BC a definite part of the Scythians, with Partatua at their head, was installed on Urarṭian territory, perhaps in the south, from where they carried out military raids into Asia Minor and elsewhere, without infringing on the Assyrian state.

It seems clear that Partatua was the king of a group of Scythians which penetrated Hither Asia before the remainder of the Scythians.[25] Another group settled in Mannea, for which there is direct evidence: one of the divination enquiries asks: "Within this period, will the Scythian troops, which are dwelling in the region of the Manneans and have gone to the boundary of the Manneans' land, make plans and come out from the pass of Hubushkia to the city of Harrania (and) the city of Anisu[26] and will they come from the Assyrian frontier and plunder much spoil and booty?".[27] It is not entirely clear from this fragment where exactly in Mannea the Scythian troops are residing, but since there is mention of the pass of Hubushkia, one may suppose that they were based north or north-west of Lake Urmia, in an area which belonged at that time to Mannea.[28]

The Scythians to the north and west of Mannea were the allies of the Manneans. At the head of this group of Scythians was probably Ishpakai, whose defeat Esarhaddon announced summarily: "I overcame the people of Mannea, the unruly Qutians, I defeated with weapons the troops of Ishpakai, the Scythians, their ally which did not save them".[29] One must imagine that Ishpakai was the leader or king of the group of Scythians located on Mannean territory. The fall of the alliance of the Scythians and the Manneans should probably be assigned to a final phase of the events on the Assyro-Mannean frontier.[30] From this point the Scythians directed their actions to the south, supporting the Medes against Assyria, and to the west, in the region of Hubushkia, where they probably tried to make contact with the Cimmero-Scythian units on Urarṭian territory. The Manneans also took part in these Scythian plans, a fact which also emerges from the letter of Bel-ushezib to Esarhaddon: "As the king wrote to his troops, saying "Enter the land of Mannea, but the whole force should not enter, let the cavalry troops and the mercenaries enter. The Cimmerians who said: "The land of Mannea is at your disposal, we have kept our feet off it (i.e. we will not intervene, Y.Y.)" - it could well be lies, they are a race of fugitives, and do not know the oath of the gods nor treaties. Let chariots and carts be stationed either side of the pass, (then) let the troops go in with the horses and mercenaries, and plunder the spoils of the plain of Mannea, and come (back) and take up their station in the pass"." The writer of the letter then proposes making an incursion while the guard follows the actions of the Cimmerians, and if they enter the country, they would then be halted.[32] This text shows that some Cimmerians were to be found outside the region of Mannea, where the Scythians of Ishpakai were established. Assuming that the term Cimmerian in the texts of Esarhaddon implies Scythian,[33] these would have to belong to another detachment of the nomads, installed on the territory of Urarṭu under the leadership of Partatua. Furthermore, according to the fragmentary part of the letter, the Assyrians "entered once or twice and plundered, and the Cimmerians *[...]* did not come. The force *[...]* entered, against the towns of the land of Mannea...".[34] Probably the Cimmero-Scythians on Urarṭian territory remained faithful to their promise and the treaty with the Assyrians. Nevertheless, Esarhaddon regularly observed the actions of the Manneans, so as to have timely warning of the birth of any alliance between them and Urarṭu, where the presumed camp of the Cimmero-Scythians was. This is shown by the letter from Assur-ushallim to Esarhaddon:[35] "As for the guards which were placed on the fortresses of Urarṭu, of Mannea, of Media and of Hubushkia, about which the king my lord wrote to me: "Give them strict instructions not to neglect their guard and to pay attention to the refugees in their vicinity, and say that should a fugitive flee to them from Mannea, Media or Hubushkia, they should place him at once in the hands of a messenger to bring him to the crown-prince, and if he has any information you should speak with the crown-prince".[36] From the continuation of the letter one sees that the Mannean scribe, evidently in the service of the guard, has to write down the information from the report of a refugee, and then the liaison chief should deliver it to the king. At the end the author of the letter adds: "and now I have just sent on two refugees from Mannea to the crown-prince, one eunuch and one bearded; they have information in their mouths".[37]

One may deduce from this text that the Manneans wished to establish contact with southern Urarṭu through the territory of Hubushkia. This would seem to follow from the fact that Urarṭu is mentioned once only, while the other lands are repeated. In a fragmentary text we find a mention of a messenger, apparently Assyrian, going towards Hubushkia, then the Cimmerians, and the Manneans.[38] In spite of the measures taken, the Cimmerians penetrated little by little into the region of Scythian activity, in Mannea. On this point a letter from the crown-prince Assurbanipal to Esarhaddon gives interesting details about the location of the Cimmerians, as in the phrase: "Why are the Cimmerians neighbours?".[39] One may suppose that the Manneans had entered into contact with the Cimmero-Scythians situated on the territory of Urarṭu, and that in consequence there had begun a displacement of part of the Cimmerians into the Lake Urmia region. In the divination questions of Esarhaddon to the god Shamash the Cimmerians are often mentioned in connection with events to the east and north-east of Assyria. In one of the fragmentary questions there is the expression "the Cimmerian troops" and the name Ahsiri,[40] who was probably the king of Mannea.[41] In one fragmentary question there is anxiety about the fate of the messenger of Esarhaddon and the probable actions of the Manneans, the Medes, the Cimmerians and the Scythians.[42] In other questions the Manneans and the Cimmerians, the Medes and the Scythians are mentioned in relation to events on the territory of Media,[43] and an Assyrian expedition, which had been despatched to collect tribute in horses.[44] These facts allow us to conclude that the Assyrian sources principally reflect the ethnic names of the tribes present in the region of Mannea: the Scythians and the Cimmerians were active here, but the Cimmerians reached the area after the Scythians of the south and south-west of Urarṭu via Hubushkia. A crucial role in this transference of the Cimmerians to the Mannean region was played by the Manneans themselves, who were able to make contact with the Cimmerians despite the vigilance of the Assyrians' intelligence. In all probability, these forces remained without a leader after the fall of the Cimmerian Teushpa, and it appears that they sided with the Scythians of Partatua, proceeding together, and with the Scythians of the Mannean region.

These results show that in the 670's BC two strong centres of the Cimmero-Scythian alliance emerged to the north of Assyria - one to the south or south-west of Urarṭu with Partatua at its head, and the other to the north and north-west of Mannea with Ishpakai at its head. The first of these Cimmero-Scythian coalitions came out of the struggle with Assyria and achieved an alliance with Assyria as well as establishing amicable relations with Urarṭu, while the second coalition, as an ally of the Manneans and Medes, took an active part in the struggle against Assyria. The rear of the second Cimmero-Scythian coalition reached to the north as far as the right bank of the Araxes in the area of its confluence with the Kura. In fact, the Scythian state was born in the two adjacent territories, in Urarṭu and Mannea, but in the course of time the two states were considered to have been a single Scythian state. There were probably reasons for the birth of this tradition, but these reasons could have come into existence later. Thus, Tugdammi, according to classical traditions, was a Cimmerian, but after cuneiform sources of the time of Assurbanipal (669-631 BC) he ruled the Umman-manda, and, finally, was also king of the Sacae and the Qutians.[48] Comparing these two last titles of Tugdammi, one can determine that by the name Umman-manda one must understand the Cimmerians and the Scythians,[49] while according to the last title he was also the king of the Sacae and the Qutians, after the primary terminology, that is, of the Scythians and their allies the Manneans.[50] So, in the middle of the 7th century BC the two centres of the Cimmero-Scythian coalitions were considered as a united state, and this is the reason for the emergency of the tradition of the united Scythian state. This state, in all probability, was born during the 670's BC to the north and north-west of the districts of Mannea, and entered little by little into contact with the Cimmero-Scythian groups to the south and south-west of Lake Van. At the middle of the 7th century BC, and at the beginning of the 6th, this wide territory, which perhaps included Hubushkia as well later, close to Mannea and Urartu, was the state of the Scythians according to the ancient oriental sources.

* Translated from French; the Editors apologise for any imprecisions which may have resulted (J.N.P.).

IM = I.M. Diakonoff, *Istoria Midi* [Moscow-Leningrad 1956]

PAN = I.M. Diakonoff, *Predistoria armyanskovo naroda* [Erevan 1968]

VT = B.B. Piotrovski, *Vanskoye tsarstvo* [Moscow 1959]

1 I.M. Diakonoff, *Assiro-vavilonskie istočniki po istori Urartu*, VDI 1951/2, 3,4; IM 242ff.; G.A. Melikišvili, *Nairi-Urartu* [Tbilisi 1954] 300ff.; id., *K istori drevnei Gruzi* [Tbilisi 1959] 220ff.; VT 232ff.; E.I. Krupnov, *Drevnyaya istoria Kavkaza* [Moscow 1960] 55ff.; I. Aliev, *Istoria Midi* [Baku 1960] 218ff.

2 Cf. in Armenia the name of Cappadocia - "Gamirk", i.e. the land of the Cimmerians. The name of Sakasene is connected with the name of the Sacae in Transcaucasia.

3 IM 247-53ff.

4 I.M. Diakonoff, IM 251, supposed that Sakasene was the kernel of the ancient territory of the land of the Scythians, which gave rise to the form Šikašen in the Old Armenian sources (see *Armyanskaya Geografia VII veka*, transl. K.P. Patkanova [St. Petersburg 1877] 41 (20)). B.B. Piotrovski, VT 254, places the state of the Scythians in the Urmia region in conformity with the written sources. According to I. Aliev, *Istoria Midi* 226, the state of the Scythians was born in the wide territory between the Caucasus Mts. and Lake Urmia. A.M. Khasanov, *Sotsial'naya istoria skifov* [Moscow 1975] 219, places the centre of the Scythian state in eastern Transcaucasia. After E. Cavaignac ("A propos du début de l'histoire des Mèdes", in *Journal Asiatique* 246 [1961] 156), the Scythian state included at different times Sakasene, the Caspian, northern Armenia and Cappadocia. While there are differences in the precise location of the state, most scholars take Sakasene as its centre. Moreover, according to the cuneiform sources, the centre of the Scythian state, of which we shall speak below, lay in western Asia. Also the location of Sakasene in the region of Kirovobad is in need of further precision: according to Strabo (II,1,14; IX,8,4; XI,14,3-4), Sakasene should be sought behind the Araxene plain. He states (XI,14,3-4): "the plain of the Araxes, where the Araxes flows as far as the frontiers of Albania, emptying into the Caspian Sea. Behind this plain is located Sakasene, which also borders on Albania and the River Cyrus". With this information, one can locate Sakasene in the region of the River Araxes, south of the confluence of the Kura, at the junction of the territories of Balasakan and Caspiana. Šikašen of the Armenian sources was to the west of this region in the province of Utii (the Barda region of contemporary Azerbaidjan). According to our localization Sakasene is situated on the road used by the Scythians in their displacement southwards towards Mannea, and does not stand in any direct relation with the state of the Scythians.

5 IM 253; G.A. Melikišvili, *K istori drevnei Gruzi* 230. The Cimmero-Scythians left no traces in Transcaucasia, where they had been.

6 IM 251.

7 V.B. Vinogradov, *O skifskikh pokhodakh čerez Kavkaz, Trudy Čečeno-Inguškovo naučno-issledovatel'skovo Instituta* IX [Grozny 1964] 21ff.; Dž. A. Khalilov, *Arkheologičeskie nakhodki "skifskovo" oblika i vopros o "Skifskom tsarstve" no territori Azerbaidžana*, in *Problemy skifskoi arkheologi* [Moscow 1971] 183-7.

8 See B.B. Piotrovski, *Arkheologia Zakavkazia* [Leningrad 1949] 114ff.; VT 237ff.; G.A. Melikišvili, *K istori drevnei Gruzi* 224-5; IM 251-4; E.I. Krupnov, *Drevnyaya istoria Severnovo Kavkaza* 63-75.

9 IM 259.

10 V.V. Struve, *Khronologia VI v. do n.e. v trude Gerodota*, in VDI 1952, 60-78; IM 293ff.; Claudio Mazetti, *Konets assiriskoi deržavy i assiroskifskie otnošenia*, in VDI 1979/4, 23.

11 Herodotus, I, 103.

12 E.G. Klauber, PRT No. 16, 29-30.

13 The second part of the text repeats the same question in almost identical words.

14 Strabo, I, 3, 21, names Madyes as the chief of the Cimmerians, and the

displacing of the Treres of Asia Minor is attributed to him.

15 Herodotus, I, 103, reports that the troops of Scythians under the direction of king Madyes, the son of Protothyes, appeared when Cyaxares was besieging Nineveh.

16 Moses of Khorene, *History of Armenia*, Bk. I, Ch. 13, cites Mades Niukar, conquered by Aram, whom one may identify with the king of Urarṭu of the middle of the 9th century BC, Aramu. Mades is approximately the name of the Scythian king Madyes, the son of Protothyes, after the Armenian source. At first I.M. Diakonoff considered the name Mades as a word signifying a Mede (IM 352, n. 1), later he took it simply as a reminiscence of the Scythian Madyes (PAN 185, n. 296). Moses of Khorene relates that Mades devastated Armenia for two years: clearly there are preserved in Armenian popular tradition the military actions of Madyes in Asia Minor, close to the land of Arme, from whose name it is considered (VT 124; PAN 234, n. 114) that the name of Armenia is formed, and which lay to the south-west of Lake Van in the region of Shupria. But there is a chronological error in the account of Moses of Khorene: Madyes-Mades was active about two centuries after Aram-Aramu.

17 V.B. Vinogradov, op. cit. (see note 7), places the land of the king of the Scythians Partatua in the Caucasus, which does not follow necessarily from the content of the Esarhaddon text. The doubts of Vinogradov and Dž. Khalilov (op. cit. in note 7) as to the existence of the Scythian state in the territory of northern Azerbaidjan are based on the inadequate archaeological data, which were stressed by Diakonoff himself (IM 251).

18 Moses of Khorene, *History of Armenia*, Bk. I, Ch. 23.

19 Gr. Kapantsian, *Istoriko-lingvističeskie raboty* [Erevan 1956] 150-1; VT 124-7.

20 Herodotus, I, 103; Strabo, I, 3, 21, see note 16.

21 VT 77; PAN 139 and esp. 150.

22 Cf. G.A. Melikišvili, *Nairi-Urartu* 314.

23 L. Waterman, RCA I, No. 434, p. 300-01.

24 J.A. Knudtzon, AGS No. 48:4, 7-10.

25 J. Aro, "Remarks on the practice of extispicy in the time of Esarhaddon and Assurbanipal", in *La divination en Mesopotamie ancienne et dans les régions voisines* [Vendôme 1966] 114.

26 The reading of the city name Anisu is based on the text ABL 173:8 (= RCA I, No. 173, p. 116). The location of Harrania and Anisu is not known, but after this text they are on the Assyrian frontier.

27 AGS No. 35:4-9, p. 130.

28 In view of this text it is presumed that at this date the frontiers of Mannea reached as far as Hubushkia (IM 265).

29 D.D. Luckenbill, *Ancient Records of Assyria and Babylonia*, II, 517 (p. 207); 533 (p. 213).

30 I.M. Diakonoff, IM 260, 272, supposes that Ishpakai died at the end of 673 BC, after which the actions of the new king of the Scythians, Partatua, began. However, according to the statements in the royal inscriptions

Ishpakai died in 672 or at the beginning of 671 BC, and Partatua had begun his activity at the same time as Ishpakai.

31 RCA II, No. 1237 (pp. 358-61); R.H. Pfeiffer, *State Letters of Assyria* [New Haven 1935] No. 329:9-22 (pp. 223-5).

32 Pfeiffer, op. cit. No. 329: rev. 7-8, 15-18 (p. 224).

33 The mention of the Cimmerians with the Scythians in the texts of Esarhaddon in the region of Mannea and Media suggested to I.M. Diakonoff (IM 265) that the sources understood Scythians also under the name Cimmerians.

34 Pfeiffer, op. cit. No. 329: 23-rev. 1-3 (p. 224).

35 RCA, I, No. 434:9-rev. 7 (pp. 300-01); Pfeiffer, op. cit. No. 15 (pp. 14-15).

36 IM 274; this document dates between 672 and 669 BC; it was probably composed in 672-671, when, according to our theory, Ishpakai died. The contents of this document show that the Manneans were making efforts to establish liaison with the Cimmerians across the territory of Hubushkia, but Esarhaddon wanted to prevent this with the help of his guard.

37 RCA I, No. 434:18-23 (p. 300); Pfeiffer, op. cit. No. 15 (p. 14).

38 AGS No. 38: rev. 8-9 (p. 135); Klauber, in PRT p. LIX, restores also the name of the Cimmerians in the lacuna (l. 10). Esarhaddon therefore was wondering whether his messenger would be captured by the Manneans, the Cimmerians, or the others in the region of Hubushkia.

39 RCA II, No. 1026:11 (pp. 216-7). The document is a report from the crown-prince Assurbanipal to Esarhaddon and perhaps to be dated 672-671 BC.

40 AGS No. 24:2, 4 (p. 114).

41 Cf. IM 281-3.

42 AGS No. 25:9-10, rev. 10-11 (p. 115).

43 PRT No. 20:4-5 (p.34); No. 22:5-9 (p. 40).

44 PRT Nos. 4, 7, 8, 38.

45 The fall of Teushpa goes back to 679-78 BC (IM 236; G.A. Melikišvili, *K istori drevnei Gruzi*, 228). Later, in 676-74 BC, the Cimmerians crushed the state of Phrygia in central Asia Minor.

46 B.B. Piotrovski, VT 233, distinguishes two regions of Asia where the Cimmerians resided: in Cappadocia and in Mannea. Cf. also Klauber, PRT p. LVIII. Following the data of the Assyrian sources and of Moses of Khorene we may localize the residence of the Cimmero-Scythians with Partatua at their head in the territory of the land of Arme in the Shupria region. The same Assyrian sources permit us to locate the kernel of the Scythian state in the land of Mannea more exactly in its north and north-western parts.

47 Strabo, I, 3, 21; Streck, Asb., II, 280.

48 H. Tadmor, *Tri poslednikh desyatiletia Assiri*, in *Trudy XXV Meždunarodnovo kongressa vostokovedov*, I [Moscow 1962] 241, called attention to this title for the first time, which is in the publication of R.C. Thompson, "The British Museum Excavations at Nineveh, 1931-1932", in AAA 20 [1933] 88:146.

49 Cf. IM 73ff.; VT 234.